Grass-roots Democracy
in India and China

Grass-roots Democracy in India and China

The Right to Participate

Editors

Manoranjan Mohanty
Richard Baum
Rong Ma
George Mathew

SAGE Publications
New Delhi ▪ Thousand Oaks ▪ London

First published in 2007 by

 Sage Publications India Pvt Ltd
B-42, Panchsheel Enclave
New Delhi 110 017
www.indiasage.com

Sage Publications Inc
2455 Teller Road
Thousand Oaks, California 91320

Sage Publications Ltd
1 Oliver's Yard, 55 City Road
London EC1Y 1SP

Published by Tejeshwar Singh for Sage Publications India Pvt Ltd, typeset in 10/12 Aldine 401 BT by Star Compugraphics Private Limited, Delhi and printed at Chaman Enterprises, New Delhi.

Library of Congress Cataloging-in-Publication Data

Grass-roots democracy in India and China: the right to participate/editors, Manoranjan Mohanty . . . [et al.].
    p. cm.
  Includes bibliographical references and index.
    1. Political participation—India. 2. Political participation—China. 3. Democratization—India. 4. Democratization—China. 5. Comparative government. I. Mohanty, Manoranjan, 1942–

JQ281.G73   323'.0420951—dc22   2006   2006031047

ISBN: 10: 0-7619-3515-0 (Hb)   10: 81-7829-667-5 (India-Hb)
        13: 978-0-7619-3515-5 (Hb)   13: 978-81-7829-667-8 (India-Hb)

Sage Production Team: Abantika Banerjee, Gayatri E. Koshy, R.A.M. Brown and Santosh Rawat

Contents

I. Institutional Structure and Local Participation

III. Comparative Reflections

List of Tables

List of Abbreviations

ABC	Agricultural Bank of China
ACWF	All China Women's Federation
ATRs	Action taken Reports
BJP	Bharatiya Janata Party
BPL	Below Poverty Line
BSP	Bahujan Samaj Party
CEO	Chief Executive Officer
CPC	Communist Party of China
CPI	Communist Party of India
CPM	Communist Party of India (Marxist)
CSS	Centrally Sponsored Schemes
DDC	District Development Councils
DPC	District Planning Committee
DRDAs	District Rural Development Agencies
DRP	District Resource Persons
DWCRA	Development of Women and Child in Rural Areas
FPCs	Funding the Poor Cooperatives
GDI	Gender Development Index
GP	Gram Panchayat
HPF	Hire Purchase Finance
IRDP	Integrated Rural Development Programmes
JD	Janata Dal
KCP	Karnataka Congress Party
KRP	Key Resource Persons
LDA	Local Development Association
LDF	Left Democratic Front
LSGIs	Local Self-Governing Institutions
MFIs	Microfinance Institutions
MLAs	Members of Legislative Assembly
MLCs	Members of Legislative Councils
MOA	Ministry of Agriculture
MOCA	Ministry of Civil Affairs
MPLADS	MPs Local Area Development Schemes
MPs	Members of Parliament
NABARD	National Bank for Agriculture and Rural Development
NBFCs	Non-banking Finance Companies

NBFIs	Non-banking Financial Institutions
NCP	Nationalist Congress Party
NDA	National Democratic Alliance
NGOs	Non-Government Organisations
NHGs	Neighbourhood Groups
OBCs	Other Backward Castes
OECD	Organisation of Economic Cooperation and Development
ORS	Open Recommendation and Selection
PAP	Poverty Alleviation Programmes
PBC	People's Bank of China
PPC	People's Plan Campaign
PRC	People's Republic of China
PRIs	Panchayati Raj Institutions
RBI	Reserve Bank of India
RCCs	Rural Credit Cooperatives
RCF	Rural Cooperative Foundations
ROSCA	Rotating Savings and Credit Organisations
RRBs	Regional Rural Banks
SCP	Special Component Plan
SCs	Scheduled Castes
SDA	Sanchuan Development Association
SEC	State Election Commission
SETC	State Economic and Trade Commission
SFC	State Finance Commission
SGSY	Swarnajayanti Gram Swarozgar Yojana
SHGs	Self Help Groups
SIRD	State Institute for Rural Development
SPB	State Planning Board
ST	Scheduled Tribes
TAR	Tibet Autonomous Region
TDB	Taluk Development Board
TP	Taluk Panchayat/Parishad
TSP	Tribal Sub Plan
TVEs	Township Village Enterprises
UDF	United Democratic Front
UPA	United Progressive Alliance
VCs	Villagers' Committee
VP	Village Panchayats
VRA	Villagers' Representative Assembly
VTC	Voluntary Technical Corps
WCP	Women Component Plan
WTO	World Trade Organisation
ZP	Zilla Panchayat/Parishad

Preface

While the world is talking about the rise of China and India as the fastest growing economies, it is important to have a deeper look at the internal dynamics of these two most populous societies of the world. With longstanding civilisations as well as great social diversity, these post-colonial societies are currently engaged in unique experiments in social transformation both in vertical and horizontal ways. This volume is an attempt to capture the meaning of that experience. It is the product of a joint project of scholars from India, China and the United States who have closely studied the grass-roots political experience in India and China from an interdisciplinary perspective. The thrust of this project is to bring out the nature of the process of democratisation, which is characterised by many similar elements in both countries, especially the trend of expanding demands for participation and complex power structures interjecting them.

The volume takes up issues of institutional structure and local participation and the dynamics of local governance in the emerging socio-economic environment including the issues of gender, ethnicity and religion in the local political processes. Some of the contributions present comparative perspectives while the others are based on case studies. The institutional structure has undergone many major changes both in India and China in the recent years. In the case of India, the Seventy-third Amendment of the Indian Constitution in 1993 introduced mandatory panchayati raj in rural India and in the case of China, the Organic Law of 1998, which provided for competitive elections at the village level, have initiated new political processes at the local level. The chapters bring out the extent to which political participation has been facilitated and institutional innovation has evolved in both the countries. There are case studies from minority regions as well as other areas, which add important cultural and ethnic dimensions to institutional dynamics.

The context of economic reforms in both the countries has generated new challenges for local institutions, both in terms of integrating the local market with the global economy as well as affecting the choices of local population, including the local producers. The comparative essays on microfinance and the political economy of the rural areas present important insights on this question. This is especially evident in the research findings on gender, caste, ethnicity and class relations in the Indian and Chinese villages. To what extent the new democratic processes in the villages have reduced ethnic subordination, caste hierarchy and gender injustice or have generated new elements of class or other forms of domination, has been investigated in comparative perspective.

This volume contributes theoretical insights to the emerging field of local governance and local democracy based on case studies and comparative analysis. Reconceptualising local democracy as a substantive process of interconnected socio-political transformation where the right to participate is a fundamental right at every level starting from the grass-roots level is a theme that emerges from this volume. India–China studies are acquiring greater significance in the contemporary world. It is hoped that studies like the present one with empirical and comparative approach can enrich that body of knowledge in the field of democratic theory and development policy.

Acknowledgements

This collaborative effort involving four institutions in three countries owes its success to a number of individuals and agencies. We first of all thank the authorities and staff of the four institutions: Institute of Sociology and Anthropology, University of Beijing, Center for Chinese Studies, University of California at Los Angeles, Institute of Social Sciences (ISS), New Delhi and the Institute of Chinese Studies (ICS), Centre for the Study of Developing Societies (CSDS), Delhi. The ISS, through its Eastern Regional Centre at Kolkata organized the international conference in January 2003 where this project took its initial shape. All the participants remember the warm hospitality in Kolkata and the rich deliberations in which many eminent scholars from the city took part. We particularly record our gratitude to the Chief Minister of West Bengal, Mr Buddhadeb Bhattacharya who inaugurated the conference and the Panchayat Raj Minister Mr Suryakanta Mishra who gave the valedictory address. We thank Mr Buddhadev Ghosh of ISS and his colleagues in Kolkata for taking great pains to make the conference a success.

This project and the conference received funding from the Ford Foundation, Beijing which supported travel support to the Chinese participants. The scholars from the US were supported by a grant from the Pacific Rim Research Programme of the University of California. The Indian participants were supported by the ICS out of the grant from the Ford Foundation, New Delhi. The ISS supported the organization of the conference. The follow up work on the volume was carried out at the ICS under the grant received from the Ministry of External Affairs, Government of India under the ICS programme of Comparative Development Studies. We express our sincere thanks to all of them.

ICS Director Patricia Uberoi has been a constant source of support for this effort. Swargajyoti Gohain, Research Associate at ICS has worked hard helping in the preparation of the manuscript for publication. All the authors have received research assistance from a number of sources for their respective studies. We take this opportunity to express our sincere appreciation to all of them. We have benefited from many scholars who have read earlier versions of these papers and made useful suggestions. The authors and editors are, however, responsible for the inadequacies remaining in this work.

Introduction
Local Governance, Local Democracy and the Right to Participate

MANORANJAN MOHANTY

Two Perspectives on Local Government

Aspirations for grass-roots democracy have acquired universal recognition during the past quarter century. In recent years, however, local self-governance has emerged as the new mantra of the forces of globalisation and liberalisation. There are two divergent perspectives on local governance: one sees it as an arena for transforming an unequal local society into a democratic community; while the other treats it as an agency or a channel to implement centrally-formulated policies and programmes. The former evokes the ideas of Gandhi, trying to reinvent the vision of *gram swaraj* or village-level self-rule or villagers' self-determination in the course of people's struggle for freedom. Mao Zedong's notion of the rural people's commune involved a comparable notion of self-reliant villages engaged in a process of 'liberation' or human transformation, both personal and social. Their perspectives differed, however, over such things as the role of individual autonomy in the process of liberation and the principal socio-political obstacles to liberation at the local, national and global levels. The Maoist approach focuses on mechanisms of governance and stresses implementation of policies involving local institutions, local groups and local people in general. While Mao Zedong's approach is tied to the politics of transformation, the Gandhian approach is embedded in a framework of self-management. Though neither of these perspectives has been institutionalised in their own countries, they remain as reference points for any discourse on grass-roots democracy.

Taking the concrete experience of local governance processes in the contemporary world, we can notice a tension between two kinds of practices in local governance, local governance as self-management and local governance as an instrumentality of the centre. The Chinese local governance model operates in a unitary centralised polity where the local institution is not only an instrument of central authority, which provides resources to it, but is also an agency of legitimation of the system and its rulers. The Indian local democracy perspective, on the other hand, implies that the local level exercises a degree of clearly-defined autonomy, has control over its own resources and possesses a constitutionally-guaranteed sphere of power. Thus, the local government shares power with the other levels in a multi-layered federal framework in which each layer possesses dignity and autonomy.

In socialist systems as well as liberal democracies, the agency character of the local government was conspicuous until recently. In China, the centralised leadership of the Communist Party of China (CPC) did not allow the local institutions to exercise autonomy either during the commune period or during the subsequent period of economic reforms. In India, the concept of panchayat went deeper due to Gandhi's influence and the legacies of the freedom struggle. But the development strategy and the pattern of party politics in India did not permit substantial decentralisation of power in India either. Only with the growth of democratic consciousness among people all over the world during recent years has there been a drive to make local governments autonomous arenas. There are new social forces in the countryside, as a result of economic growth and educational development, making demands through political as well as communication channels. The right to self-governance was always implicit in the theory of democracy though the debate between the votaries of direct democracy and representative democracy had gone on. The assertion of democratic rights by people at the grass-roots level everywhere has given the debate a new focus. The right to participate in social affairs and political decision making has emerged as an important right. Now that rulers seem to have little control over this trend, there are efforts in all countries to permit the introduction of institutions of participation at the village level. But it is important to investigate to what extent the rulers even now seek to manipulate local institutions in a variety of ways to maintain central control. This is a new stage of the movement for democracy at the local level.

Recent Initiatives in India and China

In this evolving environment, both China and India have taken recent steps to promote mandatory democratic elections in the recent years—India under the Seventy-third Constitutional Amendment in 1993 and China through the Grass-roots Democracy Law under which elections have been held every three years at the village committee level since 1998. This initiative needs to be seen against the backdrop of the different experiences in the two countries in the sphere of rural development. The Chinese policy during the people's commune period as well as during the reforms had stressed equitable restructuring of land relations—collective ownership of the earlier years giving way to the Household Contract System after 1978, under which land was distributed among families in proportion to the number of the adult members a family had. In China the emphasis has been on the enhancement of the incomes of peasants through the diversification of agriculture and by promoting rural industries. Thus, economic or material conditions for the advancement of local democracy have been the focus in China. In India, on the other hand, rapid agricultural growth was achieved through the Green Revolution in many parts of the country, which brought prosperity to some sections in rural India. In order to promote social welfare for the poor and build infrastructure in the countryside, centrally-sponsored rural development schemes were the main focus of state policy for all these years. For decades, the panchayats operated as formal bodies according to the whims and discretions of the state governments in India. There were some exceptions to this practice in West Bengal, Kerala and Karnataka. In the 1990s, after the new law came into force, the panchayats became representative institutions with constitutionally-stipulated elections every five years and reservation of seats for women, Scheduled Castes (SCs), Scheduled Tribes (STs) and also Other Backward Classes (OBCs) in some states. The question to ask is whether even after the new versions of the statutory panchayats came into being, did they nonetheless remain the main agencies for implementing these schemes. In other words, were the local bodies retained mainly as instruments for carrying out central plans or had they become a layer of democratic self-governance exercising power in a defined sphere of activities at the local level. On the whole, we see that local governance through the Communist Party apparatus and the village committee in China was geared towards generating local resources for economic development and raising people's incomes while in India it worked as a method of management of received resources while providing an arena of social representation and political competition, albeit in a limited way.

The initial experiences of the new phase of movement towards local democracy in India and China give interesting indicators of social change. For example, the practice of women's reservation has produced a political dynamic of its own, dispelling substantially the myths of the 'proxy woman' and showing the emergence of autonomous assertion of women's rights as well as feminist perspective on social development. This process is not yet so conspicuous in the Chinese countryside, where women's rights have been subordinated to the commitment to steadily raising the income of the household and the village. Competitive politics in India has percolated to the village level, making even small groups important for electoral politics even though, legally, party politics is not allowed in village elections. In China, this kind of trend has taken the shape of either factional politics within the CPC or pressure group politics involving powerful entrepreneurs trying to influence decisions at the village level. The diversity of political experience is as wide in India as in China depending on the level of economic development and political mobilisation. Wherever a political party or group is well organised and carries popular support, it uses the local institutions more effectively to pursue its objectives, as in West Bengal, Kerala and Karnataka. In China's coastal provinces, competing interest groups use the party forum to pursue their economic goals through various channels including the local institutions. In all cases, though, the newly-mandated institutions have provided new opportunities for open debates during elections, checks and balances over one another in political and economic decision making, seeking accountability and transparency including the campaign for the right to information in India at every level and a variety of political possibilities in the pursuit of people's democratic rights. However, the journey for realising local democracy may only have begun.

This volume is the product of a collective research effort by scholars drawn from India, China and the US, who aim at analysing the experiences of grass-roots political processes of India and China in a comparative perspective, keeping some theoretical questions relating to participatory democracy in mind. Our chapters together point at the significance of the dynamic relationship between political institutions and the socio-economic processes both of which have a value of their own. Thus the volume, while focusing on the recent institutional developments in rural governance in India and China, also looks at them in terms of the consequences that they imply for various sections of society. The chapters are divided into two parts, one focusing on institutional dynamics and the other on the emerging socio-economic issues. The concluding chapter puts these studies in a wider political economy perspective and speculates on future possibilities keeping in view the recent debates on the causes of turbulence in the countryside in both the countries.

I

Part One deals with the changes in the institutional structures at the local level and the dynamics of people's participation in decision making in India and China. This consists of one comparative chapter, and one chapter each on China and India which spells out the basic structure of village self-government and provides a historical overview of local political processes in China during the pre-reform period and since the reforms, and in India, prior to the Seventy-third Amendment and thereafter. Then there are three case studies each, from provinces of China and states of India, which bring out specific issues of power dynamics at the local level. The study from Sichuan shows how local people in Buyun mobilise themselves for institutional change by organising competitive elections at the township level while a non-governmental group in Qinghai has succeeded in exercising some autonomy even within the present political structure. In Inner Mongolia too, a degree of participatory politics among the minority nationality is visible. The Indian case studies from Maharashtra, Kerala and Karnataka too present interesting findings. While in Maharashtra, the statutory reservation of seats has brought greater representation for the deprived sections of society, in Kerala, such achievements as well as greater exercise of power at the local level were due to the people's development campaign. Karnataka presents yet another case of early initiatives by political leaderships in the late 1970s and the 1980s to promote local democracy.

George Mathew (Chapter 1) provides a comparative study of the village committees of China and the panchayats of India, two significant innovations in grass-roots democracy in these two societies. It traces the emergence of the village committees to the period when collectivisation ended, through a series of developments such as the Hezhai experiment, in which a group of villagers tried to set up a body to manage local affairs, which became the model on which the 1987 trial implementation of the Organic Law for Villagers' Self-Governance was based, and which later became national legislation in 1998. Similarly, the Indian experiment in grass-roots governance achieved genuine success only with the Seventy-third Constitutional Amendment in 1993 that provided for mandatory elections, representation for women, SCs and STs. However, Mathew, like other contributors, argues that panchayati raj in India has been considerably hampered by the interventions of the Members of Parliament (MPs), Members of Legislative Assemblies (MLAs) and the local bureaucracy. He believes that much more needs to be done to enhance the statutory powers of panchayats. He makes some recommendations for improving grass-roots democracy in India and China, such as overcoming skepticism among government officials regarding local self-rule, reducing corruption and ensuring greater representation of women, especially in China.

D. Bandyopadhyay, Saila Ghosh and Buddhadeb Ghosh (Chapter 2) attempt to give a historical explanation for the poor functioning of panchayats in present day India. By looking at the history of grass-roots governance in Bengal, the authors point out that rural self-governing institutions in the colonial period were mere tools of the central government whereby the British could propagate the myth of local governance in the aftermath of the 1857 mutiny and yet maintain the stranglehold of imperial rule. They show that this trend continues even today, for there has been almost no attempt, even after the Seventy-third Constitutional Amendment partially devolved power to local government institutions, to allow the panchayats to develop into powerful and autonomous institutions of self-government. In most of the states of India, they continue to remain subservient to the local bureaucracy and local politicians despite the fact that in West Bengal, Karnataka and Kerala, the state governments had devolved more power to the panchayats

We then turn to a historical overview of local government in China. Zhou's chapter (Chapter 3) is a study of villagers' participation in state building in China between the years 1949 and 1999, focusing especially on a comparison between the first 30 years and the subsequent 20-year reform period. The nature of villagers' participation in matters of local governance has changed with the shifting relations between state and society. Zhou writes that immediately after the establishment of the People's Republic in the early-1950s, peasants were actively involved in the major state-building activities, and state power was extended to every corner of rural society. In the mid-1960s, however, during the Cultural Revolution, there arose a conflict between state and society, when villagers loyal to Chairman Mao Zedong rebelled against local government officials, who were branded as followers of Liu Shaoqi. In the late-1970s, there were wide ranging administrative reforms defining the role of villagers in local governance, and the first Organic Law for Villagers Self-Governance in 1987 provided a framework for increased participation of villagers in local governance. During the 1990s, grass-roots administration was further streamlined facilitating people's participation at the village level.

The dynamics of the actual institutional structure under the Organic Law of 1998 for competitive elections at the village (*cun*) level, comparable to panchayats in India, and not at the township (*xiang*) level, comparable to block or panchayat samiti in India, is discussed in Chapter 4 by Tony Saich and Xuedong Yang. They take a close look at the attempts to raise the level of competitive elections from the village to the township in the now famous case of Buyun Township in Sichuan Province. Even though it was finally stalled as a result of the policy decision by the Jiang Zemin regime to keep local democracy limited to the village level, they give much evidence of institutional innovations in the direction of democratic change. There have been similar attempts in some other parts of China after Hu Jintao assumed the leadership of the CPC. But his regime too has been unwilling to allow competitive elections at the township or other higher levels.

Richard Baum and Xin Zhang (Chapter 5) cast a look at the relationship between local government and local associations and argue that in some cases local non-governmental organisations (NGOs) are able to function relatively independently of the state in initiating and carrying out local development projects. They support this argument by putting forward a case study of the Sanchuan Development Association (SDA), a rural NGO in Qinghai, China. The main objectives of the SDA are to implement educational development and poverty alleviation projects. Because of these apolitical goals and also because a major portion of its funds come from international agencies, the

SDA has been able to function without interference from the local government. Further, since the leaders are recruited locally, the SDA also has credibility among and cooperation from the local population. This study shows how areas of autonomous action can be carved out at the local level even though the institutional structures may have concentrated powers in the hands of the party and government leadership at the next higher level.

We next turn to the experience of local government in some minority nationality areas, which may illustrate the significance of self-governance more clearly than elsewhere. Rong Ma's study (Chapter 6) looks at the impact of recent reforms on the life of the people of the grasslands in Inner Mongolia, one of the autonomous regions of China. His descriptions of the workings of one Hurqige *Gaca* (brigade) under the commune-brigade system established in China in 1959 provide valuable field data on micro-level sociopolitical experiences. Developments arising from administrative reforms, such as flow of outside migrants and seasonal labour, the policy of redistributing livestock after the collapse of collectivisation and so on, led to major changes in livelihood patterns, family size and land holdings, fertility rate and overall community life.

Among the Indian case studies, Rajendra Vora (Chapter 7) conducts a comparative study of the composition of village panchayats in Maharashtra, before and after the enactment of the Seventy-third Constitutional Amendment, which laid down certain provisions for seats to be reserved in political bodies for SCs, STs, OBCs and women. This study, based upon a survey of the Latur and Aurangabad districts of Marathwada, the most economically backward region of Maharashtra, and where the Maratha clan is most populous, shows that the panchayats have become more representative in character after the Seventy-third Amendment, mostly because the Backward Caste candidates are now elected from the reserved seats in their caste category, and the post of sarpanch, in particular, is being held by an increasing number of Backward Caste members. This trend is especially remarkable in a society where previously, land ownership and high-caste membership used to be the eligibility criteria in practice for a person to be elected as sarpanch. This chapter also tries to understand the particular context in which the Seventy-third Amendment Act was passed. It begins by pointing out that the Act was passed in the political period of liberalisation where this Act was one way by which there could be a withdrawal of state power by bringing local bodies and NGOs to the forefront, and this is especially valid in the case of Maharashtra which was one of the first states to adopt liberalisation. In other words, this move for decentralisation may not so much be a step towards participatory democracy as for enforcing measures of globalisation through local agencies. Yet, the very process of statutory elections and social representation has generated its own dynamics of democratic decentralisation.

Isaac (Chapter 8) also looks at the structure of panchayati raj institutions (PRIs) in Kerala, calling attention to the appropriation of planning and developmental functions by the political elite in the absence of more decentralised forms of governance; he deals with an important exception to this, in the case of the 'People's Plan Campaign in Kerala in 1996, which achieved a devolution of both authority and resources to local self-governing institutions. This campaign was based on a four-pronged approach that aimed to shift budgetary authority to the local self-governing institutions (LSGIs), to devolve planning functions to the LSGIs, to mobilise civic society in social development (he mentions the role of the Kerala Sastra Sahitya Parishad or the Peoples' Science Movement in this regard) and to institutionalise the campaign's objectives through appropriate legislation. Despite criticisms of corruption and delivery failure levelled at the campaign, the author argues that this campaign was in keeping with Kerala's long history of equitable distribution. It has resulted in the increased participation of women and Backward Caste members in the local institutions.

Tracing the evolution of Karnataka's panchayati raj system through three phases, namely; 1959–87; 1987–93; and 1993 onwards, B.S Bhargava and K. Subha (Chapter 9) draw attention to the important role of local leaders, who have proved to be both an enabling and a disabling factor in the evolution of a genuine panchyati raj. Their enabling role is seen in the initiatives of local leaders leading to panchayati reforms; for instance, the Athanur all-women panchayat was formed through the enterprise of a popular *zilla* panchayat leader. Yet, the proper implementation of the panchayat's functions is hampered by the lack of awareness, education and communication skills of the local leaders. The authors also suggest that an 'organic linkage' between NGOs and PRIs should exist for effective grass-roots governance, for the NGOs can help significantly in motivating villagers to vote, in training and educating local leaders and so on. Despite the comparative success of panchayati raj in Karnataka, the authors recommend few more reform measures, such as curbing the practice of middlemen, instilling a pro-development/pro-panchayati raj mindset among bureaucrats, improving the election machinery and making the concept of panchayat popular through satellite and radio programmes.

II

Part Two comprises a set of comparative chapters on local political economy including studies on social differentiation and gender issues. Some of these are further highlighted in the case studies from India and China.

The Andhra Pradesh study by Haragopal and Sudarshanam covers both tribals and non-tribals while the Chinese case studies by Shengmin Yang, Shaoying He, Changjiang Yu and Tanzen Lhundup are from the non-Han minority nationality areas in Xinjiang, Yunnan and Tibet. The two rare empirical studies on Tibet present a unique picture of a syncretic local polity of party, state and monastery. The volume does not have an equal number of case studies on the tribal areas from India, even though the tribal population is nearly the same as that of China's minority population, that is, 7.5 per cent and 8 per cent respectively. The new stage of panchayati raj has been slow to evolve in the Scheduled Tribal areas after the Panchayats (Extension to the Scheduled Areas) Act of 1996 was first passed by the Indian government, and not all the state governments have enacted their corresponding laws yet. There are of course constitutional provisions in India protecting tribal customs and providing for special support for development of tribal areas.

While new political processes have produced new political arenas of negotiation and competition in both India and China, Kellee Tsai's comparative study (Chapter 10) shows that the main sources of finance for economic development in the villages are still located in the informal network of moneylenders in both countries. Her paper is a valuable contribution to the debate on the centrality of microcredit in rural development. She argues that microfinance is not a substitute for informal finance tied to local hierarchies that manipulate markets and resources for investment. In view of the much-publicised campaign for self help groups (SHGs) where women seemed to have made gains in many parts of India, Tsai's argument has a special significance. The rural poor need much more than microfinance to enjoy their right to decent livelihood and dignity.

Fei-Ling Wang (Chapter 11) provides the social context for political and economic initiatives in China and India, respectively. In this comparative study of the role of social institutions, and especially of stratification systems or 'institutional exclusion', in the author's terms, he shows how socio-economic processes constrain equitable economic development in India and China. The difficulties with population mobility due to the *hukou* household registration system in China and the pervasive caste system in India have affected the nature and pace of industrialisation and urbanisation in both these countries. In India, the process of socio-economic development has been less successful in comparison because of the sharp division between the rich and the poor, a division that the traditional caste system has served to buttress. Grass-roots democracy cannot succeed until such exclusionary processes are not addressed.

The gender dimensions of development are the subjects of Bidyut Mohanty's paper (Chapter 12). She gives special attention to the role of the state in recent years in improving the life conditions of women by involving a 'critical mass' of women in local governance. This was done by statutorily ensuring at least one-third representation for them in local bodies. She points out the positive impact of having women representatives in the rural panchayats of India, an effect of the Seventy-third Constitutional Amendment, and explores the need for such gender sensitive legislation in China. It is especially needed because the overall status and achievements of women have been adversely affected by the market reforms, despite the many gains that Chinese women experienced after 1949. She considers the SHGs a positive programme of the panchayats in making some productive capital available to women in the villages. Despite the phenomenon of 'proxy women' (that is, women acting as proxy for their men) or the persistence of illiteracy and ignorance, recent initiatives have resulted in increased awareness among women, besides enhancing life expectancy and female literacy. We see the evidence of this process in several case studies from India and China.

M. Vanamala's study (Chapter 13) of a village in Andhra Pradesh, on the other hand, brings out the deficiencies in the SHG programme. She throws light on the loopholes in local development programmes such as the SHGs that are mainly due to certain socio-economic factors. The absence of such factors in China, such as a caste system, basic livelihood insecurities and distress migration have led to successful rural industrialisation and improvement of general living standards. She argues that there is greater gender injustice in India compared to China, which is evident in the increased levels of family violence, prostitution and dowry demands. The relative assessment of status of women in India and China as well as the net effects of reforms on women continue to be subjects of debate.

David Zweig and Chung Siu Fung (Chapter 14) focus on the relationship between democracy and economic development in rural China. They explore the nature of democracy in China's villages in order to discover the extent to which elections are truly democratic and the extent to which democratic procedures have been institutionalised. Asking whether ordinary villagers view electoral reforms as necessary or as something manipulated by Communist Party members, they shed new light on the role of local elites in the democratic process in rural China. Based on a survey of two provinces—Heilongjiang and Anhui—their chapter shows that with the advent of political reforms, village elections are becoming more competitive and institutionalised with more and more multi-candidate elections and a higher turn out of voters, indicating a growing degree of acceptance of the legitimacy of the election process by the rural masses. However, with respect to the question of the relationship between economic development and democracy, they observe that party cadres in China's richer villages tend to be less democratic than their counterparts in low and middle-income villages. Finally, their chapter visualises the need for the formation of a non-party elite at the village level to counter the centralism of the Communist Party.

Such a competitive process is already in operation in India but with many gaps in practice. G. Haragopal and G. Sudarshanam's study (Chapter 15) of panchayati raj in Andhra Pradesh looks at the 'unfinished' process of democratisation in India, which has led to many gaps between the promise of grassroots democracy and the actual performance of community development programmes. They examine the implementation of the Seventy-third Constitutional Amendment in Andhra Pradesh by focusing on the structure and functions of panchayati raj bodies, such as the *gram sabha, gram panchayat, mandal parishad* and *zilla parishad*; and describe changing trends in local society due to the workings of these bodies. They confirm increased political awareness among women, SCs and STs, and among the masses in general about their own rights vis-à-vis government institutions and political leaders. This new level of awareness is due to the statutory representation of weaker sections of society in local bodies. Yet, much of the older negative trends persist, such as powerful caste–class pressures, centralised elements of state power and greater dependence by the state on coercive instruments to suppress peasant uprisings and other forms of mass protest. In this connection, they note that institutions of local governance have existed in many traditional societies, often based on cultural norms that were inequitable.

Choice of the term 'panchayat' was criticised by B.R. Ambedkar on the grounds that it connoted the appointment of five males from the upper castes to decide the affairs of the village. But the Indian Constitution and laws have given the term the democratic meaning of villagers' self-governance—even though socio-political factors still inhibit their fuller realisation. In their view, such constraints do not seem to be so pervasive in China, ostensibly making the possibilities of participatory grass-roots governance greater there. However, new trends of class formation in China may have already created a local elite in China's countryside who is also trying to manipulate the emerging local institutions of grass-roots democracy.

But institutional initiatives and democratic consciousness display their own dynamic method of functioning in local culture and economies, as the case studies from China and India show. Shengmin Yang's case study (Chapter 16) of the Tashikuergan Tajik Autonomous County in Xinjiang, inhabited by the Tajiks, demonstrates how, among some peoples in China, the extended family, which is a traditional unit for maintaining social stability, functions even today in maintaining social order and in managing economic and political cooperation within the village. The influence of the family in major collective activities among the Tajiks is significant mainly due to the inhospitable terrain they inhabit and the environmental pressures they face on a daily basis. This greatly limits government intervention in everyday affairs, for government agencies can hardly provide the emotional anchorage needed for a strenuous lifestyle such as theirs.

Similarly, Shaoying He (Chapter 17) gives us an ethnographic study of the workings of the *kaxie* system, a traditional system of governance in Nanduan Village, populated by the Lahu ethnic people in the Lancan Autonomous County in Yunnan Province. He traces major changes in Lahu society since the mid-1980s, in an effort to ascertain whether (and in what ways) these changes have contributed to grass-roots democracy in China. The kaxie system, which is like a village council led by a kaxie or 'master of the village' (comparable to the 'pradhan' in north India), has been maintained over the ages and in recent times has been functioning, together with the village committee, as the lowest agency of administration under communist leadership in China. The kaxie members have traditional politico-religious functions and are elected by traditional rituals rather than being chosen by the modern voting procedures. They are paid in kind instead of being given an honorarium in cash. But in the modern context, there is mutual cooperation between the kaxie and the Communist Party functionaries at the local level and this, according to the author, has led to better relations between the state and the minority peoples of China. But the embedded tradition in the functioning of the kaxie system also shows that grass-roots democracy has a long way to go in such societies.

The Tibetan case studies, which look very familiar to observers of Indian society, show what a long distance the movement for grass-roots democracy has yet to cover. Tanzen Lhundup (Chapter 18) makes an attempt to understand the impact of social changes on the local governance institutions in Tibet through empirical analysis of villagers' self-government in three villages in Nedong County under Lhokha Prefecture and Drayab County under Chamdo Prefecture. Starting from the establishment of the Tibet Autonomous Region in 1956 and the subsequent move to involve peasants in local governance in 1959, there have been a number of political changes in Tibet. In conformity with the special treatment given to minority nationality areas in China, the people's commune system was belatedly introduced into Tibet in 1966, the township system in 1982 and the Organic Law in 1992. At present, while village committees are active in promoting economic development, they also play an important role in literacy, public works, conflict management and census-taking operations. However, the advanced age and low level of education of the committee members operate as constraints on effective local governance. Moreover, women have yet to acquire a political role in local governance in Tibet. The lack of adjustment between the local culture and conditions of Tibet with the system of villagers' self-government creates a major bottleneck. Yet, the author argues that the local governance structures have in recent years served increasingly to integrate Tibet with the People's Republic of China.

Changjiang Yu (Chapter 19) goes a step further in studying the interaction between party, state and culture in profiling the experience of one village outside Lhasa. In this regard, he looks at the functions and interactions of the three main forces operating at the grass-roots level in a Tibetan village in China, namely the local unit of the CPC, the village committee, which is the unit of administration at the village level and the Tibetan Buddhist monastery. He is especially concerned with the role of religion in maintaining the stability and continuity of the social ethos in the face of rapid developmental changes and argues for the necessity of coexistence of religion and the secular forces of party administration for healthy development. This is a kind of trinity of power, which has parallels in many parts of India as well. But there is no single pattern of power sharing that is common to any two countries. Indeed, to succeed in fulfilling the material, political and spiritual needs of people by enabling them to participate in the trilateral process of the party, the local government and monastery (or church or temple) have to evolve mechanisms of participation that take into account all dimensions of popular demand.

Right to Participate

These studies show the rich variety of local forms and developmental stages at which the movement for grass-roots democracy stands at this moment in time. The case studies from India and China may also mirror the broader global picture, as people in many societies are engaged in questioning and confronting systems of centralised power and authority. These experiences show that a new civil right that was always inherent in the concept of democracy is taking shape in the contemporary era, namely, the right to participate. Social movements in the second half of the twentieth-century challenged the centralised state both in liberal democratic systems and in established socialist regimes. That was when the idea of grass-roots democracy emerged as a virtually universal value. As democratic consciousness grew among all groups and respect for the dignity of individuals and groups became a shared value throughout the world, democracy continued to acquire new meaning. Decentralisation of power and self-governance at every level of society and polity became an essential part of democratic theory, facilitating the realisation of the creative potentiality of individuals and groups everywhere. The Indian experience reveals that while constitutional guarantees of the decentralisation of power were necessary for political participation, they were not adequate without requisite social and economic conditions at the grass-roots level. The Chinese experience proves that deferring political participation in the name of carrying out economic reconstruction to provide basic necessities and comforts at the local level can create serious socio-political inequities. Therefore, decentralisation has to be not only in the realm of political power but also in economic development. Both India and China inherited centralised state structures at the time of independence. Their rulers believed they could use the state apparatus as well as political agencies such as the Congress Party in India and the Communist Party in China to bring about economic development, social change and political consolidation of nationhood. That strategy led to many positive results. But half a century later, common people were asserting their right to be heard, their right to participate in affairs of the state and society. This was taking place when yet another powerful trend of centralisation was on the rise—the force of globalisation that sought to integrate the market worldwide. Those who controlled capital and communication technology on a global scale emerged as new elites with concentrated power. Globalisation redefined decentralisation as a top–down process which effectively fuelled the global market economy. Elites of India and China had joined this process of globalisation even as the bulk of their people were anxious to pursue their right to livelihood and dignity. In this situation, grass-roots democracy meant not only providing institutional guarantees for participatory decision making but also exercising choices in adopting appropriate strategies for equitable and sustainable development. The Indian case suggests that while doing so, there is a need for guaranteed institutional representation of deprived groups. The assured proportion of representatives of the SCs and STs and one-third for women is recognition of that need, although by itself this does not ensure the fulfillment of their rights. Thus, the experiences of India and China with grass-roots democracy in recent years present challenging questions for understanding the notion of the right to participate, as well as for understanding emergent trends in democratic theory in the twenty-first century. It is hoped that in their empirical richness and diversity, the various chapters in this volume will provide a useful source of empirical material on, and insight into, the possibilities of leading local governance into participatory democracy, if not gram swaraj.

Appendix 1
Local Structures in Contemporary India and China

India	China		
		Province	
State		Rural	Urban
District			
	County (*xian*)		City (*shi*)
Sub-division	....		District (*chu*)
Block/Taluka (panchayat samiti)	Township (*xiang*) (People's Commune till 1979)		Town (*zhen*)
Panchayat	Village (*cun*) (Production brigade till 1979)		Town (*zhen*) (Village level)
Ward	Work group (Production team till 1979)		

I

Institutional Structure and Local Participation

1 Local Government System in India and China
Learning from Each Other

GEORGE MATHEW

With the holding of the direct village elections, China has made definite strides towards what has been officially termed as socialist democracy. Today villagers' committees (hereafter VCs) have emerged as enduring organs of self-government in rural China. Nearly 80 per cent of the villages across China have elected their VCs through a democratic process in which more than 600 million rural voters have taken part. These elections, in the words of a senior official in the ministry of civil affairs, that covered 31 provinces, municipalities and autonomous regions, are a 'quiet revolution in the country side' which may not have received as much publicity as China's entry into the World Trade Organisation (WTO) or Beijing winning the bid for the 2008 Olympic Games (Wang Jinhua, 2002: 10).

India's passage of the Seventy-third Amendment making the panchayats (village councils) and municipalities constitutional bodies at the district level and below, was also acclaimed as a 'silent revolution'. This chapter briefly surveys the history of the VC in China and panchayats in India and looks into the critical issues specific, as well as common, to both the countries in the process of developing and strengthening local democracy.

The Origin and Development of Villagers' Committees in China

The VCs in China were originally provisional organisations of the rural communities. When they were formed in early 1981 in two Guangxi counties— Yishan and Luocheng—these committees comprised village elders, community-minded individuals and former cadres. In their formative stage, the VCs were sustained mainly through the voluntary spirit of the rural people and were neither acknowledged nor supported by the local authorities. According to Kevin J. O'Brien and Lianjiang Li, the term 'villagers' committee' initially appeared in Luocheng in spring 1981 (O'Brien and Lianjiang, 2000: 465).

The origin of the idea of village self-governing institutions and the way it was practiced in China in the early-1980s points to a unique rural political experience. This was truly an initiative from below that was later encouraged and legitimised by the government. In the beginning, the VCs were elected informally and their responsibilities were limited to amicably managing the social affairs of the natural villages. Villagers' committees at this stage, as observed by O'Brien and Lianjiang Li, were free-standing and relatively autonomous non-governmental bodies that did not take part in the allocation of state resources. The activities of the Guangxi VCs had later drawn the attention of the central leadership. The most impressed was Peng Zhen, the then vice-chairman of the National People's Congress Standing Committee. And in December 1982, owing mainly to Peng Zhen's suggestion, VCs were written into the Constitution as elected, mass organisations of self-government (Article 111). Later in 1983, a Central Committee instructed that the elected VCs should be set up in the rural areas. It further directed that they should actively promote public welfare and assist local governments, and cautioned that prevailing local conditions should guide the process of their implementation (*The Chinese Law and Government*, 1986–87: 36).

Until then the townships had been the basic units of government administration in the rural areas. They operated under county governments and each of them had jurisdiction over about a dozen villages. In 1958, the townships were replaced by people's communes, which in the process of collectivisation combined rural government administration and management of production as well as economic affairs. Henceforth each village became a 'production brigade' that was divided into several 'production teams'. Land, animals, farm machines and all other means of production became collective property. Commune members had to work round the year in their production teams for earning 'work points' that were recorded daily, on the basis of which they got a small income in cash and kind at the end of the year. Before this, Chinese families could own a piece of land to grow vegetables for their own consumption or for sale if there was a surplus. But during the 'Cultural Revolution', as Wang Jinhua comments, these so-called 'private plots' were seen as 'remnants of capitalism' and in many communes, were confiscated to 'uproot those material conditions that prevail against socialism' (Wang Jinhua, 2002: 10).

However, the 'household contract responsibility system', which was introduced later under Deng Xiaoping's reforms, restored, in principle, farm land to individual households. It would be worthwhile to note here that this new system was initially created by a group of 'commune members' in a poverty-stricken village in Fengyang County of Anhui Province. Reduced to impoverishment, members of 18 families sought to escape their difficult life situation by breaking away from the commune system. Subsequently, they voluntarily came together to be part of a new system by putting their fingerprints on a written pledge to that effect. This document has now been kept in the Museum of Chinese History as a vivid testimony to the local initiative from below for change.

As the people's communes collapsed owing to enormous social pressure and a compelling need for economic management, the question that was raised involved the agency that would eventually take charge of the village's public affairs. Public affairs cover a range of issues from irrigation to a credible mechanism for settlement of disputes between families and individuals.

In this context, it would be relevant to mention the Hezhai experiment to throw more light on the origin of the VCs. The Hezhai 'production brigade' in Hezhai Village in Guangxi's Yishan County had six 'production teams', with a total of 85 households. At the initiative of Wei Huanneng, the leader of a 'production team', the villagers tried to set up a body that could manage the local affairs in the wake of the power vacuum created by the collapse of the commune. Acting upon this idea, they elected a group of village leaders through a secret ballot and this group was designated as the 'Hezhai Villagers' Committee'. According to Wei Huanneng, 'The committee was founded on the free will of the villagers . . . and it serves the needs of the villagers' (quoted by Wang Jinhua, 2002: 12). The Hezhai VC organised itself to build two bridges and a road. It also worked out a set of rules for the management of public affairs and the official copy of rules was signed by all as a pledge of their support.

Wei Huanneng and his fellow villagers were pioneers of a 'revolution' that was eventually to sweep entire rural China. It is reported that the local government got wind of what had happened in Hezhai Village and sent officials to investigate. Their findings were sent to China's highest authorities in the form of the Guangxi Report that impressed the central leadership, most notably Peng Zhen. With the inclusion of the VCs in the revised Constitution of the People's Republic of China, VCs became legal entities although their organisation and functions were clearly defined by a law. In November 1987, the Standing Committee of the National People's Congress adopted the Organic Law of the Villagers' Committees for trial implementation. This was the fundamental law for the grass-roots organisation in the countryside. By the end of 1987, VCs had been set up in 14,737 former 'production brigades' in the Guangxi Zhuang Autonomous Region, allowing autonomy to a total of 5.8 million former commune members.

As this discussion suggests, it was the disintegration of the communes and the production brigade that paved the way for village democracy in China. Later, the notification of the CPC in 1993 effectively struck down the village offices set up by the township government. By then, the central authorities had resolved to improve democracy along with economic reforms. That is to say, socialist democracy and economic reforms had gone hand in hand in the 1990s in China. The Organic Law on the Villagers' Committee approved by the Fifth Session of the Standing Committee of the Ninth People's Congress (4 November 1998) can be regarded as a milestone legislation. It defined

VCs as 'a self-governance organization at the grassroots level for villagers' self-management, self-education and self-service. Democratic election, decision making, management and monitoring are the principles of the villagers' committee'. Some important elements of the 1998 Organic Law are:

a) It is the village committee's responsibility to develop public services, manage public affairs, mediate civil disputes, help maintain social stability and report to the people's government villagers' opinions, requests and suggestions.
b) The rural grass-roots unit of Chinese Communist Party (CCP) should work under the Charter of CCP and play a core role in leadership. Under the guidance of the Constitution and other laws, the unit should also support and ensure villagers in developing self-governance activities and performing democratic duties.
c) The governments of township, minority township and town may guide, help and support village committees, but must not intervene in affairs that are in the purview of the village committee.
d) On the other hand, village committees should help the governments of township, minority township and towns in all ways of work.

The studies on the VCs in the last 10 years have shown that there are many important achievements to their credit. Today, VCs are chosen through direct multi-candidate elections although 70 per cent of them belong to the Communist Party. One cannot agree more with Robert A. Pastor and Qingshan Tan's report on the VCs accomplishments.[1] Unpopular incumbents have been voted out; officials have been frightened by the elections into improving their behaviour; ordinary people who never experienced democracy today participate in election meetings, they vote and even run for office. Yet, village democracy in China has a long way to go before VCs emerge as truly autonomous and lasting statutory bodies.

Institutions of Local Self-Government in India's Villages

Panchayats in the Post-Independence Period

In spite of its history, the nationalist movement's commitment to panchayats (village councils) and Gandhiji's unequivocal propagation of the ideal of village rule, the first draft of India's Constitution did not include a provision for panchayats.

The argument of those who pleaded for the inclusion of village panchayats in the Constitution finally prevailed only in a modest measure. A provision was included in the Directive Principles of State Policy of the Constitution, which is not mandatory.[2]

The Gandhians considered panchayats both a means as also an end and sincerely believed in their immense potential for democratic decentralisation, devolving power to the people. They had the basic conviction that village panchayats could play an important role in social transformation and in the implementation of development programmes. But the panchayats were not given the constitutional status and recognition they deserved, because of the disdain for panchayats among the urban and the rural elites and this has remained the same ever since. Whatever genuine attempts were made for the devolution of power, these interests saw to it that the attempts did not succeed. A break from this negative approach took place after about four decades. This was mainly because of the unrelenting pressure of peoples' quests for meaningful democracy at the grass-roots level, demands for people's involvement in development, decentralisation and devolution of funds, functions and functionaries from the centre (federal level) to the villages and towns.[3]

Need for Constitutional Support

It is well established that constitutional support and legislative measures are necessary for bringing about social change, but they are not a sufficient condition to achieve the goal. Our experience in the 55 years since independence bears witness to this fact. This is true of democratic decentralisation as well. Of course, one can argue that there was no constitutional support for local self-government below the state level till December 1992, and therefore, no state government took the process seriously.

Although state governments were not compelled to establish full-fledged panchayati raj without constitutional mandate, some states like West Bengal, Karnataka and Andhra Pradesh had gone ahead, as far as they could, in the devolution of powers to the panchayats. However, they had felt that concentration of power at the centre was working as a serious impediment. For instance, in 1985, Abdul Nazir Sab, the minister for panchayati raj and rural development in Karnataka under the Janata government, had stated that 'without a constitutional amendment guaranteeing the "Four Pillar State", our efforts may not be as fruitful as we desire' (Sab, 1986: 53). In 1985, he pleaded with intellectuals to ponder over this question and to initiate a public debate on the necessity of a constitutional amendment. There was a growing realisation that it was the lack of constitutional support that had led to the sad state of affairs in several states as far as local governance was concerned.

The Asoka Mehta Committee (1977) made the first official recommendation for including panchayati raj in the Constitution in keeping with its approach that panchayats should be regarded as political rather than mere developmental institutions. This Committee also favoured participation of political parties in panchayat elections with their symbols.

The panchayats that arose, post the recommendations of the Asoka Mehta Committee, gave more powers to the local bodies and their orientation was more political than developmental and therefore evoked widespread enthusiasm both in their implementation as well as their working. The remarkable enthusiasm among the ordinary people in West Bengal and Karnataka for panchayati raj strengthened the moves to incorporate constitutional provisions for it.

It may be mentioned here that in the mid-1980s, the idea of district government came into vogue.[4]

The Seventy-third Constitutional Amendment

It was against this backdrop that on 15 May 1989, the Constitution (Sixty-fourth Amendment) Bill was drafted and introduced in parliament. Although the 1989 Bill in itself was a welcome step, there was serious opposition to it on two basic grounds due to its political overtones. The objections were that (i) the bill overlooked the states and was seen as an instrument of the centre to have direct control over the panchayati raj institutions and (ii) it imposed a uniform pattern throughout the country instead of permitting individual states to legislate the details, keeping in mind the local circumstances. There was an outcry against this bill not only by political parties but also by intellectuals and concerned citizens.

Although the Sixty-fourth Amendment Bill got a two-thirds majority in the Lok Sabha (the lower house), it failed to meet the mandatory requirement by two votes in the Rajya Sabha (the upper house) on 15 October 1989. The National Front government introduced the Seventy-fourth Amendment Bill (a combined bill on panchayats and municipalities) on 7 September 1990 during its short tenure in office but it was never taken up for discussion.

By this time, all political parties through their statements and manifestos had supported a constitutional amendment for strengthening panchayats and a pro-panchayati raj climate was created in the country. In September 1991, the Congress government introduced the Seventy-second (Panchayats) and Seventy-third (Municipalities) constitutional amendment bills, which were referred to a joint select committee of the parliament. The Lok Sabha passed the two bills on 22 December 1992 while the Rajya Sabha passed them the next day.

They came into force as the Constitution (Seventy-third Amendment) Act 1992 on 24 April 1993 and Constitution (Seventy-fourth Amendment) Act 1992 on 1 June 1993 after ratification of more than half the state assemblies, assent by the president of India and their publication in the *Gazette of India*.

The main features of the amendments were:

a) Panchayats and municipalities were defined as 'institutions of self-government'.
b) Gram sabhas (village assemblies) comprising all the adult members registered as voters became basic units of the democratic system.
c) For all states with a population above 2 million, the panchayats would have a three-tier system at village, block/*taluk* (intermediate) and district levels and seats at all levels would be filled by direct election.
d) Seats and posts of chairpersons of the panchayats at all levels were to be reserved for SCs and STs in proportion to their population. One-third of these necessarily had to be women.
e) Not less than one-third of the total number of seats were to be reserved for women. One-third of offices of chairpersons at all levels were to be reserved for women.
f) The term of the local bodies was five-years and elections to constitute new bodies to be completed before the expiry of the term. In the event of dissolution, elections were to be held compulsorily within six months.
g) Each state would have an independent election commission for superintendence, direction and control of the electoral process and preparation of electoral rolls.
h) Panchayats were to prepare plans for economic development and social justice in respect of 29 subjects listed in Eleventh Schedule. A district planning committee was to consolidate the plans prepared by the panchayats and municipalities.
i) Funds were to include grants from state and central governments, revenue of certain taxes collected and retained and the revenue it raised.
j) A finance commission in each state was to determine the principles on the basis of which adequate financial resources would be ensured for panchayats and municipalities.

These amendments to the Constitution brought about a fundamental change not only in the realm of local self-government but also in India's federal character. This was succinctly put by Nirmal Mukarji:

> The amended Constitution requires the states to constitute panchayats as institutions of self-government not only for villages but also at intermediate and district levels. Consequently, there will, henceforth, be three strata of government: the union, the states and the panchayats. A more radical change is difficult to visualise. Its implications are far-reaching (Mukarji, 1993: 1807–12).

This journey from Lord Ripon's idea (1882) of 'local self-government' to the concept of 'institutions of self-government' as set forth in the Seventy-third Constitutional Amendment, took more than a century.

The Scenario after the Constitutional Amendment

For the panchayati raj institutions to function as institutions of self-government, the essential prerequisites are (i) clearly demarcated areas of jurisdiction; (ii) adequate power and authority commensurate with responsibilities; (iii) necessary human and financial resources to manage their affairs; and (iv) functional autonomy within the federal structure. Since the constitutional amendment opens up possibilities for fulfilling these conditions, the new panchayati raj was seen as the 'third tier of governance'.

The most fundamental change that has come about in Indian democratic polity is that the democratic base of the Indian polity has widened. Before the amendments, our democratic structure through elected representatives was restricted to the two houses of parliament, 28 state assemblies and two assemblies of union territories (Delhi and Pondicherry). And they had just 4,963 elected members.

Now there are 594 district panchayats, about 6,000 block/*tehsil*/mandal panchayats at the intermediate level and 250,000 gram (village) panchayats in rural India where about 70 per cent of India's population lives. Urban India, with about 30 per cent population, has 101 city corporations, 1,430 town municipalities and 2,009 *nagar* panchayats. Today, every five years, about 3 million representatives are elected by the people through the democratic process, out of whom more than 1 million are women. Women head about 200 district panchayats, more than 2,000 block/tehsil/mandal panchayats at the intermediate level and about 85,000 gram panchayats. Likewise, more than 30 city corporations and about 500 town municipalities have women chairpersons. A large number of hitherto excluded groups and communities are now included in the decision-making bodies. As SCs constitute 14.3 per cent and STs 8 per cent of the Indian population, about 700,000 elected members, that is nearly 23 per cent of the total membership of the rural and urban local bodies, will be from these two groups.

Another important aspect is that these amendments are bringing about significant changes in India's federalism. India is on the move to become a multilevel federation with elected local bodies at the district level and below. Of course, although there are several technical issues ahead and the elected local bodies have no legislative powers in the strict sense of the term and the Union and states constitute the de jure federal India, the qualitative change that has come about in the Indian federal structure has far reaching consequences making the local bodies the third tier of governance.

The initial 10-year period has not been altogether disappointing. Given the severe social and political constraints—social inequality, caste system, patriarchy, feudal setting, illiteracy, uneven developments—within which it had to function, there are several aspects one can be proud of.[5]

Today elections to the local self-government institutions every five years have become a norm although in the initial years almost all the states irrespective of the party in power had defied the constitutional provision with all the power at their command. As the civil society organisations took the initiative to fight the anti-constitutional approach of the states by filing public interest litigations (PILs), the judiciary at different levels effectively intervened.

State Finance Commission

By far the most novel provisions that brought the local government institutions in the scheme of fiscal federalism are the setting up of state finance commission (SFC) every five years in every state for reviewing the financial status of the panchayats/municipalities and for recommending measures to improve the same by restructuring, if necessary, the state-local fiscal relationship. In making these provisions, it was rightly assumed that the financial viability of the rural and urban local bodies cannot be ensured only by assigning tax, duties, tolls and fees, as by their nature they are less elastic and less buoyant. Transfer from the states' revenue as well as grants-in-aid would thus be necessary to supplement the finances of the PRIs and the municipalities. It is through such mechanism that the vertical imbalance (the mismatch between the revenue earning power and functional responsibilities of a unit of government) and horizontal imbalance (unequal development of areas falling under the jurisdiction of different governmental units) can be corrected in a federal polity (Institute of Social Sciences, 2001).

Almost all the SFCs by now have submitted their second reports. Andhra Pradesh, Tamil Nadu, Kerala and Rajasthan have constituted the third SFC. The reports of the SFCs have not been uniform in respect of their approach, coverage and methodology adopted for making recommendations. Some SFC reports such as those of West Bengal and Karnataka have been hailed because their approach, unmistakably, was towards creating institutions of self-government.

Whatever may be the omissions and commissions committed by the SFCs, their first reports have been successful in creating the concept of a divisible pool between the state and the local bodies, almost similar to the pattern of transfer of central revenue to the states. Some SFCs have identified innovative parameters for distribution of divisible pool funds among different local bodies in order to ensure horizontal equity.

However, in some states, the SFCs did not submit their reports in time; there was heterogeneity in the approach of different SFCs; the periods covered by the reports were not the same. Moreover, some states did not submit to the respective legislatures the report on action taken on the SFC recommendations even after the lapse of one year or more after the submission of the report.

Taking all these factors into consideration, the First Round Table of Ministers In-charge of Panchayati Raj held in Kolkata, 24–25 July 2004, had resolved that:

> A schedule, to be determined by each State Government/UT Administration, of the time-frames within which State Finance Commission should prepare their reports; for the submission of State Finance Commission recommendations, along with Action Taken Report (ATRs), to the Legislature; and for the executive to act on recommendations/ATRs endorsed by the State Legislature (Ministry of Panchayati Raj, 2004: 4).

District Planning Committee

Decentralised planning is also an essential activity of local governments in India as envisaged in the Seventy-third Constitutional Amendment. The district planning committee under Article 243ZD is mandatory 'to consolidate the plans prepared by the panchayats and the municipalities in the district and to prepare a draft plan for the district as a whole'. The draft plan so prepared will have to be forwarded to the state government, obviously for its consideration and approval.

A significant role that may be played by the DPC in the existing framework of the PRI–municipality system is one of rural–urban integration in the preparation of district plans. This institutional arrangement may work at the micro level of the village and town. But when it comes to the level of a district, the distinction disappears. A plan for the whole district has to combine both rural and urban areas. In the Indian context, the district is considered a meso level, but there are many districts in the country whose population may be more than 2 million. Planning technique applicable at the micro level of the village or small town may not suit the planning exercise for the whole district. Many functions that towns perform as seats of industry, trade and commerce, providers of services, higher education, communication, etc., have to be taken into consideration, even while a district plan aims at economic and social sector development of the rural areas. Similarly, planning for urban areas has to take into consideration the situation of the rural hinterland they serve.

The DPC is the only body in the decentralisation scheme of the Constitution where at least one-fifth of the total members can be nominated.

The manner of choosing the chairperson of the committee has been left to the state legislature. Several states ministers and not district panchayat presidents head the DPCs. In fact, as many as six states (Gujarat, Madhya Pradesh, Orissa, Maharashtra, Tripura and Uttar Pradesh) have nominated a minister to head the committee thus undermining the position of the elected members of PRIs and municipalities, including the chairpersons of zilla parishads. Nomination is a convenient tool that may be used by the state government for political expediency and to load the committee with political heavyweights to weaken the role and position of the zilla parishad. There is every possibility for DPCs to emerge as strong power centres outside the PRI–municipality system. The DPC has not been constituted in all the states. But where it has been constituted, there have been distortions. For instance, in Tamil Nadu, the law provided that the collector would be the chairperson of the DPC and the chairperson of the district panchayat would be its vice-chairperson. After protests were lodged against such a preposterous arrangement, the decision was reversed. Apart from Kerala, no state has fully-functional DPCs.

In this context the recommendations of the Round Table of Ministers In-charge of Panchayati Raj held in Mysore, 28–29 August 2004, attracts our attention. They include the following guidelines:

a) In every state, wherever DPCs do not already exist a district committee shall be constituted by the end of the current financial year and that all states must make provision, by law, for the functions relating to DPCs.

b) The district planning must take into account: (i) resource endowment of the area; (ii) felt needs of the people; (iii) relative absorptive capacity.

c) Village, intermediate and district panchayats must prepare the perspective five-year plan and annual plans for their respective jurisdiction. The same exercise should be undertaken in the municipalities of each district. The DPC should 'consolidate' the plans prepared by the panchayats and municipalities, rather than prepare the district plan of its own accord or of its own volition.

d) In order to fine-tune the plans prepared at different levels, as also to undertake the consolidation of plans in the DPC in a technically acceptable sense, state governments may specify institutions, organisations and individuals, who may assist the panchayats, municipalities and DPCs in preparing plans of a technically acceptable nature.

e) To facilitate such planning, the state government may indicate to each level of the panchayats and municipalities, 'the extent and type of available resources, whether financial or otherwise' (Ministry of Panchayati Raj, 2004: 7).

But very little has been done after adopting these resolutions to bring the DPC to the centre stage and make them vibrant institutions of local government. Nonetheless, the fact that constitutional bodies like the state election commission (SEC), state finance commission (SFC), etc., in all states are now firmly in place is in itself a great achievement. The SECs have taken up the panchayat elections seriously giving a lot of credibility to the grassroots level democratic process. In some states like Bihar, UP, Uttaranchal, Maharashtra and Gujarat, SECs have gone a step further. Taking the cue from the Supreme Court order of 3 May 2002 relating to the right to information of electors regarding criminal antecedents, assets and liabilities of the candidates, the state election commissioners have issued orders in conformity with the Supreme Court order. After all, the voters in the panchayats and municipalities also have a right to information about the candidates.

The last 10 years have also witnessed a steady progress as far as the inclusion of excluded sections of our population in the decision-making process from the village to the district levels are concerned. Women have got the maximum mileage. Today more than 1 million women are elected to these bodies every five years and more than three times that number are contesting elections. This is no mean achievement in a hierarchical and male-dominated society like ours. The common refrain that it is the menfolk in the families who control the women elected members may be partly true but studies show that the situation is rapidly changing. One-third of all panchayats and municipalities at various levels have women presidents. As years go by, the number of women getting elected from general constituencies is also increasing. The SCs and STs are also securing their due share in the local bodies.

As local self-government bodies have come into existence throughout the country their functioning has come under scrutiny. A congenial climate for taking governance to the doorsteps of the people is slowly being created. A major achievement of this process is that patronage and clienteles are slowly shifting from traditional castes and families to political parties and ideologies.

Many states, taking advantage of the prevailing situation, have gone in for innovative and creative experiments in local governance, planning and rural development. The People's Plan Campaign (PPC) in Kerala is an illustrative case in point. However, the balance sheet at the end of 10 years is rather bleak. It is an irony of sorts that the very hands that created the new panchayats and municipalities are now trying to render them dysfunctional, if not kill them. As a result, in many parts of the country the silent revolution has turned into a 'bloody' revolution (Mathew, 2001).

Neither MPs nor MLAs are giving the panchayats and municipalities their due. In fact, the MPs and MLAs are trying to appropriate the local self-government institutions' legitimate space. The MPs Local Area Development Schemes (MPLADS) and the MLA's funds running into millions is a betrayal of the local bodies. After creating panchayats to prepare plans and to implement the schemes for economic development and social justice, why should the MPs and MLAs get millions of rupees from the exchequer for local area development? Definitely, it is aimed at marginalising and debilitating these constitutional bodies.

Another glaring case is the eagerness on the part of MPs, MLAs and the bureaucracy to spend outside the panchayats all centrally-sponsored schemes (CSS) budget and to keep the district rural development agencies (DRDAs) alive and kicking. The task force on PRIs of the Planning Commission (December 2001) has observed that the state governments as well as central ministries have not taken any concrete step to integrate PRIs in their strategy or planning of the implementation of CSSs and the programmes are 'invariably implemented through vertical bureaucratic formations'. The political leaders and bureaucracy prefer it as it is 'materially' advantageous for them and their supporters. The plan outlay for 2000–2001 for the 29 subjects in the Eleventh Schedule under CSS has been to the tune of Rs 3,157.587 million. Rather than strengthening the panchayats they are pointing a finger at them saying: all is corrupt in the panchayat system. But the politician–bureaucrat clique forgets the fact that they have themselves created the role model for them. How can we create islands of honesty and integrity in the vast ocean of corruption and duplicity?

The chorus about the incompetence and inefficiency of the panchayats is trumpeted all the time. But what has been done to improve their efficiency? Practically none. Is it because of lack of funds? No. Not only do we have enough resources, but the multilateral and bilateral agencies too are ready to invest in the human capital development. But the central and state governments are least interested. Look at another area. We have the State Institute for Rural Development (SIRD) in each state that should have been centres of training and capacity building for the panchayat members and functionaries. But these SIRDs are the most neglected organisations, least equipped for this vital task.

The way the ministry of rural development handles the panchayati raj leaves much to be desired. When there is a critical need for a full division in the ministry to monitor and guide the quarter million gram panchayats, 6,000 panchayat samitis and 600 zilla panchayats there is no officer of a secretary's rank for panchayati raj, leave alone a joint secretary. Joint secretaries hold additional charge of this department. The turnover of officials in the ministry who had some responsibility for PRIs is amazing. The prime minister recently said that Article 243 must be further amended to make it sharp and effective in the light of the recommendations of the Justice Venkatacheliah Commission to review the Constitution. But no one who matters has taken it seriously. No state government is taking the SFC recommendations with the importance it deserves. At another level, the SECs, which are independent constitutional bodies, are working under severe limitations. The state governments try to twist their arms whether it is with regard to delimitation, declaring the election dates or other related issues. The DPC, which is a trailblazer in the planning history of India is either not in place or is constituted in name only. There is no panchayat cadre till today in the states nor has any step been initiated to develop one. Interdepartmental struggle is going on without any clarity or idea as to what the relationship between officers and staff of the line departments is to the elected local bodies.

One wonders whether the MPs and MLAs really understood the full meaning and its structural implications on the polity when they approved the two constitutional amendments. Now that they realise its full potential to give power to the people, taking away a lot which they had amassed since independence, every attempt is made to thwart the process of panchayats from blossoming into 'institutions of self-government' and the de facto third tier of governance.

Ten years is a short journey. The panchayats have not worked wonders but a small beginning has been made. This, despite the efforts of the MPs and MLAs who have worked overtime to undermine them.

Common Issues for India and China

The Pull of Centralisation

Both in China and India, centralisation of authority has been a deep-rooted political tendency whose historical origin can be traced back to the process of state formation in both the countries. In China, it appears that the party and government officials had got used to the old system of top–down 'vertical leadership' or commandism from above. Because of this, the officials take VCs suggestions with a grain of salt. When the 'production brigades' were gone along with the people's communes, the party and officials were concerned about the 'power vacuum' in the system of government administration in the countryside. They looked with skepticism at the form of self-government exercised by the rural population. Their prediction was that it would give rise to anarchism. If the people were able to manage their own affairs, what would become of the township governments?

This view which was so prevalent among the party cadres, prompted governments in the Guangxi Zhuang Autonomous Region to install the so-called 'village offices'—agencies of township governments, presumably to 'streamline' rural government administration and prevent a possible rise of 'anarchism' in the countryside. But VCs had already been in place and were legalised under the Constitution. To bypass this 'legal barrier', governments allowed VCs to exist only at the 'production team' level.

Ironically, Guangxi, home to the country's first VC, turned out to be the first to install 'village offices' to replace VCs. Government authorities in other parts of China followed suit and, for a time, VCs seemed in danger of coming to an end. But in 1993, the central authorities intervened decisively with a central committee directive to township governments across the country not to set up 'village offices'. In its document No. 7 circulated for the year, the highest party authority decided that 'village offices' run counter to desire of the rural population for self-government, on the grounds that more often than not, they intervened in matters that should have been handled by villagers themselves. Besides, the financial burden on the rural people grew wherever 'village offices' were set up.

In response to the call of the party central committee, work began throughout the Chinese countryside to disband 'village offices' while helping people to restore or set up VCs. Guangxi was again ahead of the entire country in accomplishing the task and had disbanded all the 'village offices' by the end of 1995. The neighbouring Yunnan Province was the last to do so. The last batch of 'village offices' ended there in the first half of 2001.

All the doubts and suspicion of the party and government officials about local self-government in China are applicable to India also. Vertical authority through line departments is the reality in India too. But decisive intervention by the central government, as it happened in China, is lacking in India. Centralisation is convenient for politicians and the bureaucracy; it is the preferred mechanism for them to govern rather than to encourage decentralisation.

Violence

In the recent past, various studies on the elections in China has brought to light the instances of abuse of power, criminal activities and violence in some localities, perpetuated by rich villagers or clans, party cadres, village leaders and entrepreneurs. It is natural that social conflict would take place when power is transferred from one centre to another through elections (see Gamer and Shou, 2000; Gray, 2000).

Amy E. Gadsden in a study on 'Grassroots Elections, Grassroots Challenges' has argued that eight provinces, where instances of social contradictions had been reported between clans or factional groups, were formed of failed elections and/or the breakdown of village government. The clan problem is rarely discussed in detail. Most provinces simply refer to the 'disturbing' (*ganrao*) influence of clans and family groups. In one Shaanxi village, a minority clan within one village collectively protested the outcome of an election, organising more than 40 people to go to the county office to register complaints. Elections exacerbate the accumulated grievances that exist between clans or factions, resulting in violence and injuries (Gadsden, 2000).

In India, in spite of more than half a century of active democratic process at all levels, violence during and after the elections are common. In the six-phase panchayat elections held from 11 April to 30 April 2001 in the state of Bihar, 96 persons, including a magistrate and several candidates lost their lives. Bloodshed, dishonouring women, torturing lower caste people, abusing the posts held by poor and weaker sections are common in the panchayats and even in town municipalities. The author's study of the state of Madhya Pradesh in north India, is an example of this continuing problem in India (Mathew and Nayak, 1996, also see Mathew, 2001).

Corruption

The question of corruption in China at the village level was rather puzzling. During my visit to Shanyong and Lioning provinces in 1992 and 1993 to repeated questions regarding checks and balances to curb the possibilities of corruption and nepotism, the standard answer was that there was no corruption. At that time, the chances of corruption had been minimal because of the regimented economic control but it cannot be said with certainty that that is the case now or will be the case in the future after liberalisation. Party leadership at the local level becoming a source of corruption through contracts and the market economy is a reality that cannot be ruled out.

After 10 years, when I visited Beizhuangtou Village, Liqio Town, Shunyi County in early November 2002, a farmer, Guan Rong stated that corruption is a major issue. Anybody who wanted to get land on rent for cultivation had to pay bribes at different levels, which included money as well as wine.[6] Corruption was a major concern in the just concluded 16th National Congress of the Communist Party too.

In India, corruption at the local self-government level is of utmost concern. Some describe this as decentralisation of corruption. The unholy nexus of politician–official–contractor is the main cause for the perpetuation of corruption. It is important to note that in India several mechanisms are in place both from the side of the government and through people's initiative to check corruption at the panchayat and municipal levels. However, corruption is systemic and it cannot be dealt with segmentally.

Women's Participation

In China, there is no reservation for women in elected bodies. In the VCs, there are just one or two women representatives and in most cases they appear to be more of a goodwill gesture towards them than a guarantee of women's rights in local power sharing. I did not come across a single woman chair-person of a VC during my visits to China in 1992 and 1993, whereas during my third visit in 2002 to Beizhuangtou Village, a woman chairperson received me. But as in India, individual cases of women reaching positions of power are not rare. The vice-chairperson of the standing committee of Lioning Province in 1993 was Chen Suzhi. She was an outstanding leader in her sixties. Chen Suzhi was formerly a governor of the province. In the reception hosted by her we were told that Suzhi began her career in a machine factory and in 1977 became part of the provincial government as the official in-charge of industry and transportation.

It is generally felt that there is a gulf between theory and practice in the matter of women's equality. In the elections, at some levels, there is only one vote for the household in China and it goes without saying that this vote is exercised by a male member of the household. In most VCs, the woman members handles women's welfare, family planning and allied subjects. At the same time it must be said to the credit of these few women representatives in the committees that they are articulate, bold and have a lot of leadership qualities. They read more than one newspaper, magazine or weekly, and are aware of the developments in their township, county, province and the nation. Women's literacy in China, unlike India, is on par with that of men. Most of them have read up to the sixth or seventh class. Commendable efforts have been made by the All China Women's Federation (ACWF) and motivated individuals to change the prevailing situation against women's involvement in community and governance. In Qianxi County, Hebei Province, the leader of the local women's federation has actively sought to increase women's representation in VCs through voter education and leadership training for women (Howell, 2002: 50).

According to a study by Jude Howell, in global terms China ranks relatively high on the scale with regard to female participation in politics and government with 21 per cent of National People's Congress deputies being women. Jude Howell uses the term 'state derived feminism' for the practical strategies used to enhance women's status and participation in public life (Howell, 2002: 43–48).

The absence of women's participation in a sizeable number in the VCs is a major concern of many groups in China. These groups as well as senior government officials I interacted with pointed out the achievements that India could record in this connection.

In India, the compulsory one-third reservation of seats for women has opened up many possibilities. There are many success stories of several women getting elected from unreserved seats; in several states more than one-third seats in the panchayats have gone to women. The day is not far when this will be the case in the state assemblies and the parliament. India is heading for a 50 : 50 male to female proportion in elected bodies tomorrow, if not today.

Democratic Norms

An ideal democratic election must have four steps: an open nominating process; opportunity to share views with the public through campaigning; secret voting; ballots and counting must be strictly monitored. Robert E. Gamer and Huisheng Shou in a study of local elections have concluded that 'most village elections allow for one or two of these steps. Some allow all four. But in every reported case, the party at some level retains some control over the outcome of elections' (Gamer and Shou, 2000: 57).

Although India with its long history of democratic election observes all the norms, booth capturing, manipulations, etc., have not totally disappeared. In fact, some states are very vulnerable in this respect. However, the election commissions at the centre and states, the multi-party system and an increasing political and democratic awareness put a brake to these tendencies.

One thing stands out. The basic level of democracy, with which China is struggling, will have a far-reaching consequence for the Chinese democratic structure. It may even go beyond everybody's expectations and even those of the party leadership. Both China and India have a lot to learn from each other be it in the field of local democracy, women's participation, economic development or in combating corruption.

Notes

1. My visit to Beizhuangtou Village, Liqio Town, Shunyi County, 50 km from Beijing, in early November 2002, was an eye opener. After the VCs came into existence through people's participation and private initiatives, the village has developed remarkably. Guan Rong is a farmer in this village. He grows vegetables and corn, rears fish, etc. He has taken land on rent for five years. He makes a profit of 100, 000 yuan per annum after paying rent and meeting other expenses. His wife has a shop in the town selling vegetables and sweets. His 21-year-old son studies in a boarding school. He, like the other 200 village families, has a well-built spacious house.

   Guan Rong took me to the VC office. All three members in the committee are party members. The chairperson is a woman, Mei Gui Fang, a well-disciplined party member for the last 20 years. She got elected in the 2001 VC elections. Fang was courteous but refused to engage in a discussion with me about the working of the VC because I had no written permission from the central party or the government.

   The VC office, almost like a panchayat house in Indian villages, exists alongside the party office and the public announcement room. The entire complex had only one picture —that of Mao Zedong in black and white. The village has small industries. But what attracted me most was the school, which has 17 students in the age group of 3–6 years. Incidentally, the village population is about 600; the one-child norm is strictly observed. I presumed that the VC managed the school. But it turned out that it was a private initiative. A lady, Liu Yang Rong, who runs it, said she charges an annual fee of 500 yuan (Rs 2500) per student. Her husband runs a paint manufacturing unit near the village. She voted in the last VC elections and in her opinion VCs do a lot of good things but they commit mistakes too.

2. Article 40 reads: 'The state should take steps to organise village panchayats and endow them with such power and authority as may be necessary to enable them to function as units of self-government.' There is another place in the Constitution where 'local government' is mentioned. Schedule Seven, List II (State List) item 5 reads: 'Local government, that is to say, the constitution and powers of municipal corporations, improvement trusts, district boards, mining settlement authorities and other local authorities for the purpose of local self-government or village administration.' Obviously, this is a curious way of defining local government without giving due place to panchayats.

3. The central government and the state governments since the mid 1950s had been appointing high-powered committees to look into the working of the panchayats and recommend ways and means to improve their functioning. Mention may be made of the Balwant Ray Mehta Committee of 1957 and the Asoka Mehta Committee of 1977. The discussions and debates such measures generated led to the building up of a positive social climate for radical measures to establish local governments on a firm footing.

4. This was mainly because of the dissenting note of E.M.S. Namboodiripad, twice chief minister of the state of Kerala and the leader of the Communist Party (Marxist) to the Asoka Mehta Committee Report and the writings of Nirmal Mukarji on the subject during this period. In fact, it was Nirmal Mukarji who introduced for the first time the concept of 'district government'. The relative success of zilla parishads in West Bengal and Karnataka also gave the much-needed boost to the district government approach.

5. I have written on this in 'Ten Years On', *The Hindu*, 27 December 2002.

6. Several studies have shown that there is corruption in the local self-government system. For instance, see Gray (2000: 74).

References

Gadsden, Amy E. 2000. 'Grassroots Elections, Grassroots Challenges'. Paper presented at the international symposium on 'Villager Self-Government and Rural Social Development in China', p. 45, Beijing, 2–5 September 2000.

Gamer, Robert E. and Huisheng Shou. 2000. 'Township Elections and the Transformation of Local Power Structures'. Paper presented at the international symposium on 'Villager Self-Government and Rural Social Development in China', Beijing, 2–5 September 2000.

Gray, Robert Peter. 2000. 'Cadre Corruption, Village Elections and Chinese Soap Operas—The Communist Party's New Conception of Rural Citizenship'. Paper presented at the international symposium on 'Villager Self-Government and Rural Social Development in China', Beijing, 2–5 September 2000.

Howell, Jude. 2002. 'Women's Political Participation in China: Struggling to Hold Up Half the Sky', *Parliamentary Affairs*, p. 50. London: Hansard Society.

Institute of Social Sciences, 'Consultation Paper on the Working of the Constitutional Provisions (Part IX) for Decentralisation—Panchayats', New Delhi, 2001.

Mathew, George. 2001. 'Panchayati Raj and Human Rights'. International Council on Human Rights Policy: Geneva.

Mathew, George and Ramesh C. Nayak. 1996. 'Panchayats at Work: What it Means for the Oppressed', *Economic and Political Weekly*, 13 (27): 1765–71.

Ministry of Panchayati Raj, Government of India, 'A Compendium of Resolutions of the Seven Round Tables of Ministers-in-Charge of Panchayati Raj (July–December 2004)', p. 4.

Mukarji, Nirmal. 1993. 'The Third Stratum', *Economic and Political Weekly*, 28 (18): 1807–12.

O'Brien, Kevin J. and Lianjiang Li. 2000. 'Accommodating "Democracy" in a One-Party State: Introducing Village Elections in China', *The China Quarterly*, 162: 465.

Pastor, Robert and Qingshen Tan. 2001. 'The Meaning of China's Village Elections', in Larry Diamond and Ramon H. Myers. *Elections and Democracy in Greater China*. Oxford: Oxford University Press.

Sab, Abdul Nazir. 1986. 'Towards a Four Pillar State', in George Mathew (ed.), *Panchayati Raj from Karnataka Today: Its National Dimensions*, p. 53. New Delhi: Concept Publishing Company.

The Chinese Law and Government. 1986–87. 'Circular on Separating Government Administration and Commune Management and Setting up Township Government', Beijing: The CPC Central Committee and State Council, 19 (4): 36.

Wang Jinhua. 2002. 'Village Autonomy: A Quiet Revolution in Rural China', *Human Rights*. Beijing: China Society for Human Right Studies, 4: 10.

2 Dependency versus Autonomy

The Identity Crisis of India's Panchayats[1]

D. BANDYOPADHYAY, SAILA K. GHOSH AND
BUDDHADEB GHOSH

Local Government under British Rule

The Myth of Local Self-government in British India

The apologists of British rule in India generally aver that whatever might be the deficiencies of colonialism, it was the colonial government which had introduced several modern institutions on which the post-colonial state could rebuild itself. According to them, the local self-government institutions set up by the imperial government provide one such example, because it was that government, which, for the first time in India, created a forum for participation of people in the public sphere. Such a position is untenable. For, the local government institutions created by the imperial state were, no doubt, locally based, but they were far from self-governing units of administration. In fact, they had been instrumental in the crystallisation of a particular mindset and administrative system, which have stifled the possibility of the emergence of genuine local self-governing institutions based on democratic participation. Before we elaborate this point further, let us have a quick look at the various stages through which the so-called institutions of 'local self-government' had evolved during the British rule. We shall cite the specific case of Bengal, which then included the permanently settled areas of Bihar and Orissa.

Local Government in Bengal

The first step towards the introduction of local government in rural areas of Bengal was taken in 1870 by way of constituting a new type of village panchayat under the Bengal Village Chowkidari Act. The objective of this panchayat was to collect local tax for maintaining village *chowkidars* and had nothing else to do in respect of providing services at the local level. A full-fledged policy statement with regard to the setting up of local self-government units came in 1882 with a government resolution passed by Lord Ripon, the then viceroy of India. Ripon's resolution contained democratic principles with respect to the setting up of local government institutions and associating people in them to provide civic services. But when the Bengal Local Self-Government Act was passed in 1885, it had little correspondence with the lofty principles of the resolution. The Act envisaged the constitution of a district board at the top and union committees below for a group of villages. At the middle or subdivision level, there was the provision for setting up of local boards. The members of the district board were indirectly elected by the local boards. Members of the local boards and union committees were elected, but the electorate was very restricted. Provisions were made for accommodating government officials both in the district boards and the local boards. As a matter of fact, the real authority was exercised by them. The district magistrate was the chairman of the district board. The system continued till 1916 when the rules were changed for the appointment of non-officials as chairmen, on an 'experimental basis'. The local boards were made agencies of district boards with no autonomy of their own. In fact, the local boards were soon found to be redundant and they were abolished altogether in 1936.

In 1919, the Bengal Village Self-Government Act was passed. It contained provisions for the formation of elected union committees for a group of villages. They were called union boards. Members of the union boards were elected, but the electorate consisted of only ratepayers. Thus, only property owners had voting rights. Women as well as the poor were denied the right to vote. The functional jurisdiction of union boards was quite wide. Apart from civic functions, it included the responsibility of construction or maintenance of roads and ferries, establishment of primary schools and libraries and promotion of cottage industries. However, the resource base of union boards was very weak. Property tax was the main staple of the revenue of these bodies. In the impoverished agricultural economy of the villages, the scope of this tax was severely limited. There was no system of sharing provincial revenue with the local government institutions, as 'local taxation for local development' was the time-honoured principle of British rule. To top it all, salaries of chowkidars and *dafadars* were taken from the union board's revenue. Therefore, the boards suffered perpetually from lack of resources. Accordingly, they did not have the capacity to perform the developmental functions as stipulated in the Act. Besides, the boards had to function strictly under the control of the district bureaucracy, so that they did not cause any problem for the imperial rulers. Thus the union board was a far cry from any genuine initiative towards the introduction of self-government. The position of the municipalities in the urban areas was no better insofar as the representative character, autonomy and financial viability of these institutions were concerned.

The Motive of the Raj

A question may be raised as to why the British rulers took any interest at all in setting up these institutions. For a satisfactory answer, we need to understand the complexities of British rule in India and also, the time and context in which these institutions were started. Attempts to introduce local government institutions started soon after the annexation of India by the British Crown.

It was a time when the trauma of the uprisings of 1857 was still fresh in the minds of the colonial rulers. It was also the time when the business of governance passed almost in its entirety to the provincial governments. As the arm of the government stretched to the remotest parts of the countryside, the local communities lost whatever power they had in managing their own affairs, if not on a democratic basis, at least on the basis of some caste or communal norms.

It was at this historical juncture that the British invented a form of 'modern' local government for the country. There were several compulsions for this. The first and foremost was a fuller political and economic integration. Second, it was necessary to build a reliable information system extending right up to the villages, because even after 1857, there were sporadic peasant movements in different parts of India. The chowkidari panchayats, and later the union committees and union boards, made it possible for the state to penetrate deep into the countryside and simultaneously put in place a reliable information system. It is interesting to note that one of the obligatory functions of the union boards was to keep the district magistrate informed about the law and order situation of the villages. Similarly, the dafadars had to report to the officer-in-charge of the local police station on a regular basis. All these could be ensured without putting any additional burden on the state exchequer.

The local government institutions in the villages also helped the imperial government to recruit a new group of collaborators in the countryside apart from the erstwhile permanently settled zamindars. They came from the ranks of big intermediaries and the traders-cum-merchants-cum-moneylenders whose economic power had been increasing over time and increased further now because of the commercialisation of agriculture. These groups came to enjoy additional power and prestige by virtue of their position as elected representatives in different tiers of the newly introduced rural local government structure. By becoming a part of the imperial system of governance to which the local government institutions were integrated, their distance from the people was now complete. It is an irony that technically though, they were representatives of the citizenry, in reality, they were the new patrons in a crystallised network of patron–client relationship of which the imperialist rulers were the highest patron. They not only emerged as powerful but also as legitimate mediators of both public and private affairs of people in the countryside.

Colonised Local Government

It should also be noted that the period we are talking about was the period of full blown imperialist exploitation of India, when the Indian countryside was being opened up both as a source of commercial crops and raw materials on the one hand and as markets for British merchandise on the other.

For this, peace had to be maintained in the countryside. But it was also a period of imperial expansion outside India and imperialist wars in different parts of Asia. The finances for these were borne substantially by the Indian exchequer. These were in addition to other administrative expenses and the so-called 'home charges'. Against the continuously increasing demands the budgetary resources were limited and inflexible. Land revenue had already reached its highest point. The rates could be increased further only at the risk of upsetting the imperial apple cart. The customs, excise and other duties had also to be kept at a minimum level lest they adversely affected the British industrial and trading interests. But the public facilities and infrastructure had to be maintained and improved. The information-communication system had to be developed and maintained for administrative, commercial and military purposes.

Against these contradictory sets of demands, the local government provided a satisfactory solution. The purpose was never to democratise local governance. The new innovation helped the provincial governments to divest themselves of a few expenditure items, which were now transferred to the local government. Cess was levied on provincial taxes and the local governments were allowed to impose local taxes to cover such expenditure. But while the local government's powers extended all over the locality and over all the people living in the locality, the franchise was strictly restricted to the local magnates and their compatriots. It created a situation in which the traditionally entrenched rural elite could join forces with the newly emerging economically-powerful sections in the countryside—the merchants, money-lenders and the *jotedars*—and further consolidate their position in the rural society through the new local government platforms and also through their intimate nexus with the imperial rulers. These sections began to get liberal support and patronage from the district administration. As a consequence, the stranglehold of the high and mighty in the countryside became far more oppressive. The system, in fact, consolidated the bureaucratic rule of colonial government even further. To flaunt these institutions as precursors of modern rural self-government in India is a travesty of truth. That apart, they created a system and conditioned the thinking of local governance in such a manner that they continue to thwart local democracy in India even after independence.

It needs to be noted that the institutional framework of local government introduced in India by the British Raj was not the outcome of an orthogenetic process. It was imposed from above. As a consequence, these institutions remained loosely grafted to the indigenous rural society. They did not have any linkage whatsoever with the existing social institutions and community-based organisations. They were, indeed, looked at with an eye of suspicion by the local people. A colonial government can integrate the colonised people and their institutions only bureaucratically. And that is what they did. The key words of such an arrangement are control and subjugation, as people are considered 'subjects' and not 'citizens'. The institution of rural local self-government bred within such a framework, therefore, did not have either autonomy or a representative character. As such, they remained distant from the people and created little enthusiasm among them. The people never considered these institutions as their own, which, if not totally unnecessary, were, in substance, extrinsic to their life process. The old community based self-governing institutions and the newly created and superimposed bodies of local government failed to develop any creative relationship.

This tradition of viewing local government institutions as non-autonomous appendages of a higher level government and as superimposed bodies on an essentially bureaucratic local administration persists even after nearly six decades of independence.

Local Government in Independent India

Local Government in the Constitution

At the time of independence, the Indian rulers did not think it necessary to build new institutions or to reform the existing ones for governing the local. Hence, they could not develop an appropriate concept of local government that could be integrated with the governments at the national and state levels. The question as to whether democracy should be extended or not to the governance of the stratum below the 'state' was not considered at all. This explains why local governments received such shabby treatment in the original scheme of the constitution. In fact, it was equated with any 'local authority' as defined in the General Clauses Act (see entry 5 of List II of Seventh Schedule of the Constitution).

Those who gave us the original Constitution had retained an entrenched administrative system in the districts and at the levels below the district. There was also a strong pressure to retain the pre-independence system in independent India. The system was so deep-rooted in the elitist understanding that it seemed to be immutable, at least for the time being. On top of it, as already explained in the previous section, the local self-government institutions in the districts and in the villages had a weak foundation and were accustomed to serve under the surveillance of the local bureaucracy. The political leaders of the country found it difficult to think of an alternative system under which the representative institutions at the local level could take part in governance independently. Additionally, it should be remembered that the most important goal that the early political leaders of free India set for themselves was the task of building the nation. Hence, the uppermost concern in their minds was to maintain the unity and integrity of the country. This concern was so great that the Indian constitution retained a strong unitary bias, even though in form it created a federal structure. Where even the autonomy of the states was unreasonably curbed, the question of decentralisation at the local level did not arise.

The pressure to retain the existing system of district governance also came from other sources. Dr B.R. Ambedkar who represented the Dalits, strongly argued against the empowerment of village panchayats, as, according to him, the landed gentry of the upper castes would invariably dominate them and these institutions would be utilised for perpetuating the exploitation of the lower-caste people and the poor. It is an irony of history that Dr Ambedkar, who was one of the principal architects of the liberal democratic framework of the Indian Constitution, found himself in the company of those who did not find any incompatibility between bureaucratic district administration and democratic governance. Such was the complexity of the historical legacy left by the imperial rulers.

The Ideology of Panchayat Raj

By retaining the existing system of district administration, the Indian constitution makers ignored not only the political principles of liberal democracy from which they borrowed substantially in drafting the Constitution, but they also chose to turn a blind eye to the rich body of thought developed by Indian thinkers on the question of organising the polity of free India. There were two streams of thought that emphasised the need for decentralised and participatory governance. One was that of M.N. Roy, the philosopher-revolutionary, who developed an alternative model of a democratic framework for the country after rejecting the Westminster model of representative government. Roy noted that under the system of representative democracy as practised in the West, power gets concentrated in the hands of a few and most people, being reduced to 'atomised individuals', are deprived of any power to control the actions of the state. He felt strongly that 'to be real, democracy must be direct'. In the constitution he drafted for free India, Roy envisaged the creation of a network of 'local people's committees in villages, towns and cities' to discharge the local-level functions of government and to exercise control over the local bureaucracy.

Roy's ideas, however, remained confined within a very small group of his followers drawn from the urban intellectuals. But when Gandhiji developed his concept of gram swaraj based on the refreshingly new meaning he gave to the concepts of 'individual freedom' and 'democracy', it became difficult for the leaders of the Congress to ignore the call he gave to establish panchayat raj. Not that they subscribed to the idea, but they did not oppose it publicly, given the moral influence Gandhiji exerted on the minds of the people.

Gandhiji's panchayat raj effectively meant self-rule of the village community, leaving minimal functions to the governments of the provinces and the centre. There was a strong anarchic element in Gandhiji's conceptualisation of organising the Indian polity based on communitarian principles where power does not flow from the top to bottom, but travels from the village communities to the districts, and then upwards to the provinces and the centre.

Response of the Political Elite and its Effect

Gandhiji's gram swaraj was too radical for the constitution makers to accept as a guide for practical policy. Even the ideas of M.N. Roy did not create any impact upon them. Their minds, as mentioned, were working in a different trajectory. Hence, in the battle between the ideology of panchayat raj and the forces of the entrenched system of district administration, the political elites sided with the latter. This led to a situation where the country had a democratic form of governance at the national and state levels and bureaucratic governance at the district and sub-district levels. This contradiction between democracy at the top and bureaucracy at the bottom created serious distortions in the functioning of Indian democracy.

First, the scope of enriching the practice of democracy through participation at the local level of governance was stifled because bureaucracy was not made accountable to the local people. A wide chasm was also created between people and representative governments at the higher levels. As such, the MLAs/ MPs slipped into the role of linkmen between people and the governmental machinery. They began to neglect their constitutional role as legislators and started devoting more energy in meddling with local administration. The unintended consequence of this was the emergence of groups of people at the local level whom Rajiv Gandhi termed the 'power brokers' who drew their strength from the MLAs/MPs and the parties they represented. They played the role of middlemen to reach the state's benefits meant for the masses. It was a situation where an ordinary villager could not approach the state, represented by the most proximate district administration, as an empowered and autonomous individual, but needed a patron to intervene on his behalf. Thus appeared on the scene the spectacle of political clientelism, which is being reinforced continuously.

Second, the Indian state after independence emerged as a developmental state. It made many interventions for social and economic development and also entered in an unprecedented manner in the production of public goods and services. There was no dearth of well-meaning schemes for the villages. But those were conceived at the top and implemented by the local bureaucracy with no accountability to the people. People were only at the receiving end. They had no say in determining what should be done for their development or how the fruits of development programmes should be distributed or even how they should be monitored. The system created a situation in which at the cutting-edge level, administration appeared to the people as unresponsive and unsympathetic, signifying continuity of the colonial tradition.

Politics of Panchayati Raj

Even though Gandhiji's vision of organising the Indian polity was not shared by the political elite, several attempts were made to make the institution of panchayat functional. However, none of these attempts was directed to correct the distortions in the functioning of Indian democracy. The motives were different and the panchayati raj institutions continued to be superimposed upon the existing bureaucratic local administration.

As is well known, the first major attempt to institutionalise panchayats came from the report of the Balawant Rai Mehta study team (1957). Its terms of reference had nothing to do with the question of rural local government. Its brief was to assess the performance of the community development programme of India and to suggest measures for improvement. But the Mehta team found that the programme of community development could not succeed unless people rallied behind it. Panchayats, which were representative institutions of the local people, would be in a better position, the committee thought, to generate people's support for the programme. This realisation prompted them to suggest a three-tier panchayat system for the country.

The point to be noted here is that the basic motive for the support given to the panchayats was to enlist in a very limited way people's participation in a programme conceived and directed by the central government. Legitimising a central government-led development programme was the hidden agenda behind the move. In the process, if the rural local government institutions were even slightly empowered, then the limits of their operations were to be determined by the requirements of the programme. It is not, therefore, surprising that of the three tiers of panchayat, the Mehta team made the intermediate tier, namely the block panchayat most powerful, marginalising both the gram panchayat and the zilla parishad, because it was the block that was the focal point of community development programme. It is also worthwhile to note that the necessity of a central programme of rural development led to the earmarking of a geographical space for making a new administrative unit to implement the programme. In the interest of the programme again, this newly-created administrative unit, namely the block, was converted into the boundary of one of the tiers of the rural local government structure. Thus, even the definition of 'local' was determined by a bureaucratic fiat and was not left to the 'imagination' of the community. Even though Nehru termed Balawant Ray Mehta's three-tier panchayats as panchayati raj or governance by the self-governing institutions, the whole attempt appears to be manipulative in nature, its main purpose being to legitimise the programme of a centralised developmental state. There was no attempt to replace the bureaucratic administration by democratic governance at the bottom level even for development purpose.

The forces in favour of centralisation of political power were so strong that even the little concessions given to these first generation panchayats were not tolerated for long. The system collapsed in almost all the states, except Maharashtra and Gujarat, soon after Nehru's death in 1964. The idea of panchayati raj was once again revived following the report of another Government of India committee headed by Asoka Mehta. Incidentally, this committee was the first panel consisting of many eminent persons to examine exclusively the question of institutionalisation of panchayats. Two interesting points require to be noted here.

First, the committee was set up by the first non-Congress government at the centre. The coalition of several opposition parties, which came to power, had promised to pursue some populist ideas. Decentralisation and extension of local democracy formed part of them. But they did precious little to achieve this goal except appointing a committee for panchayats. Second, only three states, namely West Bengal, Andhra Pradesh and Karnataka, accepted the recommendations of the committee seriously and established and empowered the panchayati raj institutions. In West Bengal and Andhra Pradesh, where regional opposition parties had just come to power after dislodging a long rule of the Congress, there was a definite political design to create power centres at the local level. For West Bengal, panchayats became a convenient means to extend the influence of the left parties in power. Besides, they were under the constant threat of being overthrown by the central government. The left parties thought that by capturing the rural local government institutions they would be in a better position to initiate a political struggle against any arbitrary use of constitutional power under Article 356 by the central government. In Andhra Pradesh, similarly, N.T. Rama Rao, who won the election on the strength of his charisma, was in urgent need of consolidating the influence of his party in the countryside. Panchayats were useful institutions for the purpose. In none of these states, was there an agenda of decentralisation of governance by allowing the panchayats to develop into powerful and *autonomous* institutions of self-government.

Only in Karnataka, it seems, there was a genuine attempt to build autonomous local government institutions in the villages and in the districts. The state even came up with the idea of district government. However, the experiment was short lived, as the party, which launched this radical programme, was voted out of power and the new regime went back to the old system.

Constitutionalising Panchayats

In 1992, the most important development in the career of India's local government institutions took place when these were given constitutional status through constitutional amendments. The Seventy-third and the Seventy-fourth constitutional amendments declared the three-tier panchayati raj institutions and the municipalities respectively as institutions of self-government, implying their right to be treated as autonomous institutions. The amendments also made mandatory provisions to hold regular elections to these bodies and gave directions to the state legislatures to devolve powers and responsibility to them, so that they could discharge certain local level governmental functions in respect of development in an autonomous manner. Initiated by the then prime minister, Rajiv Gandhi, in the mid-1980s, these constitutional amendments marked the terminal point of a process. They reflect an attempt to initiate basic change in the administrative system at the district level and below, from a non-representative, autocratic and bureaucratic administration to a representative and responsive elected system of governance. Since such an idea was first mooted by Rajiv Gandhi and was placed before the conference of chief ministers by him for obtaining consensus, it would be appropriate to examine briefly the reasons that prompted him to suggest such a radical reform measure.

The manifest reason was of course his search for an efficient delivery system. Initially he thought that the outreach of the government's development programmes could be enhanced and the leakage or misuse of huge resources for rural development curbed if panchayats were put in place as supplementary to the existing administrative structure. Later, after he toured the entire country, met the local leaders and interacted with the district magistrates in several regional seminars, he gradually realised that the district administration needed a systemic change—a change from bureaucratic district administration to democratic governance at the district level and below.

When Rajiv Gandhi became prime minister, he was a greenhorn in the political arena, which is why he could take an independent view untrammelled by the compulsions of electoral politics and stridently advocate for local democracy. Had he been a die-hard politician within the Indian political system of clientelism, he probably would not have come up with such a radical reform proposal. However, it would be too simplistic to assume that his advocacy for local democracy was inspired only by his convictions. In converting his conviction into practical policy of the state, political exigencies probably also played a major role.

The 1970s and 1980s witnessed a series of movements in different parts of the country based on ethnic, religious or linguistic assertions of regional communities who had developed a feeling of alienation from the mainstream Indian politics. There were militant movements in the north-east and in Punjab. The demand for Gorkhaland was raised in the north of West Bengal and the tribal communities of Bihar were agitating for a separate state of Jharkhand. There were demands for separate states in central India and in the hilly region of Uttar Pradesh. It was becoming difficult for the state's enforcement machinery to resist these movements and disturbances. The Indian republic was under stress and it became clear that power had to be shared with local communities, as it was beyond the capacity of the centralised state machinery to ensure enforcement of its writ by coercive power alone. The autonomous local government institutions with sufficient power, responsibility and resources were considered to be a safety valve for preventing such separatist tendencies. The thinking of the political elite on the question of maintaining the unity and integrity of the country thus turned a full circle. At independence, centralisation was considered as a means of keeping the nation safe. In mid-1980s, the danger of such policy for India's multicultural society became apparent and a need was felt to share power with the communities at the grass-roots level.

Added to this, there were considerations of power politics. In the mid-1980s, the Congress was out of power in many major states, even though it was in power at the centre. The opposition parties, which held the state governments, were mounting pressure for more administrative and fiscal powers for the states. Their opposition to accept the centre's decisions affecting the states without obtaining consensus was causing sufficient irritation to the central government. The prime minister's position as the supreme leader of the nation was in danger, as many stalwarts among the state-based leaders were asserting their views forcefully on national issues. It is possible that panchayats were sought to be constitutionalised with the hope that the autonomous local self-government institutions would create similar problems for the ruling parties of the states, as these bodies also would claim devolution of powers and resources from the states. The objective, therefore, was to create alternative power centres within the states. In fact, this possibility cannot be ruled out for two reasons. First, even though Rajiv Gandhi and his party advocated decentralisation at the local level, nothing was done for devolving more powers to the states. Even such small steps as reducing the number of centrally-sponsored development schemes in the areas constitutionally reserved for the states were not taken. Second, the central government tried to establish direct linkages with the district collectors or the panchayati raj bodies bypassing the state governments for the implementation of centrally-sponsored development schemes. The agenda behind such unusual move was quite clear—empower the local government institutions and marginalise the states in order to establish the hegemony of the centre, as it would be impossible for the numerous grass-roots institutions of this vast country to challenge the central authority.

Whatever may be the motive, constitutionalisation of the panchayats and municipalities in 1992 undoubtedly happen to be the most important landmark in the history of local democracy in India.

The Position of Panchayats after the Seventy-third Constitutional Amendment

In Article 243D 'panchayat' has been defined as an institution of self-government. In Article 243G, direction has been given to the state legislatures to endow the panchayats with 'such powers and authority as may be necessary to enable them to function as institution of self government'. Article 40 also endorses the principle of endowing village panchayats with such 'powers and authority' as would be necessary to enable them to function as institutions of self-government.

Constitutionally the panchayat has not been conceived as an appendage of the state government functioning merely as its agent for implementing its policies and programmes. The panchayat is entitled to have adequate 'power and authority', so that it can function independently and without any outside interference. In fact, the Constitution has taken the position that the panchayat must have an exclusive set of functions and they would be enabled to discharge such functions autonomously. 'Power and authority' over such set of functions imply not only 'authority' to discharge such 'functions', but also power to access the administrative and financial resources to enable them to discharge those functions independently. If in Article 40, which is a part of the directive principles of state policy, this view of the panchayat is in the nature of a guiding principle that may or may not be accepted by the legislature, in Article 243G mandatory direction has been given to the state legislatures to treat panchayats as autonomous institutions. Not only this, the Constitution has also given these local government institutions the crucial mandate of preparation of plans for 'economic development and social justice'.

Thus the Seventy-third Constitutional Amendment envisages 'devolution' type of democratic decentralisation, and not the 'deconcentration' type of administrative decentralisation under which the superior body retains various types of control including the power of withdrawing the power and authority given to a lower body. Accordingly, some observers noted that with the Seventy-third Amendment, a 'third stratum of governance' at the local level had been institutionalised (see Mukarji, 1993).

However all the acts, excepting the one of Kerala, passed by the state legislatures to conform to the requirements of the constitutional amendments have chosen to deny the status of self-government to the panchayats. In fact, except the mandatory constitutional provisions, these panchayat acts of different states have nothing new to offer. Like before, they visualise panchayats as nothing more than a local authority, which will exercise such delegated power and authority as may be given to them by the state acts or rules or executive orders. Even such delegated power could only be exercised by panchayats, subject to the bureaucratic control of the state government. There is no attempt at devolution type of transfer of functions, functionaries and financial resources from the state government to the panchayats. True, every act gives lists of a wide range of functions to be performed by the panchayats. But no exclusive functional area for these bodies is carved out. They are merely 'permitted' to work within the functional domain of the state, subject to such conditions as the state government may deem fit to impose. Moreover, financial and administrative resources necessary to discharge such functions continue to remain with the state government and are not transferred to the panchayats. In the absence of these resources, the lists of functions that every panchayat act religiously provide remain sterile. Going against the spirit of the Constitution, the panchayats are used by the state governments only as their 'agencies' to implement some of their development or welfare schemes.

Thus, what is singularly absent in the state acts as well as in the policies of the states is the question of 'autonomy' of the panchayats, which is at the centre stage of conceptualisation of the institution in the Constitution. Only in the state of Kerala, has there been a genuine attempt to develop the institutions of self-government for local governance. In no other state is there any evidence of realisation of the fact that the panchayats of the Seventy-third Constitutional Amendment are qualitatively different from the rural local government institutions of all previous generations. Although the amendments hold the promise of replacing the system of bureaucratic local governance by autonomous and representative institutions of local government, this promise has not been fulfilled as the state governments refuse to share power and resources with the panchayats.

Identity Crisis

What then are the panchayats? Constitutionally they are institutions of self-government. In reality they are not. It is true that the state governments do not have unfettered right over these institutions, as they used to have previously. There are mandatory provisions in the Constitution as regards direct election to all the three tiers, obligation to conduct election every five years, reservation of seats and the positions of chairpersons in all the tiers for women and SC/ST communities, constitution of state election commission and state finance commissions, etc. But in respect of devolution of functions, the Constitution left the matter to the discretion of the state legislatures, the Eleventh Schedule being only in the nature of an indicative list of functions that could be transferred to these bodies. The states have taken advantage of this and have chosen to keep the 'powers and authority' of panchayats unaltered. The dependence of the rural local government institutions on the superior government, which was a characteristic feature of these bodies during the British rule, remained unchanged after independence and still continues to be substantially so even after the coming into force of the Seventy-third Constitutional Amendment. The Constitution gives them autonomy. But this is a *de jure* position. As far as *de facto* position is concerned, they are, at best, nothing more than an agency of the state governments. Thus the panchayats of India suffer from an *identity crisis*. This crisis of identity results from our colonial mindset of treating the local domain as a dependent domain not fit for self-rule. The clientelist political culture of the country derives its strength from such a mindset.

Subservience of Panchayats: A Historical Legacy

Being burdened with a historical tradition of subservience, the panchayats do not yet seem to have taken cognisance of the contradictions effectively. They have been brought up in a culture in which spontaneous local initiatives and demands have been viewed with an eye of suspicion by the political and administrative authority. This has created, over time, a dependency syndrome, which has inhibited even the formation of a local political will for more power and autonomy for local government.

It is necessary to remember that the panchayats did not come into existence out of a popular demand and through a popular movement. It was a 'gift' from the top, superimposed on a very powerful and historically-structured system of bureaucratic, non-accountable, non-responsive and autocratic district administration. In the colonial days, the district officer, variously known as the collector, the district magistrate or deputy commissioner, represented the imperial crown. He was, and even now is, in the minds of the common people, a *'chota raja'*—a prince. The populace of the district had no other option but to consider themselves as subjects vis-à-vis the 'prince'. Thus a relationship of the 'ruler' and the 'ruled', the 'overlord' and the 'subject', the 'patron' and the 'client' came to be structured over time. This has been so ingrained in the popular mind in the rural areas that the concept of panchayats as autonomous institutions of self-government failed to take roots in their minds. The situation did not change much after independence, because rather than promoting a democratic culture, the elected representatives have preferred to project their image as a new set of magnates to the electorate they represent who can mediate between the state machinery and people both officially and unofficially. Thus instead of one, two sets of patrons emerged. Their goal is to perpetuate the traditional system of 'willing subjugation' of the common people to the established authority and, if possible, to reinforce it continuously. There is thus a systematic subversion of the panchayats both overtly and covertly by the bureaucracy and the MPs and MLAs who feel threatened by the emerging leadership of the three-tier panchayat system.

The bureaucracy, particularly at the local level, accustomed to overlord, resents the prospect of being lorded over by the elected panchayat personnel. The reins of power and authority are still held by it. It is not answerable to the people it serves, but to the department of which it is a part. It manipulates the panchayats as per their needs and skillfully subverts them.

The MPs and MLAs also, through a misrepresentation of their roles, often stand in the way of the proper functioning of panchayats. In the absence of powerful elected institutions of self-government, they try to establish their claim as superior if not the sole representatives of the genuine demands of people, thereby endeavouring to firmly entrench themselves between a 'giver state' and a 'receiver electorate'. As ministers also, the people's representatives flinch from taking any significant step, which may, in any way, jeopardize the departmental prerogatives and strangleholds over departmentally-fractured developmental decisions and developmental spending. Thus, willy-nilly they become champions of the status quo, though publicly they cry hoarse against it.

Reinforcing Clientelism

The situation has been aggravated by the fact that the MPs and MLAs numbering less than 5,000 in a country of a billion, go on entrenching themselves with more perks, privileges and power. The local area development fund of MPs have increased from an initial Rs 10 million to Rs 20 million per annum. There is a proposal to enhance it to Rs 30 million per MP thus enabling an MP to spend Rs 150 million in a period of five years. The MLAs also do not fall behind. Various state governments took care to introduce the local area development funds for the MLAs. The system is both undemocratic and unethical. First, the money is spent in the constituency of the MP or the MLA at his or her own sweet will. So, if the MP or the MLA comes from a rural constituency, to get a portion of the fund the panchayat representatives will have to appeal to him or her, perpetuating a system of subservience. But that apart, the fund could have been given directly to the panchayats which have a legitimate claim on the funds earmarked for local development. That such an alternative has not even been thought of or debated in the public portrays glaringly the elitist mindset, which harbours an inherent distrust of the local-level non-elite leadership. The system is also unethical, because it amounts to using public fund for private gains. It is also unconstitutional, because it creates a situation in which the sitting MP or the MLA gets an added advantage to please the electorate over his or her rival candidates during the election, denying them a level playing field and thereby eroding the fairness of the electoral process. C. Subramaniam, the veteran parliamentarian, had strongly opposed allotment of such 'pork-barrel' funds, since they have an inherent potential for misapplication and worse. Besides, as Subramaniam noted, such type of funding leads to the involvement of the members of legislatures in executive functions and this infringes the constitutionally-mandated separation of the executive and legislative branches of government.

It is, therefore, no wonder that the state legislative assemblies failed in fulfilling the constitutional obligation of endowing panchayats with power, functions and finances to make them autonomous institutions of self-government. But it would be improper to blame the legislators or the ministers alone for this situation. They are a part of the political system, which has a vested interest in keeping the PRIs subservient. This is the reason why the issue of local democracy has not been on the agenda of public debate. Even the fourth estate, which has an elitist bias, fails to highlight the basic issues and problems of local democracy. In fact, the silence about grass-roots democracy is deafening. It amounts to an elite conspiracy intending to suppress the emergence of an authentic voice of the marginalised people in the countryside.

Local Democracy: A Possible Scenario of the Future

From 'Exit' to 'Voice' Option

Against this backdrop, certain vital questions about the prospects of grass-roots democracy confront us. Will panchayats remain as playthings in the hands of the political and the bureaucratic elite for many more decades to come? Or will they start asserting themselves more forcefully in the coming days to become genuine representative governments at the district level and below, as envisaged in the Constitution? Is there any public sphere other than the mainstream political system from where the demand for grass-roots democracy can be effectively raised?

It is not easy to provide answers to these questions, but we should take note of the fact that for the first time in the history of our republic there are now over 2 million elected representatives in the panchayat bodies, thanks to the Seventy-third Constitutional Amendment. Nearly a million of them are women, most of whom have come out of their homes for the first time in centuries to hold public offices and to participate in public activities. This has been the most effective formal step towards political empowerment of women. Many anecdotes are in currency about how women representatives have been manipulated by the male folk in the family, or by the political parties and power groups. But there are also numerous instances of women exercising political power, thereby enhancing their standing both in the society and in the family against heavy odds. With elections every five years, larger numbers of women are coming into the political arena. It is not that only those who get elected are getting empowered formally and substantively. All the women who participate in the election or in the election process are also getting empowered. The immobility of the rural society is changing, perhaps faster than many social scientists anticipate. Women so empowered are not going to let go the advantage easily. Progress made cannot be reversed. It has its own dynamics of moving forward much of which may not be immediately discernible from the outside.

Then there are reservations for SCs and STs in proportion of their population to total population. Most of the elected SC/ST men and women for the first time in generations are occupying positions of power and authority over the whole population including their exploiters and tormentors. But political power does not always match social and economic power in the countryside. So they might not have been very effective everywhere; but there is no denying that there are signs of assertion and independence. Quite a number of Dalit gram panchayat chairpersons have been murdered by upper caste/class persons for exercising their authority in favour of affirmative discrimination. But such gruesome incidents could not stifle their emerging independent spirit. In many places they are now more united and more assertive than before. The new panchayats have released a new liberalising force for Dalits, STs, women and members of the disadvantaged and economically-exploited classes. It is a new phenomenon in the political field, which is likely to have its impact on the current political equilibrium dominated by the land-owning propertied classes/castes in the countryside. Not that they are going to yield power easily. But panchayats have provided space to the politically-excluded classes and segments of society to regroup and direct their energies to carve out a position in the existing power equation in which even though they may not dominate, they would not be subservient to the upper classes/castes. It is worthwhile to remember in this connection what Mahatma Gandhi thought about the inherent strength of public opinion generated from the grass roots in an ideal system of local government. He observed in the *Harijan* (7 July1947):

> When panchayat raj is established, public opinion will do what violence can never do. The present power of *zamindars* and the capitalists and the *rajas* can hold sway so long as the common people do not realise their own strength. If the people non-cooperate with the evils of *zamindary* or capitalism, it must die of inanition. In *panchayat raj* only the panchayats will be obeyed and the panchayats can work through the law of their making.

With Hope and Not with Despair

However, the wind of liberation is not quite visible and perceptible to the outsiders as yet. In the panchayat system the most important institution for direct popular participation is the gram sabha (or *palli sabha* in Orissa, *ward sabha* in Kerala or *gram sansad* in West Bengal) where the entire electorate of the territory participate to debate and decide on the plan of activities and programmes of the gram panchayat. All over the country, attendance in these meetings has been unsatisfactory excepting in Kerala. Even in the politically-conscious state of West Bengal, average percentage of attendance in the gram sansad meetings of May 2002 varied between the high of 18 per cent in Jalpaiguri District and the low of 6 per cent in Howrah District. The percentage of women attending gram sansad meetings was dismal. It varied between the high of 3 per cent in Darjeeling, Cooch Behar, East Medinipur and Burdwan and the low of 1 per cent in North Dinajpur, South Dinajpur, Maldah, Howrah, Bankura, Purulia and Birbhum (*Panchatai Raj Samachar,* November 2002, Kolkata).

From this popular apathy, one could infer that the panchayats have not been able to create that ground swell of social and political mobilisation so necessary to bring about a significant change in the established political equation of the dominant economic, social and political forces. Prima facie, such an inference is well warranted. But one also has to look at the other side. Since the panchayats are treated as the extended arms of the state administration with very little of their own to do, due to lack of functions, finances and functionaries, people do not get enthused to attend such meetings. In Kerala, when the ward sabhas had been given the task of formulating the plan, during the people's plan campaign for the Ninth Plan, there used to be large attendance in such meetings. Women also participated in large numbers. It seems that given a worthwhile creative task to perform, people would respond in large measure. Kerala's example gives one the confidence that if assigned an appropriate task, gram sabhas would be attended by a large number of persons. But for that, proper sensitisation and campaigning are also necessary. Non-governmental organizations have a role to play in this context. In Kerala, the Kerala Shastra Sahitya Parishad (KSSP) played a critical role in mobilising people, particularly women, in ward sabha meetings where area plans were debated and tentatively formulated. Elsewhere NGOs have hardly performed or been allowed to perform this function in an organised manner over a wide area. Since all NGOs are not likely to be co-opted by the existing political and administrative system, it can be expected that they would play such roles increasingly in the coming years.

There is no doubt that the central and state governments are currently exercising, in a sense, usurped powers and functions, which belong to the different tiers of panchayat under the principle of subsidiarity. The political establishment at the centre and the states, cutting across political lines, would not part with these powers easily. But the panchayats are also exerting their rights. The classic case of Perumatty gram panchayat of Kerala cancelling the license granted to the Coca Cola comapny for its plant in Plachimada on the grounds of overexploitation of ground water is now well known. A gram panchayat in Goa prevented Du Pont from establishing a plant in its area in spite of all other clearances. A lady chairperson of Bhanduvencheri gram panchayat in Tamil Nadu stopped mining operation in her panchayat as it adversely affected the groundwater level of the area. Some tribal gram panchayats of Royagoda District of Orissa have restricted giant national and multinational corporation combines from starting mining operations in their area. There is every possibility that through the political parties, beholden to moneybags, the industrial and commercial magnates would try to emasculate the panchayats and make them non-functional, sterile and parastatal entities. In this conflict of interest between the elite and the non-elite, one has to remember that the latter have tasted some power. However insignificant it might look from the metropolis, for them it is significant. Chances are that they would hate to lose even this little advantage.

Today panchayats are acting as mere spending agencies implementing only some centrally-sponsored or state-sponsored straitjacketed program-mes with little autonomy of their own. With financial crisis overtaking both the central and state governments, such funding may become scarce in future. In such a situation, even to maintain a modicum of services, panchayats have to raise their own resources. If they so succeeded, the members of the gram sabha/gram sansad would like to know how the taxes collected from them were being spent. This may lead to a ground-level mobilisation for trans-parency, accountability and autonomy in local governance.

The winds of change are also blowing from another direction. The central-ised state machinery of the country is clearly in stress. It is becoming very clear that a faceless and non-responsive bureaucracy alone cannot govern the countryside. The state machinery is being increasingly forced to involve the local community in providing basic services like primary education, primary health care, environmental protection and even in local resource mobilisation as well as community policing. The need for participatory local-level devel-opment planning is being increasingly felt, after experiencing failures of centralised planning to respond to the grass-roots realities. On the other hand, social activists concerned with such vital issues as rural livelihood, food security, natural resource management, child rights and gender justice are raising demands through the civil society institutions for community em-powerment and transparent and participatory government at the local level. The marginalised people in the villages are no more meek spectators of the sufferings caused to them by arbitrary decisions of the centralised state ma-chinery. They are raising protests against the construction of big dams, which make thousands of poor families homeless or against arbitrary commercial forestry, which denies the rights of the local people to minor forest produce. All these are significant developments and clearly point out that a public sphere outside the main political system is emerging.

Summing Up

Our analysis clearly shows that from Ripon to Rajiv Gandhi the tendency of the ruling classes has been to control in various ways the potentially explosive countryside through shades of local democracy without reforming the bureaucratic framework of local governance. Even after the Seventy-third Constitutional Amendment, things have not changed radically because the same historically-powerful forces are still in operation. They are out to deprive the panchayats the autonomy that has constitutionally been bestowed to them. They have denied the panchayats the 'three Fs'—functions, finance and functionaries. As a result, the panchayats have largely remained ineffective. People's participation in them has not gone beyond the formalism of voting. But, at the same time, it seems that a process of political and social churning has started for which panchayats are increasingly providing an institutional base. This may lead to the grass-roots level demand for closing the gap between the *de jure* and *de facto* position of the panchayats. The social activists are also clamouring for community empowerment and local autonomy. Panchayats are, thus, emerging as a new force field where diverse forces and different types of players are contending. There is a possibility that the coming years will see the Indian political discourse being structured to a considerable extent around this conflict. The outcome of this conflict is still uncertain, still embedded in the future.

Note

1. An earlier version of this chapter was presented at the International Seminar on 'Local Governance in India and China: Rural Development and Social Change' held at Kolkata on 5–8 January 2003. The seminar was organised by the Institute of Social Sciences, New Delhi in collaboration with the Institute of Chinese Studies, New Delhi, Institute of Sociology, Peking University and the Centre for Chinese Studies, University of California, Los Angeles. The authors thank Niraja Gopal Jayal, Raghabendra Chattopadhyay and David Zweig for their valuable comments.

References

Mukarji, Nirmal. 1993. 'The Third Stratum', *Economic and Political Weekly*, 28 (18): 1807–12.
Roy, M.N. 1944. *Draft Constitution of Free India*. Kolkata Renaissance Publishers.
———. 1947. *New Humanism*. Kolkata: Renaissance Publishers.

3 Rural Political Participation in the Maoist and Post-Mao Periods

XIAOHONG ZHOU

Analytical Framework

Peasants in China have long been active in politics. Even before 1949, the Chinese Communist Party (CCP)'s slogan, 'Emancipate the peasants to become masters of the state', encouraged many to take part in the fight against the Japanese and the Guomindang. In the 1930s and 1940s, peasant organisations were established in areas controlled by the CCP. These organisations allowed the poorer peasants to take charge of various local affairs. Peasants even gained the right to vote, as the CCP experimented with different forms of elections and methods of democratic decision making. Areas of Shandong, Hebei, Shanxi and Henan, for example, instituted a preliminary form of secret ballot, called 'the broad bean method'. Illiterate peasants dropped beans into bowls placed behind candidates in order to select local officials through a majority vote.[1]

Over the past 50 years, various experiments have been carried out to promote rural participation and self-governance. Such experiments have attracted much attention from scholars both inside and outside China. Since the British journalist David Crook's observations on elections in the north China village of Ten Mile Inn in 1948, numerous articles and books have been published on the subject of villagers' participation. This chapter intends to explore the same issue, but from a new perspective. Previous studies have focused on the period after 1979. The period after 1987, in particular, when the system of 'villagers' self-governance' was formally adopted, has received a great deal of attention. John Burns's *Political Participation in Rural China*, compares participation in the period before 1949 to the Maoist period, but only addresses the post-Mao period up to 1985. His analysis does not therefore discuss the current period of villagers' self-governance.

Our research looks at rural participation over the last 50 years, from 1949 to 1999, and focuses on a careful comparison between the first 30 years and the 20-year reform period. I examine the issue of rural political participation by looking at the dynamic interactions between state and society. This study draws from two sources of data (Zhou, 1998). First, I use official documents, government records, statistics and field interviews collected in Zhouzhuang Township of Kunshan Municipality in Jiangsu Province. Second, I also draw upon official documents issued by various local governments and by the central government over the last 50 years as well as secondary literature.

1949–78: The Construction of State Control and its Subsequent Reconstruction Through Peasant Participation

From the 1940s onwards, the Communist Party has mobilised peasant participation in peasants' associations and local elections in order to seize political power, as well as to carry out social transformation. One of the first campaigns effectively organised poor peasants to participate in land reform. Between 1953 and 1958, during collectivisation, peasants were mobilised to establish producers' cooperatives and people's communes. These campaigns extended state power to every corner of rural society, sometimes forcibly (Zhou, 1998: 162–73) and different areas experienced different levels of peasant backlash.[2] These campaigns, however, also incorporated principles of voluntarism and mass participation. Policy documents from 1953 not only contained directives for establishing state control but also emphasised the right of peasants to participate in democratic decision-making processes.

Peasants experienced new opportunities for participation during the Great Leap Forward. During this period, many peasants were selected for non-agricultural jobs. Some of them were sent to the cities to produce iron and steel, together with urban workers. Some were responsible for running the canteens of the people's communes. Others worked as factory managers or replaced school principals, denounced as rightists. According to the recollections of interviewees as well as documents from that period, these unprecedented opportunities did, in fact, excite poor peasants about their new lives under the CCP regime.

But in the 1960s, all the organisations of state power that had extended their reach into local communities underwent a dramatic transformation. In the wake of the Great Leap Famine, Mao's prestige was shaken. The economic and political system continued to diverge from his ideal path of socialist construction. Mao found that in order to stabilise post-famine China, he had to stabilise his position within the party. In September 1962, he announced the slogan, 'Never forget class struggle'; at the same time accusing various people within the party of disagreeing with his views (Bo, 1991: 1070–1104). In 1963, under this slogan, the party commenced the Socialist Education Movement and the 'Four Cleans' Movement in the villages.

From the very beginning, local cadres, as agents of the state within the villages, were victims of the conflict between state and society during the movement. Mao and Liu Shaoqi, as the heads of the party and government respectively, had very different goals for the movement and very different opinions about the role of local cadres. Many local cadres, who had diligently carried out the directives of the state by implementing collectivisation and compelling villagers to turn over their grain to the state were now sought to be implicated as agents of the landlord class. As Huang Zhongzhi stated, 'Chairman Mao skillfully transformed the struggle against his political opponents within the Party into class struggle' (Huang, 1998: 48). Everyone was either on the 'revolutionary path' led by Mao or on the 'counter-revolutionary path' led by Liu Shaoqi. After 1966, large-scale rural political participation became Mao's method for reconstructing the nation by destroying those taking 'the counter-revolutionary path'.

Local cadres had the worst of this mandate for mass villager participation. Villagers had grown to resent local cadres, because of their role as agents of the state and because of their 'eat a lot, take a lot' behaviour. Although villagers had previously used complaints, big and small character posters and demonstrations to protest against cadre abuse of power, now, since they had the official support of the party, their protests became much more open, and in some cases, physical, as villagers released their long accumulated dissatisfactions (Li, 1998; Zhou, 1998: 202).

Villagers in the 1950s had been encouraged to participate in social reforms that overthrew the old social and economic order, thereby contributing to the process of state-building and state expansion. But in the 1960s, villagers were told to turn and attack local officials in the very organisations that the villagers had helped the state to build. This kind of participation escalated during the Cultural Revolution. According to Mao, the entire government structure had become dominated by Liu Shaoqi and other 'capitalist roaders'. The masses were therefore justified in attacking the government and replacing existing government organisations with new ones—the revolutionary committees. These committees were characterised by the large-scale participation of workers and peasants at different levels. For a relatively lengthy period of time, ordinary citizens participated in the management of factories, communes, government offices at different levels and even in national leadership. Wang Hongwen, an ordinary worker, and Chen Yonggui, a peasant, rose to become the party's vice-chairman and vice-premier of state affairs.

Mao's plan for national reconstruction was not limited to only the governmental power structure. After the establishment of the revolutionary committees, he further encouraged the idea of using the masses to restructure the upper levels of state administration. Education was targeted for reform, partly in order to control the chaos that had erupted in many schools, but

also partly because Mao had always believed that education was the fundamental tool for capitalist domination.

In August 1968, Mao made a pronouncement about educational reform:

> The realisation of the revolution of education must be led by the workers, must
> have the participation of the workers . . . .The workers' propaganda teams must
> stay in schools for the long term and must participate in the struggle and the tasks
> of criticism and reform of the entire school. In villages, the most reliable allies of
> the workers are the poor, lower, and middle peasants, and they should manage the
> schools (Yao, 1968).

Within a few months after Mao's directive was announced, close to a million workers and peasants organised 'Workers' and Peasants' Mao Zedong
Thought Propaganda Teams'. These teams were stationed in Beijing University and Qinghua University, as well as hundreds of universities and hundreds
of thousands of high schools, middle schools and elementary schools
throughout the country (Chen, 1969). In Kunshan County, Jiangsu Province
in 1968, 81 workers formed propaganda teams and took over 17 middle and
elementary schools in the county seat and townships. Under their guidance,
1,788 poor, lower and middle peasants took over 530 rural, middle and elementary schools. By the end of 1971, this number had risen to 2,321 people
and 539 schools (see China Kunshan County Committee, 1975). Moreover,
in many areas of China, including Zhouzhuang, peasants were also involved
in the training of urban youth as agricultural specialists.

While in 1958, peasants and workers had served as school principals; they
had overseen mainly rural schools, and it had been a limited trial. In 1968,
however, administration by workers and peasants was not limited to a few
schools but extended to all aspects of school management. Under the Maoist
directive, 'The period of education should be reduced, education should be
revolutionised', education everywhere was restructured.

Educational reform focused on two main areas. First, administrative power
was given to the peasants. Directives from above emphasised that 'The masses
should take over the battle of education, using Marxism and Mao Zedong
Thought as tools for the rule of the masses, for the complete destruction of
the capitalists, and for the construction of a basic guarantee of a socialist educational system' (ibid.). An October 1968 editorial in the *People's Daily* urged,
'Break through tradition, put schools under the unified leadership of the
people's communes, propaganda teams, and revolutionary committees'.[3] Substantively, according to the recollections of one of the elementary school
prin-cipals in Zhouzhuang, control over teachers' salaries was moved from
the county education bureau to the brigade. The brigade then paid the teachers
in an example of administration by peasants.[4] In addition, the hiring and

firing of local teachers had to go through the process of 'discussion by peasants, administration by the brigade revolutionary committee, formalisation by the county revolutionary committee' (Li and Lin, 1981: 123).

Villagers were also given the right to reform the curriculum for elementary schools. In many areas of China, brigade party secretaries began taking political study classes, while the chairmen of the poor peasants' associations held classes on class struggle. Barefoot doctors taught medical courses and old peasants who had worked as tractor operators, forestry workers, or village electricians taught courses on industry and agriculture. This situation continued until about 1978.[5] While these educational reforms have come in for considerable ridicule over the last 10 years, such experiences did, in fact, give peasants the opportunity to learn and practice leadership skills. In Zhouzhuang Township, some of the younger members of the propaganda teams with higher levels of education stayed on to become teachers in local schools.

Like schools, health bureaus were targeted as one of the 'disaster areas' dominated by the capitalist class. At about the same time that Mao Zedong thought propaganda teams were sent out to schools, various hospitals and clinics also experienced similar reforms. In accordance with Mao's directive, 'Put the focus of medical work in the village', some 10,000 members of propaganda teams belonging to the Suzhou District were sent to Zhouzhuang Township's rural health clinics. The 'health revolution' involved breaking the chain of command between county public health bureaus, commune clinics and brigade clinics. Instead peasants were to run the health care system(see Suzhou Special District Revolutionary Committee, 1969). Second, peasants with some education were to be trained as barefoot doctors. Kunshan municipality's Number 71 Commune, in the suburbs of Shanghai, trained 64 peasants to become 'real' peasant doctors (*History of Shanghai 71 Commune*, 1974). Third, large numbers of doctors from cities and towns were sent down for the double purpose of allowing them to be educated by the peasants while at the same time serving the medical needs of the masses.

In addition to education and health work units, peasants participated in restructuring the state's economic and finance offices. Peasants reformed existing credit cooperatives and state supply stores or simply established their own. Peasants also participated in the management of collective assets in order to curtail the wasteful behaviour of local cadres (Zhouzhuang People's Commune Revolutionary Committee Inspection Team, 1969).

Many early forms of democratic self-governance date from this period. Before the Cultural Revolution, in order to control the rural economy effectively, the state established various types of credit, purchasing and marketing cooperatives as well as state purchasing and marketing stores. Although some of these institutions drew on villages or commune-brigades for investment, they were directly supervised by the state's economic ministries and constituted an extension of the state's system of control. The main credit co-operative, for example, was under the control of the state bank, while the main supply and marketing cooperatives were under the control of province and city bureaus. During the Cultural Revolution, in accordance with the at-tack on Liu Shaoqi's 'revisionist economics,' these organisations were con-sidered bureaucratic organisations, subject to wholesale destruction and reconstruction (ibid.). Between 1969 and 1971, 14 peasant-managed credit cooperatives were established in the Zhouzhuang commune and led by brigade party branches (Zhouzhuang Agricultural Bank, 1971). In the so-called five-star brigades, which were the earliest to establish these kinds of credit cooperatives, peasant revolutionary committees also organised peasants into smaller financial management committees. Peasant representatives in these financial committees oversaw the operation of local banks, credit cooper-atives and tax bureaus (Zhouzhuang People's Commune Revolutionary Com-mittee Inspection Team, 1969). Likewise, peasants now directly managed purchasing and marketing cooperatives, which had originally reported to higher-level bureaucratic offices (Shandong Jimo Xian, Wanshan Commune, Fangjia Brigade 1975: 30–33).

While villagers participated in restructuring the state's financial and eco-nomic bureaucracies, the state also renewed pressures for the democratic management of financial affairs. As previously mentioned, in the early years of the cooperatives, the party had emphasised the principle of democratic management. After the Great Leap Famine, in September 1961, the 10th plenary meeting of the 8th Party Congress promulgated the 'Revision of the Rules on Work of People's Communes,' which established the insti-tutions of the commune representative assembly, the brigade assembly, and the brigade representative assembly. The new rules stated that all the important issues should be decided by these assemblies, rather than by a small group of local cadres (Zhonghua Remin Gonghe Guo Guojia Nongye Weiyuan Hui, 1981: 628–29).

Another way of instituting democratic management of local finances was by fixing dates for the publicising of commune and production team accounts. In 1970, the Beicai Commune in Shanghai's Chuansha County, for example, established peasant economic supervision teams which demanded that 'the accounts of production teams be posted on a wall, every single expenditure be reported to commune members every month, and detailed income and expenditure information be reported orally every five to ten days' (Chuansha County, 1974: 149–56). In Zhouzhuang, the Number Two team of the Wangdong Brigade also established a complete set of regulations on democratic financial management. These stated:

> Any loans from the collective must obtain approval. For loans of more than five
> yuan, approval must be obtained from the economic supervision team. For loans

of more than 20 yuan, approval must be obtained from all of the commune's members. Every single expense must be verified by the commune's members, and accounting books must be publicized on fixed dates (Agricultural Bank of China, 1971).

In accordance with the Dazhai model, the Xigou Brigade in Shanxi noted, 'When there's an issue, it must be discussed with the masses. All important expenses must go through the discussion and decision of peasants.'[6] Other reforms banned local cadres from borrowing money from the collective as well as urging them to return the money they had already taken from the collective.[7] The Zhouzhuang Commune, for example, ordered 19 commune-level cadres to return within three years, the money they had previously taken from the collective (Zhouzhuang Commune Party Committee, 1975).

These attempts at extensive reforms led Mao and the party to revise their view of local cadres as agents of capitalism, who were now seen as mass representatives who had made some errors, but were now subject to the system of democratic financial management. The rights of peasants to make decisions about collective assets and the collective economy were now in place, and 'the bad influence of capitalism was halted'. Local cadres, however, remained unhappy. Cadres in Chuansha County near Shanghai raised the question, 'We ourselves come from the peasant masses, so why do we need to be supervised by other peasants?' Complaints like these showed not only that grass-roots leaders lacked a basic sense of democracy, but also that they were bristling under a policy that stripped away much of their authority.

This process of mobilised rural participation illuminates not only how Mao tried to gain tighter control over grass-roots society, but also how local society was able to reshape the state. Although Mao initiated this restructuring because he greatly distrusted cadres in the government bureaucracy, it also allowed a considerable degree of villager participation. Once permitted a voice, villagers expressed their unhappiness with the degree of state control.

1979–99: The Relaxation of State Control and the Growth of Local Autonomy

Since the late 1970s, the structure of Chinese society has changed dramatically. After Mao's death, legitimation of the concept of people's communes weakened considerably. The spread of the household contracting system eventually resulted in the collapse of the communes. Following this collapse, the grip of the state over society loosened, and weakened local governments found themselves unable to carry out their responsibilities. Villages, especially in backward areas, were trapped in a state of disorder.

Confronted with these problems at the grass-roots level, the state began deliberating on how to fill the organisational power vacuum left by the dissolution of the people's communes. At that time, the state could draw on party and governmental organisational resources.

Even during the Cultural Revolution, the party organisation had never really been paralysed. In 1982, the party re-emphasised the need to strengthen the role of the party in grass-roots-level organisations in the minutes from the National Working Conference on Villages (Zhonggong Zhongyang Wenxian Yanjiu Shibian, 1982:1061). Between 1983 and 1985, the upper half of commune administration was transformed into township governments, but the lower half of commune administration—composed of brigades and teams— was not able to recover from the changes wrought by the household responsibility system. The state had two choices. The first was to invest in the strengthening of formal state structures at the local level. The second was to unload part of the responsibility for organisational re-building to local communities and allow them to implement self-governance and institute village democracy.

Already occupied with numerous tasks of reform, the state selected the second option. From the beginning of the 1980s, with the encouragement of the central state, localities in China began experimenting with different forms of village self-governance. In November 1987, not long after the 13th Central Committee Meeting promoting socialist democracy, the 6th National People's Congress promulgated the Organic Law of Village Self-Governance. This law established the key principles of village self-governance and paved the way for the institution of local self-governance across the entire country. Since then, most areas of China, including Zhouzhuang Township, have experienced more than 10 years of self-governance and four rounds of elections for village committees. In Zhouzhuang, an election took place in 1998, about a month after the Organic Law was revised in November of that year.

The Organic Law contains the key principles for village self-governance and villager participation in grass-roots rural society. The four main principles are democratic elections, democratic village decision making, democratic management of the village and democratic supervision of local cadres. Many areas have singled out the principle of democratic supervision of local cadres in particular. Villagers had long been dissatisfied with the parasitic nature of local cadres, or what they called 'eat a lot, take a lot' behaviour. As discussed in the previous section, this dissatisfaction was the core motivation behind much villager participation during the Maoist period.

We will discuss rural political participation in the post-Mao period in terms of each of the four principles outlined in the Organic Law. Direct village elections constitute a dramatic change from the appointment of local cadres during the period of people's communes. Elections are the first step toward the actual exercising of villagers' rights outlined in the Organic Law. Their development will also determine whether or not the village committee will be able to become relatively independent of the central state and truly act as an organisation of self-governance. Village elections are the bedrock of village self-governance.

Through an examination of village elections, we will also be able to examine changes in the relationship between the state and grass-roots-level society. Many scholars have, therefore, focused on assessing the quality of elections and just how democratic they really are. In order to evaluate how democratic village committee elections are, we need to examine the following issues: whether local cadres do in fact derive their political authority from villagers; whether all villagers have equal opportunity of being elected to office; and whether all villagers do in fact have a right to vote, which they voluntarily exercise. From our observation of the fourth round of elections in December 1998, the first and third issues have been resolved satisfactorily in Zhouzhuang. Cadres are elected to office, based on the number of votes they receive. Actual election procedures followed the guidelines laid out in the Organic Law. Elections are direct and competitive. Secret ballot and ballot booths have been established and moving ballot boxes have been removed.

As for the problem of whether villagers have an equal opportunity of getting elected, the situation is relatively complicated. According to the 12th Item of the Organic Law, any village resident who is over 18, regardless of nationality, race, sex, profession, family origin, religious belief, level of education, economic status and duration of residence, excepting those deprived of political rights (such as convicted criminals), has a right to be elected to village office. According to the law, as long as you are a resident of the village (that is, your household registration is of the village), you have the right to stand for office.

In actual elections, however, villagers and the village party branch are locked in a tug-of-war over village administrative power. The recent revision of the Organic Law has changed the rules of the game and shifted the centre of gravity toward the villagers. The 14th regulation of the newly revised Organic Law states, 'All villagers have the right to nominate candidates for the village committee directly'. This mandate for direct nomination of election candidates should lead to a decline in the influence of local party and township officials over elections. Research in Zhouzhuang indicates that the new guidelines have already put the township party committee and village party branch in a hot seat. Zhouzhuang's assistant party secretary in charge of village elections admitted, 'Because this year we implemented direct nomination of villagers, we found it very difficult to handle the election process. For example, if villagers do not nominate anyone, then we cannot force them to proceed with the election process. So now our position is, "We cannot but intervene in the election process, but we can't intervene too much".' [8]

Thus, although the right to vote has been given to villagers, the village party branch together with the township party committee and government still dominate the process of nominating candidates for village elections in many areas, including Zhouzhuang. According to interviews with officials, township governments intervene in two cases: when local cadres have trouble implementing official directives or when they have a conflict with the village party secretary. Thus, even though Gaoyong Village's original village committee chairman Gao Guolin secured the nominations of 280 out of 450 households, he ultimately was not allowed to become a candidate.[9]According to local officials, these kinds of situations require intervention and 'guidance'. In other words, people who are acceptable to both the villagers and the party replace unacceptable officials. Despite these examples, however, the majority of candidates are nominated household by household, and as the assistant township party secretary says, 'Essentially, candidates are determined by the number of votes they get'.

From Zhouzhuang's perspective, the issue of the nomination process results from a conflict between the interests of villagers and the interests of the state. When villagers and the state have the same interests, it does not matter how candidates are nominated. It is only when there is a difference in interests that the question of how to nominate candidates becomes a key issue. Two methods have evolved to resolve this conflict. Taiyuan and Lishu counties, in Jiangsu and Jilin provinces, have instituted 'haixuan' elections, while Hequ County in Shanxi Province has implemented the 'two vote system'. In haixuan elections, officials are not allowed to determine the candidates. Instead, villagers directly vote for whom they want on the village committee, thereby preventing the township government from offering their suggestions on who should be selected as candidates (Lin, 1995; Zhang, 1998). In the 'two vote system', villagers first participate in a vote of confidence in the village's party members. Party members who do not win a majority are eliminated from standing for office in the village party branch. Party members then elect fellow party members who have not been eliminated, to party branch positions and the position of party secretary. In this way, ordinary villagers may hold members of the party branch accountable for their decisions in governing the village (Li and Xiong, 1998).

Zhouzhuang's actual electoral procedures are still dominated by local party officials and still lag behind the most democratic elections. But as long as the state continues to push for villagers' self-governance and village democracy by holding village committee elections every three years, the balance of power will no doubt continue to shift toward villagers.

Next, we discuss the issue of democratic village policy making and management. By themselves, village elections are relatively infrequent events. Only if villagers in their daily lives are able to make decisions about major issues that affect their interests, do elections become a significant milestone in the long-term process of democratisation. Participation in village policy making and management are two related ways in which villagers exercise their democratic rights. On the other hand, they are both implemented in practice by a single body, the village discussion assembly or villagers' representative assembly (VRA).

Compared with its significant progress in the institution of democratic elections, Zhouzhuang still has a long way to go before village decision making and management become truly democratic. The Organic Law does, however, require that issues involving villagers' interests must be discussed and decided by the villagers' representative assembly. Officials of Zhouzhuang Township and upper-level leaders of Kunshan County also continuously emphasise that village committees should practice democratic decision making and management.

Because there are too many people in a village, for them all to participate directly in making decisions about village affairs, the village VRA exercises decision-making power on behalf of the villagers. Zhouzhuang's VRA consists of five different types of members: (i) one representative whom every 10 households select; (ii) village committee officials; (iii) village party branch officials; (iv) village small group leaders; and (v) village representatives to the township people's congress. We can see from this formal organisation that Zhouzhuang's VRA is essentially consistent with the regulations of the Organic Law.

In the actual operation of the VRA, however, participation by representatives is not entirely voluntary, or bottom up. Moreover, party cadres often do the work of the VRA themselves, thus preventing VRA meetings from taking their course. The assistant township party secretary admitted, 'Using the form of the VRA to make village policies democratic, is far from standardised procedure. Decisions are mainly made by the party branch.' When we interviewed some VRA representatives in Zhouzhuang's villages and asked them why they often failed to attend meetings, we received some very interesting answers. One representative commented, 'The VRA is all party members, I don't feel comfortable sitting in there.' Another said, 'When a meeting is called, the meeting is called a meeting of party cadres. How can I have the face to go?'

Although the VRA has not been systematised yet, this does not mean that there are no democratic aspects in villagers' self-governance. The collapse of the people's communes means that village governments now have no way of controlling all of a village's economic production and the daily lives of its residents. In addition to making decisions about household production and employment, villagers have some opportunity for expressing their own views about public affairs. In the words of Yunnan Village's chairman, Pu Yulin, 'Now our job is very difficult. Except for when villagers want to build a house or apply for a business license, they don't listen to you, and you can't do anything about it. In fact, the problem is not just that they don't listen to you, but it is you, who have to listen to them.'

One example that shows how villagers are able to effect changes in village policies is in the establishment of private enterprises in Yunnan Village. Originally, village regulations prohibited private enterprises from engaging in certain industries such as printing and textiles, in order to avoid competition with the village's collective enterprises for resources and markets (Zhou, 1998: 243). But in the past few years, villagers have continuously raised objections to these regulations. On various occasions, villagers have taken the report of the 15th Central Committee to the village party secretary and chairman in order to point out that the local policies of the village are in conflict with the spirit of the central government's support of private enterprises. As a result, the party secretary and chairman came to feel they could no longer defend their position. They not only opened the printing industry and other industries to competition from private enterprises, but proceeded to contract the village's collective printing press to private entrepreneurs. We can see from this example that villagers are now able to express their opinion about village issues. While their input may not always have an impact, their effect on the actions of the party branch and village committee is certainly growing.

Progress in democratic administration of the village is also mixed. The Kunshan municipal government emphasises, 'Every village should set up their own system for different conditions and use village charters and the rules for self-governance to implement a rule of law within the village.' Numerous villages have also established general principles as well as detailed rules and procedures to govern the village.

Both villagers and the village committee think, however, that following a rule of law is very difficult. Obstacles to setting up a rule of law lie in three areas: the party branch, the villagers and the township. Quanwang Village illustrates how, even in the best of circumstances, the party branch remains above the law. Quanwang is the township's model village for implementing a rule of law. All the formal institutions have been set up, including a village charter as well as rules and guidelines for the villagers' representative assembly, for the work of the village committee, for transparency of village finances, for village elections, for democratic management and so forth. The village committee chairman complained, however, that 'most village power is still in the hands of the party secretary. The party secretary determines the three-year plan for village economic development. All economic decisions are still made by the party secretary.'

Even when village cadres are committed to implementing a rule of law, however, villagers may not be willing to comply. Quanwang's village head also commented that because villagers no longer depended on village officials, not only was collecting village fees extremely difficult, but it was difficult to enforce the village charter. And assuming that both village officials and villagers were willing to implement a rule of law, the behaviour of township officials would still present a problem. In many situations, decisions about village affairs cannot be made by the village itself. For example, even though Quanwang's village rules stipulate that approval for housing construction and the setting of family planning targets should be under democratic management, in reality, these are all decided by the township.

Chinese scholars frequently discuss the contradiction in the village committee's dual roles. The village committee is responsible for responding to the demands of both higher levels of government and villagers. The ways in which they negotiate between the two can be very complex. For example, many note that the village committee acts to enforce many government directives, but they do not pay attention to the fact that the village committee is not able to secure the cooperation of villagers in implementing these directives. The village committee often cannot really accomplish the tasks assigned to them. In Zhouzhuang, the village committees often have no way of collecting the state agricultural tax and other local fees (fees for the public goods fund, public employment fund and management fees) from villagers who have jobs in the transportation sector or who work elsewhere.

The third issue we discuss is the problem of democratic supervision of village cadres. Democratic elections imply that democratic supervision is based on each individual supervising the village committee by exercising his or her rights to remove members from office. In this way, democratic supervision has a mass participatory character. But in order to supervise their officials effectively, villagers have to be familiar with the internal operations of village government. The Organic Law states, 'Village committees must implement transparency of village financial affairs.' Village tasks can be divided into two categories: administrative tasks and financial tasks. At the local level, not only may financial supervision take place more frequently, but it can also be more important.

From our observations in Zhouzhuang, village committees have implemented measures for the democratic supervision of village cadres and for financial transparency, following the state's regulations fairly closely. From 1991 onwards, Kunshan City required that townships establish a set of model villages. These villages would guarantee financial transparency, establish a bulletin board for information about village affairs and finances, and institute a box for villager comments. In 1997, the Municipal Bureau of Administration and the Municipal Party Committee's Village Work Bureau also established test sites for implementing transparency of village affairs (Kunshan Municipal Civil Affairs Bureau, 1998). They also created procedures for establishing transparency of village affairs, the forms that transparency should take, and a timetable for carrying out these regulations. Zhouzhuang's Quanwang and Yunnan villages, for example, posted information about the party's activities, the hiring and firing, promotion and demotion of cadres, investment and the status of village public projects, village expenditures, land use, family planning targets, and the official salaries of the party secretary and village committee chairman on bulletin boards for everyone to see. For example, in 1998, Party Secretary Yuan Meishen of Yunnan Village had an official income of 23,000 yuan, while the village committee chairman Pu Yunlin brought home 21,000 yuan.

Again, the status of the party branch and party secretary present a problem. As outlined in existing regulations, democratic supervision only applies to the village committee. In Zhouzhuang and most villages, however, it is the party secretary that has control over decisions about village assets. The party secretary therefore remains outside of democratic supervision [10] Villagers and village committee chairs have commented on the difficulty of supervising the party secretary. Most village committee chairmen and village accountants know better than to ask the party secretary about his accounts. When the accountant of Gaoyong Village in 1988 confronted the party secretary about the reimbursements and invoices he had submitted, the accountant was summarily replaced.

As many have discussed, the central problem of instituting villagers' self-governance is the relationship between the village committee and the party branch. When this problem cannot be resolved, villagers' self-governance and democratic supervision cannot be truly accomplished, and the elected village committee head is not really in charge. If this situation persists, villagers lose confidence in democratic elections and the system of villagers' self-governance. But judging from the past 10 years of villagers' self-governance, we have a basis for confidence in the possibility of resolving this problem. Just as the party branch has withdrawn from the process of nominating candidates for village elections, the party branch will eventually retreat from direct intervention in village economic and social affairs. Likewise, the party secretary will become unable to make decisions about village affairs and finance outside the realm of democratic supervision. When the time comes to re-allocate village power and resolve the conflict between the party branch and villager self-governance, then the separation of state and society will be realised.

Discussion and Summary

We can see from the previous discussion that, although rural political participation has taken similar forms in the Maoist and post-Mao periods, it has had very different implications for state–society relations in the two eras. Rural participation in the Maoist period differs from participation in the reform period in terms of political context, including the central government's motivations for encouraging villager participation and the scope of participation.

Comparing rural participation in these two periods allows us to see very different dynamics at work in the interaction between state and society. In the Maoist period, rural political participation reached its height in 1958, with the establishment of people's communes. Communes constituted a total restructuring of Chinese rural society. 'First, larger, and second, collective' and 'politics and society are one' were the two distinct principles behind the people's communes. In initiating the creation of people's communes, Mao consistently supported the thorough restructuring of economic and social life.

After their formation, the communes strictly enforced the dictates of the state and organised production according to the needs of the state. Moreover, the state used the institution of the communes effectively to limit the freedom of individuals in rural society. Due to the commune's control of property rights over land and resources for production, it was able to directly control all of the commune's economic activities and allocation of labour and capital. With this power, it was able to monopolise the movement and trade of materials and products. Tight restrictions were also placed on labour mobility. As a result, peasants were unable to leave the commune.

Using these kinds of social and political institutions, state power was extended in every direction down to the local level of the villages. After losing the foundation for autonomous economic activity, members of grass-roots-level rural society found it impossible to oppose the state and pursue their own interests. Under these conditions, social forces could exert influence only in two kinds of situations. The first was when state strength and legitimacy were weakened. After the Great Leap Famine, for example, household contracting and rural markets experienced resurgence in various areas. Second, society was able to act autonomously, when Mao attempted to use the power of society to restructure the state. Participation in the Maoist period occurred in these situations.

After 1979, however, rural society experienced a monumental change, originating in implementation of the production contracting responsibility system. On the surface, the production contracting system simply gave villagers control rights over production. In reality, however, this reform led directly to the collapse of the entire commune system. The state has retreated substantially from grass-roots rural society. Not only have the rights to manage village affairs been given to the villagers themselves, but state power at the township level has also changed from very rigid control to a more elastic control. Villagers acquired control rights over production, the opportunity for social mobility, and the power to participate in village governance. Even though village democracy is, as in the Maoist period, a top–down initiative from the central government, villager participation itself is voluntary and not compelled.

Second, the central government's motives for promoting rural participation have been different in the two periods. In the Maoist period, party leaders used rural participation first to expand state power. As discussed earlier, the earliest political participation was before 1949. From the 1930s up to land reform and collectivisation in the early-1950s, the motivation for Maoist mobilisation of villager political participation was very simple, 'Destroy the old, create the new.' After the revolution, this task was seemingly finished. Mao then took advantage of the tensions created by the expansion of the state to re-direct rural participation toward criticising and transforming existing state institutions and representatives.

In the post-Mao period, motivations for mobilising peasant political participation are completely different. Just in terms of economic efficiency, others have calculated that transforming the original brigades and teams into the 700,000 or so financially self-sufficient villages that exist now saves the state between 63 and 175 billion yuan in state cadre wages. Therefore, implementing villagers' self-management has definitely been advantageous from the perspective of the state's budget. China's leaders were concerned about the over-centralisation of power. Because of this, in 1981, the sixth plenary meeting of the 11th Central Committee passed the 'Decisions relating to several historical problems since the establishment of the nation', which announced, 'At the grassroots level, direct democracy should be gradually implemented (see Zhonggong Zhongyang Wenxian Yanjiu Shibian, 1982: 841). For the party, this decision did not seem too drastic because the grass-roots-level party organisational structure was still fairly strong. The state thus loosened its direct and strict control over grass-roots society and decided to use more macro-level controls and directives. From their point of view, villagers' self-governance would maintain social stability and increase the state's financial revenue by allowing local governments to carry out the state's administrative functions.

Villagers in grass-roots society have responded actively to this weakening of the state and the devolution of power. In other words, even though villagers' self-governance in the post-Mao period was a top–down initiative from the central government, villagers' participation is quite genuine. After 1979, the turning over of production control rights created new interests among farmers, which formed the core of their positive response to the central government's push for village democracy and self-governance. Although villagers' self-governance originated from poorer areas, today villager participation is strongest in developed areas. Not only have initiatives for villagers' self-governance benefited from the state's top–down efforts, but, in contrast to the Maoist period, they have also obtained a bottom–up response from grass-roots society.

Finally, rural political participation differs between the two periods in its specific areas of involvement. During the Maoist period, the main purpose of rural participation was to realise Mao's goal of destroying the old government and establishing the proletariat as the rulers. Peasants participated at all levels of government when given a mandate to restructure state institutions. Vertically, rural political participation ranged from the production team, the brigade, the commune and the county all the way to the province and the central government. Horizontally, participation extended across many different areas—culture, education, health, and finance. After the Cultural Revolution, some among those designated poor peasants were selected by the party to take positions of responsibility at the levels of commune, district and even as high as the central government. Ironically, even though the state had succeeded in extending its organisational structure all the way down to the village, peasants who attained positions of power were able to reconstruct this same organisational structure.

During the Maoist period, the demands voiced by participants were highly influenced by the state. An individual's opportunity to participate had little to do with his level of education, knowledge, ability, experience, or sense of responsibility and much more to do with his political and family background. Moreover, because at the time, political participation occurred within the boundaries demarcated by the state, the people best able to participate were a minority mobilised by the party due to their class or political background. This political power offered to peasants, like Chen Yonggui, was given only to a few, not offered in general to allow peasants the opportunity to make decisions about their own lives.

In contrast to the Maoist period, rural political participation in the post-Mao period has gradually strengthened and the rural population has obtained the right to self-governance. In order to reduce its financial burden of managing rural localities, as well as satisfy rural demands for control over their own economic and social activities, the state voluntarily reduced the areas and extent of its control and gave the power back to the villagers themselves. Unlike the Maoist period, rural political participation is limited to managing the daily administration of village affairs. But because the state has withdrawn to a large degree from direct involvement, participation in the reform period is more substantive and more heterogeneous than it was in the Maoist period. The difference between the Maoist and post-Mao periods can be described in one sentence: in the Maoist period, villagers who could not even decide their own fate were able to influence the fate of the state, but in the post-Mao period, villagers have gained control over their own fate.

We have already seen that the Organic Law has few restrictions on what form participation takes. The very words 'villagers' self-governance' suggest how broad a scope popular participation now occupies. Participation is not restricted to any particular class or political background and it allows individuals to take advantage of their education, experience, ability, sense of democracy and concern of social affairs. In fact, it is these criteria that are coming to define candidates for public office.

Although in the 50 years between 1949 and 1999, rural political participation has often been initiated from the top down, the significance of participation in the reform period is very different from that of participation in the Maoist period. Rural political participation in the post-Mao period has occurred in the context of a changed relationship between state and society. It is not a simple extension of participation in the Maoist period, and it is thus likely to experience a brighter fate.

Notes

1. The English journalists Crook and Crook recorded in detail this unique type of Chinese elections. Candidates sit in a row with bowls placed behind their backs. Every villager above the age of 18 is allotted seven broad beans. Villagers then vote by placing their beans in the bowls. Village officials are thus selected in this manner. See Crook and Crook (1959).
2. It is worth noting this kind of resistance did not come from displaced landlords or the rich peasant class, as is often claimed, but from the poor and middle peasants with good political background. See Chen (1997). In addition, during research, we discovered that after establishing the higher levels of Zhouzhuang's brigade in March 1957, five areas and 13 brigades engaged in a total 26 protests by a total of 1,709 participants. Participants included demobilised military, politically-active peasants and frustrated lower and middle peasants. See Zhouzhuang Township Government, 1 June 1957, 'The Report on Zhouzhuang Township's Protest', from files in Zhouzhuang Township's archives.
3. The so-called 'single-line leadership' system meant that the county educational bureau directed the district central school, which directed the township, which in turn directed the village schools. 'Zhejiang Chunan County, Jiukang Commune Educational Inspection Report', 18 October 1968, Beijing: Remin Ribao.
4. According to a 6 February 1999 interview with Liu Jishi. The 'Ma Zhenfu case' took place in a Henan Province village middle school. In this case, the suicide of a student believed to result from school pressures was seen as a path of the property class.
5. See *History of Shanghai 71 Commune* (1974: 160–62); Remin Ribao, Red Flag, 1968, *The Revolution of Village Education Must Depend on Lower and Middle Peasants: Record of the Experience of the Development of Educational Revolution in Yingkou County Shuiyuan Commune*, Beijing: Red Flag, No.3. See also interview with Zhouzhuang Township Jiang Xingyi. See Suzhou

Special District Revolutionary Committee, 'Suzhou Special District Educational and Health Revolution, Conference on Sharing Experience Record', Kunshan Municipality archives, 13 July 1969.

6. 'Emphasize the hard work, carry out democratic finance'\(Taiyuan, *Shanxi Ribao*, 8 April 1972).

7. At the time, when Zhouzhuang Commune's five-star brigade's revolutionary committee member Jiao Yisheng's house collapsed, he had no means to borrow money from the production brigade. See Kunshan County People's Commune Revolutionary Committee, 29 December 1969, 'Fengshou Yihou Zeme Ban?' (After the harvest what should we do?), *Zhouzhuang Jianxun*, no. 2.

8. Interview with Zhouzhuang Township assistant party secretary, Zhuo Jianxing, 6 February 1999.

9. According to interviews with former village committee chairmen of Gaoyong Village and Quanwang Village in Zhouzhuang Township, Gao Guolin and Zhao Xiaomao respectively, taken on 8 February 1999.

10. According to interviews with officials and villagers in Zhouzhuang Township taken between 5 to 12 February 1999.

References

Bo, Yipo. 1991. *Ruogan Zhongda Juece yu Shijian de Huigu*. Vol. 2. Beijing: Central Party School Press, pp. 1070–1104.

Burns, John P. 1988. *Political Participation in Rural China*. Berkeley: University of California Press.

Chen, Guang. 1969. 'The Importance of Organizing Mao Zedong Workers and Peasants' Propaganda Teams', Hong Kong: Chinese University of Hong Kong Services Centre.

Chen, Huikang. 1997. Jiangnan Nongcun de Yichang Biange: Tongan, Wangting Xiang Nongye Hezuo Hua Yundong Yanjiu. Ph.D. dissertation, Suzhou University.

Crook, Isabel and David Crook. 1959. *Revolution in a Chinese Village: Ten Mile Inn*. London: Routledge.

Huang, Zhongzhi. 1998. *Village Class Struggle during the Revolution*. Beijing: Social.Sciences Press.

Li, Lianjiang and Xiong, Jingming. 1998. *Cong zhenfu zhu dao de cunmin zizhi maixiang minzhu xuanju*, 50. Hong Kong: 21st Century.

Li, Peiliang and Zhaojia, Liu (eds). 1981. *People's Communes and Village Development: The Experiences of Taishan and Doushan Communes*. Hong Kong: Chinese University Press.

Li, Ruojian. 1998. 'An Examination of Cadre Behavior During the Great Leap Forward', in *Hong Kong Social Sciences Academic Report*, 13, Hong Kong.

Liu, Aili. 1995. 'Democracy, Culture, Wealth, Taicang Muncipality, Villagers' Self-Governance Suo Guo Feng', 2, Beijing: Zhongguo Shehui Bao, 12 December 1995.

Yao, Wenyuan. 1968. 'The Workers Must Lead Everything', *Red Flag*, 2.

Yong, Xu. 1997. *Zhongguo Nongcun Cunmin Zizhi*. Wuhan: Huazhong Shifan Daxue Chubanshe.

Zhang, Jing. 1998, 'Lishu xian cunweihui huan jie xuanju guancha', 50. Hong Kong: 21st Century.

Zhonggong Zhongyang Wenxian Yanjiu Shibian. 1982. *San zhong quan hui yilai zhongyao wenxuan xuanbian*, Vol. 2. Beijing: Remin Press.

Zhou, Xiaohong. 1998. *Recent Changes in the Social Psychology of Peasants in Jiangsu and Zhejiang*. Beijing: Sanlian Press.

Documents

Agricultural Bank of China, Zhouzhuang Branch, Zhouzhuang Credit Cooperative. 1971. 'Zhouzhuang Commune, Wandong No. 2 Team, Gaoyong No.4 Team Report on their Financial Situ-ation', Zhouzhuang Township archives, 15 September 1971.

China Kunshan County Committee. 1975. 'Regarding the Improvement of Strengthening Workers' Propaganda Teams, Notice of the Construction of Poor Peasants' Management Committee', files from Kunshan Municipality archives.

Chuansha County, Beicai Commune, Carry out Economic Democratic Inspection. 1974. 'Poor, Lower and Middle Peasants Should Grasp Collective Economic Property Rights: Chuansha County Beicai Commune Carry out Economic Democratic Inspection', *Remin Gongshe Zai Yaojing: Shanghai Suburbs Communes's New Experience*. China: Shanghai Remin Press.

History of Shanghai 71 Commune. 1974. Shanghai: Remin Press.

Jingjiang Daxing Commune Revolutionary Committee. 1968. 'Revolution of Agricultural Specialists and Agricultural Education', Beijing, *Red Flag* 5.

Kunshan County People's Commune Revolutionary Committee. 1969. 'Fengshou Yihou Zeme Ban?' (After the harvest what should we do?), *Zhouzhuang Jianxun*, 2, 29 December 1969.

Kunshan Municipal Civil Affairs Bureau. 1998. 'Quan min guance zu zhi fa, renzheng tuijin nongcun jicheng, minzhu jianshe', Kunshan Muncipality document from the Bureau of Civil Affairs, 10 October 1998.

Remin Ribao. 1968. *The Revolution of Village Education Must Depend on Lower and Middle Peasants: Record of the Experience of the Development of Educational Revolution in Yingkou County Shuiyuan Commune*. Beijing, *Red Flag* 3.

Shandong Jimo Xian, Wanshan Commune, Fangjia Brigade Poor, Middle and Lower Peasants Leadership Group. 1975. 'Poor, Lower and Middle Peasants Management of Sales and Purchasing Learn from Experience', in *The Completion of Village Sales and Purchasing Stores*. Beijing: China Finance and Economic Press, pp. 30–33.

Suzhou Special District Revolutionary Committee. 1969. 'Suzhou Special District Educational and Health Revolution, Conference on Sharing Experience Record', Kunshan Municipality archives, 13 July 1969.

'Zhejiang Chunan County. 1968. Jiukang Commune Educational Inspection Report'. Beijing: Remin Ribao, 18 October 1968.

Zhonghua Remin Gonghe Guo Guojia Nongye Weiyuan Hui, Ban Gong Ting. 1981. *Collection of Important Documents about Agricultural Collectivization, Vol. 2,* Beijing: Central Party School Press, pp. 628–29.

Zhou, Xiaohong. 1998. 'Chinese Farmers in the Process of Modernization', Nanjing: Nanjing University Department of Sociology Monograph.

Zhouzhuang Agricultural Bank, Zhouzhuang Credit Cooperatives. 1971. 'Financial and Credit Cooperative—Investigation of Conditions and Report', Zhouzhuang Township archives, 7 September 1971.

Zhouzhuang Commune Party Committee. 1975. 'Emphasize Party's Fundamental Path, Encourage Households to Return Loans' (Jianzhi dang de jiben luxian, zhua hao chaozi hu de huan kuan), Zhouzhuang Muncipality archives, 16 January 1975.

Zhouzhuang People's Commune Revolutionary Committee Inspection Team. 1969. 'A Poor and Lower Class Take Power over Credit Cooperative: Zhouzhuang Commune Five-Star Brigade Inspection Report', Zhouzhuang Township archives, 9 April 1969.

Zhouzhuang Township Government. 1957. 'The Report on Zhouzhuang Township's Protests', from files in Zhouzhuang Township's archives, 1 June 1957.

4 Selecting Within the Rules
Institutional Innovation in China's Governance[1]

TONY SAICH AND XUEDONG YANG

Following the Fifteenth Party Congress (1997), there was not only a consolidation of the villagers' election programme but also an increased interest in reforming township government. A small number of localities took General Secretary Jiang Zemin's comments to extend the 'scope of democracy' at the grass-roots level and to establish a 'sound system of democratic elections' for grass-roots organs of power as a green light to experiment with township elections (Jiang, 1997). Subsequent reports of the first direct election of a township head in Buyun, Sichuan Province, stirred great interest within China and abroad that this might mark the extension of direct elections from the village to the township level.[2] However, the Buyun model was rejected as unconstitutional and, to date, higher-level party and state leaders have not sanctioned the direct election of township leaders.[3] The focus on direct township election has also obscured and often run counter to a significant and apparently more enduring innovation in widening the process for selection of township leaders, open selection and recommendation (OSR—*gongtui gongxuan*).[4]

While it is now generally accepted that village elections are legitimate and necessary,[5] dealing with township government, on the other hand, is more complex and deeply contested. Most importantly, the township forms the lowest level of state administration and its officials rank as state cadres. Their appointment, evaluation and approval procedures are decided within a set of relations between the township people's congress and the county congress, the party committee for the township and that at the county level.[6] Township leaders come under the party's *nomenclature* list meaning that the party must oversee and sanction even those leaders who are to be elected.[7] The township is thus an organ within the party and state networks and is the key interface between state and society. By contrast, villages are not part of the state structure and directly elected villagers' committees were established in an attempt to fill the administrative vacuum caused by the dismantling of the commune and brigade structures in the countryside. In the early to mid-1980s, village management had either collapsed in many parts of rural China or was operating policies that were at variance with state demands on villagers. As Daniel Kelliher pointed out, the starting point for gaining acceptance for villagers' committees was to accept that there was a political crisis in the countryside that probably could only be resolved by allowing the villagers enhanced capacity for self-government (Kelliher, 1997: 31–62).

Despite the reformers' hopes that the level of direct election would be raised to the township, one cannot apply the same logic here. Moreover, the vested institutional interests opposing change are stronger.[8] Support has come from within the people's consultative conference system and the Ministry of Civil Affairs (MOCA) that oversees the village elections. In March 1998, the MOCA official in charge of elections drafted a document suggesting that township elections might be carried out if conditions were ripe. This was rejected by the politburo, though Wen Jiabao among others was said to have supported the idea during discussions at Beidaihe (He, 2002: 11–12). This did not kill the issue, however, and at the March 1999 Chinese People's Political Consultative Conference session, 35 members of an agricultural subcommittee proposed that the Legal Work Committee of the National People's Congress (NPC) should study and introduce a law to promote direct election of township leaders (*South China Morning Post*, 9 March 1999). The request went unanswered and in April 1999, Zhang Mingliang, the then official in charge of village elections at the MOCA, stated that once uniform conditions were in place in the villages, direct elections could be initiated for the townships. However, as he acknowledged, elections were still not functioning properly in 40 per cent of villages and this could be a long wait. Even Premier Zhu Rongji gave the proposal for township elections his support at a news conference in March 2000 (*Renmin Ribao*, 16 March 2000, p. 1).

One major institutional barrier to this is that township elections would not, presumably, fall under the domain of MOCA but more likely under the people's congress system. This would require establishing principles and understanding within an entirely different administrative system. Apart from contravening current legal provisions for the township people's congress to appoint the township head, it would fundamentally challenge the control of the local party apparatus. It is perhaps unsurprising that to date neither township leaders nor the people's congress system have expressed enthusiasm for direct township leader elections. Baogang He's survey of 115 township leaders in Zhejiang found that over 77 per cent found direct elections premature, while a survey of 536 township leaders found 55 per cent declaring them premature, with a further 19.8 per cent considering them unsuitable (He, 2002: 7–8). However, given the lack of any official promotion, it may also be considered surprising that one in five township leaders would support elections.

The NPC under Li Peng has not supported expanding the scope of direct elections. A number of provinces including Guangdong sent requests to the

NPC to conduct elections but all were rejected (*Yazhou Zhoukan* [Asia Week], 8–14 February 1999). Shenzhen, in particular, was particularly keen in late-1997 and early-1998 to push ahead with direct township elections. It hoped to experiment with two townships in 1998 as a prelude to subsequently electing all township heads. Shenzhen has been keen to maintain its place as a pacesetter and its officials have sought to claim that it would be right for it to be at the forefront of political reform as well as economic reform through the 1980s and early-1990s. However, the senior leadership in Beijing was not so supportive and the general office of the NPC put a brake on reform attempts in Shenzhen.[9]

It appears that not only Li Peng but also Jiang Zemin is no supporter of direct township head elections[10] and in July 2001 a central committee document tried to call a halt to experimentation by declaring that the direct election of township heads was unconstitutional and contrary to the Organic Law on Local People's Congresses and People's Governments.[11]

To date, party preference has been to deal with issues of government transparency rather than accountability at the township level. Thus, in June 1998 a joint central committee and state council circular recognised that government reform should be encouraged for the 45,000 towns and townships stating that the party should 'seek proper ways to introduce the practice of open administration in government bodies at the township level'. This has become an increasingly common practice in provinces such as Fujian, Hunan and Shanxi, which are at the forefront of making township revenue and expenditures public and having an open system for government construction contracts. In Guangxi, townships have established supervisory groups to oversee administration. Such groups include members of the people's congress, delegates from the party committee, the disciplinary and control commission, retired cadres and villagers' delegates (see Liu, 2000: 72).

The Sixteenth Party Congress (2002) did not offer hope for progress on the direct election of township heads but rather stressed the need to tighten party control to maintain social stability. In fact, the sections in Jiang's report to the congress on political restructuring dealt only with regularising the party's relationship with various state institutions and mass organisations. Jiang stressed that the 'party commands the overall situation' and regarding the people's congress specifically, he noted that these were to ensure that party's views become the 'will of the state' and that 'candidates recommended by party organizations become leading cadres of the organs of state power through legal procedures' (Jiang, 2002). Such an emphasis is not likely to accommodate elections in which candidate choice and selection are taken out of the control of party organisation departments. It seems likely that Jiang's view was influenced by both the attempts of the China Democratic

Party to register in various provinces and the fear that campaigning may be taken advantage of by Falungong members (He, 2002: 2).

This has not resolved, however, how the party deals with enhancing legitimacy at the township level and finding candidates who will enjoy a modicum of local support. Before the circular was issued, in 1998 three townships experimented with the direct election of township heads with all three wishing to claim the title of the first in China to democratically elect a township leader. These were Buyun and Nancheng in Sichuan and Dapeng in Shenzhen. The Dapeng election was deemed to fall within the current regulatory framework and the Nancheng election was closely controlled by the provincial organisation department, but Buyun was deemed unconstitutional.[12] However, this has not marked the end of experimentation more broadly nor put an end to township elections within the Suining Municipality, where Buyun is located. In addition to the direct election in Buyun, Suining's Shizhong (Central) District has experimented with other innovative measures to broaden civic engagement and increase competition in selecting township leaders, including the party secretary and township head. In particular, Shizhong was praised for developing a process within existing regulations that 'increased transparency and competition in promoting cadres'.[13] The term used by the local organisation department is 'open recommendation and selection' (gongtui gongxuan).[14] Unlike the direct Buyun election, this process does not contravene existing regulations and is more acceptable as it ensures a strong role for the local party and state institutions.[15] ORS is also used for the selection of party secretaries thus opening up the process to ordinary party members rather than restricting appointment to higher-level party officials. A degree of competition replaces secretive appointment from above.

In the following sections, we discuss the four main approaches adopted to date for the selection of township leadership. We concentrate mainly on ORS. In the conclusions we make some tentative observations about how the experiments impact on China's on-going institutional transformation and the tension between maintaining a Leninist organisational framework while seeking to broaden participation to enhance legitimacy.[16]

New Methods of Township Leadership Selection

As noted earlier, the situation of the township is completely different from that of the villages where direct elections, with the exception of party leaders, have been institutionalised. Township cadres working on the lowest rung of the state ladder are recruited and paid by the state and are employed full-time. Village leaders are part-time and are compensated for their work out of the village's own finances. The social structure of the township is naturally more diverse than that of the village, making community-based politics more complex while population size, geographic spread and employment mix makes the construction of participatory politics within the existing framework more difficult. It will require more careful institutional design, as well as political and financial support.

During the 1990s, it was clear that in many areas problems arose between local administrations and society and the township had been the focal point for unrest and conflict. The townships have many demands placed on them by higher-level authorities with little independent capacity or incentive to carry out programmes that will benefit the local society. This weakens the capacity for comprehensive development by township governments. One set of Chinese researchers has even referred to the responsibilities of the townships being 'dismembered' by the county. Most government agencies at the township level actually receive contracts for their work from the county and this undermines the township's capacity to coordinate the work of their functional agencies as the administrative power in the township region does not belong to the township (Xueju et al., 1994: 5). Many of the quotas or tasks handed down are obligatory and township leaders are reprimanded and their promotion chances diminished by poor performance. Failure to meet one of the hard targets negates good performance in all other areas. This is referred to as 'one ticket override' (*yipiao foujue*). Failure to meet this target results in public criticism, fines, transfer or demotion for the party secretary and township head.[17]

However, the township does not have adequate financial resources to carry out its mandated obligations and its financial relationship to the county is not defined sufficiently clearly after the 1993–94 tax reforms. Thus the townships position is weakened further as it lacks not only power but also the necessary finances to carry out its mandates. With the various agencies under the direction of the county, township governments have little or no power to decide personnel arrangements, financial revenue and expenditures and the allocation of materials to the county branches in the township. For example in Laiwu (Shandong Province), only five staff in 28 township government offices were under the leadership of the township government. This had led some to dub the township government as a 'big title' (*paizi xiang*), 'many responsibilities' (*zeren da*), 'with little power' (*quanli xiao*) and 'difficult to deal with' (*banshi nan*) (Dai et al., 1991: 115–16).

The resultant system that comes from this contracting arrangement with limited financial resources is a 'pressurised system' (*yalixing tizhi*). This is defined as the 'management mode of dividing up tasks and the system of conducting assessment by giving material awards adopted by the political organization at the county or township level in order to develop the economy and attain the targets set by the higher authorities'.[18] Essentially, the party and administrative organisations at the county level divide up the tasks and set the targets for the organisation and individuals at the lower levels and require them to accomplish them within a prescribed period of time. There are usually one, three and five year contracts. The higher level makes its decision on political and economic rewards and penalties for organisations and individuals at the lower levels according to how well they have accomplished these tasks.[19]

This results in a number of specific problems. First, the burden of debt of townships has a tendency to increase. This has been compounded in recent years in some areas by the problems that the township and village enterprises have run into. Most townships cannot support the provision of an adequate level of public goods and services. Indeed, in many townships revenues are insufficient to cover the salaries and expenses of officials. One national survey conducted in the late-1990s showed that in a medium-sized county with a population of around half a million and with 5,000 administrative staff, 60 per cent had their salaries covered by financial revenues. Thirty per cent had to raise their salaries themselves and 10 per cent found their salary by fining farmers directly. At the township level, 35 per cent of their salary was collected directly from farmers (Guo, 1998: 34–35). With so much of the revenues tied up in salary and benefits for local officials, it is not surprising that a common name for township finances is 'eating finances' (*chifan caizheng*). Despite the unreliability of finance, most township governments are overstaffed as it still represents one of the best alternatives for employment and it does offer the opportunity for extraction.

Last but not least, these factors have created frictions between local officials and farmers. The burden of revenue collection is passed onto the farmers in the form of illegal fines and levies, commonly referred to as the 'three arbitraries' (*san luan—luan shoufei*—arbitrary taxation, *luan fakuan*—arbitrary fines and *luan tanpei*—arbitrary expropriation) (see also Wedeman, 2000: 400). At the same time that they are confronted with the inadequacies of the local administration, many farmers have become more aware of their rights through the mass media, the popularisation of laws and regulations and from the migration to the cities. With the existing system not providing any formal effective channels for redress of grievance, the end result has often been violence, blockading townships or attacking township officials.[20]

The recognition that township governing structures are failing them seems to be behind party leaders' willingness to allow limited institutional experimentation to improve transparency and accountability and to restore authority and legitimacy. Thus, there is recognition of the need for institutional innovation to deal with these problems and this might even provide the possibility for further political restructuring of local government. However, this process will not be allowed to proceed without strong oversight and hence the capacity for far-reaching change remains circumscribed.

A few innovators have focused on the process of the selection of township heads. Yet, the options within the current administrative framework remain limited as the power of appointment of the township head lies with the people's congress. In fact, the reality is that the candidate must be first nominated by the party committee at the next higher level (county or municipality). The process is not multi-candidate. Due to the lack of transparency, this places enormous discretionary power in the hands of the party committee and often in those of the party secretary at the higher level. This places the selection procedure in a black box and distorts the incentives for one to become a township head. It is common for prospective candidates to spend most time catering to the whims of their superiors with little incentive to work for the people for the latter have no say in the process of selection. This has been the reason behind the increasingly commonplace practice of 'selling and purchase of official posts' (*maiguan maiguan*). Sayings such as these have become commonplace in the countryside: 'if you bribe your superior 10 to 20, 000 yuan, you have just checked in. If you offer him 30 to 40, 000 yuan, you have registered for promotion. If you give him 80 to 100 000, you will get promoted' (Rong Jingben et al., 1998: 315).

Yet, county party authorities also have a stake in ensuring that their choice for candidate will be popular and will enjoy some modicum of a popular mandate. This would help strengthen the party's legitimacy at the local level and would help it to rejuvenate itself by incorporating members who enjoy local credibility. In addition, as in the villages, it is expected that this will help in better implementation of unpopular policies. This train of thinking has legitimated experimentation with the selection of township heads. To date, there have been four main methods.

Direct Election of Township Head

According to current regulations, direct election of a township head by the local residents is illegal. Despite this a few townships have held direct elections, the most widely publicised example being Buyun Township in Suining Municipality, Sichuan. A few weeks earlier, Nancheng Township in Qingshen County, Sichuan, also held a direct election for the township head and deputy.[21] However, because of the influence of the Buyun experiment, we shall focus on this here and refer to Nancheng where relevant.[22]

The entire process in Buyun took about two months, from preparation to the actual voting. In November 1998, the party committee of Shizhong District in Suining decided to hold direct elections in Buyun, a small township far way from the municipality.[23] It appears that the district party committee made the decision without consultation with the higher levels and drafted an electoral constitution for direct elections.[24] This outlined the process for nominating candidates. In addition to organisations (political parties, social organisations, and mass organisations), 30 voters could endorse a candidate for nomination. In Buyun, as in Nancheng, the party placed itself clearly in control of the selection mechanism. The Leadership Group for the Work of Direct Election of Buyun Township was, according to Joseph Cheng, under even stronger party control than the group that oversaw the election of deputies to the township people's congress, while the Buyun Election Committee was headed by the party secretary. All of the village-level direct election leadership groups were headed by village party secretaries (Cheng, 2001: 120–21, 136–37).

Following the endorsed procedures, 15 candidates were nominated, some of whom were members of the township party and government leadership while others had no party affiliation or any leadership position.[25] These 15 candidates were then considered by a joint electoral committee consisting of 162 members who would make a final selection of two candidates. The committee was drawn from village heads, village party secretaries and three village representatives from each of the 10 villages, members of the township party committee and other leaders from the township party and government organisations. The candidates had 20 minutes to make a campaign speech and a further 10 minutes for questions and answers. The final two were a schoolteacher who was not a party member and a village committee head who defeated those with posts in the party and government administration.[26] To ensure that the district authorities were not entirely by-passed, they used their constitutional right of nomination to propose that the Buyun Party Committee deputy secretary, Tan Xiaoqiu, be added to the list of final candidates.

The voting date was fixed for 31 December 1998 giving the candidates about a week to visit the 10 villages and the central marketplace to campaign.[27] During this phase of the campaign, the official nominee, Tan Xiaoqiu, although not a township native, enjoyed a distinct advantage being escorted from village to village by an official motorcycle entourage that was supplied by the township. This must have given the impression of official support to the villagers. Yet, the voting was quite close and Tan Xiaoqiu won with 50.19 per cent (3130) of the votes cast.[28] Tan Xiaoqiu thus became the first directly elected township head to take office. He took his oath of office on 4 January 1999 after the township congress had approved the voting.

As noted here, the election became a focal point of brief discussion before it was declared unconstitutional. This method has not been used since. The election also contained a number of other innovative measures including not arranging the candidates in alphabetical order on the ballot sheets. One-third of the ballot sheets had each candidate as the first name to ensure fairness since if people simply voted for the first name thinking that this is what they were supposed to do, it would not unduly distort the results. In addition, photographs of the three candidates were exhibited at the voting booths in order to help illiterate voters identify their candidate.

'Three Ballot' Election for Township Head

While Buyun was carrying out its election, Dapeng Township in the Longgang District of Shenzhen was preparing its own election for a township head. [29] The method chosen resembles the *haixuan* principle (literally meaning from the sea) used in village elections that allows candidates to be put forward by local organisations or groups of individuals. The method is also based on that of the 'two-ballot system' that has been experimented with for the election of village party secretaries. [30] In this process, party members and villagers or villagers' representatives vote in the first round to decide who will be candidates for a second ballot within the party itself. All party members vote to elect the party secretary from the candidates presented. This process is often referred to as a 'poll test' or 'democratic recommendation'. It provides a chance to test the credibility of candidates among the broader populace while ensuring that the party itself keeps control over the final outcome. When this process is moved to the township level it becomes a 'three ballot' process. The main reason for this is that the township head must be 'elected' by the people's congress after a two-round process of recommendation. Thus, a third ballot is necessary.

In Dapeng the election process lasted around four months. The Party Committee of Longgang District decided to hold the election on 18 January 1999. The electoral jurisdiction with 5,300 eligible voters, of whom 5,048 voted, was divided into 17 recommendation districts (*tuixuan qu*) on the basis of township party and government institutions, township enterprises and villagers' committees. The voters nominated 76 village leaders to be preliminary candidates. The Dapeng Township Party Committee then reviewed the qualifications of six nominees who had been recommended by over 100 voters. Five were then proposed for the next stage, one was excluded as he was over 50 years of age and thus disqualified in terms of the recommendation requirements. Campaign speeches and question and answer sessions were held on 27 January after which a group of 1,068 representatives voted for the candidate to be put forward as township head. [31] The incumbent township head, Li Weiwen, won 76 per cent (813) of the votes and was recommended as the only candidate to the township congress. There was then a delay before the final election was held by the congress on 29 April. Two reasons caused the delay. First, delegates to the new congress were elected on 9 April and it was felt that new rather than old delegates should approve the vote. Second, Dapeng submitted a report on the township election to both the Guangdong People's Congress and the NPC for their approval. The final vote of the township congress was unanimous (45 votes) in its support of Li as township head.

The election was widely promoted by the Shenzhen authorities as an institutional breakthrough that was consistent with current regulation. Shenzhen also held a national meeting to disseminate the experience of Dapeng as a model for others to follow. This was consistent with discussions in Shenzhen about their need to become an experimental political reform zone to follow their status as an experimental economic reform zone.[32] However, it seems that the experiment will not be continued.[33] From a participatory viewpoint, there are clear drawbacks in this process. First, the representative group clearly does not select the township head and furthermore it cannot represent all of the voters. The fact that there is only one candidate provided to the congress rather than multi-candidates weakens the competitiveness of the final election. Last but not least, the desire to remain within the existing regulations seriously circumscribes the extent to which the election can be considered genuinely democratic.

'Two Ballot' Election of Township Head

This method was adopted in Zhuoli Township, Linyi County in Shanxi province in 1999.[34] This area is well known for its two ballot village party election (see Li, 1999), from which the two ballot township election method is derived. But in addition to the township head, it is also used for the party secretary and chair of the people's congress. With selection of a new township leadership pending, the county leaders wanted to get some feedback from public opinion about the current leadership.

As a result, the party committee of Linyi County drafted the 'Implementation Plan for Opinion Polls in Zhuoli Township on Leading Officials' on 10 April 1999. Between 10–16 April, the county and township made their preparations and a work report conference was held on 16 April. At this conference, the incumbent party secretary, the township head and the chair of the presidium of the people's congress presented their work to 500 representatives.[35] There was no opportunity to raise questions. Two days later (18 April) a vote was held with some 9,000 voting at 17 different polling booths. Voters were presented with three choices for each candidate: have confidence in (*xinren*), have basic confidence in (*jiben xinren*), or no confidence in (*bu xinren*). Any candidate who received less than a 50 per cent level of support in the first two categories was not to be recommended by the township as a candidate for the next party and people's congress elections. In fact, all three gained sufficient support.

Although this system is commonly referred to as a 'two ballot' system, the second ballot is not public (Shi, 2000). The township election does not follow on directly from the first vote. The result of the first vote is only used as reference for the county leaders to consider when appointing the new leadership at the township level. It is also difficult to know the role the work report meeting actually plays in the first ballot. While all eligible voters are entitled to vote to evaluate the township leaders, they were not entitled to listen to their presentations.

These three methods of election all try to broaden the scope of participation in the selection of township leadership and seek to provide some feedback on the views of villagers. The direct election method in Buyun and Nancheng is the most open and competitive with the party guiding the process rather than being the decision maker. The latter two methods that fall within the current regulations are weaker in providing a direct link between voter preferences and outcomes. Both rely on the choice by a few on behalf of the whole. This may lead to disillusionment with the process of feedback. Essentially people are mobilised to vote for a process that boils down choice to a single candidate and that is in any case only in the form of a recommendation. In this context, it is interesting to look at the fourth method (ORS) as a way to provide better inputs within the framework of existing regulations.

Open Recommendation and Selection

The precise origins of this method are unclear.[36] As far as we are aware, however, the Shizhong District of Suining Municipality in Sichuan first implemented it on a systematic basis. The Shizhong District organised its ORS during the first half of 1998 and in addition to the township head, the process also involved the selection of the party secretary.[37]

Clearly ORS is not an election but rather a process that uses some electoral procedures to enable a representative group broader than the township people's congress to have a strong role in the selection of the candidates. It is different from the traditional way of party selection of officials through the *nomenclature* as it entails a higher degree of openness and competition. However, it is more open than competitive. Consequently, the ORS method can be viewed as a transitional institutional process situated between the conventional process of party nomination and congress ratification and a direct election. It is more open and competitive than traditional practice but is less open and competitive than a direct election in terms of public participation.

In late-1997, the Shizhong District Party Committee launched a plan to accelerate the reform of its cadre system, recognising that the current system did not meet the demands of the more complex environment. They decided that the reforms should ensure the recruitment of more highly-qualified officials and encourage more participation. In January 1998, the fourth party plenum of Shizhong District presented its work report that included an outline of the ORS method. Initially, it was the party's intention to use the ORS only for a limited number of appointments to its functional bureaus and it did not include township heads.

In May 1998, an event occurred in Baoshi Township that changed the minds of the district party leaders. Both the party secretary and the township head were removed from office because of corruption and it appeared that a further 20 township officials were involved, including the chair of the township congress.[38] Given the strong economic growth in the township, the leadership had been regarded highly by the district authorities. This judgment was now called into question and district leaders began to see that there were problems with the traditional closed system of appointment. In addition, because of the host of problems left behind by the disgraced leadership, they had trouble finding a suitable candidate who was willing to work in Baoshi.[39] Consequently, the Shizhong District Party Committee decided to extend the ORS method to the position of Baoshi Township head.[40]

Not surprisingly, such a decision was contentious. Some district leaders felt that as the use of ORS to select a township head in Sichuan was unprecedented, it would be risky and might lead to unforeseen problems and failure. The organisation department that was to oversee the process lacked experience and the necessary skills to operate the selection. It had to try to learn quickly from others while, at the same time, developing some new measures to deal with problems as they emerged. There was also suspicion among the general public that the process might not be as open and competitive as was suggested and that the party might have already secretly decided upon the candidate, in line with usual practice. Some of the remaining township officials were also unhappy with the turn of events, as they had anticipated automatic promotion, something that would now be challenged by the implementation of the ORS. Despite this opposition and uncertainty, at the end of May, the decision was made to move forward.

On 12 May 1998 the District Party Committee adopted a formal decision to hold the ORS and a leading group was established to oversee the process. Although the district organisation department implemented the selection process, others were represented in the leading group and did participate in the process. Members of the leading group were drawn from the discipline and inspection committee, the propaganda department, the standing committee of the people's congress, the people's political consultative conference and the district government. This helped build an initial consensus and reduce opposition to the process.

The formal procedure began on 25 May with a process of public application. In addition to nominated cadres, party secretaries and village heads in certain townships were allowed to apply if they met certain basic criteria.[41] Of the 69 who applied, 67 were considered to be qualified and in June they wrote a three-hour examination. This open process resulted in about half the candidates not being on the state's payroll.[42] The top six candidates from the written examination then had an oral examination on 22 June. The oral examination was held in front of a group of 149 Baoshi representatives who whittled the list down to two after all six had finished the question and answer session.[43] The two remaining candidates were then recommended to the township congress for final selection. This selection was held on the same day. Xiang Daoquan, who was only 29 years old at the time, was elected with 46 of the 49 votes of the township congress delegates.[44]

The district leadership was pleased with the outcome of this experiment and this gave them both the confidence and the experience to extend its application. Importantly, higher-level authorities did not criticise the ORS and the provincial organisation department invited representatives from Shizhong to present their experience at a provincial conference.[45] The ORS was also reported in detail by the *Sichuan Daily* and on Sichuan television. The District Party Committee then decided to extend the ORS to the township party secretary and this process began in September 1998. Dongchan and Lianhua townships were chosen as the trial sites. In addition, they also organised the open selection of the township head in Hengshan.

The basic procedures for the selection of the township head and the party secretary are essentially the same. Here we shall describe the four-stage process for ORS for the township party secretary.

Stage One: Application and Qualifications   A set of criteria were established for all potential applicants of which the most important were that they should have at least a college degree, an administrative rank of at least deputy section head (fuke) and be born after 30 September 1958 (thus, be under 40 years of age). The requirements for party secretary were more stringent than those for township head as village officials were allowed to participate even though they do not enjoy a formal bureaucratic rank. Despite seemingly strict criteria, there were 99 applicants for the two positions revealing a relatively large pool of candidates.[46]

Stage Two: Written Examination   This was considered the most objective phase of the selection process. A special group established by the organisation department was responsible for designing the examination and it made secret visits to other counties for this purpose. All the questions were kept confidential until the exam and covered areas such as Deng Xiaoping theory, theory of a market economy, public administration, leadership, laws, science and technology, history, official documents, contemporary politics, essential agricultural work and agricultural production. The highest possible score was 150 points. The questions were structured in different ways. For some questions it was necessary to fill in the blank spaces, others were multiple-choice while yet others required short reasoned judgments. The case method was also stressed with two cases presented. One case involved investigation by the leader into flood prevention work while the other concerned a case of the villagers suing the government. These were realistic cases for the aspiring leaders to grapple with. In 1998, the Yangtze River area suffered from serious flooding and Sichuan constitutes the vital up-stream area. Thus, flood prevention is an important part of local government work touching on questions of security, development and livelihood. Sichuan has also become well known for the severity of its rural disturbances in recent years with numerous cases of conflict between the farmers and the local government. Thus, we can see that the written examination did contain some substantive issues that were based on possible real life situations. Review of the written examination led to the selection of the top six candidates who then participated in the oral examination. The organisation department also set up for them a two-day investigation of the relevant township.[47]

Stage Three: Oral Examination   This phase more or less resembled a campaign speech with a representative group voting to make a final selection of candidates after listening to speeches and raising questions. Naming this group proved difficult under the existing institutional arrangements and the local organisation department simply decided to call it a defense meeting.[48] The voting process was called 'democratic recommendation' (*minzhu tuijian*). The representative groups, of course, widened participation from traditional methods and comprised: heads of the district party committee, the district government, the people's congress and people's political consultative conference, the heads of various government entities, township-level cadres (party members), village officials (party members), village party members and heads of district-level sectors. In the Lianhua Township, the number of members in the representative group totalled 278.

There were four questions of which one was known and could be prepared ahead of time. The other three questions were not made known. Voting took place following the oral examination with the two candidates who received the highest number of votes were recommended to an enlarged meeting of the standing committee of the district party committee.

Stage Four: Nomination and Announcement   The enlarged meeting respected the results of the vote and thus the candidate who had the highest number of votes was nominated as township party secretary and this was announced on the spot. However, the process for confirmation of the party secretary and township head is different. The party secretary needs to be approved by the higher-level party committee while the township head needs to be elected by the people's congress. Eventually Xia Xiandong and Tang Kunlun were elected party secretaries of Lianhua and Dongchan townships with 122 and 321 votes respectively.

ORS as a Mechanism for Broader but Controlled Participation

Clearly ORS broadens the scope of participation in selection of local leaders in contrast with traditional methods but it retains the Leninist concern for control of the process, should anything deemed untoward happen. Two institutional adjustments are made to broaden participation. First, the criteria for application are lowered. In the case of township head, village officials and lower-ranked cadres (below deputy section chief *fuke*) are permitted to participate. Having a farmer's status is not a barrier to being able to compete for a formal bureaucratic position that is financed out of the state's budget and which oversees a larger geographic terrain than the village. A larger number of younger officials can participate because the requirement for level of bureaucratic rank is lower than usual.[49] For example, among 67 applicants in Baoshi, there were 20 (29.9 per cent) cadres ranked at that just below that of deputy section chief, namely at *gu* level, with another 28 (41.28 per cent) who were ordinary cadres or village officials. In terms of age, the number of applicants under 33 years formed the majority (41 or 61 per cent).

The second institutional innovation is that the voting by the representative group is decisive. This modifies the party's dominance of the entire selection procedure of the township head. Under the old process, the organisation department would provide a name list for the party standing committee should positions in a township become vacant. The standing committee of usually seven to nine members would then convene to discuss the recommended candidates. A meeting of the party secretaries would usually precede this meeting.[50] This meeting is the quintessential bargaining and deal-making session where a basic consensus is formed after people horse trade their favorite candidates. The decision is then presented to the standing committee that is highly unlikely to raise criticism of the proposed choices. The final decision is approved and issued in the name of the standing committee. The process is then shifted from the district to the township level. The candidate for party secretary will then be elected party secretary by the township's party congress while the township head will be elected by the people's congress.

Beginning in the 1990s, this traditional process began to be modified with adoption of the process of 'democratic recommendation'. This meant, in practice, that the organisation department called together some staff from a work-unit to request an evaluation of their head. However, this process was more one of form than content as the evaluation did not necessarily have an impact on the decision of the higher level. The work of a township head could potentially affect all in the township but virtually none had input on their appointment. This is also the case with 'democratic recommendation' as it is an internal process and excludes the villagers themselves.

This is different with the recommendation group in the ORS process even though the old name of 'democratic recommendation' is retained. First, it is the representative group and not the standing committee that makes the final decision on the candidates. Second, more ordinary cadres participate in the group and not just the district's leading cadres. For example, in Baoshi ordinary cadres comprised 68 of the 149 representatives (45.6 per cent). If we include the number of ordinary cadres who were township congress delegates then the total would top 50 per cent. This is the same with ORS for the party secretary. Village officials play a decisive role in the final selection because they dominate the representative group. In Lianhua there are 198 village officials (about 71 per cent) out of a group total of 278. In Dongchan there were 237 (about 61 per cent) village officials out of a total of 388 in the group. This means that any person who wishes to win the election must gain the support of the village-level officials. Without this support, no candidate could emerge as a winner even if she/he did well on the written examination and was the preferred choice of the higher-level authorities.

The size and structure of the representative group makes it hard for the party to influence the voting. This can be seen by analyzing the voting behaviour of the representative group (see Tables 4.1 and 4.2). The distribution of the votes is interesting with an obvious divergence between the district-level and village-level officials in terms of their choice of candidate. We should keep in mind that all members of the standing committee of the party are

Table 4.1
Voting Results for Lianhua Township

Candidate Number	Candidate Name	Total Votes	Village Votes	Township Votes	District Votes	Votes Won	Ranking
		278	198	48	32		
1	Xia Xiandong		87	28	7	122	1
2	Liu Yongjun		41	24	5	70	3
3	Guo Dejin		29	17	14	60	5
4	Yuan Jie		8	0	3	11	6
5	Duan Jijiao		62	14	3	79	3
6	Hu Yongguang		40	12	15	67	4

Source: Organisation Department of Shizhong District, Suining Municipality.
Note: Please note that the number of votes in the columns do not add up to 100 per cent as each selector could vote for two candidates if they wished.

Table 4.2

Voting Results for Dongchan Township

Candidate Number	Candidate Name	Total Votes	Village Votes	Township Votes	District Votes	Votes Won	Ranking
		388	237	107	44		
1	Yi Pengfei		145	57	21	223	2
2	Liu Anzhong		0	4	0	4	6
3	Sun Hongjun		39	14	2	55	4
4	Tang Kunlun		164	44	23	231	1
5	Zhang Jiawu		46	20	32	98	3
6	Liu Yang		17	22	2	41	5

Source: Organisation Department of Shizhong District, Suining Municipality.
Note: Please note that the number of votes in the columns do not add up to 100 per cent as each selector could vote for two candidates if they wished.

district-level cadres. In Lianhua, almost half of the 32 district-level cadres voted for Yuan Jie (15 votes) but Yuan received only 8 votes from the village-level officials. By contrast, Xia Xiandong received a total of 87 votes even though he received only 7 district-level votes. He still won in Lianhua Township. In Dongchan the contrast is even clearer. The eventual winner, Tang Kunlun, won 164 of the 237 village-level official votes (over 60 per cent), while only 23 of the 44 district-level cadres voted for him. The candidate in the third place, Zhang Jiwu, received 32 votes from the district-level cadres but only 46 votes from the village level. Given this situation, it is difficult for the party to manipulate the results of the election.

When we compare the voting behaviour of the village-level officials and the township cadres, we find much greater congruence. In Lianhua, Xia Xiandong polled the highest vote among both the village and the township officials, while in Dongchan, Tang Kunlun received the highest village vote and was second to Yi Pengfei for the township votes (44:57). Two cases are not sufficient to make any robust conclusions but we can make one tentative suggestion about these voting outcomes. The main reason for the convergence is probably that township cadres maintain close working relationships and interact frequently with village officials. This means that a consensus on the candidates is more likely between township and district than between the district and the village. In the villages, the candidate's practical capabilities rather than their speech-making capacity is considered more important. By contrast, district-level cadres might pay more attention to a candidate's rhetoric and their alignment with the policies of the party and the Shizhong District in particular. Some villagers commented that they preferred a person they saw as honest, credible and modest even if they were not a good public speaker. They felt that it was easier to communicate with such a person.

However, this does not mean that the party has foregone its control and its Leninist predisposition is still apparent. We are not dealing with open representation but a process of a controlled opening to gauge public receptivity to proposed candidates. The last thing the party wants is to put forward a slate of candidates that will be rejected by those they will be overseeing.[51] The representative group is much smaller than the potential voter pool. It is elite rather than popular participation. It is limited within the system and is not inclusive, with most representatives being drawn from among officialdom at different levels.

It should also be remembered that the party controls the selection of the township heads even though it cannot decide directly who the candidates are let alone which candidate will win. The party exerts its influence in at least three ways. First, it is the only rule maker for the ORS and monopolises the privilege of setting the criteria for application, reviewing the applicants, designing the examinations and drafting the voting procedures. The party can manipulate the criteria on age, education level and years of work to limit the scope of applicants to find those potential officials who fit with its defined needs. In this case, there was a need to provide younger and better-educated officials. As the rules were institutionalised, in fact, the criteria for application were tightened. Thus, in Baoshi Township the party allowed all cadres below the fuke level to participate but this was limited in the 'Interim Provisions' of 3 November 1998. The provisions both raised the years of necessary work experience as well as the level of administrative experience. It was deemed that the candidate should hold a *guji* position, have a college diploma and have at least five-years' work experience. If the applicant was a farmer, he or she should have worked as a party secretary or village head for more than three years.

Second, the party can still move the township officials elected by ORS at will. Xiang Daoquan, the township head elected in Baoshi was moved to Hengshan Township to be party secretary after just one year in office. This showed that the party was not bound by the desire of the representative group, especially not that of its local participants. Whatever it may be, the ORS process is not an institution to promote democracy. Its primary role is to increase the talent pool and vet effective cadres. This could undermine the longer-term effectiveness of the process. In fact, some cadres in the organisation department were also concerned about the speed with which Xiang was moved. They felt that local residents would not believe that the ORS was effective and that township heads might not devote themselves to their work sufficiently if they thought that they could still be moved at will. Some villagers and Xiang himself thought that it would have been better to work longer in Baoshi as he had become familiar with the township and as he had been elected for the job.

Last but not least, most officials are still party members meaning that their ties of loyalty are still to the party organisation rather than the local community. Most applicants are party members. For example, in Baoshi, 52 of the 67 (77.6 per cent) of the applicants were party members while only two applicants came from the other ('democratic') political parties.

Concluding Comments: Institutional Innovation and Economic Development

At first glance, it may seem strange that these innovations have taken place in Suining, a small municipality in the west of China that lags economically behind the more developed areas of the east. More conventional wisdom on the relationship between economic development and political reform would suggest that Suining is an unlikely candidate to be a pioneer of political reform.

Of course we are dealing with institutional innovation rather than democratisation but it is still interesting to note that a number of key innovations in China since the 1970s have occurred in economically less developed areas. Two prominent examples from rural China are the household responsibility system and the villagers' committee elections. The former was initiated in a poor village in Anhui Province in 1978. The village election programme began in two Guangxi counties in late-1980 and early-1981. Both these experiments led to the development of a national policy and made a decisive contribution to change in rural China.

In poorer areas, the impact of a crisis is likely to be felt first and this can cause innovation by the local government. This was the case with Suining. Both general factors and some specific causes explain Suining's decision to undertake institutional innovation. First, local governments in many poor areas lack the revenue to meet basic public needs or to respond to crises. This can create the need to innovate with existing institutions. Opening up the political system or broadening public participation is likely, however, only to be a last resort. Second, local communities in poorer areas may be less driven by interest groups and the forces of pluralism. This may facilitate consensus building about alternative solutions. Third, innovation initiated by the government might be accepted more readily. Local societies might not have much information about alternatives, especially if migration is not particularly significant. Under these circumstances, the combination of remoteness would allow for more experimentation, as it does not fall under such strict scrutiny from the political centre. At the same time, the innovation is liable to be within existing institutional frameworks as access to information on alternatives will be limited.

In the specific case of Suining, the economic scandal caused by the corruption of local cadres pushed the district leadership to reconsider the method through which they selected township officials. The fact that the ORS was successful in Baoshi led them to broaden the process to other townships and to the selection of the party secretary. The use of the ORS for the selection of the party secretary is more significant than that of township head because it opens up the internal operations of the party to a broader albeit limited public. Even though participation was limited, the oral examination and the structure of the recommendation group did result in most inhabitants knowing a lot more about prospective candidates than would normally be the case.

Leadership is also important in promoting or resisting change.[52] In many localities, an insightful and strong-willed individual leader can play a crucial role in initiating and implementing reform. This was clearly the case in Shizhong with Zhang Jinming, the former party secretary who has now been promoted to vice-mayor of Suining Municipality. She played a key role in initiating and sustaining the momentum for the ORS. Importantly, she had experience outside of Suining having worked in the Sichuan provincial committee of the Youth League and been an intern in the Ministry of Foreign Trade and Economic Cooperation in Beijing. Her enthusiasm and continued support for reforming the traditional cadre system enabled the trial sites to complete the work and the success in these areas then gave confidence to other district leaders to persist with the reform.[53]

Regional competition also played a role in pushing ahead innovation. Some scholars have argued that competition among local governments wishing to improve economic growth has been a major force promoting fast economic growth (see Goldstein, 1995: 1105–31; Rawski, 1995: 1150–73). While political innovation is much riskier than economic, it is not without competition. Localities can be willing to act as trial sites for experimentation because of potential recognition and benefits higher levels might bestow on them. If experimentation is successful, local leaders might be promoted more quickly. In Suining, the ORS process attracted attention from the Sichuan Provincial Party Committee and also some scholars based in Beijing. Zhang Jinming, as noted earlier, made a presentation to the provincial organisation department in September 1998 that promoted the experiment. Through discussions with the scholars at present, she became aware that Dapeng in Shenzhen was planning to hold a direct election for township head. As a result, she decided to speed up the process for the direct election in Buyun to ensure that it would be the first in China. Cadres in Suining were very proud to be known as the first to hold a direct election while those in Shenzhen were disappointed by the news that they had been beaten.

Crisis might produce a one-time experimentation, but it is more difficult to ensure sustainability of a new institutional innovation. Once the perceived crisis is past there is a tendency to set aside the innovation. However, in the case of the ORS, momentum has been maintained. A September 2001 document issued by the Sichuan Provincial Organisation Bureau required all counties, with the exception of those in minority autonomous regions, to carry out the ORS method of selection in at least one-third of the townships by the end of that year.[54] While this process has been accepted at the provincial level, and even here there is uncertainty about institutionalising the representative group, it has not been adopted as national policy. National policy has favoured a similar process called 'open selection' (*gongkai xuanba*). However there are two principal differences. First, in general 'open selection' is only used for the position of deputy. Second, if some head positions are selected through this process, it is within functional sectors and not within the administrative organs.

The ORS is just one of the innovations that have been introduced to reform the cadre system since the Fifteenth Party Congress (September 1997) and we can expect more with the rising concern about corruption within party ranks. Party leaders are worried about a drift of qualified party members out of leading party and state positions to the foreign and private sector where not only is the pay higher but also promotions can be more rapid. Within this context, the use of selection methods such as the ORS is seen as a way to improve promotion chances for younger people. Under the traditional system, it is difficult for a person under 40 or 45 years of age to head a township. In Suining, many township heads are below 30 and the youngest head was only 26-years-old at the time of selection. However, some older cadres have not been so pleased with the outcome and have tried to obstruct its implementation. Many cadres working in the county-level administration who are around 45 years old may now find it difficult to gain promotion or may have to retire early.

It offers new opportunities to the individual while providing the party with the chance to unearth good local talent. Individuals can make a case for selection without having to rely solely on currying favour with existing leaders. One deputy party secretary of Shizhong commented that he was surprised to find so many talented people in the district. It has allowed the organisation department to have a better sense of which qualified candidates enjoy a broader credibility. Some of those who did not win in the final vote have subsequently been considered good enough for promotion elsewhere.

However, in terms of institutional design, the ORS has a number of shortcomings. First, the application criteria are still restrictive in setting age, education and administrative ranking requirements that limit the scope of applicants. Second, there are problems with the technical implementation of the voting. For example, there are no voting booths that provide privacy and there is no open count of the vote. Third, higher levels can still remove those elected during their term of office.

The development of a process such as the ORS represents a local attempt by the party to deal with what a number of observers see as a process of institutional decline resulting from economic reforms.[55] It is an attempt to deal with the evolving reality at the local level and to improve the quality of the officials that are appointed to key posts. Certainly, there was a demand with over 60 applicants for each position, revealing that in a poorer area such as Suining, a job in the bureaucracy is considered a good thing.[56] It also provides the party with feedback from society about the kinds of individuals that it is selecting and in this sense provides a modicum of democratisation within the local party apparatus. The ORS allows more party members at the grassroots level to participate in the choice of party secretaries at the next higher level. In fact, they dominate the representative group. This process can help broaden the base of the party's legitimacy at the local level.

This does not mean that the party's Leninist predilection has been abandoned nor is there any indication that processes such as the ORS are seen as a stepping stone to direct elections at the township level. The organisation department remains in control of the reform of the cadre system and the relationship between the representative groups, the people's congress and the party committee remain unclear. The party will still guide the process of selection and, as we have seen, can still remove or transfer those selected whenever they choose to do so. Senior party leaders have vacillated on the question as to whether direct elections at the township level would be a good thing or not. On balance they have tended to resist this move. The Central Secretariat of the CCP issued a document in September 2001 that called for the postponement of the experiment with township elections as the existing legal framework did not provide adequate legitimacy for this.[57] However, while the centre vacillates, local governments and party institutions have to find real solutions to the problems that confront them. Perhaps the biggest problem is that of legitimacy of the governing organs themselves. This would suggest that we might see more local institutional innovation that tries to walk the fine line of broadening civic participation while retaining Leninist organisational control.[58] This may seem a contradiction in terms but without any clear direction from the centre, the only solution for localities lies in the already existing institutional guidelines, within which the grey areas may be exploited to enhance local representation.

Notes

1. The fieldwork for this article was conducted by Xuedong Yang in Suining in September 2001. The authors would like to thank Zhang Jinming (former district party secretary,

currently vice-mayor of Suining), Yang Huadi (deputy party secretary of Shizhong District), Ma Shengkang (director of the organisation department of Shizhong District), Liu Hui (deputy director of the organisation department), Xiang Daoquan (former head of Baoshi Township, currently party secretary of Hengshan Township), Tang Kunlong (party secretary of Dongchan Township) and other local officials. They provided much information about the direct election in Buyun and about the process of 'public recommendation, public election' (gongtui gongxuan) system. Unless otherwise stated, the information in this chapter is drawn from discussions with them. We would also like to thank Li Fan who provided much useful information on the specifics of the Buyun election. However, the authors alone are responsible for the ideas expressed here. Xuedong Yang presented an earlier version of this article at a panel on local democracy in China held at the Fairbank Centre on 3 December 2001.

2. The election was widely covered by the international press (see articles in the *New York Times*, *South China Morning Post* and *Washington Post*) following a report in China's adventurous newspaper *Nanfang Zhoumo* (Southern Weekly) on 15 January1999. The most complete overview is the three-part series by Fan Li in *Ming Bao* (11, 12 and 13 February 1999). The Fan Li articles are translated in Foreign Broadcast Information Service, *Daily Report: China*, 16 February 1999. See also Li et al. (2000).

3. The election was first criticised as unconstitutional in an article by Zha Qingjiu that appeared in the authoritative *Fazhi Ribao* (Legal Daily), 19 January 1999 ('Minzhu bu neng chaoyue falu' [Democracy Must Not Overstep the Law]). The direct election of township heads should not be confused with the direct election of representatives to the local people's congress. Up to the county level, delegates to the people's congress have been elected directly since the system was restored in 1980. See Womack (1982: 261–77) and Jacobs (1991: 171–99). For new procedures that were introduced permitting direct elections up to the county level see 'Election Law', in *Zhonghua renmin gongheguo falu ji youguan fagui huibian 1979–1984*. The law was revised in 1986.

4. Recent articles on the issue of township elections include Li (2002: 704–23); Cheng (2001: 104–37); He (2002) and He and Lang (2001: 1–22).

5. This was confirmed in November 1998 with the passage of the Villager Committees Organisation Law of the People's Republic of China, see *Renmin Ribao* (People's Daily), 5 November 1998, a translation can be found in *BBC Summary of World Broadcasts: the Far East*/3380.

6. For a general analysis of the complex relationship of horizontal and vertical control within the Chinese administrative system see Unger (1987: 15–46).

7. For the nature of this process related to the people's congress at the township level see Manion (2000: 764–82).

8. On institutional opposition from the people's congress system and the party's organisation bureau see He (2002: 10–11).

9. Interviews with Shenzhen party leaders, July 2001.

10. According to Lianjiang Li, Jiang told Anhui delegates at the 2001 NPC session that the villagers' committee elections should not be extended upwards (Li, 2002: 704).

11. Document No. 12, July 2001, 'Zhonggong zhongyang guanyu zhuanfa "Zhonggong quanguo renda changweihui dangzu guanyu quanguo xiangji renmin daibiao dahui huanjie xuanju gongzuo youguan wenti de yijian" de tongzhi' (Notice of the Central Committee of the Chinese Communist Party on Transmitting 'Suggestions of the Party Group of the Standing Committee of the NPC on Certain Questions Concerning the Election of Township Level People's Congresses').

12. The Nancheng election was held on 5 December1998 while that in Buyun was held on 31 December 1998. Thus, while Nancheng may claim the title of the first such election

since 1949, the moral highground lies with Buyun. As Lianjiang Li notes 'it was freer, fairer and more competitive in almost all aspects than the earlier Nancheng election' (Li, 2002: 714–15). For an extensive account of the Nancheng election, see Li Fan (2002: 376–88).

13. Yu (2002: 16). This programme is organised jointly by the China Centre for Comparative Politics and Economics under the Translation Bureau of the Central Committee and the Comparative Research Centre for the Party under the Central Party School. Among other winners that were related to elections were: Qianxi County in Hebei Province for its direct election of delegates to Women's Associations and Guangshui Municipality (Hubei) for its 'two ballot' election for party secretaries at the village level.

14. Nanbu County in Sichuan Province has also used this system but only for deputy heads. See Liu (2000: 73).

15. The Buyun election breaches Article 101 of the State Constitution that states 'Local people's congresses at the different levels elect and have the power to recall, at the corresponding level, governors and deputy governors, mayors and deputy mayors, heads and deputy heads of counties, districts, townships, and towns'. Further, the Organic Law for Local People's Congresses and Local People's Governments reiterates these powers of appointment and removal of personnel.

16. While the account by Joseph Cheng on the Buyun and Dapeng elections is essentially descriptive, Lianjiang Li's analysis takes the optimistic view that the new leadership may be more amenable to acceptance and that the international community can play a role in protecting grass-roots experiments. We are more circumspect and view ORS as a viable way of broadening participation while resisting direct elections.

17. For more on this system see Edin (2000), Rong Jingben et al. (1998), Saich (2002) and Whiting (2001).

18. Rong et al., 1998. Xuedong Yang is one of the co-authors of this study. For more on the pressurised system see Yang (2000: 13–24).

19. It is rare to use financial penalties for officials at the township level, as their salaries are considered too low. However, a failure to meet priority targets will lead to demerits on file, possible transfer and certainly to future financial gains forgone.

20. On the rural unrest see Bernstein and Lu (2000: 742–63).

21. For information see www.dajun.com.cn/xiangzhenxuanju.htm. Li Fan, 'A Brave Experiment with Electoral Reform in China; the Direct Election of a Township Head in Nanchang Township'.

22. For further details of the Buyun election, refer to Cheng (2001: 118–30) and Li (2002: 710–19). We shall just highlight the key aspects here.

23. Buyun has a population of around 16,000 living in an area of 32 square km. Another 4,000 people work outside of its jurisdiction. The average per capita income is 1636 yuan. It is less developed than other townships in the district. There are 10 villagers' committees in the township. Nancheng has a population of 19,000 in 14 villages. The process in Nancheng was somewhat longer but interestingly began with a questionnaire circulated to 750 households of which 723 responded. The survey found that over 95 per cent of party officials and 85 per cent of the general public thought that election of deputy township heads would be beneficial. As a result of this the county and Nancheng set up groups to oversee the elections. At both levels the group was headed by the party secretary.

24. Suining shi Shizhongqu gongkai xuanba xiang (zhen) renmin zhengfu xiang (zhen) zhang zanxing banfa (taolun gao) (Suining Municipality Shizhong District Temporary Method for the Open Election of Heads of Town and Township People's Governments [Discussion Draft]), 3 November 1998.

25. Six who were members of the election committees withdrew from these positions and at a review held on 14–15 December, the election committee found all candidates acceptable.

26. In Nancheng,10 individuals were proposed of whom two declined to run. Unlike in Buyun the candidates were screened by the Nancheng township party committee and the county organisation department rather than a specially constituted body. The three candidates selected made short speeches at a meeting in the local primary school and did not answer questions. The meeting was for a select group of township and village cadres, heads of party cells, election representatives and congress delegates (Li, 2002: 378).

27. It is estimated that almost all of the inhabitants heard the various speeches and 650 raised questions. The questions ranged across topics such as agricultural production, farmers' burdens, taxation, market building, environmental protection, family planning, social security and the construction of village roads and education.

28. The total number of eligible voters was 11,347 of whom 3,700 were working outside the township. The total number of votes cast was 6,236. Of those who had remained behind to vote, 81.5 per cent cast a vote, giving a voter turnout rate of 54.95 per cent. Shizhong's party secretary had insisted that the winning candidate had to receive over 50 per cent of the valid votes and that over 50 per cent of eligible voters had to vote. Tan just made it on both counts (Li, 2002: 714).

29. Dapeng has a population of around 50,000 spread out over 82.81 square kilometers. The per capita income is 4900 yuan. There are six village committees and two residents' committees. For a detailed account see Cheng (2001: 113–17) and Li (2002: 91–95).

30. For details see Li (1999: 103–18).

31. The representatives comprised all party members within the township, township and village officials and household representatives. As there are 1,500 households in the township, not all would have been represented. However, the numbers are unclear, as some of the categories may have overlapped.

32. Discussions with Shenzhen party leaders, July 2001.

33. According to information provided to a colleague of ours from a leader of the organisation department of Longgang District, August 2001.

34. Zhouli has a population of 13,228 spread over an area of 48.05 square km. There are 8 villagers' committees and the average per capita income is 2450 yuan. See also Li (2002: 71–78).

35. These included township government cadres, village party cadres and members of villagers' committees and some village delegates. The Linyi Party Committee also invited a number of other guests to listen to the meeting and to disseminate its ideas. These included cadres from higher levels, some scholars and some reporters.

36. In part this derives from the fact that local officials often lack the resources to promote innovation. However, it also stems from the fact that some local officials do not wish to disseminate such experimentation widely in order to prevent undue attention and pressure from higher levels.

37. The case mentioned by Liu Xitang in Nanbu County, Sichuan, occurred four months after that in Shizhong. In addition it only covered the position of township deputy-head. However, the process was extensive with selection to find 178 deputy heads for 79 townships, although the final number selected was 175 (Liu, 2000: 73). Liu is an employee of the MOCA. While both Cheng and Li mention this process (2001: 710–11; 2002: 118–19 respectively), they do so only as a prelude to the Buyun election and do not discuss it as an independent, on-going process.

38. For an account see Hu (2001: 2).

39. As discussed later, there were plenty willing to fill the post but the district leaders were concerned about their suitability and credibility.

40. Such a shift can be deciphered from the decision issued by the party in May. In addition to the township head (*zhengke*), the other eight positions are all at the deputy level (*fuke*). Interviews with local leaders in Shizhong in September 2001 confirmed this. See also Shizhong District Party Committee, 'Guanyu gongkai tuixuan Baoshi zhen renmin zhengfu zhenzhang houxuanren de jueding' (Decision on the Open Election of the Deputy Township Head of the Baoshi People's Government), 12 May 1998. The same day the Shizhong District Open Election Work Leading Small Group Office issued 'Suining shi Shizhongqu gongkai taxman Baoshizhen renmin zhengfu zhenzhang houxuanren jianchang' (Suining Municipality Shizhong District General Guidelines for the Selection of the Deputy Township Head of the Baoshi People's Government). See Fan (2002: 80).
41. The most important were that they had to be born after 1 June 1960, have graduated from high school and be in good health. There was no requirement concerning official position.
42. See also, Li (2002: 711).
43. This group included all 49 township congress delegates, 68 officials from the villages and the township and 32 officials from the district level.
44. Xiang was actually fourth after the written examination. The person who was first after the written exam was placed last after the oral examination.
45. This was at a meeting on organisational work in the countryside held in September 1998. The Shizhong Party Secretary talked at the meeting about the ORS method.
46. There were 69 candidates for the township head positions, of whom two were considered unsuitable. There were 76 candidates for the Hengshan township head election, of whom four were deemed unsuitable (Fan, 2002: 82).
47. Obviously two days is too short for the candidates to get to know the township where they might work. It is also too short a period of time for the township residents to interact with the candidates. This was later recognised by the district authorities who stipulated in the 'Interim Provisions for the ORS for Township Heads of the Shizhong District of Suining Municipality' that the time for investigation in the township should not be less than seven days. This was drafted on the basis of the first three experiments. The original regulations requiring two to three days can be found in Fan (2002: 86–91).
48. In the three experiments there was no definitive process for stipulating how the representative group should be formed and what its composition should be. The 'Interim Provisions' state clearly that the total number of representatives must exceed 1 per cent of the township population (it was to exceed 1 per cent in large and medium townships and 2 per cent in small townships). The total number of cadres from the district level was not to exceed 10 per cent of the representatives.
49. In county-level politics, it normally takes five or more years to be promoted from fuke rank to zhengke (that is, township head). This means that it is very difficult for an official ranked below fuke to be able to jump up to the zhengke level.
50. The party statutes do not stipulate that such a meeting be held but it has become common practice. It provides a strong institutional mechanism for the party secretary to monopolise the power of decision making.
51. As Manion notes when looking at the process for electing people's congress delegates, the system is designed to align preferences of selectorates and electorates. The party wants to select candidates that can win an election and thus enhance the party's own legitimacy (Manion, 2000: 780–81).
52. For more on this see Yang (2000).
53. Others confirm this in their analysis of the Buyun election. Baogang and Youxing noted, 'In the course of making the decision, Zhang Jinming, the party secretary of Shizhong District, played a key role. She not only has a pioneering spirit but is also open-minded and

is good at theoretical analysis. Her determination finally promoted the direct election in Shizhong District' (2000: 125–360).

54. Organisation Bureau of Sichuan Province, 'Zhonggong Sichuan shengwei zuzhibu guanyu zuohao xiang (zhen) cun huanjie xuanju gongzuo de tongzhi' (Announcement of the Organization Bureau of Sichuan Provincial CCP Committee Concerning Implementing Smoothly Elections for Change of Leadership in Towns (Townships) and Villages), 6 September 2001.

55. See, for example, Pei (1997: 11–49) and Walder (1995: 1–24).

56. In part, this highlights the fact that the local state is too large in most localities. It might also point to the fact that many feel that not only the official benefits of office holding are good but also the unofficial perks are attractive.

57. There seems to be some confusion about this document and its status. Officials who are familiar with the document said that while the document had been issued in the name of the Central Secretariat, it had not been drafted by the Secretariat but rather by officials in the National People's Congress. They claimed that it did not necessarily reflect the intention of the party as the drafters were not familiar with the process of the elections at the township level and had just heard a number of complaints about the process. The complaints had formed the basis for their draft.

58. As Baogang He has noted recently, experiments have continued in provinces such as Henan, Guangdong and Shaanxi where they use less politically contentious terms such as 'confidence votes' or 'extensive opinion polls'. He (2002: 5).

References

Bernstein and Xiaobo Lu. 2000. 'Taxation Without Representation: Peasants, the Central and the Local States in Reform China', *The China Quarterly*, 163: 742–63.

Cheng, Joseph Y.S. 2001. 'Direct Elections of Town and Township Heads in China: The Dapeng and Buyun Experiments', *China Information*, 1: 104–37.

Dai, Junliang. et al. 1991. *Zhongguo xiangzhen zhengquan jianshe gailun* (Outline of Township and Village Government). Beijing: Renmin chubanshe.

Edin, Maria. 2000. *Market Forces and Communist Power: Local Political Institutions and Economic Development in China*. Uppsala: Uppsala University Press.

Goldstein, Stephan M. 1995. 'China in Transition: The Political Foundations of Incremental Reform', *The China Quarterly*, 144: 1105–31.

Guo, Wei. 1998. 'Jiakuai xianxiang jigou gaige, cong yuantou shang jianqing nongmin fudan' (Speed Up Organizational Structure Reform at the County and Township Level and Reduce the Farmers' Burdens from the Very Beginning), *Liaowang (Outlook Weekly)*, 43: 34–35.

He, Baogang. 2002. 'From Village to Township: Will China Move Elections One Level Up', East Asian Institute, National University of Singapore, Background Brief, No. 126.

He, Baogang and Lang Youxing. 2000. 'Predicament in Buyun: A Study of the First Direct Election of a Township Head in China', *Ershiyi shijie* (The Twenty-First Century), 64: 125–36.

———. 2001. 'China's First Direct Election of the Township Head: A Case Study of Buyun', *Japanese Journal of Political Science*, 2 (1): 1–22.

Hu, Shubao. 2001. 'Buyun zhixuan diaocha baogao' (An Investigation Report on the Buyun Direct Election), *Beijing yu fenxi* (Background and Analysis), 25: 2.

Jacobs, J. Bruce. 1991. 'Elections in China', *Australian Journal of Chinese Affairs*, 25: 171–99.

Jiang, Zemin. 1997. 'Hold High the Great Banner of Deng Xiaoping. Theory for an All-Round Advancement of the Cause of Building Socialism with Chinese Characteristics into the 21st Century', *Beijing Review*, 40 (40): 10–34.

Jiang, Zemin. 2002. 'Build a Well-Off Society in an All-Round Way and Create a New Situation in Building Socialism with Chinese Characteristics', http://english.peopledaily.com.cn., 8 November.

Kelliher, Daniel. 1997. 'The Chinese Debate over Village Self-Government', *The China Journal*, 37: 31–62.

Li, Fan. 2002. *Zhongguo jiceng minzhu fazhan baogao, 2000–2001* (2000–2001 Report on the Development of Grassroots Democracy in China), pp. 376–88. Beijing: Dongfang chubanshe.

Li, Fan. et al., 2000. *Chuangxin yu fazhan—xiangzhenzhang xuanju zhidu gaige* (Innovation and Reform: Reform of the System for Election of Township and Town Heads). Beijing: Dongfang chubanshe.

Li, Lianjiang. 1999. 'The Two-Ballot System in Shanxi Province: Subjecting Village Party Secretaries to a Popular Vote', *The China Journal*, 42: 103–18.

———. 2002. 'The Politics of Introducing Direct Township Elections in China', *The China Quarterly*, 171: 704–23.

Liu, Xitang. 2000. 'Guanyu Xiangji Minzhu Fazhan De Diaocha Yu Sikao' (An Investigation of and Thoughts on the Development of Township Democracy), *Jingji Shehui Fizhi Bijiao (Comparative Economic and Social Systems)*, 2: 72.

Li, Xueju, Wang Zhenyao and Tang Jinsu (eds). 1994. *Zhongguo xiangzhen zhengquan de xianzhuang yu gaige* (The Current Situation and Reform of Power in Chinese Villages and Townships). Beijing: Zhongguo shehui chubanshe.

Legal System Work Committee of the Standing Committee of the National People's Congress (ed.), 'Zhonghua renimin gongheguo quanguo renmin daibiao dahui he difang geji renmin daibiao dahui xuanju fa' (Election Law for the National People's Congress and the Various Levels of Local People's Congresses in the People's Republic of China. 1986,in *Zhonghua renmin gongheguo falu ji youguan fagui huibian 1979–1984 nian* (Collection of Laws and Related Legal Regulations of the People's Republic of China, 1979–1984), pp. 67–76. Beijing: Falu chubanshe.

Manion, Melanie. 2000. 'Chinese Democratization in Perspective: Electorates and Selectorates at the Township Level', *The China Quarterly*, 163: 764–82.

Pei, Minxin. 1997. 'Racing Against Time: Institutional Decay and Renewal in China', in William A. Joseph (ed.), *China Briefing 1995–95*, pp. 11–49. Armonk, NY: M.E. Sharpe.

Rawski, Thomas G. 1995. 'Implications of China's Reform Experience', *The China Quarterly*, 144: 1150–73.

Rong, Jingben. et al. 1998. Cong yalixing tizhi xiang minzhu hezuo tizhi de zhuanbian (The Transformation from a Pressurized System to a Democratic Cooperative System). Beijing: Zhongyang bianyi chubanshe.

Saich, Tony. 2002. 'The Blind Man and the Elephant: Analysing the Local State in China', in Luigi Tomba (ed.), *On the Roots of Growth and Crisis: Capitalism, State and Society in East Asia*, pp. 75–99. Milan: Annale Feltrinelli.

Shi, Weimin. 2000. *Gongxuan yu zhixuan: xiangzhen renda xuanju zhidu fazhan* (Public Elections and Direct Elections: Studies of the Electoral System of Township Congresses). Beijing: Zhongguo shehui kexue chubanshe.

Unger, Jonathan. 1987. 'The Struggle to Dictate China's Administration: The Conflict of Branches vs. Areas vs. Reform', *The Australian Journal of Chinese Affairs*, 18: 15–46.

Walder, Andrew. 1995. 'The Quiet Revolution from Within: Economic Reform as a Source of Political Decline', in Andrew Walder (ed.), *The Waning of the Communist State: Economic Origins of Political Decline in China and Hungary*, pp. 1–24. Berkeley: University of California Press.

Wedeman, Andrew. 2000. 'Budgets, Extra-Budgets, and Small Treasuries: Illegal Monies and Local Autonomy in China', *Journal of Contemporary China*, 9 (25): 498–511.

Whiting, Susan H. 2001. *Power and Wealth in Rural China: The Political Economy of Institutional Change*. New York: Cambridge University Press.

Womack, Brantly. 1982. 'The 1980 County-level Elections in China: Experiment in Democratic Modernization', *Asian Survey*, 22 (3): 261–77.

Yang, Xuedong. 2000. 'Liyi fenhua he baohu—xiandaihua yu shichang jincheng zhong de Zhongyuan nongcun' (Diversification and Protection of Interests: Zhongyuan Country-side in the Process of Modernization and Marketization), *Zhongguo shehui kexue jikan* (Chinese Social Sciences Quarterly) Spring: 13–24.

Yu, Keping, (ed.). 2002. *Zhongguo difang zhengfu chuangxin 2002* (Innovations in Chinese Local Government). Beijing: Shehui kexue wenxian chubanshe.

5 'Civil Society' Revisited
The Anatomy of a Rural NGO in Qinghai

RICHARD BAUM AND XIN ZHANG

Since the onset of the post-Mao reform movement two decades ago, China has witnessed the emergence of thousands of societal associations. Many of these operate at the sub-national level, including business and professional groups, community and social welfare associations, scholarly societies and a host of other social organisations.

Much of the early Western research on social organisations in post-reform China focused on the question of whether such groupings reflected the emergence of a 'civil society' that might eventually challenge the monolithic political control exercised by the communist party-state. Initially spurred in the late-1980s by democratic transitions in the Soviet Union and Eastern Europe, scholarly interest in the possibilities and prospects of civil society in China were generally informed by the historical emergence of a 'public sphere' and pluralistic *'pouvoirs intermédiaires'* in the democratic development of the West (Baum and Schevchenko, 1999). In the view of many Western analysts, state–society relations in a Leninist polity such as China are characterised by chronic conflict. Civil associations represent organised societal interests that are seen to be in conflict with a repressive state. Constituting an organised barrier to the party-state's efforts to penetrate and control society, associations necessarily present a threat to state domination.

To escape such domination, associations must, it is argued, strive for autonomy. In this zero-sum perspective, civil society and associational life, representing a strong force for emergent pluralism and (eventually) democratisation, inevitably come in conflict with the monolithic political imperatives of the Leninist state. In this titanic clash, either the state must triumph or society will. No 'third road' exists.

In the event, the initial wave of Western optimism that greeted the prospect of an emergent civil society in China lost much of its luster in the aftermath of the 1989 Tiananmen crackdown. With the coercive suppression of autonomous student unions and affiliated organisations of workers and other occupational groups after 4 June, researchers searching for civil society-type associations uncovered precious little evidence of associational autonomy or contestation vis-à-vis the state (Nevitt, 1996; Pearson, 1994; White et al., 1996). What followed was a 'healthy skepticism' about the plausibility of such an approach drawn mainly from Western history (Chamberlain, 1998: 69).

Attempting to fill the void left by the ostensible collapse of the civil society model, various analysts began to employ 'corporatist' models to capture the continued dominance of the Leninist party-state while acknowledging the pluralising socio-economic changes induced by market reforms (Baum and Schevchenko, 1999: 348). Two main types of corporatism were posited: 'state corporatism' and 'societal corporatism'. Common to most state corporatism analyses was the assumption that the party-state continues to dominate associations indirectly through such devices as organisational sponsorship, leadership co-optation and licensing. The currently influential notion that Chinese associations form part of an evolving state corporatist system of control and interest intermediation suggests that these associations have as a key function the exertion of a modicum of political supervision and control over their members (Unger, 1996; Unger and Chan, 1994). However, recent case studies suggest that although incorporated Chinese associations may be viewed as supporting the status quo (for example, by promoting the state's developmental goals and by helping the state carry out socio-economic functions), many of them do little to promote statist political control over their members (Saich, 2001).

'Societal corporatism' models, on the other hand, stress the interest articulation function of associations (Unger and Chan, 1994). Focusing on 'bottom–up' societal representation in contrast to 'top–down' state control, these models may overstate both the internal coherence of various socio-economic interests and the role of associations as effective channels of communication and exchange (Yep, 2000).

In conducting empirical investigations of various types of social organisation that emerged in post-reform China, scholars devoted most of their attention to new business and commercial associations. Researchers investigating these associations and their relationships with the state found something rather different from what would have been expected based on zero-sum state–society models. The terms used to describe these relationships vary widely. Kang (1999) calls business associations *'banguan banmin'* (semi-official, semi-civic); Unger (1996) refers to them as 'a hybrid of socialist corporatism and clienteles'; Pearson (1994) refers to 'the merger of state and business'; Solinger (1992) speaks of 'business–state collaboration'; Yep (2000) and Wank (1999) note the existence of 'symbiotic relations' with the state; while Foster (2002) refers to associations as 'embedded within state agencies'. The common characteristic of all these descriptions is that they represent mixed, hybrid types, that is, they lie between the two polar extremes of complete associational autonomy and total state domination.

We thus seem to find ourselves floating between two extremes. At one end is an idealised Western model of an emergent civil society that exaggerates the drive of Chinese associations toward full autonomy from, and contestation with, the state. At the other end is a corporatist model that views associations as creatures of the state, operating in the thin guise of vehicles for articulating group interests.

In an attempt to close this conceptual gap, Foster (2001, 2002) proposed an organisational-function model to capture the complex relationships that exist between Chinese associations and the state. In this view, various stakeholders in social organisations, namely, the central state, local governments and the association's members, regard the association instrumentally as a means of pursuing of their own particular interests. Different stakeholders have distinctive views of the functions and utility of a single association. For the central party-state, an association may be seen as useful for mobilising specific societal groups or strata to facilitate the implementation of state policies within a controlled organisational environment; for local governments, on the other hand, the same association may be viewed as a source of local entrepreneurship and revenue generation; while for its members, the association may represent opportunities for (or constraints on) the pursuit of individual and group interests. The idea that an association may be viewed through multiple functional lenses is an improvement over simple zero-sum models of state–society relations.

The present chapter seeks to contribute to the literature on functional associations in post-reform China by examining the case of a single local organisation—the Sanchuan Development Association (SDA) of Guanting Township, Minhe County, Qinghai Province. Unlike most research sites selected for study by Western scholars, which tend to be clustered in urban coastal areas (Guangzhou, Shanghai, Yantai, Xiamen and Tianjin) or relatively affluent rural communities (Xiaoshan, Wenzhou, Zhoushan and Yiwu), Guanting lies in a poor, remote mountainous region of northwest China. Unlike most local associations studied by Western scholars, the SDA is neither a business group nor a trade association. Also unlike most previously studied associations, the SDA is only loosely and intermittently linked to the state.

This chapter is based on the findings of the authors who spent three weeks in Guanting and its associated villages in the summer of 2002 and personally accessed the historical records of the SDA and interviewed leading members of the association.

The Sanchuan Development Association (SDA)

The Sanchuan Development Association (Sanchuan Fazhan Cujinhui) is a young, well-functioning NGO in northwest China. Its main organisational objective is to propose, fund and implement locally-based poverty alleviation projects. From its inception in September 1996 through February 2002, the SDA initiated 86 development projects and raised RMB 4,102,023 yuan in project funds (roughly US$ 500,000), mostly from outside donors, including several international philanthropic foundations. The most important projects sponsored by the SDA have been in the areas of education (school construction, purchase of educational supplies and equipment), water supply for humans and livestock (well-digging, large above-ground concrete water-tanks, rainwater collection cisterns), solar power utilisation (purchase of solar cookers), hygiene and health care (village clinic and toilet construction), animal husbandry (pigsty projects, sheep raising), manpower training (grass-roots development practitioner, English language instruction, computer literacy, new-technology agriculture) and preservation of local minority culture (video filming and archiving, video transmitting). To date, the SDA has concentrated its efforts in Minhe County, a Hui and Tu (Mangghuer) minority autonomous county located in the eastern sector of Qinghai Province, across the Yellow River from Gansu Province. This area lies between high mountains and valleys, with primitive, inconvenient transportation. Farm productivity is very low, especially in the country's mountainous regions, due to the prevalence of hard, clay-like löess soil, the steepness of cultivated slopes, the scarcity and uncertainty of rainfall and the frequency of hail. Winters in Minhe are long and cold. The average family income in this part of Qinghai is less than US$ 100 per year.

The work of the SDA was initiated in 1996 by Zhu Yongzhong, a Mangghuer middle-school teacher living near Guanting Township in southern Minhe. Attempting to organise poverty-alleviation work in the dozen or so rural villages around Guanting, Zhu recruited a core group of members from among his friends and relatives as well as fellow school teachers in the area. Initially run on a small, informal basis, the association grew larger with the addition of new members recruited through participation in projects initiated in their home villages. In 2001, the SDA applied for and received official recognition as a legal social organisation (*shehui tuanti*).

Among the 15 current core members of the SDA, most are local teachers. Only the office manager is paid by the SDA, while all the others work on a voluntary basis. Zhu Yongzhong still receives his salary as a teacher from the village middle school where he once worked. This income gives him a modicum of security against the financial uncertainty of the SDA. He maintains his paid position as a teacher largely because officials in his school and in the local school district recognise the importance of his work with the SDA; indeed, they have relieved him of all teaching responsibilities and encouraged him to devote full-time to the association—even though such paid secondment may be technically illegal.

The SDA's first delegate convention in 2001 was attended by 55 members, among whom were 16 local teachers, one retired doctor, one TV reporter, two township officials and 35 ordinary villagers. Two SDA members work for the local township government, while the retired doctor is a former local cadre. Like director Zhu, the doctor, reporter and all the teachers receive their regular salaries from the government. None are paid by the SDA.

The main sources of funding for SDA projects are grants from international philanthropic organisations abroad and foreign embassies in China. Smaller amounts have also been raised through donations from private sources (see Table 5.1).

Table 5.1
Sources of Funding for the SDA (September 1996–February 2002)

Source of Funding	Amount of Funding (yuan)	Percentage
Foreign Embassies in China	1,790,851	43.66
International Organisations and Funding Agencies	2,207,424	53.81
Personal Donations and Other Sources	103,748	3.53
Total	4,102,023	100

Source: 'A Brief Table of the Foreign Funded Projects' provided by the SDA (2002).

The biggest donors (in terms of funding amounts) are: The Trace Foundation (813,390 yuan), the British Embassy (794,675 yuan), the Royal Netherlands Embassy (446,072 yuan), Kadoorie Charitable Foundations (449,800 yuan), the Canada Fund (333,041 yuan) and the Bridge Fund (138,486 yuan). External funding usually take the form of donations in kind or cash grants for the purchase of materials and equipment. The SDA generally solicits unpaid labour contributions from those villages that stand to benefit directly from a given project (for example, most local construction and infrastructure development projects). It also raises supplemental funds from the local government (for example, for some education projects).

All projects are developed based on proposals initiated by local SDA members. The association then works with the local community to expand and refine the proposals, which are ultimately translated into English and submitted to potential donors and sponsors.

One key to the success of the SDA in raising external development funds is its creative use of the Internet to locate and cultivate appropriate funding sources. Working in close collaboration with an expatriate American ESL (English as Second Language) teacher, Dr Kevin Stuart, who teaches English at the Qinghai Teacher's College in the provincial capital of Xining, Zhu Yongzhong has managed to cobble together an international support network involving half-a-dozen or more philanthropic organisations. Working from his own apartment with two modem-connected personal computers (PCs), Stuart instructs Zhu's and his students how to surf the 'net' in search of development funds. The students—among them several Tibetan and Mangghuer youths from Minhe and adjacent counties—are encouraged to develop their own proposals for funding projects in their native villages. The synergetic combination of local, grass-roots rural entrepreneurship and global, Internet-based funding support is the defining hallmark of the SDA's remarkable success.

Once funding is secured, SDA members work in cooperation with members of the local community to elect a local project management committee to oversee each project. Typically, such a committee will consist of one or two SDA members,[1] a village committee director or party secretary, local village representatives (usually chosen from among potential project beneficiaries) and experienced local labourers (generally those experienced in construction). Overall financial management is the responsibility of the SDA, though management of individual projects is dispersed and decentralised. The SDA uses the funds at its disposal to purchase necessary construction materials and members of the project management committee manage the finances of each project. This seems to be a more effective method than the alternative of simply having the SDA give cash to local villagers and then supervise all financial management from above. The reason given for this preference for decentralised financial management is that the villagers (as potential beneficiaries) have a strong incentive to monitor the behaviour of SDA members, while the SDA members, by virtue of their greater experience in procuring resources and raw materials, have superior knowledge of the price, availability and quality of building materials. Zhu Yongzhong readily admits that in actual practice there is seldom much fuss made over financial issues, as the price and quality of most raw materials are well known to the villagers themselves.[2]

One special advantage of the SDA is that as a genuinely '*minjian*' (civic) organisation, it is not perceived by local villagers as an association dominated by 'bureaucrats' or 'outsiders'. With its roots entirely in the local community, its members are deeply familiar with local conditions and the needs of the local populace. As noted in the SDA's promotional brochure, all but one of the SDA's members 'are from rural villages in Qinghai and were reared in the most ordinary circumstances. Poverty is thus not an academic or "development-jargon" abstraction but, rather, something that was personally experienced throughout childhood in all of its ugliness and which continues to be a reality for relatives of group members' (SDA, 2001). And since the very raison d'etre of the SDA is the alleviation of poverty and the improvement of local economic conditions, it has no direct conflicts of interest with either the local community or the local government. The local government clearly tolerates the activities of the SDA (since it brings valuable funding to the local community) and in some areas, for example, educational development, it actively cooperates with the SDA in building philanthropic bridges to the global community.

Another important comparative advantage enjoyed by the SDA is that Zhu Yongzhong and Kevin Stuart have a relative monopoly over certain resources vis-à-vis the local government. For example, their fluency in English enables them to maintain regular personal contact with international funding agencies and foreign embassies alike—contact that could not be duplicated by non English-speaking local authorities. This linguistic advantage is further enhanced by their advanced computer skills and their efficiency in navigating the Internet. As a window to the world outside, the SDA also maintains a sophisticated, bilingual website containing a complete account of the association's history, objectives, current activities and accomplishments.[3]

The SDA has an additional advantage in that its core members are a cohesive group of local teachers who are generally better educated, more affluent and more cosmopolitan in outlook than most local villagers and government officials. They are open to new things and ideas and take a broad view of the outside world. The importance of their links to educators and others outside their Guanting Township headquarters is revealed by the fact that four years ago the Minhe County Education Bureau—the SDA's official sponsoring unit (*guakao danwei*)—gave its approval to the association's proposal to invite native foreign speakers of English to come to Guanting as volunteers during the summer months to teach English to local middle-school students. Insofar as the county authorities place a high priority on improving the test scores (and hence the educational and social mobility) of Minhe's minority nationality students, this was clearly a win–win proposition for the Education Bureau as well as for the SDA.

Significantly, it was under the auspices of this voluntary English teaching programme that the authors of this paper travelled to Guanting in the summer of 2002, at Zhu Yongzhong's invitation, as part of a delegation of 11 UCLA students and three faculty members. The UCLA group spent three weeks in Guanting under Zhu's overall coordination, teaching intensive conversational English to teenagers in six local village schools. The 200 local students who participated in these summer classes had been thoroughly pre-screened and hand-picked by the SDA's teachers through intensive on-site qualifying examinations administered to more than 500 youngsters throughout southern Minhe County. Importantly, the invitation to foreigners to teach English in Guanting had initially been advertised on the Internet by Kevin Stuart on the H-ASIA listserv, the professional Internet forum for teachers of Asian history. It was in response to this advertisement that the first co-author of this paper initially visited rural Qinghai in the summer of 2001. Thus did the SDA's entrepreneurial leaders bring global resources to bear, helping to fill local development needs in Guanting Township (see Appendix 5.1).

In terms of formal organisational accountability, the SDA is nominally obligated to submit an annual report on its activities to its sponsoring unit, the Minhe County Education Bureau. According to our interviews, however, the Education Bureau is largely indifferent to this requirement. Nor does the SDA's official 'registration management agency' (*dengji guanli jiguan*), the Minhe County Civil Affairs Bureau, rigorously exercise supervisory authority. Consequently, the SDA appears to enjoy substantial local autonomy—certainly a good deal more than most associations discussed in the literature.

From our observations and interviews with SDA members, it seems clear that the association actively seeks to keep local government from interfering in its activities. That was said to be the main reason why Zhu and his associates delayed more than four years before registering their association as a legal social organisation. In fact, the decision to register with the County Civil Affairs Bureau came not in response to members' desire to become an official association, but rather at the behest of the donor of the SDA's largest project. The donor had requested to deposit funds directly in the association's bank account. But the SDA could not open its own bank account without first becoming an officially registered social organisation. So they finally registered in 2001, five years after the birth of the association.

One key reason given by SDA leaders for trying to maintain their organisational autonomy is that they harbour strong doubts about the local government's ability to efficiently manage development projects. An SDA member told the authors that when one township government spent RMB 200,000 yuan of a Hong Kong donor's funds on a construction project similar to one undertaken by the SDA, the donor was unhappy about the final cost. Reportedly, the SDA could have done the same job for about half the money by relying on locally-volunteered (rather than paid) labour and by economising on the purchase of materials. This conviction—that the association can do things faster, better and cheaper than local government—is clearly stated in the introduction to a recent summary of the SDA activities: 'SDA also hopes to demonstrate to local government that projects can be done at relatively low cost and high quality as well as demonstrating the advantages of consulting with local communities and taking into account their opinions while, at the same time, requiring a significant local contribution. This has been the model successfully followed for several years by SDA' (SDA, 2001).

SDA: Civil Society or Societal Corporatism?

It is clear from the above description that the SDA lies on the 'highly autonomous' end of the state–society associational continuum. The group's origins, activities and selection of leaders are almost entirely 'societal' in nature. Its resources are mobilised, allocated and managed largely independent of government control (though not without local government consent). And the SDA, finally, has important, unique resources—including a near monopoly on English language skills and Internet capabilities and a network of relationships with foreign donors—that can be used as a shield against potential state penetration. In Zhu's own words: 'We don't expect much from the government, so we have our own freedom'. The principal associational characteristics of the SDA are summarised in Table 5.2.

Table 5.2
Associational Characteristics of the SDA

Origins	Socially Initiated
Bureaucratic Affiliation	No visible bureaucratic affiliation; the legal sponsoring unit has no effective control over the SDA.
Constituencies	Self-organised members.
Leadership	Self-selected, charismatic leadership; no government appointment.
Functions	Social development, including planning and goal-setting, resource mobilisation and resource management, provision of services.
Financial Sources	Largely dependent on external funding, especially from foreign sources such as Western embassies in China and international philanthropic foundations and international NGOs.

In each of these respects, it would be difficult to label the SDA as an 'incorporated association' or a 'co-opted association' (Foster, 2001). Nor does it fit the 'state corporatism' model. At the same time, however, there is little to indicate any desire on the SDA's part to actively contest the state's sphere of socio-political domination. The goals and methods of operation are also by no means inimical to local government interests. It neither constrains the state nor negotiates the terms of its survival with the state. Although the SDA is officially sponsored and duly registered with the county government, there is no direct or meaningful higher-level supervision of its operations. By the same token, the SDA has done nothing in the way of attempting to control local bureaucracy or make claims on local government—two of the eight defining characteristics of Esman and Uphoff's 'local development association' (see Table 5.3).

Table 5.3
Eight Functions of Local Organisations

Planning and Goal-setting	SDA (weak)
Conflict Management	No
Resource Mobilisation	SDA (strong)
Resource Management	SDA (weak)
Provision of Services	SDA (strong)
Integration of Services	SDA (weak)
Control of Bureaucracy	No
Claim-making on Government	No

The SDA clearly prefers to avoid dealing with the state altogether. When necessary, however, it will cooperate with local government agencies to protect its projects and facilitate its development objectives. In some cases, the SDA sought to secure additional resources from local government (township and county level government) to supplement project funding secured from external sources. In other cases, especially certain educational projects, the SDA utilises its connections with local teachers groups and with the educational establishment in Minhe County. The most recent educational project involves training local teachers in new teaching methods. The project was co-sponsored by the SDA and the local education bureau. In large SDA projects, including those involving school or building construction and infrastructure development, the association also needs to cooperate with villagers' committees to organise the local labour contribution and to establish a project management committee.

Although the SDA intermittently cooperates with local government, it is not an intermediary association standing between local citizens and the state. In a practical sense, it acts more as an intermediary between external funding sources and the local community, with local government consigned to the role of an interested bystander. Esman and Uphoff (1984) state that: 'The development of vigorous local organizations has important implications for extending the outreach of public administration and for improving the performance of government agencies and personnel.' To date, the SDA has not performed such functions. It does, however, fulfill other functions posited by Esman and Uphoff: 'Local organizations, by aggregating the demands and resources of private citizens, can also supplement and make more effective the efforts of individuals in the private sector, representing their needs more pervasively and helping to solve local problems in more appropriate ways' (Esman and Uphoff, 1984: 22).

Somewhat paradoxically, the very success of the SDA raises questions about its future viability as an autonomous NGO. For the first several years of its existence, the association flew under the state's radar, as it were, avoiding co-optation and manipulation by not drawing attention to itself. However, its very success in attracting foreign donors to Guanting has raised its profile significantly, rendering its continued operational autonomy more problematic.[4]

Potential problems fall into three categories. First is leadership. The association is clearly dependent on Zhu Yongzhong's charismatic personality and leadership skills. At present there is no one else in the association who could succeed him. Indeed, in many important respects, Zhu Yongzhong is the SDA. Being virtually irreplaceable, his departure from the association, for whatever reasons, would call into question the association's long-term viability.

Second is the question of the sustainability of the SDA's development strategy. Thus far, the association's major development projects—construction of schools, bridges, water wells, cisterns, outhouses and the like—have been largely self-contained and directed toward improving the quality of life enjoyed by local residents. They have not been designed primarily to maximise self-sustaining local economic growth. For example, little consideration has been given to the idea of using start-up funds to create new, commercially-viable economic enterprises. Increasingly, however, foreign donors are treating the goal of commercial viability as a precondition for assistance. Would such a change in the SDA's strategy—which would comport well with the community development models currently favoured by the international aid community—distort the motives and incentives of local residents, as has been shown to happen in other, similar cases?[5]

On the other hand, if what local communities need most is mainly start-up funds to initiate public infrastructure projects, a strategy of floating small commercial loans (under appropriate public management) might constitute a more sustainable pathway to long-term development. Then, the SDA's role might go beyond attracting outside funds to include resource management, conflict management and true intermediation between government and citizenry. If the SDA should begin to move in this direction, it would necessarily come into closer, more regular contact with local government, and would thus be subject to greater state scrutiny and regulation. Under such conditions, it would be impossible to maintain the degree of organisational autonomy that was a vital key to the SDA's early success.

The third long-term concern is that of internal financial management. For any group managing such large amounts of money, internal financial management is a problem. In the SDA's written reports to its donors, every purchase, down to the last nail or screw, is clearly itemised, and with corresponding receipts attached. However, in the absence of scrupulous financial management by trusted SDA officers like Zhu Yongzhong and his associates, these documents could easily be fabricated, making it difficult to monitor the actual use of donor funds. Since the ultimate overseers of SDA financial management are the international donors themselves, who are ill-equipped to directly monitor the association's internal finances, any change in the SDA leadership or development strategy could well undermine the well-established pattern of reliance upon trusted individuals to safeguard the SDA's financial integrity.[6]

The Role of Local Organisation in Rural Development

In the decades following World War II, development theorists generally emphasised the key transformative roles played by central governments and non-local agents of change. Local communities were generally viewed as backward, parochial, undisciplined, 'peripheral' and conservative—predisposed to consume rather than to save and invest, and needing to be 'penetrated' in order to become part of the modern nation state (Esman and Uphoff, 1984: 47). By the 1970s, scholars had begun to appreciate the importance of building local institutions in generating developmental energy and dynamism. The traditional wisdom that regarded underdevelopment as a 'gap' either in physical capital or in technology was challenged by the idea that institution-building could be more crucial in promoting development than mere transfers of technology and physical resources. By the late-1970s, emphasis was being placed on the importance of participatory local organisations as intermediaries between government and citizens (or clients). Local organisations thus took on expanded significance, in both theoretical and practical terms, as important bridges (both horizontal and vertical) linking individual households and villages with larger enterprises and communities at the regional and national levels.

Esman and Uphoff (1984: 289) and others (for example, Griffin and Ghose, 1979: 382) treat local organisation as an important factor in rural development. In their view, poverty alleviation through rural development requires a large number of small, labour-intensive investment projects utilising 'appropriate technologies' dispersed through the countryside. This implies that plans for rural development should be made locally, by those who will implement them, benefit from them and bear their major cost. Under favourable conditions a large number of local organisations could emerge, for example, forming around a technology (irrigation cooperatives), acting as interests groups (women's organisations) or class-based groups (small farmers' association). Ideally, such organisations should operate independent of government, yet, have ready access to it. The government should regard local organisations as partners in rural development, for example, as sources of ideas and information; as places where priorities can be hammered out; and as recruiting grounds for 'barefoot' doctors, engineers, village leaders and local government personnel. In this way, they argue, it should be possible to approach the ultimate objective wherein planning for the poor gives way to planning by the poor.

Evaluating the SDA

Within Esman and Uphoff's tripartite typology of local organisations (1984: 61–65), the SDA represents a typical 'local development association' (LDA). Local development associations are characterised by being area-based and multifunctional, drawing legitimacy less from formal charters than from expression of community needs. The other two major organisational types are 'cooperatives' (characterised by the pooling of resources by members, more limited group targeting and the provision of services of a more private nature) and 'interest associations' (defined by the common occupational or economic interests and functions of members). Locating the SDA within this analytical framework, and for heuristic purposes, we summarise its defining characteristics in Figure 5.1.

Figure 5.1
Variables Affecting the Contribution to Rural Development.

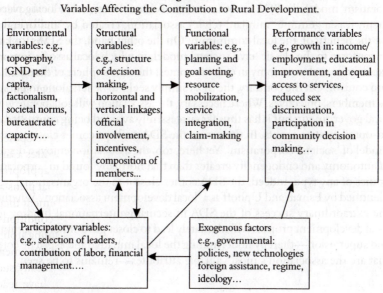

Source: Esman and Uphoff (1984: 69).

Based on the (admittedly limited and impressionistic) evidence available to us, we next attempt to evaluate the SDA in terms of the functional and performance variables specified in Esman and Uphoff's framework. The eight major functional variables are assessed in Table 5.3, while the five key performance variables are evaluated in Table 5.4.

Table 5.4
Performance Variables

Economic gains through increased agricultural and/or non-agricultural production and/or income.	SDA (weak)
Social benefits in terms of education, health, nutrition, water supply, transportation and/or other public facilities.	SDA (strong)
Equity effects, resulting from increased income, assets and/or access to services for the poor.	SDA (strong)
Reduced discrimination on the basis of sex or other ascriptive categories, so as to increase social opportunities for women and/or other disadvantaged social groups where discrimination has existed.	SDA (weak)
Participation in decision making at the community and/or government level.	SDA (weak)

Conclusion

The SDA does not fit neatly into any of the conventional analytical categories used to describe contemporary Chinese associations. Unlike the 'state corporatism' model, the SDA is not a creature of either the central or local government; it is a genuine 'minjian' (civic) association, created by, and operated for the benefit of, the local community. On the other hand, the SDA also fails to conform to the classic 'civil society' model, in which local associations are expected to seek autonomy in order to contest the state's sphere of domination and control. On the contrary, the SDA simply seeks to be left alone to pursue its members' objectives. Where necessary, the association will collaborate with local government; but it has thus far successfully avoided being controlled or co-opted by state agents. In this sense, the SDA perhaps comes closest to the model of 'societal corporatism'. Yet here, too, the association enjoys a degree of autonomy and endogeneity greater than that normally found in corporatist bodies of any type. Indeed, the SDA comes closest to the organisational type identified by Esman and Uphoff as a 'local development association'. Whether the extraordinary success of the SDA in securing international funding for local development projects will ultimately lead to closer governmental scrutiny and supervision—thereby undermining the local initiative and esprit de corps that are the association's most valuable attributes—remains to be seen.

Appendix 5.1
The SDA's Original Advertisement for English Teachers

Date: Thu, 28 Jun 2001 06:34:40 -0400
Subject: H-ASIA: English Teaching in the PRC
To: H-ASIA@H-NET.MSU.EDU
            H-ASIA

****

From: Kevin Stuart <ckstuart@public.xn.qh.cn>

Volunteer English Teaching in Northwest China

What? Teaching English to Mangghuer (Tu) middle school students

Where? Sanchuan Culture Center, Minhe County, Qinghai Province, PR China

When? 15 days in August (specific time to be established as teacher's schedule permits)

Who? 10–15 local Mangghuer middle school students. The Mangghuer are one branch of the larger Monguor (Tu) nationality in China. Deeply influenced by Tibetan Buddhism, as well as certain indigenous religious traditions, their language is primarily an archaic Mongol dialect, although Chinese lexical items are rapidly entering the language.

Why? Few Mangghuer speak English and are thus able to enjoy the benefits that a knowledge of English is capable of encouraging. This program is intended to develop a small group of bright Mangghuer students who have learned some English in middle schools, but lack oral practice opportunities.

Cost? The foreign teacher's transportation cost from Xining to the Sanchuan Culture Center and room and board while at the center will be paid for. There is no 'salary' as such.

Work? Four hours a day/60 hours oral English teaching total.

Other? The foreign teacher will live and board at the Sanchuan Culture Center. The teacher will have a room with bed and desk. S/He will share a kitchen with volunteer members of the Project Group. If s/he is interested in local poverty alleviation projects, which an active group is engaged in at the Culture Center, s/he is welcomed to participate. The time period for instruction could be altered, depending on the teacher's schedule.

Contacts? Kevin Stuart and Zhu Yongzhong

(Mr.) Zhu Yongzhong
Sanchuan Culture Center
Guanting Region
Minhe Hui and Mangghuer (Tu) County
Qinghai 810801

Tel: 0972-595114
Mobile: (0)13997031008
E-mail: yzhzhu@public.xn.qh.cn

Kevin Stuart, Ph.D.
Nationalities Department
Qinghai Education College
Xining 810008

Tel: 0971-6166015
Mobile: (0)13639786060
E-mail: ckstuart@public.xn.qh.cn

Notes

1. In many cases, Zhu Yongzhong is the general supervisor, assisted by a local SDA member.
2. One may, however, question the general applicability of this management method, since there is a potential for conflict of interests in the fact that potential local beneficiaries receive unencumbered resources via the SDA. That is, it is problematic whether the recipients of largesse delivered by the SDA would stringently monitor and criticise those 'benevolent' SDA members who brought the funding to them in the first place. Thus, the strongest supervisory incentive should reside in the donors themselves. In private conversations with one of the present co-authors, Zhu admitted: 'At the moment, our "authorities" are the donors'. In order to satisfy the donors, Zhu—and the entire SDA—have worked very hard to improve the quality of their reportage, making extensive accounting, audio and video records of each project available to patrons.
3. The website URL is: <http://www.qinghaisanchuandpwg.org>.
4. During the summer of 2002, a steady stream of foreign visitors descended on Guanting to observe the good works of the SDA, including US Ambassador Clark Randt. Thus alerted to the popularity of the SDA, local government officials sought to exploit the publicity windfall by claiming credit for SDA's success, thereby demonstrating their 'progressive leadership' to higher-level authorities. Whether this will serve to insulate the SDA from future bureaucratic interference and manipulation or, on the contrary, render it more vulnerable to predatory, rent-seeking behaviour by local officials remains to be seen.

5. Esman and Uphoff (1984) record cases of low organisational performance where local associations have become dependent on external funding.
6. This is not intended to question the integrity of other SDA members, but merely to point out the inherent potential for corruptibility in any weakly-monitored organisation.

References

Baum, Richard and Alexei Schevchenko. 1999. 'The "State" of the State', in M. Goldman and R. MacFarquhar (eds), *The Paradox of China's Post–Mao Reforms*, pp. 333–62. Cambridge, MA: Harvard University Press.

Chamberlain, Heath B. 1998. 'Civil Society with Chinese Characteristics?', *The China Journal*, 39: 69–81.

Esman, Milton and Norman Uphoff. 1984. *Local Organizations: Intermediaries in Rural Development*. Ithaca and London: Cornell University Press.

Foster, Kenneth W. 2001. 'Associations in the Embrace of an Authoritarian State: State Domination of Society?', *Studies in Comparative International Development*, 35 (4): 84–109.

———. 2002. 'Embedded with State Agencies: Business Associations in Yantai', *The China Journal*, 47: 41–65.

Griffin, Keith and Ajit Kumar Ghose. 1979. 'Growth and Impoverishment in the Rural Area of Asia', *World Development*, 7 (2): 361–83.

Kang, Xiaoguang. 1999. 'Transfer of Power: The Evolution of China's Power Structure during Transition' (*Quanli de zhuanyi: zhuanxing shiqi zhongguo quanli geju de bianqian*). Hangzhou: Zhejiang People's Press.

Nevitt, Christopher E. 1996. 'Private Business Associations in China: Evidence of Civil Society or Local State Power?', *The China Journal*, 36: 25–34.

Parris, Kristen. 1999. 'The Rise of Private Business Interests', in M. Goldman and R. MacFarquhar (eds), *The Paradox of China's Post–Mao Reforms*, pp. 262–82. Cambridge, MA: Harvard University Press.

Pearson, Margaret. 1994. 'The Janus Face of Business Associations in China: Socialist Corporatism in Foreign Enterprises', *The Australian Journal of Chinese Affairs*, 33: 25–48.

Saich, Tony. 2001. 'Negotiating the State: The Development of Social Organizations in China', *The China Quarterly*, 161: 124–41.

Sanchuan Development Association (SDA). 2001. 'Sanchuan Development Association', manuscript.

———. 2002. 'A Brief Table of the Foreign Funded Projects' (June), manuscript.

Shue, Vivienne. 1994. 'State Power and Social Organization in China', in J. Migdal, A. Kohli and V. Shue. Cambridge (eds), *State Power and Social Forces: Domination and Transformation in the Third World*, pp. 65–88. Cambridge: Cambridge University Press.

Solinger, Dorothy. 1992. 'Urban Entrepreneurs and the State: The Merger of State and Society', in Arthur Lewis Rosenbaum (ed.), *State and Society in China*, pp. 121–41. Boulder: Westview Press.

Unger, Jonathan. 1996. '"Bridges": Private Business, the Chinese Government and the Rise of New Associations', *The China Quarterly*, 147: 795–819.

Unger, Jonathan and A. Chan. 1994. 'China, Corporatism, and the East Asian Model', *The Australian Journal of Chinese Affairs*, 33: 29–53.

Wank, David. 1999. *Commodifying Communism: Business, Trust and Politics in a Chinese City*. Cambridge: Cambridge University Press.

White, Gordon. 1993. 'Prospects for Civil Society in China: A Case Study of Xiaoshan City', *The Australian Journal of Chinese Affairs*, 29: 63–87.

White, Gordon, Jude Howell and Xiaoyun Shang (eds). 1996. *In Search of Civil Society: Market Reform and Social Change in Contemporary China*. Oxford: Clarendon Press.

Yep, Ray. 2000. 'The Limitations of Corporatism for Understanding Reforming China: An Empirical Analysis in a Rural County', *Journal of Contemporary China*, 9 (25): 547–66.

6 Changes in Local Administration and their Impact on Community Life in the Grasslands of Inner Mongolia

Rong Ma

During the past half century, the local administrative system in China experienced several fundamental changes. These changes were accompanied by the political movement for regime change, civil wars and efforts by the central government to penetrate the remote border regions. In 1911, the Qing dynasty was overthrown in a national revolution movement. Between this year and 1949 (the founding year of the People's Republic), different administrative systems prevailed in different parts of China, such as the Dalai Lama and Kashag government in Tibet, several Mongolian princedoms in Inner Mongolia, Hui warlords in Ningxia, Gansu and Qinghai, and Shengshicai warlords in Xinjiang, besides the People's Liberation Army under the leadership of the Chinese Communist Party and the Army of the Republic under the Nationalist Party. In the early-1950s, the People's Republic re-established its administration over the whole of China, except Taiwan, Hong Kong and Macao. Inner Mongolia became an autonomous region in 1947 when northeastern China was under the control of the Communist Party. Before 1947, the areas now under the administration of Inner Mongolia Autonomous Region were under the control of several different regimes. In the southern parts of its agricultural areas, the Republic government had established three provinces: Rehe, Chahar and Suiyuan. In its northern areas, several Mongolian princes controlled the grasslands with a traditional league-banner system.

Until now, most studies of the grassland areas of China have focused on climate, animal husbandry and ecology, and a few studies have looked at the changes in social systems, administrative transition and policy implications in nomadic community life. Due to the strong administrative control on all aspects of Chinese society, reforms in the system and policy implications should be considered the most important factors in understanding the societal, economic and demographic changes in contemporary China. The Institute of Sociology and Anthropology at Peking University organised a series of field surveys in several locations in Inner Mongolia to study the system reform, local administration adjustment and their impact on local community in grassland areas. Hurqige Gaca in Eastern Wuzhumuqin Banner is one of these research sites.

Based on the case study of Hurqige Gaca, a former brigade, this chapter focuses on examining the reform process of the administration system, its impact on the ownership of animals, right of using pastures, management of animal husbandry, migration patterns and the subsequent impact on community life in the grassland areas of the Mongolian steppe.

Introducing Inner Mongolia

The Inner Mongolia Autonomous Region is located in northern China (see Figure 6.1). The area of this region is 1.18 million square kilometers. According to the 2000 national census, the total population of Inner Mongolia is 23.8 million. In 2000, among the total population of Inner Mongolia, 17.1 per cent were ethnic Mongols, 79.2 per cent were Han, 2 per cent Manchu, 0.9 per cent Hui, 0.3 per cent Daur and 0.5 per cent others. Grasslands in Inner Mongolia consist of 0.9 million square kilometers, over one fourth of the total area of grasslands in China.

The relevant literature on grasslands in the social sciences has been reviewed in one of the chapters of *Grasslands and Grassland Sciences in Northern China* (Ma, 1992: 121–32). A Swedish journal *Nomadic Peoples* published a special issue on 'Pastoralism in Mongolia' in 1993. This issue collected 17 articles that provided information on the nomadic life in grasslands.

Figure 6.1
Map of Inner Mongolia Autonomous Region

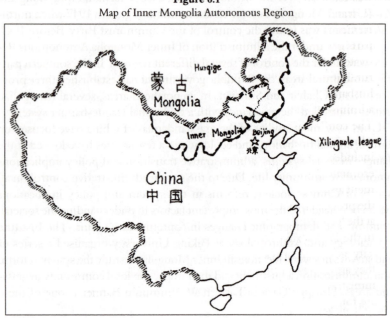

According to these previous works and the author's personal field experiences in grasslands, the administrative system and ownership system have played a very important role in economic activities and in local community life. In order to study the changes in the local administrative systems in Inner Mongolia, some points need special attention:

a) The native residents in the grasslands of Inner Mongolia have been ethnic Mongolians for centuries and their traditional economic activity has been animal husbandry (Jagchid and Hyer, 1979). However, from the beginning of the twentieth century, many Han farmers have migrated to Inner Mongolia and cultivated grasslands for agricultural production. This process was enforced by the Qing dynasty. The Qing emperor intended to increase the population density in the northern frontier areas in order to build up the national defense against Russian invasion (Ma, 1987). The Han population in Inner Mongolia has increased from 1 million to 18.5 million during the past century. The area of cultivated land in Inner Mongolia increased to 5 million hectare by 1991. Gradually, the Mongolians became the minority group in Inner Mongolia and the expansion of cultivation reduced the traditional areas of pasture of the ethnic Mongolians.

b) The commune-brigade system was established in China in the late-1950s. The management of land use, cultivation and animal husbandry was carried out under the policies of the government administration (Liu and Zheng, 1979). The system reforms in the early-1980s brought tremendous systemic changes in grassland areas as well as in the other parts of China. The communes and brigades disintegrated and all cultivated land, animals and parts of pastures were redistributed among rural households. Nowadays, pasture use and management of animal husbandry in grassland areas are no longer under the control of the administration.

c) The commune was the lowest tier of the government in the Chinese administrative system. The Chinese administrative system in general included the governmental institutions at four levels: the central government, provincial (autonomous region) government, county government and commune government. There is a 'prefecture' level between the provincial level and county level, but the governmental institutions at the 'prefecture' level are only the agency of the provincial government. In the 1980s, 'city' governments were established all over China; these 'city' governments were previously 'prefectures' or 'counties', therefore they are classified as 'prefecture-rank city' or 'county-rank city' in the administrative rank system. Beijing, Tianjin, Shanghai and Chongqing are four 'municipalities' directly under the central government.

d) In the past two decades, because of the government policy of opening the trade doors of China to the world, as well as the entry of Chinese pastoral products in the international market, the price of pastoral products (meat, wool and specially cashmere) have increased rapidly. Therefore, the income of herdsmen has also increased rapidly. Yet, many herdsmen intend to increase their number of animals and to exploit the pasture as much as possible (Ma and Pan, 1993). One of the reasons is to get a higher income. A second reason is that they were afraid that pasture and animals would be taken away from them again during future policy changes.

This brief review of the events of the past several decades brings to focus the chain of cause and effect that has been underway: first, government policies in China strongly regulated the local administrative and ownership systems. Second, these systems (the commune system or new 'household responsibility system') directly regulated and indirectly affected land use, agricultural and livestock production of local communities, which in turn had a strong impact on the life patterns and migration of local residents. The chain indicating the process of social-economic-cultural transition in contemporary China can be summed up thus—Policy adjustment of the central government→the changes in local administration→the changes in ownership and management systems of economy→the changes in community organisation and people's life patterns. This study has tried to answer the following questions: What were the major changes in the administrative system in the past five decades? What was the response of the residents to these changes? What is the result of these changes regarding migration, land use and peoples' lives? How were the community leaders selected? What have been the main functions of these leaders? What has been the relationship between administrative changes and local economic development?

Findings on these major aspects will provide important insights in understanding the changes in local economic activities and people's life and their relation to the changes of the Chinese administrative system.

The Research Site

Hurqige Gaca (a former brigade) is located in Shamai Sumu (a former commune), East Wuzhumuqin Banner (at county level), Xilinguole League (see Figure 6.1). The Gaca is along the China–Mongolia border and is considered one of the best pastures in this region. The administrative boundary of this Sumu and Gaca has been stable since 1961. In 2000, the total area of Hurqige Gaca was 869 square kilometers (or 97,363 hectare).

By the end of 2002, there were 128 households and 650 officially registered residents in this Gaca. But among them, 15 households and 108 residents no longer really live in the Gaca or work in pastoral production. They had left the Gaca after animal redistribution in 1983 and most of them now live in county town and are engaged in other economic activities as private *lobar* or businessmen. All residents living in the Gaca in 1993 were native Mongolians and several Han migrant families moved back to Gaca in early 2000, since they received some new pastures. Among those who live in Sumu or county town, about 30 per cent are Mongolian migrants and 60 per cent are Han migrants who moved into Hurqige in the 1950s and 1960s. A new phenomenon is that about 10 per cent of them are old native Mongolians who bought houses in the county town to take care of their grandchildren in banner schools because the Sumu's primary school was closed in 2001.

The net annual income per capita of Shamai Sumu (including Hurqige Gaca) was 3375 yuan in 2001 (see Table 6.1), a little lower than the average level of the herdsmen in the whole banner (10,033 yuan).[1] By the end of June 2002, there were 1,478 horses, 1,185 cattle and 67,983 sheep and goats owned by the herdsmen of Hurqige Gaca.[2] Although this Gaca has a lower than average income in East Wuzhumuqin Banner, it still represents a pure pastoral area with a relative higher income level in Inner Mongolia because this Gaca has a large and better pasture per capita compared with other animal husbandry areas.

Table 6.1
Basic Statistics of Hurqige Gaca

Year	Number of Households	Population	Number of Horses	Number of Cattle	Number of Sheep/Goat	Annual Income Per Capita (yuan)
1962	49	253	–	–	–	126
1963	59	315	–	–	–	110
1972	85	438	–	–	–	180
1979	77	415	1,698	1,442	11,051	179
1982	74	406		4,191	21,113	295
1984	75	442		4,665	18,084	817
1989★	88 (63)	481 (369)	1,746	3,175	28,180	2,318
1990	88 (65)	486 (385)	1,707	3,553	29,017	1,503
1991	91 (67)	504 (408)	1,706	4,040	32,625	2,126
1992	91 (71)	516 (407)	1,852	4,356	31,948	2,679
2002	128 (113)	650 (542)	1,478	1,185	67,983	3375★★

Source: Information collected from Gaca records and field interviews.
Note: ★The numbers in parentheses are the number of herdsmen households and people.
　★★This is the net annual income for the whole Sumu, the level of Hurqige Gaca's income should be higher.

Another important reason for choosing this Gaca as our research site is that I had spent five years during 1967–73 as a herdsman in this Gaca. In the summer of 1992, 1993 and 2002, my colleagues and I visited this community thrice. Many old people have already passed away; those of our age are going to have their grandchildren. Pastures, hills, valleys and sand dunes are still the same, but there are many new brick and tile-roofed houses instead of tents. People now own their animals and have the right to use assigned pastures, and their standard of living has also improved tremendously (see Table 6.1 for the increase of income).

I visited this community and interviewed 42 households in the summer of 1992, interviewed 110 households in 2002 and covered almost all the households registered in this Gaca including those who lived in Sumu and banner town. From the local government, we also obtained the relevant statistics of population changes and livestock production.

Changes in Local Administrative Systems

The 1947–61 Period

The area of today's East Wuzhumuqin Banner was under the rule of the Mongolian prince Demuchukedonglupe until 1947. In that year, the Inner Mongolia Autonomous Region was established. The prince's army lost in the battles against the PLA and some of his soldiers escaped to the Republic of Mongolia. After the establishment of the new banner government under the leadership of the Communist Party in 1949, the new government sent a work-team of communist cadres to Hurqige Valley in 1952. The team taught the herdsmen to read and write and established an administrative unit ('Seventh *Bage*') in this area. The bage was directly under the banner government in the administrative set-up. As an old herdsman recalled, there were about 40 households and less than 10,000 animals in Hurqige area at that time. The pastures were not fixed and native herdsmen still enjoyed nomadic life patterns.

The government then called to organise 'mutual aid group' among the herdsmen for the cooperative management of economic activities in the belief that this would help the poor herdsmen to improve their income by sharing the work. The poor herdsmen could take joint responsibility for the upkeep of their animals (sheep, goats, cattle and horse) to save labour. Again, six 'mutual aid teams' ('*gaote*') were organised in 1956 voluntarily soon after that the pastures became fixed. A fixed organisation needed a fixed 'territory'. One 'gaote' consisted of eight households and less than 800 sheep. Animals could 'move' within the 'territory' of the 'Seventh Bage', whose boundary was decided by the banner.

In 1957, the 'cooperative movement' was introduced in this area and in 1958 all animals became the property of 'cooperatives' by paying off their owners in following years. In 1961, Shamai Commune was established, consisting of three brigades (Hurqige was one of them).

The Commune-Brigade System during 1961–83

During this period, the local unit of administration was the commune-brigade system. In Mao Zedong's opinion, the commune was the ideal organisation to carry out all socio-economic functions at the bottom level of Chinese society. Therefore, the commune authority was a combination of several key positions. Each key officer was in charge of one important function, such as party affairs, administration, management of economic activities, people's militia, the activities of three 'mass' organisations (Youth League, Women's League, Association of Poor Herdsmen), inspection of discipline (against corruption, crime, etc.).

The Association of Poor Herdsmen played a very important role in the land reform movement of the late-1940s. It became important again during the 'Cultural Revolution' in the 1960s when the formal commune and brigade authorities were criticised, but it lost its political influence when 'getting rich' became accepted in the 1980s.

The authority at brigade level also played similar functions, that is, political, administrative and economic management. The brigade cadres took orders from commune authority and organised meetings in the brigade to implement the government policies and the plans prepared by the authority. For example, the brigade enforced projects to protect grasslands, to improve the breed of animals, to prevent and control animal diseases and also enforced the family planning programme, collection of tax and so on. During the commune period, the brigade organised many economic functions as a collaborative unit. The brigade had its storage houses, dining place, tractors, carts (with four horses) and so on. The brigade also had a manager to take care of the storage houses, a cook to take care of dinner, a carpenter to repair brigade properties, two cart-drivers to take care of carts, two tractor drivers to drive a tractor and a book-keeper to take care of the accounting. The brigade at times also organised works assigned by upper authorities such as the construction project of local roads or some works of its own needs, such as the construction of new office houses, new sheepfolds and so on. The brigade also paid for the welfare of herdsmen (see Table 6.2).

Since Hurqige is located at the China–Mongol border area, border vigil was also a function of the brigade's people's militia. This was organised by the brigade authority and the brigade paid the herdsman work points for their duty.

One interesting phenomenon we observed in the 1960s was that, although brigade leaders usually had the authority to assign work to brigade members,

Table 6.2
Expenditure Structure of Hurqige Brigade (1978–82) (in yuan)

Year	Livestock Expenditure	Sideline Expenditure	Others	State Tax	Accumulation Fund	Public Welfare Fund	Distribution among Households
1978	8,445	16,279	5,738	6,073	13,221	4,958	90,450
1979	12,606	25,858	204	6,190	7,250	2,993	87,050
1980	11,670	31,389	5,797	–	9,636	3,576	94,009
1981	3,252	18,020	4,830	–	9,794	3,638	93,762
1982	1,369	14,351	11,656	–	20,970	10,485	119,782

the major decisions in animal husbandry management were made at the meeting of all household heads by the end of each year. In this meeting, household heads (usually old and middle-aged males) sat together to discuss the pasture assignment of the next year, animal adjustment, change in brigade cadres, brigade construction projects, etc. The party secretary and brigade chief joined this meeting as ordinary household heads. The atmosphere of these meetings was like that of traditional tribal meetings of nomads. This was very different from the brigade meetings I attended in agricultural areas.

The New Sumu-Gaca System Since 1983

In 1983, the commune-brigade system disintegrated all over China. This administrative reform resulted in several significant changes. First, the former commune-brigade system was converted into the Sumu-Gaca system. The new administrative system in other agricultural areas is called the 'xiang'[3] (or town at the Sumu level) committee of village residents (at the Gaca level) system. 'Sumu' and 'Gaca' are the traditional terms in Mongolian social organisation, which were borrowed by the new system in the 1980s.

The officers at the xiang (town or Sumu) level still have political and administrative functions, but have fewer roles in organising herdsmen's economic activities. Although the names have been changed, people still use the old names for the local administration. They call Sumu the 'commune' and Gaca the 'brigade'.

Second, all animals and pastures (cultivated lands in agricultural areas) were distributed 'equally' among all brigade members. But in some brigades such as Hurqige, the herdsmen decided to have different standards of animal redistribution for 'native herdsman' and 'migrants'. Thus, 30 sheep, 3.5 cattle and 3.5 horses per capita were allocated to native Mongolians; and 10 sheep per capita, three cattle and three horses per household to the in-migrants (including five Mongolian in-migrant households who spoke the Mongolian language but came from an agricultural area far away).

Third, the pastures within the brigade 'territory' were distributed among herdsmen according to the size of their animals. In 1983, many migrants who received a small number of animals and small piece of pasture left the Gaca and moved to nearby towns. In 1998, the pastures of Hurqige Gaca were redistributed again. Every native herdsman received 2541 *mu* or 169.4 hectare. The others (migrants and their children) received as 50 per cent of the total pastures given to the natives.

The procedure of cadre election at the Gaca (brigade) level under the new Sumu-Gaca system is the same as that during the commune period. After the disintegration of the commune-brigade system, the brigade cadres no longer earn work points, instead they receive subsidies (300 yuan monthly) from the brigade. Hurqige Brigade still keeps about 600 sheep as brigade property. Some poor herdsmen take care of these sheep and submit a part of their earnings to the brigade. Now the brigade leaders do not have the responsibility of managing the economic activities of the brigade. If the banner and Sumu authority do not call them for meetings, they may stay at home and take care of their own animals. The function of these community leaders is quite limited now.

The Election of Commune (Sumu) and Brigade (Gaca) Leaders

There has been a dual system in the Chinese authority system since 1949 with both the party system and the administrative system operating simultaneously. However, since 1949, the party has been leading the administration in all matters and this has been the major characteristic of the Chinese political system. These two systems are now joining to a high extent in practice.

The Structure of Commune Authority and its Election

A commune has a Communist Party Committee (CPC) to lead in political functions. A commune Party Committee usually has seven to nine members. The secretary of this committee is the top leader in the commune. The other members of this committee take other key positions in the commune government. The second member (always the deputy secretary) is the chief of the commune management committee, which mainly performed the functions of administration and economic management. (Under the planning economic system, management of economic activities is a function of the government). The third member is the secretary of the 'commission for inspecting discipline', and the fourth member is the chief of the 'section of people's militia'. The other members take care of the Women's League, Youth League, etc.

All Party Committee members have a government position and all people working in a commune government are government officers (cadres) who receive salaries and other allowances from the government.

In the normal procedure of selecting commune CPC members, the banner government nominates the candidates, and the party members of the commune cast their vote after which the winner of the election has to be approved by the banner government. Sometimes the banner government directly appoints a member of the CPC and this appointment is accepted at the next party member meeting.

Within the administrative system, the banner government can directly appoint or transfer any officers in commune government.

The Structure of the Brigade (Gaca) Authority and its Election

The cadres at brigade level are not government officers or employees. During the commune period, they earn their work points while receiving limited subsidies from the brigade. In the administration at a brigade level, there are usually five full-time cadres consisting of the party secretary, a chief of brigade, a commander of people's militia company, a bookkeeper and a manager. Two other cadres (a secretary of the Youth League and the chief of the Women's League) are 'part-time' cadres. A full-time cadre receives work points generally assigned to a strong male labourer (10 points per day in Hurqige). A part-time cadre receives his/her 'cadre' work points according to the meetings attended and period of training completed. Both full-time and part-time cadres at the brigade level participate in agricultural or pastoral work.

The cadres at brigade level are selected through a similar procedure. Based on recommendations of the herdsmen and party members in the brigade, the Commune Party Committee nominates the candidates. Party members elect the party secretary and herdsmen elect the brigade chief and other cadres.

During our stay in Hurqige in the 1960s and 1970s, we found that the brigade leaders enjoyed a high reputation among herdsmen. They hailed from poor herdsman's families, had joined the Communist Party in its early period and did not exploit the advantages of their positions. The brigade party secretary, Big Bandalagqi, was a monk from a poor herdsman's family. Since he had many children and earned only 10 points a day, the living standard of his family was obviously below the average level. But he joined us in hard work like an ordinary herdsman. By doing this, he earned the respect of the whole brigade.

After the commune-brigade system disintegrated in the early-1980s, the Gaca leaders can only receive some subsidies from the Sumu and Gaca, that situation made these positions less attractive. But Gaca leaders still have some power in distribution of government resources such as welfares, loans and other resource allocation. When we went back later in the 1990s, we found that in the selection of the local leaders, father–son ties played a significant role. The son of the former brigade party secretary, Bandalakqi, became the vice Sumu chief in 1992, and then became a vice leader of a banner government bureau in 2002. The current brigade party secretary is the son of the former brigade chief and the current brigade chief is the son of the former commander of militia. The fathers' reputation helped the sons to win the elections. Because the older leaders were still alive, they could also provide advice to the younger leaders.

The Impact of the Changes in Administrative System on Community Life

Changes in Migration Patterns

Under the commune system, both the commune and brigade had to oversee the collective economic activities. They needed migrant labour for the non-herding chores. Therefore, several migrants entered Hurqige between 1962 and 1983.

In-migration (1962–83) Three Han farmers and their families moved to Shamai Commune to work in its repair and handicraft workshop in 1962. When the 'Cultural Revolution' disturbed the work order in the commune workshop (consisting of carpenters, cobblers, felt-makers, etc.) in 1967 and the workshop crashed financially, some workers from the commune workshop joined three brigades and became brigade members. This action was voluntary on the part of these workers and the commune government arranged it. Among them, three came to Hurqige Brigade.

During the 'Cultural Revolution', migration control in this remote region was loosened. The local cadres were made subjects of political charges and they were unable to enforce the relevant regulations. Further, the commune-brigade system organised some 'collective work' (drilling wells, building houses, mowing grass, transportation and farming production) under its work assignment system. The native Mongolians were not used to such work and communes and brigades had to absorb migrant labourers from agricultural areas. The migrants earned 'work points' like the other herdsmen and shared the income of the brigade that was almost totally from livestock production.

In 1967 and 1968, 52 'intellectual youth' came to Hurqige Brigade from Beijing. They were middle-school students and were sent here for 're-education' under the national policy at that time. They were organised into 10 groups and each group was assigned a flock of sheep (around 2,000 sheep and goats), together with another herdsman household at the beginning. After one year, they became experienced herdsmen. These students left Hurqige gradually for different reasons (such as illness, attending university, new job assignment, family reunion).

Both the farmer in-migration and the Beijing student in-migration to Hurqige were the results of the system and policies of that time. These in-migrants contributed to the change in political structure of the local community. For example, one of the Mongolian migrants became a chief of the Association of Poor Herdsmen and was very radical in politics. The 52 Beijing students also had a lot of influence on the dress, diet, language and customs of the native Mongolians.

Out-migration (1984–85)   Except for the three Mongolian households, most in-migrants now live in the Sumu or county town and are engaged in other activities. They left Hurqige in 1983 or 1984 after the animal redistribution.

There were two 'kinds' of households in Hurqige during the commune period in terms of their relationship with livestock production. One worked with a flock of animals (sheep or cattle). This group was composed of native Mongolian herdsmen. Members of the other group were engaged in activities such as gardening, cooking for the brigade office and school, carpentery, driving carts and tractors and engaged in other seasonal work assigned by the brigade such as drilling wells, building houses, mowing grass, etc.

The second group was of in-migrants whose in-migration became possible in pastoral areas only under the former commune-brigade system. The native herdsmen did not prefer hard labour or work that involved living in work sites far from their families. When under the commune-brigade system, the government requested the local pastoral community (commune and brigade) to organise some collective activities, the local herdsmen rejected this. Under the commune system, the commune and brigade cadres had the power to arrange official in-migration (to get residential registration), and thus, the in-migrants came in to undertake the government collective activities. The work point distribution system led to the in-migrants sharing the herdsmen's work. Therefore the herdsmen tolerated in-migration to a certain extent. Generally, most of the income of the brigade came from livestock produce (such as selling animals and wool).

After the redistribution of animals, however, in-migrants could neither live on the small number of animals nor could they get work assignments from the brigade to earn 'work points'. Therefore, they left Hurqige and moved to the Sumu or county town for other opportunities. However, they all still register Hurqige as their official residence.

New Trend of Seasonal Migration   Since each household now has a flock of sheep, a flock of cattle and some horses, the households with less labourers face problems in taking care of these different animals. One solution is to maintain a large family, which include the married children. This was contrary to the commune system, where newly-married couples established their own households as soon as possible so that they became eligible to apply for a flock of animals and become 'livestock households'. If they remained with their parents, they had to participate in other collective activities to earn work points. The flock assigned to the parents only offered a certain amount of work points.[4] But after the animal redistribution, we found some 'big' families in Hurqige. In 1993, there were eight households with eight to nine members, five households with 10 or more members. There was no big household such as this, before 1983. Big households had obvious disadvantages in the commune system but had their advantages in the new household responsibility system.

The second solution is for two or three kin-households to live together or near each other and combine their animals into one flock for more efficient herding. This is an effective way to save flock force, especially after the size of the flock became much smaller compared to flock size under the commune system. Combining their animals in grazing does not mean that the ownership of animals has to change.

A new phenomenon appeared in Hurqige and other pastoral communities recently. In 1993, in Hurqige, where labour is scarce, four households hired outsiders to take their animals to graze. In 2002, 80 per cent of Hurqige households hired migrant herdsmen to take care of their animals. Most of these employees live and eat in their own tent, earn 200 yuan plus an ewe and a lamb (or two sheep) per month. All these 'hired livestock workers' are Mongolians from poor areas in other banners or leagues far away from Hurqige. This new pattern can be called 'seasonal migration'. The earliest migrants came in 1986 and the trend became popular in the 1990s.

Impact on Pasture Use Patterns

The brigade 'territory' became fixed in 1956. After the commune-brigade system was started in 1961, the management of pastoral production and pasture use began a new pattern. Each household engaged in pastoral production only needed to take care of one flock of animals, either sheep or cattle. The brigade assigned two herdsmen to take care of about 1500 horses of the whole brigade. The community still followed the lifestyle of nomads (Li, Ma and Simpson, 1993: 69).

After the disintegration of the commune-brigade system and all the animals and pasture had been redistributed among residents, several important changes took place in the people's life pattern in Hurqige: (a) Nomads became settled residents. Each household received a piece of grassland according to the size of its members (2,541 mu or 169.4 hectare per capita), so that a household of five could have a large area of 850 hectare grasslands. They built fences around the lands, drilled wells, built houses and sheepfolds. This piece of land became its 'territory' (Li, Ma and Simpson, 1993: 69).

(b) The animals of each household became diversified. Instead of taking care of only one kind of animal, each household now had four kinds of animals; cattle, houses, sheep and goats. This had several results (i) the size of the flock became much smaller; (ii) a household needed more labourers to take care of different animals. In order to save labour, some relatives started to live next to each other and to combine their animals into a common flock for grazing; (iii) each piece of pasture came under the management of a household. The animals of a household should not cross its border. In order to reserve grasslands for use in spring, all herdsmen fenced their grasslands as much as possible; (iv) they also built houses for their own residence and pens and sheds for their animals in the spring camp (see Table 6.3).

Impact on Family Size and Fertility

The new system of pasture management has had some impact on the fertility pattern of local herdsmen. In this purely pastoral area, the income of herdsmen is totally dependent on the number of their animals and the quality and small size of pastures limit the number of animals. There is no way for a newly-established household to obtain a piece of pasture from the Gaca nowadays. When a herdsman's son gets married and establishes his own household, the father has to split his animals and pastures and give the young couple their share. The young couple will soon have their own children and then the pasture of one household will become smaller and smaller by generation. So Hurqige's herdsmen have begun worrying about their growing population.

Before 1990, there was no restriction on childbearing in Hurqige and the nearby pastoral communities. But since 1991, the local government has had a more strict regulation for 'family planning'. One couple now can only have two children within a four-year interval. In 1992, two families were fined (one for 3000 yuan and another for 4000 yuan) because the interval of their children's births was less than four years. In our conversation with these herdsmen, we had the impression that most of them accept the policy of 'two children', because they are worried about the problem of surplus labour force that might arise five to 10 years later in this community. The herdsmen worry about the future of their children, for their children do not speak good Mandarin, have less education and urban experience and so face difficulties in finding jobs in towns or cities.

The social changes in Hurqige Gaca in the past 50 years in terms of administration, ownership, herding patterns, migration patterns, fertility and cultural interaction are given in Table 6.4.

Table 6.3

Expenditure Structure of Hurqige Gaca (1985–92) (in yuans)

Year	Total Expenditure	Animal Medicine	Forage	Repairing	Other Productive Expenditure*	Grassland Fence	Pen/shed	Well	House	Tent
1985	177,839	350	500	80	6,166	3,900	5,700	4,200	5,410	–
1986	237,427	10,622	1,650	6,220	24,120	12,476	10,415	5,910	7,965	–
1987	321,972	6,464	12,745	2,200	10,340	71,000	42,143	5,920	28,090	861
1988	398,598	12,364	23,670	6,572	49,085	56,100	11,186	500	79,810	12321
1989	446,199	22,668	15,100	13,210	62,380	22,500	27,670	–	189,943	5414
1990	580,183	21,775	21,960	11,480	199,200	–	37,100	300	149,600	1486
1991	383,015	20,198	35,700	26,440	22,680	–	12,470	–	126,700	4309
1992	624,068	20,385	20,650	17,321	21,090	–	47,165	2,100	188,087	5196

Gaca Collections

Year	Animal Prices	Pasture Management Fee	Gaca Management Fee	State Tax
1985	23,323	15,725	9,236	11,180
1986	42,299	20,032	–	12,548
1987	55,077	8,730	–	5,500
1988	41,929	9,562	8,354	23,059
1989	22,143	14,157	–	36,310
1990	34,796	13,714	9,559	51,229
1991	35,614	6,440	10,215	60,959
1992	16,110		5,194	

Note: *A large proportion of this expenditure has been used to buy tractors, motorcycles, jeeps, generators and other machines.

Table 6.4

Social Changes in Hurqige Brigade/Gaca, East Wuzhumuqin Banner, Inner Mongolia, in the Past 50 Years

Year	Households/ Animals	Administration	Ownership/Tax Payment	Herding Patterns	Migration Patterns/ Channels to Sell Products	Family Formation and Fertility	Cultural Changes/ Education/Health Care
Before 1947	30–35 < 8000	Mongol price domination on traditional organisation	Private animal, public pasture/ taxes and labour duties paid to prince	Circulation within banner, by prince's permission, might circulate to neighbouring banners in periods of heavy snow	No migration allowed/a few seasonal Han traders came to banner towns to buy pastoral products	No marriage registration, most were co-residence and some single women with children.	Traditional Mongol nomadic lifestyle/ no school/ no clinic
1947–54	35–42 10,000 (1953)	Banner government established in 1947 by the Party Committee	Private animal, public pasture/no taxes	Circulation within nearby areas within banner	No migration/ products sold to 'gong-xiao-she' (collective trade enterprises)	As above	As above
1955–56	42–45 12,000 (1956)	Local administration established at xiang and gaca level	Private animal/ 'new Suluke' cooperative system	As above	As above	As above	As above/xiang had school and clinic with private doctors

(*Table 6.4 contd.*)

(Table 6.4 contd.)

Period	Population	Ownership	Pasture/Herding	Residential registration	Marriage	Culture/Customs
1957–60	45–49 18,000 (1960)	As above	Collective ownership of animals; collective pastures/tax paid to government	More restricted to local pastures	Residential registration started in 1959; two Mongolian in-migrants made their entry/products sold to gong-xiao-she	Marriage registration started in 1960; only monogamy since 1961; still some single women with children	Some farmer's customs came with migrants (house, clothing, diet, etc.)/xiang had school and clinic, private doctors
1961–83	49–74 25,300 (1982	Commune-brigade established in 1961; 'commune period'	'class' division in 1964; collective ownership; members earn work points	Herding within brigade; group works' need labour; the goal of 'grain self-sufficiency' prevalent	Entry of 7 Mongol migrants, 9 Han migrants, 52 Beijing students, 5 league students/products sold to gong-xiao-she	Small households for livestock assignment	Interaction among three 'cultures': Mongol nomads, Han farmers and urban students/brigade school/commune hospital 'barefoot doctors'

(Table 6.4 contd.)

(*Table 6.4 contd.*)

Year	Households/ Animals	Administration	Ownership/Tax Payment	Herding Patterns	Migration Patterns/ Channels to Sell Products	Family Formation and Fertility	Cultural Changes/ Education/Health Care
After 1983	74–91 (71) 38,000 (1992)	Sumu-Gaca system established in 1983	Both animal and pastures are private/tax paid to government	Circulation within private pastures; animal size controlled; care taken of pastures	Former migrants left; some keep contact for service work; seasonal herders hired/products sold in market; gong-xiao-she still exists	Larger household for labour division; reduced fertility	Less use of Mandarin, but retention of some Han/ agricultural customs (house, motorcycle); no Gaca school, private clinic

Summary

In Inner Mongolia, the policies for the ownership and management systems have gone through several significant changes since 1949. The first change was that the government distributed the animals and lands of landlords and herd lords among the poor farmers and herdsmen in the late-1940s. The second change was the establishment of collective productive units, step by step, in the 1950s, and the third change was the disintegration of commune-brigade system and redistribution of animals and lands among the residents in 1983. Such changes in the administrative system had a tremendous impact on ownership of animals and land, which in turn had an impact on economic activities and community life. The findings of this study has been summarised as follows:

(a) Under the different administrative systems, officers and community cadres played different functions. During the commune system, officers and cadres not only carried out administrative functions, but were organisers and managers of economic activities as well. Under the new system, cadres in brigade manage only tax collection and other administrative functions.

(b) Commune-brigade system fixed the 'territory' of each brigade and the new 'household responsibility system' fixed the 'territory' of each household. Now Mongolian nomads have acquired settled households, similar to individual farm owners in the Western countries.

(c) The commune-brigade system organised some collective works, which attracted in-migrants, both Mongolians and Han from poorer areas to the grasslands. The disintegration of the commune-brigade system gave the migrants no longer the opportunity to earn 'work points', since they could not live on the reduced number of animals they received in redistribution, they moved out of the community. The migration pattern has been closely related to the policy and system in this community.

(d) The procedure of cadre election has been kept the same under different systems since the majority of local community members have been stable and close to each other. They are enclosed in a wide network by blood and marriages. The sons of old generation cadres often assume their fathers' positions by winning the election.

Notes

1. The highest annual net income per capita by Sumu in East Wuzhumuqin Banner in 2001 was 9,405 yuan, the lowest one was 3,138 yuan. Shamai Sumu (where Hurqige Gaca is located) had an income of 3,375 yuan. The average level was 4,948 yuan for the whole

banner. Generally, the residents living in a Sumu site have a lower income than herdsmen in a Gaca.

2. The difference between these numbers and the numbers by the end of 1992 indicates the number of survivors among the new born animals in the past spring.

3. For the difference between xiang and town, please refer to the relevant literature (Ma, 1991: 90–113).

4. Generally, 10 points for taking care of a flock of sheep at day time, eight points for watching over them at night, eight points for a flock of cattle at day time and six points for watching over them at night.

References

Chang, K. et al. 1956. *A Regional Handbook on the Inner Mongolia Autonomous Region*. Seattle: The Far Eastern and Russian Institute, University of Washington.

Gerletu (ed.). 1988. *Grassland Resources in Xilingele League*. Hohhot: Press of Inner Mongolia Daily (in Chinese).

Jagchid, S. and P. Hyer. 1979. *Mongolian Culture and Society*. Boulder: Westview Press.

Li, Ou, Rong Ma and James R. Simpson. 1993. 'Changes in the Nomadic Patterns and its Impact on the Inner Mongolion Steppe Grasslands Ecosystem', *Nomadic Peoples*, 33: 63–72.

Liu Jingping and Zheng Guangzhi (eds). 1979. *Introduction to Economic Development of the Inner Mongolia Autonomous Region*. Hohhot: People's Press of Inner Mongolia (in Chinese).

Ma, Rong. 1987. 'Migrant and Ethnic Integration in Rural Inner Mongolia'. Ph.D. dissertation, Brown University.

———. 1991. 'The Development of the Small Towns and their Role in the Modernisation of China', *Social Sciences in China*, 22 (1): 90–113.

———. 1992. 'Social Sciences', in *Grasslands and Grassland Sciences in Northern China*. Washington D.C.: National Academic Press.

Ma, Rong and Pan Naigu. 1993. 'Social and Economic Development of Semi-agricultural and Semi-pastoral Areas in Inner Mongolia: A Survey of Fu Village', in Ma Rong and Pan Naigu (eds), *On Development of China's Frontier Regions*, pp. 82–139. Beijing: Peking University Press (in Chinese).

Si Qing and Hu Zhixiao (eds). 1983. *General Situation of the Inner Mongolia Autonomous Region*. Hohhot: People's Press of Inner Mongolia (in Chinese).

7 Village Panchayats in Maharashtra

Rajendra Vora

Maharashtra, a state of Marathi-speaking population was carved out of the Bombay Province in 1960 and since then it has been seen as a typical example of a dominant caste thesis. The Marathas, a middle-peasantry caste accounting for around 30 per cent of the total population of the state, dominate the power structure in Maharashtra. In no other state of India do we find a caste as large as the Marathas. In the past years, scholars have turned their attention to the rural society of Maharashtra in which they thought the roots of this domination lay. Anil Bhatt conducted a study of politics in Akola District (Bhatt, 1963) while B.S. Baviskar examined the role of cooperatives in Ahmednagar District (Baviskar, 1969). Mary Carras tried to understand factionalism in the politics of four districts: Poona, Ratnagiri, Akola and Aurangabad (Carras, 1972). D.B. Rosenthal analysed politics and cooperatives in two districts—Poona and Kolhapur (Rosenthal, 1977). These scholars found that politics in Maharashtra is dominated by the Marathas because of their numerical strength and their control over agricultural wealth, cooperatives and panchayati raj—a three tier system of rural government. V.M. Sirsikar's survey of leaders from the districts of Satara, Aurnagabad and Akola revealed that the Marathas are disproportionately represented in the leadership of these districts (Sirsikar, 1970). Village studies have also shown how Marathas came to acquire dominance. Lee Schlesinger's study of Apshinge Village in Satara District (Schlesinger, 1988) or Anthony Carter's work on Girvi Village, Satara (Carter, 1975) and Orenstein's village study (Orenstein, 1965) brings to the fore the dominance of the Marathas in the village power structure.

The Politics of Aggregation

However, it must be noted that the Marathas have maintained their ascendancy by accommodating diverse castes and communities in the power structure of the state. Y.B. Chavan, the first chief minister of Maharashtra believed in the 'politics of aggregation', which meant bringing together multiple castes and communities under the leadership of the rich Maratha peasantry. It was a pluralist model of power whereby various social sections were co-opted in the network, which ultimately stabilised and cemented the authority of the high-class Marathas. Chavan claimed that his regime was a rule of the *'bahujan'*, which literally meant rule by those who are in majority, that is, the Marathas, the Backward Castes and SCs. He expected judiciousness and tolerance from the Maratha elites towards other social groups so long as they did not question the Maratha hegemony and thought that the Marathas must create a sense of partnership and involvement towards SCs. They must work towards the building of a homogeneous rural social elite (Lele, 1982: 32–35). These ideas of Chavan have had a major influence on the political process of the state at all levels. Today the politics of aggregation has percolated down to the level of village panchayats.

The Bombay Village Panchayats Act of 1958 reflected Chavan's outlook. It made provisions for the reservation of seats for SCs and STs in the village panchayats. The number of reserved seats was decided by the collector of the respective district. Village panchayats in Maharashtra are governed by this Act and function within the framework of zilla parishads (district councils) and panchayat samitis (sub-district councils) created by the Maharashtra Zilla Parishads and Panchayat Samitis Act of 1961, based on the recommendation of the committee on democratic decentralisation constituted by the state government in 1960.

The 1958 Act also made provisions for the reservation of seats (two) for women in each village panchayat. Women's participation in public affairs has a long history in Maharashtra. The idea of women's panchayat was recommended by the Committee on the Status of Women in India in 1974. However, Nimboot, a village in Pune District of Maharashtra had successfully implemented this idea as early as 1962. Women candidates won the panchayat elections against the male candidates and it must be noted that out of 13 members only six were Marathas, while six were from other backward castes (OBC) and one belonged to the SC category. The all-women panchayat of Nimboot remained in power for a full term and achieved many successes with the cooperation of the menfolk (Darekar, 2002: 12–13). In the late-1980s, the Shetkari Sanghatana (farmers' organisation) took the lead in mobilising rural women. At its session held in 1986, the organisation supported greater leadership of women and proposed all-women panels for the zilla parishad (district council) elections (Omvedt, 1990: 23–22). But these elections were postponed by the government. The village panchayat elections, however, were held in 1989. The women panels formed by the organisation captured power in eight villages. In three other villages too, women panels came to power. Maharashtra was among the first few states to accept the recommendation of the National Perspective Plan for Women in 1990, and in 1999–2000, was among the first to reserve 30 per cent seats for women in the local government bodies in urban and rural areas (Moghe, 1997: 5). Women thus entered the village councils and the panchayati raj in Maharashtra even before the provisions of the Seventy-third Amendment were implemented.

A study conducted by N.R. Inamdar in 1962 showed how the Village Panchayat Act of 1958 and the politics of aggregation had influenced the social character of the village panchayats in Maharashtra. In the four villages in Pune District where he had conducted his survey, at least one member in each panchayat belonged to the SC category. One panchayat had a member belonging to the ST community since that village had a sizeable ST population. In three panchayats there were two members each who belonged to the OBC category even though there was no reservation for that category in the 1958 Act. The panchayats of two villages out of the four also had women members. In one village there was a Brahman member. This study thus validates the observation that the village panchayats of Maharashtra represented diverse social groups long before the Seventy-third Constitutional Amendment came into force and that the Marathas continued their hold by following a policy of co-optation and accommodation in the local power structure.

In what manner and to what extent has the Seventy-third Amendment changed this picture? In order to answer this question, I have presented the findings of a survey of eight village panchayats with reference to their social composition before and after the implementation of the Seventy-third Amendment in Maharashtra. I have drawn my data for the pre-amendment period from a study on the relationship between land ownership, caste and power in 48 villages of Maharashtra conducted by my department at Pune University. In this chapter I have reported findings from only eight villages where a post-amendment survey was conducted. The first study carried out in 1992 found that the land ownership was the determining factor to get into a position of power in the village and that non-Maratha peasantry castes acquired power in the village basically due to their hold over agricultural wealth expressed in the ownership of land. The study revealed that the domin- ant castes (Maratha and non-Maratha) of the respective villages were internally dominated by certain lineages or clans (Vora, 1999: 217–18). The post- amendment survey was conducted in 2002 in eight villages in Latur and Aurangabad districts of the Marathwada region. The most numerous caste in this region are the Marathas who constitute around 45 per cent of the population, which is quite high compared to the state average of 30 per cent. The Marathas are the single largest land-owning caste found in all the districts of the Marathwada region and they control 65 per cent of seats in the legislative assembly and also hold 60–70 per cent positions in zilla parishads, panchayat samitis and cooperative institutions of the region (Birmal, 1996: 36–46). Due to its contiguity with Andhra Pradesh and Karnataka, Latur District has some vil- lages that have a large population of Lingayat and Reddy castes from these states. Since the region was earlier a part of the Muslim princely state of Hyderabad, districts such as Aurangabad have a large Muslim population even in the rural areas. In the selection of these two districts, two tehsils (sub-districts) from each district and two villages from each tehsil, care was taken to ensure that one belonged to the least-irrigated tract and the other to the most irrigated.

Eight Village Panchayats

The findings of these two surveys of eight villages are presented here in the form of 16 tables. Two tables are devoted to each village, the first of which gives the distribution of panchayat members from 1960–62 according to their caste, clan, gender and the land they own. The second table of each village gives the distribution of panchayat members elected after the Amendment came into force with reference to their caste, clan and gender. The two tables of each village thus give a comparative picture of the social composition of that panchayat in the pre-amendment and post-amendment period. Each table also mentions whether a member belonging to a particular community/clan became an office holder—*sarpanch* and *upsarpanch* (chief and deputy chief) of the village panchayat.

Sukarni in the Udgir Tehsil of Latur District is a Maratha village where most of the land and the power are in the hands of Marathas (see Tables 7.1 and 7.2). Among the Marathas, the Sukane clan shares power along with other Maratha clans. The OBCs, SCs and Muslims also send their representatives to the panchayat. Land-owning Reddy clans were also elected to the

Table 7.1
Sukani (1960–92)

Caste	Land (hectare)	Clan	Number of Members	Percentage	Officers	Percentage
Maratha	179.50	Sukane	11	35.48	3 + 2 = 5	45.45
	132.17	Mule	06	19.35	0 + 3 = 3	27.27
	22.49	Kondagale	05	16.12		
	00.00	Jadhav	04	12.90	1 + 1 = 2	18.19
	10.72	Ghose	02	6.45	1 + 0 = 1	9.09
	11.06	Awalkode	01	3.22		
	40.80	Patil	02	4.45		
		Total	31	100.00	5 + 6 = 11	100.00
Matang (SC)	3.78	Gotmukle	08	61.53		
	3.98	Kedale	05	39.46		
		Total	13	100.00		
Reddi (SC)	27.54	Adarge	01	50.00		
	38.59	Karkure	01	50.00		
		Total	02	100.00		
Komti (OBC)	00.00	Motewar	01	100.00	1 + 0 = 1	100.00
		Total	01	100.00	1 + 0 = 1	100.00
Muslim	4.70	Shaikh	01	100.00		
		Total	01	100.00		
		Grand Total	48	100.00	6 + 6 = 12	100.00

Table 7.2
Sukani (1997)

Caste	Clan	Number of Members	Office-holders
Maratha	Sukane	1	
	Jadhav	1	
	Patil	1	1 + 0 = 1
	Total	3	
Matang (SC)	Kedase	2 (W-1)	0 + 1 = 1
	Total	2 (W-1)	
Dhangar (OBC)	Bhavate	1	
	Total	1	
Lawar (OBC)	Poparait	1 (W-1)	
	Total	1 (W-1)	
	Grand Total	7	

Note: Number of women members is indicated by W-1/2.

panchayat. The SC members owning some land could send their representatives to the panchayat. The panchayat had two women members in each term. In 1997, a Matang (SC) became the upsarpanch but otherwise the panchayat composition remained almost the same. In Handarguli in Udgir Tehsil of Latur District we find that Maratha and Lingayat clans are dominant and they basically share power among themselves. The number of backward castes and SC communities were represented in the panchayat during 1960–92. In 2000, the number of women representatives went up to four; one of them was an SC and the upsarpanch was a Lingayat woman. Khuntegaon from Ausa Tehsil of Latur District is a Reddy village where the Kolhe clan of Reddy control most of the land and also the panchayat. Other Reddy clans and OBC and SC land-holding clans share power with them. In 1997, the social composition of the panchayat did not change much. Karanjgaon, a village from the same tehsil is a typical Maratha village dominated by three Maratha clans. Land-owning Brahmin clans as well as land-owning SC and OBC clans also shared power. In 1997, all the three Maratha clans continued to maintain their hold. The strength of women members has gone up from two to three and a woman from the dominant Maratha clan had assumed the position of sarpanch. Wahegaon in Gangapur Tehsil of Aurangabad District is a village dominated by Maratha clans but Mali (OBC) clans have come to occupy second position and a SC clan having sizeable landholdings also shares power with them. Things have changed as far as women are concerned after the Seventy-third Amendment. Their numbers in the panchayat have increased to eight and an OBC and a SC woman have been elected to the position of surpanch and upsarpanch respectively. In Nevargaon Village in the same tehsil, two Maratha clans own most of the land and control local power. Land-owning clans from the OBC, SC and Muslim communities have been able to send representatives to the panchayat and have also occupied at one time or another sarpanch/upsarpanch positions. During 1995–2000 this picture changed basically with respect to the representation of women belonging to various OBC and SC communities. Mangrul is a village in Sillod Tehsil of Aurangabad District. In this village three Maratha clans, two Dhangar (OBC) clans and one Muslim clan controlled the local power structure from 1960 to 1992. After the implementation of the Seventy-third Amendment, the number of women members from different communities went up to seven and a Dhangar woman became the sarpanch and another woman of the same community occupied the position of the upsarpanch. The last village surveyed was Bharadi in the same tehsil. Two Maratha clans control the panchayat of this village but they have to accommodate Muslim and some OBC clans. A Kalal clan plays an important role in this panchayat. In 1995–2000, the numerical strength of women members increased to seven, which included two Muslim women.

A close and careful reading of these tables lead us to the following observations. These panchayats were composed of multiple castes and communities even though Marathas have had their hold over these bodies. The land-owning castes of the backward category used to send their representatives to the panchayats. Land ownership was one of the deciding factors for entry into the panchayats. Khutegaon Panchayat was basically controlled by the Reddys because they were the main land-owning community of the village. Minority communities like the Muslims could find a place in the panchayats in Bharadi and Mangrul due to their sizeable population and also due to their control over land. Village politics was dominated by a few clans of the land-owning caste groups. Scheduled caste candidates who could go to the panchayats belonged to the land-owning clans, such as Dusing in Nevargaon or Satpute in Karajgaon. The sarpanch and the upsarpanch, who play a crucial role in the panchayat, came from the Maratha caste, SCs, OBCs, Lingayats or Reddys and also from the Muslim category in these villages during the period 1960 to 1992. If we take a count of non-Maratha sarpanches in these villages the figure comes to 19. There was not a single instance of a SC member holding that position. However, it was not uncommon for women to become the sarpanch. Sukani had elected a Maratha woman to that post in 1988, while Wahegaon had elected a SC woman member for the post of upsarpanch in 1983. It was easier for candidates belonging to the land-owning castes and communities to secure the post of sarpanch or upsarpanch. Since SCs neither owned sizeable land nor could effectively combat the traditional hurdle of untouchability, they could not aspire for the post.

The Seventy-third Amendment has changed this picture to a certain extent. The second table of each of the eight villages surveyed reveal that for certain marginal sections the opportunities to enter the panchayat bodies have increased, thereby making panchayats more representative than those in the earlier era (see Tables 7.3–7.16). The candidates from OBC category who used to be elected from open seats are now mostly being elected from the reserved seats for their caste category. The SC and ST candidates could find

Table 7.3
Handarguli (1960–92)

Caste	Land (hectare)	Clan	Number of Members	Percentage	Officers	Percentage
Maratha	129.01	Bhosale	12	46.15	1 + 2 = 3	37.5
	102.73	Patil	09	34.61	4 + 1 = 5	62.5
	00.00	Jadhav	02	7.69		
	00.00	Belapure	01	3.84		
	22.28	Mane	01	3.84		
	00.00	Mote	01	3.84		
		Total	26	100.00	5 + 3 = 8	100.00
Lingayat	89.78	Dhuppe	07	50.00	0 + 1 = 1	20.00
	67.19	Kalawane	03	21.42	0 + 1 = 1	20.00
	19.93	Kore	03	21.42	2 + 0 = 2	40.00
	10.80	Nihure	01	7.14	0 + 1 = 1	20.00
		Total	14	100.00	2 + 3 = 5	
Matang (SC)	0.83	Kamble	06	66.66		
	00.00	Waghmare	02	22.22		
	00.00	Mane	01	11.11		
		Total	09	100.00		
Mahar	00.00	Kamble	05	83.33		
	00.00	Gaikwad	01	16.66		
		Total	06			
Vasudev (OBC)	10.35	Pendharkar	05	100.00	0 + 1 = 1	100.00
		Total	05	100.00	0 + 1 = 1	100.00
Dhangar (OBC)	22.90	Shelke	01	20.00		
	11.06	Sule	03	60.00		
	8.85	Zole	01	20.00		
		Total	05	100.00		
Muslim	3.25	Pathan	04	100.00		
Chambhar (SC)	00.00	Gaikwad	03	100.00		
Koli (OBC)	00.00	Khotewad	02	100.00		
Lohar (OBC)	1.77	Poplaim	01	100.00		
Sali (OBC)	00.00	Sinangarwad	01	100.00		
Reddi (OBC)	18.00	Chimandar	01	100.00		
Mali (OBC)	00.00	Kshirsagar	01	100.00		
		Grand Total	78	100.00	7 + 7 = 14	100.00

Table 7.4
Handarguli (2000)

Caste	Clan	Number of Members	Office-holders
Maratha	Bhosale	3 (W-1)	
	Total	3	
Lingayat	Dhuppe	1	
	Bolgave	1 (W-1)	0 + 1 (W) = 1 (W)
	Total	2 (W-1)	
Matang (SC)	Kamble	2 (W-1)	
	Total	2 (W-1)	
Dhangar (OBC)	Gudde	1	
	Total	1	
Dhor (SC)	Poul	1	
	Total	1	
Koli (ST)	Kotewad	1	
	Total	1	
Muslim	Shaikh	1	
	Total	1	
Rangari (OBC)	Ambekar	1	
	Total	1	
Koshti (OBC)	Huddwar	1 (W-1)	
	Total	1 (W-1)	
	Grand Total	13	

Note: W = women members.

a place in earlier panchayat bodies because of the policy of reservation but now their proportions have increased. Only two women used to be there in the panchayats of the pre-Seventy-third Amendment days. Their number has certainly increased to raise their proportion to 33 per cent. But the most significant development that has taken place due to the amendment is with regard to the position of the sarpanch. In Maharashtra 33 per cent of such positions are reserved by method of rotation for the women, SCs, scheduled tribes and backward class of citizens which basically include other backward castes and communities.

According to the calculation of the State Election Commission, there are 27,571 village panchayats in the 31 districts of the state and therefore in all 223,750 seats. Out of these, 25,192 seats are reserved for SCs. The total of 8,281 of these are reserved for women belonging to the SCs. The total number of reserved seats for STs is 30,730 out of which 9,857 are reserved for women of this category. For backward class citizens, 53,831 seats are reserved and out of those 22,340 are reserved for women of this class. In the category of general seats there are 113,997 seats and 30,074 of those seats are reserved for women. If all seats reserved for women from all categories are put together the figure comes to 70,562. These figures, which present the overall scenario of the state, speak for themselves. The way the reservation policy has been implemented at the local government level is beyond anybody's imagination. The real gainers, as the figures show, are no doubt women—women belonging to all categories.

Table 7.5

Khutegaon (1960–92)

Caste	Land (hectare)	Clan	Number of Members	Percentage	Officers	Percentage
Reddi (SC)	247.95	Kolhe	14	48.27	3 + 1 = 4	50.00
	37.14	Kasle	5	17.24	2 + 0 = 2	25.00
	18.02	Khutwad	3	10.34	0 + 1 = 1	12.50
	13.95	Mogale	3	10.34	1 + 0 = 1	12.50
	4.73	Nalle	3	10.34	–	–
	5.33	Giri	1	3.44	–	–
Dhangar (OBC)	1.26	Shelke	5	50.00	0 + 3 = 3	75.00
	13.85	Pandhre	2	20.00		
	9.64	Patil	1	10.00		
	34.70	Mahanwar	3	10.00		
	43.01	Sudke	1	10.00	0 + 1 = 1	25.00
Mahar (SC)	4.65	Kamble	4	57.14		
	1.09	Sarawate	2	28.57		
	4.92	Gawali	1	14.28		
Maratha	00.00	Chinchole	2	50.00		
	34.36	Pawar	1	25.00		
	80.16	Salunkhe	1	25.00		
Gosawi	00.00	Giri	1	100.00		
		Grand Total	29	100.00	6 + 6 = 12	100.00

Table 7.6

Khutegaon (1997)

Caste	Clan	Number of Members	Office-holders
Reddi (SC)	Kolhe	1	0 + 1 = 1
	Kasale	1	
	Bhojane	1	
	Total	3	
Dhangar (OBC)	Shelke	1	
Bandgar (OBC)	Mahanavar	I (W-1)	
Mahar (SC)	Kawale	1	
Matang (SC)	Gaikwad	1 (W-1)	
Maratha	Pawar	1	1 + 0 = 1
	Salunkhe	1 (W-1)	
	Grand Total	9	

Note: W = women members.

Can this change be considered as a tranformative phenomenon so far as the rural power structure is concerned? What is the larger context of the new panchayat raj introduced by the Seventy-third Amendment? How do we historically place this Amendment? Let me formulate plausible answers to these questions.

Table 7.7
Karajgaon (1960–92)

Caste	Land (hectare)	Clan	Number of Members	Percentage	Officers	Percentage
Maratha	185.35	Dalve	15	36.58	1 + 1 = 2	20.00
	144.33	Jadhav	13	31.70	2 + 0 = 2	20.00
	101.88	Patil	06	21.95	2 + 3 = 5	50.00
	37.61	Nagrale	02	4.87	0 + 1 = 1	10.00
	37.87	Wakase	01	2.43	–	–
	0.00	Yedule	01	2.43	–	–
		Total	41	100.00	5 + 5 = 10	100.00
Mahar (SC)	43.65	Satpute	08	88.88	–	–
	00.00	Kamble	01	11.11	–	–
		Total	09	100.00		
Mali (OBC)	27.77	Gawli	1	100.00	1 + 0 = 1	100.00
		Total	1	100.00	1 + 0 = 1	100.00
Brahmin	18.15	Joshi	1	100.00	0 + 1 = 1	100.00
		Total	1	100.00	0 + 1 = 1	100.00
		Grand Total	52	100.00	6 + 6 = 12	100.00

Table 7.8
Karajgaon (1997)

Caste	Clan	Number of Members	Office-holders
Maratha	Dalve	4 (W-1)	1 (W-1) + 0 = 1
	Jadhav	1 (W-1)	
	Patil	1	0 + 1 = 1
	Total	6 (W-2)	
Mahar (SC)	Satpute	1	
	Total	1	
Mali (OBC)	Gawali	2 (W-1)	
	Grand Total	9 (W-3)	

Note: W = women members.

Historical Context

The dominant sections of Indian society never considered parliamentary democracy sufficient enough to generate a belief in the legitimacy of the Indian state and along with distributing power between the centre and constituent regional units, also made constitutional provision for the decentralisation of power, even if only as a directive principle. While many important directive principles remained on paper, Article 40 concerning organising the panchayat system was taken up on the agenda by Nehru's government in 1957 and by 1959–60, panchayat raj was established in many constituent states.

Table 7.9
Wahegaon (1960–92)

Caste	Land (hectare)	Clan	Number of Members	Percentage	Officers	Percentage
Maratha	577.88	Manal	12	69.69	6 + 1 = 7	70.00
	236.27	Hiwale	09	27.27	0 + 3 = 3	30.00
	43.34	Karbhar	01	03.03	–	–
		Total	33	100.00	6 + 4 = 10	100.00
Mali (OBC)	84.11	Bhadke	05	31.25	1 + 0 = 1	50.00
	76.83	Darunte	05	31.25	0 + 1 = 1	50.00
	35.16	Kalamkar	03	18.75	–	–
	14.08	Chatekar	01	6.25		
	00.00	Dewle	01	6.25		
	13.31	Teherkar	01	6.25		
		Total	16	100.00	1 + 1 = 2	100.00
Mahar	137.67	Parkhe	14	87.50	0 + 1 = 1	100.00
	00.00	Chitte	02	12.50		100.00
		Total	16	100.00	0 + 1 = 1	
Dhangar	146.45	Tagare	06	85.71	0 + 1 = 1	100.00
	00.00	Butte	01	14.28		
		Total	07	100.00	0 + 1 = 1	100.00
Chambhar	4.66	Udmale	01	100.00		
		Total	01	100.00		
		Total	73	100.00	7 + 7 = 14	100.00

Table 7.10
Wahegaon (1995–2005)

Caste	Clan	Number of Members	Office-holders
Maratha	Manal	4 (W-1)	0 + 0 = 0
	Hiwale	5 (W-2)	1 + 0 = 1
	Total	9 (W-3)	
Mali (OBC)	Bhadke	2	
	Darunte	1	
	Kalamkar	2 (W-2)	1 + 0 = 1 (W)
	Gadhekar	1 (W-2)	
	Suse	01	
	Total	7 (W-3)	
Mahar (SC)	Parkhe	6 (W-2)	0 + 1 = 1 (W)
	Total	6 (W-2)	
	Grand Total	22 (W-8)	

Note: W = women members.

It was a question not only of creating legitimacy in the eyes of people but also in the eyes of the local elite. The social character of the dominant classes, in fact, necessitated some kind of panchayati raj. There was a perceived and actual distinction between the dominant classes at the national level and those at the regional and local level in terms of economic class and castes. In order to seek the support of the rich peasantry castes it was felt necessary to expand the network of power to include them in it while also making their local

Table 7.11
Nevargaon (1960–92)

Caste	Land (hectare)	Clan	Number of Members	Percentage	Officers	Percentage
Maratha	690.68	Pawar	22	52.38	3 + 4 = 7	63.63
	248.12	Walture	13	30.95	3 + 1 = 4	36.36
	6.02	Chavan	02	4.76		
	11.50	Dike	02	4.76		
	19.34	Bhusal	01	2.38		
	50.91	Wane	01	2.38		
	0.81	Deokar	01	2.38		
		Total	42	100.00	6+5=11	100.00
Mahar (SC)	126.11	Dusing	05	100.00		
		Total	05	100.00		
Matang (SC)	14.30	Kangare	05	100.00		
		Total	05	100.00		
Bhilla (ST)	10.89	Gaikwad	02	100.00		
		More	01	33.33		
		Total	03	100.00		
Dhobi (OBC)	23.17	Aghade	02	66.66	0 + 1 = 1	100.00
		Nidhe	01	33.33		
		Total	03	100.00		
Nhavi (OBC)	19.38	Pawar	03	100.00		
		Total	03	100.00		
Wadar (NT)	0.82	Gaikwad	02	100.00		
		Total	02	100.00		
Kahar (OBC)	71.21	Pandhure	02	100.00	1 + 0 = 1	100.00
		Total	02	100.00		
Muslim	60.38	Shaikh	02	100.00	0 + 1 = 1	100.00
		Total	02	100.00		
Dhangar (OBC)	38.13	Kakde	01	100.00		
		Total	01	100.00		
Marwadi	00.00	Dule	01	100.00		
		Total	01	100.00		
Teli (OBC)	11.63	Chothe	01	100.00		
		Total	01	100.00		
		Grand Total	70	100.00	7 + 7 = 14	100.00

Table 7.12
Nevargaon (1995–2000)

Caste	Clan	Number of Members	Office-holders
Maratha	Pawar	5 (W-1)	1 + 2 = 3
	Walture	2	3 + 1 = 4
	Dike	1	
	Total	8 (W-1)	
Mahar (SC)	Dusing	1	
	Total	1	
Matang (SC)	Kangare	1 (W-1)	
	Total	1 (W-1)	
Bhilla (ST)	Gaikwad	1	1 + 0 = 0
	Pawar	1 (W-1)	
	Khaire	1 (W-1)	
	Total	3 (W-2)	
Dhobi (OBC)	Aghade	1 (W-1)	
	Nidhe	1 (W-1)	
	Total	2 (W-2)	
Kahar (OBC)	Pandure	1	
	Total	1	
Dhangar (OBC)	Kale	1	
	Total	1	
Teli (OBC)	Chothe	1	
	Total	1	
	Grand Total	18 (W-6)	

Note: W = women members.

power more decorative than real. The local elite from the rich peasantry castes were taken up at a point from where they would be able to aspire to move towards a higher level. In one sense it was seen as an apprenticeship whereby the best among them could be picked up at an appropriate time.

If the Congress leaders at the centre worked as arbitrators for the regional elite, the regional elite in turn became arbitrators for the local elite. If Nehru wanted the support of the regional elite, the regional elite sought the following at the local level. Panchayat raj, the term coined by Nehru thus worked as an ideology that conferred legitimacy on the liberal democratic structures by creating political linkages between the regional and local administrative units.

This model of political linkages and notional power at the local tier in effect strengthened the regional elite to such an extent that they started challenging the high command at Delhi. With Indira Gandhi's coming to power this pyramid was shaken for the first time. Indira Gandhi's populism had no use for panchayat structures or layers of power. Her strategy basically targeted the poor and minorities and therefore, it had little significance for the rich peasantry caste elite. During her regime we see that many developmental

Table 7.13
Mangrul (1960–92)

Caste	Land (hectare)	Clan	Number of Members	Percentage	Officers	Percentage
Maratha	69.95	Barde	08	30.76	1 + 0 = 1	25.00
	192.24	Dhormare	07	26.92	1 + 0 = 1	25.00
	167.88	Khelewane	07	26.92	1 + 1 = 2	50.00
	00.00	Gawli	01	3.84		
	16.72	Palode	01	3.84		
	3.34	Kawle	01	3.84		
	7.90	Agale	01	3.84		
		Total	26	100.00	3 + 1 = 4	100.00
Dhangar (OBC)	51.92	Borde	05	41.66	0 + 0 = 0	
	103.04	Warpe	05	41.66	1 + 2 = 3	100.00
	77.97	Dudhe	01	8.33		
	64.94	Hase	01	88.33		
		Total	12	100.00	1 + 2 = 3	100.00
Muslim	86.43	Shaikh	06	100.00	2 + 0 = 2	100.00
		Total	06	100.00		
Mahar (SC)	21.41	Damodhar	03	75.00		
	40.39	Borde	01	25.00		
		Total	04	100.00		
Chambhar (SC	11.41	Katkar	02	100.00		
		Total	02	100.00		
Brahmin	1.27	Joshi	01	100.00		
		Total	01	100.00		
Nhavi (OBC)	00.00	Bode	01	100.00		
		Total	01	100.00		
Bairagi (OBC)	3.81	Vaishnav	01	100.00		
		Total	01	100.00		
Sonar (OBC)	23.24	Bute	01	100.00		
		Total	01	100.00		
		Grand Total	54	100.00	6 + 3 = 9	100.00

schemes for the benefit of the rural population were organised without giving any important role to the local political elite. Centralisation of power within the party and within the government became the dominant theme in her era. The local elite became subservient because their leaders at the regional level themselves were relegated to the background. It was no wonder that the panchayat raj became less effective and probably lost even the notional power.

It was only during the Janata phase that the panchayati raj institutions again figured in the political discourse. The Janata experiment was effected mainly by the backward and peasantry caste elite at the regional and local levels and therefore was more concerned with the decentralisation theme. The Asoka

Table 7.14
Mangrul (1995–2000)

Caste	Clan	Number of Members	Office-holders
Maratha	Barde	2	0 + 1 = 1
	Dhormare	2 (W-1)	
	Kawale	1 (W-1)	
	Khelawane	2	
	Total	7 (W-2)	
Dhangar (OBC)	Borde	2 (W-2)	
	Warpe	1 (W-1)	0 + 1 (W) = 1 (W)
	Hase	3 (W-1)	1 (W) + 0 = 1 (W)
	Total	6 (W-4)	
Muslim	Shaikh	1	
	Total	1	
Mahar (SC)	Borde	2	
	Total	2	
Brahman	Joshi	1	1 + 0 = 1
	Total	1	
Teli	Misal	1 (W-1)	
	Total	1 (W-1)	
	Grand Total	18 (W-7)	

Note: W = women members.

Mehta Committee's report on panchayati raj (1978) reflected this social and political character of the Janata Party. The pro-decentralisation and pro-peasantry caste Janata politics was juxtaposed with the pro-centralisation and populist regime of Indira Gandhi. But the Janata experiment failed, thus giving another term to Indira Gandhi's revived populism in 1980.

In the late-1980s, Rajiv Gandhi once again brought the panchayati raj on the government agenda. His strategy of technological revolution with centralism had no place for regional power, but wanted, however, direct access to village elite. Rajiv Gandhi's technological revolution took his image to the villages through television while his Sixty-fourth (Constitutional) Amendment Bill of 1989 aimed to reach the panchayats directly, bypassing the regional elite. It would have been an overhead shoot. But that Amendment did not come through.

After that came the Seventy-third Amendment that not only gave constitutional status to the panchayat raj institutions but also made them politically and financially self-reliant and autonomous. I need not dwell upon the provisions of the Amendment since they are already discussed elsewhere in this book. However, what I intend to do here is to contextualise the Seventy-third Amendment so that we may grasp the purport of its provisions. By doing so we would be able to know why the recommendations of various commissions regarding devolution of power, autonomy and financial viability or self sufficiency were kept on hold from the early-1960s to the early-1990s and suddenly in 1992–93 they were judged worth implementing and this move secured consensual support. We would also understand why power is being transferred to the panchayats when there has not been any major agitation demanding such a transfer. The Seventy-third Amendment should be seen as a logical outcome of the new economic policy adopted by the government of India in the early-1990s. The new economic policy believes in curbing state intervention, curtailing public expenditure, downsizing bureaucracy and restoring state run enterprises to the private sector. In a nutshell, the new economic policy encourages withdrawal of the state from economic and social sectors. The devolution of power implied in the Seventy-third Amendment indirectly facilitates this process of withdrawal. The governments at the central and the regional levels want to get rid of many responsibilities and functions. In this endeavour they find a facilitator in the panchayat raj institutions. The 29 items that are brought under the purview of the panchayat raj institution include subjects such as agriculture, small-scale industries,

Table 7.15

Bharadi (1960–92)

Caste	Land (hectare)	Clan	Number of Members	Percentage	Officers	Percentage
Maratha	125.16	Mahajan	14	59.00	0 + 3 = 3	60.00
	76.90	Khomne	07	28.00	1 + 0 = 1	20.00
	55.62	Rakde	03	12.00	0 + 1 = 1	20.00
	00.00	Jadhav	01	04.00		
		Total	25	100.00	1 + 4 = 5	100.00
Muslim	16.35	Shaikh	13	76.47	1 + 0 = 1	100.00
	–	Pathan	04	23.52		
		Total	17	100.00	1 + 0 = 1	100.00
Mali (OBC)	41.08	Sonawane	04	44.44		
	17.10	Ghongte	03	33.33		
	7.86	Kale	01	11.11		
		Total	08	100.00		
Lingayat (OBC)	00.00	Mule	0.1			
Rajput	4.18	Gaur	06	100.00	1 + 0 = 1	100.00
Mahar (SC)	00.00	Shelke	03	60.00		
	00.00	Arak	02	40.00		
		Total	05	100.00		
Marwadi	17.37	Agrawal	05	100.00	0 + 2 = 2	100.00
Kalal (OBC)	51.37	Jaiswal	04	100.00	3 + 0 = 3	100.00
Dhangar (OBC)	00.00	Ghogte	02	100.00		
Nhavi (OBC)	27.04	Bidwe	01	100.00		
		Grand Total	74	100.00	6 + 6 = 12	

Table 7.16
Bharadi (1995–2000)

Caste	Clan	Number of Members	Office-holders
Maratha	Mahajan	4 (W-2)	0 + 2 = 2
	Khomane	2 (W-1)	
	Rakade	2	
	Total	8	
Muslim	Shaikh	2 (W-1)	
	Pathan	3	
	Rank	1 (W-1)	
	Total	6 (W-2)	
Mali (OBC)	Sonawane	1 (W-1)	
	Ghongate	1	
	Kale	1	
	Pandav	1 (W-1)	
	Total	4 (W-2)	
Mahar (SC)	Shelke	2	
	Total	2	
Kalal (OBC)	Jaiswal	4	
	Total	4	
Nhavi (OBC)	Bidwe	1 (W-1)	
	Total	1 (W-1)	
Lingayat	Dharkar	1	
	Total	1	
	Grand Total	26	

Note: W = women members.

infrastructure, education, health and social welfare. It indicates that the governments at the central and state levels want the local governments to share the burden with regard to these items and that has prompted the devolution of power by the Seventy-third Amendment.

Radical Potential

But this very amendment contains a radical potential to produce good results in the long run. The new panchayats could bring politics down to the villages. The villagers might collectively decide to use the instruments created by the amendment to acquire greater control over local resources and might eventually stand up against the governmental bodies at the higher level. In the western Indian state of Maharashtra, the Maharashtra Industrial Development Act has given power to the state government to acquire land for the purpose of starting industrial projects. This is being used to grab land from the villages for the benefit of multinational corporations. While developing industrial estates the government not only acquires huge tracts of land but also obtains control over resources such as water. The new panchayats and the gram sabhas might unitedly oppose such encroachment on their resources and might insist that their resources should be used for their benefit.

However, the disparities and inequalities inherent in the class and caste-based village societies hamper any possibility of forming a community at the village level. The unseen threat and concealed repression by the ruling clans of the dominant castes make it simply impossible for the masses to enter into the collective decision making in the gram sabhas. In many villages the leaders coming from the ruling clans are seen as benefactors by the villagers. In reality these so-called benefactors control the lives of the villagers who are under the impression that the leader is genuinely working for the village as a whole. What they probably do not realise is that his definition of village excludes the poor and downtrodden sections. It has been pointed out that the '*gavki*', a village collective constituted by upper-caste rich men functions along side the village panchayat in many villages. These 'gavkis' control the real power in the villages, especially where the sarpanch is a woman or belongs to the SC group (Kotwal-Lele, 2001: 4702–4). New reservation provisions should have prompted political parties to recruit more women and OBC candidates to their organisation. Instead, the parties prepared a panel of candidates of all categories to contest the panchayat elections whereby the real purpose of reservation could be defeated (Palshikar, 2002: 1280).

Nevertheless, taking politics—not the usual politics of periodical elections, of assemblies and parliament, but the politics of the empowered gram sabhas—to the villages might in course of time bring to surface the contradictions in rural society. The poorer and the downtrodden groups might thereby become conscious of their right to the local resources. If the state refuses to help them in this neo-liberal era, they might, encouraged by their numbers in the gram sabhas, demand their share in the resources which are at the disposal of the panchayats. Thus, instead of joining struggles against an abstract entity named state, they might prefer to fight democratic battles against the dominant sections in their own village.

References

Baviskar, B.S. 1969. 'Cooperative and Caste in Maharashtra—A Case Study', *Sociological Bulletin*, 18 September: 148–66.

Bhatt, Anil. 1963. 'Caste and Politics in Akola', *Economic Weekly*, 15 (34): 1441–46.

Birmal, Nitin. 1996. 'Maharashtrateel Jamin Malkai, Jat Aani Rajkiya Satta: Marathwada Vibhag, Ek Abhyas' (Land Caste and Political Power in Maharashtra: A Study of Marathwada Region), Ph. D. thesis submitted to the University of Pune, Pune.

Carras, Mary. 1972. *The Dynamics of Indian Political Factions: A Study of District Councils in the State of Maharashtra*. London: Cambridge University.

Carter, Anthony. 1975. *Elite Politics in Rural India: Political Stratification and Political Alliances in Western Maharashtra*. New Delhi: Vikas.

Darekar, Nayana. 2002. 'Nimbootchi Pahili Mahila Gram Panchayat' (First Women Panchayat of Nimboot), *Parivartanacha Vatsaru*, 16–30 September 2002.

Inamdar N.R. 1970. *Functioning of Village Panchayats*, Bombay: Popular Prakashan.

Kotwal-Lele, Medha. 2001. 'Local Government: Conflict of Interest and Issues of Legitimation', *Economic and Political Weekly*, 36 (51): 4702–704.

Lele, Jayant. 1982. 'Chavan and Political Integration of Maharashtra', pp. 29–54, in N.R. Inamdar, R.M. Bapat, P.N. Limaye, S.N. Tawale and Rajendra Vora (eds), *Contemporary India*. Pune: Continental Prakashan.

Moghe, Kinan. 1997. *Mahila Aarakshanasathi Ladha*, (The Struggle of Women's Reservation). Janawadi Mahila Sanghatana, Mumbai.

Omvedt, Gail. 1990. 'Women, Zilla Parishads and Panchayati Raj: Chandwad to Vitner', *Economic and Political Weekly*, 25 (31): 1687–90.

Orenstein, Henry. 1965. *Gaon: Conflict and Cohesion in an Indian Village*. New York: Princeton University Press.

Palshikar, Suhas. 2002. 'Triangular Competition and Bipolar Politics: Elections to Local Bodies in Maharashtra', *Economic and Political Weekly*, 37 (13): 1273–80.

Rosenthal, Donald. 1977. *The Expansive Elite: District Politics and State Policy-Making in India*. Berkeley: University of California Press.

Schlesinger, Lee. 1988. 'Clan Names, Dominance and Village Organisation: Bhosale and Kadam in Apshinge', in D.W. Attwood, M. Israel and N.K. Wagle (eds), *City, Countryside and Society in Maharashtra*, pp. 209–23. Toronto: University of Toronto Press.

Sirsikar. V.M. 1970. *Rural Elite in a Developing Society*. New Delhi: Orient Longman.

Vora, Rajendra. 1999. 'Dominant Lineages and Political Power in Maharashtra', in Irina Glushkova and Rajendra Vora (eds), *Home, Family and Kinship in Maharashtra*. Delhi: Oxford University Press.

8 Kerala's People's Plan Campaign 1996–2001
A Critical Assessment

T. M. THOMAS ISAAC

Introduction: The Logic of the Campaign

The People's Plan Campaign (PPC) in Kerala (1996–2001) was a unique experiment in democratic decentralisation. The PPC represented far more than a simple devolution of resources and powers to lower-level elected bodies. It transformed decentralisation from a mere administrative reform exercise from above into a social movement. The PPC was in effect an acceptance of the fact that sufficient institutional capacity did not exist at the local level proportional to the unprecedented scale of devolution. First, the social mobilisation was intended to empower the local bodies to draw up local plans and utilise substantial financial resources and powers devolved to them. Second, the PPC was to generate a new style of governance that is transparent, participatory and efficient. Third, it was also to create an enabling environment for the institutionalisation of the new ideals and procedures through appropriate changes in statutes, redeployment of staff, creation of an information network and so on.

Reversing the Sequence of Decentralisation Reforms
Democratic decentralisation requires changes in administrative structures, in the allocation of functions and powers and in the control of resources. All three are interrelated and need, to an extent, to be introduced simultaneously. In the technocratic model advocated by multilateral development agencies like the World Bank, decentralisation is seen as an exercise in incremental institution building informed primarily by public administration and managerial sciences.[1] Typically it is argued that certain sequenced preconditions, defined by a clear demarcation of functions among the various levels, must be met before genuine authoritative decision-making power can be successfully devolved. Administrative support structures have to be created, new organisational procedures have to be put into place, government staff have to be redeployed, a new information base has to be developed and new personnel—both voluntary and official—have to be trained. Most significantly, the devolution of financial resources has to be carefully calibrated to the absorptive capacity of the nascent institutions.

What is most problematic about this linear model of decentralisation is the assumption that the task of transforming the very mode in which the government works can be achieved through a prescribed process of introducing a discrete set of technically and managerially rational solutions. A largely frictionless and apolitical world is more or less taken for granted. But successful and sustainable democratic decentralisation has been the exception to the rule, frustrated more often than not by bureaucratic inertia—most notably the resistance of powerful line departments—and vested political interests. And the pre-conditions of capacity development have often become an alibi for not devolving resources.

Kerala certainly has its share of entrenched bureaucratic fiefdoms and political formations with a stake in the status quo. Democratic decentralisation was the cornerstone of the Administrative Reforms Committee (ARC) Report of 1958 prepared for the newly-formed state of Kerala under the chairmanship of E.M.S. Namboodiripad. It envisaged district governments with both development and regulatory functions at the district level. The vision never materialised as the Communist government was dismissed before the law could be passed. A similar effort by the left government in 1967 was also not successful. The effort to form district councils in 1980 was frustrated by dissension within the left-led coalition government. Finally, when district councils were formed in 1990, they were disempowered and disbanded by the right-wing government that followed. These bitter experiences convinced E.M.S. Namboodiripad of the importance of mass mobilisation for the successful implementation of decentralisation. E.M.S. Namboodiripad ranked democratic decentralisation as second only to land reforms after the formation of united Kerala in terms of the profound impact it would have on administration, society and economy. The success of land reforms in Kerala in the late-1960s and 1970s—widely recognised as having been the most far reaching and equity-enhancing in the subcontinent—was made possible not merely by legislation but also through a peasant mobilisation of unprecedented scale.

The reforms in Kerala reversed the linear prescription of devolution by first devolving resources and then building up the local capacity. The most dramatic step was the devolution in 1997–98 of more than 35 per cent of the annual developmental budget to local self-governing institutions (LSGIs). Before 1996–97, LSGIs received approximately Rs 200 million in untied funds. The total untied grant-in-aid devolved amounted to Rs 7,490 million in 1997–98, Rs 9,500 million in 1998–99, Rs 10,200 million in 1999–2000 and Rs 10,450 million in 2000–01. The grant-in-aid along with state-sponsored schemes constituted more than 35 per cent of the plan outlay. These sums, however, do not include funds from centrally-sponsored schemes and institutional loans to local governments. Devolving fiscal resources and control—even while the immense task of building a new regulatory environment and administrative capacity was only getting underway—had a critical strategic effect. Because local governments now enjoyed significant budgetary discretion, local planning exercises had a tangible and immediate character. This, as we shall see, has invited high levels of participation. The devolution marked a major break, a commitment from which the state government could not backtrack. This effect was ensured by the mass campaign in support of decentralisation in which millions of people participated.

Planning as an Instrument of Social Mobilisation

Another distinctive feature of the decentralisation experiment in Kerala was the central role accorded to the planning function of the LSGIs. As a statutory precondition for receiving the grant-in-aid from the government, LSGIs had to prepare a comprehensive area plan. The planning process, as prescribed by the State Planning Board (SPB), included holding grama sabhas (ward-level assemblies), the convening of village/municipal seminars to determine the priorities and the constitution of sectoral task forces in which non-official experts and volunteers directly prepared reports, formulated projects and drafted sectoral plans. The various stages of plan preparation in effect represented new participatory spaces in which citizens, elected representatives and officials deliberated and prioritised developmental goals and projects.

In order to ensure transparency and participation without compromising the technical requirements of planning, the planning process was divided into discrete phases with distinct objectives, key activities and associated training programmes. Though modifications to the sequence were made every year, the basic model inaugurated in 1997 (Table 8.1) remained the same.

A critical component of the PPC was an elaborate training programme that developed into one of the largest non-formal education programmes ever undertaken in India. In the first year, in seven rounds of training at the state, district and local levels, some 15,000 elected representatives, 25,000 officials and 75,000 volunteers were given training. About 600 state-level trainees called key resource persons (KRP) received nearly 20 days of training. Some 12,000 district level trainees—district resource persons (DRP)—received 10 days of training and more than a 100,000 persons received at least five days of training at the local level. All the elected representatives were expected to participate in the training programme at one level or another. Each round of training focused on specific planning activities. Separate handbooks and guides, amounting to nearly 4,000 pages of documentation were prepared and distributed at each round.

Table 8.1

Different Phases of the People's Plan Campaign in its Inaugural Year (1996–97)

Phase	Period	Objective	Activities	Mass Participation
Grama sabha	August–October (1996)	Identify the 'felt needs' of the people	Grama sabha in rural areas and ward conventions in urban areas	2 million persons attending grama sabhas
Development seminar	October–December (1996)	Assessment of the resources and problems of the area and formulation of a local development strategy	Participatory studies: preparation of development reports, organisation of development seminars	300,000 delegates attending seminars
Task forces	November 1996–March 1997	Preparation of projects	Meetings of task forces	100,000 volunteers in task forces
Plans of grass-root tiers—municipalities and grama panchayats	March–June (1997)	Formulation of plan of grass-root tiers.	Plan formulation and meetings of elected representatives	25,000 volunteers in formulation of plan document
Plans of higher tiers—block and district panchayats	April–July (1997)	Formulation of plans of higher tiers	Plan formulation meeting of elected representatives.	5,000 volunteers in formulation of plan documents
Plan appraisal (volunteer technical corps)	May–October (1997)	Appraisal and approval of plans	Meetings of expert committee	5,000 volunteer technical experts working in the appraisal committees

Source: Isaac and Franke (2000).

Building a New Form of Government

A local government should not be a miniature of the representative state or central governments. It has to be a genuinely different form of government in which people can directly participate in government functioning and thereby generate synergies. The objective of the PPC was not simply to draw up a plan from below. The very process of planning was conceived as a means to fundamentally transform the character and scope of participation and the nature of interest mediation. Such a transformation cannot be secured through government directives or institutional design alone. It requires the creativity and the social logic of a mass movement.

A radical transformation of the development culture of the state was a necessary prerequisite for successful participatory decentralisation. It also required basic attitudinal changes towards the development process among all the key players involved: the elected representatives, officials, experts and the public at large. Unlike scholars like Robert Putnam, who take civic culture as historically determined and given, the PPC approached it as shaped by the nature of political and civic engagement (see Putnam, 1993).[2] Many of the unique features of the state–society synergies in Kerala were facilitated by the nature of such engagement, driven by the mobilisation of lower classes. The campaign actively sought to nurture a culture that promoted democratic institutions at the local level.

Institutionalisation

The vital challenge at this juncture was to ensure that the new values and styles generated by the tide of the movement were sustained beyond the movement. This was all the more important in Kerala's highly volatile political climate, where the two political fronts more or less alternated in power. The sustainability of the new developmental culture and the decentralisation process depended on institutionalising them within appropriate legal and administrative frameworks. Institutionalisation will not occur spontaneously but requires sustained mass pressure from below to overcome the inertia and secure necessary structural changes.

Along with the decision to launch the PPC, the Committee on Decentralisation of Powers (popularly known as the 'Sen Committee', after its chairperson Satyabrata Sen) was appointed to make recommendations for a comprehensive overhaul of the legislation on local self-government, redeployment of staff and other related administrative matters. The Committee members closely interacted with the PPC in their personal and official capacity. There was a close correspondence between the approach of the PPC and that of the Committee in vision and spirit. The Committee submitted its final report in December 1997.

The PPC was to address the challenge of institutionalisation by generating pressure from below on the state government. Even under the left government, there was much disconcerting delay in bringing about necessary changes in statutes and redeployment of staff. This brought forth severe criticism even from E. M.S. Namboodiripad at a meeting of the High Level Guidance Committee of the People's Plan Campaign. Consequently, the Left Democratic Front (LDF) government comprehensively amended the existing Kerala Panchayathi Raj Act of 1994 and the Kerala Municipality Act of 1994 aiming at securing the autonomy of LSGIs and ensuring participation and transparency. A scheme for the redeployment of staff was also prepared. However, the pace of institutionalisation was never satisfactory mainly due to opposition from the line departments and compulsions of coalition politics.

The Change of State Government

In May 2001, the LDF was defeated in the elections and a Congress Party-led coalition came to power. Most observers concur that the CPI (M)'s defeat was not a judgement on the PPC. A variety of factors contributed to CPI (M)'s defeat despite the PPC. There was a consolidation of all casteist and communal groups and parties around the Congress Party-led opposition. Another factor was the severe economic crisis that the agricultural economy of Kerala was plunged into after a sharp decline in the prices of rubber, coconut and other commercial crops. The collapse of commodity prices was a direct result of trade liberalisation of the national government. It was compounded by a severe fiscal crisis of the government that led to the closure of the state treasury and a cutback in the plan outlay of the local governments.

In contrast to the scuttling of the district council reform by the United Democratic Front (UDF) government in 1991 (which we have already referred to), the new UDF government in 2001 clarified that it would continue to strengthen the decentralisation process. Two factors pre-empted a frontal assault on the PPC. One was the popularity of the PPC at the grass-root level, which cut across the political divide. The PPC had succeeded in building a bi-partisan coalition at the grass-root level in favour of decentralisation. Any efforts to erode the autonomy and authority of LSGIs would have been difficult, not only because it would have required significant legislative efforts, but also because such efforts would have alienated the Congress Party's own rank and file who, in coalition with other parties, controlled roughly half the total number of LSGIs in Kerala. The second factor was the prestige that the PPC had gained in national and international circles. In addition to significant media attention, the PPC had attracted the attention of officials from other Indian states and even figured in the remarks made by the president of India in his Independence Day address to the nation in 2000.

Nevertheless, the various acts of commissions and omissions of the state government severely weakened the decentralisation process over time. We shall take up this issue of degeneration in the third section of this chapter. For the moment, we would only point out that it took four long years for the UDF government to bring out an official critique of the PPC, and that too on the eve of local body elections in 2005 (State Planning Board, 2005). Unwittingly, the environment for such a rightist onslaught, though belated, was prepared by a controversy created by vicious attacks from the extreme left on the PPC. Unlike the right, who suddenly perceived in the PPC a CPI (M) ploy for political manipulation, the extreme left denounced it as an attempt to de-politicise Kerala and implement the World Bank agenda for development. This vicious controversy that raged for about two years (2003 and 2004) is not taken up for analysis in this chapter.[3] In the light of this criticism from the right and the extreme left, we make a reassessment of the PPC in the third section.

Before this task is undertaken, a description of the participatory plan formulation, implementation and outcome will be useful.

Participatory Formulation and Implementation

Planning in India was historically a highly insulated and top–down affair. Though guidelines were issued for district-level planning in 1969, in practise, nothing much was done with regard to area-level planning below the state level (GoI, 1969). Teams of experts drew up district or block-level plans in consultation with groups of key informants such as officials, 'progressive' farmers, representatives of cooperatives, local self-governments and so on. It is instructive to quote from the Report of the Working Group on Block-Level Planning regarding the effectiveness of direct public participation in the preparation of the plans:

First, we should be clear as to who we do have in mind when we talk of the people: their representative political institutions such as the district and *taluk* panchayats or class organisations where they exist (*khedut mandals* or trade unions), political or caste leaders or target groups. It is well known that the public is not a harmonious entity; it really comprises groups with conflicting interests. If we wish to plan for the weak, the plan may have to be imposed from above and cannot be a product from below in which 'the below' is dominated by the rich and the strong.

Second, people can make a contribution to planning only if they are presented with a well-articulated and feasible framework of approaches, objectives, measures, and alternatives. If, however, they are asked to indicate their needs in a vacuum, they are bound to put up a charter of demands, which will be far beyond the capacities of the government. (Government of India, 1978)

A number of model block and district-level plans were prepared in the 1970s by voluntary agencies and professional bodies. These plans provided important methodological experience in local-level planning. By the early 1980s, some form of district planning machinery existed in most states, but the planning process was anything but participatory. It was described by the Report of the Working Group on District Planning as follows:

> Usually, after the state budget is voted in the assembly, the different heads of departments are requested to make a district-wise break up of the outlays provided in the plan budget. This is then communicated to the districts, either by sectoral departments or by the planning department of the state. This usually takes four-five months after the commencement of the financial year. After this communication is received, the district attempts to incorporate a write up for the district-wise outlay and a document called 'district plan' emerges in this manner, which is *purely an aggregation of departmental schemes* (GoI, 1984, emphasis added).

District planning in other words was in practice detached from budgetary discretion, and as such devoid of any authoritative decision making. The major departure from this pattern took place in Karnataka and West Bengal where a conscious attempt was made to link the district-planning process to local self-governments. The Karnataka experiment was notable for the autonomy given to district panchayats in the preparation of plans and the involvement of lower panchayats in a consultative process. However, the Karnataka initiative disintegrated after a change in the state government in 1990. The West Bengal experiment has proved to be more enduring. West Bengal created a history of local democracy by organising elections for local bodies at regular five-year intervals and by constantly enhancing their powers. However, the process of planning in West Bengal has remained centred around the district, with lower tiers playing only a consultative role. The autonomy of the decentralised planning process has also been restricted by the practice of schematic or minor subhead wise devolution of funds.

This brief discussion of the theory and practice of decentralised planning in India provides a point of comparison with the decentralised planning procedures adopted in Kerala. In Kerala, the focus of decentralised planning is not the district but lower tiers, the most important being the grass-roots tier—the grama panchayat or urban municipality. There are 14 districts, five municipal corporations, 53 municipalities, 152 blocks and 991 grama panchayats in Kerala. At the block and district levels, the democratic character of planning is ensured through the involvement of elected officials and a range of citizen committees. At the municipal and grama panchayat level, the planning process is driven by direct mass participation.

Autonomous decision-making power was granted to local governments by providing untied 'grants-in-aid'. In building continuous deliberative structures, the PPC had to tackle two micro-level design challenges. The first was to create institutional forms that can correct the asymmetries of power among local agents. The second was to make local participation effective by allowing space for grass-roots intervention and deliberation without compromising the technical and economic requirements of planning.

The Grama Sabhas

Grama sabhas, the assemblies of ward or panchayat ward based voters, represented the key deliberative moment in the planning process. By law, grama sabhas had to be held at least twice a year in the initial years of the PPC. After amendments to the law in the later years, they had to be held four times a year. The first grama sabha served as an open forum in which residents identified local development problems. In the second grama sabha, plans approved by the elected panchayat council were presented to the public and departures from the original grama sabha proposals were explained. Beneficiaries for different welfare schemes were also selected at the grama sabhas.

Rousseau notwithstanding, there is nothing spontaneously democratic about a general assembly, especially in a society infected with complex and durable inequalities. The PPC's architects and activists devoted substantial time and energy to enhance the deliberative quality of these large meetings. An obvious innovation, but one that nonetheless required significant organisational effort, was the adoption of a small-group approach. In each grama sabha, after an introductory general body meeting, participants were divided into smaller groups to discuss issues and problems in-depth, each group dealing with a particular development sector. This small-group arrangement made it possible for ordinary people, particularly women, to be able to participate in discussions. A second innovation was to provide a semi-formal discussion format and a trained facilitator for each group. Working with a basic template of questions and useful planning concepts, the locally-recruited facilitator had to encourage participants to list and analyse local problems based upon their real life experiences.

Local Information Gathering

Asymmetries of information are a key source of domination in nominally deliberative institutions. Even in Kerala's social climate of a highly-politicised and a highly-literate citizenry, durable social and status inequalities and the hoarding of official expertise by state institutions have severely restricted access to useful information.

After the first round of grama sabhas in the first year, panchayats were required to make a formal assessment of the natural and human resources of the locality. The idea was to promote resource optimisation by actually comparing expressed needs with local resources. With assistance from specially trained resource persons and using techniques developed by the PCC, a series of participatory studies were undertaken in every grama panchayat and municipality. These included the collection and organisation of secondary data available in various local-level offices, the identification and mapping of local eco-zones using a transect walk technique, a review of ongoing schemes to be prepared by each local department, and a review of local history. By and large many departments were reluctant to cooperate with this plan, and this did adversely affect the integration of existing schemes with the new plans. The quality of the data, of course, varied significantly from one locality to another, but the exercise itself had the important benefit of helping individuals develop skills and tapping local knowledge.

Development Reports and Seminars

The outcome of the data collection exercises was a 'development report' for each panchayat, prepared according to the broad guidelines set by the SPB. With a five-year strategic outlook, these reports served as the basis of the annual planning exercise. Of about 75 to 100 pages in length, the reports provided a comprehensive overview of local development and included a chapter on local social history intended to underscore the role that social mobilisation could play in meeting the challenges of contemporary development. Each report had 12 chapters that assessed the current status of each sector, a critical review of ongoing schemes and a list of recommendations. An assessment by the SPB showed that majority of the reports were of higher quality than departmental planning documents and were excellent benchmarks for local development.

Because the recommendations of the development report could differ from the demands raised in the grama sabha and because demands from different wards had to be integrated into an area-wide perspective, reports were presented in development seminars. Majority of the delegates in the seminars were selected from subject groups of grama sabhas following the principle of equal representation for men and women. Local-level government officials from the relevant departments were asked to participate, as were any experts invited by the panchayat executive committee. On an average, development seminars had 231 delegates, where officials constituted 13.8 per cent, SCs and STs constituted 10.5 per cent and women constituted 22.1 per cent. Extensive preparation went into the organisation of seminars; the development report was distributed to all delegates and widespread publicity was given through leaflets, festivals, *jathas* (marches) and exhibitions. A major portion of time in the seminar was devoted to sector-wise group discussions in order to facilitate an in-depth analysis of the development reports and proposed amendments. The recommendations of different groups were then presented to a plenary session and adopted.

Task Forces and Preparation of Projects

After the development seminars, task forces of about 10 persons each were constituted to prepare project proposals on the basis of the recommendations of the seminar (in the subsequent years, task forces became the starting point of the planning process with development seminars being convened at a later stage to review the work of task forces). Each development seminar elected 12 task forces, one for each development sector. The delegates selected from the development seminars were ordinary citizens, though many had gained specialised training through the PPC. The chairperson of the task force was an elected ward councillor. In order to secure the relevant expertise as well as coordination with state structures, an officer from the concerned line department was elected as the convener of the task force.

The sustainability of a participatory institution is in large part determined by its demonstrated capacity for effective problem solving. In order to ensure a degree of quality control and effective monitoring, task forces were required to prepare detailed project proposals in accordance with a set of criteria and standards established by the SPB. Thus, all project proposals had to include a list of objectives (as far as possible in quantitative/measurable terms), criteria for the selection of beneficiaries, a time frame for completion of tasks, an organisational overview of the role of implementing agencies, a financial analysis including identification of the funding sources, a social and environmental impact review and details of the proposed monitoring mechanisms.

Plan Documents and Coordination

The fourth and final stage of the planning process was marked by the prioritisation and integration of the projects prepared by the various task forces into a plan document for the panchayat. The final form of the plan was the legal prerogative of the elected council, which had to formally vote to approve the plan. There were, however, a number of formal and informal mechanisms that ensured that elected representatives abided by the projects. Formally, the approved plan had to conform to a detailed reporting format that laid out the general strategy and objectives of the plan as well as the sectoral and redistributive criteria. Authorised projects had to be specifically linked to the strategic statement and the full text of the proposed projects had to be listed in an appendix. The fact that ward councillors participated actively at every level of the participatory process—from attendance at grama sabhas and training seminars to chairing the task forces—also helped ensure integration between participatory processes and the council's final decisions.

Since the beginning of the PPC, plan allocations were separately indicated in the state budget, with broad guidelines regarding sectoral allocations to be made by the local bodies. These guidelines had a functional (sectoral) and redistributive character and were designed to coordinate and integrate local allocations with state-level objectives. For example, in order to prevent reduction in public investment on social services and infrastructure, it was mandated that 40 to 50 per cent of the plan allocations be directed to the productive sector. Local governments were also required to spend not less than 10 per cent of the plan allocations on projects targeted at women, and exclusive earmarking of funds for SC and ST development.

Block and district panchayats started the preparation of their annual plans only after grama panchayats completed their plan drafts. The sequential ordering was intended to ensure that plans at various tiers were integrated and plans of the higher tiers complemented, rather than duplicated, those of lower tiers. A matrix-based analytical tool was developed to assist blocks and districts in the integration of the programmes of panchayats into their plans. Blocks were also tasked with integrating the different centrally-sponsored poverty alleviation schemes, which were traditionally implemented at the block level, into their plans. There was strong resistance to this move from both bureaucrats and elected representatives. In part, this was due to the genuine problems arising from the existence of separate guidelines for centrally-sponsored programmes.

Plan Appraisal

In the first year of the PPC, a review of sample projects of local bodies showed that a significant proportion of them needed modification to ensure their technical soundness and viability before being approved for implementation. In all, more than 100,000 projects had to be evaluated. The evaluation was not for selection or rejection of projects, but to rectify technical and financial weaknesses in them. This monumental task had to be completed in a short span of three to four months. The official machinery was neither capable nor willing to cope with the task.

The SPB responded to this problem by launching the Voluntary Technical Corps (VTC). Retired technical experts and professionals were encouraged to volunteer their skills for appraising the projects and plans of the local bodies. A professional or postgraduate degree or officer-level experience in a developmental sector was specified as the minimum qualification for membership in the VTC. A volunteer expert committed herself/himself to spending at least one day in a week to give technical assistance to panchayats. More than 4,000 technical experts enrolled in the VTC.

Later, expert committees were formed with VTC members and certain categories of mandatory officers at the block, municipal and corporation levels. Each expert committee had a non-official as its chairperson and the block panchayat secretary or an officer from the town-planning department as its convener. The expert committees functioned through subject committees with membership confined to those who had expertise in the concerned field. The committees were not empowered to modify the priorities set by local bodies. Their tasks were limited to providing technical and financial advice, appraising the projects and suggesting modifications where necessary. The district planning committees approved plans on the recommendations of the expert committees.

The formation of expert committees in the course of the PPC's first year was an important organisational innovation, which helped to de-bureaucratise project appraisal and technical sanction procedures. Without this mobilisation of extra-bureaucratic expertise, these tasks would have got bogged down in the line departments through inertia and outright resistance. Not surprisingly, these committees were the subject of much public debate fuelled in particular by criticisms that they were part of a partisan attempt to create parallel structures to elected bodies.

Implementation

In Kerala's traditional system of development planning, while decision making was the domain of elected representatives, implementation was the prerogative of the bureaucracy. A key rationale for making the decision-making process more participatory was to ensure the involvement of beneficiaries and the public at large during implementation. Popular involvement increased problem-solving efficiency through better and more rapid feedback and increased accountability by multiplying the points of scrutiny. The PPC evolved a wide range of new rules to maximise participation and transparency.

The financial procedure for regulating the flow of grant-in-aid funds to local bodies and specific projects was designed to ensure the involvement of officials of the transferred institutions and to maximise effective monitoring. To begin with, officers transferred to grama panchayats were held more directly responsible for financial flows. Financial allotments to local bodies were released in four instalments. All funds had to be specifically tied to an approved panchayat project or scheme and held in special accounts that were managed by the implementing officer. Actual disbursement of funds required co-authorisation from the head of the elected body.

The creation of democratically-accountable beneficiary committees was an important innovation. Instead of implementing public works through contractors, local bodies were encouraged to form committees of project beneficiaries to undertake the task. The idea here was to break the ties of collusion between contractors, politicians, government engineers and some of the politicians that had historically been the most important source of corruption. To do so, however, beneficiary committees had to become sufficiently autonomous and empowered to resist capture by rent-seeking interests. First, officially-ratified local market rates were adopted for the cost estimation of works so that beneficiary committees could execute the work with trans-parency, main-taining actual records of purchases and payments. Second, effective authority for the technical sanction of projects was shifted from department officials to block/municipal and district-level expert committees. Third, responsibility for examining finished work and authorising payment was shifted from official to non-official engineering experts from the VTC.

A major change was introduced in the procedure for selecting beneficiaries of developmental projects. In the past, beneficiary selection had been little more than a concerted exercise in patronage. Campaign rules asked grama panchayats to extensively publicise the criteria for eligibility. Notices listing the projects and the criteria had to be displayed prominently in public places as well as circulated. Applications had to be printed in Malayalam and made freely available. The rules also provided for a system for verifying statements made in the applications. Verification was conducted by designated officers or by a committee appointed by the panchayat. Finally, the list of applicants had to be presented to the grama sabha with sector-wise subject groups tasked with processing applications.

The responsibility for consolidating and finalising the priority list of bene-ficiaries received from each grama sabha rested with the panchayat. The final priority list had to be created on the basis of clearly stated norms. In no case could the relative priorities from each ward be overturned in the process of consolidation. Members of the public and the local press were free to attend the proceedings of selection. The draft list had to be exhibited prominently. All public objections had to be given consideration and reasons for rejection stated.

Critically Assessing the Campaign

What was the outcome of the PPC? The outcome may be measured on the basis of visible achievements of the Ninth Five-Year Plan. The process through which they were achieved is equally important. How deliberative was the planning process and to what degree were the activities of decentralised units effectively integrated with higher levels of planning? Given the sheer com-plexity and scale of the PPC and the inevitable teething problems, it is only inevitable that there would be many drawbacks. The institutional learning that took place does, however, hold some important lessons for our under-standing of the implementation of democratic decentralisation reforms and also for democratic politics in the country. Here, we shall briefly survey the achievements, limitations and lessons from the PPC.

Achievements

Kerala: In the Forefront of Decentralisation   Before the PPC, Kerala, with its high literacy, successful land reforms, social sector achievements, eradication of severe forms of social inequalities and vibrant associational life, and yet, lagging behind the rest of India in democratic decentralisation constituted a paradox. Today, Kerala has become a model state in democratic decentralisation. Local government plays a far greater role in development in Kerala than any other state in India.

It was the decision in 1996 to earmark 35 to 40 per cent of plan funds for local self-governments that kick-started the campaign. The most important achievement of the PPC was the sustenance of political will to maintain and even increase the scale of devolution in subsequent years, despite severe financial constraints of the state government. In other words, local governments have enjoyed a continuous and substantial flow of financial resources. Nowhere in India do LSGIs receive as much untied grants as in Kerala.

Procedures for Local-level Planning   That grama panchayats and municipalities throughout the state were given the charge of preparing local area development plans was a milestone in itself in India. Given the sheer enormity of the task and the lack of local experience and capacity, plan preparation in the first year was six months behind schedule. However, the dramatic returns of learning-by-doing were reflected in the steady shortening of the time overruns in each subsequent year. While in opposition, the present ruling parties were vociferously critical of many of the procedures adopted for planning. However, but for cosmetic changes like the change in nomenclature, the PPC has remained very much the same.

Better Choices   A major objective of decentralised planning was to match local needs and potentials to actual public expenditures patterns. A rationalisation of resource allocation based on more direct and informed inputs represents one of the two critical efficiency gains associated with decentralised planning (the second gain being the increase in accountability). There are, however, serious empirical difficulties in comparing pre- and post-campaign expenditure patterns (there are no sub-district figures available for the pre-campaign period). Nevertheless, three important general trends can be highlighted.

First, the investment priorities in the plans prepared by local bodies differed significantly from the investment priorities given in the district plans (that were formulated from above). Much greater priority came to be accorded to basic needs such as housing, drinking water and sanitation by the local bodies. In the productive sectors, there was a discernible shift towards animal husbandry, garden crops and minor irrigation. Both these shifts had significant redistributive implications. Second, in contrast to past patterns, the invest-ment priorities in the special plans prepared for SCs and STs differed signifi-cantly from the overall investment patterns. This points to an effort to take the lower income, asset and skill position of these marginalised communities into account. Third, in contrast to the one-size-fits-all logic of the past, there were significant interregional differences in the investment priorities of local self-governments.

Physical Achievements   A major criticism of the PPC was that all attention to process and participation had come at the expense of actual delivery, measured by physical achievements. This criticism was misplaced, as it failed to recognise that quality of participation was 'an independent desiderata of democratic politics' (Fung and Wright, 2003: 38). But even if building decentralised insti-tutions could be justified on the grounds of extending citizenship alone, their long-term viability, especially under the circumstances of the liberalisation of the national economy, would rely on the capacity to provide tangible de-velopmental outcomes.

An accurate appraisal of physical achievements is complicated by the prac-tical problems of aggregating local-level datasets. Nevertheless, simple measurements of physical achievements in the first four years (between 1997 and 2001) are impressive. About 460,000 houses were built, 154,000 houses were repaired, 497,000 sanitary latrines constructed, 110,000 wells were dug, 48,000 public taps were installed and 136, 000 houses were electrified. About 68,000 km of roads were laid, 132,000 sq m of school buildings, 114,000 sq m of hospital buildings and 303,000 sq m of other public buildings were con-structed. Each of these was three to four times the physical achievements of the five years of the Eighth Five-Year Plan. These achievements have spurred the state government to set a time-target, for the first time in Kerala (or for any state in India), for delivering shelter, sanitary latrines and drinking water (within 200 meters) to *all* households in the state. The universalisation of pre-primary education, improvement in the quality of education and health care centres and the completion of rural electrification were also on the mid-term strategic agenda.

Empowerment of Elected Women Representatives   The Kerala experience certainly bears out the importance of affirmative action in representative structures and suggests that the principle should be further extended to higher levels of government. But affirmative action alone is insufficient. An in-depth study of elected representatives in Kerala showed that while elected women repre-sentatives were better educated than their male counterparts (a social fact that is unique to Kerala in the Indian context), women were on an average younger, much less politically experienced and inadequately equipped with basic knowledge on rules, regulations and administrative issues. Moreover, women representatives have had to bear the triple burden of holding public office, engage in income-earning activities and undertake domestic duties. From its outset, the PPC had run a capacity-building programme targeted at women representatives. The training programme, which evolved significantly to adapt to new challenges, yielded impressive results. A self-assessment survey of elected women representatives showed that their administrative knowledge and management skills, as well as the ability to officiate at public functions and interact effectively with their constituencies improved significantly in a span of three years (Isaac et al, 1999).

An Alternative Model of Microcredit   Another important outcome of the PPC was the organisation of the SHG network-based microcredit provisioning in the state in close integration with local self-governments. The Kudumbasree neighbourhood groups (NHGs) launched in 1999–2000 in the municipal areas and 250 grama panchayats was distinguished by features that were remarkably different from the so-called 'best practices' espoused by the World Bank. Instead of the NGOs, these groups were sponsored by the local self-governments and were to have no federating structures above the local panchayat. The transition of microcredit to microenterprise was to be integrated and supported by the local plan.

The Kudumbasree NHGs were conceived as a point of convergence of the various poverty alleviation programmes and social banking initiatives rather than the replacements for them. It was also realised that neither microcredit nor microenterprise per se lead to empowerment of women. Empowerment requires a conscious intervention for which economic activities could play only a facilitating role. Further, these groups were also conceived as important community forum that could act as subsets of grama sabhas. For this purpose, all families irrespective of their economic status could be represented through one of the female members in the network.

Limitations

Sustainability and Quality of Participation   The PPC created numerous opportunities for ordinary citizens to actively participate in different phases of plan formulation and implementation. But how many citizens have made use of these opportunities? Did locally-dominant groups manipulate discussions? Were the different forums merely a means to legitimise decisions made by elites?

Every ordinary citizen, irrespective of his/her membership in political or non-political social formations, has the right and opportunity to intervene in the planning process by participating in the grama sabhas. One of the greatest achievements of the PPC was the demonstration that grama sabhas can function effectively. In the first grama sabhas of the PPC in August–September 1996, over 2 million people participated at an average of 180 persons per grama sabha. This represented 11.4 per cent of the voting population and roughly one in every four households. However, the participation rates dropped slightly in the following years. This decline in participation rate raises a serious question of maintaining high levels of participation in the long run. The same question arises with respect to the participation in seminars, task forces and other forums of the decentralisation process.

There were also significant limitations to the deliberative character of grama sabhas. To begin with, they were too large and unwieldy for meaningful deliberation, the small-group approach notwithstanding. Because of Kerala's dispersed settlement pattern, participants in grama sabhas had to travel to long distances and meetings could not be conducted for more than two to three hours. These problems did not allow for a serious discussion of the large number of complex issues that were normally included in the agenda of grama sabhas. By all accounts, middle-class participation was low and most participants were from the lower classes that were the targeted beneficiaries in most development projects.

The formation of NHGs consisting of 40 to 50 families, was a response from below to the limitations of grama sabhas. Though not formally required, NHGs were formed in around 200 panchayats. One study in 100 panchayats found that NHGs functioned as mini-grama sabhas, discussed local issues and priorities, reviewed plan implementation and selected beneficiaries (Isaac, 1999a). Neighbourhood group representatives often constituted a ward committee, which in many cases became the de facto executive committee of grama sabhas. The NHGs also took up other activities, such as conflict resolution, after-school educational programmes, health clinics, cultural activities and thrift schemes. The crowding-in effect that the PPC appeared to have had on associational life in Kerala was also evidenced in the proliferation of a variety of SHGs, particularly women's microcredit schemes (Manjula, 2000; Seema and Mukherjee, 2000). The Kudumbasree women NHGs, which we have already referred to, were conceived as subsets of grama sabhas.

Plan Integration   In a sense, the term, decentralised planning is a misnomer. What we have is a process of multi-level planning, which needs to be integrated into a comprehensive state-level plan. This was one of the most daunting challenges faced by the PPC.

In the first year of the PPC, a number of factors contributed to the weak coordination between the plans of the different tiers of local bodies and that of the state government. First, the functions of local bodies were listed in the law by subjects rather than by activities. This resulted in considerable overlap. The second was the peculiar tactic adopted in the PPC to bring about a division of activities between the state government departments and the LSGIs. The LSGIs were granted full autonomy to formulate any project that fell within their capabilities. In other words, devolution of discretionary budgeting authority introduced a de facto functional division of labour between the state government and the LSGIs. However, in the first year of the PPC, most departments insisted on continuing their traditional schemes. As a result, there was considerable duplication in the list of programmes of the government departments and LSGIs. This created considerable strain on the overstretched financial resources of state government departments and most gradually withdrew their schemes that overlapped with LSGI projects. Village roads and minor irrigation virtually disappeared from the state government's plans. Though all piped water supply schemes were by law the monopoly of Kerala Water Authority (KWA), the KWA stopped undertaking small-scale projects.

Though prescribed planning procedures called for higher tiers to take the priorities and programmes of lower tiers into account, there was little coordination in the first year (in no small part because of a shortage of time). More detailed guidelines were issued in the second year, but problems persisted. Finally, a solution to the problem of lack of integration was found in the third year through the formulation of district plans by the district planning committees (DPC).

The district plan was conceived not only as a consolidated list of projects of different tiers of local governments, but also as a comprehensive document providing a macro-perspective for the development of the district. A systematic review of the local self-government programmes with a macro-perspective identified contradictions, duplications and gaps in the ongoing programme. The DPC was then expected to formulate district-specific guidelines for the preparation of future local plans so that weaknesses can be identified and avoided and the local and state plans are integrated into a comprehensive district development programme.

In the first three years of the PPC, the planning process only provided feedback from below. In the absence of coordination from above, integration between the programmes of different tiers was inadequate and insufficient attention was given to the spatial dimension of the planning process. District plans were conceived of as providing the primary source of feedback from above. The intention, moreover, was that this feedback should not take the form of instructions or commands, but guidelines evolved in a participatory manner. This allowed for the preparation of local plans at every level with feedback from *above and below*.

Weaknesses in Agrarian Programmes   The poor quality of many projects was a glaring weakness of the planning process. Many projects were modified versions of standardised department schemes. There was often little consideration of the forward and backward linkages of the projects; fully-integrated plans were actually rare. The mechanical ward-wise allocation of funds proved tenacious, particularly in the higher tiers (blocks and districts). A number of measures were adopted to improve the quality of projects and programmes. The most important measure was to introduce subject-specific training programmes for task force members. In the third year, the training programme was upgraded and formalised into a state-wide programme linked to specialised institutions, such as the Kerala Agricultural University, the Institute of Management in Government, NGOs like the Kerala Shastra Sahitya Parishad's Integrated Rural Technology Centre and Centre for Science and Technologies for Rural Development (COSTFORD). These specialised training programmes by different institutes and training programmes undertaken by the beacon panchayats based on their area of excellence were expected to significantly improve the quality of the projects.

There were high expectations about the impact of decentralised planning on agricultural growth in the state. The introduction of decentralised planning coincided with a collapse of agricultural prices causing an unprecedented agrarian crisis. Therefore, there can be no realistic assessment of the independent impact of decentralisation in agriculture. Nevertheless, it has generally been accepted that the agricultural programmes were crop-specific, did not pay sufficient attention to land and water management, did not bring about innovations in agricultural practises and did not create new agrarian institutions. This growing realisation led to a greater emphasis on the systematic introduction of watershed-based planning as a basic tool of agricultural policy.

In the third year of the PPC, the SPB launched a scheme to assist block panchayats in mapping all the micro-watersheds and preparing master plans for each of them. The micro-watershed reports were printed and presented in special grama sabhas convened for the purpose and watershed committees were formed. Programmes in the Tenth Plan were to be based on watershed planning. Further, institutional innovations like the labour banks, which were successfully experimented in some panchayats, were given wide publicity. Microenterprises for agro-processing and value addition under the protection of regional and centralised marketing arrangements were also to be promoted.

Corruption and Nepotism   One of the most important criticisms of decentralisation was that it devolved corruption. Indeed, funnelling substantial funds without proper safeguards to localities would inevitably fuel rent-seeking behaviour and even lead to community conflicts. The mainstream media and opposition parties raised serious allegations of nepotism in beneficiary selection and corruption in project implementation. Of the nearly 30,000 beneficiary committees, it was alleged that a substantial number were led by nominees of contractors (so-called *benami* committees). State investigative agencies also pointed to irregularities in the first year's plan implementation (Isaac, 1999d).

In its own evaluation, the SPB concluded that irregularities in the first annual plan resulted more from inexperience and haste than from corruption. Even though regulations were bent, and even broken at times, there was little leakage as such. Irregular expenditures identified by the government were disallowed and with the new rules put in place in subsequent years, such improprieties declined sharply. It would not be possible to quantify the level of corruption but it is possible to make an assessment of the trend in the level of corruption by identifying its different components and analysing the plausible impact of decentralisation on them. In Table 8.2 we have listed the major types of corruption at the local level and our assessment of the impact of the PPC on corruption.

Table 8.2
Impact of Decentralisation on Different Components of Local Corruption, 1997–2001

Type of Corruption	Impact of Decentralisation	Rationale
Nepotism in beneficiary selection	Drastically reduced	Introduction of transparent and participatory beneficiary selection procedure
Corruption at the administrative sanction stage of public works	Eliminated	Administrative sanction made automatic with the approval of the plan
Corruption at the technical sanction stage of public works	Virtually eliminated	Not a single allegation of corruption raised against expert committees despite controversies that surrounded them
Corruption in the award of works to the contractors	Significantly reduced	Beneficiary committees promoted instead of contractors
Corruption during actual implementation	Reduced	Only less than 25 per cent of the beneficiary committees were benami committees. Nearly 25 per cent of the beneficiary committees were exemplary and raised substantial additional resources.
Frauds in the purchase of materials	Reduced	Better monitoring and public visibility than in the past

It is clear from Table 8.2 that the PPC had a positive and significant impact on the reduction of corruption, nepotism and leakage. When compared to the possible corruption that would have occurred if the plan grant-in-aid to the LSGIs were directly spent by the governmental departments, the significant decrease in leakage is observed.

With respect to the process of selecting beneficiaries the returns on institutional fine-tuning and increased community experience have been visible. During the first year, complaints about the selection process were registered in a majority of local bodies. The volume of registered complaints is in itself indicative of the increased transparency of the system. The traditional system was entirely based on patronage. Complaints were rare simply because the information was accessible only to the patrons and their clients. The rules for beneficiary selection have been modified in every year of the PPC and by the third year less than a fifth of panchayats were registering complaints.

The high levels of transparency in decentralisation have made corruption more visible, which in fact can be viewed as one of the strengths of the decentralisation experiment. A number of measures were initiated to strengthen accountability and check irregularities, such as the appointment of ombudsman, performance audit and social audit. An audit commission was to be formed; appellate tribunals were to be set up in every district; most importantly, a thorough overhaul of the accounting procedures of the LSGIs was to be undertaken; and accounts were to be computerised.

Programmes for Weaker Sections   The fear that the interests of SCs and STs are more readily subverted at the local level where severe caste inequality persists has often been raised by community leaders. How did SCs and STs benefit from decentralised planning in Kerala?

The Special Component Plan (SCP) and the Tribal Sub Plan (TSP) in Kerala were formulated and implemented in a decentralised manner from the mid-1980s. However, this form of decentralisation was purely bureaucratic and lacked real participation of elected representatives, let alone members of the community. Under the PPC, 75 to 80 per cent of the SCP and TSP funds were devolved to the LSGIs, which was almost entirely taken away from the hands of the bureaucracy.

The first visible impact of decentralised planning was a significant increase in the funds actually earmarked and spent for SCs and STs. Careful disaggregation shows that a substantial part of SCP and TSP were always calculated on the basis of notional flows , that is, by including general schemes that encompassed, rather than targeted, SC and ST communities. The PPC abolished this system of calculation. The SPB estimated that as a result, real resources for weaker sections increased by 30 to 40 per cent in the PPC period compared to the pre-PPC period. The SPB plan appraisal also revealed that fears of local bodies diverting funds were misplaced; except in rare instances, local bodies fully accounted for grant-in-aid from the SCP and TSP. Even though it was permissible to allocate up to 30 per cent of the grant-in-aid from the SCP and TSP for infrastructure projects, such as roads and bridges, actual expenditure under these heads was less than 20 per cent. The emphasis was on projects that could be specifically targeted at individual beneficiaries from the SC and ST communities, such as for housing, latrines and income-producing assets.

Despite these improvements, the situation regarding the TSP remained far from satisfactory. The strength of decentralisation lies in the involvement of the beneficiaries themselves in the planning and decision-making process. However, the participation of STs in the planning process was nominal. There is no panchayat in Kerala where the ST community forms a majority. It was made mandatory to convene special assemblies of the ST population to discuss and approve the TSP. An educated local youth from every tribal hamlet was selected, trained and paid an honorarium to ensure more effective tribal participation in the planning process.

Women Component Plan Gender justice was declared to be one of the major objectives of the PPC. There were special efforts to increase the participation of women in grama sabhas and promote SHGs of women. It was mandated that every project should have a gender impact statement. Besides, 10 per cent of the plan funds of each panchayat were to be earmarked for projects, where women would be the direct beneficiaries and which would be managed by women. This constituted the Women Component Plan (WCP).

The WCP for the first year did not meet the PPC's targets, both in terms of overall allocation or the relevance of projects. An obvious reason was the insufficient representation of women among trained resource persons. This problem was addressed by introducing special training programmes for women elected representatives. As a result, the effectiveness, content and scope of the WCP improved. First, more than the statutory minimum requirement of 10 per cent of the plan grant-in-aid was actually earmarked for WCP in all districts. Second, the undue emphasis on beneficiary contribution and credit provision in women development projects was reduced and more realistic patterns of project financing were adopted in the second year. Third, the quality of projects under the WCP improved. The tendency to include general sector projects in the WCP on the basis of notional (indirect) benefits to women declined and the number of projects that specifically addressed the gender status of women significantly increased.

Nevertheless, the preponderance of projects linked to practical gender needs leading to the neglect of strategic gender needs remained an area of serious concern. Projects that defied the traditional gender division of labour or meaningfully addressed the gender awareness in society were few. This situation was sought to be addressed through a mass programme of gender awareness centred on the preparation of a women status report in every panchayat. Each dimension of the status of women was to be discussed in the SHGs on the basis of their life experience with the help of trained facilitators. The discussions were to be summed up as the status report on the basis of which a critical review of women development programmes were to be carried out. As a first step towards this mass awareness programme, a preliminary statement on the status of women in the panchayat was printed and discussed in the grama sabhas. This was considered as the first step in the year-long gender awareness campaign.

Additional Resource Mobilisation   The expected additional resource mobilisation by the LSGIs failed to materialise. Due to the inadequate institutional capacity, the LSGIs were struggling to fully absorb the plan grant-in-aid from the state government. In such a situation, there was not sufficient incentive for additional resource mobilisation. In fact, it was argued that the devolution of untied plan grants has had a negative impact on the traditional tax and non-tax revenues of the LSGIs. However, an elaborate exercise in this regard by P. Shaheena did not find sufficient proof to reach such a conclusion (Shaheena, 2003). It was argued here that the deceleration in tax and non-tax revenues was largely due to an increased strain on the tax collection machinery due to delays in staff redeployment even after large-scale financial devolution. Besides strengthening the local tax system of LSGIs, there was also a case for a built-in incentive for tax collection in the fund devolution scheme.

A major weakness of the local level plans was their weak credit linkages. Both commercial banks and cooperative banks had by and large been unwilling to link official credit planning to the local planning process. The evidence in the first two years also indicated that additional local resource mobilisation from voluntary labour, donations and beneficiary contributions had fallen short of targets fixed in the draft plan. However, the fact that a number of local bodies did successfully mobilise additional resources pointed to the significant potential in tapping this source.

Institutionalisation   The significance of the institutionalisation was summed up best by the Sen Committee in the following words:

> [The] Government has relied on a Campaign approach....When lots of new things have to be done in a short time, when a distinct break with the past was necessary in the work culture, and when harnessing of experience and expertise from all sources was necessary, the Campaign approach was the only course open to the

government. This approach has been able to utilise to its advantage Kerala's traditional forte of public action for development....However, it needs to be noted that a Campaign by definition relies on volunteers who are basically social activists willing to lead from the front without any expectations of personal gains. Necessarily, the Campaign depends on informal and semi-formal systems and on the motive force of committed individuals. The momentum generated by the Campaign has pushed things along. This is the time to internalise the essential elements of the Campaign and institutionalise the procedures and systems thrown up by the process (Committee on Decentralisation of Powers, 1999: 6–7).

Even though a comprehensive report of the Sen Committee was submitted in 1999, the institutionalisation process proved to be tardy. Though legislative amendments were carried out, the rules and regulations were not amended. The budget and accounting manuals remained the same as in the pre-devolution period. As already noted, though a staff redeployment scheme was drawn up, the actual redeployment was delayed. The transferred institutions and staff continued to be under dual control. Though Information Kerala Mission (IKM) was set up for fast track computerisation of accounts and services of the panchayat, the training programmes were completed and orientation programmes for staff started, the computers could not be deployed.

A Postscript by Way of Conclusion

The discussion on the weaknesses of the PPC has brought out the strategies for rectification and strengthening of the decentralisation process that have evolved from within the campaign itself. However, the political change in 2001, when the LDF government was defeated and the Congress-led UDF came to power, signalled a downward turn in the decentralisation process. There has been much political criticism regarding the many modifications introduced in the decentralisation programme by the UDF government. The UDF policy on decentralisation has been marked by their omissions in continuing most of the strategic initiatives that emerged from the PPC. The district plans and watershed-based plans have been shelved. Instead, a programme for preparing five-year plan documents for the Tenth Plan period was commissioned. Due to inadequate training and support, this attempt was later given up. The NHG system has nearly disappeared and efforts to develop Kudumbasree NHGs as subsets of grama sabhas have been scuttled by limiting them to below poverty line (BPL) families. The grama sabhas have also become dormant. The efforts to achieve greater integration of local-level planning with the co-operative system was also given up.

Though there has been much talk on institutionalisation, very little success has been achieved under the UDF government, except in staff redeployment. Even the extent of staff redeployment has been less than what the Sen Committee had recommended and many of the redeployed technical staff has since reverted to parent departments. No new rules have been framed, or manuals prepared. Instead, the UDF government has destabilised many of the measures undertaken earlier for checking corruption and strengthening local self-governments. The ombudsman has been reduced to a one-member commission, the District Rural Development Agency (DRDA) revived, departmental control over transferred institutions strengthened, performance audit transformed into yet another version of financial audit and the State Development Council given up. A plethora of new vertical programmes have been started and parallel authorities and boards set up. The TSP was withdrawn from local self-governments, though it has been partially restored. Some of the legislative enactments to create special tourism zones and on irrigation have significantly encroached upon the powers of the local self-governments.

The fund devolution practice of the UDF government has attracted sharpest criticism. While it is true that there was a cut in plans in the year 2000–01 during the rule of the LDF, it has become a common feature under the UDF. Because of the public process of plan formulation, any arbitrary reduction in plan size creates severe strains on the public relations of local governments. By abolishing special plan accounts, local self-governments have been reduced to the status of yet another departmental appendage of the government in terms of their control over financial resources. As a result, all unspent balances in the account lapsed to the state government at the end of the financial year. During the PPC, 25 per cent of the plan fund allocations were carried into the next year by the LSGIs. This healthy practice has been given up and local governments are under pressure to spend the entire amount by 31 March under the threat of lapse. The delay in the release of funds and restrictions of fund withdrawal from the treasury makes it inevitable that a significant portion of the funds is lost at the end of every financial year. It has been argued that if lapsed funds and the funds taken back by the government at the time of closure of special plan accounts are deducted from annual allocations, the actual devolution since 2001–02 would have been significantly lower than in the PPC period. Even the formal allotment of plan grant-in-aid in 2005–06 came to only about 25 per cent of the annual plan outlay.

The net result of these acts of omission and commission is that the decentralisation programme initiated by the PPC has reached an impasse. Nevertheless, one decade of decentralisation experience in Kerala does provide powerful lessons for the country and for the state.

The most important lesson from the PPC is that it has underlined the central role of financial devolution in the decentralisation process. Financial devolution was the fulcrum around which the campaign revolved. The uncertainty and reduced flow of resources under the UDF government, thus, is a major source of concern regarding the future. The severity of the fiscal crunch faced by the state governments is inevitably going to make it difficult to devolve resources to local self-governments. Also, with a large proportion of the annual plan outlay consisting of tied projects, the state governments would find it difficult to stick to the PPC devolution ratio of 35 per cent to the LSGIs.

The second lesson is that decentralisation cannot be implemented as a mere administrative reform. The PPC played a vital role in empowering the local self-governments, creating a new ethos of governance and creating an enabling environment. A major blow struck by the UDF government was the undermining of the importance of the campaign, the formal and informal support structures, by demobilising trained resource persons, providing only minimal training programmes and dispersing the VTCs. The ending of the PPC was premature and has brought the institutionalisation process to a grinding halt.

The Kerala experience of decentralisation also underlines that even though dramatic breaks are necessary to launch the process, the decentralised administrative system would require years of experimentation to fine-tune and stabilise itself. There are no ready blueprints and any successful reform effort of this scope and depth has to be necessarily a learning-by-doing process. It is this incremental and continuous process that was disrupted after 2001. We have already discussed the numerous omissions and commissions that contributed to this disruption.

Experimentation with decentralised planning in Kerala between 1996 and 2001 created new sources of democratic authority and generated lessons that are certain to have a lasting impact. Politically, the most important lesson is that decentralisation and people's participation can and does work. Even if only a small proportion of panchayats have approximated the ideal of local planning, the demonstration effect of what is possible would continue to have profound reverberations and to be a firm basis for the rejuvenation of democratic decentralisation under a more conducive political environment.

Notes

1. For a critique of the technocratic vision, see Harriss (2001) and Heller (2000).
2. In a comparative analysis of the degree of democracy in different states in India with special reference to Kerala, Heller (2000) has argued that the structure and patterns of interest representation mediates the relationship between civil society and democracy.

3. For details of issues involved in the debate, and for a response from the perspective of the PPC, see Thomas Isaac (2005).

References

Committee on Decentralisation of Powers. 1999. *Final Report, Vol. III Part A*. Government of Kerala.

Fung, Archon and Erik Olin Wright (eds). 2003. *Deepening Democracy: Institutional Innovations in Empowered Participatory Governance*. London: Verso Press.

Government of India. 1969. *Guidelines for the Formulation of District Plans*. New Delhi: Planning Commission.

———. 1978. *Report of the Working Group on Block Level Planning*. New Delhi: Planning Commission.

———. 1984. *Report of the Working Group on District Planning*. New Delhi: Planning Commission.

Harris, John. 2001. *Depoliticizing Development: The World Bank and Social Capital*. Delhi: Left Word Books.

Heller, Patrick. 2000. 'Degrees of Democracy: Some Comparative Lessons From India', *World Politics*, 52: 484–519.

Isaac, Thomas, T.M. 1999a. 'Janakeeyasoothranavum Ayalkoottangalum: Anubhavangalum Padangalum (People's Planning and Neighbourhood Groups), Vol. 1', Kerala State Planning Board, Thiruvananthapuram.

———. 1999b. 'Gunabhokthra Samithikalude Anubhava Padangal (People's Planning and Beneficiary Committees: Lessons from Experience)', Kerala State Planning Board, Thiruvananthapuram.

———. 2005. *Janakeeyasoothranathinte Rashtreeyam* (The Politics of Decentralisation). Trivandrum: DC Books.

Isaac, Thomas, T.M., T.N. Seema, Binitha Thampy and Margaret Anthony. 1999. 'Gender and Decentralised Planning: The Experience of People's Campaign', Working Paper, Centre for Development Studies, Thiruvananthapuram.

Isaac, Thomas, T.M. and Richard Franke. 2000. *Local Democracy and Development: People's Campaign for Decentralised Planning in Kerala*. New Delhi: Leftword.

Manjula, B. 2000. 'Voices from the Spiral of Silence: A Case Study of Samatha Self-Help Groups of Ulloor', Paper presented at the International Conference on Democratic Decentralization, Thiruvananthapuram, 23–27 May.

Putnam, Robert. D. 1993. *Making Democracy Work: Civic Traditions in Modern Italy*. Princeton: Princeton University Press.

Seema, T.N. and Vanitha Mukherjee. 2000. 'Gender Governance and Citizenship in Decentralised Planning'. Paper presented at the international conference on 'Democratic Decentralisation', Thiruvananthapuram, 23–27 May 2000.

Shaheena, P. 2003. 'Fiscal Devolution and Revenue Mobilisation: A Study of *Grama* Panchayat Finances in Kerala'. Ph.D. thesis, Centre for Development Studies, Trivandrum.

State Planning Board. 2005. *Economic Review 2005*. State Planning Board, Government of Kerala.

9 Panchayati Raj System in Karnataka
Trends and Issues[1]

B.S. BHARGAVA AND K. SUBHA

The focus on rural development started with the realisation that the rural sector was underdeveloped economically, socially, politically and needed special attention from the government. Hence, the Community Development Programme was launched in 1952 covering the entire nation. Unfortunately, this programme could not deliver much. According to the observations of the Balwant Rai Mehta Committee (1957), the main factor that caused the failure of the Community Development Programme was the absence of people's participation. The Committee recommended the creation of a three-tier institutional arrangement to make people's participation meaningful and effective. Necessary legislation was to be enacted by every state to implement the panchayati raj system as a form of rural local self-government to perform developmental, administrative and political tasks. Rajasthan and Andhra Pradesh were the first states to adopt this system in 1959, followed by Karnataka and Orissa. Since then Karnataka[2] has been at the forefront of decentralisation.

However, with exceptions, the panchayati raj system had not received a fair deal since its inception (1959/1960). The panchayati raj institutions (PRIs) had not been assigned specific and sufficient powers, responsibilities as well as resources to carry out even the routine functions. Besides, elections to these bodies had not held for years on one pretext or the other. This, among other compelling internal and external factors, necessitated the need to include panchayati raj as a mandatory provision in the Constitution of India. Conferring constitutional status on this institution of grass-roots governance reaffirmed the nation's faith in the philosophy of 'democratic decentralisation'. Accordingly, provisions were made for a mandatory three/two-tier set-up of panchayati raj, conferring legal status to grama sabhas, regular five-year term elections, reservations for the weaker sections and women, an independent finance commission and state election commission. The Amendment, therefore, was intended to lay a strong foundation for 'democratic decentralisation', thereby paving the way for planning from below, a concept which had eluded the people ever since the beginning of the era of planned development.

The Constitutional (Seventy-third) Amendment Act of 1993, which was brought into force from 24 April 1993, established India's PRIs on a sound footing. The Amendment gave the much-needed impetus to the concept of local self-government, which till then suffered from lack of constitutional protection.

Evolution of PRIs in Karnataka

Before the reorganisation of the state on 1 November 1956, five different legislations on panchayati raj were in operation in different regions of the state. They were the Madras Village Panchayat Act, 1950, the Hyderabad Gram Panchayat Act, 1950, the Mysore Village Panchayat and District Board Act, 1952, the Coorg Panchayati Raj Act, 1956 and the Bombay Village Act, 1953. The Mysore Village Panchayats and Local Boards Act 1959, which was brought into force in December 1960, replaced all these acts. Elections to the PRIs were held in 1960, 1968 and 1978 under this Act.

Basically the evolution and performance of PRIs can be divided into two phases: the first phase (1959–87) and the second phase (1987–93). The various acts and amendments therein were introduced between the two phases from 1959 to 1993. The third phase is the current one (since 1993).

1959 Act

In Karnataka, the panchayati raj system started as early as 1959. The legislation which was enacted came to be called the Mysore Village Panchayats and Local Boards Act 1959 which aimed at ensuring people's participation in rural development and transferring power to them through the institutions of local governance.[3]

The 1959 Act followed partly the recommendations of the Balwant Rai Mehta Committee, which recommended a three-tier panchayati raj system. They were the village panchayat (VP), taluk development board (TDB) and district development council (DDC), the last being an ex-officio body headed by the deputy commissioner, with the presidents of the TDBs, also MLAs, Members of the Legislative Council (MLCs) and MPs as members. The indirectly elected chairpersons headed the VP/TP and TDB. The PRIs were assigned a large number of functions grouped as obligatory and discretionary. The DDC was essentially a coordinating and supervisory institution. Under this Act, about 8,411 village panchayats and 96 town panchayats, 175 TDBs and 19 DDCs were established.

The report of Asoka Mehta Committee submitted in 1978 recommended a two-tier system of the rural local government, and emphasised the need for constitutional sanction to the PRIs. Karnataka's panchayati raj legislation, drafted by the Janata Government of Rama Krishna Hegde was enacted in 1983. The Karnataka *Zilla Parishads, Taluk Panchayat Samitis, Mandal Panchayats* and *Nyaya Panchayats* Act, 1983 recognised the principle of party-based elections to the two-tier of elected office—the mandal panchayats and zilla parishads. The panchayati raj experiment in Karnataka was hailed all over the country as a major and 'bold step' in the direction of democratic decentralisation for development.

The 1983 Act

Most of the principles enunciated in the report of the National Committee on PRIs, headed by Asoka Mehta, became the basis of the Karnataka *Zilla Parishads, Taluk Panchayat Samitis, Mandal Panchayat* and *Nyaya Panchayat* Act 1983.[4] This was a radical change brought about by the Janata Party, which formed the government in Karnataka in 1983 under the chief ministership of Ramakrishna Hegde. It was implemented to prioritise rural development as a means of eradicating poverty and improving the rural economy through people's participation.

In addition to the zilla parishad at the district level followed by the mandal panchayat comprising a group of villages, the Act provided for two other statutory bodies—the taluk panchayat samiti at the taluk/block level, which was an advisory and coordinating body with no executive function and the grama sabha (village assembly) below the mandal panchayat. The grama sabha was vested with the right to prepare and approve the development programmes of the village. The grama sabha, the foundation of the structure, consisted of all those registered in the electoral rolls in a revenue village. It met twice a year and was enjoined with the review of the accounts and the performance of the grama panchayat. It had the responsibility of considering the development programmes proposed by the latter. In addition, it identified beneficiaries under poverty alleviation and the development programmes. The mandal panchayat was the first elected tier located between the village and the taluk while the zilla parishad, the second directly elected tier, was a powerful body which administered schemes and programmes developed by it. Cadres were maintained for manning the zilla and mandal parishad. Election processes started in 1986 and ended in January 1987. For the first time the elections were conducted on party lines.

Another significant feature of this Act (1983) was that it realised women were inadequately represented in the political system and an effort was made to do justice to them. Reservation of upto 25 per cent was provided in the local bodies. Women's participation in the political process took a different turn in the history of Karnataka. The lowering of the voting age to 18 years and the extension of anti-defection bill to the PRIs constitute other important aspects of the panchayati raj system.

After the first five-year tenure of the panchayats in 1992, the 1983 Act was repealed by a new act of the state—the Karnataka Panchayati Raj Act 1993, which incorporated the essential features of the Seventy-third Constitutional

Amendment and established elected bodies at the three levels—the village, taluk and district so that there is 'greater participation of the people'. The Act now provides for 33.33 per cent reservation to women unlike the 25 per cent under the 1983 Act. The first elections to the three tiers were conducted under the 1993 Act in December 1993 for grama panchayats, and for taluk panchayats and zilla panchayats in March 1995.[5]

The three-tier panchayati raj system in the state with the elected bodies at grama, taluk and district levels for increased participation of the people and more effective implementation of rural development programmes in the state are shown in Table 9.1.

Table 9.1
PRIs in Karnataka, 2000

Tiers	Number of Panchayats	Number of Seats (members)
Zilla Panchayat	27	890
Taluk Panchayat	175	3255
Grama Panchayat	5659	80114

Present Panchayati Raj System

Grama Panchayat: According to the Act (1993), normally a grama panchayat will be constituted for a population between 3,000 to 5,000. The area covered by a grama panchayat will consist of a village or a group of villages. There will be one member for every 400 persons.

The *adhyaksha* and *upadhyaksha* (president and vice president) will be elected from among the elected members. There are three standing committees, namely, (i) production committee, (ii) social justice committee and (iii) amenities committee. A secretary is appointed by the government as the administrative head of the grama panchayat. The main functions of the grama panchayat are to promote economic and social welfare, education and health. Financial powers of the grama panchayat are given in the Act itself. It is only the panchayat which has taxation powers in addition to government grants and other sources of income.

Taluk Panchayat: The Act stipulates that for each taluk there shall be a taluk panchayat consisting of local representatives, from the state legislature and parliament, one-fifth of the grama panchayat adhyakshas in the taluk chosen by lots every year (in rotation). Members are directly elected from separate territorial constituencies in the ratio of one member for every 10,000 population.

The elected members of the taluk panchayat have to choose two members from among themselves to be the adhyaksha and upadhyaksha. There are three standing committees, namely, (i) general standing committee, (ii) finance, audit and planning committee and (iii) social justice committee.

A Group-A officer of the state civil services is to be the administrative head of the taluk panchayat. Taluk panchayats are empowered to supervise the activities of grama panchayats in their jurisdiction.

Zilla Panchayat: The Act further stipulates that each district will have a zilla panchayat consisting of the members of parliament and state legislature from within the district, the adhyakshas of taluk panchayats in the district, and elected members in accordance with the scale of one member for 40,000 of the population.

The elected members shall choose two members from amongst them to be adhyaksha and upadhyaksha. There are five standing committees, namely, (i) general standing committee, (ii) finance, audit and planning committee, (iii) social justice committee, (iv) education and health committee and (v) agriculture and industries committee.

As regards finances, both taluk parishad and zilla parishad have no taxation power; they mainly depend on government grants—plan and non-plan.

The grama sabha is the soul of panchayati raj for effective functioning and transparency in decision making; it is accompanied by panchayat *jamabhandi* (social audit mechanism) where audit of accounts and works is carried out with public participation and the report is put forward before the grama sabha for further action.

Election Process: In Karnataka, after the Seventy-third Constitution Amendment Act 1993, a three-tier system was envisaged and a State Election Commission (SEC) was appointed. The SEC is empowered to deal with all major issues connected with elections to the PRIs. The purpose of the provision to appoint SEC was to ensure that the conduct of elections would be entrusted to an impartial authority. A model code of conduct is provided for the peaceful conduct of elections and strict observance of the code of conduct.

Elections to 5,640 grama panchayats were held in December 1993. They consisted of elected members each representing about 400 people. The average population of each grama panchayat was 5,300 according to 1991 Census. Of the total number of 80,627 members in all the grama panchayats, 35,305 (43.8 per cent) were women. Elections to grama panchayats were conducted on a non-party basis.

Elections to all the 175 taluk panchayats in the state were held between 13–18 March 1995, on a party basis. The offices of adhyaksha and upadhyaksha of taluk panchayats have also been reserved for different categories. Elections to all the zilla panchayats were held during March 1995 on a party basis. Likewise, the second term elections took place between 23–27 February 2000[6] to grama panchayats and on 2 and 6 June 2000 to taluk and zilla panchayats.

The number of candidates in the fray for zilla panchayat elections in 2000 was 3,071 compared to 3,612 candidates in 1995. In the case of the taluk panchayats, there were 9,860 candidates as against 11,497 candidates in 1995. The number of zilla panchayat constituencies itself had come down from 919 in 1995 to 890 this time. Likewise, the number of taluk panchayat constituencies had come down from 3,340 to 3,255. This was to increase the size of the panchayat.

Comparing the results of the zilla parishad and taluk parishad elections, there appears to be a dip or at least stagnation in the interest of people and political parties in contesting the zilla and taluk panchayat elections when compared to the last elections held in 1995, if the number of contestants and unanimously elected or unopposed members were of any indication.

In the natural course, one would expect the number of contestants to increase and the number of unanimously elected members to come down in view of the keen interest shown by the political parties and rural masses in general in the local body elections. But, in reality there has been a fall in the number of contestants this time and an increase in the number of unanimously elected candidates (38) in 2000 as compared to the 1995 scenario. On an average there were 3.9 candidates per zilla panchayat seat last time, whereas this time the average worked out to be only 3.4. In case of taluk panchayats also, the average number of candidates per seat had come down from 3.4 to 3.00.

Considering the number of those elected 'unopposed' in 1995, nearly 36 taluk panchayat members were elected unopposed. The main reasons for unopposed elections might be:

a) reservation of seats created confusion for the contesting candidates;
b) candidates did not come forward to contest due to lack of awareness;
c) political parties were dormant;
d) conciliation or compromise; and
e) rejection of nomination papers.

The number of contestants had decreased despite the number of parties remaining the same, though some of the parties were different this time. In the last elections, the contesting parties were the Janata Dal (JD), the Congress, the Bharatiya Janata Party (BJP), the Karnataka Congress Party (KCP), the Communist Party of India (CPI), the Communist Party Marxist (CPM), the Karnataka Rajya Raitha Sangha and the Janata Party whereas this time the parties were the Congress, BJP, JD (S), JD (U), Bahujan Samaj Party (BSP),

CPI, CPM and National Congress Party (NCP). The number of independents also came down from 784 to 613 in case of zilla parishads and from 2,277 to 1,889 in case of taluk panchayats.

An all-women panchayat came into existence during 1993–98 in Shimoga District, namely, the Mydolalu Gram Panchayat. During the 2000 election, three all-women panchayats came into existence. The case of the Athanur Gram Panchayat (one of the all-women panchayats) in Gulbarga District is quite reflective of the rural power structure scenario. The all-women grama panchayat came into existence in Gulbarga due to the intervention of the local elite. A popular local leader of Athanur Village, who was a zilla panchayat member, decided that only women needed to be elected to this panchayat. He convened a meeting of caste leaders and elders and indicated that it would be desirable to have an all-women panchayat, and that they should be elected unopposed. The others in the meeting agreed to this proposal. There were, indeed, others who wanted to contest (and one man had even filed his nomination papers) but they yielded to the decision of the local elite at the instigation of the zilla panchayat member. This clearly shows that it was a local leader who decided on such course of action.

It can, therefore, be said that the hold of village elders/traditional village leaders over village social institutions is still prevalent. Though the political parties have made great inroads into the remote villages, they too have to take the opinion and support of these leaders. The two are thus inter-related and together play a significant role in deciding the membership of the panchayat.

A significant factor, however, in the elections is the role of political parties. The Panchayati Raj Act clearly affirms that the grama panchayat elections should not be conducted along party lines. Naturally, political parties should not play any role either in the election or in the functioning of these panchayats. But it is evident that the grama panchayats are influenced or controlled by locally-dominant people from different political parties. The gram panchayat election in Karnataka, which was due in December 1998 and was postponed indefinitely, is an instance of the control of local leaders. Although the state government had not made a formal announcement to this effect, it was the natural outcome of a decision taken at the cabinet meeting on 18 January 1999 to incorporate certain changes in the panchayati raj structure of the state. The SEC had taken all steps in connection with the preparation of polls and issuance of notifications, but the elections, nevertheless, were postponed though the Constitution does not allow postponement of elections of PRIs.

The state decision to make toilets mandatory for a candidate in the panchayat elections also led to a stalling of the election process. The presence of a toilet became a prerequisite for any person to contest in the grama panchayats elections and its absence would be a reason to reject (disqualification) the nomination papers. This was contested and the court allowed for a conditional relaxation of this rule on 9 February 2000. All this created a lot of confusion during the grama panchayat elections of 2000.

Thus, although Karnataka was going to conduct the second term elections to the PRIs after the adoption of the Seventy-third Constitutional Amendment Act, various issues came up before the elections, creating confusion and leading to their postponement. The need was to set right these issues so that elections would be conducted on the scheduled dates. Regular and periodic elections are the only solution to ensuring greater participation of the local people. A conducive environment could be created only by 'political commitment'.

Emerging Issues and Strategies (Institutional and Functional)

The preamble to the Act (1993) expresses its basic tenet by declaring that PRIs should function as units of local self-government. Among other changes, achieving universal enrolment in primary schools, providing sanitary latrines, improving water supply, establishing health and maternity centres and social forestry are to be among the priorities at each level. Though these developmental functions had been transferred to the zilla panchayat it was seen that the zilla panchayats had not been able to give any priority to the stated development matters. Though the new system has provided membership and positions of authority in local bodies to the weaker sections namely, the SCs, STs, OBCs and women, these provisions did not lead to any significant social gains. The intended beneficiaries' access to the existing facilities, the methods of access and so on were limited mainly due to their lack of awareness. They were, thus exploited by middlemen and political brokers. Therefore, these schemes should be given wide publicity.

Another major instrument for ensuring people's participation is their organisation into community groups such as the NGOs. They have increased substantially in number in the country in recent years and have assumed an important role in rural development. As voluntary agencies, they work with the people and catalyse their development. In this effort, they focus not just on developmental programmes but also on the process of awareness building and community organisation. In Karnataka, there has been progress in bringing about a working relationship between the various government departments and the voluntary agencies in the areas of social forestry and wasteland development. The goal of such a relationship is to meet more effectively the basic needs of the rural people, such as providing fodder, fuel, timber fruits and raw material for rural artisans.

There is no doubt that the NGOs have come to play an important role in influencing the PRIs in crucial areas of development. But there is no proper 'organic linkage' between NGOs and PRIs. Very few opportunities are there for constructive cooperation between the two due to lack of proper communication and information. The NGOs could play a significant role in strengthening the rural local self-governance. Some activities on which the NGOs could concentrate are:

a) During the panchayati raj elections, they can organise and motivate people for electing only genuine representatives who can work for the people.

b) They can train and educate the elected representatives of the PRIs, specially women, SCs, STs and OBCs who have limited access to information and are new entrants to the panchayati system.

d) They can provide technical know-how on different aspects of developmental work and help in the planning and implementation of many of the panchayat programmes to make them more effective.

Reservation plays a crucial role in breaking the stranglehold of traditionally-dominant sections on PRIs. Leadership is no longer confined to a particular class, caste or gender. This reflects the strength of our democratic structures and political processes. The amended panchyati raj system has seen the emergence of a new leadership, increasingly determined by the 'achieved status' of an individual. The distinction of Karnataka is striking in the field of representation of women. The state has been following a progressive 'policy of inclusion' of the hitherto neglected/weaker sections of rural society in one form or the other from the very beginning (under the Panchayati Raj Act of 1959). Even before Seventy-third and Seventy-fourth Constitutional Amendments, it introduced and practiced 25 per cent reservation for women under the Panchayati Raj Act 1983. The Panchayati Raj Act 1993 (Conformity Act) took it further in the direction of inclusion, by implementing 33 per cent reservation to the backward classes and a rotation system for the positions of president and vice-president (20 months in case of zilla panchayat and taluk panchayat and 30 months for grama panchayats). Vokkaligas and Lingayats have been conventionally known as 'dominant castes' but the state witnessed a 'shifting of dominance' at different levels in the last few years. All these enabled the weaker sections to have access to PRIs in huge numbers and to broaden the social base of democracy.[7]

However, the skill, knowledge and correct attitude required of panchayat members are often missing in the local leaders. *They lack awareness, and hence, are not able to articulate their rights and demands in an effective manner.* Therefore, the leadership at the grass-roots level has to be strengthened through 'capacity-building' programmes. The need for training/orientation is necessary as political education is a prerequisite for their effective participation.

The concept of PRIs grew out of the failure of the community development administration in involving the people in the development process. The normative theory of decentralisation assumes that the grass-roots level elected bodies facilitate peoples' participation in local governance and are more accountable as they are nearer to the people. But, the term of the president of the zilla panchayat being 20 months has weakened the position of the elected head and strengthened the position of the administrative heads. Since they lack education and awareness, they are not able to comprehend their roles and discharge their duties effectively. Their role thus tends to be reduced to that of mere overseers who bring the local problems to the notice of the concerned officials.

It has been observed that panchayat elections have been postponed in several states violating the constitutional norms. Though Karnataka is a pioneering state in holding elections to PRIs under the new dispensation, it has not been an exception to the trend of delayed elections. The issue of postponement of elections becomes serious especially in view of the fact that the zilla panchayat is the facilitator and coordinator, responsible for integrating the plans of the taluk panchayat and grama panchayat and overseeing their functioning and allocating finances. This reflects the need for effective inter-institutional relationship. Therefore, postponement of elections should be checked at the earliest in the light of the present 'development paradigm'.

In 2000, elections to many panchayats were postponed due to ballot paper problems such as errors in serial numbers in the ballot paper, confusion over the nomination of candidates and symbol problems. These events clearly indicate that postponements on simple grounds are also taking place. In addition, elections to the different tiers of panchayats are bifurcated by holding one on time and postponing the other. This practice not only creates confusion in the administration but also deprives the development of a proper linkage between the three tiers, which is crucial for development. This demands more efforts by the SEC and sincerity on the part of the contesting candidates. The SEC should be strengthened as an independent body. All functions related to the electoral process should be under the supervision and control of the SEC. The present status of the SEC is not enough to conduct free, fair and timely elections (based on events during PR elections in 2000). The state government should intervene less and instead coordinate more with the SEC.

Today 'good governance' is the key word, yet corruption, money and muscle power continue even in the local elections scenario. It is necessary to put a ceiling on canvassing and overall election expenses on the same lines as the general elections. There is also an urgent need to curb practices such as snatching and tampering of ballot boxes, violent incidents, group clashes, booth capturing and rigging in order to have fair and free elections. It becomes even more important when we consider the hitherto disadvantaged sections of the society entering politics and the political process. Moreover, there is a need for effective and timely dissemination of information during elections in order to reduce confusion. Gazette notifications and important decisions should be made clear to the people quite in advance. Website, newspapers, pamphlets, periodic bulletins, press briefings, radio and television can be used to make information readily available for public use. This also leads to transparency in government functioning, which is the need of the hour.

An interesting development in the 2000 grama panchayat election was that more than 26 per cent of the members were elected unopposed all over the state. One reason could be that there were no candidates interested to contest from the category for which the concerned seat was reserved. It could also be said that the traditional power centres of the rich and influential prevailed upon the people not to oppose the candidates selected by them. Also, in some cases, the villagers themselves showed unity to elect their leader unanimously. Another reason could be the role of the local leaders in dissuading aspirants from filing nominations. However, this type of control over local affairs is a blow to the voter's privilege and it leads to an authoritarian polity. Trading leads to gerrymandering and results in certain interests not finding representation at all. This is not desirable and hence, it is more appropriate to have popularly elected members to represent the heterogeneous interests of the village.

When the results were announced after the village panchayat elections in 2000, all the major political parties claimed majority. It is clear that the grama panchayat elections are to be held on a non-party basis. But each party was able to identify the number of seats bagged by them. They were engaged in counting the number of winning candidates sponsored by them. It was obvious that many candidates were identified by their party affiliations. In this context, one has to question the feasibility of the system of having non-party elections at the grama panchayat level when the elections confirm the opposite, namely, that political parties are entering the remotest villages and influencing local politics. It is time to rethink the issue of non-party based elections at the village level.

On the other hand again, in many constituencies, the winning candidates were selected for contest and their style of campaigning. The parties are pushed to the background when candidates enjoying a good rapport with the villagers contest the election.

Another important phenomenon in the 2000 elections was the emergence of the three 'all-women panchayats'. From the empowerment angle, this is a positive and progressive trend. But a deeper probing revealed that it was the decision of the local political elite to have all women members. It was an unopposed election as no other candidate was allowed to contest. This practice is undemocratic as leadership is forced on certain sections of the society depriving other people of their political rights.

In rural India today, PRIs are evolving institutions and with proper inputs over a period of time they are bound to stabilise as a strong democratic base. With this aim in mind, the Karnataka government has decided to conduct training programmes for the newly-elected members of the grama, taluk and zilla panchayats. Taking into effect the problems encountered in the running of these local bodies as well as the new provisions incorporated in the 1993 Act, the following matters/issues[8] need to be considered:

a) The zilla panchayat should be strengthened financially by increasing the untied grants and by giving them powers to levy taxes and mobilise other resources such as the powers of the grama panchayat.

b) A proper coordination mechanism should be developed between the zilla panchayat and the line departments and among the departments in the district. Single line of command, effective communication and strict adherence to the guidelines of the Karnataka Development Programme can help in developing close coordination.

c) Domination of MPs and MLAs is a threat to local decision making. They should be kept outside the panchayati raj system. It is, therefore, suggested that the Karnataka Panchayat Raj Act should be amended accordingly/appropriately.

d) Though the bureaucracy provides stable leadership when the elected body is in a state of flux, the administrators have a decisive role in translating various policies and programmes of the government into reality. The efficacy of decentralised planning depends on their commitment. They must, therefore, be oriented towards the local self-governing bodies. This presupposes a drastic and purposive change in their outlook so that they identify themselves with the panchayati raj system. Placed in positions of authority and responsibility, they can reactivate the political process and create a better climate. The administrative process, therefore, needs to be reformed. This demands trained personnel with the requisite skills and a commitment to developmental goals.

e) The electorate no longer ignores the performance of the local political leaders, which implies that the work of the representatives during their tenure is of great significance. Only when they spend their time resolving the problems of their constituencies, can they rely on the support of the voters.

f) Now that the electronic media has reached most villages, serious thought should be given to developing satellite, radio and TV programmes on panchayati raj. Of late, the government has taken initiatives in this regard.

g) Special programmes to train the presidents and the vice-presidents on their roles, responsibilities and limitations should be taken up so that they develop a cordial relationship with the officials. The members should be made aware of their roles and responsibilities so that the standing committees develop as real decision-making bodies and the purpose for which they are formed, is fulfilled.

h) The election procedure seems to be reasonably efficient but a close examination has revealed some weaknesses. Effective methods of election administration have a direct impact on the accuracy and honesty of elections. A start has been made by giving due attention to the election machinery and the election process. The reforming zeal of the government in power can further strengthen this in the interest of honesty and efficiency.

i) The district planning committee should be constituted on time and it should be made functional to be effective. Adequate skill building at the district and sub-district levels on techniques of planning is necessary to develop an effective planning mechanism.

j) The target groups should be empowered to take up the programme themselves. Encouraging user groups like water users committee, an education committee for ensuring proper education and a health committee for ensuring health facilities and the like can facilitate community participation in programmes.

k) The grama sabha is the soul of the panchayat raj and the idea is to progressively strengthen its functioning to ensure full participation of the people and assure accountability and transparency. It should become a people's movement. Grama sabhas should meet regularly, failing which it should be construed as a disqualification on the part of the president. The area of the grama sabha should be such that people particularly women, daily-wage earners and the old can reach the venues of meetings conveniently. The grama sabha can be held on *shandy* (weekly market) days, so that there will be opportunity for meaningful participation of all.

Recent Developments

The Karnataka government, irrespective of political hues, has been generally responsive to the need for the necessary reforms in the panchayati raj system since its inception, and especially after the Panchayati Raj Act 1993. This is evident from the fact that it constituted a high-power committee to look into the problems in the panchayati raj system and to suggest remedial measures as early as 1995. This committee submitted its report in March 1996 and as a follow-up, necessary amendments were made in the Act. Again, in 2002, a working group was constituted to look into the problems and to suggest ways and means to take panchayati raj further for decentralised governance. Later, the government brought about another comprehensive amendment to overcome the institutional and administrative lacunae in the composition and functioning of PRIs.

Keeping in mind the many issues and problems that emerged in course of the elections in 1995 and 2000, several corrective steps were taken by the government to remove some of the drawbacks and dysfunctionalities in the functioning of the system.

Some of the amendments and correctives undertaken by the government are:

a) Establishing ward sabhas (Amendment Act 2002) with sufficient functions such as approval of the panchayat budget, programmes and development projects in ward area, selection of beneficiaries, planning.

b) Provisions have been made to see that SC, ST, BC and women participate in ward sabha and grama sabhas in stipulated percentages.

c) In order to make the electoral process clear, clean, transparent and corruption free, provisions for declaring assets of the candidates, ceiling of expenditure on election and strengthening the SEC by giving it more powers to enable it to function independently and freely for conducting elections.

d) Right to information, social audit and bringing PRIs under the purview of the lokayukta (ombudsman at the state level) have been introduced.

e) Mapping out of activities for three tiers, to be performed under 29 subjects given in the Eleventh Schedule of the Seventy-third Constitutional Amendment Act followed in the Panchayati Raj Act 1993 under three schedules, have been completed and necessary government orders have been issued.

f) The state government's decision to transfer 176 state schemes to the district sector and additional funds for implementing them. (In the 2004–05 budget, there was provision for Rs 40,000 million, an addition of Rs 8000 million over the previous year's budget for the district sector for strengthening PRIs financially.)

g) The proposal for establishing ombudsman institution in each district to contain corruption in its different forms.

Having the reputation of a high-level commitment to democratic decentralisation on the part of the Karnataka elite cutting across party lines, the various governments in the state have considered many serious proposals for strengthening panchayati raj in the state. Some of the proposals may, however, appear to be extraordinary. For example, there is a proposal to hold panchayat election for a constituency not once in five years but in ten years (two terms) with the idea of developing leadership among different communities (reserved and unreserved) over a reasonable period of time. There are other proposals which invite national attention. Considering the problems of local bureaucracy vis-à-vis control by political heads, the government is contemplating having a separate panchayati raj cadre for these institutions, thereby avoiding the problems of deputation, transfers and skill development necessary for rural development. Based on past experience, the Government of Karnataka has gone for a capacity-building programme in a big way for elected members of PRIs. This programme is conducted by Abdul Nazir Sab Institute of Rural Development, Mysore through satellite. It proposes to start training the newly-elected grama panchayat members shortly. All these positive steps are expected to transfer sufficient finances, functions and functionaries to the three-tier panchayati raj system. Being committed to decentralised governance, the government maintained the schedule of the third round of elections, which were conducted in three phases on 25 February, 27 February and 6 March 2005. During this election, some of the grama panchayat polls were postponed because the SEC found that the election process in certain grama panchayats constituencies was 'flawed' and cancelled it. Repoll was held on 20 and 26 March 2005, as ordered by the SEC and 15,189 candidates were elected unopposed. The elections to zilla panchayats and taluk panchayats, as reported, would be held shortly. During the latest election conducted for grama panchayats, the following have been observed, which are worth mentioning:

It should be noted that legally the grama panchayat elections should be held on a non-party basis. However, involvement of political parties in the campaign was visible everywhere as it happened in the past. In almost all places, the legislators were openly supporting their candidates. In some villages, of course, candidates fought the elections without any political support. On the days of voting, most candidates were seen offering meals and *tambula* (gifts) to the voters to woo them. In the camps of some candidates, the festivities matched only those of a marriage ceremony. Enthusiasm and active partici-pation of women in the elections was noticeable. Kodihalli and neighbouring Gopalapura villages are the first two villages in Mandya District in Karnataka to jointly elect an all-women grama panchayat. Women candidates were fielded for all the eight panchayat seats, which include the SC and BC seats. Seven members were elected unopposed. Polling was peaceful barring a few incidents.

Some Observations

It is evident that decentralisation has encouraged local participation. However, it is still far from the normative standards and has not led to increased efficiency, effectiveness and efficacy. This means that these institutions should be made much more participatory as involving the beneficiaries will automatically lead to improvement in the works executed. Adequate empowerment of the grama sabha is the crux of effective decentralisation (but not at the cost of the grama panchayat) as that is where people's democracy can be put into practice. It is there that the voice of the people, including the weaker sections and women, can be really heard. The elected grama panchayat must be accountable to the grama sabha, which should be convened according to the statutory requirements and government guidelines. The annual statement of accounts and the '*social audit*' report must be formally placed before the grama sabha, as also the development report relating to the preceding year and the programme for the current year, including the annual plan and selection of beneficiaries. The annual plan should be considered against the background of a five-year plan based on local priorities.

All relevant information should be systematically made available to the grama sabha in accordance with the Transparency Act and the Right to Information Act, which have been enacted in Karnataka. Full use should be made of the grama sabha to create awareness regarding the policies and programmes, which are of great relevance at the grass-roots level, so that people's participation can be progressively increased and improved. The grama sabha should be fully representative, especially of the weaker sections and women as mandated by an amendment to the Panchayati Raj Act 1993. Each separate habitation in a grama panchayat should have its own people's committees, which could be like sub-committees of the grama panchayat with suitable links with the grama sabha, to strengthen people's participation. Any user or stakeholders group that is set up should have organic links with the grama panchayat to ensure that it is not sidelined. The media should also work towards bringing about a fundamental change in the development thinking, that is, participatory human development for sustainable growth.

Since one cannot dissociate political parties from panchyatai raj, it is essential to have a 'culture of democracy' or unity among the various political parties. This means that they should incorporate groups and individuals, who have been hitherto excluded, under-represented or discriminated against, in local politics, cooperate in the development activities of the villages, take responsibility for their representatives to carry out their tasks and be accountable for their actions. The PRIs should be developed as a medium of community development and not as a power mechanism where they are treated as centres of power.

Democratic decentralisation is a remedial measure to mobilise popular voluntary participation. The PRIs, therefore, have a vital role in rural development being the only institutions to facilitate planning, participation and mobilisation of resources. The emergence of these institutions has brought governance closer to the people. Yet, we have seen that the elective base of the local self-government system is facing various pressures, stresses and strains. Popular enthusiasm and 'collective actions' should, therefore, emerge to meet the present challenges. In all probability only 'activism' can make any difference in the political orientation of the system.

The entire discussion in this chapter reveals quite effectively that Karnataka has till date, quite famously incorporated many progressive ideas and innovative mechanisms for strengthening PRIs. The commitment of the government to decentralised governance is beyond doubt. One can say confidently that the state is moving further in the direction of genuine decentralisation, that is, to make these institutions sustainable as 'institutions of self-government' as envisaged in the provision of 243G in the Seventy-third Constitutional Amendment Act 1992.

Notes

1. The authors are thankful to Mangala Nayak, research associate, Institute of Social Sciences, Southern Regional Centre, Bangalore, for assisting in the preparation of this paper.
2. Karnataka is one of the largest Indian states with a population of 5,28,50562 and an area of 191,791 sq km. A majority of the population, around 3,48,89,033, lives in rural areas (2001 Census). Again, of the total population, the share of male population is 17,648,958 and that of female population 17,240,075. Further, as elsewhere in the country, the female literacy rate of 57.45 per cent is lower than the male literacy rate of 76.29 per cent (2001 Census). Karnataka lies on the western part of the Deccan Plateau. The state is in many ways the archetypal Indian state, in natural regions, languages, faith and culture, caste and class, etc. It is especially rich in mineral wealth and one of the first states to reach electricity to all its villages. The state's capital city is Bangalore and it is known internationally as the hub of information and technology and the electronic city of India. The people of Karnataka speak different Indian languages but Kannada has been the official language since 1973. The state has 27 districts, 176 taluks and 29,406 villages. The sex ratio is 965. Among the districts in the state, there are 27 zilla panchayats, 176 taluk panchayats and 5,650 grama panchayats. A substantial increase in literacy rate can be observed during the decade 1991–2001. As against 56.04 per cent in 1991, the literacy rate has gone up to 67.04 per cent in 2001. According to the recent census, the female literacy rate has gone up from 44.34 per cent in 1991 to 57.45 per cent in 2001, whereas in the case of males, it has risen from 67.26 per cent to 76.29 per cent in 2001.
3. For details about the structural and functional aspects of the panchayati raj system under the Act of 1959, see Bhargava et. al. (1982); see also Bhargava (1984).
4. A plethora of literature is available on the panchayati raj system and its functioning under the Act of 1983 conducted by foreign and Indian scholars. Among others, two empirical studies by B.S. Bhargava and N. Sivanna (1990 and 1992) are worth noting.

5. For structural and operational aspects, especially election process and related issues, see Mathew (1994, 2000). See also Subha (1996).
6. For extensive coverage of pre, during and post phases of panchayati raj elections, 2000, based on primary and secondary data, refer the unpublished research report of the ISS (2000). Also, see, Subha et al. (2001). Also, see, Subha and Bhargava (2000).
7. For the concepts of 'dominant caste', 'shifting of dominance', 'inclusion' and 'exclusion' and their testing at the field level in Karnataka, refer to the unpublished research report of the ISS (2002).
8. In this paper, observations and findings are based on the data (primary and secondary) collected in connection with recent larger research projects/studies on Karnataka's panchayati raj system and election process at the Institute of Social Sciences, Southern Regional Centre, Bangalore.

References

Bhargava, B.S. 1984. 'Working of Town Panchayats in Karnataka: Problems and Prospects' (mimeo.). Institute for Social and Economic Change, Bangalore.

Bhargava, B.S, C.R. Bada and V.N. Torgal. 1982. *Panchayati Raj System* (in Karnataka). New Delhi: Jackson Publications.

Bhargava, B.S. and N. Sivanna. 1990. 'Emerging Pattern of Leadership in Panchayati Raj System: Case Study of a Zilla Parishad in Karnataka'. Working paper, Institute for Social and Economic Change, Bangalore.

———. 1992. 'Place and Role of Taluk Panchayat Samiti in Panchayati Raj System of Karnataka: A Case Study'. Working paper, Institute for Social and Economic Change, Bangalore.

Mathew, George (ed.). 1994. *Status of Panchayati Raj in the States of India*. New Delhi: Concept Publishers.

———. 2000. *Status of Panchayati Raj in the States and Union Territories of India*. New Delhi: Concept Publishers.

Subha, K. 1996. *Karnataka Panchayat Elections 1995, Process, Issues and Membership Profile*. New Delhi: Concept Publishers.

Subha, K. and B.S. Bhargava. 2000. 'Feminism and Political Empowerment of Women: The Karnataka Experience', *South Asian Journal of Socio-Political Studies*, Kollam, 1 (2).

Subha, K., B.S. Bhargava and Mangala Nayak. 2001. 'Women in Panchayati Raj Institutions: Political Empowerment through Capacity Building', *South Asian Journal of Socio-Political Studies*, Kollam, 2 (1).

Institute of Social Sciences (ISS). 2000. Unpublished research report. 2000. 'An Overview of Panchayati Raj Election in Karnataka 2000'. Institute of Social Sciences, Bangalore.

———. 2002. Unpublished research Report. 2002. 'Inclusion of the Excluded Communities, Panchayati Raj System and Social Cohesion: The Case of Karnataka'. Institute of Social Sciences, New Delhi.

II

Local Governance and the Emerging Socio-economic Issues

10 Imperfect Substitutes

The Local Political Economy of Informal Finance and
Microfinance in Rural China and India

KELLEE S. TSAI[1]

'[O]fficial reports of the moneylender's impending demise are much exaggerated'
(Clive Bell on India, 1990).

'The fact that these private or underground credit money houses exist and sometimes thrive in the countryside even today has revealed that farmers need them
(*People's Daily* on China, 29 November 2002).

Introduction

Developmental economists have long noted the complexity of providing effective rural credit delivery in large, agrarian countries such as India and China.[2]
Establishing and maintaining a network of rural financial institutions is expensive and managing their operations is difficult in the absence of proper
training, monitoring and incentive structures. The operational challenges of
rural financial intermediation are compounded by state development strategies
that promote industrialisation and urbanisation at the expense of agricultural
production. At the macrolevel, the notorious scissors gap between agriculture
and industry redistributes savings from rural to urban areas, thereby limiting the relative supply of rural credit. At the microlevel, this means that even
well-located rural households that have the option of keeping their savings
in official financial institutions may lack access to formal sector credit and
rely instead on a wide range of informal, curb market mechanisms.

It is in this context that governments throughout the developing world
have regarded informal finance as a negative reflection of deficiencies in the
formal financial system. In both China and India, the traditional image of
the usurious moneylender adds an additional pejorative dimension to the
official depiction of informal finance: when the poor lack access to conventional sources of credit, they are exploited by loan sharks and other illegal
curb market operators. Following this logic, the prescription thus requires
increasing state efforts to eliminate informal finance, while enhancing the
availability of state-sanctioned financial intermediaries, especially microfinance programmes devoted to poverty alleviation. Even with these policy

measures, however, small business owners and farmers continue to rely primarily on curb market finance in both China and India. Moreover, in some cases, the scale of informal finance actually increases in communities that have been targeted for a greater supply of official credit. This raises the question of why official attempts at limiting informal finance and expanding the accessibility of formal finance may have such unintended consequences. One basic reason for the persistence of informal finance is that the supply of formal finance is limited and insufficient to meet the demand for credit. A second explanation is that official state policies are not being implemented properly. In addition to these economic and state-centric explanations, this chapter argues that informal finance and formal finance are imperfect substitutes for two additional, complementary reasons: First, because credit markets are segmented by local political and social dynamics; and second, because government-sanctioned microfinance programmes are often structured in a manner that fails to serve its intended clientele. This suggests that informal finance is not simply a manifestation of weaknesses in the formal financial system, but also, a product of local political, institutional and market interactions. The analytical value in recognising these local interactions lies in their ability to explain why developmental outcomes deviate from state intentions.

The chapter proceeds as follows: The second section reviews the key expressions of formal and semi-formal finance in China and India and shows how the countries' strategies in rural financial intermediation compare with one another. Both have relied on directed credit and encouraged the growth of microfinance programmes, albeit to differing degrees. The third section outlines the main expressions of informal finance in China and India and discusses the extent to which they have been subject to state regulation. The fourth section delineates four complementary explanations for why state efforts to substitute informal finance with microfinance have not been successful and presents two local case studies from India and China, respectively, to illustrate how the combination of credit supply, local political economic conditions and institutional characteristics of financial intermediaries mediates the dynamics of rural finance.

Financing Rural Development in China and India

To understand the formal institutional context against which curb market activities have flourished, this section highlights major changes in the basic structure of rural finance. Both countries have established credit cooperatives, commercial banks, and poverty alleviation microfinance programmes in rural areas, but these formal sector institutions have not displaced informal and semi-formal sources of credit.[3]

Formal Financial Sector

After India's independence in 1947 and the establishment of the People's Republic of China in 1949, the 1950s represented a relatively optimistic and ambitious phase for both countries in establishing a national system for agricultural finance. Both newly inaugurated regimes shared the developmental goals of promoting growth without exploitation and creating grass-roots level savings and credit institutions to serve farmers.

Although India inherited a basic network of credit cooperatives from the colonial era, the Reserve Bank of India's (RBI) first decennial All-India Debt and Investment Survey in 1951 found that 93 per cent of rural households relied on informal finance (Bouman et al., 1989: 12–14). This finding inspired a strong political commitment to establishing formal sector alternatives to the curb, which was popularly viewed as being exploitative and even 'evil' (RBI, 1954). Hence, throughout the 1950s and 1960s, the government actively promoted the expansion of cooperatives 'to provide a positive institutional alternative to the moneylender himself, something which will compete with him, remove him from the forefront, and put him in his place (ibid.: 481–82)—or more generally, to enhance the availability of agricultural credit and alleviate rural poverty. In the mid-1970s, India's rural financial system went through another expansionary stage with the establishment of regional rural banks (RRBs) at the district level, farmers' service societies at the village level, and further growth of non-banking finance companies.[4] Even though the number of bank branches tripled during 1969–79, the government considered rural access to be too low at 37,000 people per rural bank branch; therefore, in 1980 another seven commercial banks were nationalised to extend their outreach in rural areas (AFC, 1988, in Nagarajan and Meyer, 2000: 172). In quantitative terms, progress has been made on this latter objective: according to the RBI, by 1998 India had a total of 64,547 RRB branches, which was equivalent to 17,000–21,000 rural citizens per bank branch.[5] But the RRBs have proven to be financially unsustainable and inefficient in loan delivery (Bhatt and Thorat, 2001).

Shortly after the founding of the People's Republic of China, the Chinese communists ordered the closure of all forms of private finance and banned popular forms of curb market financing including pawnbrokering and 'loan sharking' (Hsiao, 1971). During the 1950s, China also set up a network of rural credit cooperatives (RCCs), but unlike the cooperatives in India, China's original RCCs acted mainly as fiscal institutions that funnelled credit between the state and the people's communes rather than serving as commercial credit-granting institutions. It was not until the commencement of market-oriented reforms in the late 1970s that RCCs started to function more as grass-roots banking institutions that served rural households and collective enterprises, and the Agricultural Bank of China (ABC) was re-established to handle larger scale commercial banking activities.[6] Meanwhile, in the early-1980s, the Ministry of Agriculture established a network of rural cooperative foundations (RCFs) to serve farmers, but the People's Bank of China never considered them formal 'financial institutions' and succeeded in shutting them down at the end of the 1990s. Indeed, throughout the reform era central authorities have repeatedly waged national political campaigns to crackdown on the curb. In July 1998, China's State Council even issued formal 'Provisions on the Cancellation of Illegal Financial Institutions and Activities', which reiterated that illicit financial institutions should be banned (Xinhua, 22 July 1998, cited in Tsai, 2002a: 1).

The elimination of RCFs left about 44,000 RCCs at the township level (with about 20,000 village branches) as the only formally approved non-banking financial institution devoted to serving rural enterprises and households. Since then, central banking authorities have deliberated over how to improve their performance (Watson, 2003) and injected approximately US$ 4 billion in recapitalisation funds into the RCC system because RCCs are technically insolvent. As of mid-2003, RCCs accounted for 11.5 per cent of total savings and 10.8 per cent of loans extended by formal financial institutions, and a pilot reform scheme for decentralising their management was underway in eight provinces (*People's Daily*, 30 November 2003).

The Rise of Microfinance

Given the inability of most formal sector banking institutions to reach rural populations and the popularity of informal sector alternatives, microfinance programmes have emerged as a potential solution for bridging the gap between the supply and demand for rural finance. In both India and China, microfinance has taken the form of subsidised loans in government-supported poverty alleviation (PA) programmes and various donor and NGO-led endeavours. While the actual expressions and overall scale of microfinance differs in the two countries, the relative effectiveness of these two main forms of microfinance is similar. Specifically, subsidised microloans in government-supported PA programmes tend to have low repayment rates and tend not to reach the intended clientele; and microfinance programmes run by NGOs are more effective in reaching poor clients when loans are structured in a financially sustainable manner and use lending methodologies that are adapted to the particular economic needs of the intended clients.

Directed Subsidised Credit in Public Poverty Alleviation Programmes: Extending subsidised loans to low-income areas and households has traditionally been the first, and perhaps least effective strategy that governments use in their rural development strategies, and India and China are no exceptions (Adams et al., 1984; cf. Morduch, 2000). The Indian Integrated Rural Development Programme (IRDP) was established in 1978 with the mandate of extending microloans through the banking system to impoverished households and now regards itself as the 'world's largest programme for providing micro-loans to the poor' (Sinha, 2000: 66). In its first two decades, the IRDP extended Rs 250 billion (US$ 12.3 billion) worth of subsidised loans to approximately 55 million families who have an annual income of less than Rs 11,000 (US$ 305).[7] Given that 70 million families live below the poverty line in India, it is apparent that the IRDP has had significant outreach. In addition to the loans, IRDP borrowers also receive a cash subsidy at the time of loan disbursal equivalent to 25–50 per cent of the project cost (Nagarajan and Meyer, 2000: 170). The programme has certainly disbursed a high volume of loans, but funds have been misused via the subsidy component such that cash is diverted to local elites rather than the intended borrowers; as a result, the programme has had a repayment rate of only 25–33 per cent (Sinha, 2000: 66). Meanwhile, the RRBs and primary agricultural credit societies have not performed any better. The RRBs have been saddled with soft loans to priority sectors, while primary cooperatives have served mainly as tools of political patronage.[8] Due to the non-commercial orientation of these pro-grammes, basically all of the formal sector institutions involved in microfinance have depended on refinancing and recapitalisation by apex institutions on a regular basis (Nagarajan and Meyer, 2000: 177–79).

State-subsidised microfinance in China has had a shorter history than in India, mainly because China started poverty lending about one decade later than India. To be sure, both central and local governments in China have directed subsidised credit to particular sectors or industries, but that type of 'policy lending' has not occurred in the name of microfinance or poverty alleviation.[9] In 1986, a subsidised lending scheme for poverty relief was introduced, which targeted collective enterprises at the township and village level rather than individual households (Rozelle et al., 1998). While official interest rates on loans ranged between 8 per cent and 10 per cent, the poverty alleviation loans charged only 2.88 per cent annual interest. As is the case with most subsidised credit schemes, the loans were distributed to politically important enterprises and higher-income households and the repayment rates were about 50 per cent (Park, 1999).

Providing subsidised loans directly to households did not start until a few years into China's National 8-7 Poverty Alleviation Plan, introduced in 1993. As part of the strategy to raise 80 million people out of poverty in seven years (that is, during 1994–2000), the central government identified 592 poor counties where households would be directly targeted for subsidised poverty loans. In quite a change from the previous mode of distributing subsidised credit to local enterprises, in 1996 many of the counties adopted the Grameen Bank model of group lending whereby groups of five borrowers would mutually guarantee the repayment of their respective microloans in multiple instalments (Bornstein, 1997; Holcombe, 1995; Khandker et al., 1995). These loans ranged from RMB 1,000 to 2,000 (US$ 120–240) and they continued to be subsidised at the official PA lending rate of 2.88 per cent. Once the decision was made to disburse PA loans directly to households in officially designated impoverished counties, they were disbursed rapidly, almost quota style:

> By August 1998, official microcredit schemes were operating in more than 600 counties in 22 provinces, with the largest programs (in Shaanxi and Yunnan) reaching over 500,000 households.... In 1999, with between 30 and 40 million people still classified as poor, the central government's budget for the 8-7 Plan called for expenditures of Y24.8 billion ($3 billion), of which Y15.3 billion ($1.84 billion, or 62 per cent) was for loans funds (Conroy, 2000: 36).

By 2000, the government had disbursed US$ 775 million worth of subsidised microloans (Tsien, 2001) and by 2002 nearly US$ 3.7 billion (or half) of the central government's poverty-relief funds were going toward poverty-relief loans (Xinhua, 2 March 2002). As in the earlier model of poverty lending, however, repayment rates in these government programmes have been low, that is, less than 60 per cent. Even though the Agricultural Bank of China (a state commercial bank) took over the poverty lending programme from the Agricultural Development Bank (a policy bank) in 1998, the People's Bank of China (PBC) has not been involved in monitoring the microcredit component of the Agricultural Bank of China's operations and the loans are treated more as social grants rather than as commercial loans. In other words, the microcredit component of PA lending has been treated as one-time fixes rather than exhibiting a commitment to sustainable models of microfinance (Cheng, 2003).

Meanwhile, the PBC has been encouraging RCCs to extend microloans to rural households. As of 2002, the PBC reported that RCCs had extended a total of RMB 78.9 billion (US$ 9.54 billion) worth of microloans and that 25 per cent of all rural households in the country had received such loans (CIIC, 5 November 2002). Although RCCs report higher repayment rates than the PA programmes, as of year-end 2003, their ratio of non-performing loans was still quite high at nearly 30 per cent (SIC, 14 January 2004).

NGO and Donor-Managed Microfinance Institutions: The involvement of NGOs in running microfinance institutions (MFIs) varies significantly in India versus

China. This is due in part to differences in the policy environment for both NGOs and non-banking financial institutions. While the government of India has promoted the growth of self-governing NGOs and encouraged domestic development finance institutions to collaborate with them, China's NGOs are sponsored by a particular government unit (making them government-organised NGOs rather than pure NGOs) or established by international donors. To date, India's NGOs have had more extensive reach in microfinance than their counterparts in China, but in both countries, few MFIs are financially sustainable while the market for MFIs remains vast.

In India, microfinance NGOs have generally taken one of the following three forms: self-help group (SHG) programmes that have linkages with banks; cooperatives; or Grameen replicators (EDA Rural Systems, 1996). Organised by NGOs, SHGs consist of 10–12 people with similar socio-economic and demographic characteristics (for example, low-income women in rural areas). As of 2002, there were one million SHGs with 17 million members (Ashe, 2002, cited in Wilson, 2002: 221). The purpose of the SHGs is to help the members save small amounts of money on a regular basis, to create an internal insurance fund for members to draw on in times of emergencies, to empower the members through collective decision making, and to extend uncollaterialised loans to group members (Hannig and Katimbo-Mugwanya, 1999: 7). Since 1992, the National Bank for Agriculture and Rural Development (NABARD) has experimented with creating linkages between SHGs and banks, such that banks lend through NGOs or directly to SHGs. As of March 2003, over 444 banks were participating in microfinance linkages with 717,360 SHGs; in total, the SHG-bank linkage programme had served an estimated 7.8 million low-income households (NABARD, 2002, 2003).[10] Ultimately, NABARD hopes to reach one-third of India's rural population through the establishment of one million bank-linked SHGs by 2008 (Bansal, 2003: 24).

Aside from participating in the SHG-bank linkage model, over 500 NGOs serve as financial intermediaries themselves by brokering funds between banks and low-income borrowers. There are also a handful of cooperatives such as SEWA Bank, the Indian Cooperative Network for Women, Tamil Nadu and cooperative credit societies associated with the Cooperative Development Foundation that are involved in microfinance. Finally, about 10 organisations may be considered Grameen replicators. The largest ones are SHARE, Activists for Social Alternatives Trust and Rural Development Organisation, Manipur (Sinha, 2000: 70).

Overall, MFIs in India have not been subject to stringent regulations, especially those that are not registered as cooperatives or non-banking finance companies. Given the developmental contribution of MFIs, the RBI has not enforced Section 45S of the RBI Act, which prohibits savings mobilisation from the public without RBI permission. Furthermore, financial liberalisation since the 1990–91 economic crisis has loosened interest rate controls on microcredit, which offers MFIs in India the space to structure their loans in a financially self-sustainable manner. Whether this occurs, however, depends in large part on changing popular perceptions that low-income borrowers cannot afford commercially viable interest rates.

In contrast to the relative ease with which NGOs may register themselves and act as MFIs in India, China's policy environment is much more restrictive. All NGOs in China must have an official government unit sponsor their application to register as 'social organisations' with the Civil Affairs Bureau (Saich, 2000). As such, China does not have purely non-governmental organisations engaged in microfinance even though they may be functionally equivalent to NGOs. The introduction of the Grameen model of microfinance provides a good example of the close relationship between government entities and NGOs in China.

The replication of the Grameen model in China first came about through the individual initiative of researchers at the Rural Development Institute of the Chinese Academy of Social Sciences (CASS) and international donors; but to date, the most successful Grameen replications are managed from an office housed at CASS. With funding from Grameen Trust, the Ford Foundation, and the Canada Fund, in 1994 a small group of CASS researchers led by Professor Du Xiaoshan established the Funding the Poor Cooperative (FPC) in Yixian, Hebei (Tsai, 2002a: 200–202). To implement the project they collaborated with the Yixian county-level Poverty Assistance Bureau and the Civil Affairs Office. As of March 2003, there were three FPCs in Yixian, Yucheng (Henan) and Nanzhao (Henan) counties, respectively, and together, the three FPCs had served a total of 15,244 borrowers (Du, 2003). With repayment rates ranging from 95 per cent to 99 per cent, the FPCs are considered the best examples of Grameen-style micro-finance in China. A central part of their success has been structuring the loans in a manner that covers their operational costs, that is at 16 per cent effective interest per annum.[11] Scaling up to extend their reach and experimenting with non-Grameen lending methodologies is their next challenge.[12]

Besides the FPC Grameen replications, international donors have initiated over 200 microfinance programmes throughout central and western China (Cheng, 2003: 123). The donors have all implemented their projects with different local governmental partners. For example, the AusAid project in Haidong, Qinghai that started in 1996 collaborates with the Agricultural Bank of China and the Qinghai Commission of Foreign Trade and Economic Cooperation; the Heifer Project International has been collaborating with the Sichuan Animal Husbandry Bureau since 1985; and since 1995, the International Crane Foundation has implemented a Trickle-Up Programme in

Guizhou with the cooperation of the Guizhou provincial Environmental Protection Bureau.[13] With few exceptions, the donor-initiated programmes have been structured as projects with a limited lifespan rather than as MFIs aiming for sustainability (Cheng, 2003; IFAD, 2001: 20–21; Park and Ren, 2001). Although this may be attributed in part to the official interest rate ceilings on poverty loans, the FPCs have shown that it is possible to build in a higher, sustainable rate of interest in the Grameen model; and that rural borrowers are willing and able to pay those rates. Indeed, a study of NGO MFI clients found that the highest monthly interest rate that they would be willing to pay is 32.6 per cent.[14] This is consistent with the popularity of informal financing mechanisms (discussed next) that charge even higher interest rates.

The Informal and Semi-formal Financial Sector

As suggested already, despite the substantial expansion of rural financial institutions in both countries over the last several decades, informal finance still represents a major source of credit for farmers and petty traders. In China, a study by IFAD estimates that farmers obtain four times more credit from the curb market than from formal financial institutions (IFAD, 2001: C11) and another study of small business owners found that the curb accounted for up to three-quarters of private sector financing during the first two decades of reform (Tsai, 2002a: 36–37). In India, the 1992 AIDIS survey revealed that nearly 40 per cent of rural households continue to rely on informal finance— or more technically, non-institutional credit agencies, which include agricultural moneylenders, professional moneylenders, traders, relatives and friends, and others.[15] Table 10.1 outlines the primary forms of informal and semi-formal finance in both countries and notes the extent to which they are sanctioned or prohibited. In both countries, private transactions involving high interest rates are in violation of banking regulations, as are organisations that mobilise savings without registering with the appropriate authorities.[16] Beyond those two restrictions, however, the legal marginalisation of curb market activity has not been consistently defined or enforced. In practice, curb market actors in both China and India have proven to be adaptable despite multiple rounds of disciplinary action by financial regulators.

Grey Areas in China's Curb Market Financing
In China, the extremes of legal versus illegal forms of financing are distinguished by whether or not they are sanctioned by the PBC, which hinges on whether they mobilise savings from the general public and offer/charge interest rates above the repressed interest rate ceilings. Interpersonal lending

Table 10.1
Legal Condition of Informal Finance in China and India

Type	China	India
Interpersonal lending—loans extended among friends, relatives, neighbours, or colleagues.	Minjian jiedai—financial authorities do not interfere with casual, interest-free lending.	Interpersonal lending—financial authorities do not interfere with casual, interest-free lending.
Trade credit—merchandise credit between wholesalers and retailers.	Hangye xinyong—neither sanctioned nor prohibited.	Trade credit, forward sales.
Moneylenders, loan sharks—loans from professional and non-professional money brokers, typically at high interest rates.	Gaolidai—all high interest lending is illegal.	Mahajan and chettiar bankers—some are registered as finance companies, trusts, banks, and partnership firms.
Rotating savings and credit associations (ROSCAs)—indigenously organised savings and credit groups.	Huzhuhui, hehui, biaohui, chenghui, juhui—permitted in localities where they have not collapsed.	Chit funds–registered as companies, partnerships, and sole proprietorships.
Pawnshops—extend collateralised loans with interest. Indigenous banks, money houses, finance companies—mobilise savings and extend collateralised loans.	Diandang, dangpu—permitted when operated according to regulations siren qianzhuang, private money houses—regarded as private banks, which are illegal; most operate underground now.	Pawnshops—legal if licensed. Deal with short-term credit (hundis) combined with trade for financing trade—committees have made efforts to formalise them n.a.
Rural cooperative foundations, social organisations, mutual benefit funds—registered entities that are supposed to serve lower-income populations	Nongcun hezuo jijinhui—approved by MOA until closure by PBC in 1999. Huzhuhui, hezuo chu jijinhui (mutual assistance societies, cooperative savings foundations)—registered with MCA, but not supposed to engage in for-profit financial intermediation.	Nidhi companies, mutual benefit societies, permanent funds (mainly in Tamil Nadu)—committees have recommended that they be regulated more stringently.

and trade credit, for example, are among the most basic strategies that entrepreneurs use to deal with short-term liquidity requirements. Small business owners frequently borrow money from friends, relatives and neighbouring shopkeepers. Wholesalers may deliver goods to retailers on 10-day or even 30-day credit if they have an established relationship. Such practices are not illegal to the extent that they do not entail interest above the rates of state banks,[17] in contrast to those charged by loan sharks or private money houses. The latter are clearly illegal by PBC standards because they reflect the higher market cost of capital in a financially repressed environment. Indeed, with the sole exception of Minsheng Bank,[18] private commercial banks are prohibited in China and the PBC has launched multiple 'financial rectification campaigns' to shut down private money houses. Nonetheless, they have continued to operate underground, not only in the coastal south where private commerce is better developed, but also in northern central provinces such as Henan (Tsai, 2002a: Chapter 5).

Pawnshops straddle a finer line between being legal and not quite legal and provide a good example of Beijing's regulatory ambivalence in dealing with unconventional financing mechanisms. Their re-emergence during the reform era has been uneven and ambiguously regulated due to their usurious connotation.[19] By 1956 private pawnshops were effectively eliminated, but after the first one opened up during the reform era in Chengdu in 1987, they developed rapidly and by 1993, there were 3,013 documented pawnshops throughout the country. Most were operated by various branches of government agencies, including state banks, policy departments, tax bureaus, customs bureaus and finance and insurance companies (Li, 2000), though some simply registered as ordinary private businesses with the Industrial and Commercial Management Bureau (ICMB). The official interpretation of the 'new' pawnshops was that they differed fundamentally from the traditional exploitative ones. As explained in a Ministry of Finance report:

> It should be noted that today's pawnshops in the country are not entirely what they used to be. Pawnshops in old China took in personal effects at very low prices when the owners were poverty-stricken. However, such businesses today represent a medium for normal commodity circulation.... The new-born pawn brokering aims to serve the people and social production (Zhongguo yinhang, 1993: 240–43).

Despite this more favourable, revisionist evaluation of pawnshops, it became increasingly apparent that many were (illegally) mobilising savings deposits from the public and offering high rates of interest.[20] As a result, in 1994 the PBC was granted administrative authority over pawnshops and two years later, a PBC-led crackdown on illicit financial institutions closed over half of the registered pawnshops, leaving only 1,304 shops with PBC licenses.[21] In a further attempt to circumscribe the financial malfeasance of pawnshops, they were reclassified in 2000 from being 'financial institutions' under the PBC's authority, to 'a special kind of industrial and commercial enterprise' regulated by the State Economic and Trade Commission (JJRB, 2000). In short, over the course of the reform era, pawnshops have been legally registered in some cases, registered with the incorrect local agency in others and engaged in practices that are clearly illegal.

While pawnshops are now technically subject to central-level regulations, rotating savings and credit associations (*hui*) remain unregulated in most localities. When *hui* involve relatively small groups of people (5–10 members on average) who pool set monthly contributions and rotate the disbursal of the collective pot of money to each member, local governments usually consider them a productive form of mutual assistance among ordinary people, typically women. But if a member runs off with the collective pot early in the life of an association, the members who have not had their turn in collecting money are cheated out of their contributions. In the coastal south, a handful of high-profile cases have accumulated where various types of *hui* were exposed as fraudulent schemes organised by con artists (Tsai, 2000). The large-scale cases were not traditional ROSCAs, however, but rather, ponzi schemes that are never sustainable because they generate extremely high returns by exponentially expanding the network of investors. *Hui* collapses make headlines, but they are actually relatively rare. As such, it is only in a small handful of localities that *hui* have been banned by local governments.

The ambiguous and shifting legal status of other curb market practices listed in Table 10.1 share the attribute of being legal according to certain governmental agencies, but not sanctioned by the PBC. The establishment of rural cooperative foundations (RCFs) by the Ministry of Agriculture in the mid-1980s exemplifies this phenomenon (Cheng et al, 1998; Du, 1998). As noted earlier, the PBC never recognised them as legitimate 'financial institutions' because another ministerial bureaucracy created them. Nonetheless, by the early 1990s RCFs had been established in approximately one-third of all townships and by 1998 there were over 18,000 RCFs with over five million depositors (Holz, 2001). Since RCFs were not permitted to mobilise deposits or extend loans like formal financial institutions, they used euphemistic terms for comparable transactions; instead of paying interest on deposits, for example, they sold 'shares' (*rugu*) and extended 'capital use fees' (*zijin zhan feiyong*). Like pawnshops and other forms of informal finance, RCFs had a variety of governance structures and were more central to rural finance in some provinces than others (Park et al., 2003). Their quasi-legal status proved to be short-lived, however. As part of broader national efforts to rectify the financial system, in March 1999, the State Council announced the closure of poorly performing RCFs and the takeover of better performing RCFs by RCCs. These actions triggered farmers' protests in at least six provinces, including Sichuan, Hubei, Hunan, Henan, Guangxi and Chongqing (*AP*, 22 March 1999; *AFP*, 23 March 1999). Apart from RCFs, some de facto non-governmental financial institutions have managed to operate above ground and serve private businesses by registering as social organisations, which are administered by the Ministry of Civil Affairs. These go by a variety of names, including mutual assistance societies and cooperative savings foundations. The credit societies are supposed to be non-profit organisations that serve impoverished populations. In practice, however, they operate like RCFs or private money houses in the sense that they mobilise savings, extend credit to private entrepreneurs who may be well off, and use interest rates that are higher than that set by the PBC. These types of social organisations should be distinguished from those that are genuinely oriented toward poverty alleviation via microfinance.

Attempts at Mainstreaming India's Informal Sector

Relative to China, India has a longer history of state-directed credit for poverty alleviation, yet its formal financial sector is more liberalised and its informal financial sector, better documented and more likely to take corporate forms than those of China. These apparent inconsistencies may be attributed to the fact that India's financial policy environment has also fluctuated considerably over the years. Post-independence governments in India have been concerned about the negative effects of informal finance on rural welfare and made repeated efforts to regulate and create institutional alternatives to the curb. Indeed, what most observers would regard as informal financial intermediaries are registered under the Companies Act, 1956 or regulated by the RBI. For example, moneylenders acts at the state level regulate non-borrowing lenders, while borrowing lenders (or intermediaries) are also subject to various types of regulation.[22] Furthermore, the RBI has tracked informal financial activities in official statistics as a means to measure progress in expanding credit access into rural areas. (Table 10.2 lists the official categories of informal finance as defined by RBI and Figure 10.1 shows their relative share of the curb market over time.) The extent of curb market regulation and tracking

Table 10.2
Breakdown of Informal Finance in Rural India Over Time

Type of Noninstitutional Sources	1951	1961	1971	1981	1991
Landlords	3.5%	1.1%	8.6%	4.0%	n.a.
Agricultural moneylenders	25.2	47.0	23.1	8.6	6.3
Professional moneylenders	46.4	13.8	13.8	8.3	9.4
Traders and commission agents	5.1	7.5	8.7	3.4	7.1
Relatives and friends	11.5	5.8	13.8	9.0	6.7
Others	1.1	7.5	2.8	5.5	4.9
Unspecified	n.a.	n.a.	n.a.	n.a.	3.8
Informal credit as share of total household debt	92.8%	82.7%	70.8%	38.8%	39.6%[1]

Source: Reserve Bank of India, All-India Debt and Investment Survey, various years.
Note: 1991 figures do not add up to 39.6% even though Table 5 of the 1991–92 AIDIS report clearly states that non-institutional agencies account for 39.6% of total rural household debt.

Figure 10.1
Distribution of Informal Financing Mechanisms, India 1951–1991

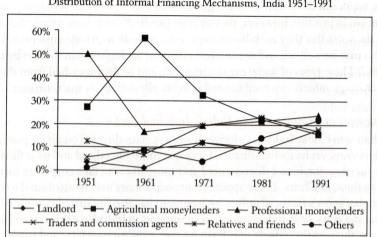

in India stands in contrast to the situation in China where many types of informal financing activities are simply banned. After taking into account sampling and non-sampling errors in the decennial surveys, the main trend is that informal credit has certainly declined as a percentage of total debt, and both professional and agricultural moneylenders have reduced their share of the curb market over time. The decline of the moneylender in official statistics reflects in part state efforts to register and regulate professional moneylenders during the 1950s. Some went underground to avoid regulation and others were probably re-classified as agricultural moneylenders or traders (Bell, 1990). In this regard, note that the first three official categories of informal lenders—landlords, agricultural moneylenders and professional moneylenders—are not necessarily distinct from one another depending on the locality. But generally speaking, landlord lenders extend credit to tenants; agricultural moneylenders primarily deal with agricultural labourers and small farmers; and professional moneylenders service a wider range of customers and may register themselves as companies, partnerships, and trusts (Ghate et al., 1992: 45).

Those in the fourth official category of 'traders and commission agents' are also known as indigenous bankers. In contrast to professional moneylenders who lend their own money, indigenous bankers broker funds between banks and their clients, who tend to be traders rather than farmers (Schrader, 1994). The Shroffs of Western India, for example, provide a short-term credit instrument called *darshani hundi* to traders who need to travel great distances to purchase inventory and transfer funds (Ghate et al., 1992: 198–200). In addition to serving as financial intermediaries, indigenous bankers are also business-people themselves.[23] Besides trading, they may operate commission agencies or hire-purchase finance (HPF) companies, which are basically leasing companies that finance automobiles and other goods over a fixed term for clients who lack sufficient cash to purchase capital goods up front (Nayar, 1992: 192–200). Even though formal sector HPFs exist, one study found that informal HPFs finance a much higher volume of vehicles than official auto finance corporations—probably because lower-income populations find the informal HPFs more accessible (Das-Gupta et al., 1989).

Forms of informal finance in the other category also include indigenous bankers who are not registered as traders or commission agents; unregistered finance corporations; non-professional moneylenders (other than those identified as friends and relatives); various types of leasing, investment, and housing finance companies; ROSCAs (chit funds) and nidhi societies. Unlike the ROSCAs in China, which are completely informal, a number of chit funds in India are registered as companies, partnerships and sole proprietorships under the All-India Chit Funds Act 1982 or the state acts (Rutherford and Arora, 1997). The state's rationale for regulating them is to increase the security of the members' contributions and to reduce the incidence of defaults. As such, organisers are required to have licenses and make security deposits with the Register of Chit Funds; the cost of collecting the pot (that is, the de facto interest rate) is capped at 30 per cent of the size of the pot; and chit funds are limited to a maximum of 60 months (Ghate et al., 1992: 197). These regulations have not had their intended effect, however. Rather than increasing the stability of chit funds in general, many organisers have gone underground and taken their members (who seek higher returns) with them.

In addition to chit funds, nidhi companies or mutual benefit societies are also an important part of the non-banking world of financial intermediation, especially in south India. Incorporated under the Companies Act 1956, nidhis mobilise savings from their members and extend loans that are collateralised with jewellery and real estate (Nayar, 1992: 197–99). When non-members wish to make a deposit or borrow from a nidhi, they take a share of the nidhi. Over the years, the state has made repeated efforts to regulate these mutual benefit societies; and an Expert Group on nidhis constituted by the Department of Company Affairs has recommended a host of additional regulations to professionalise their operations (PIB, 2002).

The Persistence of Informal Finance

State authorities in both China and India have clearly recognised the importance of formal financial institutions in rural areas, including the expansion of microfinance programmes for poverty alleviation purposes. Financial regulators have also made repeated efforts to eliminate and/or regulate/curb market activity. Why, then, has informal finance persisted and even expanded in both countries? Four complementary explanations may be derived from the perspective of supply-leading economics, state–society relations, the local political economy of markets and the institutional characteristics of lending programmes. As will be shown, the first two hypotheses capture macrolevel dynamics, while the second two have explanatory leverage at lower levels of analysis. Specifically, the economic hypothesis concerns the gap between the overall supply and demand for formal credit, and the state–society hypothesis concerns limits in state capacity to reach the intended recipients of subsidised loans and microcredit. Both the local political economy and institutional design perspectives then explain why certain groups of people do or do not receive credit at the ground level. The rationale for each explanation is discussed in more detail next.

Neo-classical Economics: A Matter of Supply and Demand

Based on the logic of supply and demand in neo-classical economics, one reason that informal finance continues to play such an important role in rural China and India may simply be because the amount of credit demanded by rural households exceeds that supplied by the formal financial sector in rural areas. Therefore, to reduce the rural population's reliance on the curb, official sources or credit should be increased. This is known as the supply-leading approach to finance and development (cf. Chandavarkar, 1992; Patrick, 1966). Table 10.2 shows that according to official statistics, the relative dominance of the curb market in rural India has declined over time with the expansion of formal credit institutions. Bell (1990) draws on two independent World Bank surveys to demonstrate, however, that the decennial RBI surveys underestimate the true scale of informal finance. This leads him to conclude:

> [A]lthough the moneylender did lose ground relative to [formal financial] institutions over the period from 1951 to 1981, he remained a very important source of finance to rural households, and the expansion of aggregate debt was almost surely so great as to imply that his volume of business grew.

In other words, despite significant increases in the supply of bank loans and microcredit (over US$ 15 billion), rural households continue to draw on informal sources of credit. A more recent study of credit rationing in rural India confirms that this is due to the combination of limited access to formal credit and continuing high demand for such credit (Swain, 2002).

In rural China, the closure of RCFs eliminated an important source of semi-formal financial intermediation, but we can still heuristically test the supply-leading hypothesis by considering the impact of the government's large-scale poverty lending programmes. Specifically, if people were turning to informal finance only because more institutionalised sources were unavailable to them, then *ceteris paribus* we would expect clients of microfinance programmes to rely on subsidised poverty loans rather than high-interest loans from the curb.[24] Yet this turns out not to be the case. In their surveys of MFI clients, Park and Ren (2001) discovered,

> [O]ver 50 per cent of households in program areas had outstanding loans from other sources, and that this percentage was similar for both members and non-members. The most common source by amount was Rural Credit Cooperatives (55% for members, 46% for nonmembers), followed by informal sources. Thus it does not appear that microfinance participants lack access to other credit sources, whether formal or informal (Park and Ren, 2001: 46).

Their study also found that the overall level of indebtedness is higher among microfinance clients and that only one-quarter of them would have engaged in income-generating activities of the same scale in the absence of these loans. This suggests that although government-sponsored microloans are not going only to rural households that lack access to formal credit, microfinance lending relieves credit constraints at the margin' (Park and Ren, 2001: 46).

Applying the supply-leading hypothesis to India and China explains in part the on-going popularity of informal finance among rural households, but it also raises a number of questions. Why is business getting better for India's moneylenders amid the expansion in formal sector institutions and the MFIs? If MFI clients already have access to RCC loans, then why are they receiving MFI loans in the first place? Examining the issue from the perspective of state–society relations helps to explain this disjuncture between the intended and actual recipients of targeted and microcredit.

State–Society Relations: A Matter of State Capacity

A second reason why increasing the official supply of credit has not translated into a matching decline in informal financial activity is because official state policies are not being implemented properly. This may occur in three main ways: First, state actors may not be distributing targeted credit properly due to insufficient knowledge of how to identify the intended clients of subsidised credit and MFI programmes. Second, state actors may intentionally divert credit from the intended recipients. Third, non-state actors may interfere with the proper disbursement of formal and MFI credit. Taken together, all three types of implementation failure could be interpreted as reflecting weaknesses in state capacity (Evans et al., 1985).

The first type of implementation failure is rooted in the conditions under which formal credit is disbursed. In both India and China, conventional commercial banks do not have institutional experience in lending to rural clients who lack an established credit history and collateral or guarantor. Therefore, the typical state response has been to require that national banks allocate a certain portion of their lending portfolios to lower-income rural households. Quota-style lending often does not achieve its substantive objectives, however, because the emphasis is placed on ensuring that a certain number of loans is disbursed, rather than on the identity and needs of the borrower.

When quota-style lending is accompanied by subsidised interest rates—which has been the case in both India and China's PA loans—the prospects of reaching the intended clientele are further diminished. Instead of reaching lower-income households, subsidised loans usually end up in the hands of local elites who do not feel obligated to repay the loans (Adams et al., 1984). This common phenomenon relates to the second implementation failure, whereby state agents knowingly distribute credit to sectors of the population that are not necessarily excluded from the formal financial system. In India a number of government interventions in rural finance have been motivated by short-term political objectives that coincide with the electoral cycle. While China's political context differs significantly from India's, targeted credit and PA loans are similarly subject to political patronage at the local level. Compared with participants in the FPCs and mixed NGO-government programmes, borrowers in the microcredit projects run by local governments tend to be much wealthier and engaged in non-cropping activities (Park and Ren, 2001). The next section shows that the *underlying reason* for this second type of implementation failure is due to local market segmentation along political and social lines.

Aside from the top–down weaknesses in state capacity discussed earlier, non-state actors may also be responsible for distortions in policy implementation (Migdal, et al., 1994). In this case, non-state actors would include private economic actors such as financial entrepreneurs and politically important constituents of society. First, the argument could be made that the curb market thrives because informal financiers are determined to evade banking regulations. In other words, no matter how much formal credit is available in rural areas and no matter how stringent the penalties are for violating state laws, a certain strata of financial entrepreneurs will always endeavour to subvert state policies. After all, informal finance persists even in advanced industrialised countries with sophisticated financial systems. The second main expression of non-compliance by societal actors may come from borrowers themselves. One could argue that lower-income farmers and rural traders boycott formal and semi-formal financial institutions to undermine their legitimacy (Selden and Perry, 2000). Thus far, however, there is no evidence for this in India and China. Instead, it is more typically the privileged slice of the population that has interfered with the implementation of PA lending policies. In India, local politicians may extend subsidised credit to the upper tier of society, but after elections, loan recovery has also proven to be difficult because 'the credit agencies' bureaucracy is reluctant to touch the influential rural elite who wield much formal and informal influence and considerable power' (Yaron et al., 1997: 102). The low repayment rates in China's subsidised PA programmes suggest that similar dynamics are in operation.[25]

Analysing the persistence of informal finance through the state–society lens takes us one step closer to explaining why state financial policies have had unintended outcomes, that is, why state-subsidised credit and microfinance have not gone to their intended recipients. But conceptualising the curb market as an inverse function of state weakness and societal strength suffers similar problems as the supply-leading hypothesis. Just as increasing the supply of government-sanctioned credit does not automatically crowd out informal credit, strethening state capacities in rural financial intermediation does not necessarily come at the expense of non-state actors such as moneylenders and wealthier households if local agents and institutions face competing political incentives. In both China and India, intrastate actors (such as local officials and bureaucrats charged with loan disbursal) are just as likely as non-state actors to distort policy implementation.

Segmented Markets: A Matter of Institutional Design and Local Political Economy

Ultimately, rural credit markets are more finely differentiated than a dichotomous trade-off between state and society. Rather than assuming the perfect fungibility of credit (whether it be formal, semi-formal, or informal), this explanation starts from the premise that credit markets are segmented even at the grass-roots level. This means that no single type of credit can meet the needs of various potential borrowers and no single type of credit is accessible to everyone (Hoff and Stiglitz, 1990). The concept of *segmented markets* typically refers to the variation in preferences among consumers in different economic strata, for example, in terms of loans for consumption versus productive purposes and the conditions of credit access such as collateral, third party guarantees and savings requirements. In other words, various forms of credit are not functionally equivalent to the borrower. Both the *institutional design and lending methodology* of different forms of credit influence the relative attractiveness of, for example, government-subsidised loans versus unsubsidised microfinance loans from NGOs versus high-interest loans from the curb. All of them have different restrictions in terms of loan size, amount, repayment terms, preferred clientele, etc. Hence, a borrower might take out a high-interest loan from a moneylender rather than a low-interest one from a government programme because the former entails lower transaction costs or because the latter requires that the loan be used for productive purposes.

In addition to supply-side differences in the institutional types of rural credit, market segmentation also occurs along political and social lines, which further distorts the way local credit markets function in practice. Far from being a pure market where prices (interest rates) reflect the relative supply and demand of different types of financing, formal and semi-formal sector credit for PA purposes often faces state-mandated interest rate ceilings and is subsidised. That is to say, even during periods of credit scarcity, the cost of directed bank credit may be extremely low. By definition directed credit cannot go to the highest economic bidder; instead, it is disbursed by credit officers. Moreover, as with any government-allocated good or resource, the distribution of subsidised credit and PA loans is political. Therefore, when PA loans do not reach the target population, more often than not, examining local political and social hierarchies may reveal where the soft loans were distributed.

Similarly, the cost of accessing informal credit also varies depending on the structure of local political and social networks. Interest-free lending only occurs among tight knit groups of people, typically close friends or relatives. Members of ROSCAs usually know one another, or at a minimum, know the organiser of one other member. The higher rates of interest charged by professional moneylenders reflect in part the higher level of risk associated with lending to clients with unconventional forms of collateral (if any). Even then, however, accessing most forms of informal finance requires some form of introduction. Local curb markets are also segmented, though not always in expected ways. The following two cases from India and China illustrate more concretely how local social, political and economic dynamics mediate the use of both formal and informal finance.[26]

Tribal, Caste and Occupational Segmentation in a North Indian Village: In a diachronic study of a south Rajasthan village that Jones (1994, Chapter 18) calls Chandrapur, we can compare the nature of the local credit market before and after a village bank was introduced. As of 1989, Chandrapur Village had a population of over 1,000 people in 200 households, within which were four main social groups engaged in different economic activities: Hindu households engaged in caste-based non-agricultural activities, Jain households prevailed in commercial and financial services, Jogis relied on income from working as migrants in Gujarat and Bombay and the Bhil population lived in the hinterland. Before a village bank was introduced at the end of 1983, Chandrapur residents relied solely on informal sources of credit. The records of a Jain shopkeeper (called B. Jain) who provided pawnbroking services revealed that even six years after the village bank was established, B. Jain's lending volume had increased by over 100 per cent in nominal terms—from

Rs 53,351 (US$ 5,455) in 1982–83 to Rs 110,818 (US$ 6,756) in 1988–89 and the annual number of loans had increased from 290 to 335, but the interest rate had remained at 3 per cent per month throughout the same period.[27] Meanwhile, the total number of pawnshops in the village increased from 15 in 1983 to 24 in 1989. Most remarkably, however, Jones found that the volume of loans extended by pawnbrokers vastly outstripped that of the village bank:

> For Chandrapur, as a whole, a tentative estimate of pawnbroking loan volume is made by multiplying Rs 110,818 (B. Jain's loan volume) by the proportions of loan volume indicated by this shopkeeper for the other 23 lenders in the village. Adding the figure to his own loan volume produces a total Rs 2,292,850 for all 24 pawnbrokers in the village: five times the loan volume advanced by the bank during 1989–89.

> A similar extrapolation from the 335 loans advanced by B. Jain, results in a total of 6,799 loans for all 24 pawnbroking businesses: 75 times the number of loans advanced by the bank in 1988–89, six years after it was established (Jones, 1994: 18–24).

In addition to the expansion in pawnbrokering, mutual finance groups emerged during the same phase. By 1991, 50 out of the 200 households in the village were participating in these savings and credit groups, and by 1992, the loan volume of mutual finance groups was comparable to that of pawn-shops and exceeded that of the village bank (Jones, 1994: 188, 189). Why did a substantial expansion in curb market activities follow the introduction of the village bank?

Each of the explanations outlined earlier offers insight into the question. First, from an economic perspective, one could infer that the overall demand for credit in Chandrapur simply increased dramatically over those years such that a single village bank could never have fulfilled the demand. Indeed, during 1988–89 the village bank accounted for only 90 out of the total of 425 loans extended in the village (Jones, 1994: 18–23).[28]

Second, irrespective of credit supply, the village bank itself was poorly man-aged and failed to carry out its intended mandate. Specifically, the Chandra-pur village bank was supposed to service a total of 17 different villages, yet Chandrapur village residents alone received over half (54 per cent) of its loans. Furthermore, even though the Bhil are Scheduled Tribe members and rep-resent a specific target group of the bank, over half (52 per cent) of these bank loans were extended to Jain borrowers who are relatively well off. It is also worth noting that in 1989, 52 per cent of the bank's loan portfolio was in arrears, and 30 per cent was past due for over three years, that is, in default. By way of contrast, during the same period 70 per cent of the loans extended by B. Jain's pawnshop were repaid in full.

Third, the local credit market was highly segmented on both the supply and demand sides. On the supply side, the lending methodology varied considerably among different sources of credit. The village bank did not offer the types of services demanded by certain groups in the community. In contrast, the popularity of pawnbroking and mutual finance groups may be attributed to their flexibility relative to restrictions associated with loans from the village bank. Villagers turned to the pawnshops to meet seasonal needs such as productive household consumption (for example, housing construction, education, migration), agricultural cultivation and ceremonial expenditures. At the other end of the income spectrum, members of mutual finance groups used them to engage in moneylending rather than consumption or productive investment purposes.

At the same time, Chandrapur's local credit market was also highly segmented along tribal and occupational lines. For example, the Jogis who are on the Scheduled Caste lists were supposed to receive targeted credit from the village bank, but due to their life cycle and consumption needs (for example, weddings and funerals), they ended up relying on pawnbroking loans from Jain shops. Meanwhile, only 23 per cent of the number of pawnbroking loans extended by B. Jain went to local villagers, while 75 per cent of the loans went to Bhil customers who focused on agricultural cultivation in tribal settlements. By 1989, Jain households themselves did not use the services of pawnshops because 'to take such a loan would involve loss of prestige with fellow Jains' (Jones, 1994: 18–27). Instead, Jains not only enjoyed privileged access to loans from the village bank, but also dominated the ownership of pawnbroking businesses and accounted for one-third of the participants in mutual finance groups, which were geared toward enhancing the volume of their informal lending activities.

In addition to intertribal and caste differentiation, informal credit markets are also segmented along occupational and gender lines. This is reflected in the participation of savings and credit groups: of the 126 people participating in mutual finance, 125 were men; and the groups were organised by professional occupation such that the Jains form the government employees' group, the blacksmith caste form the school staff group and relatively few (8 per cent) Bhil cultivators participate in mutual finance. These multiple dimensions of segmentation help to explain why the scale of informal finance actually increased after the introduction of the village bank: not only did the village bank deviate from its mission, but ironically, the fact that most of the bank's loans went to local curb market financiers (Jains) enabled them to expand the provision of informal financial services to other groups in the village.

Segmentation within a Single Surname Village in South China: While it may seem intuitive that a multi-tribal village would have a segmented economic structure and, therefore, credit markets, the case of a single-surname village in the southern coastal province of Zhejiang shows that strong internal forms of differentiation are not uncommon even in a village where everyone could be considered a relative of some sort. Lin Village is comparable in size to Chandrapur Village, but unlike the latter it appears homogenous: 95 per cent of the households share the surname Lin and the village temple, which traces the Lin lineage back to the late Qing Dynasty.[29] Despite this shared ancestry, access to various forms of credit is segmented along political, sectoral, and gender lines in Lin Village.

The political fault lines in the village are based on the three branches of Lins that originally settled in the village. The first branch was very active during the Communist Revolution and ended up with the most Communist Party members. The third branch was the most prosperous one before the Revolution and was thus subjected to considerable political persecution throughout the Mao era. For example, during the Great Leap Forward, adult members of the wealthiest household were sent to reeducation through labour (prison) camps and their spacious traditional courtyard home was tuned into the communal mess hall.[30] The privileged position of the first branch has carried over into the reform era. Even though major decisions are supposed to be made by the democratically-elected village committee, households from the first branch dominate village governance and the allocation of key resources, including access to land and credit. As such, members in the third branch have a difficult time contracting land for their businesses and accessing official sources of credit. Although members of the second branch are neither politically privileged nor persecuted, they also have disadvantaged access to various production inputs relative to the first branch.

It is important to point out, however, that the political hierarchies in Lin Village have not translated neatly into economic stratification. During the Mao era, the third branch certainly suffered more than most, but in the reform era, the second and third branches have found ways to operate private businesses without going through official channels. Given the paucity of arable land,[31] virtually every household in Lin Village operates a small factory. Interestingly, a member of the third Lin branch owns the largest of these factories with over 30 employees—yet he has never borrowed from formal sources of credit. Owner Lin explained:

It's not worth it to me to apply for a loan from a state bank or rural credit cooperative because the credit officers are dirty and rip me off given my family background. If I applied for a RMB 100,000 (US$ 12,000) loan, I would only receive RMB 60,000 (US$ 7,200) because the credit officer would pocket the other RMB 40,000 (US$ 4,800). Meanwhile, I would still be expected to pay interest on RMB 100,000.

Owner Lin explained that households from the first Lin branch were more likely to borrow from state banks or RCCs because their relatives work there. Lacking such official connections, Owner Lin nonetheless managed to invest RMB 700,000 (US$ 84,000) in his motorcycle parts factory by using RMB 100,000 (US$ 12,000) of his own savings, borrowing RMB 200,000 (US$ 24,000) interest free from his four older siblings and borrowing RMB 400,000 (US$ 48,000) at 24 per cent annual interest through moneylenders (*yinbei*). The latter loans were guaranteed by his sisters who have good credit among money-lenders in the textile sector. As of 2001, Lin still had the largest factory in town even though his family's local political status remained low.

Before Lin's motorcycle parts factory was established in 1998, there were larger collectively-owned factories in the village and each of them raised their funds in different ways. For example, at the outset of reform, there was an iron factory, which relied mainly on RCC loans because it was run by managers from the first branch of Lins. Later on, in the early 1980s, about 25 households in the second branch set up a plastics factory by pooling their savings for four years and registered it as a collective enterprise. This is called the 'wearing a red hat' strategy because the plastics factory was really privately owned— registering it as a collective gave it referential land use and tax treatment. Meanwhile, clusters of smaller household factories producing sugar, lime, paint, autoparts and textiles tend to raise their start-up and working capital in sectorally distinctive ways, except in cases where extended families are involved in more than one sector. Given the rapid industrial transformation of Lin Village in the first two decades of reform, it is unlikely that the local RCC and county-level agricultural bank could have kept up with the grass-roots demand for investment and working capital. As such, the expansion in informal financing during the reform era is not surprising. It is noteworthy, however, that the businesses that have received formal sector loans, that is, those run by the first branch, have not performed as well as those financed by the curb. This may be attributed at least in part to the tendency of local political elites to view the loans as grants rather than serious business obligations.

Gender represents the third major dimension along which credit markets are segmented in Lin Village. In contrast to the male-dominated savings and credit groups in Chandrapur, the ROSCAs in Lin Village (called *chenghui* or *hui*) are only managed by women. In China's southern coastal provinces, women dominate *hui* participation because they have better developed social networks with one another, because they are more likely to remain in town year round (as opposed to men who may engage in seasonal migration) and because men are more likely to have other financing options (Tsai, 2000). In Lin Village, a handful of middle-aged women run ROSCAs full time, but most *hui* organisers have other income-generating activities as well. The organiser with the largest volume of hui in Lin Village, for example, is a doctor who operates the village clinic from the courtyard home of the third Lin branch. At any given point in time, she runs up to five hui in the range of RMB 200,000 (US$ 24,000) each (that is, 20 members contributing RMB 10,000 (US$ 1,200 each meeting) and the interest rates run up to 36 per cent annually. Villagers find Doctor Lin to be a trustworthy organiser because as the village doctor, she knows everyone and is unlikely to flee town with their money.

The manner in which credit markets in Lin Village are segmented is only one example of how single-surname villages may be internally differentiated (Tsai, 2002b). Indeed, regardless of the particular distribution of surnames at the village-level, many other patterns of local segmentation may be identified in rural China depending on the structure of the economy, the nature of geographical constraints or resources, the extent of external versus internal migration, and the often path dependent developmental orientation of the local government (Unger, 2002; Walder and Oi, 1999; Whiting, 2001; Wu, 1998).

Finally, despite the shared popularity of informal finance, the financial landscape in Lin Village differs significantly from that of Chandrapur. While the introduction of formal finance to the latter had the unintended effect of expanding the volume of the curb, in Lin Village the formal financial institutions have always been captured by local political elites who are not especially adept at business (cf. Adams et al., 1984; Otero and Rhyne, 1994). The vast majority of commercially successful operations in Lin Village have relied on informal financing mechanisms that do not involve the first branch of Lins. This is typical of China's private sector as a whole. As of year-end 2003, less than 1 per cent of all loans extended by state banks were going to private entrepreneurs (PBC, 2004). Hence, even though there is political and economic segmentation at the local level, the expansion of informal finance in China is largely attributable to the limited supply of formal credit to the non-state sector.

Conclusion

The enduring popularity of informal finance in rural China and India may be traced to a number of complementary factors: First, formal financial institutions and microfinance programmes are often unable to meet the demand for grass-roots credit. But, merely increasing the availability of official credit may not reach the targeted population because it still needs to be disbursed in some manner. Even if the supply of official credit were sufficient, credit officers and poverty alleviation cadres charged with the task of extending loans to rural households often face local pressures and incentives for credit distribution that deviate from the original intentions of state authorities. This is especially the case when it comes to subsidised microfinance programmes because microloans are readily treated as political patronage. Meanwhile, curb market operators at the grass-roots level generally have a comparative advantage in serving rural households because they possess better knowledge about local market actors and conditions.

This is not to say, however, that informal finance trumps formal finance in either economic or normative terms, but rather, that top–down efforts at rural financial intermediation are not likely to achieve their objectives if they are not structured in a sustainable manner and implemented properly. It is no wonder that subsidised PA programmes have low repayment rates when the loans are presented as developmental side-payments. MFIs that charge sustainable interest rates, on the other hand, tend to have higher repayment rates; and while reliable estimates of repayment rates in the curb are not available, it is probably safe to say that most informal financiers face hard budget constraints. While the constant threat of bankruptcy looms over the curb, the potential promise of additional subsidies fuels targeted microcredit. That is why informal finance and microfinance are imperfect substitutes. Rather than crowding out informal finance, the infusion of public and donor funds into microfinance adds another discrete source of credit in local markets. As seen in the Chandahar case, the establishment of a village bank enabled pawnbrokers to expand their role as financial intermediaries to local populations in the Scheduled Tribe and Scheduled Caste lists. Meanwhile, the Lin Village case demonstrated that from the perspective of borrowers with lower political status, formal sector credit is actually more expensive to them than the curb. Informal and formal sources of finance are not necessarily in competition with one another because they serve different segments of local society.

Analytically, if we accept that local-level political and economic dynamics fundamentally mediate developmental outcomes, then it makes sense to transcend the conventional state–society dichotomy by disaggregating both state and society. Just as local state agents may subvert central state objectives, different segments of society may be at odds with one another. Recognising the complexity of grass-roots segmentation ultimately has implications for the local distribution of both governmental and non-governmental sources of finance. Commercial bank credit, subsidised loans, microfinance facilities and curb market financing all entail a mix of social, political and economic incentives that are contingent on local context. Only when microfinance programmes are structured according to local needs and aimed at cost recovery will microfinance hold greater potential for displacing usurious forms of informal finance.

Notes

1. Reprinted from Tsai, Kellee S. 2004. 'Imperfect Substitutes: The Local Political Economy of Informal Finance and Microfinance in Rural China and India', *World Development*, 32 9: 1487–1507, Copyright (2004), with permission from Elsevier. Earlier versions of this chapter were presented at the Workshop on 'Local Governance in India and China: Rural Development and Social Change', Kolkata, 6–8 January 2003 and the Duke University Comparative Politics Workshop, 24 February 2003. The chapter benefited greatly from the constructive input of the workshop participants. I am also grateful for the insights of Richard Baum, Anirudh Krishna, Laura Locker, Eddie Malesky, Mark Selden, Suman Sureshbabu, Sarah Tsien, Fei-ling Wang, Steven Wilkinson, David Zweig and four anonymous reviewers. They are, of course, absolved from the article's inadequacies. Financial support from the Ford Foundation Public Policy Grant Competition is gratefully acknowledged.

2. Useful compilation of the debates include Bouman and Hospes (1994) and Hoff et al. (1993).

3. By definition, informal finance refers to financial flows that occur beyond the scope of a particular country's formal financial system of banks, non-banking financial institutions and officially sanctioned capital markets. Most countries, however, also have a range of financial intermediaries that are best described as *semi-formal* because central banking authorities do not regard them as part of the formal financial system, but they may be approved by some government agency or entity. In India and China, the definitional boundaries among informal, semi-formal and formal finance have shifted due to changes in their political, macroeconomic and regulatory environments. Furthermore, each of the categories encompasses a wide range of different financing mechanisms. In this article, *formal finance* comprises not only conventional banking and financial institutions, but also officially sanctioned *microfinance* programmes, which include both subsidised and unsubsidised programmes, as well as state-sponsored and NGO-led programmes. *Informal* and *semi-formal* finance will generally be discussed together because both fall beyond the scope of standard commercial and developmental/policy-oriented financial institutions. As the chapter discusses, many forms of informal finance are subject to regulation in India, while most forms of informal finance are simply banned in China.

4. RRBs represent a hybrid between cooperatives and commercial banks; they were established specifically to serve impoverished farmers, labourers, and microentrepreneurs in rural areas.

5. By 1999 India had a total of 140,000 branches of various rural credit facilities, which is equivalent to one formal financial institution per 5,600 rural citizens (Sinha, 2000: 66).

6. In 1984 the responsibility for RCCs shifted from the PBC to the ABC. Also, the Agricultural Development Bank was established in December 1993 to handle the policy lending functions of the ABC so that the latter could devote itself to commercial banking activities.

7. During 1978–98, US$ 1 ranged from Rs 8.2 to 41.3. The conversion for Rs 250 billion is based on an annual average rate of 20.3 over that period. The figure includes repeat assistance to the same families.

8. Especially during the 1980s, nationalised banks had periodic loan *melas*, which entailed extending massive quantities of subsidised loans to targeted sectors of society without regard for their creditworthiness.

9. When it comes to subsidised loans for state-owned enterprises or collectives that employ large numbers of people, the argument could be made that propping them up has local employment and therefore, welfare implications; but in the development field, microfinance refers specifically to loans that are extended to individual, small business owners rather than larger scale corporations that have larger capital requirements.

10. Note that the participating 'banks' include commercial banks, RRBs and cooperatives. For additional information about SHGs and what is known as the 'new microfinance', see Bansal (2003), Satish (2001) and Wilson (2002).

11. For a comparison of the performance of NGO, joint NGO-government, and purely government-run microfinance programmes in China, see Park and Ren (2001).

12. Citibank has committed US$ 1.3 million to FPC via Grameen Trust for expansion (*Xinhua* 19 November 2002).

13. For a list of microfinance projects supported by international donors, see China Development Brief (1999).

14. NGO participants said they were willing to pay up to 32.6 per cent in annual interest, while participants in government-run PA programmes were willing to pay up to 21.4 per cent annually and those in mixed NGO-government programmes were willing to pay up to 20.2 per cent (Park and Ren, 2001: 45).

15. The survey found 39.6 per cent of rural households relied on 'non-institutional credit agencies' RBI (2000: Table 5).

16. Note that 'high' interest rates are defined as rates that exceed the interest rate ceilings in China and the anti-usury laws in India. These limits are in the range of 10–12 per cent year for China and 24 per cent year for India.

17. They are 'legal' to the extent that they have not been banned explicitly.

18. China Minsheng Banking Corporation was established by the All-China Federation of Industry and Commerce in February 1996. In November 2000, it went public by issuing 350 million A shares on the Shanghai Stock Exchange.

19. Communist-era references to pawnshops in imperial China condemned them as an expression of class-based exploitation. For example, Xin (1993).

20. For example, pawnshops in Xingtai, Hebei offered annual interest of 40 per cent to its depositors in 1991 (Xin, 1993). A more recent study found that some pawnshops charge monthly interest rates between 5 per cent and 8 per cent (that is, up to 72 per cent interest annually), which is how they are able to offer depositors such high rates of return (*China Online* 9 September 1999).

21. The rectification effort was not entirely effective, however. The PBC issued additional regulations throughout the late 1990s to standardise their operations and reiterate prohibitions against charging/offering high interest rates—again, to limited avail in implementation.

22. Many non-borrowing and borrowing lenders probably do not comply with the various acts. Moreover, informal moneylenders fall beyond the scope of regulation. I thank one of the anonymous reviewers for pointing this out.

23. In pre-colonial and colonial India, Multanis, Gujarati Shroffs, Marwaris, Nattukottai Chettiars and Kallindaikurichy Brahmins represented the most prominent indigenous bankers. During the late colonial period, many invested in industry and commerce (cf. Bagchi, 1972).

24. Of course, formal and informal sector loans do not have similar lending methodologies (in terms of size, length, repayment schedule, collateral requirements, etc.). But this section of the chapter only focuses on the actual financial cost of formal versus informal credit to examine the issues of access to and demand for credit, *ceteris paribus*.

25. This phenomenon is not specific to India or China (Adams et al., 1984; Otero and Rhyne, 1994).

26. The local case study from India—'Chandrapur Village' in South Rajasthan—was included in a larger project on microfinance in general. The local case study from China—'Lin Village' in Wenzhou, Zhejiang—was part of a project on informal finance and rural industrialisation in Wenzhou.

27. The US dollar equivalent of the Indian Rupee went from Rs 9.8 per US$ 1 in 1982–83 to Rs 15.1 in 1988–89.

28. Note, however, that the village bank accounted for 80 per cent of the total loan volume.

29. 'Lin Village' is a pseudonym. This case is based on fieldwork in Wenzhou, Zhejiang Province, 2000–01.
30. During my visit in 2001, faded slogans from that period could still be seen from the wooden beams. The thought-reformed family was permitted to return to their home in 1963, but as might be expected, during the Cultural Revolution much of the intricate artwork along the entryway, roof, windows and walls was destroyed or damaged.
31. Lin Village is 'all mountains and water', as the locals put it.

References

Adams, D.W., D. Graham, and J.D. von Pischke. 1984. *Undermining rural development with cheap credit.* Boulder: Westview Press.

Agricultural Finance Corporation (AFC). 1988. *Agricultural credit review: Role and effectiveness of lending institutions* (Vol. V). Bombay: AFC.

Ashe, J. 2002. *Self-help groups and integral human development.* Waltham, MA: Brandeis University/ Catholic Relief Services.

Bagchi, A.K. 1972. *Private investment in India: 1900–1939.* Cambridge: Cambridge University Press.

Bansal, H. 2003. 'SHG-bank linkage program in India: An overview', *Journal of Microfinance*, 5(1), 21–19.

Bell, C. 1990. 'Interactions between institutional and informal credit agencies in rural India', *The World Bank Economic Review*, 4 (3): 297–327.

Bhatt, N. and Y.S.P. Thorat. 2001. 'India's regional rural banks: The institutional dimension of reforms', *Journal of Microfinance*, 3 (1): 65–94.

Bornstein, D. 1997. *The price of a dream: The story of the Grameen bank.* Chicago: University of Chicago.

Bouman, F.J.A. and O. Hospes (eds). 1994. *Financial landscapes reconstructed: The fine art of mapping development.* Boulder: Westview Press.

Bouman, F.J.A., R. Bastiaansen, H. Van Den Bogaard, H. Gerner, O. Hospes and J.G. Kormelink. 1989. *Small, short, and unsecured: Informal rural finance in India.* New York: Oxford University Press.

Chandavarkar, A. 1992. 'Of finance and development: Neglected and unsettled questions', *World Development*, 20 (1): 133–42.

Cheng, E. 2003. 'Microfinance in rural China', in C. Findlay, A. Watson, E. cheng and G. Zhu (eds), *Rural financial markets in China*, pp. 120–133. Canberra: Asia Pacific Press at the Australia National University.

Cheng, E., C. Findaly and A. Watson. 1998. We're not financial organisations!: Financial innovation without regulation in China's rural cooperative funds, *MOCT-MOST: Economic Policy in Transition Economies*, 8 (3): 41–55.

China Development Brief. 1999. 2, p. 2.

Conroy, J.D. 2000. 'People's Republic of China', in ADB (ed.), *The role of central banks in Asia and the Pacific.* Manila: ADB.

Das-Gupta, A., C.P.S. Nayar and Associates. 1989. *Urban informal credit markets in India.* New Delhi: National Institute of Public Finance and Policy.

Du, X.S. 2003. Author's correspondence, 8 May 2003.

Du, Z.X. 1998. *The dynamics and impact of the development of rural cooperative funds (RCFs) in China.* Working Paper No. 98/2. Chinese Economies Research Centre, The University of Adelaide, March.

EDA Rural Systems. 1996. *India: Microfinance for the poor: An assessment of the status and efficacy of microfinance institutions and programmes.* Study prepared for the Asian and Pacific Development Centre, Kuala Lumpur.

Evans, P., D. Reuschemeyer and T. Skocpol (eds). 1985. *Bringing the state back in.* New York: Cambridge University Press.

Ghate, P., A. Das-Gupta, M. Lamberte, N. Poapongsakorn, D. Prabowo, A. Rahman and T.N. Srinivasan. 1992. *Informal finance: Some findings from Asia.* Manila: Asian Development Bank, Oxford University Press.

Hannig, A. and E. Katimbo-Mugwanya (eds). 1999. *How to regulate and supervise microfinance? Key issues in an international perspective.* Proceedings of the High-Level Policy Workshop, Kampala.

Hoff, K. and J. Stiglitz. 1990. 'Imperfect information and rural credit markets: Puzzles and policy perspectives', *The World Bank Economic Review,* 4 (3): 235–50.

Hoff, K., A. Braverman and J. Stiglitz (eds). 1993. *The economics of rural organisation: Theory, practice, and policy.* New York: Oxford University Press for the World Bank.

Holcombe, S. 1995. *Managing to empower: The Grameen bank experience of poverty alleviation.* London: Zed Books.

Holz, C.A. 2001. China's monetary reform: The counterrevolution from the countryside, *Journal of Contemporary China,* 20 (27): 189–217.

Hsiao, K.H. 1971. *Money and monetary policy in communist China.* New York: Columbia University Press.

International Fund for Agricultural Development (IFAD). 2001. *People's Republic of China: Thematic study on rural financial services in China.* Rome, Italy. Available: http://www.ifad.org/evaluation/public_html/eksyst/doc/thematic/pi/cn/cn_1.htm#2.

Jones, J.H.M. 1994. 'A changing financial landscape in India: Macro-level and micro-level perspectives', in F.J.A. Bouman and O. Hospes (eds), *Financial landscapes reconstructed: The fine art of mapping development.* Boulder: Westview Press.

Khandker, S.R., B. Khalily and Z. Khan. 1995. *Grameen bank: Performance and sustainability.* World Bank Discussion Paper No. 306. Washington, DC: The World Bank.

Li, M.Y. 2000. 'Diandangye: "jinzi zhaopai" xiexia qianhou' (Pawnshops: Future after removing the 'gold store sign'), *Hexun caijing* (Homeway Financial News), October.

Migdal, J.S., A. Kohli and V. Shue. 1994. *State Power and Social Forces: Domination and Transformation in the Third World.* New York: Cambridge University Press.

Morduch, J. 2000. The microfinance schism. *World Development,* 28 (4): 617–29.

Nagarajan, G. and R.L. Meyer. 2000. *Rural financial markets in Asia: Paradigms, policies, and performance.* Manila: ADB.

National Bank for Agriculture and Rural Development (NABARD). 2002. *Ten years of SHG-bank linkage (1992–2002).* Mumbai: NABARD.

———. 2003. Regional spread of SHGs as on 31 March 2003. Available: http://www.nabard.org/oper/oper.htm.

Nayar, C.P.S. 1992. 'Strengths of informal financial institutions: Examples from India', in D.W. Adams and D.A. Fitchett (eds), *Informal finance in low-income countries,* pp. 199–200. Boulder: Westview.

Otero, M. and E. Rhyne (eds). 1994. *The new world of microenterprise finance.* West Hartford, CT: Kumarian Press.

Park, A. 1999. 'Banking for the poor', *China Brief,* II(2), 9–15.

Park, A., L. Brandt and J. Giles. 2003. 'Competition under credit rationing: Theory and evidence from rural China', *Journal of Development Economics,* 71 (2): 463–95.

Park, A. and C. Ren. 2001. 'Microfinance with Chinese characteristics', *World Development,* 29 (1): 39–62.

Patrick, H.T. 1966. 'Financial development and economic growth in developing countries', *Economic and Cultural Change*, 14 (2): 174–89.

People's Bank of China (PBC). 2004. Financial industry's performance was stable in 2003. Available: http://www.pbc.gov.cn, January 15.

Press Information Bureau (PIB). (2002). Government of India. Export group on Nihdis recommends continuation of regulatory measures. Available: <http://pib.nic.in/archieve/lreleng/lyr2002/rmar2002/22032002/r220320022.html>, March 22.

Reserve Bank of India (RBI). 1954. *All-India credit survey*. Bombay: RBI.

———. 2000. All-India debt and investment survey (AIDIS). 1991–92—Incidence of indebtedness of households, Part I. *RBI Bulletin*. Available: http://www.rbi.org.in, 8 February.

Rozelle, S., A. Park, C. Ren and V. Bezinger. 1998. 'Targeted poverty investments and economic growth in China', *World Development*, 26 (12): 2137–151.

Rutherford, S. and S.S. Arora. 1997. *City savers*. New Delhi: Department for International Development.

Saich, T. 2000. 'Negotiating the state: The development of social organizations in China', *The China Quarterly*, 161, 124–41.

Satish, P. 2001. 'Institutional alternatives for the promotion of microfinance: Self-help groups in India', *Journal of Microfinance*, 3 (2): 49–74.

Schrader, H. 1994. 'Moneylenders and merchant bankers in India and Indonesia', in F.J.A. Bouman and O. Hospes (eds), *Financial landscapes reconstructed: The fine art of mapping development*, pp. 341–55. Boulder: Westview Press.

Selden, M. and E. Perry (eds). 2000. *Chinese society: Conflict, change, and resistance*. London: Routledge.

Sinha, S. 2000. 'India', in *The role of central banks in microfinance in Asia and the Pacific: Country studies: Vol. 2. Asian Development Bank*, pp. 61–89. Manila: ADB.

Swain, R.B. 2002. 'Credit rationing in rural India', *Journal of Economic Development*, 27 (2): 1–20.

Tsai, K.S. 2000. 'Banquet banking: Rotating savings and credit association in South China', *The China Quarterly*, 161, 143–70.

———. 2002. *Back-alley banking: Private entrepreneurs in China*. Ithaca: Cornell University Press.

Tsai, L.L. 2002. 'Cadres, temple and lineage institutions', *The China Journal*, 48, 1–27.

Tsien, S. 2001. 'International projects left in the lurch as government weighs in,' *China Development Brief*, 4 (1).

Unger, J. 2002. *The transformation of rural China*. Armonk: M.E. Sharpe.

Walder, A. and J. Oi (eds). 1999. *Property rights and economic reform in China*. Stanford: Stanford University Press.

Watson, A. 2003. 'Financing farmers: The reform of rural credit cooperatives and provision of financial services to farmers', in C. Findlay, A. Watson, E. Cheng and Z. Gang (eds), *Rural financial markets in China*, pp. 63–88. Canberra: Asia Pacific Press at The Australia National University.

Whiting, S. 2001. *Power and wealth in rural China: The political economy of institutional change*. New York: Cambridge University Press.

Wilson, K. 2002. 'The new microfinance: An essay on the self-help group movement in India', *Journal of Microfinance*, 4 (2): 217–45.

Wu, J.M. 1998. Local property rights regime in socialist reform: A case study of China's informal privatization, Unpublished doctoral dissertation, New York, Columbia University.

Xin, J. 1993. *Diandang shi* (History of pawnshops). Shanghai: Shanghai wenyi chubanshe.

Yaron, J., M.P. Benjamin Jr. and G.L. Piprek. 1997. 'Rural finance: Issues, design, and best practices', *Environmentally and socially sustainable development studies & monographs series* (Vol. 13). Washington, DC: The World Bank.

Zhongguo yinhang Beijing guoji jinrong yanjiusuo (BOC Beijing Institute of International Finance). 1993. *Zhongguo de jinrong jigou jiqi zhuyao jingying* (China's financial institutions and their primary management). Beijing: Zhongguo jihua chubanshe.

News Sources

Agence France Presse (AFP).
Associated Press (AP).
China Daily.
China Internet Information Centre (CIIC).
China Online.
Jingji ribao (JJRB—Economic Daily).
People's Daily (*PD*).
Shanghai Information Centre (SIC).
Xinhua.

Further Reading

Adams, D.W. and D.A. Fitchett (eds). 1992. *Informal Finance in Low-income Countries*. Boulder: Westview Press.
Asian Development Bank (ADB). 2000. *The Role of Central Banks in Asia and the Pacific*. Manila: ADB.

11 Stratification and Institutional Exclusion in China and India
Administrative Means versus Social Barriers[1]

FEI-LING WANG

A Tale of Two Nations

As the two most populous nations in the world, China and India indeed share much in common: Both are large and densely inhabited; both have a long history and are rich in culture and tradition; both had a backward economy and low technology development when they acquired modern statehood in the twentieth century; both are featured with a typical dual economy with massive or even 'unlimited' supply of low- and unskilled labour from the agricultural sector; and both are inspired and competing with each other to be a world class power and leader.[2]

Yet, there are also many differences that set the two nations apart. Created from the remains of the British colonial rule, India has had a functioning, however limited and criticised, political democracy for over half a century while China for the same period of time has been under an one-party authoritarian regime. China is largely a homogenous nation with over 92 per cent of its population belonging to the same ethnic group of Han, whereas India displays one of the most complicated, diversified and conflicting racial and ethnic collections in the world.[3] By the early twenty-first century, China appears to have achieved a significantly higher economic growth than India[4] (Table 11.1). Even the widely mentioned 'socialist' state of Kerala in southern India, which has had impressive achievements in areas of women's literacy campaigns, rural medical programmes and family planning, has not been an impressive model of successful economic growth or technological sophistication.[5]

It may be practically fruitful and intellectually stimulating to compare China and India for a study on any subject in social sciences and humanities. Just the issue of the seemingly puzzling relationship between political systems and economic growth in the two nations would easily sustain a whole enterprise of scholarship. Yet the linguistic and logistic difficulties and the immensity of conducting a comparative field study in both countries would make any in-depth comparative study of the two nations too daunting a task to be carried out in one single paper. Nevertheless, this chapter, utilising an analytical framework of institutional exclusion, will attempt to examine one

Table 11.1
India and China: A Comparative Report Card

	India	China	Developing Nations
Size (1,000 square km)	328.8	959.7	–
Population (million, in 1975)	620.7	927.8	2,898.3
In 1999	1,000.8	1,264.8	4,609.8
In 2015 (projected)	1,230.5	1,410.2	5,759.1
Annual growth rate (1975–99)	2.0%	1.3%	1.9%
Urban population (1999)	28.1%	26.1–33.8 %	38.9%
Urban population (1988)	27%	18.7 %	23%
Administrative units	25 states & 7 territories	31 provincial units	–
Languages	14 official	1 official	–
GDP (by PPP method, billion US$)	2,242	4,534.9	16,201.9
Annual growth rate (1975–99)	3.2%	8.1%	2.3%
Annual growth rate (1990–99)	4.2%	9.5%	3.2%
Per capita GDP (PPP, 1999)	$ 2,248	$ 3,617	$ 3,530
Export (1999, million US$)	37,598	194,931	–
Import (1999, million US$)	47,212	165,699	–
Trade balance (1999, million US$)	–9,614	29,232	
Export/GDP in 1990	7%	18%	26%
Export/GDP in 1999	12%	22%	29%
Hi-tech import/export (1999)[i]	16.6%	39%	–
Foreign direct investment/GDP (1999)	0.5%	3.9%	2.9%
Foreign exchange reserve (1999–2000)[ii]	$ 35.1 billion	$ 161.4 billion	
Annual inflation rate (1999–2000)	4.7%	–3%	
Inequality (Gini Index)[iii]	37.8	40.3 (29.3)	–
Human development index/rank (2001)	0.571/No. 115	0.718/No. 87	0.647/Nos. 49–162
Human development index/rank (1990)	0.439/No. 93	0.716/No. 64	–/Nos. 46–130
Technology achievement index (rank)	0.201 (number 63)	0.299 (number 45)	–
Gender development index/rank (1999)	Number 105	Number 76	
k-9th grade school enrollment	56%	73%	61%
People live under poverty line	35–44.2%	4.6–18.5%	–
Physicians (per 100,000 people)	48	162	–
Life expectancy (years)	62.9	70.2	64.5

(Table 11.1 contd.)

(*Table 11.1 contd.*)

	India	China	Developing Nations
Infant mortality rate (per 1,000 births)	70	33	61
Underweight children at age 5	53%	10%	–
Undernourished people	21%	11%	18%
Adult literacy rate	56.5%	83.5%	72.9%
Per capita electricity use (kw, 1998)	384	746	757
Subjective happiness index[iv]	72/100	78/100	62–77/100
Political system	democracy	one-party authoritarianism	
Military expenditure/GDP (1999)	2.4%	2.1%	–
International status	strong regional power	weak world power	

Sources: MPS 2001; Interview with Li Yining in 2001; EIU (2001, 65–74); RBI (2001, Tables 113 & 140); SSB (2001, 4); UNDP (1990, 128–43); UNDP (2001, 48–54, 142–212); World Bank (2001).

Notes:
    i. China was number 10 of the world's top 30 high-tech goods exporters in 1999 and India was not on the list.
    ii. China has been the second largest foreign exchange reserve holder (after Japan) and second largest FDI recipient (after the US) in the world since 1997.
    iii. 0 = perfect equality and 100 = perfect inequality. China's value (40.3) is the aggregate national Geni Index. The value inside the prentices (29.3) is perhaps the more accurate and applicable sectorial Geni Indices, separately calculated for the urban and rural residents in China's clear-cut dual economy.
    iv. Inglehart and Klingemann (2000). As a reference, the US has a subjective happiness index of 89/100 and Spain 79/100.

aspect of the Chinese and Indian political economy and propose one more factor that may have accounted for the different record of economic growth in China and India: how the two peoples are divided and organised internally. I will describe that, in addition to the 'universal' division between the haves and the have-nots, based on money, the Chinese and the Indians are also divided, excluded and organised along their own peculiar but profound fault lines respectively. Whereas the 1.3 billion Chinese are divided into exclusive segments by the administratively maintained PRC hukou (household or residential registration) system, the one billion Indians appear to be largely segmented and stratified by the societally-enforced caste system.

    The PRC hukou system can be viewed as a continuation of an ancient Chinese institution, the imperial hukou system. But it is qualitatively different in that it is unprecedentedly divisive and exclusive, extensive and rigid and consequential and hence a full-bloom institutional exclusion based on the officially recognised and determined criterion of *where you are*.[6] The Indian caste system is also a continuation of an ancient institution. Despite the fact that it became illegal over half century ago and there have been concerted efforts demolishing it, it continues to play great roles in the Indian political economy as a powerful institutional exclusion to organise through dividing and excluding people based on the socially and traditionally determined criterion of *who you are*.[7]

The impact of these peculiar Chinese and Indian ways of stratification and exclusion is very significant. Facing a roughly same challenge of passing the so-called 'Lewis Transition' to develop their economies in a dual economy featuring massive, even 'unlimited', supply of low and unskilled labour, China and India have scored differently in economic growth. I suggest that much of these differences results from the particular consequences of the different types of institutional exclusion China and India have had, in addition to the money-based institutional divide.

In the following pages, I will first briefly present a theory of institutional exclusion, especially the typology and impact of institutional exclusion. I will focus on a description of the peculiar Chinese way of institutional exclusion, the PRC hukou system. Then I will briefly sketch the Indian style of institutional exclusion, the caste system. Finally, I will make a comparative analysis and attempt to draw some conclusions. The hukou-based administrative control and the caste-based social barriers constituted to the peculiar conditions in which local governance and grass-roots democracy take place in China and India. A great trade-off is observable in the two countries: while the Chinese economy has been growing impressively, its local governance is still largely an exclusive domain of the ruling Communist Party and its agents and grass-roots level democracy is still creeping at the low level of villages. The Indian economy has shown a somewhat slower pace, but it has had a long record of local self-governance based on significant development of grass-roots democracy that features the prominent role of existing social groups and even the participation of lower-class people. In the long run, the Indian socio-political structure may be able to deliver a more sustained and more balanced economic growth (Huang and Khanna, 2003).

A Theory of Institutional Exclusion

Nations are all divided and organised at the same time and each nation is divided and then organised in its own different ways. Institutional division, stratification and exclusion are the standard statecrafts employed by all states to organise their people and rule. Different types of institutional division and exclusion, however, set the nations and states apart in their degrees of governing effectiveness, individual rights and mobility, and their overall records of achievements and performance.

Institutional exclusion refers to this fundamental fact of any human group: people are divided and then organised into hierarchical layers and horizontally coexisting but separated sub-groups.[8] The concept of institutional exclusion is comparable to the neo-Weberian sociological notion of 'social closure' that describes human stratification systems based on various fault lines (property, age, gender, ethnicity and educational credentials or skills) in a society. It also engages the rich literature on citizenship or membership.[9] Indeed, on the most fundamental level, citizenship and membership represent a formal and lasting form of institutional exclusion. All human groupings first identify their members and treat their own more or less equally but 'others' (outsiders or the excluded) with great differentiation. I go further by suggesting that within any nation, institutional exclusion necessarily and constantly exists to divide the same citizenry along various fault lines.

There is always an important fault line in any nation that is both divided and organised: A divide between those who are 'in' or having 'access to institutions that provide capacities and resources'[10] as well as information, and those who are 'out' or excluded from these institutionalised provisions.[11] Although life chances based on the distribution of capacities, resources and information that enables and improves human life may be affected by many non-uniform but important factors such as genetics, one human grouping (a nation in particular) must by definition have some more or less uniform and even centralised way of such division and exclusion to ensure the cohesion and viability of that grouping. The unevenly distributed capacities and resources, in turn, ultimately shape the people's sense of ranking and belonging hence forming the social and normative fabric that separates and divides everyone while linking and organising everyone all at the same time.

Primarily determined by its foundation, institutional exclusion in different human grouping and at different times can present itself very differently, producing different socio-political and economic consequences. We can easily identify the various institutional exclusions in history that were based on family rankings and lineage (the nobles versus the commoners and the various caste systems), race and ethnicity (various forms of racial and ethnic exclusion and discrimination), citizenship (fellow countrymen versus foreigners), political power (the rulers and the ruled), legality (law-abiding citizens versus outlaws and criminals), religion (the 'chosen' versus the barbarians), economic power (the rich/the haves versus the poor/the have-nots), gender (various forms of sexual discrimination),[12] linguistic and cultural differences ('Western' versus 'Eastern', for example), group association (party versus non-party members), personal skills (the educated versus the uneducated) and locational differences (community members versus outsiders). Some of these differences and dividing lines are real while many could be merely perceptional or indoctrinated. These fault lines could grow 'naturally' such as genetic characteristics, but are often created by political power that can be formed with the use of sheer force (as in the cases of war or a coup d'état) or the counting of votes (as in the case of a functional democracy).

Few societies, however, are stratified by only one fault line.[13] But in a given nation, its institutional exclusion is primarily based on one leading fault line, usually assisted by other types of less important but possibly significant differentiations and separations. Different types of institutional exclusion, although they basically perform the same roles of dividing and organising people and prioritising resource allocation, naturally have different effectiveness and legitimacy. For example, as the acceptance of property right-centred (economically-based) institutional exclusion grew after the end of the Cold War,[14] we see that gender, race or ethnicity-based institutional exclusions are increasingly becoming illegitimate and hence ineffective around the world.

The varied effectiveness and consequences of institutional exclusion in different settings and times stem from the varied bases on which it is built and the different ways in which it is enforced. By and large, there are four major types of institutional exclusion, defined by their different bases. (See Table 11.2) Type One is in which people are divided and excluded because of *who you are* in terms of their racial, ethnic, linguistic, sexual and religious differences. Under Type Two, people are divided and excluded based on *what you have* regarding their resource/property-ownership and skills. Type Three allows people be divided and excluded based on *where you are* in regard to their family associations and their physical location or birthplace. Type Four divides and excludes people based *what you did/do* or their individual work and behaviour.[15]

In short, institutional exclusion, often centres around one leading fault line and is usually assisted by other differences, divides and organises the people in any given nation. It performs very important roles in constructing and maintaining socio-political order and stability, formulating and allocating capital and other economic resources thus directly impacting economic development, affecting everyone's sense and position of rank and belonging hence determining population mobility and social stratification in a nation. Various types of institutional exclusion have varied degrees of effectiveness, legitimacy, flexibility and endurance. As a result, every sizeable human grouping must have excluded segments of its population for its polity to function, for its economy to develop and for its society to be stable. For example, humans have been long accustomed to the obvious inevitability and necessity of punishing some of their own through exclusion (imprisonment), discrimination (public humiliation and fines) and even elimination (execution) to maintain law and order. The normative question, therefore, is not how to

Table 11.2
A Typology of Institutional Exclusion

Types	One	Two	Three	Four
Discrimination & exclusion based on	Who you are	What you have	Where you are	What you do/did
Chief enforcer	state &/or society	state & society	state & society	state & society
Stability	high	low	adjustable	adjustable
Rigidity	high	low	adjustable	adjustable
Legitimacy today	low	high	low	high
Effectiveness today	generally low	high	can be high	can be high
Leading impact	racial/religious biases	classes	regional gaps	job/record biases
Restriction on internal migration	medium	medium/low	high	Medium/low
Example	caste in India	money in US	hukou in China	criminal justice systems

eliminate institutional exclusions but rather how to minimise the size and the sufferings of the excluded. Namely, the central questions appear to be what types of institutional exclusions are to be established and how they are enforced.

Implications of Institutional Exclusion in Developing Nations

Institutional exclusion is inevitable in every nation. It is very consequential to a nation's political stability, economic growth, social development and individual rights. Ethically, however, institutional exclusion produces troubling questions about equity and equality of human rights and civil rights of the citizens of the nation. Geographically-based horizontal stratification may even harm national unity over the long run. Furthermore, a society's creativity and ingenuity may be discouraged and even hindered by institutional exclusion since it reduces people' horizontal and vertical mobility that usually lead to the flourishing of exchange and competition of new ideas. In this chapter, I will only focus on the role and functions institutional exclusion may play in the economic development and urbanisation in those 'latecomer' developing nations that are commonly featured with a dual economy such as my chosen cases: China and India.[16]

No government can rule without some type of effective institutional exclusion to divide and organise people. Institutional exclusion, however, creates conditions not particularly conducive for comprehensive democratic politics featuring mass participation in the political process. This is especially true in the case where there is a rigid institutional exclusion based on some inherent and immutable differentiation (such as race, ethnicity, or gender) of individuals and sub-groups. The only possible way democracy can survive in a nation featuring a rigid institutional exclusion is to have the so-called elite democracy where only a small group of people participate in and control the political process while keeping the excluded (slaves or women or the poor, for examples) out of the political arena. It may be further hypothesised here that, due to the inevitability and necessity of institutional exclusion in any society, all functional democracies are essentially elite democracies with varied sizes and flexibility of the ruling elite groups, especially at the beginning.[17] Conversely, to demand non-exclusive and massive political participation at the very time of creating a democratic regime may be fundamentally impractical and even counterproductive.

Economically, institutional exclusion services a key role in prioritising resource allocation and the formulation or accumulation of capital.[18] It enables the state, the ruling elite, or the able citizens to accumulate capital relatively quickly, from the delayed, decreased, or even denied consumption of the excluded.[19] It also allows for segregated experiments and a protected, 'trickle-down' or 'spill-over' process of development through both the forward and backward linkages of leading industries or sectors. Institutional exclusion, which may hinder population mobility and labour flows, does not necessarily affect economic growth negatively. On the contrary, institutional exclusion is often indispensable to economic growth, especially in a market-oriented fashion. The history of economic development is, and perhaps has to be, coloured with tears, sweat and even blood, mainly of those who were institutionally excluded.

Institutional exclusion may play a special role in the economic development of those latecomer developing nations, the so-called dual economies where there is a massive or even unlimited supply of low and unskilled labour from the 'traditional', agricultural, or backward sector.[20] Such nations, suggested development economics models, are likely to have their economic development doomed in the dual economy swamp. The existence of a massive surplus of labour constitutes a key obstacle to a meaningful economic take-off.[21] Unless and until enough industrial jobs, with above-subsistence level wages, are quickly created, which requires immense investment, modern technology and new market—all of which are naturally and perpetually in short supply in these developing nations—to absorb and transform enough surplus labour with a zero or near zero marginal productivity out of the agricultural sector to turn the overall supply of labour from being unlimited or near unlimited to a normal market-regulated scarcity, the developing nations can only expect a stagnated economic growth and associated chronicle poverty and backwardness. The unlimited supply or inflow of low and unskilled labour drives the wages down to the subsistence level and the capital hard to accumulate and easy to fly, while creating problems of urban poverty, political tension and social decay. To absorb this 'surplus labour' becomes the key transition, the so-called Lewis Transition, for a dual economy to complete in order to grow out of backwardness and poverty.[22]

A jeopardy is thus formed. To quickly accumulate massive capital and to invest it to industrialise the economy becomes the key to the development of the latecomer nations, which, on the one hand, need to quickly employ the seemingly endless low or unskilled labour in an era of market economy, modern consumerism, mass mobility and equal human rights. On the other hand, these latecomer nations are usually poor and powerless on the international financial market where they only have access to a very small share of world's capital resources. Furthermore, these latecomer nations could not repeat the old story of emigrating the 'surplus' labourers like the early-industrialised nations in Europe. Indeed, after centuries of colonisation and the decolonisation in the late twentieth century, massive overseas emigration has become a thing of the past. For example, a nation of 1.3 billion and with an estimated over 140–240 million 'surplus' labourers, China now emigrates only 100,000–180,000 people a year to other countries, and 20 per cent of the emigrants are already the so-called 'illegal immigrants' who paid between $ 10,000 and $ 60,000 per head to smuggle themselves to other countries.[23]

Too many developing nations, indeed, seem to have been held up by this hopeless dual economy swamp for decades and even indefinitely. A commonly seen 'free' or uncontrolled internal migration of rural and unskilled labour to the cities tends to be enormous but often highly irrational and inefficient.[24] The massive migrant new workers in the modern sector (the cities) commonly end up in the crowded slums, earning subsistence wages indefinitely (Lewis, 1954: 193–96). They also bring down the wages of the original urban workers and often diminish profits of investors as well due to the increased pressure for more public spending funded by new taxation. At the same time, the farms neglected by the able migrants are unlikely to yield any higher income for the remaining villagers. The motivation and energy for economic growth hence are depleted since, as Lewis argued, that '*the possibility of higher individual earnings is the fuel of economic growth*' (Lewis, 1966: 273, emphasis in the original).

A stable and effective institutional exclusion may provide remedies, at the expense of equality of human rights and civil rights of the excluded, to a dual economy to allow for an accelerated economic growth and technological development. By excluding the surplus labour from the industrial urban economy and affixing them to their home villages, institutional exclusion not only performs its traditional role of capital accumulation but also breaks the dual economy's vicious cycle of diminished income due to an unlimited supply of cheap labour. A market-oriented industrial sector can achieve a high rate of growth and rapid technological advancement to allow the nation to quickly engage the world market as a viable competitor (Meier, 1984: 156–58). The key, therefore, is how to effectively and efficiently maintain and justify the large income gap among the same citizenry without drowning the growing modern/urban sector under a sea of unskilled labour.

Indeed, many development economists have long argued for the need to have balanced, planned and even controlled economic development to avoid the perpetual economic 'retardation' many developing nations are suffering from. To control urbanisation has been viewed as a key. Lewis believes that the rural to urban migration should and can be restricted to prevent the dreadful 'excessive mobility of the population' and the number and size of urban centres should be limited to benefit the whole national economy (Lewis, 1954: 145, 429; 1966: 68–75). To simply rely on a market-driven and spontaneous urbanisation to pass the Lewis Transition is viewed as undesirable and irrational, hence 'more of the rural labor must be kept and absorbed in the rural areas, and the rural-to-urban migration must be curtailed' (Meier, 1984: 166).

A model of economic development assisted by institutional exclusion is by no means ideal or even fair, but realistically it may be the only way for a latecomer nation to accelerate its growth in the information age with a globally-integrated financial market, to break the vicious cycle of backwardness and to avoid being condemned as a permanently slow follower of the developed nations. Institutional exclusion, as long as it is effective and not too costly in terms of socio-political stability and national cohesion, will thus allow the developing nation to circumvent its Lewis Transition by temporarily neutralising the problem of an unlimited supply of unskilled labour. With the right kind of government (such as a so-called 'developmental state' or a 'hard' or 'strong' state[25]) and the right kind of policy, continued adjustment of the institutional exclusion may later facilitate the spillover and trickle-down effect of the developed 'in' sector, hence mitigating and even eradicating the dual economy problem at a much higher level. Namely, with a stable and effective institutional exclusion, a developing nation plagued by a dual economy structure can achieve rapid economic growth and high technological sophistication with sustained gains in real industrial or urban wages and delayed growth of non-agricultural employment, despite the existence of an unlimited supply of unskilled labour.

In a way, the economic impact of an effective institutional exclusion in latecomer nations may be viewed as something similar to the economic impact of the Westphalia international political system since the end of the Middle Ages. The political division of the 'sovereign' nations, the citizenship-based division of humankind and the exclusion of 'foreigners' maintained by the regulation and restriction of international migration have contributed indispensably to the development of the modern capitalist market economy that has brought unprecedented economic growth and technological sophistication in the included parts of the world, primarily today's OECD (Organisation of Economic Cooperation and Development) nations.[26] The world economy has developed spectacularly in the past few centuries, but an overwhelming majority (80 per cent in 2000) of humankind still lives in less developed poor nations, excluded from sharing most of the world's achievements and products. While the developed nations have achieved a per capita annual income of over $ 25,000, over half of the world's population (three billion in 2000) lives on an income of less than $ 3 a day (G8 Okinawa Summit, 2000: i; UNDP, 2001: 144, 157). Today, the uneven distribution of income, resources, information and opportunities between rich and poor nations, maintained primarily by the politically decided citizenship-based Type Three (*where you are*) institutional exclusion, is indeed among the greatest that humankind has ever seen.[27]

The Hukou System-based Institutional Exclusion in China

Today's Chinese institutional exclusion is largely associated with the PRC *hukou zhidu* (household or residential registration system) that was formally adopted nationally in the 1950s.[28] By itself, residential registration is not inherently a form of institutional exclusion. It becomes one when the registered people are treated differently according to the different categories and locations of their registrations; and when the registered are restricted in their cross-region migration. The PRC hukou system, which requires a registration of every citizen and controls the change of the location and type of one's registration, therefore, provides perhaps an ideal foundation for a Type Three (based on *where you are*) institutional exclusion to form.

The PRC hukou system gives every Chinese a geographically-defined location and an associated socio-political status and identity practically for life. People are treated differently according to their hukou-based location and identity in almost every aspect of their lives. This system not only regulates and restricts internal migration in a very unevenly developed nation, but also treats differently categorised people differently, culminating in its *zhongdian renkou* (focal or targeted people) management scheme.[29]

The hukou-based institutional exclusion in China has deep roots in the past that can be traced back centuries and even millennia. Yet the PRC hukou system is qualitatively different from the imperial hukou system and the ROC (Republic of China, 1911–49) hukou system since it reaches an unprecedented level of rigidity, effectiveness and comprehensiveness in its role and capacity of division and exclusion. The backing of a powerful authoritarian one-party government has been the key to the stability and effectiveness of the PRC hukou system in the past half century. The hukou system still enjoys a strong institutional legitimacy in China,[30] perhaps largely because familial and locational differentiation is perhaps more 'natural' and prevalent than most other human differentiations. Unlike the similar but now disgraced and disintegrated *propiska* (registration permit) system in the former Soviet Union, the PRC hukou system is both legal and strong. With only a few reform attempts and limited alterations, the hukou system continues to be the backbone of Chinese institutional structure and fundamentally contributes to the seemingly puzzling coexistence of China's rapidly developing market economy and the remarkable stability of the CCP's political monopoly.

As 'the central institutional mechanism defining the city–countryside relationship and shaping important elements of state–society relations in the People's Republic', the hukou system 'not only provided the principal basis for establishing identity, citizenship and proof of official status, it was essential for every aspect of daily life' (Cheng and Selden, 1994: 644). One Chinese scholar believes that the hukou system fundamentally touches and determines the life of every Chinese since it comprehensively collects data of every PRC citizen, identifies and stratifies individuals and regions, controls population movement and allocates resources and opportunities (Yu Depeng, 2002: 1–2).

The PRC hukou system requires that every Chinese citizen register with the hukou authority (the hukou police) at birth. The categories of non-agricultural (urban) or agricultural (rural), legal address and location and unit affiliation (employment) and a host of other personal and family information are documented and verified to become the person's permanent hukou record. A person's hukou location and categorisation or type were determined by his mother's hukou location and type rather than his birthplace until 1998, when a child was allowed to inherit the father's *or* mother's hukou location and categorisation. One cannot acquire a legal permanent residence and the numerous community-based rights, opportunities, benefits and privileges in places other than where his hukou is. Only through proper authorisation of the government can one change his hukou location and especially his hukou categorisation from the rural type to the urban type. Simple and rigid, the PRC hukou system has been enforced forcefully for five decades and has had a deep and extensive impact on the various aspects of the Chinese society. It is China's peculiar way of organising its huge population through institutionally dividing and excluding large segments of the people.

All institutional exclusions encounter resistances from the excluded. The hukou system is no exception. But the PRC hukou system draws its extraordinary institutional legitimacy, operational effectiveness and cultural support from not only the authoritarian state power but also from the Chinese family/ clan structure, regional and community divisions, the tradition of parochial political culture and the fact that a hukou system existed in China for a very long time before the PRC. Since its early days date back to at least the Warring States era (some 2,400 years ago), the hukou system has taken various forms and performed to varied extents its function of population management, taxation, mobilisation and social control during various dynasties and also in the Republic of China. The current form of the hukou system in the PRC, however, is the most extensively built, best maintained, most effective and most influential thus far. The size of the population it divides and organises, the power and rigidity of the system and the lasting legitimacy of it certainly makes the contemporary Chinese hukou system one of the best examples of institutional exclusion ever seen.

Consequently, for the most part of the PRC history, the majority of the Chinese population, the rural residents, have been the 'peacefully' excluded under the hukou system. The much smaller urban population (only 14–26 per cent of the total population) has had qualitatively much better access to economic and social opportunities, activities and benefits, and has also dominated Chinese politics. To a lesser extent, urban residents in smaller cities and in less developed regions have also been the excluded compared to those living in major urban centres or regions more favoured by the government in terms of investment, subsidies, or policy flexibilities.

Functionally, the PRC hukou system has been the leading tool for Beijing to control the population in two crucial ways: to regulate China's internal migration and to control the politically decided targeted (*zhongdian*) segments of the population. Migration from the excluded regions, especially the rural areas, to the 'in' areas, especially the major urban centres, has been strictly controlled and practically almost impossible. Thus, a classic case of dual economy and dual society has been developing in China for the past half century. In practice, not only a legal rural–urban duality exists in China; there is also the clear presence of a metropolitan–city–town multiplicity in China's unique socio-political, economic and cultural stratification that is both vertical and horizontal. Furthermore, the hukou system allows the police to focus on a constant monitoring and controlling of the selected most 'threatening' individuals and groups in the society hence to consolidate the PRC's socio-political order. A quarter of humankind is thus divided, organised and controlled through an institutional exclusion based on their parents' location and the state-regulated association and identification. This institutional division and exclusion not only fundamentally determines much of the people's rights and benefits, but also their and their offsprings' opportunities in life.

As a consequence of the Chinese Reform since 1978, the hukou-based institutional exclusion has evolved and has been adapting in a number of important ways. Money has eroded some of the old edges of the PRC hukou system, while creating new divisions and exclusions in China between the haves and the have-nots. The rich, the powerful and the talented (the Chinese 'meritocracy')[31] have now achieved de facto national mobility granted to them by the adaptive measures of the hukou system. Controlled, limited, but practical labour mobility has also been developed for low-skilled or even un-skilled labourers (Chan and Zhang, 1999). At the same time, the PRC hukou system has facilitated both regionalism and communitarianism in the Chinese political economy. Much of the mechanisms and functions of the system like the important scheme of managing targeted people, however, remain basically intact in the early twenty-first century.

Clearly, the PRC hukou system poses serious ethical and legal questions that demand creative solutions. The hukou system has systematically created barriers against labour mobility, thus limiting the growth of the market eco-nomy in the PRC as the serious problem of underemployment continues to devastate the state-owned economy[32] and perpetuate poverty for the majority of the population living in the rural areas.[33] It has legitimised unfair treatment and frequent exploitation of the excluded population (mainly the rural residents). It contributes to the growing regionalisation of the Chinese political economy with profound consequences for the Chinese economic develop-ment, the capacity of the central government, and even the unity of the Chinese nation. Yet, to Chinese leaders, the hukou system still appears to be a familiar, effective and legitimate statecraft. Much of this system has been internalised as a part of the Chinese culture and has acquired a high degree of legitimacy, even among the excluded. In the past two decades, a somewhat adapted hukou system has made some important contributions to China's socio-political stability and a segmented but rapid economic growth and tech-nological sophistication in a marketisation of the Chinese economy. Because of these important utilities and deeply-rooted legitimacy, the hukou system, increasingly under scrutiny and criticisms now, is likely to continue in the foreseeable future.

Institutional Exclusion in India: The Perpetual Caste System

There has been well-established scholarship about India's caste system, which this chapter attempts to draw from to present a contrasting case to China's hukou-based institutional exclusion. I will briefly argue that there is a peculiar way of institutional exclusion based on the caste system in India. The caste system seems to be well accepted and deeply trenched in today's India. Naturally, just as in the case of China, India has more than one type of institutional exclusion, but the caste system services as the basis for many of its unique national characteristics. It affects Indians' daily life chances, socio-economic stratification and changes and internal migration. One can certainly never tie everything that happens in India down to the caste system, but it is without exaggeration to say that this societally-enforced Type One (*who you are*) institutional exclusion functions extensively, profoundly and continuously to affect virtually every aspect of Indian life, decades after it was declared illegal by the Indian state. The caste system has been viewed as a highly unique reprehensive of *homo hierarchicus* social structure, as opposed *homo aequalis* commonly found in today's Western societies (Louis Dumont, 1981).

The caste and sub-caste system is a race, ethnicity, language, religion and profession based, highly-cemented and permanently labelled identification of a one-time socio-economic and political stratification, as the results of military and religious conquests. Based on the supreme principle of *dharma* (law of all things) in the Hindu religion, deeply-rooted in Indian culture and evolving over many centuries (some Indian scholars believe that the four *varnas* or main caste divisions of the Indians can be traced back to 5,000 BC[34]), the caste system was created to 'denote geographical identity' and professional identity for the various social groups, to be treated discriminatorily by law and the state. To socially maintain the caste system, discriminatory 'customs, traditions and rituals were developed … [and] acquired the force of law'. The invasion by the Muslims and later British manipulation contributed to the rigidification and longevity of the caste system (Gupta, 1991: 35–44).

Under the caste system, four varnas (*Brahmans*, *Kshatriyas*, *Vaishyas*, and *Shudras*) and *avarna* (Untouchables) and as many as 1,200 complicated castes, sub-castes and 'creeds' of the five categories exist in India to socially divide the people into fixed 'clusters of families'. Each high-caste family has several permanently attached non-paid and specialised worker families, the so-called 'Scheduled Castes', to form a hierarchy for generations. At the bottom of the caste system are several kinds of sub-castes of the so-called 'Untouchables', considered spiritually, mentally, physically and socially unclean and discarded.[35] '[T]he significance of caste that more than anything else characterizes India…. Every Hindu necessarily belongs to the caste of his parents and in that caste he inevitably remains' (Pandey, 1986: 1).

The caste system has existed very extensively in India in particular, but its varied forms also can be found at different times in places like Burma, Persia, Fiji, Tonga, Samoa, Sri Lanka, parts of Africa and ancient Egypt, Greece, Japan and Rome (Hocart, 1950; McCord and McCord, 1977: 36–37). The remarkable longevity, rigidity, sharp social stratification of the caste system, however, is found in nowhere else but India (Pandey, 1986: 1–15). It is a peculiarly powerful institution to the Hindu majority of the Indian population (about 80 per cent in 2001), since it is rooted in the Hindu religious teaching and ceremonial rituals. But it also exists among the Muslims as well as other non-Hindu Indians in the subcontinent.[36]

The caste system features a clear hierarchy among the layers of inherited social identifications of the families that have different rights and privileges as well as different access to community services and provisions. The religious standing and chance in life and afterlife for the castes are also predetermined, although individuals may theoretically have some freedom to escape from fate through personal effort, especially for the afterlife. The status and division are 'given' and unchangeable according to religious teachings and folklore as well as social customs. In some communities, lower castes or sub-castes are limited even in their daily share of food and water consumption. With a highly restrictive connubiality, 'there is no mobility within the hierarchy of caste' (Pandey, 1986: 3–9).

The post-independence Indian government, created in 1947, set out to peacefully tackle the issue of caste system through legal means. The Indian Constitution prohibited discrimination on the basis of caste, abolished 'untouchability' and banned trafficking in human beings and forced labour (*Constitution of the Republic of India*, 1949, Sections 15–17, 23). It also allowed for special assistance and rights to the lower caste people, the SCs, once their status is declared and recognised by the government. The SCs have reserved seats in Parliament and state legislatures for fifty years. They also have special access to government jobs and welfare assistance as well as legal protection (*Constitution of the Republic of India*, 1949, Sections 29, 164, 330–42). By the 1980s, the Indian president recognised by declaration many SCs and STs, about 11 per cent of India's total population (80 per cent of them lived in the countryside, Gupta, 1991: 46) to be specially protected and assisted by the state. The hope is that, gradually, the lower castes can escape from the discrimination, control and exploitation by the higher classes and castes. Indeed, some studies show that, after half a century of such a political effort in the forms of special assistance (loans, college and training admissions, legislature seats and quotas in government employment), many SCs and STs (including mostly officially recognised 'Untouchables') have gained noticeable political and economic empowerment and higher social status.[37]

Yet, the gains by the SCs have not changed the position and role of the caste system itself in India. To cite just a few scholars, India's caste system seems to be a remarkably resilient, stable and powerful base for India's peculiar institutional exclusion. J.H. Hutton found in the mid-twentieth century that the caste system is 'exceptionally constant for a human institution' (Hutton, 1946: 123). Ronald Segal's conclusion in the 1970s seems to still ring true in today's India: 'A society like *India with caste system is easy to rule but difficult to change*' (Segal, 1971, cited in Pandey, 1986: 14–15, emphasis added). Rajendra Pandey found in 1986 that 'through the centuries in India, caste has remained a force despite religious and political revolutions to uproot it' (Pandey, 1986: 15). Some Indian scholars even believed that the caste system was actually 'reinforcing itself', as the socio-economic stratification in India became even more inflexible vertically and horizontally. The gap among the castes, or between the 'in' people and the excluded groups, widened and tensions among the castes increased.[38]

> [C]aste exists; whatever changes there are, these are only in the peripheral areas,' asserted an Indian scholar, 'there is continuance and reinforcement of old in new forms,... and new dimensions of stratification,.. alongwith the caste are in the process of emerging.... Caste seems to be entrenched in almost all walks of our life after Independence (Pandey, 1986: 175).

The former director of the Indian Council of Social Science Research, S.P. Agrawal, pointed out in 1991 the caste system as a 'social organization worked very well as a well-oiled smooth system'. Without a written 'ban on horizontal or upward mobility', the caste system is still giving rise to 'divisive forces' in India while it may provide some important organisational and religious services.[39] 'Brahminism' based on the caste system, argued a leftist militant pamphlet published in Bangalore in 1994, functions powerfully, breeding racism and fascism that was 'killing India'. [40] Another study by Indian scholars concluded in 1996 that Indians' caste status 'affected their ability to exercise basic citizenship rights' and the caste system remained 'India's principal category of social grouping—represents one of the most entrenched structures of domination and subordination, with an in-built system of demarcation and exclusion'.[41] 'Caste system', argued an Indian scholar in 1997, is 'the controlling mechanism of the Indian society'.[42] As many as 75 per cent of the Indian population were believed to be the low castes and excluded from most of the business and political opportunities, while the small group of top caste (Brahmans) monopolised over 70 per cent of all government jobs.[43]

By 2000, Indian watchers concluded that 'the processes of urbanization, industrialization and modernization have ... not necessarily replaced old values' of caste and class structures and dynamics in rural India. 'Caste and class nexus have penetrated into Indian politics as well as the larger society', just as it was in the mid-1970s (Selvam, 2000: ix–x). The caste system, a mainly socially-maintained division, has increasingly mingled with class structure featuring the partition between the rich and the poor, 'cooperating with each other' to provide the foundation of the political, economic and social activities for the one billion plus Indians in the new century (Selvam, 2000: 121–58, 179–89).

In 2005, a senior official of the India government, Narendra Jadhav, vividly described how post-1947 India has provided the opportunity for lower-caste people, like himself (Jadhav is a Dalit [Untouchable]), who number over 160 million members, to rise to the top of society. Yet he wrote that he is still asked about his caste today and that the caste system remains 'an inseparable part' of his life (Narendra Jadhav, 2005).

The caste-based institutional exclusion not only conditions people's social life; it also affects people's economic and social activities. One illuminative example is the sale of land property. While the higher-caste people have preference in buying land from anyone, lower caste or 'outside' families would have a hard time buying land from higher-caste families even though they may be very able farmers and have the money.[44] Less than 5 per cent of newspaper personal ads seeking mates stated 'caste creed is not a concern' in the late 1990s and hotel registration forms commonly require the guest to report his caste and creed.[45] The caste system has apparently contributed to the repeated failure of the much 'needed' population policy of the Indian government sine the 1950s (Narayana and Kantner, 1992).

Although the Indian government does not use a hukou-style administrative control of internal migration and caste-based discrimination against sojourning ruralites is illegal, India's urbanisation has been nonetheless slow and low. In the second half of the 1980s, the annual cross-state migration rate in India was only slightly higher than China's cross-province permanent migration (*qianyi*) rate of 0.196 per cent but much lower than the total internal migration, including *liudong renkou* (migrants without changing their hukou permanently) rate in China (Zha Ruichuan, 1996: 18, 86–87). India's urbanisation level was slightly below the Chinese urbanisation level in 2001 but was already twice the Chinese urbanisation level in 1970 (Gowariker, 1993: 175; MPS, 2001: 3–5). This slow growth of urbanisation without a formal government control of internal migration is perhaps due to several factors and the 'informal' but powerful restriction of the caste system is likely to be a crucial reason. As a southern India-based British scholar concluded, 'there is no meaningful internal migration in India' under a 'very alive and powerful caste system other than urban slums, beggars, and a few technical professionals'.[46] In one West Bengal block (equivalent of a Chinese township) that has nearly a quarter of a million population, we were told by local officials that anyone from outside can move in and apply for local residency and the food ration card; but 'very few people are coming or leaving'.[47]

The generally low level of industrialisation and the high degree of income inequality, combined with the caste-based exclusion and discrimination in housing and employment, have created in Indian cities some of the worst urban poverty and urban slums in the world, despite the slow and low urbanisation level.[48] In the 1980s, 20 to as much as 45 per cent of the Indian urban residents were already estimated to be living in those urban slums (De Souza, 1983: xiii–xiv). By the late-1990s, the improvement in the situation was almost unnoticeable (Misra and Misra, 1998: vol. I, 1–70).

Consequently, 'India lags behind many other poor countries in general education standards and achievement, and also in health improvement' (Joshi and Little, 1997: 219). Indeed, 'too many Indian people are sleeping on the sidewalks of the cities' and 30–40 per cent of India's rural population suffered from starvation.[49] India's urban poverty and rural backwardness, environmental degradation and poor sanitation in both urban and rural areas and widespread corruption and petty crimes empirically appear to be more serious and extensive than that in China.[50] In the exceptional state of Kerala, under a 'communist' government, weakened caste system may actually have been the key to the relatively impressive social development despite the continuation of economic and technological backwardness.[51]

The caste system, mixed with many other fault lines in the multi-ethnic, multi-lingual and multi-religious society of India, provides the foundation for one of the most delicate, decentralised, debilitating, discriminating and deepest institutional exclusions in the world. The people who are the most excluded seem to be the rural, poor, uneducated and women.[52] The fact that the caste system is alive and well and still very influential in India perhaps has been a good testament of the power of social and religious organisations and traditions in India, of the weakness and inability of the Indian government, of the lack of revolutionary institutional changes and of the function and service provided by the caste system itself in the second largest nation that features a typical dual economy structure and a burning desire to engage in international power competition.[53]

Some Indian scholars have maintained that the caste system, as a way to materially and ritually organise and rank people, can be and has been adapting in the forms of the *jati* (kind)-based political participation and social compartmentalisation and the Sanskritisation or national culture-oriented social mobilisation. All these have provided the socio-political organisation and social mobility control to the population during the modernisation process and under the Indian democracy, hence given the caste system values and utilities in its perpetual existence.[54] Others have presented interesting arguments about the uniquely formed social capital in India that is deeply and complexly related to the powerful social organisations based on the caste system. And the extensive 'caste associations' that may even serve as a 'civil society solution to development and democracy' (Krishna, 2002).

Perhaps organising a nation like India indeed requires an effective institutional exclusion in addition to the division between the haves and the have-nots. If a democratic but weak state cannot provide one, the society will simply keep its tradition of organising based on a social and racially-based institutional exclusion. The weakened and politically modified caste system in today's India, with its functions of social organisation and regulating internal migration hence providing order and social stability, could well turn out to have many 'positive' implications on India's economic growth in the future, as it may have already contributed to the Indian style of democracy especially in the rural areas where the peasants would otherwise be much less organised in their political participation and their struggle for equality (Mohanty, 2004).

Conclusion

I have attempted to show that China and India have quite different types of institutional exclusion and varied mechanisms affecting their internal migration and population mobility. Table 11.1 provided a comparison of the economic development, technological sophistication and socio-political features of China and India. A summary of these different types of institutional exclusions and the varied records of socio-economic development in the two nations are provided in Table 11.3. The institutional and performance discrepancies between the two nations certainly have many causes and some of which could be temporary and not necessarily institutional or lasting, as the Indian economy has now also picked up speed in the first decade of the twenty-first century, and the rapid economic growth in China is poised to lead to more political changes down the road. However, the role played by the different types of institutional exclusion seems to be an obviously important and lasting, if not decisive, factor.

Furthermore, I propose, as a hypothesis, that the caste type of social-based institutional exclusion has more negatives than the hukou-style residential or location-based institutional exclusion concerning the speed of economic growth, yet may have allowed for some additional platforms for local self-governance and grass-roots democracy to develop. Even though they both may serve very important 'positive' functions of capital formation, social organisation and stability, and regulation of internal migration, the two types of institutional exclusion have had different impacts on the overall development of political economy in the two largest nations. From this standpoint, I list some assertions as hypotheses about stratification, institutional exclusion and population mobility in China and India.

First, China and India have roughly the same problem of surplus labour in a typical dual economy. But the two nations have different records of

Table 11.3
In Addition to Money: Institutional Exclusion in China and India

Country	China	India
Institutional Exclusion (IE)	Yes	Yes
Common type (nationally)	II	II
Fault line	*What you have*	*What you have*
Legitimacy	high	high
Enforcing forces	market	market
Uniformity	high	high
Effectiveness	high	high
Rigidity	medium/low	high
Unique type (nationally)	III (hukou)	I (caste)
Fault line	Where you are	Who you are
Legitimacy	high	low
Enforcing forces	the state	society
Uniformity	high	low
Effectiveness	high	medium
Internal migration control	tight	medium
Performance/Implication		
Growth rate (1990–2001)	high	medium
Technological sophistication	medium	medium
Urbanisation	slow/low	slow/low
Distribution of gains	uneven	uneven
Income inequality	medium	medium
Urban poverty/slum presence	low	high
Population growth	low	high
Subjective happiness index	78/100	72/100
Formal democracy	no	yes
Local governance	weak	strong
Governance rank	high/medium	medium
HDI rank	rise	slow rise
International standing	high/rising	medium/rising

Note: China had revolutionary land reforms that destroyed the landlord class. The basis of the Chinese new rich is less rigid since it is not associated with land-based property rights but more with the ever changing political power and administrative control of the PRC hukou system. India had no meaningful land reform and the land-based entrenched rich class is hence more stable and rigid.

economic growth, social development and political systems. China has so far managed to circumvent the Lewis Transition with an authoritarian regime, with rapid economic growth and improvement of living standards. India has maintained a functional democracy and shares with China the problems of inequality and low urbanisation. But India appears to have significantly lagged behind China in other aspects of socio-economic development. A trade-off between political democracy and economic growth seems to be the case. But the real reason is perhaps the different ways the two peoples are organised and excluded, a cause that is deeper and more historical than the current form of government.

Second, money and market forces are or are becoming a major basis for institutional exclusion (Type Two of *what you have*) in both China and India. There seems to be a strong convergence of the two nations in that regard. Based on a market-oriented economy and supported by market-friendly states, the rich now enjoy the greatest vertical and horizontal mobility in both nations while the poor have the least amount of upward mobility or real freedom of internal migration. The recent economic reforms, similar in their general directions, in both countries and the subsequent and resultant high economic growth illustrate the new trend of having a market-oriented economic system.

Third, both nations have their powerful additional types of institutional exclusion: the PRC hukou system in China and the 'illegal' but powerful caste system in India. The existence of additional types of institutional exclusion may hold a key to our understanding of the two nations' varied records of political development, socio-economic achievement and international standing. In a nation with low per capita resource endowment and the problem of dual economy where the supply of unskilled labour seems to be unlimited, as in China and India, market-based institutional exclusion may 'need' to be supplemented with other types to allow for fast economic growth and technological development, while maintaining socio-political stability. However, these additional types of institutional exclusion, under the pressure of, and being replaced by, the market forces, all have demonstrated trends of weakening, localisation and signs of changes in the general direction of relaxation.

Fourth, in theory and in practice, all nations must have institutional exclusion of at least one type. All institutional exclusions create injustice, inequity and inequality to the excluded. A combined consideration of how much and how strong negatives an institutional exclusion creates for how many people versus how effective and how efficient it performs its necessary and even 'positive' functions may give us some sense in making any comparative assessment. Based on the study presented in this chapter, I suggest that the residential registration-based administrative control of internal migration (Type Three or *where you are*) may be a lesser 'necessary evil' than the genetic, ethnic, religious, or social grouping-based (Type One or *who you are*) social barriers in terms of facilitating a rapid economic growth. A Type One institutional exclusion, with its contributions to socio-political stability and local political participation, perhaps also helps to smooth and even circumvent a Lewis Transition that is 'required' for a developing country to have an economic take-off. But it appears to be less effective than a Type Three institutional exclusion, which could allow for a quick, targeted and selected adjustments of policies to enable a fuller circumvention of the Lewis Transition.

Fifth, all types of institutional exclusion can be highly rigid but they can also have certain varied flexibility. Type One (*who you are*) institutional exclusion understandably has the highest inherent rigidity that usually only grants some upward mobility to the excluded in the promised afterlife. The Type Two (*what you have*) form of institutional exclusion may have demonstrated the most flexibility historically since it sometimes can be altered by the results of an individual's able and willing effort. The existence of the entrenched urban poverty in many developing nations may have shown, however, that the division between the rich and the poor can be stubborn and rigid for generations. The rigidity of a Type Two institutional exclusion may be even more apparent if we consider the impact of 'globalisation' under which capital (and the rich) has achieved quasi-global mobility while the labour (and the poor) has not even had internal mobility. The Type Three (*where you are*) form of institutional exclusion usually is highly rigid, as the PRC hukou system has demonstrated. Yet, it could allow for 'authorised' vertical and horizontal mobility for the selected few from the excluded, as it has been the case in the PRC even before the Chinese reform released the forces of the market. Mixed and combined with the market forces, Type Three institutional exclusion has allowed more vertical and horizontal mobility than Type One, especially in regard to the 'guided' or 'directed' moves of the selected groups of people who meet the state (and sometimes the market) decided qualifications.

Finally, it seems that an effective and 'suitable' institutional exclusion or a combination of several institutional exclusions is crucial to a nation's record of development and achievement.[55] More specifically, a certain combination of Type Two (*what you have*) and Type Three (*where you are*) institutional exclusions seems to be a more effective and efficient form of institutional exclusion for a large and massively populated developing nation to rapidly develop its economy, upgrade its technology levels and living standard and still maintain its socio-political stability. Considering the higher achievement China has attained and the lower per capita natural resource endowment it has in comparison to India,[56] the socio-economic 'utility' of the hukou-based institutional exclusion in China, albeit with all its implied dreadful consequences of inequality and discrimination, is perhaps indeed quite impressive.[57] But the effectiveness and function of the administrative control of a hukou-type institutional exclusion hinges precariously on the power of an authoritarian state that makes local democracy hard to develop. The decentralised and diversified caste-type social barriers in India, on the other hand, less effective and unimpressive in 'helping' in rapid economic growth, may have had a more 'positive' effect on local socio-political stability and political participation.

Notes

1. The author wants to thank the organisers and participants of the international conference on 'Local Governance in India and China: Rural Development and Social Change' held in Kolkata, India, 6–8 January 2003. I especially benefited from the comments by Satish Agnihotri, Richard Baum, Manoranjan Mohanty, Mark Seldon, Kellee Tsai, David Zweig and the anonymous reviewer.

2. For the 'protracted' China–India rivalry, see Garver (2001: 110–37, 368–90). For a Chinese view on the Sino-Indian strategic rivalry to be a 'world leader' and the 'need to study each other carefully', see He Sen (2001).

3. For an account on the ethnic conflicts in India in general and the Sikh relationship with the Indian state in particular, see Gurharpal Singh (2000).

4. India's controversial but outspoken defense minister, George Fernandes, openly admitted in November, 2000 'China has surpassed India in basically every aspect'. Reported by the New York-based www.chinanewsnet.com. Accessed on 16 January 2001. For a Chinese response to such admission and India's 'great power ambition' see Zhang (2001): 43–46.

5. Although Kerala scores significantly better than India's national averages of life expectancy, adult literacy, infant mortality reduction and birth rate reduction, its per capita GDP and economic growth rate are actually lower than India's already low national averages. Further-more, a Hong Kong-based scholar who visited Kerala in 2001 commented to the author in 2002 that 'in terms of technological sophistication, Kerala looks like China in the 1960s and 1970s.' For a general argument that social development can be achieved with low level of economic development, using Kerala as an example, see Sen (1995, 2000).

6. For a comprehensive study of the hukou system, see Fei-Ling Wang (2005).

7. For two representative treatments of the caste system in India, see Louis Dumont (1981) and Anirudh Krishna (2002).

8. Here, 'institution' is understood as a set of 'humanly devised constraints that shape human interaction' and 'a set of rules, compliance procedures, and moral and ethical behavioral norms designed to contain the behavior of individuals in the interest of maximizing the wealth or utility of principals' (North, 1981: 201–202; 1990: 182).

9. For an elaboration on Max Weber's profound concept of social closure and its comple-mentary role to Marxism, see Murphy (1988). For a general discussion of the concept of exclusion, see Riggins (1997). For a discussion of the concepts of citizenship and exclusion, see Bader (1997) and Castles and Davidson (2000). Solinger (1999) impressively applied a citizenship analytical framework in studying China's migrant population.

10. Eckstein (1991: 346). For the consequential division between the 'in' people and the 'outsiders' in the context of Italy, see Sniderman et al. (2000).

11. It should be noted, as Solinger did (1999: 110–146), that some 'public goods' can not be realistically excludable. In China, for example, certain subsidised resources and services are also readily available to the floating peasants and temporary visitors. Yet, the non-excludable public goods, important as they can be, do not constitute much of the life-chance-shaping resources and services discussed here.

12. For a discussion on gender-based stratification and exclusion, see Blumberg (1984: 42–47).

13. Max Weber (1978), for example, explored and discussed exhaustively many of the political, economic, social, racial and cultural divides and strata in his general theory of economy and society. Many others followed the same track (for example, see Talcott Parsons, 1964).

14. The suburban versus inner city division, for example, vividly illustrates this division and exclusion in the United States. See Langdon (1997) and Duany et al. (2001).

15. Of course, in reality, the four types listed here often overlap with one another and create hybrid variations, as few nations have only one type of institutional exclusion.

16. For a fuller treatment of the implications of institutional exclusion, see Fei-Ling Wang (2005: 1–31).

17. The much-admired democracy in the Greek city-state of Athens was a good example of elite democracy for the minority of the population. It took 130 years for the American democracy to include half of the US population when women gained voting rights in the 1920s and nearly 200 years to include African Americans during the civil rights movement in the 1960s. Swiss women did not have voting rights in the long-standing Swiss democracy until as late as 1971. *Time*, 28 August 1995, p. 25.

18. Capital accumulation has always been regarded as the number one 'pushing' factor for economic development (Meier, 1984: 137).

19. In Marxian terminology, the so-called primitive accumulation of capital (Marx, 1992).

20. For a concise description of the dual-economy concept and its modifications, see Meier (1984: 151–58).

21. One group of Chinese economists and strategists declared that the serious problems of the backward rural sector was 'the most fundamental problem' for China's great power dream (Hu et al., 2000: 285–350).

22. This is what was later named as the Lewis Model of economic development, after the development economist W. Arthur Lewis. For his original treatment of the dual economy model, see Lewis (1954, 1974 and 1983). For modifications and amendments of the Lewis Model (from duality to three-dimension and varied ways of the Lewis transition), see Fei and Ranis (1997), Todaro (1969, 1999) and Schultz (1976).

23. Huang Renlong, 'Zhongguo de feifa yimin wenti' (China's problem of illegal emigration), in *Renkou yu jingji* (Population and economics), Beijing, No. 124 (January) 2001, 12–22. The 'cost' figures are reported in *South China Morning Post*, Hong Kong, 15 February 2001, p. 9.

24. Field reports from China (Wang Jun, 2001) and the author's personal interviews in Brazil (1997) and in China (2000–2001) both revealed a high degree of economic irrationality in rural-to-urban migration that inevitably creates urban slums and poverty, as well as retarding the development of an urban middle class.

25. For a discussion on such state's role of 'governing the market', see Wade (1990). For discussions on 'strong state', see Myrdal (1968) and Migdal (1988).

26. This line of thinking benefits from the insights developed by the 'world system' theorists. For the crucial role of the divided international politics in the development of the capitalist world economy and the conceptualization of the included 'core' versus the excluded 'periphery' of the world economy, see Wallerstein (1974). John G. Ruggie made a similar argument about the role of Westphalia world politics. For a study on the international mobility of capital and labor, see Sassen (1988).

27. There is perhaps no need to further describe the common knowledge of the deep gulf between rich and poor nations. The US Department of Defence's annual budget ($ 289 billion for 2000) alone is nearly three times as large as the total estimated cost ($100 billion) for providing safe water, adequate nutrition and basic education for the whole humankind (*Time*, 27 September 1999, p. 33). The 7 per cent of the world's population living in North America consumes 30 per cent of the world's energy, ('Earth Pulse–Insatiable Appetites', *National Geographic*, March 2001) and 20 per cent of the world's population living in the OECD nations have per capita productive land of 20 acres (the US has 30.2 acres) while the remaining 80 per cent only has 5 acres per person. ('Earth Pulse–We Leave More than Footprints', *National Geographic*, July 2001).

28. Money-based social divisions and stratification never disappeared in the Mao era. Money-based Type Two institutional exclusion has become increasingly prominent in the PRC in the past two decades. In addition to the money-based and the hukou-based types, another unique form of exclusive barriers is the now reduced and withering *danwei* (unit)-based divisions and exclusions. For more on the danwei system and its role, see Walder (1986), Bian (1994), Lu and Perry (1997), Wang (1998) and especially Li and Li (1996).

29. For the current status and functions of the PRC hukou system, see Fei-ling Wang (2005).

30. Here, the word 'legitimacy' refers to the acceptance, de jure or de facto, by the practically meaningful majority of the population.

31. For how the meritocracy works in China in the 1990s, see Bakken (2000: 254–76).

32. By the late-1990s, 'internal' estimates concluded that nearly 50 per cent (80 per cent in the north-east and more than a quarter in Shanghai) of the Chinese state-owned enterprises were losing money. Massive underemployment (estimated to be more than 30 per cent of the state employees) has been deemed the main cause of the problem. Author's interviews in Shanghai and Beijing, 1997–2000.

33. Conservative estimates put the 'surplus' labourers in the Chinese rural areas to be 150 to 240 million by the mid-1990s, out of about 900 million rural residents. The rural population still grows by more than 10 million every year. See Niu Renliang (1993: 145–49) and SSB (2001). As a comparison, the total rural labour force of the fifty-two countries of Africa in the early 1980s was only 117 million and the total rural labour force in the twenty-seven European nations was only 31.29 million (Wang Guichen 1988, 112).

34. Gupta (1991: 13–14). According to a Tamil Nadu-based British scholar of Indian studies, Michael Lockwood, India's upper castes, mainly English-speaking and about 5–10 per cent of the population, are descendents of the conquerors/rulers of India in the ancient times. The lower castes are largely non-English speaking and mostly illiterate. Their ancestors were either the conquered people or the escaped refugees. The lowest social groups of 'Untouchables' are the descendents of the rebels who rose unsuccessfully against the conquerors. The religious origin of the castes is used later as a ' political adornment'. Author's interviews in India, 1997.

35. They tend to have inherited low-ranking jobs such as working at the burning sites of fire burial on the banks of the Ganges River. Author's interviews in Varanasi, India. 1997.

36. Singh (1977) and Ahmad (1978). For the political favours bestowed to the lower castes by the Indian Government after 1947, many other ethnic and religious groups in India also tend to simply rename their internal socio-economic stratification as caste system. Ahmad's description of castes in the Muslims is actually applicable to other Muslim nations including the Arabic nations where a highly fixed social stratification and exclusive barriers among the layers of the population exist and often glorified by the religious establishment.

37. For the gains and progress of the SCs, see Singh (1987).

38. Pandey (1986: 167–74). By the end of the twentieth century, Indian politics in general had a turn for conservatism and the Hindu nationalist party, the BJP (Bharatiya Janata Party) came to power. Physical mistreatment of lower caste people in the hands of higher caste people was common in places like Varanasi (Banaras) and old Delhi. In some southern cities, the role of the caste system seems to be less prevalent. Author's interviews in India, 1997.

39. Gupta (1991: 7). Agrawal's view is quite representative of the Indian government's official opinion, which often tends to downplay or even dismiss the role played by the caste system in India. Many conservative and religious fundamentalist forces in India actually launched campaigns against the scheduled castes for their 'unfair' rights and power. Author's interviews in India, 1997.

40. Rajshekar (1994). Many Indian college professors and students believe that the conflicts between higher and lower castes were not diminishing but 'rising' in the 1990s. Author's interviews in Madras (Chennai), Varanasi (Banaras) and New Delhi. 1997.

41. Appasamy et al. (1996: 85). For statistical data on the caste-based socio-economic exclusion against the low-caste people, see Appasamy et al. (1996: 88–97). For examples of radical pamphlets and essays advocating revolutionary ways to destroy the 'evil' caste system published in India in the 1980s–1990s, see Ambedkar (1987), Rajshekar (1994) and the articles in the fortnightly journal *Dalit Voice*, Bangalore, various issues, 1981–97.

42. Author's interview with Badrinath Krishna Rao, in Chennai, 1997.

43. Author's interview in New Delhi and Chennai, 1997.

44. Selvam (2000: 119–20). Incidentally, this serves as a good comparison to real estate transaction in China where the PRC hukou system literally led to housing price being drastically higher for non-local buyers. In Singapore, the government subsidised housing, the HDB (Housing Development Bureau) apartments must be sold only to the government-approved buyers based on the factors of race/ethnicity, religion, age and gender.

45. Author's field notes and content analysis of the personal advertisements in English language newspapers such as the *Indian Express*, the *Economic Times*, and the *Saturday Statesman* of January 1997.

46. Author's conversation with Michael Lockwood at the Mamallapruma Relics in Tamil Nadu, 1997.

47. Author's field notes about a visit to Panchla Block, Howrah District, West Bengal, 2003.

48. The massive urban slums in major cities like Bombay (Mumbai), Calcutta (Kolkata) and Madras (Chennai) have been some of the best-known examples of urban poverty in the world. See Desai and Pillai (1990: 125–248).

49. Author's interview with P.S. Jacob and Badrinath Krishna Rao, two Indian professors of development studies, in Chennai, 1997.

50. Author's field notes in Chennai, Varanasi, Agra and New Delhi, 1997.

51. For an academic discussion of 'social inclusion' as a leading cause for Kerala's social achievements, see Heller (1999).

52. See Jayaraman (1981) and especially Den Uyl (1995).

53. For an officially endorsed Indian examination of the multi-dimensional causes of the inability of governance and changes, as reflected by the lack of success in population control and labour resource utilisation, see Gowariker (1993).

54. Gould 1988, especially his second volume.

55. Of course, to say that the existence of institutional exclusions is inevitable and even necessary does not mean we should not work to minimise the negatives, mainly inequities and inequalities, produced by institutional exclusions as well as the size of the excluded. For a discussion on the varied existence of 'social exclusion' and 'the design of policy against exclusion', see Rodgers (1995, especially 253–309).

56. For one thing, the per capita arable land in China is only 33 per cent of the world's average or 40–42.2 per cent of that in India. Hu and Yang (2000: 300) and the Washington-based National Institute for the Environment, www.cnie.org, Accessed on 19 February 2002.

57. Some readers may infer further and come to a conclusion that a heavily populated large developing nation today is better off with an authoritarian regime rather than a democracy since a Type Three (*where you are*) institutional exclusion can hardly sustain or function well in a mass democracy. I would suggest that, first, an effective role of the state in legitimising a Type Three institutional exclusion is not necessarily impossible under a political democracy, especially a common elite democracy. Second, an effective mass democracy is generally a rarity in the developing nations anyway. Third, it takes more than an authoritarian or effective state to implement a Type Three institutional exclusion. History and

social and cultural factors matter greatly. Finally, although beneficial for a nation with dual-economy to grow fast, a Type Three institutional exclusion is not the ideal or sufficient condition for socio-economic development, probably not even a universally necessary condition.

References

Ahmad, Imtiaz. 1978. *Caste and Social Stratification among Muslims in India*. New Delhi: Manohar,
Ambedkar, B.R. 1987. *Annihilation of Caste*. Bangalore: Dalit Sahitya Akademy.
Appasamy, Paul et al. 1996. *Social Exclusion from a Welfare Rights Perspective in India*. Geneva: International Labour Organization.
Bader, Veit. (ed.). 1997. *Citizenship and Exclusion*. New York: St Martin's Press.
Bakken, Borge. 2000. *The Exemplary Soceity: Human Improvement, Social Control, and the Dangers of Modernity in China*. Oxford: Oxford University Press.
Baviskar, B.S. 2002. 'Including the Excluded: Empowering the Powerless', *Sociological Bulletin*, 51, 2.
Bian, Yanjie. 1994. *Work and Inequality in Urban China*. Albany, N.Y.: SUNY Press.
Blumberg, Rae Lesser. 1984. 'A General Theory of Gender Stratification', in R. Collin (ed.), *Sociological Theory*. Jossey-Bass Inc.
Castles, Stephen and Alastair Davidson (eds). 2000. *Citizenship and Migration: Globalization and the Politics of Belonging*. London: Routledge.
Chan, Kam Wan and Li Zhang. 1999. 'The Hukou System and Rural–Urban Migration in China: Processes and Changes', *The China Quarterly*: 831–40.
Cheng, Tiejun and Mark Selden. 1994. 'The Origins and Social Consequences of China's Hukou System', *The China Quarterly*: 644–68.
Cook, Susan and Margaret Maurer-Fazio (eds). 1999. *The Workers' State Meets the Market: Labor in China's Transition*. London: Frank Cass.
De Souza, Alfred. 1983. *The Indian City: Poverty, Ecology and Urban Development*. New Delhi: Manohar.
Den Uyl, Marion. 1995. *Invisible Barriers: Gender, Caste, and Kinship in a Southern Indian Village*. The Netherlands: International Books.
Desai, A.R. and S.D. Pillai. 1990. *Slum and Urbanization*. Bombay: Popular Prakashan.
Duany, Andres, Elizabeth Plater-Zyberk and Jeff Speck. 2001. *Suburban Nation: The Rise of Sprawl and the Decline of the American Dream*. New York: North Point Press.
Dumont, Louis. 1981. *Homo Hierarchicus: The Caste System and Its Implications*, 2nd edition. Chicago: University of Chicago Press.
Eckstein, Harry. 1991. *Regarding Politics: Essays on Political Theory, Stability, and Changes*. Berkeley, CA: University of California Press.
EIU (The Economist Intelligence Unit). 2001. *Country Profile 2000: China and Mongolia*. London: EIU.
Fei, J.C.H. and Gustav Ranis. 1997. *Growth and Development from an Evolutionary Perspective*. Oxford: Basil Blackwell.
Asian Development Bank, African Development Bank, European Bank for Reconstruction and Development, Inter-American Development Bank, International Monetary Fund and World Bank. 2000. *Global Poverty Report*. Prepared for G8 Okinawa Summit.
Garver, John W. 2001. *Protracted Contest: Sino-Indian Rivalry in the Twentieth Century*. Seattle: University of Washington Press.
Gould, Harold A. 1988. *The Hindu Caste System*, Vols 1 and 2. Delhi: Chanakya Publications.

Gowariker, Vasant. 1993. *The Inevitable Billion Plus: Explorations of Interconnectivities and Action Possibilities*. New Delhi: National Book Trust.

Gupta, Shanti Swarup. 1991. *Varna, Castes and Scheduled Castes: A Documentation in Historical Perspective*. New Delhi: Concept Publishing.

Heller, Patrick. 1999. *The Labor of Development: The Workers and the Transformation of Capitalism in Kerala*. India, Ithaca, NY: Cornell University Press.

He Sen. 2000. 'Indo kai "ruanjian" qiangguo' (India relies on software to empower), in *Zhongguo guoqing guoli* (China national conditions and strength), Beijing, No. 103 (July): 39–40.

Hocart, Arthur M. 1950. *Caste: A Comparative Study*. London: Methuen.

Hu, Angang and Fan Yang. 2000. *Daguo zhanlue: zhongguo liyi yu shiming* (Great power's strategy: China's interest and mission). Shengyang: Liaoning Renmin Press.

Huang, Yasheng and Tarun Khanna. 2003. 'Can India Overtake China?', *Foreign Policy*, July–August.

Hutton, J.H. 1946. *Caste in India: Its Nature, Function and Origins*. Cambridge: Cambridge University Press.

Inglehart, Ronald and Hans-Dieter Klingemann. 2000. 'Genes, Culture, Democracy and Happiness', in Ed Diener and E.M. Suh (eds), *Culture and Subjective Well-being*, pp.165–85. Cambridge, MA: MIT Press.

Jadhav, Narendra. 2005. *Untouchables: My Family's Triumphant Journey Out of the Caste System in Modern India*. London: Scribner

Jayaraman, Raja. 1981. *Caste and Class: Dynamics of Inequality in Indian Society*. New Delhi: Hindu Publishing Corp.

Jiang, Zemin. 2001. *Lun sange daibiao* (On 'three representing'). Beijing: Zhongyang Wenxian Press.

Joshi, Vijay and I.M.D Little. 1997. *India's Economic Reforms: 1991–2001*. New Delhi: Oxford University Press.

Khan, Azizur Rahman and Carl Riskin. 1998. 'Income and Inequality in China', *The China Quarterly*, 154 (June): 221–53.

Krishna, Anirudh. 2002. *Active Social Capital*. New York: Columbia University Press.

Langdon, Philip.1997. *A Better Place to Live: Reshaping the American Suburb*. Amherst MA: University of Massachusetts Press.

Lewis, W. Arthur. 1954. 'Economic Development with Unlimited Supplies of Labour', *The Manchester School*, 22 (2): 139–91.

———. 1974. *Dynamic Factors in Economic Growth*. New York: Advent Books (1954) 1956. *The Theory of Economic Growth*. London: George Allen & Irwin.

———. 1983. *Selected Economic Writings of W. Arthur Lewis*, ed. by Mark Gersovitz. New York: New York University Press.

———. 1996. *Development Planning: The Essentials of Economic Policy*. London: George Allen & Unwin.

Li, Nan and Shuzhuo Li (eds). 1996. *Quyu renkou chengzheng hua wenti yanjiu* (Study on urbanization of regional population). Shanghai: Huadong Normal University Press.

Lu, Xiaobo and Elizabeth J. Perry (eds). 1997. *Danwei: The Changing Chinese Workpalce in Historical and Contemporary Perspective*. Armonk, NY: M.E. Sharpe.

Ma, Hong and Mengkui Wang (eds). 2001. *Zhongguo shichang fazhan baogao, 2000–2001* (China market development report 2000–2001). Beijing: Zhongguo Fazhan Press.

Marx, Karl. 1992. *Capital, Volume 1: A Critique of Political Economy*. London: Penguin Publishers.

Matthews, Mervyn. 1993. *The Passport Society: Controlling Movement in Russia and the USSR*. Boulder, CO: Westview Press.

McCord, William and Arline McCord. 1977. *Power and Equity: An Introduction to Social Stratification*. New York: Preager.

Meier, Gerald M. 1984. *Emerging from Poverty*. New York: Oxford University Press.

Migdal, Joel S. 1998. *Strong Societies and Weak States: State-Society Relations and State Capabilities in the Third World*. Princeton: Princeton University Press.

Mishra, Anil Kant. 1998. *Rural Tension in India*. New Delhi: Discovery Publishing.

Misra, R.P. and Kamlesh Misra. 1998. *Million Cities of India: Growth Dynamics, Internal Structure, Quality of Life and Planning Perspectives*, two volumes. New Delhi: Sustainable Development Foundation.

MPS (Ministry of Public Security). 2001. *2000. Niandu Quanguo fengxianshi renkou tongji ziliao* (Statistical information of the population by cities and counties in the PRC, 2000). Beijing: Qunzhong Press.

Mohanty, Manoranjan. (ed.). 2004. *Class, Caste, Gender*. London: Sage.

Myrdal, Gunnar. 1968. *Asian Drama*. New York: Oxford University Press.

Narayana, G. and John Kantner. 1992. *Doing the Needful: The Dilemma of India's Population Policy*. Boulder CO: Westview.

Niu Renliang, Laoli. 1993. *Yongyuan shiye yu qiye xiaoli* (Labor force: Underemployment, unemployment, and enterprise efficiency). Beijing: Zhongguo Caijing Press.

North, Douglass. 1981. *Structure and Change in Economic History*. Norton: New York.

———. 1990. 'Institutions and a Transaction-Cost Theory of Exchange', in James Alt and Kenneth Shepsle (eds), *Perspectives on Positive Political Economy*. New York: Cambridge University Press.

Pandey, Rajendra. 1986. *The Caste System in India*. New Delhi: Criterion Publications.

Parsons, Talcott. 1964. *Social Structure and Personality*. New York: Free Press.

Rajshekar, V.T. 1994. *Brahminism: Father of Fascism, Racism, Nazism*. Bangalore: Dalit Sahitya Akademy.

Reserve Bank of India (RBI). 2001. *Handbook of Statistics on Indian Economy 1999–2000*. New Delhi: RBI.

Riggins, Stephen Harold (ed.). 1997. *The Language and Politics of Exclusion: Others in Discourse (Communication and Values)*. London: Sage.

Rodgers, Gerry, Charles Gore and José B. de Figueiredo (eds). 1995. *Social Exclusion: Rhetoric, Reality, Responses*. Geneva: International Labor Organization.

Ruggie, John G. 1983. 'Continuity and Transformation in the World Politics: Toward a Neorealist Synthesis', *World Politics*, 35–32 (1983): 261–84.

Sassen, S. 1998. *Globalization and its Discontents*. New York: New Press.

Schultz, Theodore W. 1976. *Transforming Traditional Agriculture*. New York: Arno Press.

Segal, Ronald. 1971. *The Crisis of India*. New York: Penguin Books.

Selvam, Solomon. 2000. *Caste and Class in India in the late Twentieth Century*. New York: Edwin Mellen.

Sen, Amartya. 1995. *Inequality Reexamined*. Cambridge, MA: Harvard University Press.

———. 2000. *Development As Freedom*. New York: Anchor Books.

Sharma, Bal Krishna. 1999. *The Origin Of Caste System In Hinduism And Its Relevance In The Present Context*. Nepal: Samdan Publishers.

Singh, Gurharpal. 2000. *Ethnic Conflict in India: A Case Study of the Punjab*. London: Macmillan.

Singh, Harjinder (ed.). 1977. *Caste among Non-Hindus of India*. New Delhi: National Publishing House.

Singh, Soran. 1987. *Scheduled Castes of India: Dimensions of Social Change*. New Delhi: Gyan Publishing House.

Sniderman, Paul M., Pieranngelo Peri, Rui J.P. de Figueiredo, Jr. and Thomas Piazza. 2000. *The Outsider: Prejudice and Politics in Italy*. Princeton: Princeton University Press.

Solinger, Dorothy J. 1999. *Contesting Citizenship in Urban China: Peasant Migrants, the State, and the Logic of the Market*. Berkeley, CA, University of California Press.

Soros, George. 2002. *George Soros on Globalization*, New York: Public Affairs.

SSB (State Statistics Bureau). 2000. *Zhongguo Tongji Nianjan 2000* (China statistical yearbook, 2000). Beijing: China Tongji Press.

———. 2001. *Zhongguo Tongji Nianjan 2001* (China statistical yearbook, 2001). Beijing: China Tongji Press.

Todaro, M. 1969. 'A Model of Labour Migration and Urban Unemployment in Less Developed Countries', *The American Economic Review*, 59 (1): 138–48.

———. 1999. *Economic Development*, 7th Edition. London and New York: Longman.

UNDP. 1990. *Human Development Report*. New York: Oxford University Press.

———. 2001. *Human Development Report*. New York: Oxford University Press.

UNDP. (United Nations Development and Planning) and World Bank, World Resources 2000–2001. Oxford: Elsevier Science, 2000.

Wade, Robert. 1990. *Governing the Market: Economic Theory and the Role of Government in East Asian Industrialization*. Princeton: Princeton University Press.

Walder, Andrew G. 1986. *Communist Neo-Traditionalism—Work and Authority in Chinese Industry*. New Haven, Conn: Yale Press.

Wallerstein, Immanuel. 1974. *The Modern World-System: Capitalist Agriculture and the Origins of the European World-Economy in the Sixteenth Century*. New York: Academic Press.

Wang, Fei-Ling. 1998. *From Family to Market: Labor Allocation in Contemporary China*. New York: Rowman & Littlefield.

———. 2005. *Organizing through Division and Exclusion: China's Hukou System*. Stanford, CA: Stanford University Press.

Wang, Guichen. 1998. New Theory on Reform of China's Rural Areas. China Social Sciences Publishing House.

Wang, Jun. 2001. 'Dushi lide chunzhuang' (Villages in the cities), Tianya (Frontier), *Haikou*, 1, 2001: 58–69.

Weber, Max. 1978. *Economy and Society*. Berkeley, CA: University of California Press.

West, Loriane A. and Yaohui Zhao (eds). 2000. *Rural labor Flows in China*. Berkeley CA: Institute of East Asian Studies.

World Bank. 2001. Country Data, updated on the World Bank web site at: http://www.worldbank.com/data/countrydata/countrydata.html. November, 2001.

Yu, Depeng. 2002. *Chengxiang shehui: cong geli zouxiang kaifang—zhongguo huji zhidu yu hujifa yanjiu* (Urban and rural societies: from separation to open—A study on China's hukou system and hukou laws). Jinan: Shangdong Renmin Press.

Zha, Ruichuan et al. (eds). 1996. *Zhonguo disici quanguo renkou pucha ziliao fengxi* (Analysis of the data from the fourth Chinese national census), two volumes. Beijing: Higher Education Press. 1996.

Zhang, Wenmu. 2001. *Zhanlue yo guanli* (Strategy and Management). Beijing: No. 3.

12 Women and Local Power in India and China

Revisiting the Ghosts of Manu and Confucius

BIDYUT MOHANTY

Introduction

The status of women in India and China have continuously been redefined with the evolution of the great civilisations. Brahminism, and later on the industrial revolution, as well as the freedom struggle influenced the status of women, one way or the other, in India. However, the dominant ideology, namely, patriarchy, continued to be a major influence in determining the subordinate role of women in India.

Similarly, China was also influenced by Confucianism and a radical political revolution, which in turn influenced the status of women dramatically. If Confucianism suggested a subordinate role for Chinese women, Mao Zedong, the leader of the Revolution said, 'Women constitute half of the sky'. Hence, they should be given egalitarian position. Yet, Chinese women continued to remain in a subordinate position though their status is a shade better in terms of access to health care services, employment opportunities and education than those in India.

The last three decades of the twentieth-century saw tumultuous changes. For example, international organisations like the UNO have compelled national governments to take proactive roles. In addition, the role of the market has become a guiding force in both the countries in terms of access to education, health care and to earning of livelihood though the intensity of the reforms is much higher in China than in India.

The proactive role of the state has led to, among other things, the enactment of two progressive legislations known as the Constitution (Seventy-third and Seventy-fourth Amendment) Acts, 1993 in India. We will restrict our analysis to the Seventy-third Amendment, meant for rural areas only. One of the objectives of this Act has been to mainstream women in the decentralised decision-making process. There is a provision of reserving *at least* one-third of the total seats for women both at the membership as well as the level of the functionaries in the local government institutions. As a result, 5 million women have become active in grass-roots politics in the rural areas directly and indirectly within a span of 10 years. Panchayats are village councils which are political institutions for participatory decision-making at the grass-roots level through which many rural development schemes are implemented. Some of these schemes create opportunities for high degree of social mobilisation. The panchayats are instrumental in implementing the schemes meant for poverty alleviation in the rural areas. These institutions are also responsible for the overall development of the village through a participatory process. Women, being part of the governance, have benefited from these schemes as implementers as well as beneficiaries. At a time when the developing market forces are eroding the role of the political institutions, the Swarnajayanti Grameen Swarozgar Yojana (SGSY) brings in a comparative advantage to women who can avail this with their traditional skill and locally-available cheap raw material. Women deal with locally available raw materials to manufacture products of daily use and sell them in the market. Membership in the panchayats has changed women's self-perception for the better. The status of women in India has in turn been enhanced because of their participation in panchayats, since, being partners in the decision-making process, they engage themselves in service delivery. Indicators like reduction in the incidence of poverty, increase in female literacy rates and life expectancy at birth within a span of 10 years of their participation encourages us to see a positive relation between the two.

On the other hand, in China, the inroad of market forces is more marked and the achievement of women under the protection of the state are, in fact, declining, leading to further discrimination against women. One plausible way to integrate women into the decentralised decision-making process is to have reservation of seats at the local government level. Since Chinese women have better access to health care and education as well as to the job market than women in India to begin with. Their representation in the local government would consolidate their position in society, as they would be in a position to have a say in the decision-making process at the local level.

In order to test this hypothesis, we will first discuss the status of women in India. The impact of the Seventy-third Constitutional Amendment Act on women, including the process of social mobilisation, will be taken up after that. We will also discuss the status of Chinese women in terms of access to education and health care, particularly in the post-Revolution period. We will also take up their position in the local government institutions in the era of economic reforms followed by a summing up of the discussion.

The Status of Women in India

In India, the social status of women has been deeply influenced by the teachings of the Manu Smriti. According to the Smriti, women occupy a subordinate position to men. Several stories, folktales, rituals and the up-bringing of girl children reflect the dominance of patriarchy. A quotation from the *Human Development Report*, South Asia (UNDP, 2004: 3) epitomises the state of women in India. 'Gender discrimination in South Asia (India) is situated within deeply inquired systems of patriarchy which limit and confine women to subordinate roles'.

The discrimination against women get reflected not only in the social field (Table 12.1) but also in economic and political spheres. The carriers of the ideology are both men and women. Table 12.2 depicts some of the indicators such as literacy rate, life expectancy at birth, employment scenario, females per 1,000 males, maternal mortality, etc., which throw a dismal light on the status of women. However, there has been a marginal improvement in some of the indicators within the span of a decade. One such improvement is a quantum jump in the literacy rate from 39 per cent in the 1991 Census to 53 per cent in 2001.

But the most distressing fact is that the juvenile sex ratio in the age group of 0–6 years has shown a sharp decline from 945 in 1991 to 927 in 2001 (*Census of India, 2001*). The state-level variations are even sharper.

Commenting on the decline, the registrar general pointed out that the three-year moving average of sample registration data on mortality show that there has been a real decline in the total births of female babies (*Census of India, 2001*). The registrar general has pointed out that 'neglect of the girl could result in higher mortality at the younger ages'. He also cited 'sex-selective female abortions', 'female infanticide', etc., as factors responsible for the decline in the juvenile sex ratio.

Even though, the registrar general did not elaborate on any of those points, it is noticed that the juvenile sex ratio is one of the lowest in the states where the status of women is relatively low in terms of access to education, health

Table 12.1
Why Sons are Preferred to Daughters in India and China

India	China
Pressure from the family. Ensuring constant flow of income till parents' death.	Pressure from the family. Ensuring constant flow of income till parents' death.
Old-age security.	Old-age security.
Will carry on the ancestral legacy.	Will carry on the ancestral legacy.
Will get dowry continuously in some form or other.	Will give dowry or bride price one time only.
Will not be a helping hand if he belongs to a high-caste family.	Will be a helping hand.
Will not fragment landholding. Will enhance status in family, society.	Will get more land after marriage. Will enhance status in family, society.

Source: Chu (2001) for China.

care services and decision-taking process.[1] Those are the states which have an acute 'son preference' and neglect of girl child (Bose, 2001). Das Gupta and Bhat (1997) have gone a step further by saying that the 'intensified gender bias' is the result of fertility decline. However, Dreze and Murthy (2001) have qualified the statement by observing that the gender bias in terms of female feticide and infanticide would take place whether there is high fertility or low fertility.

The factors behind the marked son preference, as revealed in Table 12.1, are social and economic security, social rituals, dowry, etc. In sum, this analysis shows that the status of women in India is relatively low.

Government Initiatives

After independence, the Government of India did take various initiatives to improve the status of women in India though these were not as radical as those adopted by the Government of the Peoples Republic of China. (We will discuss those measures in the next section.)

The government initiatives can be characterised as 'women in development', 'gender and development' and finally 'rights-based development'. The details of these approaches have been discussed by many (*Human Development in South Asia*, 2001; Mohanty and Mahajan, 2004).

Suffice to say here that the Government of India passed a piece of progressive legislation in 1993 to enable the presence of a 'critical mass' of women in the decentralised decision-making process. This enabling measure can be characterised as the facilitator of the 'rights-based approach' to women's empowerment. In the next section some of the features of the panchayats will be discussed.

Panchayati Raj Institutions

The Constitution (Seventy-third Amendment Act) was originally initiated by the late Rajiv Gandhi as the Sixty-fourth Amendment but got defeated in Parliament. It was passed after the death of Rajiv Gandhi during the tenure of Narasimha Rao. Since the Act was a landmark in the history of local government or the panchayati raj system, it is worthwhile to narrate some of the salient features of this Act. First of all, the new panchayati raj system has a three-tier system, namely, village panchayat, block panchayat and district panchayat. The size of the population determines the size of each tier.

In each tenure about 532 district panchayats, 5,912 block panchayats and 2,31,630 gram panchayats are formed in which around 3 million elected representatives interact (Mathew, 2000).

The most important feature of the Act from women's perspective is the reservation of at least one-third of total seats for women both at the membership level and at the level of functionaries. Another landmark of this Act is the importance given to the gram sabha or the village assembly, having adults of the panchayat as its members. The panchayat acts as an executive body and the gram sabha acts as the watchdog to which the panchayats are accountable. The panchayats have a separate finance commission as well as an election commission (Mathew, 2000). Twenty-nine subjects ranging from agriculture to family welfare and poverty alleviation have been devolved to the panchayats. Almost all the schemes meant for poverty alleviation such as the Swarnajayanti Gram Swarozgar Yojana (SGSY), the Gram Samridhi Yojana, etc., are routed through the panchayats, though money is subject to sanction from the central government. The main chunk of the panchayat's income is utilised on infrastructure (construction of small irrigation structures, source of drinking water, roads, repairing of community buildings, etc.) and implementing welfare schemes (old-age and widow pension, maternity benefits, etc.). In principle, the panchayat has complete flexibility in allocating these funds (Chattopadhyay and Duflo, 2004).

For the first time, incidentally, the Eleventh Finance Commission (meant for allocating finances to local bodies in different states) has devoted one chapter for panchayat's finance. It has recommended an amount of Rs 80,000 million for all the panchayats in the country. This amount is meant for five years! Even though it is highly inadequate and fulfills only a fraction of the requirements, it is worthwhile to note that the Commission has given due emphasis on the index of decentralisation. Incidentally, the amount of money given to each village panchayat varies from state to state. For example, in West Bengal a gram panchayat gets on an average Rs 1.5 million per year but in a state like Rajasthan it gets only Rs 60, 000. In Kerala, on the other hand, panchayats were given 35 to 40 per cent of the plan funds to work with. In terms of the financial resources it amounted to Rs 1,025,000 excluding the grant from the central government in one year only (Isaac, 2003). Interestingly, the new government at the centre has been reiterating the importance of panchayati raj institutions in furthering rural development (*The Economic Times*, 2004).

At the same time, it is worth mentioning that the real fiscal decentralisation in terms of deciding to spend money their own way and augmenting local revenue is still not with the panchayati raj institutions (Sethi, 2004).[2] In a nutshell, even though the states are yet to share their power with the panchayats, a beginning has been made for involving all villagers in the decentralised decision-making process (Pal, 2002).

Impact of the Panchayats on the Lives of Villagers

The first and foremost impact of the Seventy-third Amendment Act has been the widening and strengthening of the base of participatory democracy. Because of reservation a large number of women have been elected from the lower socio-economic strata (Buch, 2000). Further, at least 90 per cent of the ward members are from low socio-economic backgrounds and those of higher categories are from the high caste/class. Almost all the states have conducted elections at the panchayat level. Some states have conducted the elections for the second time. About 3 million elected representatives have been elected to these political institutions of which about 1 million are women as mentioned earlier.

The most significant impact of the legislation has been to bring 5 million women to active politics within a span of 10 years (Buch, 2000). We are interested to know the impact of the large number of women emerging at the level of grass-roots politics, which will be taken up at a later stage. (The arithmetic of 5 million women can be explained in the following manner. First of all, in each tenure 1 million women get elected. Second, for each seat two to three women on an average contest the election. Thus all together 5–6 million women participate in the political process.)

Yet another impact of the PRIs is the reduction of the poverty ratio from 38 per cent to 26 per cent and a slight increase in the rate of urbanisation by 2 per cent between 1991 and 2001 (Government of India, 2002) At least a major part of these results can be explained by the implementation of schemes meant for poverty alleviation through panchayats. It is interesting to note that within a span of two years, between 1999 and 2001, about Rs 35,793 million were allocated, out of which 72 per cent was utilised. About 2.4 million *swarozgaries* (self-earners) were assisted of which 44 per cent were women (Government of India, *Annual Report, 2001–02*). This formed a significant portion of a total sum of Rs 97,650 million, which were allocated for rural development, rural employment and poverty alleviation programmes for the financial year 2001–02 (Government of India, 2001–02). Unfortunately, the total allocation of financial resources to rural development is not restricted to panchayats, but the schemes routed through these institutions are better targeted, as is pointed out a little later in this chapter.

There are debates regarding the role of decentralisation in reducing the incidence of poverty in a particular area. Johnson (2002), who has reviewed the existing literature on the subject, is of the opinion that there is a weak relationship between decentralisation and the reduction in poverty. Johnson also cites other studies to show that the panchayats provide space for marginalised sections of the people to articulate their needs. Further, it is also observed that the panchayats' decisions are not restricted to class (Johnson, 2002).

On the other hand, experts have shown that the panchayats were responsible for reducing the poverty ratio in India (Bardhan and Mukherjee, 2004). Bardhan and Mukherjee have done extensive empirical research in West Bengal. They have pointed out that panchayats in West Bengal have targeted land reforms, delivery of agricultural mini-kits, initiating employment programmes and access to credit—all of which have led to poverty alleviation. They have analysed the performance of 89 villages and the time period extends to 20 years. In addition, it may be pointed out that the marginal increase in urbanisation is most likely due to lack of significant scale of distress migration to the city.

After discussing the general impact of the PRIs, we will turn our attention to the specific impact of PRIs on women.

The Impact of Panchayats on Women

The sources of data are:

a) A longitudinal study of 235 elected women representatives in 22 panchayats spread over three districts of Orissa keeping different locales in mind, with an objective of monitoring and capacity building for leadership roles. The project spanned five years. This was taken up by the Institute of Social Sciences, New Delhi.

b) Observation of an annual programme marking 24 April as Women's Political Empowerment Day, which has been celebrated by the Institute for the last 10 years.[3]

Institutional Impact: Engendering Development

According to various micro-studies including our own observations from the field, about 80–90 per cent women attend the panchayat meetings regularly (Buch, 2000; EKATRA, 2003). Given their sheer numbers, one might conclude that democracy has become more participatory than before, at least at the grass-roots level. This argument is strengthened by the fact that the socio-economic background of these women showed that the majority of them come from the lower-income group, particularly in the case of membership at the village panchayat level. Insofar as the effective participation of these women is concerned, it is noticed that if they get outside support in terms of NGO intervention, women's groups, or any other social or political movement, the women become relatively more vocal. Their knowledge about the functioning of the panchayats increases (Kumud Sharma, n.d.).

Social Mobilisation

At this point a reference can be made to the implementation of an important scheme, namely, the SGSY through the panchayats and its impact on the poor in general, and poor women, in particular. The main features of the scheme are that it lays stress on a few select activities in each developmental block and attends to all aspects of these activities ranging from availability of raw materials, upgrading skills to marketing. The main objective of the scheme is to augment a sustainable income of the swarozgaries (self-earners) through this investment. A major component of the scheme was in operation since the 1980s in the form of Development of Women and Child in Rural Areas (DWCRA) and had created some successful groups in Andhra Pradesh. The revised scheme has borrowed a few innovative concepts from the Grameen Bank (Bangladesh) such as flexibility in payment. In addition, this scheme emphasises social mobilisation of poor in the rural areas. Several women entrepreneurs have emerged as a result (Government of India, SGSY: Guidelines, n.d.). Studies conducted on the impact of SHGs show that women's group formation, new knowledge and, moreover, group mobilisation are capable of creating an alternative to women's traditional status in the family. Group mobilisation also enables women to speak out in the village meetings (Vijayanthi, 2002). The social mobilisation created by the SGSY/SHGs gets reinforced by another factor, namely, women's participation in the political process through campaigning, addressing the meetings and going to cast their votes. Women not only take up issues relating to basic needs, such as, drinking water, availability of doctors and teachers in the villages, which are dear to them, but also general developmental activities, for example, augmenting the income of the panchayats and generating irrigation facilities for the paddy fields. The micro-study conducted by the Institute of Social Sciences referred to earlier also shows that not only are the schemes better targeted but also the knowledge about different largess such as widow and old-age pensions, availability of free rice spreads fast among the women because of the presence of women in the panchayats. The women of the neighbourhood act as 'watchdogs' in compelling the elected women to deliver at least some goods. Women of the villages can easily approach the women elected members and can get subsidised rice at any time.

Micro-studies conducted in various parts of the country (Buch, 2000; Chattopadhayay and Duflo, 2004; Datta, 1998) reveal that given a chance the elected women representatives try to engender the developmental activities. For example, in her study on 12 all-women panchayats, Datta pointed out that elected women representatives gave more priority to programmes that were 'need based' and 'sustainable'.

Sen (1983) has mentioned that the family is an arena of cooperation and conflict. It is observed that the reservation of seats in the local governments has increased the areas of cooperation at the family level. Evidence from the results of the Census of India, 2001 show that the female life expectancy at birth has exceeded that of males, thus indicating the fact that women's self-perception has changed and they look after their health and nutritional status. Similarly the female literacy rate has jumped from 39 per cent to 53 per cent within a decade. A part of this quantum jump could be explained in terms of women's excitement to become literate after getting elected (Saldanha, 1995).

Related to this issue (the impact on institutional standards) is the question of the 'proxy women'. Let us define the term proxy women. It is alleged that since many of the women are participating in the panchayats for the first time and are illiterate they depend on their menfolk for conducting panchayat activities. In other words, the women follow their menfolk without understanding the implications. Hence they are termed as 'proxy' women.

There are several issues involved here. First of all, the husbands or other male relatives shield them from the panchayat secretary and block development officers if they try to harass the women. In fact, some state governments (Uttar Pradesh and Rajasthan) have passed a rule that women elected representatives should be accompanied by their male relatives to the panchayats (Rai et al., 2001). This is because in some cases, the secretaries of the panchayats and male colleagues tried to implicate inexperienced women by asking them to sign blank cheques. Some of the women chiefs went to jail because of those acts. In many cases, no-confidence motions were passed in the panchayats against the women chiefs on false charges.

Again, even if they depend on their husbands, the power relation between husband and wife has already changed because of reservations, particularly because the husband gets a chance to come to the public sphere because of his wife, and in the process the character of patriarchy gets altered. As a result, in many low-income families the husband–wife relationship has not soured. On the other hand, the husband supports his wife and also helps her with domestic work. Even other members of the family including the mother-in-law and sister-in-law help her to complete domestic chores. The community leaders of the same caste also support the women candidates.

Besides, those who argue that the women coming to panchayats are all 'proxy' women forget to analyse their socio-economic background. Many of the women, even in places like northern India, are recruited from a white-collar background. Since they are educated and know about the working of the official system they do not remain silent in the panchayat meetings. The same critics assume that all the men who work on behalf of women are corrupt and want to grab power. But in reality it may not be true.

Finally, the 'proxy' women syndrome is seen only in the first one or two years of the tenure. Gradually, the women become independent, as studies conducted in Karnataka show (Mathew, 2002). In the process, they come to know about many modern institutions like courts, the block development office, agriculture and other offices, the existence of various officials and some times about the prime minister, chief ministers and other ministers.

Thus, we see that, contrary to popular criticism, the standard of the political institutions at the grass-roots level has not been lowered as a result of women's reservations and the development process has also been engendered to some extent. Finally, with regard to the girl child issue, the elected women in the panchayats are persuading the villagers not to eliminate the girl foetus.

Constraints

The constraints are many. The most important constraint of women's empowerment through panchayats is that they are not a homogenous category. They represent different interest groups depending on their class and caste, which get perpetuated through patriarchy. However, the one positive thing that comes out of women uniting together is access to basic services such as drinking water, health care facility and education—the practical needs. Again, in many places women are not immune to systemic corruption though as beginners they are relatively more cautious. Joining politics is still considered 'dirty' and is frowned upon. The community leaders of the village try to choose candidates who are non-performers or would toe their line. The women themselves do not come forward. It is always the family members, or party leaders who push them to contest. The selection of seats for reservations, which are done on a lottery basis and only for one term, does not provide much scope for nurturing a constituency. Even if the women perform well during the first term, the men do not allow them to contest from the same seat again. The panchayati institutions are used as an implementing agency. So the bureaucrats feel that they are the bosses and the first time leaders are there to obey them.

Violence against women has also increased. A woman chief of the panchayat was killed in one of the states because she defied her husband and called the meeting of the village assembly to discuss the agenda of the budget. In some cases, women representatives do not know that they have been elected from certain constituencies (Rai et al., 2001). Inter-caste violence has become more acute and so much so that a woman member of a *nagar palika* (township government) in an urban part of Tamil Nadu was murdered because she wanted to bring piped water to her ward. She belonged to a low-caste community. In yet another case another woman was forced by the villagers to quit her menial job because it did not suit her status as an elected representative.

In a nutshell, men support women in panchayats so long as women do not challenge them to fulfil the 'practical needs'. But men feel threatened when women try to fulfil the 'strategic needs'.

Apart from the specific constraints, the PRIs system as a whole faces several structural constraints such as limited power and resources, the absence of an appointed cadre and hence, dependence on state-level functionaries and so on. Again the panchayats are given 29 subjects that come under different departments. But the policy matters are not conveyed to the elected representatives at all. So the elected representatives cannot take decisions on their own regarding any subject, such as, agriculture, irrigation, family welfare, etc., except only in implementing schemes or acting as the spokespersons of the state governments.

Besides, there are a number of parallel structures such as the Janmabhumi Programme in Andhra Pradesh, the Vana Panchayat (Joint Forest Management), Uttar Pradesh, and Water Harvesting Management, etc., which try to ignore the involvement of the PRIs. All these systemic constraints also affect the functioning of the women in the panchayats.

On the whole, however, it can be argued that reservation of seats in the local council has provided a critical mass of women with an opportunity to empower themselves by being partners in the decision-making process.

Status of Chinese Women

Like that of Indian women, the status of Chinese women was highly influenced by Confucian thinking which was highly patriarchal Unlike Manu Smriti which was not codified, the Confucian philosophy has been well documented in the 'Book of Rites',[4] (Yue and Li, 1997).

The feudal system of arranged marriages was very important in the Chinese families to regulate the lives of women. 'Son preference' seemed to be the sole occupation of married women in the traditional set up. Keeping concubines by Chinese feudal lords is a familiar concept even in India, but it seemed that this practice was relatively more prevalent in China. However, it is interesting to note in this context that unlike in India, Chinese families accept bride price or the money and presentations given in exchange for a bride. One of the factors which affect the status of girls in India is the dowry system that involves paying money and property to the husband's family. But in China, despite the practice of bride price, the status of a son remained superior to that of a daughter. Table 12.1 gives a comparative picture of factors affecting the son preference syndromes in both the countries.

Like Indian women, Chinese women had participated in the Revolution in 1949. But unlike Indian women, who became relatively invisible after independence, the Chinese government took various steps to make them visible outside the institution of the family. A series of laws such as the Marriage Law, Electoral Law and the land reforms campaigns tried to ensure women's equality in all spheres of life.

The Marriage Law was first passed in 1950. It focused on women's rights and gender equality. The law makers wanted to do away with the prevailing feudal Confucian values in families and in society, and as women are the carriers of those values, the leaders wanted to target the women first. The law was quite comprehensive, including raising the age of marriage, sending women to school and entrusting the initiative of divorce with women, etc. It was also realised that if women stayed at home, they would perpetuate the feudal values. So they were compelled to go out and get employment in the state-owned enterprises (see Table 12.2).

The institutional deliveries were encouraged. All those measures yielded good results. The age of marriage increased from 18.52 in 1950 to 25.5 in 1992 even in rural areas. It was even higher in the urban areas. The adult female literacy rate reached 79 per cent in 2000. The gain in institutional deliveries has been quite remarkable, namely, 89 per cent in the period of 1995–2001 (see Table 12.2). Since the span of reproductive age was reduced and institutional deliveries encouraged, the maternal mortality ratio per 100,000 live births has become only 55 (Table 12.2) in contrast to India, where it is still very high.

The Marriage Act did yield good results but women had to pay a heavy price. The arranged marriages fell to 1 per cent between 1977 and 1982.[5] At the same time more than 10,000 women were killed or committed suicide in 1951 because men did not like the law and women became frustrated at their failure to execute their plans (Daiyun and Jin, 1997). Again some women, being socialised in a particular way, were unable to bear the separation. Finally, the older women and men did not like it because of its fluid situation. On the other hand, the party cadre was too busy in measures like land reforms to oversee the enactment of the law. Some of them were staunchly against the law (Diamant, 2000). Thus, it can be inferred that the composition of patriarchy had a conflicting elements. Some leaders were trying to give maximum freedom to women but others were against it.

The Girl Child

In spite of progress made by Chinese women, the fate of the girl child is not at all safe in China. Table 12.2 shows that the sex ratio of males per 1,000 females in the children's age group has increased from 1110 to 1170 between 1990–99. Das Gupta et al. (1997) points out that the juvenile sex ratios were high and have been increasing rapidly since the 1960s in China, fuelled by fertility decline and availability of sex-selective technology. They also noticed

Table 12.2
Comparative Indices of the Status of Women in India and China in 2003

	India 2001	China 2000
Sex ratio females per 1,000 males	933	937
Juvenile sex ratio in the age group of 0–6 years	927	850
Life expectancy at birth of surviving to the age of 65 (percentage of cohort 2000–05)		
Female	67.5	81.3
Male	61.9	72.7
Maternal mortality ratio reported per 100,000 live births	540	55
Births attended by skilled health personnel (1995–2001)	43	89
Total fertility rate per woman 1970–75	5.4	4.8
2000–5	3.0	1.8
Life expectancy at birth		
Female	64.0	72.9
Male	62.8	68.6?
Adult literacy rate 15+		
Female	46.4	78.7
Male	69.0	92.5
Seats in parliament (percentage of total)	9.3	21.8
Women in government at the ministerial level, 2000 (percentage of total)	10.1	5.1
Work participation rate Rural	28	
Production		43.4
Construction		18.4
Mining		25.6
Finance and insurance		41.5
Real estate		33.7
Health, social welfare		56.5
Education		43.1
State control		36.1
Unemployment		52.6
Rural	28	
Agriculture	85	
Organised sector	18.1	
Services	56.5	
Manufacturing	20.6	
Work participation rate female 2002 (1)	42.4	45.2
Gender-related development index	103	71

Source: Various statistical year books of China; Government of India (2004) Economic Survey, Ministry of Finance, Economic Division; Major Figures on 2000 Population Census of China complied by the Population Census Office under the State Council Department of Population Social Science and Technology, Statistics, National Bureau of Statistics of Peoples Republic of China; UNDP (2004).

that the influence of 'son preference' declined with urbanisation. However, the authors felt that urbanisation is no panacea for this evil and that, in this case, attitudinal change will play a more important role. Just like in India, Chinese society still has a fascination for sons. In this case Das Gupta's concept of 'intensification of gender bias' due to family planning, referred to earlier, is quite applicable.

Attane (2002) has drawn our attention to another aspect of the neglect of the female child. She noticed that the resistance to the family planning programme (and hence son preference) is strongest in the regions having a large number of female agricultural workers. According to her, the presence of such a large unskilled labour force indicates the low status of women. In these areas the rural families resort to three types of methods, namely, selective abortions, female infanticide and under-reporting of births (Attane, 2002).[6]

Chu (2001) through extensive survey in rural central China came to the conclusion that out of these three factors, female infanticide plays a very negligible role. On the other hand, the under-reporting of female child births and sex-selective abortions are much more significant in determining the increasing sex ratio.[7]

The discriminating attitude towards the girl child is reflected in families not sending their daughters to school, particularly in rural areas. Further, shortage of women of marriageable age has increased the cases of abduction and trafficking of women. The white papers published by the Government of China in the recent years, refer to issuing a notice on 'Reprisals Against Trafficking in Women and Children' in 1989. In 1991, in response to proposals by the political parties and organisations, the government drew up the 'Decision on the Strict Prohibition Against Prostitution and Whoring'. It was strictly implemented and the cases of abduction and sale of women and children were reduced by 35.2 per cent in 1992, compared to that of 1991 (Government White Papers, China, 25 August 2004).

Thus, it is noticed that the Government of China has taken various bold initiatives to raise the status of women socially and economically. These initiatives have yielded some results in terms of access to education and health services. Women have also entered the job market. However, the discriminating attitude towards women, in general, and girl child in particular, still persists more acutely in rural areas.

The Employment Scenario

Insofar as the employment scenario is concerned, it is noticed that the state has given a lot of encouragement to women's employment. Table 12.2 shows that the state units still employ 36 per cent of the total female labour force. Further, the classification shows that most of the women are employed in the soft sectors such as health, social welfare and sanitation, etc. The total participation rate has increased from 43.20 per cent in 1990 to 45.20 per cent in 2000. Like in India, women in China work mostly in agriculture and allied activities. This was particularly noticeable after men left for the cities.

The *Human Development Report* (1997) was all praise for China's achievement in the context of feminisation of poverty. It stated that 'China has made enormous progress in gender equality' vis-à-vis other developing countries. In terms of GDI measuring the capabilities of women in relation to men, China is far ahead of India.

After the household responsibility system was introduced, men migrated to cities and started working in communication, transportation, handicraft production or production for export (Yue and Jin, 1997). Women, on the other hand, not only managed the agricultural activities well but also diversified into off-farm activities. Some of them have become successful pig and chicken farmers.[8] In contrast, the city women have guaranteed employment. The wage rates unlike in rural area are relatively egalitarian. However, like women in rural areas, women in urban areas also bear the double burden of household work.[9]

Thus, it can not be said that Chinese women have achieved the same opportunities as men in the social and economic spheres though they have achieved some gains in terms of access to education and health care.

On the other hand, Rai (1994), for example, observed that in the wake of the structural adjustment programme (SAP), more women than men got unemployed. The private companies refuse to employ young married women on the grounds that they would lose money on maternal benefits and that women lack in efficiency. Again, women are encouraged to retire at the age of 45 though the longevity of women has increased tremendously and has surpassed that of men. In 1995, the China Association for Labour Studies commented on the trends of women's employment in the wake of SAP. It recommended that guidance be provided to women to take up activities which are suitable to their physical characteristics (Mohanty, 1998).

Further, as early as in 1984, young women constituted 70 per cent of those waiting for employment. At that time a company which advertised for 351 workers recruited only 82 women during the early days of reform. It shows the attitude of private companies towards the capabilities of women. In the case mentioned here, however, the All China Women's Federation fought against this and managed to raise the percentage of women's recruitment to 20 per cent (Yue and Jin, 1997).

Local Government in China

Local government institutions or village committees became popular, particularly in rural areas, in the 1990s. Like panchayats, the village committees[10] have elected members.[11]

Diamond and Myers (2000) observed that China had gradual reforms in the sphere of decentralisation for the last 20 years but still the 'inhibited political centre tightly controls the society'. These reforms have not been 'robust enough' to produce the first political 'break through' by which 'inhibited political' centre 'delegates greater autonomy to the four "market places"— economic, political, organisational and intellectual life' (Diamond and Myers, 2000).

Oi and Rozelle (2000) show that wherever the villagers have a clear stake in the village economy with very little or almost no financial support from outside the village, the elected committee is 'likely' to have greater power vis-à-vis the party leaders. Otherwise the non-elected members, namely, the party leaders, have a definite say.

Pastor and Tan (2000) on the other hand, have observed that the party village secretaries usually serve or chair the village election committee that supervise village elections. Thus they exert considerable influence over the outcomes of the elections at the village level.

With regard to financial allocations, it has been noticed that the central government has been adopting a policy of 'carrot and stick'. The local governments are given special project funds, grants and loans, provided they come up with matching grants (Christiansen, 2004).[12]

Thus it can be inferred that because of reforms, the local government institutions have autonomy regarding tax rights at least in some areas. Hence these institutions have become 'engines of growth'.

On the other hand, Tsui and Wang (2004) suggest that the local governments are less autonomous and are subjected to vertical bureaucratic control.

On the whole, however, it seems that unlike in India, the economic reforms have created some space for local government institutions to act as engines of growth because these institutions enjoy taxing rights.

Women in Local Government

Unlike India's progressive legislation, China does not have a similar kind of legislation to allow a 'critical mass' of women to be present in the local government institutions. As Howell (2003) pointed out, in spite of progressive official ideology and 'long established state women's organisation', Chinese women still have not got adequate representation in political institutions.

She pointed out that unlike in other countries, the women's movement in China is not independent (of course recently the All China Women's Federation has been taking an independent stand). In other words, China suffers from 'state-sponsored feminism'. During the Cultural Revolution too, women were encouraged to take an active part in the economy and politics and their status became better than that of the feudal society (Edwards, 2000). However, the vigorous campaign to raise the status of women in society and in the economy did not match a similar campaign to include them in the political decision-making process. In 1992, for example, the percentage share of women in the politburo was only 6.4. The picture at the local level was not very different. According to Edwards (2000), earlier women were elected to local councils through a quota system. But after market reforms started, the quota system was abolished and they could not compete with men from open seats. At the top level of leadership, the wives of Chinese leaders have been appointed. In general, Edwards reported that Chinese women leaders are assigned soft portfolios like health, education, etc. (Edwards, 2000). She also talked about the factors responsible for such low participation as well as the reasons for women holding such soft portfolios. The author pointed out that women are still overburdened with domestic as well as public responsibilities. In addition, the feudal ideology still lingers on in the minds of the political leaders.

Insofar as the percentage of women in different political institutions is concerned, various estimates are available. For example, statistics collected by the All China Women's Federation indicate that women make up 36.2 per cent of the public servants in the party and government organs. But in each of the 31 provinces, autonomous regions and municipalities of China, at least one woman leader is present. (Wen and Yue, 2002).

Howell (2003), on the other hand, points out that there has been a 'virtual ceiling' on women's participation in political institutions. The percentage varies between 21–22.6 per cent.

The picture in a village committee is no different. Customarily, there has been a provision of inducting at least one woman in the village committee as mentioned earlier. But that provision gets flaunted with the slightest provocation. According to Wu Qing (2003), an outspoken deputy to the Municipal Peoples Congress of Beijing, out of the total 1,117 village surveyed, 24 villages had no women leaders in the party branches. According to her, women constitute only 16 per cent of the total village heads.[13] However, caution has to be used while using this data because neither has she elaborated on the survey nor is the source available. But one thing is quite certain that in spite of state-sponsored feminism, women do not figure significantly in politics both numerically or qualitatively.

The functioning of elected women representatives shows a mixed picture. In some places it is revealed that the party personnel try to intervene and reduce the significance of elected members. Since profit is the sole motive, male migrants are preferred to women for land allotments. In places the party cadres resort to physical violence towards women leaders.

It was also evident from the sharing of experience in the training camp that the patriarchal attitude among male colleagues is still prevalent. Male colleagues do not approve of women rising in their careers. One of the leaders present in the workshop narrated how her male colleagues tampered with her birth record and showed her as being older than her actual age. As a result her promotion got stalled. After that episode she decided to join a training school to teach young women leaders about the a b c of politics. Women do not get much encouragement even from their family members to join politics. In the workshop women said that young women were encouraged to marry early and look after the family well. They were not supposed to challenge the elders in the family. Interestingly, the woman official from the Ministry of Civil Affairs who came to deliver lectures in the workshop talked about the role models of women leaders and said that they should not only look after their in-laws at home but should behave properly in public places. In other words, family in China still plays a very important role in determining the status of women in society despite the fact that many progressive measures have been taken to overcome the restrictive family values. Appendix 12.1 gives a glimpse of the kind of difficulties women leaders face and the kind of help they need.

At the same time, some of the elected women representatives spoke about their achievements. The activities included working for land rights, helping families with family planning, augmenting the income of villages, helping villagers participate in the export markets through diversification of agriculture. Interestingly, some, like those in India, got school buildings, roads, etc., constructed, managed natural resources, fought against pollution, etc. Some of them have started small enterprises with the help of microcredit programmes.

On the whole it can be pointed out that the percentage of women present in the village committee is very low though the state is more sympathetic to women's cause. Even though women are capable,[14] they are not allowed to function in the village committee because a 'critical mass' of women is not present. Thus, even though China has a positive attitude towards women's issues, the policy towards village committees is not gender sensitive. In addition, by not allowing adequate women's representation in the local government institutions, such as village committees, these institutions are yet to become democratic.

Conclusion

The status of women in India and China has undergone several changes. The dominant ideologies of the Manu Smriti and Confucianism still hold a significant influence on the women's status in both the countries. Women of both the countries participated in the freedom struggle and Revolution. But after that Indian women were relegated to the background till 1971. In India, the government initiatives to improve the status of women started only after 1975. In China, on the other hand, the government took various measures including the passage of the Marriage Law, Land Reforms, etc., to dismantle the feudal values cherished by the Chinese families and society and raise the status of women. As a result, the access to education, employment, health care was much better for Chinese women than for Indian women. Several indicators, such as female literacy rate, life expectancy, maternal mortality, age at marriage, work participation rate and finally gender development indicators are much better in China compared to India. However, insofar as the juvenile sex ratio is concerned, both countries present a dismal picture indicating the inferior status of the girl child in both countries.

One of the government's initiatives to raise the status of women in India was to ratify a progressive legislation called the Seventy-third and Seventy-fourth Constitutional Amendment Acts, in 1993. Through these acts, the panchayats or village councils and municipalities in the urban areas got a new lease of life. There are 3 million elected representatives who take charge of planning and implementing the appropriate development agenda for their villages and towns as well as cities even though there are financial and functional constraints.

One of the important clauses of these acts is the reservation of seats for women amounting to not less than one-third of the total seats. It has resulted in the presence of about 1 million women per tenure of five years.

Even though some of these women are participating for the first time in politics, some of them have participated in social movements, political movements, white-collar jobs and SHGs. In addition, several NGOs have been working with those elected women representatives. Because of all these interventions, it has resulted in not only 'numerical presence' but also 'representation'. In many places these elected women representatives are trying to alter the priorities of economic and political life. Being a 'critical mass' of women, they are influencing the attitude of the community leaders. The attitudinal change has been made possible because of women's reservation in local government, which, in turn, has led to 'social mobilisation'. The successful SHGs contribute to this mobilisation. In addition, these groups provide financial support to the contestants (Kaushal and Kalia, 2003). Women being present in local government has resulted in changes in terms of literacy, life expectancy and reduction in poverty.

On the other hand, these women are subjected to various forms of violence and indignity. The status of the girl child is still not good and she faces acute violence even while in the womb.

In contrast, women in China, in spite of having access to education and health care, do not have much presence or representation in the village committees, which are the equivalent of the panchayats in India. Unlike panchayats, the village committee is much more powerful for these committees can genuinely set the agenda for development since they can augment financial resources. However, women's representation in these committees is minimum. The party cadres and male elected members always try to undermine the functioning of the women elected representatives. The state-sponsored feminism manifested in the All China Women's Federation is unable to raise the ceiling of women's participation even at the grass-roots level. In the age of globalisation, the emergence of new elites, with new institutional arrangements and new sets of consciousness will soon compel the government in China to yield to the new situation as it has happened in India.

Appendix 12.1
The Charter of Village Women Cadre's Network

(Passed by the participants of the Second Seminar on Promoting Rural Women's Ability to Participate in Politics on 17 September 2003)

a) Aim: To promote the communication between women village heads and party branch secretaries across the country, provide information about rural women's involvement in politics and carry out various suitable activities among members of the network at appropriate time.

b) Definition: Women village heads of the network indicate village party branch secretaries and director of the village committee.

c) Organisational form: The network is an NGO, charging no fee for membership. The network has a council composed of 7–9 persons. Two years for a term and one meeting of all council members.

d) Condition for joining the network: Women village heads can join the network on their own accord without any fee. Each member of the network must subscribe to five copies of the *Rural Women* magazine. The network will use the magazine as a platform to exchange experiences, publicise relevant activities and information.

e) The contents of the network's activities: To open a column for women village heads in the *Rural Women* magazine to communicate what they have learned as village heads, reflect on problems they have met when making decisions, discuss the theory on rural women's participation in politics. The network will publish four issues of the newsletter every year, which will be distributed to every member of the network.

f) The obligation of network members: To recommend people to join the network and contribute to the 'Women Village Head' column and actively participate in the activities organised by the network and make suggestions for the network.

The network is set at the location of the magazine, *Rural Women*, which appoints a staff member to do some routine work, contact members of the network, edit and publish the newsletters as well as supply articles for the column of 'Women Village Heads Forum'.

Notes

1. Ashish Bose (2001) has analysed the data given in the Second Round (1997–99) of the *National Family Health Survey*, in terms of response of women to various indicators to assess their status. For example, when asked as to who took decisions regarding, 'own health care', 72.6 per cent of total women from Kerala said that they decided themselves. But only 36.6 per cent of the women in Madhya Pradesh agreed with them. Bose, however, observes that the 'son preference' cuts across boundaries of region, caste, class in Indian society though it is very acute in the northern states in which the juvenile ratios are low and declining. Various state governments have introduced schemes like 'cradle babies' to discourage sex-selective abortions. The Chinese government has also been trying to encourage the survival of the girl child quite seriously.

2. The study conducted by the World Bank (2004) showed that only two states, namely, Kerala and to some extent Karnataka, have devolved the financial and administrative power to the panchayats.

3. The author has been conducting this programme since 1994 with the objective of creating awareness among the elected women representatives at a national level and providing a forum to learn from each other's experiences. For two days, about 350 elected women representatives from all over India, congregate in New Delhi along with NGOs, academics, parliamentarians, human right activists and government officials. They deliberate on a specific theme out of 29 subjects given to them in panchayats and suggest recommendations to overcome the difficulties, which they face in dealing with such issues. The author compiles and edits the proceedings and disseminates them to the elected women representatives later on. This creates an ongoing interaction. Feedback from the field shows that women who come to this programme go back as changed persons, with more self-confidence, being encouraged by shared experiences and armed with useful strategies.

4. The Marriage Act was revised again in 2001. Along with the right to divorce, the revised Act had other clauses such as prohibition of bigamy, notorisation of property, prohibition of domestic violence, etc.

   In 'Book of Rites' it was mentioned that 'A Woman is a submissive person, submitting to her father...submitting to her husband after marriage, submitting to her son after husband dies', quoted in Daiyun and Jin (1997: 164).

   Similarly, the document clearly specifies under what circumstances women can be divorced. The quotation given here sounds quite familiar in the Indian context because similar sayings that determine the status of women are also prevalent in India.

It is important to note that the categories of work used by two governments are not comparable. The categories used by the Chinese government are perhaps indicative of a more diversified economy and hence more vulnerable to the vagaries of market forces.

5. The proportion of arranged marriages have been quite small in the cities but 80 per cent of the population who live in rural area are more traditional and they do not believe in the new system of marriage. Nonetheless, a new form of marriage developed known as the 'mercenary marriage' or arranged marriage in disguise. Of course this form of marriage was developed partly to escape from the rising bride price (Daiyun and Jin, 1997).

6. Ashish Bose made an interesting observation as to how the one child policy might have led to son preference and this in turn would have led to a kind of socialisation process of a non-accommodating nature. As a result, the army might also have become very aggressive (Bose, 1991).

7. The Chinese government has introduced various schemes to prevent sex-selective abortions.

8. In spite of women's visibility in economic activities, they are still over-burdened. Croll while reviewing Laurel Bossoen's book, *Chinese Women and Rural Women* (Rowman and Littefield Publishers, 2002), wrote ' ...study adds significantly to our understanding of foot binding and its eradication, and of ways in which despite a succession of shifts and new opportunities, division of labour within the family and village primarily remain gendered' (Croll, 2003: 220).

9. It will be worthwhile to report here that the mushrooming of eating places particularly in big cities try to fulfill the much-needed respite from the household drudgeries to some extent. Similar eating places have sprung up in the state of Kerala, India also.

10. O' Brien and Li (2000) pointed out that the first election to village committees started in 1931–34. They have traced the history of elections to village committees till recent years. In contrast the first panchayat elections were held in Rajasthan and Andhra Pradesh only in 1959 after the passage of the Balwant Rai Mehta Committee Report (Mathew, 2000).

11. George Mathew elsewhere in the volume has talked about the 'Organic Law' as well as the structure of village committees in China.

12. An opposite view has been expressed by Dorothy J. Solinger (1996) referring to the case of Wuhan City where the central leadership did not favour its expansion even though the inland city did possess the required growth potential.

13. On 14–16 September 2003, the International Republican Institute (IRI) in collaboration with the authorities of *Rural Women*—a monthly magazine, had organised a training camp for a group of grass-roots women leaders for capacity building. This training camp was organised in Beijing. The section on the functioning of elected women representatives in China is heavily dependent on the speeches delivered by the women leaders themselves as well as by the expert like Professor Wu Qing, editor of *Rural China*, officials from the civil affairs ministry, advisor to CIDA, etc.

14. That women in China had challenged patriarchy during the pre-1949 period is evident from these remarks given by Vincent K. Pollard in 'Women and Girl Children First I or Not? Law, Society and Marriage Policy in Revolutionary China, 1931–1949', in http://mcel.pacificu.edu/easpac/.

'By the same token rural Chinese women who began participating in Communist Party sponsored meetings in the middle 1904s "signaled the whole village that they had ceased being the property of their husbands and fathers". In so doing, many of these women "destroyed links to their families" and quickly "formed a central part of the shock troops that the cadres used to destroy traditional power in villages".'

References

Attane, Isabelle. 2002. 'China's Family Planning Policy, An Overview of Its Past and Future', *Studies in Family Planning*, 33 (1).

Bardhan, P. and Dilip Mukherjee. 2004. 'Poverty Alleviation Efforts of Panchayats in West Bengal', *Economic and Political Weekly*, 39 (9).

Bose, A. 1991. 'Demographic Trends in India and China', *China Report*, 30 (1).

———. 2001. 'Promoting Health and Family Planning through Panchayats', in Bidyut Mohanty (ed.), *Women and Political Empowerment* 1999, Women's Political Empowerment Day Celebrations on Panchayats. Women and Family Welfare, ISS, New Delhi.

Bossen, Laurel. 2002. *Chinese Women and Rural Women*. New York: Rowman and Littefield Publishers.

Buch, Nirmala. 2000. 'Panchayats and Women', in George Mathew (ed.), *Status of Panchayati Raj in the States of India*. New Delhi: Concept Publishing House.

Chattopadhyay, R and Esther Duflo. 2004. 'Impact of Reservation in Panchayati Raj: Evidence from a Nationwide Randomised Experiment', *Economic and Political Weekly*, 39 (9).

China Association for Labour Studies. 1995. *Women and Employment in China*. Beijing.

Christiansen, Flemming. 2004. 'Book Review of Yangzhong. 2003', *Local Government and Politics in China, Challenges from Below*. New York ME Sharpe: Armonk.

Chu Junhong. 2001. 'Pre-natal Sex Determination and Sex—Selective Abortion in Rural Central China', *Population and Development Review*, 27 (2).

Croll, Elisabeth J. 2003. 'Book Review', *The China Quarterly*, 173.

Das Gupta, M., Jiang, Zhenghua, Xei Zhenming Li Bohua. 1997. 'The Status of Girl Child', in 23rd IUSSP General Population Conference', Symposium on Demography of China. China Population Association: Beijing.

Das Gupta, Monica and P.N. Mari Bhat. 1997. 'Fertility Decline and Increased Manifestation of Sex Bias in India', *Population Studies*, 51.

Datta, Bishakha. 1998. *And Who Will Make Chapatis? A Case Study of All Women Panchayats in Maharashtra*. Calcutta: Stree Publications.

Diamant, Neil J. 2000. 'Re-examining the Impact of the 1950 Marriage Law: State Improvisation, Local Initiative and Rural Family Change', *The China Quarterly* (March).

Diamond, Larry and Ramon H. Myers. 2000. 'Introduction: Election and Democracy in Greater China', *The China Quarterly*, Special Issue on *Elections and Democracy*, 162 (June).

Dreze, J. and Mamta Murthy. 2001. 'Fertility, Education and Development: Evidence from India', *Population and Development Review*, 27 (1).

Edwards, Louise. 2000. 'Women in the People's Republic of China: New Challenges to the Grand Gender Narrative', in Louise Edwards and Mina Roces (eds), *Women in Asia, Tradition, Modernity and Globalisation*. Ann Arbor: The University of Michigan Press.

EKATRA. 2003. *Women and Governance, Reimagining the State*. New Delhi: EKATRA.

Government of India. 2001. *Provisional Population Totals*. India Registrar General: New Delhi.

———. 2001–02. *Economic Survey*. New Delhi: Ministry of Finance.

———. 2002–03. *Annual Report*. Ministry of Rural Development: New Delhi.

———. (n.d.) *SGRY: Guidelines*. New Delhi: Ministry of Rural Development.

Howell, Jude. 2002. 'Women's Political Participation in China: Struggling to Hold Up Half the Sky', *Parliamentary Affairs*, 55 (1).

———. 2003. 'Challenges for Female Political Participation in China', Valedictory Speech Delivered in a Conference on 'Women and Politics in Asia' NIAS and Halmstad University, 6–7 June 2003, Halmstad University, Sweden.

Human Development Report. 1997. *Human Development Report*. United Nations Development Programme, New York: Oxford University Press.

International Republican Institute. 2003. Briefing Materials for Symposium on 'Promoting Rural Women's Participation in Politics', Beijing China (14–18 September 2003).

Isaac, Thomas. 2000. 'The Status of Panchayati Raj in Kerala', in George Mathew (ed.), *The Status of Panchayati Raj in India*. New Delhi: Concept Publishing House.

———. 2003. 'Women Elected Representatives in Kerala (1995–2000): From Symbolism to Empowerment', Paper presented at the workshop on 'Women's Empowerment through Seventy-third Constitution Amendment Act', Institute of Social Sciences, 20–21 October 2003, New Delhi.

Johnson, Craig. 2002. 'Decentralization and Poverty: Exploring the Contradictions', *The Indian Journal of Political Science*, 63 (1).

Kaushal, Avdhash and Bindu Kalia. 2003. 'Uttaranchal: Betrayal of Grassroots Democracy', *Panchayati Raj Update* (March).

Mathew, George (ed.). 2000. *The Status of Panchayati Raj in India*. New Delhi: Concept Publishing House.

———. 2002. *Panchayati Raj: From Legislation to Movement*. New Delhi: Concept Publishing House.

Mohanty, Bidyut. 1998. 'Women and Family', in Tan Chung (ed.), *Across the Himalayan Gap, India's Quest for Understanding China*. New Delhi: Gyan Publishing House.

Mohanty, Bidyut and Vandana Mahajan. 2004. 'Women's Empowerment in the Context of the Constitution (73rd and 74th Amendments) Acts 1992: An Assessment'. A Workshop Report, New Delhi: Institute of Social Science, (mimeo).

Mohanty, Manoranjan and Mark Selden. 2003. 'Reconceptualizing Local Democracy: I & II Preliminary Reflections on Democracy, Power and Resistance', *Panchayati Raj Update* (April and May).

Mohbub Haq, Human Development Centre. 2000. *Human Development in South Asia 2000: The Gender Question*. Karachi: Oxford University Press.

O' Brien, Kevin J. and Lianjiang Li. 2000. 'Accommodating "Democracy" in a One State: Introducing Village Elections in China', *The China Quarterly*, 162 (June).

Oi, Jean C. and Scott Rozelle. 2000. 'Elections and Power: The Locus of Decisioin Making in Chinese Villages', *The China Quarterly*, 162 (June).

Pal, Mahi. 2002. *Swarnajayanti Gram Swarozgar Yojana, Evolution, Assessment and Future Prospects*, Kurukshetra (June).

Pastor, Robert A. and Qinshan Tan. 2000. 'The Meaning of China's Village Elections', *The China Quarterly*, 162 (June).

Rai, Manoj, Malini Nambiar, Sohini Paul, Sangeeta Singh and Satinder Sahni (eds). 2001. *The State of Panchayats: A Participatory Perspective*. New Delhi: Sanskriti.

Rai, Sirin. 1994. 'Gender Issues in China: A Survey', *China Report*, 30 (4).

Saldanha, Denzil. 1995. 'Literacy Campaigns in Maharashtra and Goa, Issues, Trends and Direction', *Economic and Political Weekly*, 30 (20).

Sen, A.K. 1983. 'Conflict in Access to Food', *Mainstream*, 21 (8).

Sethi, Geeta (ed.). 2004. *Fiscal Decentralisation to Rural Governments in India*. The World Bank, New Delhi: Oxford University Press.

Sharma, Kumud (n.d.). 'From Representation to Presence, The Paradox of Power and Powerlessness of Women in PRIS', Occasional Paper. CWDS: New Delhi.

Solinger, Dorothy, J. 1996. 'Despite Decentralization: Disadvantages, Dependence and Ongoing Central Power in the Inland—the case of Wuhan', *The China Quarterly*, 145 (March).

The Economic Times, 30 June 2004, Delhi Edition.

Tsui Kai–Yuen and Youqiang Wang. 2004. 'Between Separate Stoves and Single Menu: Fiscal Decentralization in China', *The China Quarterly*, 177 (March).

UNDP. 2004. *Human Development Report*. New Delhi: Oxford University Press.

Vijayanthi, K.N. 2002. 'Women's Empowerment through Self-Help Groups: A Participatory Approach', *Indian Journal of Gender Studies*, 9 (2).

World Bank. 2004. *Fiscal Decentralization to Rural Governments in India*. Washington, D.C.: The World Bank.

Wen, Chihua and Ruifang Yue. 2002. 'Rural Women Sample State Affairs', *China Daily*, 14 May 2002.

Wu Qing. 2003. Theme Paper at the Symposium on Promoting Rural Women's Participation in Politics, September 14–18, International Republican Institute, Beijing (mimeo).

Yue, Daiyun and Li Jin. 1997. 'Women's Life in New China', in Barbara J. Nelson and Nirja Chowdhury (eds), *Women and Politics World Wide*. New Delhi: Oxford University Press.

13 Gender, Work and Power in an Andhra Village

M. VANAMALA

Introduction

This chapter is an attempt to look at the role of self-help groups (SHGs) in the changing developmental context in rural India, and to compare this with the Chinese experience of rural development. Industrialisation in India failed to employ local forces of capital, leading to the local surplus capital being diverted to unproductive, usury-seeking sectors. On the other hand, in order to fulfil local needs of industry, outside capital and labour, and outside female labour in particular, were brought in resulting in the under use of local labour, which, in turn, resulted in a helpless struggle for survival for the majority of the families in the surrounding villages of the industries. Thus, the concept of SHGs or locally-formed groups of rural women was initiated by the village panchayats, mainly to promote the cause of women's development and welfare. This chapter is an empirical study of the experiences of this initiative in a village called Muttangi, in the context of the changes wrought by global and industrial forces in rural India.

Historical Background of the Village

Muttangi is located in Medak—a backward district in Andhra Pradesh. It was selected for the study as it has experienced industrialisation twice on both its boundaries. During the 1970s, the district was selected for industrial development under the industrial policy of 'Backward Region Development'. Indira Gandhi contested from this district with the political slogan of '*Garibee Hatao*'. During the 1990s, this district was marked as an export promotion zone (EPZ) and infrastructure was developed for the promotion of exports.

Muttangi is 40 km away from Hyderabad—the capital city of the state—on the national highway leading to Mumbai and 10 km away from the mandal or zonal headquarters. The village has been expanding rapidly during this decade and the number of voters also increased from 2,000 to 6,000. During

Acknowledgements: I place on record my deep felt gratitude to Professor G. Haragopal for commenting on this chapter. I also thank Mr Dileep of the Department of History, University of Hyderabad, who helped me in collection and tabulation of data. But for him I would not have completed this work.

the late 1970s, the main occupation of the people was cultivation in an area of 1,226 acres spread over 253 households. Industrialisation brought rapid changes in the village, particularly in cultivable land during the 1990s. Out of the total cultivable land, 55 per cent of it has been converted to non-cultivable land. Out of this, 30 per cent was sold to land traders. These traders were from outside the village. About 23 per cent of the land became an industrial base and about 5 per cent became polluted with industrial waste.[1] This major shift of cultivable land disturbed the interlinkage between different agricultural activities. For example, the fall in cultivable land caused a fall in livestock, grazing activity, a fall in fodder cultivation, rural transport and making of conventional agricultural tools and implements. It also caused a fall in agriculture-related activities like cane work, pot making and sheep rearing. These adverse consequences of the loss of agricultural land had a more disastrous impact on women than on men, as displaced women were less mobile and had fewer avenues of employment in the new job market. This, in turn, led to a swelling in the ranks of housewives. These processes are presented in the following discussion.

The Process of Inclusion

The relatively greater loss of cultivable land by some social groups than others in the village widened the disparities in the size of individual holdings.[2] This gave rise to new systems in land cultivation. The cultivators who lost more land were looking for lease-in land. The landowners who were cultivating land with outside labour on an annual basis were looking for lease-out contracts, mainly to escape from the high cost on male agricultural labour. These two factors suited each other and gave rise to an informal tenancy system. Compared to self-cultivation, this system of cultivation[3] was cheaper for landowners and it also helped the cultivators who worked on their own land to utilise their unemployed female family labour fully. The resulting increase in the scale of production helped them to diversify their livelihood activities. It also helped them in upholding the family prestige as their women could now work as family labour instead of as hired labour, which has lower status than the former in this society. This is one illustration of the process of 'inclusion' associated with development, which meant that women were included in the family enterprise. However, though inclusion could provide full work to women, it also affected their freedom. As family labour is unpaid, it curtails the freedom of women without giving them any personal advantages. These trends are evident from the following case study.

> Bhoo Laxmaih is a backward caste and adopted son of Gandiah. Gandiah was an attached child labourer with the village officer during the 1950s. Bhoo Laxmaih

succeeded his father as '*kaval kar*' (watch man) in the office of the '*patwari*'. He has five sons and five daughters-in-law. Except for the second son and daughter-in-law, no other member has any education or skills. Bhoo Laxmaiah owns just 01.20 acres of dry and 00.02 acres of irrigated land. This land was not sufficient to fully engage all his unemployed family members. He leased in nine acres of land from three extended families (of ex-patwari Sreenivas Rao). This leased-in land has helped Bhoo Laxmaiah in many ways—one, to use his family's labour, specially female labour, intensely for cultivation; two, to enlarge the scale of agricultural production; three, to mainain bullocks and other agricultural implements; four, to make agriculture viable and profitable; five, to diversify the agricultural activities into dairy. The leased-in land helped Bhoo Laxmaiah protect his status as 'kaval kar'. The outside wage work for his daughters-in-law is regarded as being of a low status on account of his own status as a government employee. But Bhoo Laxmaiah perceives his status as different from his own caste people. This is on account of his relations with power and production activity.

The Process of Exclusion and Deskilling

The data on occupational details shows that industrialisation by nature is associated with the 'exclusion' of some sections. In the 1970s, hired labour constituted 70 per cent of the village labour and was one of the predominant occupations of the village. Female family labour constituted 20 per cent of the total labour force during the same period. These two types of labour came down to 13 per cent and 3 per cent respectively by 1999. During the two-decade period of 1979 to 1999, the number of types of occupations available for women came down from 16 to nine by 1999. This marked decline in employment opportunities resulted in 'deskilling' in some of the activities. The dual processes of 'exclusion' and 'deskilling' were the consequence of the disruption of the link between different agricultural activities caused by the decline in cultivable land. For instance, fall in cultivable land and agricultural production led to a fall in the number of cattle used in cultivation. This adversely affected the demand for cane basket making and pottery, because cane baskets were used extensively in removing animal dung, feeding animals, lifting agricultural produce, preserving agricultural produce and seeds for the next crop, sieving and cleaning grains. Cane mats were used as sidewalls for carts and rural transport. The demand for cane and pots was also adversely affected when the industries began the manufacture of plastic and steel vessels and other substitutes. The demand for cane products also suffered with the tightening of forest rules. All these factors resulted in the 'deskilling' of cane and pottery workers.

Occupations like wool spinning were also adversely affected by the encroachment on agricultural land. Less cultivation meant a reduced demand for manure, leading to a reduction in the breeding of goats and sheep.[4] The decrease in grazing land and pollution of drinking water by industrial waste further compounded the difficulties of sheep and goat breeding.

The scarcity of water also led to the disappearance of caste services like washing (*dhobi*), which was traditionally a female activity. The male members of the dhobi households set up 'dhobi kits' for ironing clothes in the business centre, an option that was not open to women. This caused a shift of work from women to men. This type of 'exclusion' was due to the 'masculinisation' of activities resulting in a loss of place for women in traditional occupations. The new market had no potential for development of alternative employment avenues. However, women were forced to continue with activities associated with birth, death and puberty in the household as the male members would not undertake this unhygienic, undignified 'dirty work'.

Emergence of New Labour Institutions

One of the major changes brought about by industrialisation was the phenom-enon of 'landed labour'. When the male workers of the households preferred to work in the newly set up industries, it resulted in a lot of fallow land and thus in 'landed labour'. The rise in the costs of production on cultivation led to many more men turning to industrial work. The adoption of bore well technology in cultivation was a critical turning point in this respect. This technology needed expensive inputs like diesel and electricity. Cultivation needs both male and female labour to work on different activities. But with the increasing shift of male agricultural workers to industry, fallow land and 'landed labour' began to rise steadily. The rise in prices of other inputs like fertilizers and pesticides aggravated this process (Vanamala, 2003).

The rapid increase in female agricultural labour consequent to the increase in cultivable fallows added to the existing surplus labour. Against this local trend, the new market inducted new female contract labour groups from outside which competed with the local female labour. This adversely affected the work opportunities of local female labour and pushed women either to 'distress employment'[5] or to being housewives. Added to these problems of work opportunities, the institution of outside contract created hostile relations between local labour and the landowners and many landowners started opting for outside labour. These factors have initiated a 'downward spiral of agri-cultural wages'. However, the conditions of the women working in the contract labour groups were also not all that favourable. Contract work is more stressful as the contractor keeps trying to reduce the number of days of work compared to time-rate work in order to reduce the emoluments.

All these trends led to very interesting changes in the local labour market. To overcome the problem of outside contract labour, the local female labour have been forced to adopt a system of female labour groups to hire small pieces of available land for work. They distribute the wages paid in lump sum among themselves. The survey indicates that a worker could hardly earn Rs 6 per day, for four hours of group-work. This is one indication of how hard the local female labour has been hit by the opening up of the labour market. The contradiction of workers facing less work and yet trying to increase their bargaining power by forming work groups shows how much they are struggling for survival.

The female workers also tried to strengthen their positions by expanding and diversifying their village-based non-farm activities. But these activities are termed distressed[6] (see Appendix 13.3) employment as they are season based, ritual based and occasion based and hence 'fleeting' and derive neither regular income nor command a proper market price. To overcome this problem, women also started taking up 'multi-non-farm activities', such as home-based dairy, tailoring and business activities (see Appendix 13.2). As most of these activities were home based, the female labour in all these cases became 'domesticated'.[7]

Employment Opportunities in the Industries

As the new industries preferred migrant labour to local labour, it resulted, as pointed out earlier, in massive unemployment of the local labour. The data on employment in industries from the village shows that industries could provide work for a mere 5 per cent of the village workers. Less than 1 per cent of female workers could enter the industries (Appendix 13.5) and that too, as casual, informal, flexible and feminised and low-paid workers. The insecure employment of the male members in the family shifted part of the economic burden to the women, and forced them further to take up work at any wage level.

The Social Scenario

The changes brought about by the forces of industry were perceptible not only in the rural labour market but also in the rural social life. For instance, with the increasing demand for land for purposes other than cultivation, the vulnerability of women has also been increasing more than proportionately. This is forcefully seen in the increase in dowry. Increased dowry, in turn, forced the households towards further sales of land holdings. The data (Appendix 13.1) shows that land sales to meet marriage expenditures and dowry demands constitute as high as 30 per cent of the total land held.

The increase in dowry, on the other hand, indicates deterioration in the status of women in society.

Quality of Life of Women

When the status of women in general is low in a society, it also weakens their chances to improve the quality of their lives. This study observed that at the household level in the village, domestic labour and childcare continues to be wholly the responsibility of women, leaving them with no time to develop their creative abilities. These entrenched values of inequalities that exclude men from domestic work has led to undignified living conditions of women in the family. For instance, in most of the working class houses, the kitchen (where only women work) is located outside the main living quarters in order to protect the house from firewood smoke. This kitchen is a low-roofed thatched hut without side walls and is generally built beside the cattle shed. These huts do not have sanitary facilities and are not connected with protected water lines. Hence, the women inhabiting these spaces experience unhygienic, undignified and stressful living conditions. Added to these, there are no medical facilities in the village. The villagers believe that witchcraft is the cause of ill health and even today, the mid-wife is called in to deal with delivery and maternity cases. These factors add to gender imbalances in society. The male and female ratio is 1.57:1 in the village.

The migrant labour that entered the village in search of industrial work was another cause of domestic crises in the village. Extra-marital relations, bigamy and prostitution have been on a steep rise. Liquor trade and consumption have also gone up several times.[8] There has been gradual erosion of close family ties, which is reflected in the conflicts that break out when the household expenditures have to be shared between the members. All these have affected women the most.

Power Structure in the Village

Field observations have noted the perpetuation of an unquestioned power structure in the village for more than four decades. The institution of 'patwari' (a post for the maintenance of land records) in the 1960s, the village grama panchayat (revenue) office from 1970s to 2000 and the office of the Grameen Cooperative Bank, the public distribution system and temple property have been under the control of an extended Brahmin family. Apart from these economic powers, this family is vested with the social authority to settle family disputes of the villagers, as the sarpanch is also a member of this family. Thus, this extended Brahmin family has power over all the key facets of village life and it actively tries to perpetuate its hold on local society by promoting certain rituals and practices that reinforces their authority in the village. For instance, the family arranged a meeting of the well-known religious leader

Ganapathy Sachhidanada Swamy who told the villagers that 'for maintenance of peace' in the village, some more temples needed to be constructed. This family also involved all the villagers in the temple activities, lifting the 'ban' on SCs entering the temple in the process. The levels of illiteracy, ignorance, inequalities and backwardness among the common villagers also contributed to the perpetuation of this systemic power.

However, by 2002, there was a change in the political power. But this political power was much more degenerate and 'vulgarised' than the earlier feudal power exercised by the Brahmin family. The present elected representative—the sarpanch—Narsimha Reddy, who was a supervisor in the electricity department, became very rich by entering into multiple businesses in the new urbanised surroundings of the village. It is believed that he strategically bought it with village money and his unethical practices.[9] The means he is said to have adopted to win the election shows a deterioration in the overall political set-up and it also proves that if surplus capital is not directed properly, it finds its own lanes and by-lanes. When the goal of improving the quality of life of the common people do not figure in the political agenda, capital may be said to have lost its direction.

Self Help Groups and Women's Development

There was a worldwide shift in the development paradigm in the 1990s in order to improve the quality of life of women in rural India. This paradigm conceived of extending microcredit to village women to cover all aspects of their self-employment. For this purpose, women have to organise themselves into SHGs, which are formed around political, religious/cultural issues that can become support structures for microenterprises and other work-based issues. The overall aim of this programme is to raise every family assisted with microcredit, above the poverty line. The Government of India conceived of the Swarnajayanti Gram Swarojgar Yojana (SGSY) as a holistic programme of microenterprise[10] for planning activity clusters, building of infrastructure and technology, credit and marketing (Government of India, Ministry of Rural Development, New Delhi, The Guidelines SGSY, n.d.). This new approach expects to achieve 'empowerment of women', realisation of equality, welfare, conscientisation, organisation, sustainable democratic development and governance. This approach is expected to result in the transformation of the unequal relations between men and women and in the greater participation of women in wider society.

The concept of SHGs incorporated in the SGSY has been drawn from the successful model of Bangladesh's Grameen Bank, which promotes microcredits. It was also influenced by programmes like the 'Global Microcredit Campaign', the World Bank's concept of 'social capital' for the eradication of poverty and so on. The SHGs in India were floated as 'collateral credit groups', in a context where the commercial and cooperative banks moved away from lending microfinance on the grounds they would face the high risk of defaulters and high operational costs. The Seventy-third Amendment of the Indian Constitution and its SGSY programme strengthened the microcredit programme in the rural areas.

The District Rural Development Agency (DRDA), National Bank for Agriculture and Rural Development (NABARD) and NGOs were made responsible for training the women in SHGs Statistics show that 5.7 million women members have been drawn into 400,000 SHGs in Andhra Pradesh.

Bankability of the SHGs

The members of SHGs save a minimum of Rs 1 per day and deposit it in a bank located in the region. The stipulated period for SHGs to become eligible for a bank loan is a six months saving period.[11] The bank should extend a loan amount ranging from two to four times of the savings of an SHG on collateral security. The SHGs from a group of villages converge into a 'federation' that operates under a bank. This bank has a specified area for its services called the 'service area federation'. The federation helps in mobilising higher-level credit, as the number of members and amount of savings of a federation are higher than that of the SHG. Each member of the federation pays a Rs 10 membership fee. A facilitator/promoter is elected from among the members of the federation to coordinate its activities. The facilitator's duties include the collection of savings, loans and deposit.

However, the eligibility of SHGs to be promoted to a federation depends on the discretion of the bank and recommendation of the group leader. Therefore, all SHGs are not the members of a federation.

The state provides funds under central assistance as matching grants (funds sponsored under central welfare schemes, such as the SGSY) for starting microenterprises.

Institutional Arrangements

A new institution called the 'nodal office' is formed to implement the development programmes of the SHGs. The position of nodal officer[12] is an additional charge entrusted to an officer working in one of the government departments for district development. He is made in-charge of a mandal to coordinate the development activities.[13] This organisation is floated as a parallel institution to the mandal praja parishad and grama panchayat to function with the new development programmes.[14] However, this has disturbed the link between the development programmes and the village elected representatives. The grama panchayats are also now starved of funds. Against this backdrop, this study looked into the SHGs in Muttangi and attempted a close look at the development programmes and their impact on the living conditions of women.

The Case Study

The programme of SHGs was started in Muttangi in 1999[15] with around 27 groups. Ideally, each group should consist of 15 members but there are many groups which have less than 15 members. Each member contributes Rs 30 per month towards the saving account. These savings amount to Rs 450 per group per month. A group becomes eligible for a bank loan after pooling the savings for six months. A revolving fund of Rs 5,000 per group is released from the DRDA.[16] The savings of the groups, bank loan and revolving fund together are used by the groups to lend among their own group members at an interest rate of 2 per cent per month. The group members are expected to pay back the loan amount taken from their own savings to the savings account of the bank so that the money becomes eligible to be lent out again.

The new development activities include raising nurseries, keeping the village clean and planting trees (called the Janma Bhoomi, clean and green programme). Meetings are arranged at the mandal level to discuss these programmes. Participation in all these meetings is compulsory to become eligible for a bank loan. The respondents, however, expressed that the issues discussed in the meetings were not useful for promoting their skills and general awareness or for starting any enterprise for employment. It is evident that these development activities do not generate employment.

Although the financial assistance for village-level development programmes is drawn from the pool of central assistance fund, the villagers think that these programmes are sponsored by the state government, for the central assistance is diverted to the state as implementation money for development programmes. This becomes evident from the data on the savings of SHGs and financial assistance of the government presented in Table 13.1.

Table 13.1
Stipulated Savings of SHGs of the Village

Total Number of Groups in the Village	Number of Members in each Group	Total Members in Village 1×2	Contribution by each Member Rs p.m.	Total Contribution Rs p.m. 3×4	Contribution Per Year from Village Rs
24	15	360	30	10800	1,29,600

Source: Mandal office, Patancheru.

Field observation shows that the groups are encouraged to save more than the stipulated minimum of Re 1 per day per member with the promise of more loans and matching grants. The actual amount saved, however, depends on the saving capacity of each group. The following are the details of the savings of the groups (corpus fund), bank loan and the revolving fund released by the state (see Table 13.2).

Table 13.2
Details of Amount Granted to the SHGs during 1999 (in Rs)

Savings of SHGs	Revolving/ Matching Grant (Rs)	Bank Loan (Rs)	Total Corpus Fund	Total Members	Per Capita (Rs)
2,03,530	55,000	89,500	348,030	300	1,160

Source: Mandal office, Patancheru (the data for other years is not documented).

The data in Table 13.1 shows that the estimated total contribution of the SHG members in the village is Rs 10,800 per month.

The data in Table 13.2[17] shows that 300 members were assisted by the village during the year 1999 (only one year's data is available at the mandal office). The total savings by these members should work out to Rs 9,000 per month. But the data in Table 13.2 shows that the amount of savings is Rs 2,03,530. This explains that the amount of savings is much higher than the stipulated amount of Re 1 per person per day. It is observed in the field that the SHGs are encouraged to save more than the stipulated minimum of Re 1. Thus, higher savings are mobilised under the guise of creating scope for higher loans and matching grants. This explains that the actual amount saved depends on the financial capacity of the members in each group. The data shows that when a matching grant or revolving fund of Rs 55,000 and a bank loan of Rs 89,500 was released, the amount of savings of the SHGs was about three times the amount extended by the bank (Table 13.2). But according to the programme structure, the bank loan should be three to four times the savings of the SHGs. So what is happening is exactly the reverse of what was planned.

There are also other ways in which concealed swindling of the funds take place. The bank cannot legitimately impose any interest on the SHGs, as the savings amount of SHGs is treated as collateral security for the loan to be released by the bank. But the commercial banks impose an interest of 13.5 per cent per annum to the SHGs on the loans extended by them. This rate of interest is almost two times to that of the rate of interest imposed by NABARD to commercial banks. NABARD gives loans to commercial banks at the rate of 7 per cent for the purpose of extending it to SHGs. The SHGs in turn lend this amount at the rate of 24 per cent among their own group members. Thus, a multi-tiered swindling is in place. Yet another form of swindling is seen in that the SHGs are not allowed to repay the loan amount earlier than the stipulated period of 36 months, and have to pay the interest for the whole of this period. This clearly demonstrates that the credit extended are only to promote regular usury earnings of the banks from the SHGs. The entire programme of the SHGs has turned into a usury seeking business at different levels starting from NABARD, to the commercial banks and the SHGs. The usury seeking agenda certainly cannot promote the development of women.

Field Experiences

It is observed from the field data that out of the sample of 77 SHG members, more than 58 per cent of them diverted the funds in the sense that they have not used the credit amount for starting a new enterprise. As the total corpus fund of Rs 348,030 extended to 300 members, works out to Rs 1,160 per capita, the members responded that such a meagre amount is not sufficient for starting any new enterprise. The members who did not divert the amount constitute 42 per cent. These members have used the amount in their already existing units of occupations. Among them, more than 62 per cent have invested on family based and not on individual female-headed enterprises. The data also reveals that most of the members who availed of the loan are not from the 'very poor' families. This explains that the banks have excluded the poor and deserving sections. They preferred financially better off family-based enterprises, for it ensured them an 82 per cent regular loan repayment. Therefore, the regular repayment of loans should not be mistaken for an overall improvement in the economic status of the SHG members, and should be recognised for what it is—the result of a strategic selection of enterprises by the banks. The family-based units that are preferred by banks do not give any financial freedom to its women workers. That is, these units do not help in 'empowering' women, as was expected. The occupational details of the SHG members are a testimony to this trend.

Out of the 77 sample SHG members, 62 per cent are in occupations of business and agriculture or are housewives. Another 28 per cent are engaged in physical labour, 4 per cent are workers in the factory, and 6 per cent have individual tailoring units. Except for a meagre 6 per cent, the remaining 94 per cent do not have independent income-earning units. This trend can hardly influence any intra-household relations.

The data shows that 57 per cent of SHG members are illiterate. Among the SHG leaders the figure is 38 per cent. These leaders depend on other literates for writing the accounts of their group. Although the groups were formed four years back, there has been no effort to promote the skills, training and literacy of the members. This shows that there is hardly any scope for the democratic transformation of society towards equality as has been envisaged in the objectives of the SHGs. The concept of the SHGs itself clearly mentions that sustainable development is possible only with the promotion of skills among these women. The data on occupations and field observations have already revealed that hardly any step has been taken by the government in this respect. However, the field experience shows that women in the village exhibited a lot of enthusiasm for learning skills.[18] This shows that there is lack of commitment on the part of the authorities in integrating women with development.

However, this study has also uncovered a positive aspect of the SHG programme. Survey has revealed that 63 per cent of the SHG members have been attending the meetings regularly. The men, out of economic compulsion, cooperate and allow the women to come to these meetings. This has given the women the confidence to question the lapses and also unfulfilled promises of the government. Women are also criticising family violence. Thus the SHGs have evidently contributed more to a change in social attitudes than to economic development. All these go to show that the SHG programme has the potential of becoming a great social force and for paving the way towards greater women power.[19] However, this social force needs to be directed and organised properly.

Women's Development in China

After having looked at the Indian experience of women-oriented development, it may now be helpful to look at the micro-level experience of China in the same area. Several studies indicate that China has experienced phenomenal development in rural areas and that the condition of women in China has not only improved considerably but is far better than in many parts of the world, including India.

It is observed that rural industrialisation has been the engine behind China's recent economic miracle (Chong Chor Lau and Yusheng Peng, 2000: 3). The rural sector has been most dynamic and has grown at an annual rate of 27 per cent during the last two decades. Today this sector has become the largest employer, employing one-fifth of the work force and contributing more than the urban industries in taxes. The workers in rural industries are more productive and earn more profits than their urban counterparts (Chong Chor Lau and Yusheng Peng, 2000).

Rural industries have also contributed to the social development of the villagers. The price of agricultural commodities too have been subsidised and according to many scholars, this was made possible by the changes initiated in the structure of industries, and in the state policies on the industrial and agricultural sectors (Chong Chor Lau and Yusheng Peng, 2000). These changes, along with the initial endowments, changed the socio economic scenario in China. Some of the major policy measures, as observed by scholars, are given next.

Structural Changes in Industries

Between 1978-84, individual[20] and private enterprises[21] were encouraged, but the Township Village Enterprises (TVEs)[22] continued to exist side by side. By the mid 1980s, TVEs were either owned by the collectives or co-operatives which were outside state control and planning. To give impetus to their growth, several incentives were introduced by the state from 1988 onwards. The TVEs have also developed strong links with local governments.

Policy Changes in Industries

The state policy focused both on agriculture and foreign trade in the 1978 reforms. The earlier restriction on farmers not to engage in non-farm activities was lifted. Therefore, farmers could now enter all types of economic activities like agriculture, mining, construction, manufacturing, machinery, industry, transport, communication, commerce and services.

Policy Changes in Agriculture

In the reforms, the state adopted the system of individual cultivators on a long-term (15–20 years) lease basis, in place of communes. The farmers had to contribute a fixed percentage of output to the state. These changes in policy were accompanied by reforms in the price mechanism. The prices of agricultural products were increased by 25 per cent. This in turn raised productivity and output of agriculture to more than eight per cent (8.8 per cent). This further resulted in a growing pressure on the state for permission to utilise the spare labour and cash savings for industrial use. The capital accumulated by the communes in the earlier period further led to the communes joining the call for industrialisation in the late-1980s.

Initial Collective Accumulation

Rural industrialisation or the growth of TVEs during 1978 was associated with agricultural growth and savings. Agricultural savings were the main source of the accumulated collective capital. (Yusheng, 1999). It was observed by scholars that surplus labour, proximity to cities, agricultural output per capita significantly contributed to the industrial growth rate (Yusheng, 1999) and that education (at least up to junior high school) would help in bringing higher industrial returns (Yusheng, 1992).

It is also worth mentioning in this respect, that the unit family system, a highly educated labour force, low fertility rate among the workers and more egalitarian relations especially between gender and age groups, helped in building rural industries in China.

Microcredit in China

The Funding for the Poor Cooperative (FPC) programme in China is a replication of the Grameen programme of Bangladesh. The microfinance system, its operation and management have been so designed that they are adaptable to local circumstances and culture in rural China. The staff of the microfinance operators was trained in Bangladesh, where this system has been successfully implemented. The NGOs in China who have been providing microcredit to the poor have approached the government for the formulation of a new legal framework, which would suit the changed circumstances following market reforms.

The most revealing fact about the changed fortunes of women in rural China is that some members of SHGs in the village have started schools. The women members of SHGs expressed their satisfaction that they could educate their children with the microfinance extended to them. However, these trends need to be probed further (Grameen Connections, 2001).

Conclusion

This discussion on China shows that growth in the primary sector is a prerequisite for local industrialisation as it alone can lead to local savings and local surplus capital which can be used for rural industrialisation. Second, the state can also play a significant role in encouraging rural industries by its policy decisions and a close connection between the local government and industries go a long way in promoting industrialisation. Last, sound human capital, well-educated families, egalitarian relations between the sexes; all contribute to the promotion of local industries in China.

In India, on the other hand, the lack of political will to promote egalitarian growth proved detrimental to developmental interests in local society. The high-levels of illiteracy, pauperisation and ignorance of villagers have been a major cause behind the failure of the development policy. Lack of proper direction and utilisation of local surplus led to unproductive investment in real estate business and marriage expenditure, thereby rendering local labour vulnerable to the open market forces. Development programmes like SHGs too failed to generate a rounded development of women because of the deeply embedded socio-economic inequalities and the patriarchal ideology governing the functions of state, capital and familial relations in society.

Appendix 13.1
Particulars of Land Sale

Year of Land Sale	Total Land Sold	Sales to Industry		Sales to Real-esestate Business		Sales to Agriculturists		Sales to	
Year	Acres	Number	Acres	Number	Acres	Number	Acres	Villagers	Outsiders
1973–74	12.19	nil	nil	nil	nil	9/6	12.19	6	nil
1974–75	11.13	nil	nil	nil	nil	5/8	11.13	8	nil
1975–76	7.21	nil	nil	nil	nil	10/5	7.21	5	nil
1976–77	9.29	nil	nil	nil	nil	5/6	9.29	6	nil
1977–78	Nil	nil	nil	nil	nil	nil	nil	nil	nil
1978–79	13.02	nil	nil	1/6	13.02	nil	nil	nil	6
1979–80	Nil	nil	nil	nil	nil	nil	nil	nil	nil
1980–81	32.52	7/2	6.25	2/7	26.27	nil	nil	nil	19
1981–82	34.55	21/3	26.12	1/3	1.32	2/1	7.11	1	23
1982–83	Nil	nil	nil	nil	nil	nil	nil	nil	nil
1983–84	2.04	nil	nil	nil	nil	2/2	2.04	2	nil
1984–85	4.01	nil	nil	nil	nil	5/5	4.01	2	nil
1985–86	9.37	1/4	1.13	4/13	6.03	5/2	2.21	2	17
1986–87	Nil	nil	nil	nil	nil	nil	nil	nil	nil
1987–88	13.15	nil	nil	nil	nil	15/17	13.15	17	nil
1988–89	8.03	nil	nil	14/6	1.00	7/5	7.03	5	6
1989–90	3.20	1/1	3.20	nil	nil	nil	nil	nil	nil
1990–91	0,34	nil	nil	1/4	0.34	nil	nil	nil	1
Total	160.05	30/10	36.70	53/3	47.98	65/57	75.37	54	72

Source: Collected from MRO Office, Patancheru.

Appendix 13.2
Survival Struggles—Combinations of Female Multiple Activities

(income in Rs per annum)

Activities	1	2	3	4	5 = (3 + 4)
	Rs aipm	No.mwa	Rs tipa Agri	Rs tipa Non-Agri	Rs tipwpa Agri + Non-Agri
Tailoring and knitting	650	4	–	2600	5600
Agricultural labour	–	–	3000	–	
Tailoring	650	4	–	2600	11,600
Bangles business	1500	6	–	9000	
Tailoring and knitting	650	4	–	2600	10,600
Cultivation	–	–	8000	–	
Dairy	2000	12	–	24000	30,000
Animal grazing	–	–	6000	–	
Cane work	800	8	–	6400	9,400

(*Appendix 13.2 contd.*)

(Appendix 13.2 contd.)

Activities	1	2	3	4	5 = (3 + 4)
	Rs aipm	No.mwa	Rs tipa Agri	Rs tipa Non-Agri	Rs tipwpa Agri + Non-Agri
Agricultural labour	–	–	3000	–	
Broom stick making	100	8	–	800	3,800
Agricultural labour	–	–	3000	–	
Leaf plate making	1500	2	–	3000	6000
Agricultural labour	–	–	3000	–	
Cane work	800	8	–	6400	33,400
Dairy	2000	12	-	24000	
Agricultural labour	–	–	3000	–	
Selling pots	100	2	–	200	4200
Cultivation	–	–	4000	–	

Note: Rs aipm: average income per month; nomwa: number of months work available; Total income per annum from farm; tipa: total income per annum; tipw: total income per worker. For grazing imputed value is assigned.

Apendix 13.3
Non-farm Female Employment

Activities	Sample Number	Average Income (Rs per Month)	Work Available (in Months) per Year)	Annual Income of Sample (3.4)	Average Hours of Work per Day	Total Number of Workers in Village
Attendant	01	625	12	7500	08	01
Fair price shop	01	1500	12	18000	06	02
Four mill supervisor	01	1500	12	18000	03	03
Rice mill	01	1500	0	6000	10	03
Vegetable business	03	1050	12	12600	05	03
Grocer	03	1733	12	20796	13	12
Bangles	01	1500	06	9000	10	01
Tailoring	08	650	04	2600	05	13
Snacks	02	1250	12	15000	07	02
Quarry	02	1500	12	18000	10	03
Laundry	01	1500	12	18000	10	01
Dairy	04	2000	12	24000	08	12
Leaf plate	01	1500	02	3000	08	04
Brooms	01	200	08	1600	06	01
MatsΦ	01	200	02	400	04	06
Potter	01	200	03	600	01	03
Mid-wife	01	100	–	300	04	01
Cane work	02	800	08	6400	06	02
Total	35	9,308	8	181796	07	73

Appendix 13.4
Non-farm Male Employment and Income in the Village

1	2	3	4	5	6	7
Activities	Sample Number	Per Head Income Rs per Month	Work Avaialable in Years per Month	Annual Income of Sample	Average hrs of Work per Day	Total Number of Workers in Village
Dairy*	01	2000	12	30000	06	04
Tailor	01	1200	08	9600	10	04
Attender	01	800	12	9600	08	04
Carpenter	01	500	06	3000	08	01
Rice mill	01	2500	04	10000	10	02
Quarry	02	1500	12	18000	10	03
Toddy	02	1200	08	9600	10	05
Piggery	02	100	12	1200	05	02
Sheep & goat	02	8000	12	96000	14	20
Mutton	01	2000	12	24000	08	02
Hotel	02	1800	12	21600	14	02
Drivers	05	1000	12	12000	14	30
Riksha	01	400	12	4800	12	10
Hair cutting	02	3000	12	36000	13	10
Washing	01	300	12	3600	03	06
Total	25	26,300	10.5	289000	10.00	105

*for grazing Rs 6000 is imputed.

Appendix 13.5
Industrial Workers from the Village

	Workers in Village	No. of Workers in Private Industries	Percentage of Industrial Workers among Village Workers
Male	1770	83	4.6
Female	1599	8	0.50
Total	3369	103	3.05

Notes

1. The effluents let out from the industries polluted the surface and groundwater. The Pollution Control Board has marked this region under 'Red alert, danger zone' indicating that the water from this region is not for use. The Supreme Court has ordered the state to

supply drinking water to villages under this zone free of cost. But the water authorities are collecting the water cess charges. These charges exceed the total revenue amount of the village.

2. The land retained by the households is skewed. The land to man ratio for SCs and BCs is 1:1.9 and 1:1.7 acres respectively, while in the case of Forward Castes (FCs), it is 1:5 acres. The land that yields two crops is mostly owned by the FCs. This adversely affected the employment and income of the female members of the SCs and BCs, as agricultural wage labour is recruited more from these social categories.

3. The upper caste landed households, in order to protect their land, established connections with the households who were loyal and had been working for generations in the office of the *'patwary'* (keepers of land records) and later in the office of the grama panchayat as watchmen. These landed households also have their own people as 'officials' in the village panchayat. The powerful connections of the landed gentry are used to facilitate subsidised agricultural credit, inputs and information to tenants to make tenancy attractive and cheap. To attract tenants, the landed/officials also help the sons of tenants get placement in industries. It is noticed that these tenants are largely from BC families.

4. There are 20 *'kuruva'* families whose occupation is sheep rearing. At present, only six families rear sheep. The shepherds no longer graze the sheep in the fields for natural manure as they did before industrialisation due to the increase in sheep theft. They sell them once a year during the Dassera festival to slaughterhouses.

5. The land owners preferred outside contract workers over village labour to avoid the hassles of village labourers bargaining for higher wages. The landowners complain that 'the local labour do not maintain timings to take up work in the field. The local labour bargain for wages in kind which was an old practice'. To accommodate all these complaints, village women formed themselves into groups to work on a contract basis for piece-rate work in the village. This set in the process of 'distress employment'

6. These activities are characterised as distressed non-farm activities as they earn an income lower than minimum wages. Women are much more vulnerable in this respect.

7. This refers to 'pushing the productive activity into home'.

8. A toddy society has been formed in the village. Everyday, about 80 to 100 bags of toddy are sold. Each bag consists of 24 bottles and each bottle costs Rs 3.50. So this works out to an income of $100 \times 24 \times 3.50 =$ Rs 8400 everyday. The annual income from toddy works out to Rs 3,066,000.

9. Mr Reddy, a candidate supported by the 'Telangana Rastriya Samity', which is a regional party, manipulated and managed different sections of the society with different means and money. For example, he distributed clothes, cooking vessels to the poorest sections of the village. He also purchased autos for some SC youth and brought up the mistakes of the former sarpanches of the village in public to stop them from contesting in the 2001 panchyat elections.

10. The objective of the holistic microenterprise programme of 'Swarnajayanthi Gram Swarojgar Yojana' is to bring every assisted family above the poverty line in three years. It covers all aspects of self-employment, namely, organising the rural poor into SHGs, building their savings capacity, planning activity clusters, building up infrastructure, technology, credit and marketing (Government of India, Ministry of Rural Development, New Delhi, The Guidelines SGSY, n.d.)

11. Following the scheduled norms such as (i) holding regular monthly meetings (ii) maintaining accounts (iii) continuously practicing thrift (iv) rotating the corpus generated and (v) making the group eligible to get bank loans. It has been observed that any group requires at least four days training in a year. Training is given in areas like group management, conducting of group meetings, accounts and bookkeeping and mode of accessing the government schemes and bank finance.

12. The interaction in the field revealed that the nodal officer is an officer who is loyal to the ruling party, though this fact needs further probing.

13. The heads of different government departments at the district level such as health, education, social welfare, civil supplies, etc., will be appointed by the district collector to the post of nodal officer for a mandal. It is an additional charge for him.

14. The new development programmes refer to the programmes floated by the Telugu Desam government.

15. The SHGs of the village were located within the cooperative structure. To avoid the cost of service they were shifted to the commercial banks with the name 'Service Area Federations'.

16. The data recorded in the Mandal office shows that there is convergence of the services of the state and centre. No separate allocations of matching grants for lending to SHGs by the state has been made as was promised.

17. The data is documented only for the year 1999 in the mandal office, Patancheru. The total number of members, the total amount under revolving fund, bank loan and savings have been documented.

    This data is used as only example.

18. As part of survey, the author formulated groups of women who were willing to learn skills on payment. The response was immense. The author introduced these groups to a skill promotion organisation 'SETWIN'.

19. One group purchased an auto and gave it to a member, whose husband began operating it. But he was a drunkard and refused to give his earnings to his wife for repayment of the loan taken with the collateral security of the group. Hence, the auto was taken back and a driver was hired to drive the auto. The driver pays regularly. Thus, collective force won in the fight against patriarchy.

20. Which have less than eight outside workers.

21. Which have eight or more workers

22. These are the enterprises run by former communes, including towns and districts authorities.

References

Associate Programme Co-ordinator, Centre for Cooperative and Rural Development. 2003.

Bhatia, Navin and Anju Bhatia. 2002. 'Lending to Groups: Is it Worthwhile?', *Yojana, The Great Concern*. New Delhi: The Indo-German Social Service Society.

Chong, Chor Lau and Yusheng Peng. 2000. 'Explaining China's Rural Industrialization: The Roles of Social Capital, Human Capital and Economic Fundamentals', *China Report*, 36 (3): 1–38.

DWCRA & Women Empowerment. 1999. 'A Success Study of Self Help Movement in Andhra Pradesh'. Department of Panchayat Raj and Rural Development, Government of Andhra Pradesh.

Galab, S. Chandrashekhar Rao N. 2003. 'Women's Self-Help Groups, Poverty Alleviation and Employment', in C.H. Hanumantha Rao and S. Mahendra Dev (eds). Andhra Pradesh Development: Economic Reforms, Challenges Ahead. Hyderabad: Centre for Economic and Social Studies.

Grameen Connections, Internet, undated.

Mohanty, Manoranjan. 1995. 'Power of History: Mao Zedong Thought and Deng's China', *China Report*, 31(1): 1–7.

Naithani, Pankaj. 2003. 'Microfinancing the Self Employment Activities: A See-Saw of Ideas', *The Great Concern*, 28 (1): 50.

Peng, Yusheng. 1992. 'Wage Determination in Rural and Urban China: A Comparision of Public and Private Industrial Sector, *American Sociological Review*, 57 (2): 198–213.

———. 1999. 'Agricultural and Non-Agricultural Growth and Inter-Country Inequality in China, 1985–1991', *Modern China*, 25 (3).

Sinha, Sanjay, John Samuel and Benjamine Quinones htt//www.asiasociety.org/speeches/microcredit.*html The Great Concern*, 28 (1): 12.

Vanamala, M. 2003. 'Impact of Industrialisation on Female Employment', Report submitted to ICSSR, New Delhi.

'Workers on SHG-Bank linkage' (NIPCCD), *The Great Concern*, 28 (1): 53.

14 Democracy, Good Governance and Economic Development in Rural China

DAVID ZWEIG AND CHUNG SIU FUNG

Introduction

Within a decade of the decollectivisation of rural China (1978–83) and the enormous economic boom that decollectivisation generated, rural China began to fall on hard times.[1] Particularly after the urban reforms of 1984 and rapid urban economic growth in the mid- to late-1980s, rural China's economic conditions deteriorated. The price scissors between urban and rural goods, which had narrowed in 1978–83, expanded significantly. As many as 20 per cent of rural villages lacked any real political authority. In the 1990s, local taxes and fees, imposed by cash-strapped rural cadres, created political hostility and social conflict that threatens the Communist Party's grip on power in the countryside.[2] As a result, the number of rural protests increased almost four-fold between 1993–99.[3]

In response to these challenges, China's leaders, egged on by younger reformers, have sought to introduce greater democracy and mechanisms of good governance into rural China (Li and O'Brien, 1999). These include village elections, village contracts, village assemblies and transparent financial management within the villages. These reforms, they hope, will increase villagers' willingness to invest in capital construction projects, such as new roads, under the assumption that if their own elected officials call on them to do so, they will do so (Wang Zhenyao, 1998: 239–56). Moreover, it is hoped that more economic growth and greater democracy will promote political stability. Thus, their support for democracy remained highly instrumental and not an end in itself; so long as democracy strengthened state power and national economic growth, it would be supported.

Conceptual Perspectives on Democracy and Economic Development

This chapter assesses several assumptions underlying the promotion of democracy and good governance in rural China.[4] A most common argument in the political science literature is that economic development leads to democratisation. Quantitative and qualitative studies generally confirm this relationship (Bollen, 1980; Rueschemeyer et al., 1992; Diamond, 1992). For Huntington, 'few relationships between social, economic, and political phenomena are stronger than that between level of economic development and existence of democratic politics' (Huntington, 1991: 311). Nevertheless, the Latin American experience in the 1970s and 1980s suggests that, while middle levels of economic development are conducive to democratisation, both poverty and higher levels of economic development could generate authoritarianism (O'Donnell, 1979).

In rural China, the relationship between economic development and democracy may also be curvilinear. In very poor communities, local governments cannot afford ballot boxes and villagers may be too busy making ends meet to care about good democratic procedures.[5] At the other end of the economic spectrum, the most industrialised and collectivised villages have the financial wherewithal to resist democracy. Oi and Rozelle found that the competitive nature of elections decreased in the top decile of villages in terms of their levels of industrialisation. However, in the other 90 per cent of villages, they found no relationship between economic development and electoral politics (Oi and Rozelle, 2000: 513–39). In this vein, Guangdong Province was the last major province to introduce village elections. Perhaps middle-income regions, where numerous private businesses want less intrusive leaders and more transparent polities, are where we find the socio-economic roots of democratisation and a positive relationship between economic development and democracy. Still, Rong Hu's research in Fujian Province found greater participation and more competition in wealthier villages, which also did a better job of instituting various election laws (Hu, 1999).

Our Research Questions[6]

In light of this discussion, the key questions driving this study are:

a) Is rural China democratic? Did the level of democracy increase as the system improved and as villagers became more aware of the opportunities democracy affords them? How institutionalised are 'democratic procedures', such as secret ballots, multi-candidate elections, public nominations and village contracts?

b) Are villagers satisfied with economic development alone, or do they believe that democratic reforms are necessary even if there is good economic growth? Do they see elections as efficacious, fair and competitive, or do they feel that the local power elite can manipulate the outcomes? Does enhancing democracy, through more democratic nomination systems, increase government legitimacy?

c) What is the relationship between economic development and democracy? Are richer areas, or richer people, more supportive of democracy?

Are cadres in wealthier areas more or less supportive of democracy? Does the emerging rural middle class support democracy or resist it? If the answers to these questions are positive, continued economic growth could transform rural politics.

d) Finally, has democracy affected the local elite? Have elections led to leadership turnover? How do local elites perceive electoral politics? Does the ballot box discipline cadres so that democratically elected cadres are less prone to misbehave; that is, does democracy lead to good governance?

Methodological Issues

With the cooperation of a research centre in China, we drafted two detailed surveys, one for villagers and another for cadres. Due to financial and political limitations, however, the survey was carried out in 1999 in two provinces, Heilongjiang and Anhui, with two counties selected in each province and 30 villages selected in each county for a total of 120 villages. In each village we selected 20 villagers at random, for a total of 2,400 villagers. We also pinpointed 237 individuals who ran their own businesses—approximately two in each village—whom we categorise as entrepreneurs and treat as the emerging middle class. Finally we interviewed 360 cadres, including from each village the party secretary, the current director of the villager committee and one other cadre who did not hold either post. About 20 per cent of informants were women.

Unfortunately, we could not collect time series data on the elections. Election data only reflected the village's most recent election. Thus we cannot talk about how elections or better governance over time changed popular political attitudes. Moreover, the elections in Heilongjiang Province all occurred in 1996–97 (with only one in 1998), before China's National People's Congress passed a law announcing its preference for direct nomination by villagers. Fortuitously, in Anhui, all the villages held elections in 1999, with about half of them following the haixuan system, or other forms of direct nominations by villagers.[7] Thus, though we have no time series data, we can still try to assess whether better democratic procedures—in the form of more direct nominations—affected villagers' attitudes towards the government and political reforms. Still, we must recognise that we cannot show causality—it is possible that areas introduced more democratic forms of nominations because the people and/or locals supported greater democracy.

The Context of the Village Study

All 120 villages were predominantly agricultural, with little variation in demographic or socio-economic characteristics of two Anhui counties.

Per capita income for the two counties as reported in *Anhui Provincial Yearbook, 2000* was RMB 2,182 (Anhui A) and RMB 2,201 (Anhui B), while the provincial average was RMB 1,900.[8] In Helongjiang, the per capita income in one county in 1999 (Heilongjiang A) was RMB 2,637, but the second county, Heilongjiang B, was significantly poorer, with a per capita income of RM 1,227 (Zhongguo Tongji Chubanshe, 2001c: 439) and significantly below the provincial average per capita income of RMB 2,165. In terms of per capita income as derived from the village records, the two Anhui counties and Heilongjiang B were relatively similar. Anhui A and B had a mean income of 1,983 and 1,827 respectively, while Heilongjiang B had a mean per capita income of 1,877. However, Heilongjiang A had a mean per capita income of 3,273.[9] This pattern also holds true for per capita income, measured by the number of household appliances. In the two Anhui counties, 79 per cent and 84 per cent of all households had three household appliances or less. In Heilongjiang B, 64 per cent of villagers had three items or less, while in Heilongjiang A, the richest country, 58 per cent of villagers reported having three household items or less.

Education levels also varied. The mean number of years of schooling of the Anhui counties was 5.1 and 5.7, while in Heilongjiang, the richer of the two counties had a mean score of 6.8, while the poorer county had a higher mean of 7.2. There was also greater inequality in the level of individual schooling in Anhui than in Heilongjiang, as measured by the standard deviation.

As outlined here, the political context of the survey varied between the two provinces as well. Both counties in Anhui held their elections in 1999, after the National People's Congress passed the new Organic Law, while most Heilongjiang elections were held in 1996–97. As a result, nominations in Anhui were far more democratic (see Table 14.1).

The Practice of Democracy in Rural China

So, how well established are democratic institutions in these communities? Indicators of the level of democracy include voting rates, secret ballots, multi-candidate elections, a village contract, whether the villagers felt that village leaders were publicly sharing financial records with them and how many times elections had been held in the community (see Table 14.1).

Almost 70 per cent of villagers reported that their community had multi-candidate elections,[10] a much higher rate than that reported by numerous observers for the 1995–97 period.[11] However, our survey occurred in the summer of 1999, after the spring 1999 reform of the Organic Law on Village Elections by the National People's Congress. Over 79 per cent of villagers reported that their village used secret ballots. Similarly, 91.4 per cent of our villagers reported satisfaction with the level of transparency of the village's financial reports, while 78 per cent of villagers reported that their leaders had

Table 14.1

Measures of Democratic Procedures, by Province, 1996–99

	Percentage of Villagers Reporting	
Procedures Employed	Heilongjiang	Anhui
Voting Rate	84	85
Villages with Multi-candidate Elections	66	74
Villages with More Democratic Nominations★	23	47
Secret Ballot	80	79
Election Speeches	26	19
Village Contracts	88	68

Source: Survey in rural China, summer 1999.
Notes: ★ from Robert A. Pastor and Qingshan Tan (2000: 490–512) (see endnote 12).

signed a contract with the villagers, both important steps in improving local governance. On the other hand, candidates made speeches before the election in only 22.4 per cent of the cases. According to Pastor and Tan, since villagers know the candidates intimately before the election, there is little need for campaigning (Pastor and Tan, 2000). Still, if elections were really competitive, candidates should want to make speeches to differentiate themselves on important policy positions from their opponents.

We also had results on how candidates were nominated and broke those responses into two categories: more democratic nomination (MDN) systems and less democratic nomination (LDN) systems. The MDN category included villages using the haixuan system—which the Ministry of Civil Affairs posits as the fairest nomination system; those whose villagers nominated candidates directly; self-nominations; nomination by a unified group of villagers; or nominations by representatives of the households. Nominations by organisations, such as the party committee, the election committee, the villager representatives assembly, nominations by 'powerful or privileged people in the village' and people 'who did not know' how the nomination occurred, fell into the LDN.[12]

In our overall sample, 43 per cent of villagers reported that their village used more democratic nomination systems, but in Anhui Province, which held its elections in 1999, the share of MDN elections was significantly higher. In this chapter we compare the findings of these two cohorts, in part because we believe that MDN villages and villagers who live in MDN villages, represent a more democratic trend and we wish to see how that trend affects attitudes and beliefs about local politics.[13]

Our villages' voting rates were rather high—86 per cent of villagers reported voting in the villager committee elections—but this is the easiest medium through which people can participate. Also, 21 per cent of people had encouraged other people to vote, 13 per cent had nominated candidates, while another 10 per cent of villagers reported voluntarily participating in the meeting of the villager assembly or the village party committee. Only 10 per cent of villagers reported not participating in any form of political activity at all.

Elections as a Source of Support for the Government

What were the villagers' attitudes towards elections? If they saw elections as fair and competitive and felt that the CCP or other administrative forces were not too influential in determining electoral outcomes, the elections may become legitimate and help stabilise the political system. However, if they felt that the local power holders could control electoral outcomes, democracy would remain formalistic and yield few positive political outcomes.

For example, people may feel that party officials control the electoral outcome through manipulating candidate selection. So, we asked villagers— '*what do you think of the CCP's level of influence over elections?*' Surprisingly, only 10 per cent saw the party's influence as 'very great'; 22 per cent saw the CCP having 'a certain level of influence'; 22 per cent saw it having 'not much influence'; while 21 per cent saw it having 'no influence'. Finally, 21 per cent said that they 'did not know'. Even if we assume that those who selected 'did not know' were afraid to say that the CCP had too much influence, 43 per cent did not feel that the CCP had very much influence.

Similarly, we asked people to respond to the statement: '*If a ministry or bureau wants to control the election, they need not control the voting but instead can control the selection of candidates*'. The responses? 'Totally agree'—6.5 per cent; 'relatively agree'—18 per cent; 'don't agree much'—21 per cent; 'totally disagree'—20 per cent; 'don't know'—27 per cent. Thus, 41 per cent of respondents felt that outside forces cannot control candidate selection or electoral outcomes. In Anhiu Province, villagers in MDN villages were even more likely to 'totally disagree' (25 per cent) or 'disagree' (21 per cent) than villagers in LDN villages, whose scores were 'totally disagree'—19 per cent and 'don't agree much'—15 per cent (total 34 per cent) (MLA, p = .01).[14]

Overall, villagers saw an increase in the level of competitiveness and fairness of the most recent elections as compared to the previous election. In our survey, 15 per cent of villagers saw the level of competitiveness as being 'very intense', 40 per cent saw it as being 'relatively intense', while 22 per cent saw no change. Only 6.6 per cent saw the recent elections as 'not intense at all'. Similarly, 18 per cent saw the most recent election as 'fairer', 41 per cent saw it as 'a little fairer' and 21 per cent saw no change. Only 6.5 per cent saw the most recent election as 'a bit less fair' or 'far less fair' than previous ones.

These findings were particularly true in villages with more democratic institutions. Based on a multi-variate analysis, the best explanations for 'level of perceived fairness' was whether villages allowed voters two or more ballots—villages that allowed some voters two or more ballots were seen to be very unfair—and whether there were more candidates than positions. In Anhui, when we asked rural inhabitants to rank the level of fairness of the electoral process, 70 per cent of villagers whose village used more democratic nomination systems selected 'fairer' or 'a bit fairer', while only 52 per cent of LDN villagers did so (p < .001). Therefore, in villages that had more democratic nominations systems, villagers also saw more fairness in the electoral process.

Table 14.2
Perceived Level of Fairness in MDN and LDN Elections, Anhui Province, 1999

Perception of Elections	MDN Villages (in per cent)	LDN Villages (in per cent)
Became Fairer	18	13
Became a Bit Fairer	52	39
No Change	10	19
Became a Bit Less Fair	7	6
Became Far Less Fair	3	3
Don't Know/No Response	10	20
Total	100	100

Source: Survey in rural China, summer 1999.
Notes: 1. When we calculate the MLA value, we put the 'don't know/no response' between 'no change' and 'became a bit less fair' category.
2. MLA, p=.001.

Similarly, villagers who reported that their village selected candidates through a more democratic nomination process also saw the electoral system as more competitive, another boost for the system's overall legitimacy. Thus 20 per cent of MDN villagers saw the level of competition under the MDN systems as 'extremely intense', versus 11 per cent of villagers in LDN villages. And when we combine 'extremely intense' and 'comparatively intense', villagers in MDN villages holding these views comprise 78 per cent, while 52 per cent of villagers in LDN villages held similar views (p < .001). Given that the Anhui elections were held two to three years after the Heilongjiang ones, and after promulgation calling for reform of the electoral nomination, it is possible that more democratic procedures makes people see the electoral system as more competitive and fairer.

Elections strengthen villager support for government policy. When asked to respond to the statement: '*After several rounds of elections, the villagers are more supportive of government policy than before*', 23 per cent of villagers strongly agreed with this statement, 43 per cent agreed somewhat, 11 per cent disagreed somewhat and only 4 per cent strongly disagreed. (19 per cent did not know or did not answer.) Moreover, villagers who reported that their candidates had been nominated through more democratic systems were more likely to see a

Table 14.3

Perceived Level of Competitiveness in MDN and LDN Elections, Anhui Province, 1999

Perception of Elections	MDN Villages (in per cent)	LDN Villages (in per cent)
Extremely Intense	20	11
Relatively Intense	58	41
No Change	5	15
Not Very Intense	5	6
Not Intense at All	1	1
Don't know/No response	11	26
Total	100	100

Source: Survey in rural China, summer 1999.

Notes: 1. When we calculate the MLA value, we put the 'don't know/no response' between 'no change' and 'not very intense' category.

2. MLA, p=.001.

relationship between elections and support for government policy. Of villagers in MDN villages, 72 per cent 'strongly supported' or 'relatively supported' this statement, while 58 per cent of villagers in LDN villages held such a view (MLA, p=.001).

Some villagers believed that elections brought bad influences. So increased democracy could contribute to political or social instability, as some oligarchs assert. However, 61 per cent of our villagers do not believe elections are harmful; only 11 per cent feel this way, while 28 per cent selected the 'don't know' option.

Would villagers be satisfied with good governance—without greater democracy—and could good economic development ameliorate aspirations for greater democracy? In response to the statement—'*If the existing cadres are capable and trusted, there is no need for democratic elections*', 12 per cent agreed strongly and 24 per cent agreed somewhat, 33 per cent disagreed somewhat and 22 per cent disagreed strongly (9 per cent did not know or had no response). Thus good governance alone is not sufficient for 55 per cent of our villagers—they want democracy. Similarly, when asked to respond to the statement: '*as long as village economic development is stable, there is no need to increase the level of democracy*', 33 per cent strongly disagreed and 32 per cent disagreed somewhat. Only 7 per cent agreed strongly, while 14 per cent agreed somewhat (14 per cent didn't know). Clearly, most villagers cannot be bought off by capable leaders and economic growth; they want more democracy.

Elections, Democratic Values and Economic Development

A truism of political development is that stable economic development, without significant inequality, is highly correlated with democratic development.

As more rural inhabitants, particularly in the wealthier coastal or suburban areas, become more prosperous, might the demand for democratic procedures and higher levels of political participation increase? To answer this question, we need to know if wealthier villagers held stronger democratic values.

We combined villager responses to a series of four questions about democracy, elitism and electoral politics to create one variable we call 'the democratic idea'. (See Appendix 14.1 for the list of questions and the villagers' responses to those questions.) We stratified the responses into four categories, running from *not democratic* to *very democratic*. We also asked villagers to describe their income relative to other people in their village, selecting upper, upper-middle, middle, lower-middle and lower. Table 14.4 shows the results of this cross-tabulation, while Figure 14.1 shows the curvilinear relationship between the perceived level of wealth and democratic values.

Table 14.4
Democratic Idea by Perceived Level of Wealth (in percentage)

Democratic Idea	Perceived Level of Wealth					
	Lower (n = 250)	*Lower -middle* (n = 435)	*Middle* (n = 1415)	*Upper -middle* (n = 419)	*Upper* (n = 102)	*Total* (n = 2621)
Not democratic	41	28	26	29	38	28
A bit democratic	42	50	47	41	43	46
Democratic	9	14	16	17	13	15
Very democratic	8	8	11	13	6	11
Total	100	100	100	100	100	100

Source: Survey in rural China, summer 1999.
Note: MLA, p = .003.

Interestingly, the very wealthy (upper) are almost as non-democratic (38 per cent) as the poorest or lower income group (41 per cent) and comprise even a smaller share of the most democratic group (6 per cent) than the poorest villagers (8 per cent). The most democratic people are those who see their wealth as 'middle' or 'upper-middle', while those who see themselves as 'lower middle' fall in between. These findings are statistically significant.

These findings employ the individual's wealth relative to villagers in their own village, rather than the village's overall wealth. But which communities are likely to be democratic—rich ones, poorer ones, or average ones? As mentioned earlier, Oi and Rozelle found a negative relationship between competitive elections and the level of industrialisation. However, in their data, the incidence of contested elections decreased only in the wealthiest 10 per cent of villages (Oi and Rozelle, 2000: 537). Otherwise, the level of economic development did not affect their measure of democratisation.

Figure 14.1
Democratic Idea by Perceived Level of Wealth (in percentages)

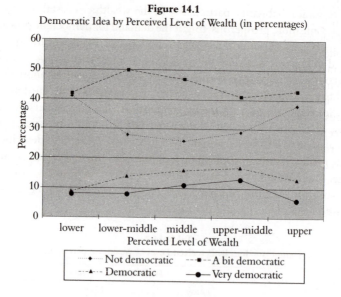

Our data, though tentative, also suggest that richer villages, based on per capita income from village records, are less democratic. While 62 per cent of villagers in wealthier villages reported that their most recent election had involved more candidates than positions, 72 per cent of middle-income villages and 76 per cent of poorer villages reported multi-candidate elections (p < .001). Similarly, while 64 per cent of villagers in poorer villages saw the most recent elections as more competitive, only 44 per cent of villagers in wealthier villages expressed such views.[15] Also, while speeches may not be that important in village elections, 26 per cent of villagers in poorer villages reported having had speeches, while only 21 per cent of those in richer villages said that there had been speeches.[16]

Also wealth did not correlate with democratic values. When asked to respond to the statement—'*so long as there is stable economic development, there is no need to promote greater democracy*'—villagers in richer villages were more likely to 'strongly agree' and 'agree' (24 per cent) than villagers in poorer (17 per cent) or middle-income villages (22 per cent) and the finding was statistically significant (p < .006). Similarly, people in wealthier villages were more likely to believe that the wealthy should have more right to speak out on village affairs (p < .001)—what might be seen as an elitist view of democracy—and they strongly agreed with the statement—'*because I know what's happened in the village, I have the right to participate in village affairs*'. Here, 34 per cent of villagers in wealthier villages 'strongly agree' with that statement, while only 22 per cent and 17 per cent of villagers in poor and middle-income villages respectively, strongly agree. Again, the finding was statistically significant ($p < .001$), and again, middle-income villages were more democratic.

The cadres' attitudes towards democracy also vary according to the village's per capita income (Table 14.5). Four questions assessed the cadres' views about democracy and elections and we broke their responses into three categories—non-democratic, democratic and very democratic. We also divided village income into richer, middle-income and poorer. In richer villages, 25 per cent of cadres fell into the 'non-democratic' category, while only 16 per cent and 13 per cent of cadres in poor and middle-income villages held 'non-democratic' views, respectively. Similarly, only 24 per cent of cadres in richer villages expressed 'very democratic' ideas, while 38 per cent and 40 per cent of cadres in poor and middle-income villages respectively, expressed 'very democratic' values—a very big difference.[17] These findings suggest that as villages get wealthier, their cadres are likely to become less democratic.

Table 14.5
The Cadres' Attitudes Towards Democracy by Village
Income Per Capita (in percentage)

	Village Income Per Capita			
Attitudes Towards Democracy	Poor (n = 108)	Middle (n = 129)	Rich (n = 123)	Total (n = 360)
Not democratic	16	13	25	18
Democratic	46	47	51	48
Very democratic	38	40	24	34
Total	100	100	100	100

Source: Survey in rural China, summer 1999.
Note: MLA, $p = 0.01$.

Finally, what kind of villages and who within them are most likely to demand good governance? We asked villagers—'*if you heard that village cadres were considering instituting an unfair measure (cuoshi), what would you do?*' Based on their selection from a list of options, including collective or individual action, as well as no action, we gave each villager a total score. The individual scores varied based on their relative income, showing that richer villagers (62 per cent) were much more likely to consider action than poorer (44 per cent) or middle-income ones (55 per cent, MLA=.00). Similarly, when asked if they had taken actions to solve problems facing their village, richer villagers were again more active. Of the 14 per cent of our entire sample who had taken some concrete action, richer villagers had acted more often (16 per cent) than middle-income (14 per cent) or poorer villagers (11 per cent). The measure of linear association was .008. Therefore, perhaps it was the richer villagers—who are better connected, particularly with the local party leadership—in poorer villages—where there were economic problems—who were most likely to consider taking action in response to unfair policies. This finding suggests that if cadres misbehave, wealthier villagers are most likely to challenge those actions. Still, despite the fact that they are more likely to take action, it is important to remember that these same richer villagers possess less democratic values.

Democracy and the Emerging Entrepreneurial Class

Another law of political development is that an emerging middle class is critical for democracy (Moore, 1967). With the growing influence of the rural private sector, the emergence of a new middle class might abet demo-cratic development. Newspapers, magazines and some scholars report that villagers elect entrepreneurs because they believe they are most capable of promoting the village's economy.

However, our localities did not have many factory owners. In our total sample, only 2 per cent of villagers reported that their family's main income came from wage labour. Nevertheless, interviewers in each village identified two entrepreneurs, yielding a total of 237 individuals, whose views we can compare with non-entrepreneurial peasants. These people were significantly richer than other villagers, both in terms of the self-identification of their level of wealth (the lower mean of 2.4 versus 3.2 reflected greater relative wealth) and in terms of the number of household appliances they possessed (mean of 4.4 versus 2.8).

But, do their views and attitudes about politics differ from the average peasants? First, they are much more aware of political phenomenon, discuss politics more frequently and are more willing to voice their opinion on issues than average villagers. In fact, 28 per cent of them report 'often' discussing political and economic issues, while only 14 per cent of other villagers do so. This may be because they are more educated and more likely to have a party member in their family. They are also more willing than other villages to discuss issues with the party secretary and to participate in the village repre-sentative assembly's meetings, but they are not more likely to discuss issues with the village director, perhaps due to his more limited influence. Maybe they know where the real power lies.

In terms of values, they are no more democratic than other villagers, except for their response to one question—'*as long as the village economy is stable, there is no need to increase the level of democracy*'. The data in Table 14.4 about the relationship between the 'democratic idea' and level of perceived wealth, reflect the position of entrepreneurs somewhat, in that 47 of the 237 entre-preneurs or 20 per cent declared their income as upper level, which placed them in the least democratic group. Still, 88 or 37 per cent of them fall into the upper-middle income group, which was the most democratic cohort.

Compared to other villagers, our entrepreneurs voice greater support for good governance and political procedures that limit the local elite's ability to manipulate the local economy and intervene in their private economic affairs. They are more likely than regular villagers to think that publicly displaying the village's financial records is good for economic development,[18] and to think that a contract between the villagers and the local cadres improves villager–cadre relations.[19]

Yet villagers do not want entrepreneurs to serve as village director.[20] When they were asked to select who should be elected from a list of possible candidates—villagers could choose more than one response—only 7 per cent selected entrepreneurs, less than those who selected normal villagers (*putong nongmin*) (8 per cent) or cadres (17 per cent). Also, when asked to respond to the following statement: '*entrepreneurs who are good at business and have money are the best candidates for village director*', a total of 71 per cent of villagers 'totally disagreed' (38 per cent), or 'disagreed' (33 per cent), while only 13 per cent 'relatively agreed' (9 per cent) or 'totally agreed' (4 per cent). Villagers may fear what Putnam called the 'agglutination' of political and economic power, seeing this process as threatening local democracy.[21] This finding also suggests that in these localities it will not be easy for entrepreneurs to crack into local politics through democratic means.

Democratising the Rural Elite?

Has democracy and elections affected the local elite? Have elections led to significant turnover? Does the fact that elections are becoming more competitive change elite behaviour towards villagers? Do elections serve as a monitoring mechanism limiting cadre misbehaviour?

Is there a 'Power Transition' Underway?

To what extent have local elections led to a restructuring of power in the countryside? In our villages, elite turnover increased significantly between 1996 and 1999. The percentage of village leaders taking office for the first time increased significantly year to year, from 37 per cent in 1996 to 43 per cent in 1997, reaching 53 per cent in 1999.[22] Much of this turnover in 1999 occurred in our Anhui villages, where the introduction of more democratic nominations led 25 per cent of cadres to decide not to run for re-election (see Table 14.6). Also, when Anhui village directors ran again for office, they lost approximately 50 per cent of the time. Rural elections are changing the people who hold political power.

Table 14.6
Getting Re-elected, MDN and LDN Village Directors, Anhui Province, 1999

	MDN Village Directors		LDN Village Directors	
	No.	%	No.	%
Previous director, ran for office and re-elected	7	25.0	15	46.9
Previous director, ran for office but not re-elected	14	50.0	13	40.6
Previous director, did not run for office	7	25.0	4	12.5
Total	28	100	32	100

Source: Survey in rural China, summer 1999.
Note: Chi-square test, p = 0.173.

Second, elections are pluralising political authority in the villages under study. While the village party secretary in 1996–97 often also held the post of director of the villager committee, in the 1999 elections this phenomenon ended almost entirely. Thus in 1996 and 1997, the party secretary held both posts in 32 per cent and 46 per cent of the cases respectively, but in 1999, the same person was elected to both posts in only one of 49 cases.[23]

But even though there is now a clearer division of labour and authority between the two top posts in the village, an authoritarian leadership strata may still hold power, making the division of authority somewhat pro-forma. Why do we say this? Even though a clear division of posts occurred in Anhui, the director of the village committee is now frequently the deputy secretary of the village party committee. While in Heilongjiang in 1996–98, 20 per cent of people elected as director of the village committee were also the vice party secretary, in 1999, 53 per cent of the newly-elected directors in Anhui were also vice party secretary. These newly-elected village leaders may be invited to become the vice party secretary to insure that key decisions are made in a committee run by the village party secretary.

What about non-CCP members who are elected to the villager committee or as director of that committee? Are they a source of democratic values within the local elite? According to Jakobson, in 1997, 44 per cent of village committee members nationwide were not party members. She also quotes Wang Zhenyao to the effect that 30–50 per cent of village committee directors were not party members when they won the election, but were recruited into the CCP in a few weeks (Jakobson, 2000).

Our survey documents this trend, as 25 per cent of village committee directors reported that they had joined the CCP before becoming a cadre, while 54 per cent of them had become a cadre and then joined the party. This latter group, then, was recruited into the CCP after attaining local elite status.

However, the pattern for the village party secretaries was reversed: 48 per cent of them had joined the CCP before becoming a cadre.[24] The finding suggests a different mobility track for party secretaries and village committee directors—with the former having much deeper roots in the CCP—which could lead to different values and attitudes.

The Values of Local Cadres

Despite the different mobility tracks, village party secretaries and village directors share similar attitudes on most issues, reinforcing the argument that a village-level oligarchy exists. On our democratic scales, there were no statistically significant differences between these two groups. We would have hypothesised that on issues, such as democratisation or elections, their differing experiences should have led to different views. Nevertheless, since many village directors in our survey were nominated by local organisations or elected through only partially democratic procedures, their views may not differ so much from local party elites who may have influenced their selection. In fact, they were no more worried about losing office if they could not resolve local problems than the party secretary, suggesting that they felt well protected by the local power structure.

Still, elite turnover has had some impact on the values of local leaders. In particular, cadres who had simultaneously held both posts were less democratic on a number of dimensions than cadres who held either the post of village party secretary or director of the village committee. In terms of their response to the question measuring democratic predilections, of the 22 officials who had held both posts, 32 per cent fell in the 'non-democratic category', while only 20 per cent of party secretaries and 14 per cent of village directors did so. Similarly, only 23 per cent of those holding dual posts fell in the very democratic group, while 36 per cent of party secretaries and 34 per cent of directors of villager committees did. On questions related to democratic process, these 'village emperors' were also less democratic. They were much more likely to believe that wealthier people should have more right to speak out on public affairs; they were less likely to disagree with the statement that '*if the economy is good then there is no need to promote democracy*'; and they were much more likely to agree that '*only people with special skills should have the right to hold office*'.

The most democratic group was the local non-party elite who were members of the village committee. As Table 14.7 shows, they were least likely to believe that the wealthy should have more say in public affairs or to believe that only people with special knowledge should have greater influence on decisions. Also, they were less likely to believe that good economic development mitigates the need for greater democracy. If these villagers move into leadership positions, the future local elite could become more democratic. Still, one wonders whether they will be able to enter the elite if they maintain those attitudes or whether they would maintain those attitudes after they gain real power.

Table 14.7
Attitudes Towards Democracy among Different Types of Cadres

(No.)	Party Secretaries (122) %	Village Directors (97) %	Other cadres who are CCP members (103) %	Other madres who are not CCP members (38) %
Wealthy people should have more say in public affairs than poorer people.				
Strongly agree	20	10	13	8
Agree	24	33	22	18
Disagree	21	24	35	32
Strongly disagree	33	31	30	40
As long as development of the village economy is stable, there is no need to increase the level of democracy.				
Strongly agree	4	4	3	3
Agree	5	4	8	3
Disagree	23	21	24	24
Strongly disagree	67	69	65	71
Only people with special knowledge and abilities have the right to speak at times of decision making.				
Strongly agree	24	12	18	16
Agree	25	32	36	21
Disagree	26	34	25	29
Strongly disagree	22	21	19	29

Source: Survey in rural China, summer 1999.

Central leaders frequently call on local cadres to be less rapacious and 'lighten the burden of the peasants'. Given the fact that the state has made this exhortation on an almost annual basis since 1978, the centre clearly needs a new mechanism to monitor cadre behaviour. Do elections discipline cadres and help the state monitor local misbehaviour? According to Li and O'Brien, the Fujian Provincial Bureau of Civil Affairs convinced the provincial Discipline Inspection Committee to support village elections 'when the commission realized that corruption tended to be lower where well-run village elections took place'(O'Brien and Li, 2000: 481). If this is generally true, elections could decrease rural instability that is triggered by cadre malfeasance.

What did our survey show? Both villagers and cadres believed that elections had a positive effect on cadre behaviour. In Anhui, 48 per cent of villagers from MDN villages believed that village elections could improve the cadres' haughtiness or rudeness, while only 41 per cent of villagers in LDN villages held these views.[25] Villagers from MDN villages were more likely to be satisfied with the level of transparency of the village's financial records, with 64 per cent of them being either 'very satisfied' or 'satisfied', while only 47 per cent villagers in LDN villages held these views (MLA, p = .001). This finding occurred because villages that introduced direct nominations were also more likely to make their financial records public. That meant that 29 per cent of citizens in LDN were 'not satisfied' and 6 per cent were 'extremely dissatisfied'.

This more favourable attitude towards how officials allocated village finances was reconfirmed by other questions. Villagers in MDN villages expressed greater satisfaction with how funds that they contributed to the village were used—44 per cent being 'very satisfied' or 'satisfied'—while only 30 per cent of villagers in LDN villages felt this way (MLA, p = .001). Importantly, 25 per cent of villagers in LDN villages were flatly dissatisfied (the bottom scale on this question) as compared to only 15 per cent of MDN villagers.[26] Still, villagers in MDN villages were not more likely to believe that elections could end the problems of 'random taxes or assessments' (*luan shou fei*) or prevent cadre corruption, a position echoed by Bernstein and Lu (2003).

Cadres say that elections make them more responsive to villagers' interests, a positive force for political stability and democracy. Cadres in our survey were more likely than peasants to believe that elections make them more likely to resist taxes and fees from the upper levels. While 14 per cent agree completely, 41 per cent agree somewhat with this point (so a total of 55 per cent are in agreement), while for cadres, 31 per cent agree completely, 50 per cent agree somewhat (making a total of 81 per cent). On the other hand, if true, their relations with higher-level officials get complicated if they respond to villagers' demands and protect the villagers' interests (Li, 2001).

Ironically, elections may make it more difficult, not easier, for village directors to promote economic development. Cadres in MDN villages were more likely to have faced a situation where villagers refused their requests to contribute to a proposed development project (36 per cent) than LDN directors (19 per cent) (MLA, p = .14).[27] We also asked the village directors to agree or disagree—on a four point scale—with the statement: '*Democratic elections make villagers more willing to contribute money to the village accumulation fund*'. Village directors in MDN villages tended to disagree with this statement (their mean score was 2.5) while directors in LDN villages were inclined to agree with it (mean score 2.1).[28] Thus directors in MDN villages were less likely to believe that elections persuade villagers to contribute to local economic development—a major expectation of central advocates of rural democracy. While the process of local capital accumulation may have become more democratic, democracy may not be helping economic development, despite the fact that local governments need to accumulate capital if they are to build roads and other forms of infrastructure that promote economic development.

Conclusion

Like many other studies of democracy in rural China, this study will not make sweeping or definitive generalisations. Data from four counties simply do not permit that. Our findings remain suggestive. Part of the problem lies in the fact that good indicators of democracy, stability, economic development or good governance are not easy to collect. Though few analysts want to confess to the limitations of their data, because it would call into question their findings, we must admit that surveying rural China on political variables is costly and very difficult.[29] We, therefore, should not give up case studies, or in-depth interviews, although a research strategy involving case studies and surveys would be optimal.

Still, democratic procedures based on some indicators seem fairly well established, and responses to our questions suggest that there was some strengthening of democracy in rural China in the late-1990s. As villages moved from having organised groups nominate candidates and increased the role of individuals in this process, the democratic environment improved. Villagers have a strong sense of fairness on this issue, and in our survey they clearly express a willingness to contemplate political action if cadres act unfairly. Little wonder cadres who cheat on elections worry about getting called onto the carpet.

But are wealthier localities more prone to adopt democratic principles and procedures? Our data do not allow us to make that statement. In fact, our data suggest that neither wealthier villagers nor villagers in wealthier villages are stronger advocates of greater democracy; even though they are more likely to take action against cadre malfeasance, the very wealthiest villagers are not repositories of democratic principles. Rather, those in the upper-middle income bracket may be the most democratic citizens in rural China. Similarly cadres in the wealthiest villages were the least democratic of our entire sample.

Democratisation apparently makes it more difficult for cadres to convince villagers to contribute to local development projects, and to the extent that this situation undermines economic development, it may be a negative result of democratisation. Admittedly, local cadres often do not allocate funds in a way that is beneficial to economic development. But if they are disciplined by elections, then granting responsive or responsible officials the authority to create collective goods could promote the local economy.

It is also not so clear from our data that elections are constraining cadre misbehaviour, though the direct nomination process in Anhui may have had that effect. Cadres say that elections keep them in line; but they know the politically correct responses—that is how they got to be cadres. Moreover, few of them expressed great concerns that they might lose their jobs if they could not solve the villagers' problems. And, they are under great pressure to conform to the demands of the township leaders (Alpermann, 2001: 45–67). Still, elections may encourage them to resist the demands for fees and taxes from upper levels.

Finally, despite the increasing institutionalisation of democracy, the changes underway within the local elite suggest relative political constancy. The old party secretaries, who also held the post of village director, are gone and a real division of authority emerged between the village director and the village party secretary. But as long as village directors are recruited into the CCP and are becoming the vice party secretary, the challenge to the CCP's authority posed by elections remains limited. We are not yet seeing the emergence of a '*dang wai*', or the rise to power of any cohort of like-minded individuals outside of the ruling party who could coalesce into a stable opposition. Only if the non-party elite become village directors, all the while resisting pressures or blandishments to join the CCP, could this process materialise. But our data suggest that this type of major political transformation is not happening yet.

Appendix 14.1
Measuring the Democratic Idea

We asked villagers to respond to a series of questions that could tap into their democratic predilections. We asked the following statement—'*Only people with specialised knowledge and ability have the right to speak during periods of decision making*'. Almost 45 per cent of villagers disagreed with this statement—27.6 per cent 'disagreed' and 17.3 per cent 'strongly disagreed', while over 30 per cent 'somewhat agreed', 12.1 per cent 'strongly agreed' and 9.1 per cent selected the 'don't know' option.[1] A second question confirmed the views of Li and O'Brien on the use of petitions by villagers as a means of political expression. In response to the statement: '*If villagers disagree with local policies, they have the right to petition the higher levels*', 81.4 per cent 'strongly agreed' (41.1 per cent) or 'agreed somewhat' (40.3 per cent), while only 8.8 per cent 'disagreed' (6.4 per cent) or 'disagreed strongly' (2.4 per cent).[2] Only 6.6 per cent of villagers had no opinion on this issue. The third statement focused on whether poor people had the right to speak out on village-level policies. It stated: '*People with good economic conditions have more right to speak out on village policy as compared to people with poor economic conditions*'. Only 7.3 per cent of villagers 'strongly agreed' and 17.6 per cent 'somewhat agreed'. Instead, 35.2 per cent 'disagreed somewhat', 29.2 per cent 'totally disagreed' and 12.9 per cent either did not know or did not answer. Clearly, people in these villages do not think that the rich should dominate the decision-making process. Finally, villagers strongly disagreed with the argument often proposed by politically influential Chinese that Chinese people accept non-democratic politics if they can make money.

This is a common reason given in Hong Kong for the slow pace of democratisation. But in response to the statement: '*As long as the village economy shows stable development, there is no need to raise the level of democracy*', only 21.0 per cent 'strongly agreed' (6.6 per cent) or 'agreed somewhat' (14.4 per cent), while 63.4 per cent 'disagreed somewhat' (32.3 per cent) or 'strongly disagreed' (33.1 per cent). Finally, 10.3 per cent 'didn't know'. Clearly, the oligarchs are wrong; even if there is good economic development, villagers in these communities still wanted more democracy.

Since each of the four statements can be a good indicator of democratic values, those who 'strongly supported' the above statements received a score of –2 for each one, while those who 'agreed somewhat' received a score of –1. Those who 'disagreed somewhat' received +1, while those who 'strongly disagreed' scored +2. By combining each person's score on all four questions, we gave them an overall score on the 'democratic ideal' and positioned them on an anti- versus pro-democratic continuum.

Notes: 1. Selecting 'don't know' is a common choice in surveys in the PRC. In fact, one can study these responses to explain who is more likely to select this option. In many cases it reflects a lack of political awareness. See M. Kent Jennings (2000).

   2. Even local cadres expressed strong support for the villagers' right to petition higher-level officials if they disagreed with 'local policies.' The question, though, is how they all defined 'local policies.'

Notes

1. On rapid rural industrialisation, see Jean C. Oi (1999). For a more general overview of rural reform, particularly in Jiangsu Province, see David Zweig (1997).
2. For an excellent study of 'peasant burdens', see, Thomas P. Bernstein and Xiaobo Lu (2003).
3. Data from the Fourth Research Institute of the Public Security Ministry shows a jump in the number of protest from 9,709 in 1993 to 32,000 in 1999. Li Lianjiang in his seminar, 'Do Villagers Trust the Central Government', Hong Kong University of Science and Technology, 30 October 2002.
4. On China's democratic development see Suzanne Ogden (2002).
5. See Amy Epstein (1997: 418) and Tianjian Shi (1999: 425–42).
6. Most of the funding for this research came from the United States Institute of Peace, with further support coming in the form of a Direct Allocation Grant from the Hong Kong University of Science and Technology, with funds coming from the Research Grants Council, Hong Kong.
7. According to the 'haixuan' system, anyone possessing their democratic rights can run for office. Then, through a series of ballots, the number of candidates is cut until only two or three candidates remain. These candidates compete for the post of village director.
8. See Zhongguo tongji chubanshe (2001a), p. 589 and *Zhongguo tongji chubanshe* (2001b), p. 332.
9. Either the villages selected were not representative of the county overall, which we doubt, or reported income by the local governments is quite different from that reported by the statistical yearbooks.
10. In most villages, villagers gave mixed reports as to whether or not the election had been democratic. Some villagers, perhaps women or migrant workers, simply did not know what types of procedures had been used in the most recent elections. So any village where

over 65 per cent of the 20 informants said that there had been multi-candidate elections was considered as having undergone a multi-candidate electoral process.

11. O'Brien and Li cite estimates by the US State Department, Tianjian Shi's nationwide survey and their own survey, with most estimates falling between 10–30 per cent. See O'Brien and Li (2000).

12. Within the same village, villagers had very different memories of how the election had transpired. So we used a 50 per cent rule, whereby if more than 50 per cent of villagers reported nomination forms that fell into the more democratic category, we scored the village as MDN. In five villages, nine or ten villagers reported that their village had used 'haixuan', but 10 to 11 people in the same village said that either they did not know, or that some local organisation had nominated the candidates. Our view is that if 50 per cent of villagers did not know what system was used then it was not a well-functioning democratic system and, therefore, we scored it as a less democratic nomination system.

13 For an in-depth analysis of these two cohorts, see David Zweig and Chung Siu Fung, 'Do New Institutions Create New Politics? The Impact of '*Haixuan*' or Direct Nominations for Village Elections on Elite and Villager Attitudes', Paper presented at the International Symposium: 'Villager Self-government and Rural Social Development in China', Ministry of Civil Affairs and the Carter Centre, 2–5 September 2001, Beijing.

14. MLA refers to the Mantel-Haenszel test for linear association and is a good statistical test of linear relationships of Likert scales.

15. It is worth noting that 41 per cent of villagers in wealthier villages felt that there had been no change. Therefore, if their previous elections had been relatively competitive, this finding says nothing about the real level of competition.

16. Part of these results may be due to the fact that one of our Heilongjiang counties was significantly richer than the Anhui counties, but had held its elections two to three years earlier. Therefore, the county affect may explain this difference. However, there was very little variation in voting rates among the four counties, suggesting that wealth, rather than locality, had some influence. Similarly, more of Heilongjiang's villages reported having had speeches than Anhui's.

17. The relationship between these two variables was significant at the .003 level.

18. While a smaller percentage believe that it 'really speeds up economic development' (16 per cent versus 18 per cent), many more think that it 'speeds up development' (62 per cent versus 47 per cent). The Mantel-Haenszel measure of linear association was .02.

19. Of entrepreneurs, 76 per cent believe that the charter has a 'big influence' or 'some influence' versus 65 per cent for regular villagers (MLA = .00).

20. Baogang He, who studied elections in wealthier parts of China, particularly Zhejiang Province, found that 15–20 per cent of village directors were entrepreneurs. See Baogang He (2002: 55–89).

21. Agglutination occurs when elites have power on more than one dimension, that is, political and economic power. Robert D. Putnam (1975).

22. In 1998, there were only three elections in the villages we sampled and in two of them the director of the villager committee was elected for the first time.

23. According to Jakobson, in 1997 only 2 per cent of village directors nationwide were also party secretaries. Perhaps our two Heilongjiang counties were unique (Linda Jakobson, 2000). Recent reports, however, suggest that the CCP favours fusing these posts again because competition between these officials was destabilising. Personal communication, Kevin O'Brien, January 2004, Hong Kong.

24. Unfortunately, we used the term 'cadre' rather than village director in the questionnaire, so it is unclear what was entailed in the term 'cadre'. If they held a village post before being elected village director, they might already have been a party member when they ran for the post of village director.

25. Chi-square test, p = .017.
26. Nevertheless, it is worth reporting that 53.1 per cent of villagers in MDN villages and 57.7 per cent of villagers in LDN villages selected 'don't know' when asked who decides how the funds are spent in the village.
27. We report this finding, even though it is not statistically significant. But given that we only have a total of 60 cases in Anhui, the value of the MLA is quite suggestive.
28. Despite our small sample size of 60 villages, the finding was significant at the .08 level.
29. Bruce Dickson organised a conference entitled 'Surveying China', which addressed many of these issues, including the difficulty of finding good and reliable Chinese co-researchers, the high costs of surveys, getting local-level support for carrying out the survey, and problems of measurement.

References

Alpermann, Bjorn. 2001. 'The Post-Election Administration of Chinese Villages', *The China Journal*, 46 (July 2001): 45–67.

Bernstein, Thomas P. and Xiaobo Lu. 2003. *Taxation without Representation in Rural China: State Capacity, Peasant Resistance, and Democratization*. New York: Cambridge University Press.

Bollen, Kenneth A. 1980. 'Issues in the Comparative Measurement of Political Democracy', *American Sociological Review*, 45, 2: 370–90.

Diamond, Larry. 1992. 'Economic Development and Democracy Reconsidered', in Gary Marks and Larry Diamond (eds), *Re-examining Democracy*. pp. 93–139, Newbury Park: Sage.

Epstein, Amy. 1997. 'Village Elections in China: Experiments with Democracy', in Joint Economic Committee, Congress of the United States (ed.), *China's Economic Future: Challenges to US Policy*. pp. 403–22, Armonk: M.E. Sharpe.

He, Baogang. 2002. 'Village Elections, Village Power Structure, and Rural Governance in Zhejaing', *American Asian Review*, 20, 3 (Fall 2002): 55–89.

Hu, Rong. 1999. *Cunmin zizhi jiagou xia de cunmin weiyuanhui xuanju: Fujian sheng 1997 nian ge'an yanjiu* (Village elections within the framework of village autonomy: Research on case studies from Fujian Province). City University, unpublished Ph.D. thesis, 1999.

Huntington, Samuel. 1991. *The Third Wave: Democratization in the Late Twentieth Century*. Norman, Oklahoma: University of Oklahoma Press.

Jakobson, Linda. 2000. Lecture at the Division of Social Sciences, Hong Kong University of Science and Technology.

Jennings, M. Kent. 2000. 'Missing Data and Survey Research in China: Problems, Solutions, and Applications', Paper prepared for conference on 'Surveying China', George Washington University, Washington, DC, 9–10 June 2000.

Li, Lianjiang. 2001. 'Elections and Popular Resistance in Rural China', *China Information*, 15, 2: 1–19.

Li, Lianjiang and Kevin O'Brien. 1999. 'The Struggle over Village Elections', in Merle Goldman and Roderick MacFarquhar (eds), *The Paradox of China's Post-Mao Reforms*. pp. 129–44, Cambridge, MA: Harvard University Press.

Moore, Barrington . 1967. *The Social Origins of Dictatorship and Democracy*. Boston: Beacon Press.

O'Donnell, Guillermo A. 1979. *Modernization and Bureaucratic-Authoritarianism: Studies in South American Politics*. Berkeley: University of California Press.

Ogden, Suzanne. 2002. *Inklings of Democracy in China*. Cambridge, MA: Harvard University Press.

O'Brien, Kevin J. and Lianjiang Li. 2000. 'Accommodating 'Democracy' in a One-Party State: Introducing Village Elections in China', *The China Quarterly*, 162 (June 2000): 465–89.

Oi, Jean C. 1999. *Rural China Takes Off*. Berkeley: University of California Press.

Oi, Jean C. and Scott Rozelle. 2000. 'Elections and Power: The Locus of Decision-Making in Chinese Villages', *The China Quarterly*, 162 (June 2000): 513–539.

Pastor, Robert A. and Qingshan Tan. 2000. 'The Meaning of China's Village Elections', *The China Quarterly*, 162 (June 2000): 490–512.

Putnam, Robert D. 1975. *Political Elites*. Englewood Cliffs, NJ: Prentice Hall.

Rueschemeyer, Dietrich, Evelyne Huber Stephens and John D. Stephens. 1992. *Capitalist Development and Democracy*. Chicago: University of Chicago Press.

Shi, Tianjian. 1999. 'Economic Development and Village Elections in Rural China', *Journal of Contemporary China*, 8, 22 (1999): 425–42.

Wang, Zhenyao. 1998. 'Village Committees: The Basis of China's Democratization', in Eduard B. Vermeer, Frank N. Pieke and Woei Lien Chong (eds), *Cooperative and Collective in China's Rural Development*, pp. 239–56. Armonk: M. E. Sharpe.

Zhongguo Tongji chubanshe. 2001a. *Anhui tongji nianjian, 2000* (Anhui Provincial Yearbook). Beijing.

———. 2001b. *Zhongguo tongji nianjian, 2000* (China Statistical Yearbook). Beijing.

———. 2001c. *Heilongjiang tongji ninanjian, 2000* (Heilongjiang Statistical Yearbook). Beijing.

Zweig, David. 1997. *Freeing China's Farmers: Restructuring Rural China in the Deng Era*. Armonk, NY: M. E. Sharpe.

15 Grass-roots Democracy
The Working of Panchayati Raj Institutions in Andhra Pradesh

G. Haragopal and G. Sudarshanam

Introduction

Andhra Pradesh is one of the largest states in the Indian Union. It comprises the Telugu-speaking people who were one of the earliest to demand a linguistic state as they were separated and put under two different political systems—the Andhra region under colonial rule and the Telangana region under feudal princely rule in the eighteenth century (1776). The separate existence for about two centuries left its own impact on these two regions. It was only in 1956 that the two regions were merged to form the present state of Andhra Pradesh. This merger was based on the assumption that language constitutes one of the crucial elements in the democratic reorganisation of people of a multi-lingual and highly-pluralistic society.

The rural social structure, notwithstanding the reorganisation of the state on a linguistic basis, remained authoritarian and hierarchical. The medieval feudal order and the subsequent colonial rule did not touch the basic structure as they proved to be useful in facilitating 'orderly' appropriation of the surplus. The mainstream freedom movement that began in the late nineteenth century and gained momentum in the first half of the twentieth century challenged the colonial dominance but did not question the feudal structures. Barrington Moore Jr. in his very significant work characterised the freedom movement as an attempt at a peaceful transition of the society, which provided a linkage between the peasantry and bourgeoisie through non-violent means. The Gandhian paradigm with its emphasis on swaraj that included grama swaraj with self-sufficient villages also did not question the basic structures of power, property and privilege in the rural society. In a way, it was this approach that left the rural feudal structure largely intact. The transfer of power from the British to Indian rulers changed the form of power but not its content. It is this unfinished process of democratisation that posed a real challenge to the post-independent Indian democratic experience and experimentation.

The concepts of community development, democratic decentralisation, democratisation of governance, local self-government, participative development, empowerment of people, panchayati raj are all expressions and experiments that are a continuation of democratisation at one level and institutionalisation of the growing democratic consciousness at another level. However, some of these concepts and concerns are contradictory. The contradictions arise primarily from the premise that the Indian democracy is based on the sovereign power of the people and empowerment of the people through decentralisation. India is a formal democracy in search of the substance. This chapter is an attempt to take stock of the present state of democratisation at the grass-roots level with a focus on Andhra Pradesh.

Historical Roots of Democracy

Immediately after independence, there was talk of a community development approach to accelerate the process of change and to involve the rural people in this grand project. Several studies indicate that there was something intrinsically wrong with this project. To cite Barrington Moore, 'the intellectual and institutional antecedents of Community Development Programme do not have the remotest connection with Marxist Socialism' (Moore, 1977: 392). He observes that it carried three elements: first, Gandhi's faith in an idealised version of the Indian village as the most suitable community for civilised man, second, the American experience with agricultural extension service and third, the influence of British paternalism and more specifically, the movement for village uplift (Moore, 1977: 392). This combination did not prove to be effective.

As the community development programme aimed at community participation in the growth and change process, there was no other means except involving the people. But in less than a decade, all the evidence indicated that there was a wide gap between promise and performance. The failure of the programme was attributed to the lack of popular enthusiasm and direct popular participation in the developmental process. This, in turn, was attributed to the bureaucratisation of the programme, which involved neither the people nor their representatives. This led to the appointment of the famous Balwant Rai Mehta Committee, which recommended the three-tier panchayati raj institutions. In retrospect, one may say that the failure of the community development programme was largely on account of a rigid socio-economic structure, which was not conducive for any collective or community action. That the village people constituted a community was by itself a faulty assumption. Any Indian village is a 'community' of divided communities rooted in undemocratic social relationships conditioned by an inegalitarian economic structure and social institutions. Any attempt of democratisation without transforming these basic relations was bound to be futile. Therefore, any attempt at democratisation should start with transforming these relationships. The community development experiment did not address these questions, nor talk of altering them. The Chinese experience, in this respect, was of a totally different kind.

In Chinese history, while there was feudalism comparable with that of India, it was different in the sense that there was a competitive and commercial element. It had patronised a bureaucratic class based on some form of merit. This class was used to extract the agrarian surplus and was also allowed to be corrupt. Barrington Moore maintains that the absorption of ambitious persons into the extractive mechanism, in a way, halted the emergence of a commercial or entrepreneurial class that threatened the privileges of the landlord class. However, the commercial class that did emerge gradually, allied with the Western forces who threw their military and diplomatic forces in favour of this class, giving rise to the comprador class. There was also opposition to this hybrid class who were condemned 'as servants of the foreign devils destroying the foundations of Chinese society' (Moore, 1977: 201).

The frequency of peasant rebellions in China is well known. Barrington Moore points out that for China, this was 'the main instructive contrast with India where peasant rebellions in the pre-modern period were relatively rare and completely ineffective and where modernization impoverished the peasants at least as much as in China and over a long period of time' (Moore, 1977: 202). He further adds that in China 'many villages rigidly excluded outsiders from membership. The reason was simple; there was not enough land to go around' (Moore, 1977: 212). Although there was community feeling among the land owning peasantry, the relations within the peasant family was subjected to petty despotism made necessary by a brutally cramped existence. Moore conjectures that 'the Chinese peasant family had built into it a highly explosive potential to which the Communists in due course were to set the spark'. It is also a striking observation that the cohesiveness of Chinese peasant society appears to have been considerably less than that of other peasant societies and had to depend very heavily on the existence of sufficiency of landed property. In contrast, in India 'the caste system provided a niche for landless labourers and tied them into the division of labour within the village, while its sanctions depended for their operation less directly on the existence of property' (Moore, 1977: 223). Dr Ambedkar went one step further and characterised it as 'division of labourers and not division of labour'.

The Communist Party used the old and tainted leadership at times, but created new organisations among the poor peasantry and even among the women—the most oppressed group in Chinese society. Moore observes that 'in their programs of local economic self-sufficiency, as shown in the establishment of cooperatives and in many other norms they presented the peasants with concrete alternatives to submission and starvation' (Moore, 1977: 226). This is very significant in understanding the grass-roots reorganisation of rural China. A landmark action was 'to unite the poor peasants, agricultural labourers and middle peasants and ...neutralise the stand of the rich peasants so as to isolate the landlords' (Moore, 1977: 226).

It was also important that 'the land was redistributed not to the family as a whole, but to each member on an equal share basis, regardless of age and sex. It is also striking that the Communist Party broke the village apart at its base, obliterating the connection between landed property and kinship. This released powerful antagonisms across class lines as well as those of age and sex. In a way this bitterness provided the wherewithal in reordering the relationship between the landlords and peasants, tenants and the rent collectors, victims and the local bullies and the young and the old (Moore, 1977: 227).

It is in this historical backdrop that the experience with grass-roots democracy needs to be appreciated and understood while the Indian experience represents persistence of the traditional structures and the relationship, in China a serious attempt was made to alter them. The grass-roots institutions in China, therefore, have had the advantage of being grounded on altered relationships whereas the Indian grass-roots institutions are not products of change but continuity. The irony is that it was these institutions that were expected to bring the necessary change. The following sections of the chapter deal with this unfolding Indian experience with the process of democratisation.

The First Panchayati Raj System

Andhra Pradesh was one of the first Indian states to introduce the panchayati raj system based on the recommendations of the Balwant Rai Mehta Committee. The three-tier structure of decentralised local self-government was created in the year 1959. The lowest tier is the grama panchayat. The members of the grama panchayat are elected by all the voters of the village. It is headed by a sarpanch and upasarpanch, who are elected indirectly by the members of the grama panchayat. There is a grama sabha, where all the voters of the village are members. The grama sabha is a body where all the important issues of the village are discussed and so it provides an opportunity for villagers to participate in the process of decision making.

The panchayat samiti is the second tier, which is organised for a group of villages. All village sarpanches are the ex-officio members of the panchayat samiti. The members of the panchayat samiti elect the president and the vice-president of this samiti.

The third tier of the panchayati raj is the zilla parishad. The area of the zilla parishad is coterminous with the revenue district. All the presidents of the samiti are ex-officio members of the zilla parishad and they in turn elect one chairperson and one vice-chairperson from among themselves.

This was the structure of democratic decentralisation created for the rural areas. These panchayati raj bodies are responsible for the various developmental programmes that are required at different levels. The important functions of panchayati raj bodies are to look after agriculture, irrigation, animal husbandry, public health and several other functions. These elected bodies are helped by a number of officials appointed for different purposes.

Panchayats are given certain powers to collect taxes from the people and also receive state and central grants for various activities. This system continued up to 1986, with slight changes made with regard to the mode of election to different levels of panchayati raj bodies, reservations for certain disadvantaged sections of the community such as SCs, STs and women, etc.

In 1986, however, certain major changes took place under the Telugu Desam government. In the place of panchayat samitis, mandal parishads were created. The mandal parishads are much smaller units compared to the earlier panchayat samitis. This reform was taken up with an objective of further decentralisation of power and for bringing the panchayati raj bodies closer to the people. The slogan given at that time was 'taking the administration to the doorsteps of the people'. Under these reforms, reservation for SCs, STs, BCs and women was further increased.

Several reforms were brought out from time to time with regard to the size of the different levels of panchayati raj bodies, the mode of elections of members to these bodies, etc. But in spite of these efforts, the panchayati raj institutions continued to suffer from lack of autonomy to take their own decisions, bureaucratic domination over these bodies, centralisation of powers at the state and central governments, lack of financial resources, irregular conducting of elections to these bodies, etc. The political leadership at the state and central levels were not interested in giving powers and funds to these bodies. These bodies were further weakened by the introduction of a number of centrally-sponsored schemes for rural development in the 1970s and 1980s. An attempt to strengthen the panchayati raj bodies in the early-1990s began with a move to amend the Constitution that would give more powers and functions to the panchayati raj bodies, ensure regular elections and greater representation of the weaker sections of the community. This resulted in the Seventy-third Amendment to the Constitution in 1992. Andhra Pradesh too changed its Panchayati Raj Act in 1994 to incorporate the provisions of the Seventy-third Constitutional Amendment.

Post-Seventy-third Amendment Developments

The Andhra Pradesh Panchayati Raj Act, 1994 enacted on 21 April of the same year replaced the Andhra Pradesh Gram Panchayats Act, 1964 and the

Andhra Pradesh Mandala Praja Parishads, Zilla Praja Parishad and Zilla Pranalika Abhivrudhi Sameeksha Mandals Act, 1986. The 1994 Act provided for a three-tier structure—a grama panchayat at the village level, mandal parishad at the mandal level and zilla parishad at the district level. The word 'praja' in the erstwhile mandala praja parishad and zilla praja parishad has been dropped in the new act.

Grama Sabha

Under the 1994 Act there shall be a grama sabha at the village level comprising all the voters. It must meet at least twice a year under the chairpersonship of the sarpanch. The grama sabha considers all matters relating to the annual statement of accounts of the grama panchayat, its report on administration, development programmes of the village, new schemes and tax proposals.

Grama Panchayat

A grama panchayat comprises five to 21 members depending upon the population of the village. The members of the grama panchayat are directly elected by the grama sabha. For this purpose the village is divided into wards and one member is elected from each ward.

Provision has also been made for the reservation of seats in the grama panchayat for persons belonging to SC and ST categories in proportion to their population by rotation. Similarly, one-third seats are reserved for BCs and another one-third for women (including seats reserved for women in each of the reserved categories).

Each grama panchayat is headed by a sarpanch who is directly elected by the voters of a village. His term of office is five years. The upasarpanch is elected by the grama panchayat. The post of sarpanch is reserved for members belonging to the SC and ST categories on a rotational basis and in proportion to their population in the state. Similarly, one-third of the posts in the state are reserved for BCs and another one-third for women. The sarpanch exercises control over the village executive officer and the village development officer and he is held responsible for the implementation of the decisions of the grama panchayat. The commissioner of panchayat raj exercises control over the grama panchayats.

The grama panchayat discharges obligatory as well as optional functions. The important functions include maintenance of government roads and buildings, primary education, cooperatives, agricultural development and housing. However, the number of functions that a grama panchayat performs depends on its financial condition.

The grama panchayats are also vested with taxation powers. The compulsory taxes are house tax and surcharges on stamp duty. They can also collect advertisement tax, vehicle tax, entertainment tax and profession tax. In addition, they receive grants from the state government, the zilla parishads and the mandal parishads.

Mandal Parishad

The Act provides for the formation of a mandal parishad for each mandal. A mandal parishad consists of members directly elected from the territorial constituencies consisting of a population between 3,000 and 4,000, the members of the Lok Sabha and MLAs representing a constituency, which comprises wholly or partly the mandal, as well as any member of the Rajya Sabha who is a registered voter in the mandal. One person belonging to the minorities is also to be co-opted by the elected members. The elected members of the mandal parishad alone are eligible to contest or vote in the election to the offices of president/vice-president of the parishad.

Seats are reserved for SCs and STs in proportion to their population in the mandal and by rotation between different constituencies. One-third of the seats are reserved for BCs by rotation. Similarly, one-third seats are reserved for women. This includes one-third seats allotted to women in each of the reserved categories (The reservation for BCs in the panchayati raj bodies was later enhanced from one-third to 34 per cent for the state as a whole.) The elected members of the mandal parishad elect their president and vice-president from among themselves. Posts of mandal presidents in the state are reserved for SCs and STs in proportion to their population. One-third of the posts are reserved for BCs and one-third for women.

The important functions of the mandal parishad are community development, agricultural development, animal husbandry and fisheries, rural health and sanitation. Other areas of work include land development, irrigation, roads, electricity, education, anti-poverty programmes, women and child welfare.

The grants given by the state and the central governments under various schemes, the mandal parishad's share in the land cess and other taxes, contribution given by grama panchayats, income from remunerative enterprises and per capita annual government grant are the important sources of a mandal parishad's revenue.

Zilla Parishad

The 1994 Act provides for a zilla parishad for each district (except the district of Hyderabad). Zilla parishads consist of the members elected by the voters from territorial constituencies (the area of a mandal is considered a territorial constituency), members of the Lok Sabha and the Legislative Assembly representing the constituency which falls partly or wholly in the district, and members of the Rajya Sabha who are registered voters in the district. Two members belonging to the minorities are co-opted by the elected member of the zilla parishad.

The chairpersons of the district cooperative market society, the *Zilla Grandhalaya Samithi* and the district cooperative central bank, as also the district collector and all the presidents of mandal parishads in the districts are permanent invitees to the meetings of the zilla parishad but without the right to vote.

The chairperson and vice-chairperson of the zilla parishad are elected by the elected members of the zilla parishad from among themselves. Of the 22 zilla parishads in the state, four posts of chairpersons are reserved for SCs, seven for BCs and seven for women.

The chief executive officer (CEO) for the zilla parishad is appointed by the state government. He attends the meetings of the zilla parishad but is not entitled to vote. He is responsible for the implementation of the resolution of the zilla parishad and its standing committees and has to supervise its activities.

Every zilla parishad has seven standing committees to oversee the following departments: (i) rural development, (ii) planning and finance, (iii) agriculture, (iv) education and medical services, (v) women's welfare, (vi) social welfare and (vii) public works. The chairperson of the zilla parishad is an ex-officio member of the standing committees. The other members are nominated by the chairperson. The vice-chairperson is also an ex-officio member. The district collector has a right to participate in the meetings of all standing committees but without voting rights. The decisions of the standing committees have to be ratified by the general body of the zilla parishad.

The more important functions of the zilla parishad are examining and approving the budgets of the mandal parishad in the district, distributing funds allotted by the governments to the mandals in the district, coordinating and consolidating the plans of mandals and preparing a district plan, executing the plans and schemes, supervising the activities of mandals and establishing and maintaining secondary, vocational and industrial schools.

The important sources of income of the zilla parishad are central or state government funds, grants coming from various bodies to develop villages and small-scale industries, share of the land cess, local cess, state taxes, income from enterprises, endowments or trusts administered by the zilla parishad, contributions from mandals and annual grants from the government at the rate of Rs 2 per person residing in the district.

The grama panchayat, when resolving to abolish an existing tax or reducing its rates, needs the prior approval of the commissioner. In the case of the mandal and zilla parishad there are no taxation powers. Their sources of income consist of funds of institutional schemes and programmes and a prescribed share of taxation and fees.

The Act of 1994 does not provide for a no-confidence motion against the sarpanch of a grama panchayat because the voters directly elect him. But a motion expressing no confidence in the president or vice-president of the mandal parishad, or the chairperson and vice-chairperson of the zilla parishad can be initiated by giving a written notice to the prescribed authority, signed by not less than one-half of the total members of the respective bodies. If the motion is carried with the support of not less than two-thirds of the total members, the commissioner shall remove him from office.

The Two-Child Norm

Section 19 of the Act, which gives a list of the disqualification in the case of a candidate, includes disqualification of candidates who have more than two children. However, the birth of an additional child within one year from the date of commencement of the Act will not be considered a basis for disqualification.

Government Control

The government can cancel or suspend any resolution of the grama panchayat or mandal parishad or zilla parishad if it feels that the said resolution abuses the provisions of any Act. The government may suspend a resolution on the recommendations of the district collector. The government may also dissolve a grama panchayat, mandal or zilla parishad on grounds of incompetence or misuse of power. The government also has powers to dismiss heads of panchayati raj bodies at all the three levels and to stipulate that such persons cannot seek re-election for two years from the date of their removal. Thus, the Act gives considerable powers to the government to control the panchayati raj bodies. Besides, the Act seems to have placed more authority upon the executive officers than the political heads of the panchayat bodies for proper functioning of the latter. Even in respect of convening meetings of grama, mandal and zilla panchayats, executive officers of the respective bodies have the power to convene such meetings if they are of the view that the former have failed to follow the statutory requirements in this respect.

Working of the Institutions: The Issues

This discussion indicates the varied attempts made to empower the grass-roots institutions in Andhra Pradesh. All these attempts did not meet with success. Although it would be unfair to say that they were a total failure, the experience has been a mixed bag. We notice some encouraging trends representing the brighter side but there are also trends, which are darker and depressing. The encouraging trends include: (i) greater mass consciousness, (ii) shift in power relationships, (iii) infrastructural development. The darker side includes (i) the continued stubbornness of the social and economic structure, (ii) proliferation of parallel institutions, (iii) the centralised nature of state power and (iv) increasing presence and rise of instruments of coercive power of the state.

Among the brighter trends, most noteworthy has been the emerging voice of the ordinary people. On an average, a common man today is more critical of the role of leaders, more articulate and also in certain cases, very assertive. In the early-1960s, the ordinary masses used to be passive and acted more as mute spectators to development. Studies show that the grama sabhas, the primary units providing for direct participation of the people, were neither regular and nor did people evince any interest in attending them. The situation today is different. On the question of the frequency of holding of grama sabhas and levels of participation of people, the elected representatives say that 'there is wide spread apathy'. But if one probes further they also remark that 'holding grama sabha is a big headache'. To the question as to why it is a headache, they reply that 'people have a big list of demands ranging from drinking water, roads to regular electric power supply. Given the resources and powers of the panchayat, one cannot meet the unending demands of the people'. But the fact that the masses have begun to voice their demands is one indication that a change has been taking place on the ground level.

Here is an instance that is very revealing. In one of the backward villages, in the most backward district of Andhra Pradesh, a former sarpanch and the present sarpanch were attending a health camp organised by a memorial trust. Towards the close of the health camp, some of the villagers waiting for a health check up were turned away on the excuse that the doctors were pressed for time. Among them, four middle-aged Dalit women turned aggressive and insisted that they would not leave the place until the doctors attended to them. When both the former and present sarpanches appealed to them, the four women said in one voice that in the next panchayat elections they would not vote for them. When the sarpanches said that they could discuss the matter in the next grama sabha, they remarked:

> You divide the poor people and make us quarrel among our selves. Why don't your representatives ever pressurise the government for sanctioning a regular primary health centre? Where will the poor people go? Who will make the demand for the hospital except we, the Harijans?

This incident, in a way, epitomises the changing mood and consciousness of the rural people.

Another trend that is noticed is the shift in the overall power relationships in the villages. The studies in the 1960s on the social base of panchayat leadership showed that it was drawn essentially from the dominant caste groups—Reddys and Kammas. There was hardly any representation from the other communities. By the late-1960s, rural India and more so, rural Andhra Pradesh started witnessing unrest of the poor, as their basic problems remained unresolved. Rural institutions were drawn into the turmoil. As a result, the entire panchayati raj system came under terrific strain and the upper strata grew apprehensive of the potential of these institutions to trigger off changes. Consequently, in the 1970s, the institutions were suspended giving rise to special clientele-centric development agencies with a focus on small farmers, SCs, STs and women, which were wholly manned by the appointed officers drawn from the regular bureaucracy. A study conducted in the 1970s revealed that while the rich were against these institutions, the poor were indifferent. The peasantry drawn from the BCs alone supported the revival of these institutions. In the late-1970s, when the institution of mandal—a middle tier covering a smaller population and area was suggested—it was almost a response to this class of the peasantry. It was also seen that the social profile of representatives elected to these institutions was now different from the earlier situation. The statutory provisions of reservations to varied social categories of people were both an acknowledgement of this change and also institutionalisation of the changing balance of power relations.

This class of peasantry was looking for greater access to infrastructure. The development thrust, by and large, has been on building of roads, construction of buildings, increase in power supply, access to agricultural inputs, markets, credit from the banking sector and so on. This development, however, has been uneven. But whenever it expanded the middle castes, particularly artisans, and toddy tappers, who have had earlier market connections, gained greater share in power and wealth. These castes and classes have come to assume considerable importance in the contemporary power structure and there is an intense competition among the political parties for this social base and for including them in the overall power structure. This cannot be viewed as a qualitative change in the process of democratisation as it excluded not only the landless agricultural labourers but also millions of small and marginal farmers. This has led to increasing tension at multiple points, calling for institutional changes and balance of power.

It is this increasing consciousness of the marginalised sections and the failure of the government to cope with it that represents the darker side of the process of democratic decentralisation. The larger economic and social structure underwent some quantitative change but not qualitative change. The social institutions like caste and family and the institution of property, not only remained largely intact but have also become far more influential.

The assertion of patriarchy and the propertied, upper castes has been assuming different forms. As a result, democratic decentralisation involving community or popular participation remains more formal than real. This is evident from two very powerful trends. For instance, the reservation of positions at all levels did bring in persons from the marginalised sections like the Dalits, BCs and women. There is evidence to show that BCs better placed on the socio-economic ladder are able to wield relatively more influence, but not others. Instead of contributing to the elevation of the other disadvantaged sections, particularly Dalits, this change led to more organised oppression as the newly emerging forces joined the ranks of the powerful and the propertied. In fact, after the last general elections there was a spate of attacks and atrocities on the Dalits in which the physical involvement of the backward communities was far higher than the upper castes and classes. In a way, this has come to provide a base for the emerging authoritarian and autocratic forces.

The Dalits and women who entered the public space through reservations have neither been able to assert their share in the power structure nor are they in a position to articulate their interests. There are many observations indicating that the dominant leaders in the rural areas hold the real reins of power over the direct 'elected' Dalit representatives. There are also instances where old customs and even the body language of subservience have not changed. The Dalits sit on the floor while the other upper caste members sit on chairs. In most cases, Dalit members are not the emerging organic repre-sentatives but are simply those nominated by the powerful upper strata, who may even choose their own servants or illiterate labourers working in their fields for these positions at times. Such Dalit representatives say 'how can we sit on the chair in the office when we have to live at their feet [metaphor for sub-servience] outside'.

Similar is the experience with women representatives, who are also ruled from behind the scenes by their sons, husbands, brothers or the local dominant leaders. This has given rise to expressions such as *sarpanchpati* (the husband sarpanch). There are also instances where women representatives sign on the dotted line without even understanding the content of the matter. The women's overall position, however, is not as dismal as it is with the Dalits. This is partly because women representatives are also drawn from the upper strata. Rural women leaders are often articulate, assertive and even aggressive. In such cases they are able to take up development works, which are of wider concern for the people and particularly for women. If one draws the balance sheet, representation for women did introduce an element of tension between the growing feminist consciousness and patriarchal values. The evidence sug-gests that the power of patriarchy is such that it is in a position to constrain the enlargement of democratic consciousness and more so, its institutional expression.

Another constraint on the growing democratic consciousness comes from the process of globalisation. The new economic reforms have been emphasising on democratic governance, decentralisation, transparency but they have also simultaneously introduced the concept of stakeholder or users association—client-centric organisations. As a result, in every village we find water users associations, *vana samrakshana* (forest conservation) samitis, women SHGs, educational committee of parents and so on. These are all loose organisations that have nothing to do with the panchayat. The very concepts of stakeholder or users associations are excluding and not inclusive. This is leading to the consolidation of interest groups against the panchayats whose power, at least in principle, is based on village interests and power drawn from the citizens. Thus, forces buttressed and patronised by the global agencies are leading to further fragmentation of village life.

The important reasons for the persisting problems of the panchayati raj institutions are: the increasing suspicion on the part of the rural leadership about the local bodies and their functionaries; the overall tendency for centralisation of power; the growing socio-economic inequalities due to recent reforms; privatisation of public services such as health, education, agriculture, animal husbandry, etc., which are primarily the function of panchayati raj bodies; non release of grants by the state and also inadequate financial resources available to local bodies; creation of special agencies like the DRDA, the Integrated Tribal Development Agency (ITDA) and placing them outside the purview of panchayati raj institutions; and the creation of SHGs and assigning them development programmes by neglecting panchayati raj institutions (Balaramulu, 2002: 662).

In Andhra Pradesh there are 11 types of parallel bodies or SHGs, which consists of 5,85,501 committees and 1.705 million members in all groups such as water users associations, watershed committees, van samrakshan samitis, DWACRA groups, tribal development committees, 'Janmabhoomi' (motherland) habitation committees, etc. The financial transaction of all these groups is about Rs 28,798.8 million (Balaramulu, 2002: 663). Several committees are working at the village level undermining the importance of panchayati raj bodies. According to Balaramulu:

> The major problems with the self-help groups are: they are guided and controlled by the Government and they do not have any authority in preparing the plans and implementation of programmes. The political parties are using them to accommodate persons who are politically unemployed. There is political interference in the implementation of the programmes (Balaramulu, 2002: 664).

Janmabhoomi, a major programme undertaken by the Telugu Desam government, is another encroachment into the functions of the panchayati raj bodies. Though the stated objective of 'Janmabhoomi' was to bring the government to the doorstep of the people and ensuring peoples' participation in development through '*shramdhan*' (voluntary labour), in reality, this is yet another activity where government officials and nodal officers take the lead role.

In Andhra Pradesh, particularly in the Telangana region, there are ongoing tribal and peasant movements, which are, in one form, a continuation and intensification of the democratic process. These are assertions outside the formal institutional framework indicating the fragile nature of institutions and their incapacity to absorb the growing consciousness. The police wield so much of unquestioned and arbitrary power that the elected representatives are reduced to mute spectators. There are instances when the police arrested and detained a mandal president in Karimnagar District and they brought the hand-cuffed president to hoist the national flag on Independence Day and took him back. In Adilabad District, the police assaulted a lady mandal president because she was settling the civil disputes resulting in the loss of 'extra income' for the police. A husband of a sarpanch in a district of Warangal languished in a jail on the charges that he was an underground activist. The sarpanch appealed to the district authorities and even publicised through a press conference the fact that it was a case of mistaken identity and that the police should release her husband. But she has been crying in the wilderness. These are only a few instances symptomatic of the growing crisis in the rural areas. As the state has come to depend more and more on coercive instruments, power is shifting from the developmental and democratic institutions to coercive organs of state power, which are located completely outside the so-called self-governing institutions.

Thus democratic governance through greater devolution of power to the grass-roots institutions is not sufficient to bring about genuine participation of the local people. The need of the hour is to implement broader structural changes in society. Though the process of societal change has been started, there is a long way to go before the goals of participatory democracy and equitable social structures are achieved. The institutional changes and the social movements in Andhra Pradesh as elsewhere in the country are no doubt contributing to that process.

References

Balaramulu. 2002. 'Participatory Development: The Experience of Andhra Pradesh', *Indian Journal of Public Administration*, 4 (October–December): 655–88.

Government of Maharashtra. 1989. 'Annihilation of Caste', in *Dr Ambedkar's Writings and Speeches*, Vol. 1 (compiled by Vasant Menon). Bombay: Government of Maharashtra.

Haragopal, G. and G. Sudarshanam. 2000. 'Andhra Pradesh', in George Mathew (ed.), *Status of Panchayati Raj in States and Union Territories of India*, pp. 45–58, New Delhi: Institute of Social Sciences.

Jain, L.C. 1985. *Grass without Roots*. New Delhi: Sage.

Kumar, A. Vijay and E. Sudhakar. 2003. 'Role of Panchayat Secretary in Andhra Pradesh', *Indian Journal of Public Administration*, 3, April–June: 201–11.

Maheshwari, S.R. (ed.). 1984. *Administrative Reforms*. New Delhi: Indian Institute of Public Administration.

Mathew, George. 1995. *Panchayati Raj: From Legislations to Movement*. New Delhi: Concept Publishing.

Misra, B.B. 1983. *District Administration and Rural Development in India*. New Delhi: Oxford University Press.

Mohanty, Manoranjan and Mark Selden. 2003. 'Reconceptualizing Local Democracy: Preliminary Reflection on Democracy, Power and Resistance', *Panchayati Raj Update*, April–May: 6–7.

Moore, Barrington. 1977. *Social Origins of Dictatorship and Democracy*. Harmondsworth, London: Penguin.

16 The Environment, the Family and Local Government among the Tajik People

Shengmin Yang

The natural environment tends to have a certain degree of influence on human social organisation. When a people's production capabilities are comparatively low, and when they find themselves in hostile environmental settings, this influence tends to be stronger. Under such conditions, people have little choice but to adopt forms of social organisation that can effectively help them struggle against these tremendous environmental pressures. One such form of social organisation is the extended family.

On the other hand, local governmental representatives have rather little influence on areas where people have to cope with harsh environmental conditions. For the government agencies may not always know how to deal with natural hardships. In such localities, therefore, the development of local government is often quite slow. The Tashikuergan Tajik Autonomous County, a place inhabited by the Tajik people of China, is an example of this sort of county.

Between 1992 and 2001, I conducted field research in this county on four separate occasions. This chapter is an attempt to draw upon my research in order to discuss the tripartite relationship between the environment, the family and local government, as it has unfolded in the Tajik areas of western China.

The Tajik people of China have a total population of 41,028 people (in the year 2000), of which 96 per cent (39,493) live in Xinjiang Autonomous Region (Province) (Census of 2000, China.). Located on the Pamir Plateau, the Tashikuergan Tajik Autonomous County has a history that extends back more than 2000 years. Ta County is 484 km across, 329 km north to south and has a total land area of 25,000 square km. To its south-west, it borders Tajikistan, Afghanistan and Pakistan, forming a boundary, which stretches some 888 km. It is one of China's most remote counties.

The Environment and the Economy

Tashikuergan is situated on the eastern slope of the Pamir Plateau, at an average of 4000m above sea level. The local territory contains a number of snow-capped mountains that rise to a height of over 7000m, as well as a scattering of some 5000m tall mountains where snow accumulates throughout the year.

The rivers freeze over regularly, the terrain is criss-crossed by gullies and ravines, the roadways are rugged, and even the mountain valleys tend to rise to above 3000m above sea level. It is the archetypal mountain plateau. The climate here is dry and cold, with an average yearly rainfall of 69 mm. Frost covers the ground for all but 75 days out the year and there is 37 per cent less oxygen in the air than in the plains. The terrain is exposed and bare in many places, plant life is sparse, there are no trees and the amount of usable land is limited. In all, 71 per cent of the land is barren mountain terrain, 9 per cent is covered by frozen rivers and the remainder is farmland and man-made grassland.

In its history, Ta County has been the site of numerous natural disasters. Most common are blizzards, windstorms, ground freezes, floods, rockslides and avalanches. According to statistics dating back to 1957, the area has suffered exceedingly low, disaster-level temperatures on an average of once or twice every year. Other forms of natural disasters have taken place about once every three to five years, mid-level disasters have happened once every five to seven years and large-scale natural disasters have taken place once every seven to 10 years. In 1999 alone, a blizzard and a flood affected over half of the county's farmers and froze to death nearly 30,000 heads of cattle. In all, more than 500 families lost their homes, land and livestock, and were left with nowhere to turn.

The farmland in Ta County is located in narrow, unfertile areas prone to frequent soil run-off. The grassland is found mainly in the more barren, high-altitude areas. Its capacity to raise livestock is thus relatively low. The county is isolated from roadway transportation, lying some 1,765 km away from the autonomous region's capital of Urumqi. The closest city, Kashgar, is 294 km away, a trip that used to take locals one month to travel during the first four decades of the twentieth century. Although, roads were paved for automobiles following the 1940s, they are often damaged and cut off by rockslides. Within the territory, residents gather in pockets in between the nine mountains of the region. In between these mountains, there is snow throughout the year, which makes it difficult for residents to travel back and forth. Among the 64 villages within the county, there are still 25 with no access to roads and 30 with no access to electricity. Horses are still the primary means of transportation, thus separating the county centre from the furthest villages by about a six-day journey.

The economy of the area is essentially one of self-sufficiency and semi-self-sufficiency. Cattle farming is the primary occupation¹and agriculture is the secondary occupation. Cattle farmers raise sheep, mountain goats, yaks, scalpers, horses, donkeys, and camels. In 2000, the total amount of livestock came to 161,700 heads, or an average of five heads per person. Cattle farming in the area is still done in the traditional, nomadic style. Pasture land is divided seasonally into those used during spring, summer, autumn and winter. The pastures are separated from each other by anywhere between a few dozen to 100–200 km of mountain road, making the move from one area to another very difficult. Due to the mountain climate and the infertility of the grassland, the growth of livestock is quite slow. Sheep, for instance, need between two and three years before they can be sold in the market and in some places, six to seven years before they reach maturity. This, of course, has a negative effect on the rate of production.[2]

Due to these harsh environmental conditions, socio-economic development among the Tajik people of China has proceeded quite slowly. According to statistics from 2000, the average income for the county was RMB 600 per person and 75 per cent of the farmers fall beneath the poverty line set by the Chinese government. From the perspective of per capita income, Ta County is the poorest in all of China.

The Slow Establishment of Local Governance

In ancient times, Tashikuergan was a small kingdom of the Tajik people. In the eighth century, this kingdom was wiped out. The Tang Dynasty stationed troops in the area, established military garrisons and converted the territory into a militarily-controlled administrative district. Nevertheless, the county's internal affairs continued to be autonomously run, a situation that lasted for more than 1000 years. In the eighteenth century, the county once again fell under central control, this time under the Qing Dynasty. It reappeared on the map under the name Silekuer Hui-zhuang, with a total population of 500 households. The Qing government promoted the local Tajik leader to the level of *boke,* a hereditary position charged with managing the local courts and tax collection. In 1884, the province of Xinjiang was established and divided into administrative sub-units called *fu* and counties. By that time, the Qing government had eradicated the hereditary system of rule throughout Xinjiang and replaced it with a county magistrate system where local officials were appointed directly by the provincial government. In Silekuer, however, the Qing did not establish a county. Instead, it maintained the earlier system of hereditary rule and left the area's internal affairs to the autonomous control of the local leaders. This system lasted till 1926, after which it was eliminated. At this time, the Republican government established a county, within which there were 27 townships (*zhuang*). The county governor appoints the head of the zhuang from among the local Tajik leaders. And thus was created the sub-county form of local administrative structure: the *xiang.*

In 1952, the government in Xinjiang undertook reforms, convened the people's representative congress, the villager representative meetings, established peasant associations and put into effect a four-level administrative system encompassing the county, area, xiang and sub-village levels.

The county and area chiefs were appointed by the provincial government, whereas the xiang and village chiefs were elected from the villager representative meetings. Following 1958, the administrative system changed once again, this time to a four-tier system encompassing county, commune, large production unit and small production unit levels. The head of the communes was appointed by the county government, whereas the heads of the large and small production units were elected positions. Among the four levels, the small production team was what we here could call 'local government', as it was the basic unit of production and distribution. In 1983, the government set in place the production responsibility system. Land and pastures were reallocated to each family, thus once again turning the family into the basic unit of production. Following 1984, the administrative system changed to a four-tier system encompassing the county, xiang and village-level people's committees as well as the so-called 'natural village' administrative unit. (Natural villages are quite small and one can think of them in essence as 'sub-village level' administrative units.) The xiang director is appointed by the county government. The chairman of the village committee is an elected position.

Although the functions of the xiang government has grown over the course of the 90 years since the establishment of county-level administration, the socio-economic influence of local government structures in Tashikuergan County has been much less than in other areas. Most significantly, the local government in the county is out of joint with the area's economic life and types of production organisation. Since Tashikuergan County is the poorest in the entire country, the government has basically done away with most forms of tax collection. Moreover, there is no industrial enterprise in the county. What this means is that the government is left with little to manage except for such matters as local public security, education and public construction works, all of which have little connection with the everyday life of its citizens. Tajik society, for instance, is essentially a crime-free and violence-free society, leaving the local public security administration with nothing to do. As for education, the entire county has only 16 elementary schools (one per xiang) and one middle school. Public works, furthermore, is limited mainly to the agricultural off-season, when the local government brings together the residents from each village to repair flooded-out dirt roads, to mend canals and to engage in various other forms of temporary work. This is to say that the xiang government has not been able to influence much the lives of the local people.

Over the past 50 years, the local government in this area has been treating economic development and the improvement of living standards as their prime responsibilities. To that end, the following three methods have been employed:

a) Budgetary requests to the central government. At present, the central government gives the county more than RMB 50,000,000 each year, equalling 30 times the administrative income of the county itself. This money, however, has been used mainly towards the living expenses of bureaucrats at the various levels of government, school staffs and provisional economic aid to farmers in times of natural disasters.

b) Enlarging the amount of land under cultivation. There is currently three times as much farmland as there was 50 years ago.

c) Enlarging the amount of livestock. Over the past 50 years, the total number of livestock has increased by more than a factor of 6.

These methods, however, have not yet helped the Tajik people escape poverty. (Over the past 50 years, one should point out, the population has also increased by more than a factor of two.) To the contrary, it has increased the speed and intensity of pasture degradation, soil run-off and natural disasters.

The Importance of the Family

To the present day, the one thing that has provided the Tajik people a reliable shelter against their harsh natural environment, is the traditional extended family. Hence, Tajik culture places supreme importance on the protection, stability and coherence of the family.

For the Tajik people, the family is a kind of stronghold, forming for the individual a type of miniature society which encompasses the realms of production, consumption, education, security, emotion and love. One's immediate family, extended family and neighbours carry out all livelihood and production activities. Certain aspects of this form of production organisation, namely, its strong internal coherence and the importance of relationships built on trust, are fundamentally different from those of other organisational forms. The extended family and the community are built upon the foundation of ethnic relations and the individual rarely subscribes to any other authority outside the extended family.

The Tajik people traditionally permit most forms of inter-relational marriage, except those between siblings. In fact, the marriage of close relations has traditionally been very popular as a way to strengthen territorial links, for the Tajiks have not migrated for thousands of years. Those unable to find an appropriate match within their close relations often marry within their own village. The Tajik people have a popular saying, 'One does not cross the mountain to find a mate, nor cross the river to plant a field.' As a result, people from the same sub-village and the same village are, for the most part, relatives. Among the Tajik people, relations between husband and wife are quite stable. The marital relationship, moreover, is not purely a relationship between individuals. Rather, it represents the relationship of two families. Therefore, divorce is regarded as highly shameful, as is the abandonment of children and the failure to take care of the elderly.

The patriarchal large family is the traditional family structure of the Tajik people. Normally, the male head of the household acts as the head of the family and arranges the production labour of each of the other family members. Respect for the head of the household and respect for the elderly are traditional moral concepts, which the Tajik people have always sought to preserve. For instance, if children divide up family property while the mother and father are still alive, they are likely to become the object of public scorn. If the father passes away, the mother takes over as the head of the household. Following the mother's passing, the oldest son assumes control. The extended family encompasses a few nuclear families and each of these nuclear families cooperates in carrying out the duties of production. In turn, the extended family provides daily goods for each nuclear family. Thus, the extended family is the fundamental unit of production. All the members are very close and work in harmony.

In addition to the cooperation that takes place within the extended family, Tajik people are also quite close to their relatives and neighbours. This form of cooperation is quite common in the field of production. In the sub-village (cun), if any one family needs to build a house, repair a canal, or arrange weddings or funerals, relatives, friends and neighbours will offer help, without expectation of remuneration (except, perhaps food and drink). Members of the community cooperate during the spring planting and the autumn harvest as well. On the pastures, people assist one another by herding each other's cattle. In times of personal misfortune and natural disasters, everyone is likely to come forward to give assistance. Because of this, although Ta County is Xinjiang's poorest county, it is still consistently the county in Xinjiang with the lowest crime rate. Relations by blood and by shared locality have constituted the principal forms of social relations, as well as the primary type of social structure and social order for thousands of years, and this has helped preserve their existence.

The Example of Waqia Xiang

In July 2001, I conducted fieldwork in the xiang of Waqia in Ta County. The situation in this xiang serves well as a representative illustration of the current condition of the Tajik people, both in terms of production and lifestyle. From it, we can better understand how and why the Tajik people rely on the extended family and the community.

Waqia Xiang is situated in Tashikuergan County in mountainous area approximately 80 km east of the county centre. The total area of the xiang is about 2,500 square km and is bordered on both sides by mountains—to the east lies the Kalabaderike Mountains and to the west the Kuitidaier Mountains. The two mountain ridges extend to more than 5000m above sea level, the uppermost 500m of which is an area of permanent snow and no vegetation. The mountain ridges form a natural boundary between Waqia and the neighbouring xiang of Datong to the east and Yategunbaizi to the west. In the valley between the two mountains flows the Waqia River, which is approximately 30m wide, with a typically low flow rate and with depths of only 30–50 cm. The river periodically runs dry, except in cases of melting snow and heavy rainstorms, at which point its waters can rise rapidly to the depth of a few meters. Under such conditions, the Waqia River often causes large-scale erosion and run-offs. The narrow valleys located on the banks of the river lie at 3,310m above sea level. The valley is a little over 50 km long and is home to seven of the village's sub-villages, with a total of 406 households and 2,393 people. (In 1949, the xiang had just over 70 households, with about 400 people.) Except for one Kyrghiz household, all of the people in Waqia are Tajik. In 2000, the average per capita income was RMB 579, which falls below the official poverty line set by the Chinese government.

This mountain village is semi-agricultural and semi-pastoral and takes cattle farming as its economic mainstay. The xiang contains 1,023,240 mu^3 of pasture, all of which is rather barren mountain terrain, with very low capacity to sustain livestock. The pasture land is divided up into four sections, one for each season and located at different altitudes of the mountain. In all, the county possesses 15,488 heads of livestock, of which 12,365 are sheep and the remaining are cows (1,397), horses (196), yaks (778), donkeys (656) and camels (96). There is an average of 6.4 heads of cattle per person. Although this number is fairly low, it already exceeds the pasture's capacity to sustain them. The village has 5,216 mu of land under cultivation, about 2.1 mu per person. The farmland is in the mountain valley, where the villagers plant mainly barley, peas and corn. One portion of the yield serves as food for the village and the other as cattle feed. Due to run-off, the infertility of the land and the mountainous climate, the rate of production for such foodstuff averages only 103 kg, with a total production rate of 518,162 kg (about 204 kg per person). From February to May of each year, however, farmers must supplement the cattle feed with larger amounts of grain, each sheep needing approximately 10–20 kg and every horse needing about 150 kg of feed. After setting aside the grain needed for livestock feed, every person's average share of grain does not even reach 100 kg. Because of this, every year the village must purchase a large amount of grain to fulfil its requirement. If we calculate the average amount per person, we find that farm and livestock products are not plentiful. On top of that, when the villagers need to buy daily goods, they have no choice but to sell their own wares. Since the village is quite far from the nearest marketplace, direct exchange of commodities is very popular. Villagers often trade their livestock with merchants from outside the village in exchange for the items they need.

After 1983, the village's land and pasture were divided among individual households, but production activities in the area continued to be a matter of mutual assistance among different families. Here, I can draw upon my interviews with Baikeli Aisha and his family, whom I spent time with during my fieldwork. The Baikeli family's production activities during the course of one year offer us insight into the matters discussed thus far.

The Baikeli Family

Baikeli Aisha is 52-years-old and his family has six members: four sons, one daughter, and himself. His wife has already passed away. The family owns 98 sheep, 20 yaks, one cow, one camel and 1,218 mu of pasture land. Specifically, they have 274 mu of winter pasture, 634 mu of summer pasture, 310 mu of spring and autumn pasture and 5 mu of grassland. Besides this, they have 14 mu of farmland (4 mu of which has already been destroyed by floods) where they plant either peas or barley. Their production activities are mainly agriculture and cattle farming.

Agriculture   Every year, in April, the spring season begins. On about 1 April, the village begins to repair the canals. First, residents collectively repair the village's canals, which have dried out, a task that takes approximately three–four days. Afterwards, they help repair each individual family's canals. At the same time, they have to move the donkeys to the spring, autumn and summer pasture land, which is atop the mountain some dozens of kilometers away. Then they have to collect the manure, which has accumulated in the pasture, transport it back and, after stamping the soil, spread the manure. Because the land in the region is very rocky, it leaks water very quickly. So, every year, villagers must irrigate the land 12–13 times, without which crops will grow poorly. In the dry season, the river often runs dry, forcing farmers to irrigate the soil only about seven or eight, resulting in poor harvests. On the other hand, when rain water and snow are at high levels, rockslides and mudslides often bury the farmland. In the beginning of every spring season, therefore, the family must go into the fields and remove the rocks and small stones that have collected. At their worst, these rockslides have been known to destroy farmland. Out of the 14 mu of pasture, which was distributed to the Baikeli family in 1983, for example, 4 mu have since been carried off by rockslides. From the beginning of April to the end of August, the family has to irrigate its land at least twice every month. Amidst all this, they still have to repair canals, cut hay and loosen the soil. In the middle of August, they begin to harvest the peas, a task that lasts until the end of the month. In the beginning of September, it is the time to harvest the barley, which again carries on till the end of the month. Following the end of September, the family starts to collect manure. First they take manure produced by the sheep, cows and donkeys (all of which are raised in the house) and prepare it for use in the following spring season. By mid-October, the year's farm work is basically complete. In the year I visited them, Baikeli Aisha's family's 10 mu of land was dedicated completely to growing barley and produced a total of 1,000 kg—just enough to feed the livestock. As for the family's six members, all their food had to be purchased. Every year, his family needs to buy 1,300 kg of flour.

Herding During the winter months, herders and their livestock live in the winter pasture land. Here, snow begins to fall in October, quickly killing off the grass, and in January, the temperature falls to 30 degrees below zero Celsius. To maintain the livestock, they must rely mainly on the original collection of hay and grain. In the beginning of May, the family begins the process of moving to the spring pasture land, located atop the mountain. The spring pasture is 30 km away from the village and is already equipped with living quarters. Before moving, however, the family must first climb the mountain and repair their spring home, as well as prepare wood for heating and cooking. When moving, the family first takes their grain, bedding and clothes, cookware and production tools, using donkeys, horses, or camels to ship them up the mountain. This job typically requires 10 or more donkeys or three camels. So one has to rely on relatives and neighbours for help. During the move, the family rises early and arrives late in the evening. Afterwards, the family still has to move its livestock up the mountain. On the journey, the sheep, cows and horses all need to be alternately set out to graze and thus a number of families have to divide up the work. Thus, in every pasture there are always a few families living together and cooperating. In 1983, when the government divided up the pasture land, they did so in accordance with the requirements of the villagers; it ensured that the pasture land of relatives and neighbours were adjacent. When setting livestock out to graze, relatives and neighbours use their pasture lands collectively, often gathering the same kind of animals together and herding their own as well as others' livestock together. The Baikeli family's spring pasture land is connected with those of their relatives in five other households. In the winter pasture, eight households live together, out of which four are related and the rest are neighbours. In the summer pasture, there are 12 households together, among which two are related and 10 are either neighbours or people from the same village.

Since ancient times, the tradition among the Tajik people has been that each village uses its pasture land collectively. To the present day this tradition has basically remained the same. In the beginning of May, if the area is afflicted by a spring frost, or if the prairie grass still has not grown, they will take the hay from their farms in the village and ship it up the mountain. In the spring, they set the livestock out to pasture for one month and on about 1 June, move to the summer pasture. Here, the Baikeli family lives in a *yurt* (tent). The summer prairie is more than 40 km away from the village, located more than 4000 m above sea level. During July and August, the family must return to the valley to harvest the grass, dry it and then prepare the livestock feed for the following winter. The Baikeli family's 5 mu of grassland can produce 1,500 kg of hay. In addition, they must buy 3,000 kg more each year before there is enough to get the livestock through winter. In the summer prairie land they set the livestock out to pasture for about three months. When September comes, they travel down to the autumn prairie land, which lies about 20 km from the village. In the middle of November, they return to the winter pasture land. The winter prairie land is in the valley, about 7 km away from the village. The livestock stay there for about five-and-a-half months. Over the course of these four seasons, the herders also have to repair and maintain their houses, which are made out of either stone or unbaked clay bricks. Because temperatures in summer are warm, families can live in yurts and do not have to spend time making these mud-brick houses. Thus, every family on the prairie must build a total of at least three houses. The Baikeli family has one house in each of the spring, autumn, and winter prairie lands. Each year, the family sells 20 sheep (for about RMB 5,000–6,000) and four calves (for RMB 6,000), using the money they earn to buy grain, hay and to send one son to attend school.

In this Tajik county, every household engages dually in farming and cattle farming. As such, they must simultaneously take part in a number of labour-intensive activities. Each family must, at the same time, have one son managing the farm fields and two sons on the prairie herding the livestock and transporting materials. In addition, the family also needs at least two women in the house and on the prairie land to prepare meals, clean clothes, feed the baby animals, take care of the elderly, raise the infants, shear the wool and milk the livestock. When the time comes to move to a different pasture, to repair houses, or to harvest, the family needs even more labourers. They are subject to immense pressures and in order to survive must battle with nature. For every individual, there is no alternative but to rely on the household and for every household to rely on relatives and neighbours.

The Relationship between Villagers and the Local Government

The government of Waqia Xiang has a xiang director, co-director and about 50 political cadres whose salaries are paid by the county. Their relationships with the villagers are best described as one of inattentiveness. The villagers of Waqia are connected to their xiang government by means of the village committee (large production unit). The entire xiang has a total of five village committees, each of which is composed of four people who are elected from among the residents of Waqia. These positions rotate once every three years. Every year, each committee member receives RMB 650 in the form of a salary subsidy. This money is acquired from the villagers on a household-by-household basis, with each household giving between RMB 56–100 per year. In accordance with state guidelines, the village committee manages family planning programmes, public security and organises the villagers in the repair of canals and roadways. Beyond this, the economic and everyday lives of the villagers are essentially autonomous, having very little connection with either the village committee or the xiang government. In reality, their mode of production, their production organisation and their natural environment has been fundamentally the same for the past hundreds of years, making it little wonder that the Tajik people have maintained traditional family structures, social relations and customs.

In his research on ancient Chinese society, G. William Skinner has contended that administrative capitals are the by-products of economic centres. As one moves further away from these economic centres towards border areas, the level of reliance on commercial products goes down and the level of reliance on self-sufficiency goes up. As this reliance on self-sufficiency increases, the extent of government control in the area decreases in direct proportion (Skinner, 1974).

While theorising on the relationship between modernisation and the political power of the state, Anthony Giddens and Mingming Wang (Giddens, 1985; MingmingWang, 1988) have claimed that for state power to penetrate into the local society, it must be founded on an increase of the rate of material production, the diffusion of industrialisation in all sectors of society and the replacement of a society based on communal-style relations with a society based on citizenship. These theories can all help us understand and explain the relationship between Tajik communities and local government in the region.

Notes

1. Statistics of 2000 by Livestock Department of Ta County, 66 per cent of the GDP of the county is from livestock.
2. In the oases of Talim of Xinjiang, sheep reach maturity in eight months.
3. Mu = 0.07 hectare.

References

The Census Office of China State Council. Census of 2000, 2002, Beijing: China Statistics Press.

Skinner, William G. 1974. 'Cities Hierarchies of Local Systems', in Arthur Wolf (ed.), *Studies of Chinese Society*. Chicago: Stanford University Press.

Wang, Mingming. 1988. 'Chinese Xiang and Town Government: In a View of the Relationship between Country and Society', *Chinese Social Sciences*, 24: 21.

17 The Evolution and Function of the Kaxie System of the Lahu People in South-west China

SHAOYING HE

The Lahus and Nanduan Village: An Introduction

The Lahu people are an ethnic group with a long history and splendid culture. As recorded in literature, the Lahus are descendents of the ancient Qiang people, who lived in the areas of Gansu and Qinghai. According to some historical materials, this people first appeared as a unitary group in the Tang Dynasty (619–907 AD). In the late Song Dynasty (960–1279 AD), the Lahus emigrated southward from the Erhai area along two routes. In Ming Dynasty (1368–1644 AD) and the Qing Dynasty (1644–1911 AD), they settled down in the forests by the sides of the Lancang River and Yuanjiang River, which run through vast territories of Simao, Lincang, Xishuangbanna, Yuxi and Honghe. They also scattered in some places of Myanmar, Vietnam, Laos and Thailand. The population of the Lahus in China was 50,000 in 1950s, but reached 411,746 in 1990, according to the statistics of the national census of 1990. In addition, about 200,000 Lahus live abroad.

Lancang in China, as a region with the world's most concentrated Lahu inhabitants, is the only 'Autonomous County' established for the Lahus. The county homes 200,000 Lahus, accounting for a half of the total population of the Lahus in China. Nanduan Village (22°02' North Latitude, 99°35' East Longitude) is located in the southern end of Nuofu Township in the southwest of the county neighbouring Myanmar. It consists of 10 smaller villages sharing a population of more than 2,000. The village office is situated in this village. Nanduan had 49 households, 254 people in 1995, and 54 households, 249 people in 1999, with a negative population growth. Currently, there are 450 mu (30.02 hectares) of ploughland, yielding 330 kg of grain per capita. Calculated in cash, the annual average income of the villagers is presently RMB 649. In 1995, when I did my fieldwork in the village, a tea-processing factory was set up, since the area of tea plantation has been expanded (as a matter of fact, besides grain production, tea has become an important source of income of the villagers). In the same year, the County's Water Conservation

Bureau invested RMB 110,000 and built a waterworks, pumping and channelling drinking water into each household. The villagers, who earlier had to walk miles to carry water, also contributed both money and labour to the project.

During the last five years of the twentieth century, while China's economy boasted a high growth, the economic development of Nanduan Village remained slow and the gap between rich families and poor ones (a general index of urban and industrial growth) was fairly small (see Appendix 17.1: Annual Statistics of Domestic Economy in Nanduan Village). Even at present, this condition is rife in over 60 per cent of China's territory, where ethnic minority people are living. The analysis of it produces unique characteristics that differ from those of other places, such as, the Han Chinese settlements. However, what is most conspicuous in Nanduan is the ancient kaxie system that coexists and functions side by side with the grass-roots village committee of the Chinese Communist Party (CCP) regime.

The Lahus' Kaxie System: In Historical Process

Kaxie is a transliteration into Chinese, of the Lahu characters 'ka', which means 'village' or 'residence block' and 'xie' which means 'master' or 'local authority'. Thus, kaxie originally indicates 'master of a village' or 'chief of a certain population'. Kaxie is also called *kaxiepa*, which has the same meaning as kaxie, that is, the 'master of a village' or the 'chief of a certain population'. This connotation helps shed light on the origin of the institution. It might be safe to say that the kaxie system originated in the time of tribal civilisation and has experienced a long process of evolution over time.

The kaxie institution might have descended from a pattern of military-democracy, for villagers elect their kaxie democratically. The kaxie's period of office depends on his own capability and prestige among the villagers, and if villagers wish it, a kaxie's term of office can be renewed. The responsibility of a kaxie in early times was to head his fellow villagers in primitive productions such as hunting and collecting in daily life and to command his people in wartime. The primitive structure of the kaxie system might have been simple. But, with the population growing over time and relationships to other ethnic groups getting more complex, it became a compelling need for the Lahu people to select a head who could supervise production, solve disputes, maintain social order, bridge relationships with neighbouring villages and ethnic groups, and who was simultaneously capable of dealing with conflicts with other peoples as well as coordinating economic activities. Hence, a kaxie had to shoulder a greater burden than before and was required to possess the qualifications concerned. Consequently, subtle changes have taken place in the relationship between a kaxie and his villagers. Besides performing the functions of a kaxi, he enjoys certain preferential treatment in the village because of the fact that he has been empowered by the Lahu society. For example, during festivals and especially in the new year, villagers usually come to visit the kaxie. As a general practice, the kaxie and especially the senior villagers receive respectively a piece of the fleshy 'back meat' if a wild animal is trapped. This is a cultural relic handed down from the ancient time of Lahu Presbyterianism that has survived through history in Lahu society. Specifically, those considered as having both ability and moral integrity by the elders are considered for candidature for the post of kaxie. Presbyterianism maintains deep influence on the ethnic group of Lahu and the elders are regarded as symbols of wisdom. Some old sayings are even now still popular among the Lahus such as 'The junior will know nothing if the senior speaks less'; 'An old hand is a good guide and an old man knows about the past'; 'An elder knows the truth and thus a kaxie learnt to judge'. There are stories of how kaxies solicited the elders for advice in the settlement of cases. Even today in the Lahu areas, in keeping with the tradition of the kaxie system, people must consult a prominent elder or a former kaxie for advice before a new kaxie can be elected. Moreover, any renewal or removal of a kaxie's before the end of his term depends largely on 'a simple word of the elders'. Briefly, Presbyterianism is an essential characteristic of the kaxie system of the Lahu people.

Modern Development and Characteristics

The origins of the Lahu's kaxie system is yet inexplicable, but if we trace it back to the 'Guizhu Tributary System' of the Qiang people's descendents and the religion Mahayana, we may find some link between the kaxie system, Mahayana and the Guizhu tributary system. The tributary system came into existence during the period of the Tang Dynasty (619–907). Since Mahayana had a great impact on Lahu society and its ideology in the late Ming Dynasty (1368–1644) and early Qing Dynasty (1644–1911), it might have helped in passing down the 'Guizhu tributary system' and even transformed it into a political-religious kaxie system and consequently, formed a kaxie nominating system—an 'Esha Buddha' (Wang and Shaoying, 1990),[1] in which a kaxie could be directly ordained. Besides functioning as a traditional kaxie (village master), a nominated kaxie works simultaneously in managing village and Buddhist affairs. In other words, a nominated kaxie is a living Buddha or an appointed guardian of Buddhism in his village, being responsible for both religious rituals and political activities.

The political-religious kaxie system consisted of four levels of institutions. As the religious head, the kaxie was in charge of preaching the Buddhist scripture and tenets in every first, fourth and eighth month of the lunar year on the one hand, and on the other hand, as the political head, had to help the elected kaxies arrange seasonal activities such as teaching, spring ploughing, farming, cereal cropping and storing. The kaxie was elected by the villagers and appointed by the Buddhist monk on the basis of the former's moral merits such as goodness, unblemished record of no quarrels with others, good command of Chinese, eloquence, sense of justice and concern for the masses. The inheritable system was extrusive in some areas. When a kaxie died, one of his sons, who needed to be wise and competent, would be selected to succeed him. If the dead had no sons, his brother(s) or others could be selected as candidates (The Simao Prefectural Committee of the Nationalities, 1990: 346).

In the political-religious kaxie system, the kaxie was directly subject to the Buddhist monkhood, being responsible for teaching Buddhism and for managing the production and livelihood in his village. That is to say, he took charge of Buddhist affairs and civil service on the Buddhist clergy's behalf. Evidence of this are old sayings commonly heard in Lahu villages such as: 'A village has a master, a family has a host'; 'the master grieves over the village's losses, the host grieves over the family's misfortune'; 'master is worried if his villagers do things wrong'; 'the village's dirtiness is the master's shame'; 'master is concerned about the villagers, villagers are concerned about the master' and so on. This indicates that 'political-religious syncretism' characterised the kaxie system in the early times of development. This combination, which used to reinforce intercommunication, accumulate manpower and material resources used for fighting against the rule of other ethnic groups, accords with the common aspiration of the people, and in some sense, promotes the social productivity of the Lahus. On occasions such as the annual gatherings in temples, Buddhists, depending on their financial circumstances, made offerings of rice, soybean, sesame or money to the Buddha. Those who owned little just brought firewood as offerings. People were all willing to lend a hand in activities such as preparing firewood, pounding rice, milling, etc. With the increase in production, people became more enthusiastic to offer grain, which served partly as food for the monks and partly as aid for people in need. Even now, well-known stories are told about the golden times of the 'political-religious syncretism', which is a valuable contribution to Lahu culture (The Simao Prefectural Committee of the Nationalities, 1993: 279).

The kaxie system prevailed for a time in the Lahu areas (current Shuangjiang, Ximeng, Menglian and Lancang). In Lancang County, the ancient custom still exists today. For instance, in the area of Nanduan, which was the last destination of Mahayana, people even today call their religion 'Nanduan Buddhism', in an attempt to be different from others. Nanduan Buddhism provides us with an analytical base to understand further the ancient kaxie system of the Lahus.

Kaxie and their Responsibilities

The Lahu people believe that a village must have a 'village heart'. So one may often see a village stake standing in the center of a Lahu village. Every village has four gates and four kaxie (or *aduoagua*) residing separately in the four directions. The kaxie, the *zhuoba*, the *foxiepa* and the *zhangli*, all of whom are elected by the villagers, make up the membership of the kaxie. The kaxies' duties depend on their capability, morality and willingness, with different members playing different roles. The kaxie normally administers the civil services of a village. There are, however, some exceptional cases where one person occupies several different positions. Acting as the village priest, the zhuoba primarily engages in ceremonies performed in the village fair, village stake and manages Buddhist prayers for the common weal of the village and its production. The foxiepa takes care of the temple facilities and public properties. The zhangli is a man who arranges activities of making and repairing the villagers' farming tools. These personnel symbolise respectively the village gods, Buddhism and the divine merit of tools. In some of the Lahu festivals, such as the *kuo* (spring festival), the new rice festival, the kaxie or former kaxies receive collective new year visits from the villagers. In return, the kaxie offer good wishes by fastening 'blessing threads' on the visitors' wrists. At present, the zhuoba and kaxie are replaced more frequently. Replacement of these posts take place because sometimes the position holders are too old or because some momentous natural disasters like poor harvests have come to the village. In such a situation, the villagers usually request re-election for a better zhuoba and kaxie. Let me turn to the necessary qualifications of a kaxie and the voting procedure of a candidate.

A kaxie candidate must have the following qualifications. First, he should not be younger than forty years of age. In the traditional viewpoint of the Lahus, a person younger than forty years cannot receive any presents from his fellow villagers because of his immaturity and inexperience. Only a man older than forty, according to the Lahus, 'behaves as a man and is able to foster his children well'. Second, according to the rules and conventions of the ethnic group and the village, an intended kaxie must not be involved in any sexual scandals and must simultaneously be fair and kind. Third, a kaxie candidate should be rich or wealthy. Usually, if a villager is facing difficulties such as a lack of money to pay the indemnity fine for some offence, the kaxie is expected to indemnify the concerned villager with his own money otherwise he will be derided. People would most likely say, 'He only knows how to get presents, but is not ready to do his duties well'. In older times, a kaxie would not be elected from a family with a small labour force. Fourth, a kaxie must be courageous and should not evade responsibility. Fifth, a kaxie should have good knowledge about Buddhism, rites and farming. Sixth, he must not be involved in any case of divorce.

Traditionally, the election for kaxie is held on a chosen date and the outcome must be announced publicly. The Lahu people in Nanduan area adopt the approach of 'thatch stalk picking egg' to elect a new kaxie (the zhuoba is selected in the same way). In this method, a ritual is held at the temple. Two bowls (one filled with rice and the other half-filled with water) are placed on the underside of the village god's stake. Then the presiding monk picks up an egg, breaks it and slides the contents into the bowl with water. Each of the candidates takes a thatch stalk and breaks it at one end to make a hook-shaped tip and then places it against the side of the bowl. The monk covers the bowls with a dustpan cover and scatters some rice over the cover while chanting. Half an hour later, he removes the dustpan cover and tries to pick the egg in the bowl with the hook-tipped thatch stalks made by the candidates. The candidate whose stalk hook hooks the egg white is believed to be the divinely ordained kaxie. In some places, while a kaxie is being elected, people conduct a ritual of lighting a candle or burning a joss stick; if the candle keeps burning to its end, the chosen kaxie will accept his post, otherwise, he will reject it.

People in Nanduan Village are enthusiastic about voting in the Communist village committee elections. The voters' turn-out in a recent election was 90 per cent and over 90 per cent of the voters were satisfied with the outcome (The Simao Prefectural Committee of the Nationalities, 1993: 122). However, the Lahus in Nanduan Village have greater enthusiasm in voting for kaxie members, believing that the elected would be the harbinger of favourable weather and happiness for the village, since his election has divine sanction.

The major responsibilities of a kaxie are to maintain village order, safeguard villagers' production and provide civil services. The kaxie acts as a problem solver, mediator and intervener in cases such as breaking the social moral code, robbery, stealing, pillaging, maltreating elders, incest, damaging of crops by livestock, disputes over land, marital conflicts, neighbourhood conflicts, troubles from intemperance, confrontations between villages or between the villagers and residents on the other side of the border. The kaxie must fulfil his job justly and the solutions are reported faithfully to the village office and then to the upper departments of the administrative organisation. If there are cases violating the national laws of the country, the violators as well as their cases will be passed over to the related judicial organs, according to the laws. The kaxie system functions positively under the overall governance of the Chinese government.

A kaxie today neither has financial privilege nor is paid a fixed salary. He receives a piece of pork (as thick as two folded fingers, locally called 'kaxie's present') cut down from a pig's neck when a villager slaughters a 'new year pig'. When receiving the gift, the kaxie cannot take it with his hand, but has to let the giver place it on the table (which is covered with a blanket or thick cloth symbolising the power of the kaxie) called the 'kaxieay'. It is said that 'aya' is Buddha's 'zhikezhila' (assistant) and the elected kaxie will be provided with an 'aya table'. When the kaxie deals with momentous matters such as affairs concerning Buddhism, regulations of the ethnic group, village rules and even foreign affairs, the 'aya table' is used as a display table with presents to consecrate to Buddha. The presents are not for the kaxie himself, but are meant for the gods. On Lahu's 'kuoshi' (the second day of the Lahu's new year, or the second day of the first month of the Chinese lunar year), all the villagers gather at the kaxie's place in the evening. There are dances and prayers to the Buddha and their gods, and then the 'kaxie's presents' are shared among all the villagers. The kaxie may sometimes present, in return, glutinous rice buns to those who come to pay him a new year call. During the new year period, the zhuoba leads his fellow villagers in the general prayer for a prosperous new year. On new year's day or other festivals, the kaxie also give presents to neighbouring villages as a friendship gesture.

With swift changes taking place all over the world, the system of kaxie has vanished in many places. But in the areas mentioned in the previous sections, the existing kaxie system still functions well in the daily lives of the Lahus. Apart from the responsibilities mentioned earlier, the kaxie also plays a very active social role by cooperating with local governmental agencies, that is, the village office and village committee. They organise people to build their homesteads, instil among villagers discipline and obedience to laws, encourage villagers to report criminal acts such as drug abuse and drug traffic. They also make efforts to coordinate the relationship between the cadres and the masses and the relationship between the masses and the locally-stationed troops.

A kaxie is considered as being endowed with power by deities and the masses. He has total authority to deal with inter- and intra-villagers' disputes and is empowered to handle 'foreign affairs' on behalf of the village. The settlement is normally reached by means of reconciliation and compensation. More interestingly, the kaxie, who delivers the compensation, always executes the adjudication in question. Other incidents, for example, such as felling trees or cutting grass in the divine hill, regarded as immoral acts, are solved customarily through fines executed by the kaxie. Nowadays, when the kaxie's adjudication is considered inequitable, the victim may turn to the village committee for settlement. The village committee normally discusses the matter again with the kaxie rather than giving an independent adjudication. If the person concerned is still not satisfied, he can lodge an appeal to higher courts. However, this has never happened so far in Nanduan Village. The Nanduan community has a relatively sound social order.

Since Nanduan is situated along the China–Myanmar border and the cross-border residents are Lahu people who have been living in the same area for decades, the kaxie of Nanduan Village has had to mediate in disputes between villagers on both sides and has even taken care of some internal affairs of a village in Myanmar. During my fieldwork, I fortunately happened to be witness to an incident where some of the neighbouring Myanmarese villagers were sent to appeal to Kaxie Lizhagei for a judgement and to offer personal intercession in a case where one of their buffaloes had trampled the corn fields of a Chinese Lahu village. However, the kaxie and the village director do not undertake criminal or serious civil cases like stealing cattle, illegal cutting, etc. These have to be transferred to the county government of Lancang or the counterpart on the Burmese side.

Owing to the 'political-religious syncretism' of the kaxie system, some original religious activities have gradually evolved into historical and cultural traditions of the people in both content and form (see Appendix 17.2: Background of Lahu Beliefs). The Buddhist monk, zhuoba, jiali are all religious leaders in the current kaxie system and play very important roles in village affairs. Dalisi, the current Buddhist head monk was elected by the villagers just after his predecessor died of illness in 1999 and his previous position of kaxie was given up to his son Lizhagei the same year. A Buddhist head monk's major responsibilities are arranging joss sticks and candles at the temple, serving Buddha on the villagers' behalf, leading the villagers in welcoming the gods during the celebration of festivals, arranging the village sorcerer's dance to entertain the gods, leading the villagers in bidding farewell to the gods once the festivities are over, presiding over the ritual of electing the kaxie, zhuoba and jiali, taking charge of various Buddhist ceremonies and prescribing villagers' behaviour with Buddhist scriptures and handling cases of violation of the regulations. The main job of a zhuoba is to be in charge of the 'village heart', consisting of the village stake and village god, for the 'village heart' represents the collective idea and will. The zhuoba deals with cases such as violation of the village regulations, leading villagers to repair temples, building village gates, changing the village stake, distributing offerings and so on. The zhuoba is also considered to be the one who can communicate with supernatural forces and can deliver villagers' wishes to the divine and issue messages on the divines' behalf. He is, therefore, a medium between man and the divine. The major job of the jiali, a term that originally meant 'black smith', is to make iron farm tools and hunting tools. The jiali, in the mind of the villagers, is the 'protector' of Lahu society and is a living force. The current jiali is not an ironsmith, but he is in charge of all blacksmiths in the village, deciding when to make or repair farm tools.

The Village Committee and the Kaxie System: A Comparison

As shown in the previous section, the kaxie system plays an important role in Lahu society, particularly from a historical point of view. After the People's Republic of China was founded in 1949, the power of the kaxies, as well as the function of the system was weakened by centralisation and even abolished in the anti-rightist Great Cultural Revolution (1966–1976). After the death of Mao Zedong, Deng Xiaoping and his successor Jiang Zemin initiated a series of rural reforms in which the decision-making power of the CCP and its government was decentralised gradually down to the grass roots. As a result of decentralisation and decollectivisation, two new governmental agencies—the village office and the village committee—were established, replacing the leadership of the Maoist production brigade and the production team. Moreover, as a result of decentralisation and decollectivisation, individualism and pragmatism have emerged in the rural areas of the country. This makes the post-Mao household responsibility system a challenge to the local governments and cadres. Problems such as how to organise and promote production well, how to manage effectively local resources and how to solve local social problems and conflicts, came to be included in the political agenda of the village offices and committees.

Things are more complicated in the areas occupied by ethnic minority groups such as the Lahus in Nanduan Village. There is a realistic need, politically and economically, for local governmental agencies to seek and elect rural leaders for, in specific situations, local rural leaders are more capable of handing local affairs than local political offices and committees. Thus, from the mid-1980s onwards, the kaxie system began to revive in Nanduan Village and the other neighbouring villages. The villagers elect their kaxie, zhuoba, jiali and so on by traditional methods such as the 'thatch stalk picking egg', thereby forming a new self-governing kaxie organisation. The village office and committee in Nanduan neither reject nor support publicly the organisation, but they try to cooperate with the leadership of the kaxie organisation in their governance of local farming and ethnic affairs. This helps the members of the office and committee restore the state–society relationship, on the one hand, and bridge the gap between the Han and the minority people, on the other hand. In this way the communist grass-roots democracy has become localised.

In Nanduan Village, Lizhalun, the Buddhist monk's son has been elected as kaxie, Li Laosan as the zhuoba and Li Bao as the jiali. They work well with the members of the village committee and office. The village office of Nanduan presently has a four-member staff, including a party branch sectary, a village director, a copy clerk and a military secretary, whose individual monthly salary is RMB 300. The village committee of Nanduan Village consists of a director, a villager, a vice-director, an accountant, a storekeeper and a women's director, jointly managing various affairs with the villagers' kaxie system. These committee members do not have fixed salaries unlike the members of the village office. Every year they share 600 kg of paddy withdrawn or retained from the villagers. As the 'chief' or 'master' of the village, Lizhalun—the kaxie—works together with Li Zhabo—the village committee director. The director regards the kaxie as a member of the committee and thus invites Lizhalun to divide the paddy equally with the members of the committee. However, according to Luo Zhasi, who is the village director and belongs to the village office, the kaxie cannot enjoy the same treatment as the village committee members because the kaxie system has not been legitimised by the government. Despite it all, however, the kaxie members are acknowledged and supported by all the villagers.

In Nanduan, villagers elect all the committee members through a voting arranged by the local township government and the village office. But there is always much ambiguity in the election procedure. A village committee has no fixed work schedule. The members sometimes have three or four meetings a month; and sometimes they do not have any activities. The village committee of Nanduan Village performs the following major duties:

a) Publicise and enforce projects such as family planning, land contracting and management, prohibition of illegal cutting.

b) Implement policies and decisions from the county, township and village authorities, and organise labour for common projects.

c) Make agricultural decisions relating to taxes, fees, etc. Whenever an important decision is to be made, for instance, the committee will assemble an overall villagers' meeting to counsel with the villagers.

d) As to how much grains or money should be withdrawn and retained, for instance, the village committee will deal with villagers' defaults or violations to the laws or rules and make a budget in advance on the items of expenses and then declare the apportionments at a villagers' meeting.

While the village office and village committee are political as well as economic instruments of the communist hierarchic bureaucracy, the kaxie system looks more like a cultural as well as religious organ of the Lahu folk society, though it is a political tool to some extent. The communist scheme works at the macro levels of the village organisation, while the kaxie scheme operates at the micro and bottom levels of the Lahu community. Though the two schemes function well side-by-side, there are indeed some subtle differences between the two institutions. Comparatively, the kaxie scheme emphasises more in-group affection through emotional manipulation of the masses. We may find good support for this argument if we have a glimpse at the culture of the Lahus. According to *Lahu Zu Wenhua Daguan* (A Grand View of Lahu Culture, Yunnan Provincial Committee of the Nationalities, 1999: 74), the following 12 clauses are unwritten but underpinning conventions of Lahu society:

a) A person convicted of homicide pays with his life.

b) Injury to others is to be fined and the offender ordered to offer therapy to the wounded and provide for all the needs of the victim for life if disabled.

c) A pilferer is to be fined twice the wealth he steals and ordered to repair roads or bridges.

d) A man committing fornication with a married woman is to be fined. If he cannot afford the fine, his pigs and cattle are to be slaughtered and enjoyed in a feast by all the villagers, while he is ordered to clean the village.

e) An arsonist blaming others is to be thrown into fire.

f) A monk committing adultery faces the death penalty.

g) One releasing secrets about residence and migration is to be killed.

h) One cutting trees at headwaters is to be fined and made to clean the village.

i) One ruining the divine house and divine woods is to be fined. If he cannot afford it, his cattle are to be slaughtered and enjoyed by the villagers. All expenses are to be those of the wrongdoer.

j) Whenever the tribe is bullied and humiliated by another tribes, all tribe members are to fight unconditionally. Those withdrawing halfway are to be driven out of the village and their property confiscated.

k) Family hosts, both the man and the woman bears responsibilities and have to respect the old and take care of the young.

l) The old are to be responsible for preventing the young from wrongdoing and bad manners.

These conventions have a long history and some of them have even become village norms and regulations, commanding obedience from villagers. In reality, they may be readjusted or changed adaptively under specific circumstances. Here is a 10-clause written village charter I noticed in Nanduan Village:

a) Drug abuse is to be prohibited and abusers, if caught, to be handed to official authorities.
b) Gambling is forbidden and gamblers, if captured, are to be fined.
c) No dallying with women.
d) No pilfering, no fighting, being friendly to each other.
e) No cheating, everyone needs to be honest.
f) Being loyal to parents, respecting the senior, being polite to the headman, being obedient to the elders and always maintaining courtesy.
g) No cutting the trees at the headwater and in the divine woods, no mowing in the headstream hills and divine hills.
h) Cattle not allowed to enter tea gardens or to graze in others' fields.
i) Everyone to join in in the cleaning at traditional Lahu festivals and in welcoming gods to spend the new year in the village.
j) Marriage to be of choice, but 'chuan gunian' (dating) not to be allowed during busy farming seasons.

Conclusion

It is evident that apart from the village committee, that is, the officially-institutionalised village authority, there exists an unofficial but parallel power centre, the kaxie system. This system is a social organisation of the local people, though the government never accords it public recognition. The existence and operation of the kaxie system undoubtedly fills up to some extent the power vacuum in the state–society relationship. In this respect, the system is not only a traditional or cultural outcome of the Lahus, but also an institutional and organisational organ for an otherwise voiceless rural society. However, the kaxies are not 'gentries' or an oligarchy in China, but 'social actors' in the context of modern political science. They are not only like the agents of the communist party and its government, but somewhat like spokesmen of the grass roots of Lahu society. The parallel apparatus of the village committee and the kaxie system are, in fact, mutually complementary and interdependent. Though I cannot comment on how strongly or effectively they pass on the voice of the grass roots of the Lahus, it is clear that they represent a new social force of the Lahu people. However, despite institutional changes and democratic components in the kaxie system, the system is still attached with religious and tribal features. This implies, partially at least, that grass-roots democracy in China still has a long way to go.

Appendix 17.1
Annual Statistics of Domestic Economy in Nanduan Village

Date: November 23rd, 1995 Unit: RMB¥

| No. | Name | No. of Family Members | General Income | | | | | Total (Per Family) |
			Livestock Product	Byproducts	Forestry	Stock Raising	Parergon	
1	Napi	8	/	350	380	/	280	1,010
2	Zhabo	7	115	230	380	1,100	260	2,085
3	Xiaobiao	6		40	380	/	70	490
4	Xiaozhaluo	7	650	150	360	800	170	2,130
5	Luozhaluo	4	420	70	320	600	90	1,500
6	Dazhanu	4	/	50	320	800	60	1,230
7	Lisi	4	350	140	380	500	160	1,530
8	Naduo	9	1,350	85	380	1,400	130	3,345
9	Yapu	4	120	120	380	150	130	900
10	Zhatuo	8	/	130	380	/	270	780
11	Zhanuzhaluoba	4	75	100	360	110	164	809
12	Nage	6	1,800	600	360	1,990	110	4,860
13	Zhanuzhasiba	5	/	/	360	/	10	370
14	Laosan	7	/	80	360	/	150	590
15	Zhanuzhayiba	9	850	60	320	1,400	130	2,760
16	Nalie	5	/	/	360	/	10	370
17	Luozhala	5	650	30	360	800	40	1,880
18	Libao	6	1,800	150	360	2,000	225	4,535
19	Naiba	2	/	/	380	/	/	380
20	Zhanai	6	890	70	360	1,400	130	2,850
21	Naxilibodan	3	/	190	320	/	220	730
22	Luoda	6	/	/	300	/	10	310
23	Dalisi	12	2,150	/	360	2,800	18	5,328
24	Zhapo	4	/	30	320	/	80	430
25	Linaxi	9	/	/	360	/	130	490
26	Zhaduo	7	2,250	320	330	2,450	480	5,830
27	Liqing	3	1,580	90	350	3,200	100	5,320
28	Nataozhu	6	/	/	360	/	20	380
29	Zhadi	6	/	180	380	/	230	790
30	Zhawa	5	270	90	380	600	100	1,440
31	Lizhalun	4	1,420	120	360	1650	150	3,700
32	Zhapodi	4	560	720	360	600	815	3,055
33	Zhae	4	350	50	360	500	80	1,340
34	Zhakabo	4	2,350	/	320	2,500	15	5,185
35	Lizhonghua	4	/	30	370	/	180	580
36	Yadu	6	360	/	360	500	/	1,220
37	Zhabo	8	450	90	370	650	100	1,660
38	Yunan	4	850	160	380	1,100	200	2,690
39	Zhasi	4	/	90	370	/	120	580
40	Nabao	2	2,750	320	320	294	450	4,134
41	Zhanvnapoba	4	210	/	320	2,050	30	2,610

(Appendix 17.1 contd.)

(Appendix 17.1 contd.)

No.	Name	No. of Family Members	General Income					Total (Per Family)
			Livestock Product	Byproducts	Forestry	Stock Raising	Parergon	
42	Xiaozhanuzhasiba	5	190	30	320	360	50	950
43	Zhapowangnanba	3	/	180	320	/	200	700
44	Xiaozhaba	4	/	90	360	/	120	570
45	Nabaolizhuping	5	650	80	360	990	160	2,240
46	Linapo	3	/	80	360	/	35	475
47	Zhamuzhu	2	/	40	310	/	50	400
48	Xiaolibo	3	/	90	320	/	185	595
49	Nayoudi	4	/	190	320	620	230	1,360
	Total	254	25,460	5,655	17,320	3,4514	7,147	91,456

Five years later, when I returned to Nanduan Village in 2000, I found that the living conditions there had remained almost the same as in 1995. The most well-off family is presently Zhanuzhayiba's. This family of 6 own 31.6 mu land which includes paddy fields, dry land and woodland. It also owns 8 oxen, 8 buffaloes, 4 pigs, 8 chickens, 15 bed quilts, 7 blankets and even bicycles, a tractor, an electric mill and a sewing machine. In 2000, the family's income included RMB 3,600 in cash and 2,400 kg grain, from which 144 kg grain would be turned in as agricultural tax, 76 kg sold to official order and 400 kg withdrawn and retained by the collective. RMB 120 is to be paid as public planning fund and educational surtax. The poorest household is Zhapowangnanba's. This family of 5 owns 26.2 mu land, which includes paddy fields, dry land and woodland; 1 pig, 5 chickens, 3 blankets and a spot of production tools and living utensils as family property. The income of the family in 2000 was only RMB 400 in cash and 1,200 kg grain, with per person cash income and grain lower than the village average. But in general, financial differentiation in the whole village is not very large. Even the families of Kaxie members (the Buddha man, Kaxie, Zhuoba and Jiali) and the director of village committee could only pay their way. The rough natural environment, backward traffic condition is part of the cause of the condition, but lacking diligent and able people is also an inducing factor.

Appendix 17.2
Background of Lahu Beliefs

As the core of Lahu beliefs, 'Esha' plays the dominant role in the Lahu society and living. This is true even in areas dominated by Mahayana, Christianity or Catholicism. 'Esha' is the sovereign god of all among the Lahus, believed to have created the universe and to dominate everything on earth. When Buddhism and Christianity were introduced to these areas, they were combined with some features of the native primitive beliefs. Seemingly, the religion of the Lahus still wears the face of primitive belief, but is completely different in content; religious creed has been completely changed. Rituals formerly hosted by Moba or presbyter have become religious activities in a Buddha house or church.

In Lahu primitive belief, Moba and Xiba were the host and deliverer of traditional culture. Now Moba and Xiba have been replaced by Zhuoba, a member of the current Kaxie System, while in some of Nanduan's neighbouring villages where people believe in Christianity, the job has been taken over by the priest. As the most active person, a Zhuoba participates in the practices of divination, evocation, sending off the spirits, offering sacrifice, driving off the evils, capturing demons, praying and practicing sorcery. In Lahu society, the position of the Zhuoba is not hereditary or a full-time vocation. Nor is it paid for its operation. A Zhuoba is knowledgeable about Lahu's history, culture, sagas, epics, and ballads and is even able to answer various questions and cure people. A Zhuoba enjoys great respects from the villagers.

There are 3 major Buddhist activities: The first time is on 1st of the first moon, when Lahu Buddhists worship Esha Buddha. Head men and Buddha men from different villages come to the Buddha village to pray with presents for the Buddha and monks. After praying, they listen to the Buddha's remarks on the weather, rainfall and the possibilities of the coming year, and they discuss Buddhist affairs. The second is on fifteenth of the fourth Lunar month, and the third on the fifteenth of the eighth lunar month, when Esha Buddha presides over the event. People listen to Esha Buddha's sermon about Buddhist rites, disciplines and farming know how and so on. In the sermon of the fifteenth of the eighth lunar month, Esha Buddha teaches about spring ploughing. If there is a draft, the Buddha will lead the people to pray for rain. On the 15th of the eighth lunar month, the Buddha will teach about autumn harvesting. If there are rainy days, the Buddha leads the mass to pray for fine days and god's blessing for a smooth harvesting. In the process of the transmission of Buddhism, native primitive belief was incorporated into Buddhism and farming techniques are taught along with preaching. As a result, Buddhism has become more and more significant in the Lahu way of life.

Note

1. A more detailed discussion can be found in Wang and He (1999: Chapter 7).

References

Simao Prefectural Committee of the Nationalities. 1990. *Simao de Shaoshu Minzu* (Ethnic Groups in Simao). Kunming: Yunnan Press of the Nationalities.
————. 1993. *Simao Lahu Zu Chuantong Wenhua de Diaocha* (A Survey of the Lahu's Traditional Culture in Simao). Kunming: Yunnan Press of the Nationalities.
Wang, Zhenghuan and He Shaoying. 1999. *Lahu Zu Wenhua Shi* (A Cultural History of the Lahus). Kunming: Yunnan Press of the Nationalities.
Yunan Provincial Committee of the Nationalities. 1999. *Lahu Wenhua Danguan* (A Grand View of Lahu's Culture). Kunming: Yunnan Press of the Nationalities.

18 Social Change and the Development of Democracy in Local Governance in Tibet

TANZEN LHUNDUP

Social Change and Tibet's Local Governance Organisations

The local governance organisations in Tibet have experienced four main historical periods, in accordance with the changes in society:

a) 1951–59, that is, from the signing of the Agreement of the Central People's Government and the Local Government of Tibet on Measures for the Peaceful Liberation of Tibet to the democratic reform (many scholars, in fact, further divide this period into two periods, namely 1951–56 and 1956–59);
b) 1959–66, that is, from the democratic reform of Tibet to the Cultural Revolution;
c) 1966–80, that is, from the period of the people's commune to the beginning of reforms and opening up; and
d) 1980 onwards, that is, from the post-reform and opening up period to the present period (some further divide the last period into two periods respectively from 1980–92 and from 1992, when the market economy was implemented, till today).

No matter how the historical periods are divided up, however, our purpose is to acquire an understanding of the impact of social change on the local governance organisations in Tibet, and this is what this chapter seeks to do.

When Chamdo was liberated in October 1950, the People's Liberation Committee of Chamdo Prefecture of the People's Republic of China was established under the direct leadership of the State Administration Council (renamed as the State Council later). This was Tibet's first government organ under the new state power in the transitional period. When Tibet was peacefully liberated in May 1951, the central government did not change Tibet's original political system in accordance with the Agreement of the Central People's Government and the Local Government of Tibet on Measures for the Peaceful Liberation of Tibet. At that time, three government organisations including the Kasha government, the Auditor's Office of the Council of *Khenpos* of Panchen Erdeni and the People's Liberation Committee of Chamdo Prefecture coexisted with each other in Tibet and governed 147 *dzongs* (*shikas*).[1]

In March 1955, the Seventh Plenary Meeting of the State Council adopted the Decision of the State Council of the People's Republic of China on the Establishment of Tibet Autonomous Region (TAR) Preparation Committee. The TAR Preparation Committee was established in April 1956 and the three coexisting government organisations were put under the leadership of the Committee, leading to a situation where several independent government organisations conjointly functioned under a centralised leadership. Starting from August 1956, the TAR Preparation Committee successively set up eight *chikyap*[2]-level offices and 71 dzong-level offices (the equivalent of prefecture-level and county-level institutions) in the whole region. On 4 September of the same year, the Central Committee of the CPC decided not to carry out democratic reform in Tibet for at least six years and the 71 dzong-level offices already established were all cancelled, except those in Chamdo Prefecture. But on 20 April 1959, the State Council announced the cancellation of the People's Liberation Committee of Chamdo Prefecture and all its subordinate organisations because of the revolt that broke out in Tibet. On 9 July 1961, the State Council decided to dissolve the Auditor's Office of the Council of Khenpos of Panchen Erdeni and thus the term of coexistence of several governments was brought to an end. In July 1959, after the revolt was suppressed, the TAR Preparation Committee adopted the Organic Rules of Peasants' Associations in all counties, districts and townships of Tibet, which stipulated that the peasants' associations of districts and townships should exercise the powers of local government organisations. In October 1959, the Tibet Affairs Committee of the CPC announced the Instructions on the Establishment of Government Organisations at all levels in Tibet and soon after, various levels of people's democratic government organisations were rapidly established throughout the region. Between 1960 and 1962, the original 147 dzongs (shikas) were combined together and reorganised into six prefectures, one municipal people's government, 72 counties, 200 districts and more than 1,300 townships.

People's Commune System

Tibet began implementing the people's commune system from 1966. Under this system, various organisations of local governance were established in the rural areas of Tibet in conformity with those in other parts of China. Besides the local administration, party and youth league organisations, there were also Young Pioneers oriented to children, people's militia oriented to young and middle-aged people, women's federation oriented to women and poor peasants' associations oriented to ordinary poor peasants. Thus the people were effectively organised together. Going entirely against their original intention of economic cooperation, the people's communes in Tibet laid more stress on class struggle and carried out ceaseless political movements. Though the people's communes in both Tibet and inland China had adopted the system of integration of government administration with commune management (which meant that communes were both economic and administrative organisations) and 'ownership by two levels of governments, taking production teams as the basis', the communes in Tibet had actually no powers. In terms of economy, production teams were units of management and accounting in Tibet and in terms of government administration, district governments were the basic units of administration, while communes were only transitional organisations playing the role of a bridge.

Restoration of Townships and District Governments

With the implementation of household-based contract system from 1979, China's new Constitution was promulgated in 1982, which renounced the organisational form of commune that integrated government administration with commune management. This Constitution stipulated that the national structure should be divided into government organisations at four levels, namely, the central government, provincial governments, county governments and township (town) governments (including autonomous township governments). In October 1983, the Central Committee of the CPC and the State Council published the Notice about the Separation of Government Administration from Commune Management and the Establishment of Township Governments. The CPC Committee and the People's Government of TAR decided to dissolve the existing commune system and to restore the people's governments of townships (towns) in the whole region (including autonomous townships and border townships/towns) from 1984. Tibet successively established 10,144 villagers' committees, eight autonomous townships, 106 border townships and three border towns in the whole region in that period.

The People's Government of Tibet had also set up agencies of county governments—district administration stations in all counties for strengthening the governing over township governments in the early period of the establishment of local governance in Tibet, following the experience of China's inland provinces. The district administration station basically oversaw the functions of township governments and this created a hindrance in the functioning of township governments. Therefore, the Tibet government adjusted the setting up of districts and townships, reduced the intermediate organs and implemented a system of township administration directly under the leadership of the corresponding counties.

In August 1987, the CPC Committee and the People's Government of TAR publicised their Decision on Strengthening the Construction of Local Governance Government Organizations in Agricultural and Pastoral Areas through a conference, following which, the original 436 districts, 2,055 townships and nine towns in the whole region were reorganised into 71 districts, 897 townships and 31 towns. The numbers of districts and townships were respectively reduced by 83.7 per cent and 56 per cent and the number of towns was increased by more than three times. Thus a system of townships under the direct leadership of counties was realised. By September 1995, Tibet had set up 71 counties, one county-level city, one county-level district, 891 townships, 32 towns and 7,539 villagers' committees in the whole region, thereby completing the systemic restructuring of local governance organisations and putting into motion a process of development.

Economic Benefits for Township Officials

A semi-sabbatical system is in place for the township officials in Tibet and these officials can enjoy the state's subsidies for their loss of working time. The living subsidies for the semi-sabbatical officials in 1959–72 were 35 kg of highland barley per month for each official in the agricultural area or 25 kg of highland barley per month for each official in the pastoral area. In 1972, TAR adjusted the living subsidies for semi-sabbatical officials to RMB 15 per month for each official in the agricultural area and RMB 20 per month for each official in the pastoral area. In 1982, the living subsidies were readjusted to RMB 25 per month for each official in the agricultural area and RMB 30 per month for each official in the pastoral area.

The Impact of Social Change on Elections at the Basic Level

The first election of the People's Congress of Tibet Autonomous Region was held in Gurum Township of Duelong Dechen County of Lhasa City in 1961. Elections became popular in the whole region from then on. In accordance with the Electoral Law of the National People's Congress and Local People's Congresses of the People's Republic of China (PRC) and the Rules for the Implementation of the Electoral Law of Local People's Congresses of Tibet Autonomous Region, Tibet began dividing electoral districts, registering electors and carrying out direct elections in townships from 1980. Direct elections were extended to counties in 1984. Town elections for the fresh term of county and township officials were carried out in 1987 and 1990 and the proportion of voters to the total population in 1990 was 85.5 per cent.

In 1987, the CPC Committee and the People's Government of TAR pointed out in their 'Decision on Enhancing the Construction of Local Governance Government Organizations':

> The system of contract-based employment and appointment shall be adopted for the employment of township officials and the officials shall be employed or

appointed after election among the existing township (town) officials, ex-servicemen and the public youth. The people's government of townships, autonomous townships and towns shall be respectively composed of the township leader, assistant township leader, town leader and assistant town leader and each term of their office shall be three years. The system of election shall be implemented for the appointment of township leaders, assistant township leaders, town leaders and assistant town leaders, who shall be directly elected by the people's congresses of the corresponding townships, autonomous townships and towns. The said officials may take consecutive terms of office when reelected but the maximum number of consecutive terms shall not exceed three. (Policy Research Office, 1987).

In December 1992, the Seventh Meeting of the Standing Committee of the Sixth People's Congress of TAR adopted the Measures for the Implementation of the Organic Law of Villagers' Committees of the People's Republic of China in TAR. These measures stipulated that the list of electors, the number of committee members to be elected, the list of candidates, the procedures and particular rules of election and the number of votes for each candidate and the result of election must be made known to the public; all candidates shall be directly recommended by villagers with no setting of limits or tone; and villagers shall directly carry out voting in accordance with the legal procedures.

The Basic Legal Guarantee System for, and the Practice of Self-government by, Villagers

The People's Government of TAR promulgated the General Rules on the Work of Villagers' Committees of Tibet Autonomous Region (Provisional) in August 1982 and the Detailed Rules on the Work of Villagers' Committees of Tibet Autonomous Region (Provisional) in August 1987. From 1987, Tibet began adjusting villagers' (neighbourhood) committees, rectified the mass organisations in charge of security and mediation under the villagers' committees and reorganised the original 10,166 villagers' committees and 37 neighbourhood committees in the whole region into 7,410 villagers' committees and 68 neighbourhood committees. Also in 1987, the People's Government of TAR promulgated the General Rules on the Work of Neighborhood Committee of Tibet Autonomous Region (Provisional).

The TAR carried out demonstration of self-government by villagers in Nedong and Dranang counties of Lhokha Prefecture first in 1993. Afterwards, the People's Government of TAR selected one township (town) in each prefecture to carry out demonstration and summary of self-government by villagers. By 1993, the demonstration of self-government by villagers had already been carried out in five prefectures (cities), 18 counties, 31 townships (towns) and 222 villagers' committees.

With the promulgation of the Measures for the Implementation of the Organic Law of Villagers' Committees of the People's Republic of China (Provisional) in TAR in December 1993, Tibet began to implement the system of self-government by villages in the rural areas. In 1998, the Organic Law of Villagers Committees of the People's Republic of China replaced the Organic Law of Villagers' Committees of the People's Republic of China (Provisional). According to the report, the new measures for the implementation of the Organic Law of the PRC are to be submitted to the People's Congress of TAR for discussion next year.

In accordance with the Organic Law of 1998 and according to the local conditions of TAR, the Twenty-fourth Meeting of the Standing Committee of the Seventh People's Congress of TAR adopted the Measures of Tibet Autonomous Region for the Election of Villagers' Committees on 20 January 2002. Composed of a total of 43 articles, the said measures stipulate the particular measures for implementing the election of villagers' committees in TAR. The main contents of the measures include the following:

Chapter 1. General Provisions (including six articles):

Article 3. Each villagers' committee shall be composed of three to five persons, including chairman, vice-chairman and the members(s). The particular number of the members of a villagers' committee shall be proposed by the people's government of the relevant township, autonomous township or town according to the actual conditions of the corresponding village and decided after discussion by villagers' conference or villagers' congress.

Article 4. The chairman, vice-chairman and member(s) of a villagers' committee shall be directly elected by the villagers participating in election. No organization or individual may designate, appoint or replace any member of a villagers' committee. The term of office for a villagers' committee is three years; a new committee shall be promptly elected upon the expiry of each term. Each member of a villagers' committee may continue to take his/her office when reelected.

Chapter 2. Election Organization Organs:

Article 7. During the election of villagers' committees for a new term of office, the people's governments at all levels shall respectively set up villagers' committee election guiding groups to direct and assist the election of the villagers' committees under their jurisdictions. The said groups mainly have eight responsibilities.

Article 8. Each villagers' committee shall set up an electoral committee, who shall be responsible to take charge of the election of the villagers' committee.

Article 9. An electoral committee's responsibilities are as follows: 1. to publicize the relevant laws, rules and regulations and answer the villagers' inquiries about election; 2. to formulate the plan of election and submit to the higher-level people's government for putting on record; 3. to organize electors and distribute electoral certificates; 4. to organize the electors to consider and nominate candidate members of villagers' committee, decide the qualifications of candidates and announce the list of candidates; 5. to decide and announce the date, time, place and method of election; 6. to preside over election meeting, organize election through voting and announce the result of election; 7. to handle the villagers' letters concerning election; and 8. to summarize and report the result of election to higher-level government and establish a file about the work of election.

Chapter 3. Registration of Electors (including five articles):

Article 11. Any villager who has reached the age of 18 shall have the right to elect and be elected, regardless of his/her ethnic status, race, sex, occupation, family background, religious belief, education level, property status and length of residence, with the exception of the persons who have been deprived of political rights in accordance with law. The age of each elector shall be calculated on the basis of the date of election. Article 15. A villagers' electoral committee shall register the electors, publicly announce the list of electors and distribute electoral certificate 20 days before the date of election. In case of any different opinion about the announced list of electors, the villagers may put forth their opinion to the villagers' committee, who shall handle the said opinion according to law within ten days after the list of electors is announced. In case the villagers still have any different opinion about the result of handling by the villagers' committee, they may place a complaint to the villagers' committee election guiding group of the county (city), who shall give a reply to the villagers within five days after receiving the complaint.

Chapter 4. Nomination of Candidates (including six articles):

Article 16. Each candidate member of a villagers' committee must satisfy the following conditions: 1. the candidate shall support the CPC, love the socialist China and the unity of nationalities and oppose separation; 2. the candidate shall observe the Constitution and the other laws, rules and policies of China; 3. the candidate shall be impartial in handling affairs, honest in performing his/her duties and warmhearted in serving the villagers; and 4. the candidate shall be familiar with the conditions of the village, have strong organization and leading ability and can lead the villagers to work for common prosperity.

Article 17. There shall be at least one woman in the members of a villagers' committee. The members of the villagers' committee of a village inhabited by a number of ethnic groups shall include one or more members from the ethnic group with a small population. The members of a villagers' committee shall have no relationship of spouse or linear relative between each other.

Article 18. The candidate members of a villagers' committee shall be directly nominated by the electors', who may nominate candidates separately or jointly.

Article 19. When nominating candidates, each elector shall fill up a list of nominated candidate chairman, vice-chairman and member(s).

Article 20. In accordance with the Decision to Temporarily Implement Equal-number Election Instead of Multi-candidate Election in the Whole Region adopted by the 24th meeting of the Standing Committee of the 7th People's Congress of TAR, equal-number election shall be adopted for the election of villagers' committee.

Article 21. After the formal candidates of the chairman, vice-chairman and member(s) of a villagers' committee are decided, the candidates names shall be announced in the order of the alphabetic letters of the Tibetan language five days before the date of election.

Chapter 5. Procedures of Election:

Article 22. A villagers' electoral committee shall announce the particular time and place of election and the method of election five days before the date of election.

Article 23. At the time of election through voting, the villagers' electoral committee shall preside over the election meeting. Two tellers, two scrutineers and two vote counters shall be elected at the meeting. The spouses and linear relatives of the candidates shall not act as teller, scrutineer or counter. For a village whose villagers live in a scattered way, additional meeting sites and voting stations or mobile vote boxes may be set up for the election of villagers' committee. There shall be more than two scrutineers responsible to supervise the casting of votes at each voting station or mobile vote box.

Article 24. The chairman, vice chairman and member(s) of a villagers' committee may be elected separately or jointly. The particular form of election shall be decided by the villagers' committee according to the actual conditions.

Article 25. Secret ballot shall be adopted for the election of villagers' committee. During election, booths shall be set up for the electors to write their votes in privacy. For the blind electors or the handicapped ones that cannot write votes, they may authorize the persons that they trust to write votes on behalf of them. Every elector shall have the right to cast only one vote during each election. The electors may vote for or against a candidate or abstain from voting. An elector that votes against a candidate may elect another elector.

Article 27. An election shall be ineffective unless more than a half of the villagers with the right to elect have participated in the election. An election shall be ineffective unless the number of votes received is equal to or less than the number of voters.

Article 29. The method of open vote counting shall be adopted for election through voting. After the end of voting, the scrutineers, tellers and vote counters shall collect all the vote boxes to the scene of the election meeting, open the vote boxes in public and then check the votes, call out the names of those voted for count the number of votes for each candidate and make a record of the votes on the spot. The record shall be put on record after being signed by the scrutineers.

Chapter 6. Dismissal, Resignation and By-election:

Article 33. The work of a villagers' committee is subject to supervision by the villagers. More than one-fifth of a village's villagers with the right to vote may put forth a joint request for dismissing a member of the villagers committee. The said request shall be submitted in written form to the villagers' committee or the people's government of the corresponding township, autonomous township or town with the cause of dismissal being clearly indicated. After receiving the villagers' request for dismissing any member of the villagers' committee, the villagers' committee or the people's government of the corresponding township, autonomous township or town shall hold a villagers' meeting or a villagers' congress to decide the matter through voting within 30 days.

Chapter 7. Legal Responsibilities:

Article 38. In case any person adjusts or changes the candidate members of a villagers' committee or specifies, designates or dismisses any member of the villagers' committee in violation of the provisions of these rules, the higher-level people's government shall correct the malpractice and impose administrative penalty on the directly responsible person according to the gravity of the circumstances.

Article 39. In case a person becomes one member of a villagers' committee by threatening, bribing, forging votes or other illegal means, the people's government of the corresponding township, autonomous township or town or the department of civil affairs of the corresponding county (city or district) government may declare this person's taking of office invalid. In case the circumstances are serious and a crime has been constituted, the judicial authority may impose criminal sanctions on this person.

Article 41. In case a person retaliates upon the villagers that have reported illegal acts during election or proposed to dismiss any member of the villagers' committee, the matter shall be handled by the people's government of the corresponding township, autonomous township or town or the department of civil affairs of the corresponding county (city or district) government. In case a crime has been constituted, the judicial authority shall give criminal sanctions to the said person according to law.

From this we may see that there is a complete legal system for safeguarding self-government by villagers in TAR. Such democratic requirements as democratic election, democratic decision making, democratic management and democratic supervision are all embodied in both the national laws and the local rules, which are the essential guarantee for the rural political activities in TAR to become more democratic and institutionalised. According to the progress of self-government by villagers in the whole country, Tibet first made experiments and then popularised self-government by villagers step-by-step in the whole region in conformity with the actual conditions of the rural areas.

Empirical Study of the Villagers' Committees (Neighbourhood Committees)

Tibet began implementing rural self-governance in the same time as the other rural areas of China, but there were some slight differences in terms of background conditions and measures of implementation. First, the local governance organisations in Tibet had undergone ceaseless adjustment and reform from the original people's commune system to district and township government system since the mid-1980s and this period was one of the periods when the local governance organisations in Tibet were being radically transformed. Second, since the implementation of the household-based contract system featured by household ownership of land use rights and domestic animals, the Tibetan government has neither collected any taxes nor carried out family planning in the rural areas. The Tibetan government had implemented all the preferential policies implemented in the other parts of China and even implemented a policy of providing subsidies for fertilizer consumption in the rural areas. Therefore, no such contradictions as the contradiction of taxation, the contradiction of family planning and the contradiction between officials and the masses that were common in the other Chinese rural areas occurred in the rural areas of Tibet in that period. On the contrary, the functions of the local governance organisations in the rural areas of Tibet were relatively weakened and even paralyzed, because the officials only cared about farming their own lands and raising their own domestic animals. Hence, when the People's Government of Tibet implemented self-government by villagers, it led to a radical change in local society.

Here, I present briefly the cases of self-government by two villagers' committees in Tibet.

Report of the Election of Shol Neighbourhood Committee of Lhasa for a New Term of Office in 1999

Preparatory Work for the Election

The preparatory work for the election involved the following steps:

a) To check and count the number of electors with the right to elect in accordance with the national unified standards. (The main standards were: the registered permanent residence of each elector shall be in the local community; an elector shall be more than 18 years old; should not be deprived of political rights; and must not suffer from any mental disease or dementia.).

b) To set up an electoral committee. (Members of the committee were LoSang, 50 years old, secretary of the Shol Neighbourhood Committee; Lha Ba, 39 years old, deputy director of the iron and wood processing plant, university graduate; Tshe Do, manager of the No. 6 company, technical school graduate; TsheRing Yang'dzom, 36 years old, assistant manager of production, junior high school graduate; and Tshe Drolma, about 60 years old, leader of the agricultural production team, illiterate.)

c) To hold a meeting of the neighbourhood committee to publicise the relevant laws, explain the procedures of election and announce the conditions of the candidates.

d) The leaders of all residents' teams and the neighbourhood committee to announce the date of formal election through broadcasting.

e) To make propaganda, cleaning and other preparations.

The Election Process

A meeting of all residents was held on the evening of 13 October 1999 for reporting the work of the neighbourhood committee over the last year.

The 3rd election of the neighbourhood committee for a new term of office took place on 16 October 1999. It was formally inaugurated by all participants standing up while the national anthem was played. The meeting worker read out the points for attention during election; the scrutinizers checked the vote box in public; voting papers were distributed; votes were cast and then counted; and the names of those voted for were called out (see Table 18.1).

During the counting, students from Shol Primary School put up performances.

The Election Results

The result was announced in the Tibetan language and the secretary of Jibenggang Office of the Government of Chengguan District read out the result in the following manner: 'Now I will read out the result of vote counting. We distributed total 977 votes today and recovered 975, and two persons did not vote. The number of voters is in conformity with the quorum and the election is valid.'

The electors also elected some residents beyond the list of candidates. The secretary read aloud:

Now, I will read out the names of the persons that were newly proposed during the voting and the number of votes for them. Tshe Do from No. 5 company, four

Table 18.1
Statistics of the Election of the Shol Neighbourhood Committee, 1999

Candidate	Affirmative Vote	Negative Vote	Abstention	Percentage
Chairman Tob Chung	953	10	12	97
Vice-chairman LoSang	958	4	13	98.25
Vice-chairman NgaWang LoSang	946	18	11	97.02
Member Kal Do	949	14	12	97.33
Member Lha Ba Drolman	956	4	15	98.05
Member Pasang Drolma	938	25	12	96.2
Member Chunda	951	14	10	97.57
Member Pasang Tshering	955	5	15	97.94
Member Mima Tshering	930	26	19	95.38

votes; Pal Jyor from the repair factory, five votes; Lha Ba from the repair factory, my vote; Renzing from the No. 9 team, one vote; SoNam Yangji from the kindergarten, two votes; Kra Sang from the kindergarten, one vote; and LoSang TsheTan from the No. 9 team, one vote. Another matter that needs to be explained is that nine votes were miswritten. It means that the electors ticked the column 'Agree' and then wrote the names of eleven persons including Bian Jue and Yang Ji beside the column. These votes are invalid in accordance with the rules.

Then, the election-leading group's leader announced the list of the successful candidates: chairman Tob Chung, vice-chairman LoSang, vice-chairman NgaWang LoSang and members Kal Do, Lha Ba Drolma, Pasang Drolma and Mima Tshering. The successful candidates came to the front to meet the masses in the order of their names in the list.

Finally, the election-leading group and the relevant leaders of Lhasa who were present at the meeting to observe and supervise the election presented *hadas* and the masses drank a toast to the successful candidates according to traditional Tibetan etiquette. The whole ceremony lasted for about 45 minutes.

Announcement of the Conditions of and the Material Benefits for Persons Retiring from the Neighbourhood Committee

SoNam YangJi who had taken charge of women's affairs and the kindergarten in the neighbourhood committee submitted an application for resigning from her post in view of her advanced age. Lha Ba, a member of the election-leading group, read out SoNam YangJi's open letter to the neighbourhood committee and the masses. The leader praised the work of three old persons applying for retirement and announced post-retirement material benefits for them, which were RMB 175 for SoNam YangJi, RMB 150 for LoSang TsheTan and RMB 120 for SoNam Doje every month. The neighbourhood committee also granted certificates of honour to the three people.

Speech by the Chairman Elect of Shol Neighbourhood Committee
In this speech, the re-elected chairman Tob Chung summarised the work of
the neighbourhood committee in the last term of office, thus:

> On behalf of the neighbourhood committee, I will report the committee's work
> in spiritual and material aspects in the last term of office to the leaders attending
> the election meeting and all the residents. We have conscientiously studied and
> implemented the spirits of the 15th national CPC Congress, the 4th Enlarged
> Meeting of the 5th CPC Congress of TAR and the relevant meetings of Chengguan
> District and completed all the important tasks assigned by the party committee
> and the government of Chengguan District and the higher-level departments. We
> have saved no efforts in publicising and implementing the relevant policies, rules
> and regulations of the CPC and the government and meticulously carried out
> elementary education in love for the country, for socialism and for the party in
> the neighbourhood committee and among the residents to make the residents
> understand and self-consciously observe the laws, rules and regulations of the
> state, enhance national unity and safeguard the reunification of the country.
>
> While implementing the relevant policies of the state with strict requirements
> on ourselves, the neighbourhood committee has made our community a united
> community with a tidy environment and complete service. The neighbourhood
> committee has fulfilled all the tasks assigned by the relevant departments, conscien-
> tiously listened to the residents' comments and suggestions, tried to bring about
> benefits to the residents in the our community, sincerely worked for solving the
> problems confronted by the poor families in the community, made all possible
> efforts to develop collective, private and characteristic economic entities and laid
> particular stress on increasing the residents' incomes and living standard and
> offering job opportunities to the unemployed. Through holding meetings of the
> neighbourhood committee or meetings of the resident's teams, the neighbourhood
> committee has carried out publicity, education and study with the young people
> as the focus and family harmony, unity between neighbours, respecting the old
> and cherishing the young and observation of disciplines and laws as the contents
> for promoting ethnical and material progress and making the residents self-
> consciously observe disciplines and laws, safeguard the reunification of the state
> and national unity and build up excellent social morals and order.
>
> The neighbourhood committee has established a contract system for sanitation
> in a designated area outside of each unit, strengthened the management of collective
> affairs, worked hard for creating a good community environment, further enhanced
> the management of various enterprises under the neighbourhood committee, tried
> to increase the quality of the managers at all levels, further improved community
> management, implemented various measures for facilitating the residents' study
> and work and opened up new channels and forms for economic growth.
>
> In the future work, we will learn from the model local governance official
> Tanzen Doji, establish a spirit of serving the people with heart and soul, devote all
> ourselves to the public interests, strive for becoming public servants satisfactory
> for the people and raise the standard of our work to a higher level.

A Typical Case of Self-government by Villagers in Nedong County

Nedong is a county under Lhokha Prefecture, TAR. In 1992, it was selected to be one of the two experimental counties for the demonstration of self-government by villagers in Tibet. The following case study provides some information about how Nedong County promoted the stability and development of rural areas through all-round implementation of self-government.

Nedong County has 10 townships, one town and 52 villagers' (neighbourhood) committees under it. The total number of domestic animals in Nedong County is about 170,000. This is an agricultural-pastoral county with agriculture taking the leading position and diversified business developing gradually.

In the past, the officials of villagers' committees were directly appointed by the CPC committees of townships or town and a village official could retain his post for several years regardless of his/her performance. This situation invited many complaints from the peasants and herdsmen. After the introduction of self-government in Nedong County in 1992, the people's governments and the local townships and towns have organised the masses to directly elect villagers' committees in accordance with the provisions of the Organic Law of Villagers' Committees of the PRC (Provisional). At the same time, the relevant rules and regulations were also improved.

In the election, the earlier backward looking and inefficient lot of village officials who falied to initiate development and to get rid of poverty were voted out. In their place, 59 young people with advanced ideas, enterprising spirits, a high educational level and knowledge of techniques were elected into villagers' committees. The system of election by the villagers has strengthened the new village officials' sense of responsibility and mission.

For example, Chode Kong Village elected Tshering Dundang as the chairman of its villagers' committee. There was only RMB 318 in the village account when Tshering Dundang took office. But after assuming office, he advanced RMB 4,000 from his own pocket for purchasing electrical poles, organised the villagers to explore crystals (RMB 40,000 has been obtained from the exploration of crystals till date) and repaired the village's old transformer substation that had been lying in disrepair for years. He also led the villagers to build an impounding reservoir with a storage capacity of 20,000 l and a 37.5 KW transformer substation for providing lighting to the villagers and meeting the need of the irrigation of more than 600 mu of farming lands. He said, 'I have to do something when I take the office of chairman. I'll be unworthy of the villagers' trust in me if I fail to do my job well'.

In the past, village officials had a say in all matters pertaining to the village, while peasants and herdsmen were in a position of passive acceptance and observation. It was difficult for the villagers' committees to implement the policies decided by them because some policies themselves were incomplete and were not fully understood by the masses. The village officials considered the peasants and herdsmen difficult to control, while the masses considered the officials too arbitrary in their decision making.

After the demonstration of self-government by the villagers, a democratic discussion system with the villagers' congress as the major form has been established and the peasants and herdsmen have been enabled to participate in the management of village affairs. According to the relevant regulations, all important matters in connection with a village (especially the affairs related to the personal interests of the peasants and herdsmen) must be submitted to the villagers' congress for discussion and no decision by a minority is allowed. A system of regular meeting of villagers' congress has also been established. For example, Gesang Village of Jieba Township has two villagers' teams, which had formed one production team in the period of people's commune.

When the policy of households' ownership of land use rights was implemented in the 1980s, the lands of the two teams were divided simply according to the distance away from each team. However, because of the great difference in soil texture, the yield of one of the team's lands was 100kg/mu less than that of the other team's lands. Therefore, the villagers of the former team wanted a re-division of lands and contradictions between the two teams occurred because the problem could not be solved promptly. In 1997, the villagers' committee of this village held a meeting of the villagers' congress to specially discuss the said matter. Following the principle that the minority is subordinate to the majority, the villagers' committee smoothly solved the dispute between the two teams.

In the past, the poor transparency of village-level finance was one of the important reasons influencing the relations between the masses and the county, township and town officials. After the implementation of self-government by villagers, every village has, according to its conditions, formulated a series of regulations on village affairs with particular stress laid on financial management and the attendance of officials. All the matters with which the villagers are generally concerned and the matters that involve the villagers' interests are made public. For example, Losang Village announces information about the attendance of village officials and financial expenditure and revenue every month. An incident about the secretary of the CPC subcommittee and the chairman of the villagers' committee of a village in Sozhug Township secretly sharing RMB 20,000 of public money was made public in 1997 and they were accordingly punished.

Such judicial organs as the court and the public security bureau of Nedong County also offer special training and education in the law, rules and regulations and the procedures for handling civil affairs to the mediators elected by various villagers' committees. This becomes necessary since civil disputes between neighbours, in households and between villagers concerning marriage, family affairs, grasslands, irrigation, farming lands and so on are unavoidable and these disputes directly influence the social relations in rural areas.

After more than six years of the implementation of self-government by villagers, the number of mediation committees in the whole county has increased from 11 in the past to 42 at present; the number of mediators has reached 175; and the rate of successful mediation has increased from 52 per cent in the past to more than 90 per cent.

The county specially organised 44 peasants' anti-illiteracy schools and the proportion of illiterate people in the country's whole population has dropped from 50 per cent in the past to less than 10 per cent. Nedong County's anti-illiteracy campaign passed acceptance by the People's Government of TAR in 1998. The organised popularisation of science and technology in the rural areas have also resulted in the peasants and herdsmen using improved varieties, chemical fertilisers, pesticides and mechanical machines in agricultural production. At present, the total area of land sowed with machines and the area of land harvested with machines in the whole county are respectively 45,000 mu and 53,000 mu. The adoption of machines has increased the peasants' income from grain production and reduced their labour costs. The per capita net income of peasants and herdsmen rose continuously from RMB 600 in 1993 to RMB 1,594 in 1998. At the same time, the collective sector of the rural economy has also witnessed rapid growth. Various villages have organised their villagers to establish enterprises, grow vegetables and participate in road and hotel construction as shareholders, thereby increasing the incomes of both the villages and the villagers. The collective incomes have been used to improve the facilities for villagers' activities and help the poorer households solve their problems of food and clothing. The chairmen of the local villagers' committees have also put an end to the traditional practice of working at home.

After six years of practice, Nedong County has worked at and developed a way suitable for it and helped popularise self-government by villagers in Tibet. After examination and verification by the departments of civil affairs of TAR and the country, Nedong County won the title of a national model in self-government by villagers in 2000.

I now put forward the case studies of two village committees.

Case 1: Village C's Self-government

Village C is located in a valley in Drayab County, Chamdo Prefecture, TAR. It is an agro-pastoral economy, with the main agricultural crops including highland barley, wheat, peas, grapes and peanut and the main domestic animals including yak, dzo, cattle, sheep and goat. Vegetable farming is also gradually becoming popular. Because of the shortage of transportation and communication facilities, village C has few connections with the outside world and away from the local political, religious and cultural centre. Since the implementation of household-based land and grassland management in the 1980s, the local people have been facing a lot of difficulties in making out a living and village C is a typical poor village.

Village C has 1,250 residents, including 650 men and 600 women. The total number of households is 186 and the number of family members in each household is 6.72. In the total population of the village there are only four junior high-school graduates and most of the villagers have only attended primary school or are semi-literate or illiterate.

The party and government organisations of village C were basically paralysed in 1983–95. Since TAR began implementing the demonstrative experiment of self-government by villagers in rural areas from 1996, village C's social order and public welfare activities were gradually reconstructed, and today, village C has a complete party organisation. The main members of the CPC subcommittee of the village include one secretary, one deputy secretary, one member in charge of organisation and one member in charge of discipline.

The members of the villagers' committee include one chairman, one vice-chairman, one clerk, one member in charge of security, one regulator and one member in charge of women's affairs. In addition, a grassland construction committee has been set up under the villagers' committee, composed of the secretary of the CPC subcommittee of the village, the chairman of the villagers' committee and five representatives of villagers. None of the members of the CPC subcommittee receive wages from the government. The secretary of the CPC subcommittee and the chairman of the villagers' committee can each receive RMB 30 of subsidy from the village funds every month.

Village C also formulated eight normative documents (for example, the Functions and Responsibilities of the Villagers' Committee, the Rules and Regulations of the Village, the Functions and Responsibilities of the Grassland Construction Committee, the Targets of Comprehensive Social Security Management etc.) in accordance with the provisions of the rules and regulations of TAR. The contents of the Functions and Responsibilities of the Villagers' Committee involve such aspects as politics, economy, science and technology, culture, education, family planning, environmental protection and undertakings for the public good. However, this village has formulated neither special documents on the openness of village affairs and democratic supervision nor rules on the procedures of the meeting of villagers' committee or villagers' congress and the range of the functions and powers of the said meetings. It has simply included the relevant provisions in the Functions and Responsibilities of the Villagers' Committee.

Case 2: Village P's Self-government

Village P is located in Markham County, Chamdo Prefecture, TAR. It is an administrative village directly under the county government. The average elevation of the village is 3,800m. This village has few farming lands but a large area of grasslands on mountain slopes. The local economy is agricultural-pastoral. The village is seated at the junction of two rivers, so that the water system and irrigation is well developed. Because it is close to the county town, the local communication and transportation facilities are developed. Forty per cent of the households have TV sets and the villagers have much knowledge about the outside world.

Village P has a total of 1,015 residents, including 375 men and 640 women. The total number of households is 153. In the whole population of the village, the proportion of persons who have attended junior high school or higher is 10 per cent; the proportion of persons that have attended primary school or higher is 50 per cent; and the proportion of semi-literate and illiterate persons is 40 per cent. The rate of illiteracy is quite high among women.

Village P has a small temple, in which there are 30 monks. At the same time, there is a privately run profit-oriented video hall, some small stores and a collectively-run small enterprise (a wood-processing plant). This village is typical of a community where traditional and modern factors blend and conflict.

The CPC subcommittee of village P is composed of three members, including one secretary, one deputy secretary and one member in charge of organisation. There are 31 Communists in the village, including seven women. The villagers' committee of village P is composed of one chairman, two vice-chairmen, one clerk, one accountant, one member in charge of security, one regulator, one member in charge of women's affairs, one medical worker and one militia leader. None of the members of the CPC subcommittee and the villagers' committee receives wages from the government. The secretary of the CPC subcommittee of the village, the chairman and vice-chairmen of the villagers' committee and the accountant, clerk and medical worker each may receive RMB 70 of subsidy every month. Each of the leaders of the villager's teams may receive RMB 25 of subsidy from the village funds every month. The subsidies mainly come from the villagers, each of whom pay RMB 5.2 every year. The insufficient part is made up by the village-run enterprises.

However, the annual total amount of subsidies for village officials is more than RMB 8,000, which is a heavy burden for the villagers. Since most of the households in the village are in a self-sufficient state, they do not have too much cash in hand and prefer to use grain and sheepskin as a substitute. The poor households are generally unwilling to contribute in either cash or kind and the village officials cannot bear to press them.

The routine jobs of the villagers' committee of village P include the following: (i) to implement various policies of the town government and publicise the laws and policies of the state; (ii) to manage the houses, warehouses and the other assets owned by the entire village and organise the villagers to build roads and dig canals for improving transportation and irrigation conditions; (iii) to mediate disputes among villagers and supervise the villagers to ensure that they send their children to school (each violator is ordered to pay a fine equal to RMB 300–500); (iv) to be responsible for the management and operation of the village-run wood-processing plant; and (v) to cooperate with the relevant departments to carry out population, economic and social statistics and census and organise and mobilise the villagers to participate in the election of the town's people's congress.

Almost all of the villagers' of village P believe in Tibetan Buddhism and there are niches for the statues of Buddha and scriptures of Buddhist gods in the homes of all families. Though some peasants are not so well off, each family's expenditure for religious etiquette and activities come to RMB 300–500 every year. There are 30 monks in the small village temple. Most of the monks are young and only a few are old and have no one to depend on. The young monks are supported by their families, while the old monks live on the villagers' donations. Sometimes, the villagers' committee donates some grain or cash to the monks. In case of illness, death or wedding, the relevant households always invite some monks to their homes to recite the scriptures. However, the monks neither participate in the mediation of disputes among villagers nor accept public posts.

The chairman of the villagers' committee of village P was once an official in the people's commune system. He enjoys a high reputation among the villagers and has rich experience in handling various matters.

The Relationship between Villagers' Self-government and the Development of Democracy

The analysis of the cases of self-government by villagers in the rural areas of Tibet shows that rural self-government by villagers is still confronted by many unfavourable factors and restrictions.

First, most of the chairmen of villagers' committees and secretaries of CPC sub-committees of the villages in Tibet are advanced in age and the educational level of the members of villagers' committees is low. According to the statistics about local governance and democratic elections in 1999 made by the Bureau of Civil Affairs of TAR, the average age of the members of villagers' committees was 40.3 years, dropping by 5.4 years from the last term. The number of female members was 3,309, rising by 1,337 from the last term and accounting for 14 per cent of the total number of members of villagers' committees (neighbourhood committees). The number of members who have received junior high school education or above, the members who have received primary school education and illiterate members were respectively 1,088, 14,714 and 7,435, respectively accounting for 4.6 per cent, 62.1 per cent and 31.4 per cent of the total members.

The villager's low educational level has directly influenced the development of economy and political democracy in the rural areas of Tibet. The educational level of rural women is generally lower than that of men. Some young and able persons do not want to act as the chairman of the villagers' committee because the committee members do not earn much but spend a lot of time in handling various matters.

Second, the system of self-government by villagers requires the implementation of democratic election, democratic management, democratic decision making and democratic supervision in rural areas. However, the Tibetan villagers' sense of their own democratic rights and participation in the management of public affairs is far from adequate. There is still a long way to go for the construction of self-government by villagers.

Third, as a new democratic political system, the system of self-government by villagers implemented in Tibet should be conscientiously popularised and summarised in conformity with the local conditions of Tibet, and the relevant rules and regulations must be standardised. The Standing Committee of the People's Congress of TAR should formulate and improve the rules on self-government by villagers as soon as possible in accordance with the relevant laws of the state and according to the actual conditions of Tibet.

In accordance with the Organic Law of Villagers' Committees of 1998, the Standing Committee of the People's Congress of TAR formulated the Measures for the Election of Villagers' Committees of Tibet Autonomous Region on 20 January 2002. It is said that the People's Congress of TAR will promulgate the new rules on self-government by villagers next year. At the same time, the rules and regulations concerning the handling of the relationship between villagers' committees and township (town) governments, the relationship between villagers' committees and the CPC subcommittees, villagers' meeting and villagers' congress should be improved, the arbitrary fines on villagers' failure to do dutiful work should be revised, policies for sending children to school and reaching a high index of scientific fertiliser use and so on should be improved in view of villagers' opinions and the actual conditions of Tibet.

There are still many deficiencies in self-government by villagers in Tibet. But from the angle of the historical course of political development in Tibet for over more than 50 years, Tibet has achieved great progress in implementing democratic politics, which is essentially different from its pre-1959 traditional social structure and system. At the same time, the new conditions of the market economy system offer new challenges and opportunities for villagers' self-governance.

First, the social structure of Tibet has witnessed profound changes. With the establishment of regional autonomy of minority nationalities and the people's congress, the Tibetan people are no longer serfs, dependent on aristocrats, temples and the government and they have obtained their due human rights. Over the past 50 years and more, the Tibetan people's consciousness of modern democracy has been strongly aroused and characteristics of the modern society, such as independence, equality, democracy and participation have become part of the people's political life. The implementation of villagers' self-governance has further provided the Tibetan people with a novel opportunity to act as the master of their own affairs and to directly participate in democratic rule. The combination of the system of regional autonomy of minority nationalities with the system of self-government by villagers has enabled Tibet to realise innovations in society and development in politics.

Second, the implementation of the system of election by villagers has enhanced the Tibetan peasants' spirit of cooperation and consciousness of independence and changed them from being passive receivers into active participants in the political system. The system is also favourable for protecting the public undertakings of a village and peasants' interests and it enables a village to achieve development under the leadership of the able people of the village.

Third, self-government by villagers is beneficial for eliminating various contradictions and ensuring the stability of rural areas. Before the implementation of self-government, the system of contract-based land and grassland operations had led to some disputes about sharing of resources (for example, forests, grasslands, etc.) as well as contradictions and conflicts between villagers and villages. But now, villagers' committees come forward to mediate or solve such problems. Villagers' committees can also organise such jobs as road building, canal maintenance and poverty alleviation or report to the higher-level authorities for carrying out the relevant work or solving the relevant problems. In the conditions of market economy, villagers' committees have played an important role in developing collective undertakings and the economy, especially in poverty alleviation.

Fourth, we must see that the People's Government of TAR has to reform its policy of imposing no tax or providing subsidies in the rural areas for the continuous progress of a market economy. The subsidies for fertiliser consumption have been revoked; the policy of centralised grain purchase has been changed into a market act; and peasants need to pay for water consumption, power consumption, rural medical service and the cost of textbooks. With the development of rural areas, there have appeared some new problems. For example, peasants need to pay for the use of the electrical mill for grinding flour whereas the traditional water-driven mill was free.

The People's Government of TAR has taken various policy measures to increase investment in the construction of township (town) governments, support the development of township collective economy, encourage university graduates to act as township and town leaders in rural areas, make more investment in rural capital construction, improve the infrastructures in rural areas through building roads and transformer substations. It has also taken steps to raise peasants' income, grant more credit funds to peasants, encourage the development of diversified business and private economy and increase the educational level of rural population by popularising compulsory education and promoting technical education in rural areas.

Social Change and Local Democracy in Tibet

A period less than 60 years is a very short moment in human history, but this period has witnessed unprecedented social change in Tibet. First, the social system of Tibet has seen an essential change from the pre-1959 political system featured by a synthesis of politics and religion into a socialist system featured by the separation of politics and religion. In the ideological sphere, Marxist ideology has replaced religion. Many important factors have influenced the development of democratic politics in Tibet. In my opinion, the most important factor is the signing of the Agreement of the Central People's Government and the Local Government of Tibet on Measures for the Peaceful Liberation of Tibet in 1951, which decided Tibet's reunification with China in 1951 and the democratic reform in 1959 and historically changed Tibet's social structure and system.

In terms of political consciousness, the Tibetan people have gradually established and formed the consciousness of being a citizen of the People's Republic of China. Tibet has set up a new authoritative political system composed of the Communist Party of China and CPC Committee, the People's Government, the People's Congress and the Political Consultative Conference of TAR. The old authoritative leaders such as living Buddhas, aristocrats, tribe leaders and government officials have entirely become history, while such persons as Mao Zedong, Deng Xiaoping, Jiang Zemin and Hu Jintao as well as the Tibetan leaders in all parts of Tibet have become new political leaders in all parts of Tibet and in the hearts of the Tibetan people.

Second, the local governance system has witnessed profound changes and Tibet has established an organisational form in line with the central government's administrative organisation. The Cultural Revolution and various political movements have made all organisations in Tibet highly integrated. Before 1959, the organisation systems in Tibet basically included the three-level system composed of *Kashag*, *Chikyap* and dzong (shika), the headman system in pastoral areas and the chieftain system in Kangqu and there were hundreds of officials operating around these systems. Now, there are CPC committees, people's congresses, governments and political consultative conferences of different levels in all parts of Tibet. In 2002, TAR established six prefectures, one prefecture-level city, 71 counties, one county-level city, 541 townships and 6,054 villagers' committees (see Table 18.2 for details).

Table 18.2
Statistics of Townships, Towns and Villagers' Committees in TAR in 2002

Area	Number of Townships and Towns			Number of Villagers' Committees (Neighbourhood Committees)
TAR	541	140	175	6054
Lhasa	48	9	28	3249 (six sub-district offices)
Chamdo Prefecture	110	28	13	1312
Lhokha Prefecture	56	24	41	553
Zhigatse Prefecture	174	27	29	1730 (2 sub-district offices)
Nakehu Prefecture	89	25	51	1232
Ngari Prefecture	29	7	8	202
Nyingchi Prefecture	35	20	5	701

Source: Statistics of the Bureau of Civil Affairs of TAR.

In 1997, the number of officials operating around this system was 67,054, including 49,410 Tibetan officials, accounting for 73.3 per cent and 17,644 Han officials, accounting for 26.3 per cent. The proportions of the officials who had received college education or above, the officials that had attended technical school or senior high school and the officials that had only attended junior high school or under were respectively 23.44 per cent, 46.02 per cent and 30.54 per cent. The proportions of the officials less than 30 years old, the officials aged 31–40, the officials aged 41–50 and the officials more than 51 years old were respectively 35.4 per cent, 34.6 per cent, 21.8 per cent and 8.2 per cent (Luobu, 1999).

Third, there are many occasions requiring elections and many channels for obtaining democratic information. Through self-government by villagers, the Tibetan villagers (residents) may directly elect their own villagers' (neighbourhood) committees as well as the deputies to the people's congresses and leaders of the corresponding townships and towns. All information are broadcast to the villagers through television, newspapers and various conferences.

Fourth, though the concept of democracy and the consciousness of social equality have been strengthened, for the limitation of educational level and the weakness of the consciousness of social equality,[3] a long-term effort is still necessary for promoting the development of democracy and the modernisation of society in the rural areas of Tibet.

Fifth, the social transformation and democratic development in Tibet must be carried out without endangering the excellent Tibetan cultures and traditions. The trend of the increasingly secularisation of the Tibetan society and religion, the challenge of adapting to the modern society and the rapid social and economic development of China are all factors that are directly influencing and pushing forward the development of Tibet.

Notes

1. These two Tibetan words correspond to the county-level administrative unit of local Tibetan Government. *Shika* means estate.
2. A title of high ranking official of the Local Tibetan government. Traditionally, there were three *chakyab* and they were sent as governors to Chamdo, Nagchu and Lhokha regions. Since 1956, the number of Chikhyab has been extended to eight.
3. The consciousness of 'social equality' means the consciousness of economic equality, the consciousness of gender equality, the sense of birth, the sense of retribution in Tibetan Buddhism, the pursuit of personal progress and so on.

References

Luobu, Jiangeun. 1999. 'Record of the Splendid Achievements of China in the 20th Century', in *The Volume of Tibet 1949–1999*, p. 572. Beijing: Hongqi Press.

Policy Research Office (ed.). 1987. *The Collection of Policy Documents*. Communist Party of TAR.

19 The Party, the Village Committee and the Monastery
Functions and Interactions of Three Institutions at the Grass Roots

CHANGJIANG YU

Introduction

One of the biggest challenges that a developing society like China faces is how to maintain a balance between development and stability. This corresponds in a sense to the traditional Sinitic concepts of the interaction between 'yin' and 'yang' (which are complementary opposite forces). The history of the micro-response of local society to the macro-social dilemma of China may be traced back to the nineteenth century, when Chinese society was gradually falling into chaos under the frequent attacks and influences from outside. After a succession of complicated changes in the last century, China finally evolved from a half-colony, half-ancient-style empire to become a socialist country with Chinese characteristics. Accordingly, grass-roots society experienced dramatic crises, reorganisations and changes. The last systemic change of grass-roots society took place around 20 years ago, when the policies of reform and opening up began. This led to drastic changes in the rural areas, such as the disintegration of the commune and production team system (1950s–1980s) and the establishment of the township and villager's committee system.

The administration at the grass-roots level of the society always plays a crucial role in dealing with the problem of maintaining stability through the process of change. As part of the general attempt to facilitate administration, the Chinese government has been trying to introduce elections among villagers at the grass-roots level since the 1980s. But practice has shown that in a heterogeneous and complex non-Western society like China, a formal pursuit of democratisation without fundamental change of the political culture of people may lead to paralysis of the basic social organisation (Song Yaowu, 2003).

'Condemned Modernisation'

A simple but significant lesson that the Chinese social elite learnt from modern history is that the only way to survive globalisation and international competition is modernisation based on economic development. Social order depends heavily on an effective economy or organised social production. There must exist, firstly, a basic level of organised production of daily necessities before other aspects of social life can be improved. However, modern economy and production are built upon a set of modern norms and order that most Chinese still find unfamiliar and require time adapting to. On the other hand, introducing new economic and social norms may involve a painful transformation of lifestyle, but it is the only way for a society to survive in a global economy. Therefore, moral and idealist goals have, at least temporarily, to give way to more pragmatic aims. And again, therefore, the administrative system has to be designed to encourage (or force sometimes, if necessary) people to adjust themselves (without any other choice) to work hard under modern social norms.

Here inevitably arises the question of modernity. Although there is not yet a general consensus about the definition of modernity (Yaoji Jing, 2001: 363–65) from a common sense view, modernity does seem to be reflected not only in the minds of people, but also in the social behaviour of individuals. There is a visible and felt difference between the developed societies and the developing societies. And regardless of the endless debate among scholars about a proper definition of modernity, people in grass-roots society are already very sure of what it is. It is simply what they feel to be the difference between their life and that of those living in the developed world; it is what they do not have and what they envy and dream of having!

Empirically speaking, the real danger and dilemma lies not in the definition of modernity, but in the big gap between the common people's expectations and the real outcome of modernisation. The social elite learn from different sources that it will be a road full of hardship and pain, but they also realise that development is a matter not of happiness or hardship, but of survival or death. Both the objective survival and subjective dream of the vast population decide that there is no way out but to take the road of a 'condemned modernization' (Yaoji Jing, 2001: 365).

Probably, if we realise that development is a matter of life or death in local perception, we may understand why local elites destroy their beautiful old style houses and develop a fetish for ugly new buildings.[1] Similarly, with enough empirical intuition, we can learn how to weigh the pros and cons of development in terms of the local mentality. This calls for an understanding of what the 'local' means in a society like China, with its own peculiar characteristics. The mainstream international academic circles (Mukherji, 2001: 163) often neglect the specific questions and characteristics of a local society. This is partly because almost all the dominant sociological theories originate in Western societies and, hence, the Western set of knowledge is naturally taken as the foundation of theory.

What should be pointed out is that the emphasis on the localisation of issues by no means supports a binary Asia–West oppositional concept. Local societies of Asian countries are not opposite to the West (Heberer, 2001: 39), but are simply not regarded as the original source of the basic concerns, categorisation and conceptualisation of sociology. We do not yet have enough knowledge from local Asian society 'sociologicalised'. There is not yet any methodological concept based on or even in reference to any Indian or Chinese philosophical treatise. Apart from some skills to deal with local respondents in anthropological approach, little local epistemology has been recognised or assimilated into the research method, even in a study purely of Asian society. Therefore, more fieldwork in grass-roots societies needs to be conducted, more local-based methods to be found and more local phenomena to be expressed effectively and meaningfully.

According to local people in China, development is all right 'as long as it works', and sometimes there is no alternative but 'to choose the lesser evil'. A centralised, elite-dominated system may be found to be necessary in order to guarantee efficient decision making so as to avoid waste of time in endless discussion or debate.

The Study

Given all the arguments discussed here, certain questions arise: what indeed is grass-roots governance in China? How does it work in reality? And whether or not it can meet the specific goal of today's China?

The current governance system of China is basically a 'Party-administration dualistic combined structure' (Gang Bai and Shouxing Zhao, 2001: 253), in which the party operates as a centralised power dispensing leadership, support and guarantee, while local administrative sectors, namely, the villagers' committee in the present time, are responsible for the day-to-day operation. With the opening up of the economy in the past 20 years, non-government forces have rapidly developed to become important players in society. In the region of this study, a manifestation of this trend is the revival and vicissitude of Buddhism as the third force besides the Communist Party and administration.

Given the specific political system of China, I choose the party branch, the villagers' committee and Buddhism as the three main forces in a grass-roots community, and attempted to study their functions and interactions. Attention is given to how these different forces are functioning under the special circumstances in China, and whether and how these forces could keep the local society stable as well as developing with a relatively low social cost.

Most studies on the roles and relationship of the Communist Party, villagers' committee and Buddhism in grass-roots society are conducted by the policy study offices of various levels of the government, which are often not fully recognised by the academic circles. But their focus is mainly on development and what could be regarded as the mainstream concerns, such as the following:

a) Relationship between the Communist Party branches and villagers' committee, especially the conflicts and solutions. There is some consensus on the reasons of the conflicts. It is a structural conflict decided by the overall political system of China and there is not yet a feasible thorough solution. The latest solution suggested by Chinese researchers is a complete combination of the Communist Party and committee system (for example, electing the head of committee only from among Communist Party members). But this suggestion is challenged by the fact that the party members are not always recognised as outstanding enough in terms of prestige or competence, especially compared with other local elites (Xianqun Fu, 2003; Gang Bai and Shouxing Zhao, 2001; Yaowu Song, 2003; Jinping Wang, 2000).

b) The relation between the state and Tibetan Buddhism. Studies in this area were for a long time deeply involved in ideological and political argument. The latest development inside China is the adaptation of socialism and Buddhism. Now, relevant projects are being carried out by several academic institutes, including the Ethnology Institute of Social Science Academy, the Social Science Academy of Tibet Autonomy, the Tibetology Research Centre of China, etc. The latest conclusion is that Buddhism could generally build a harmonious relationship with the Communist Party and socialist state at the social level, though there still is a big gap in terms of ideology and personal outlook.

c) The general relation between Buddhism and social development. The latest discussion focuses on whether Buddhism can help to realise a smooth social transformation, or block development by diverting people's attentions from secular market-oriented ambition to spiritual realisation in reincarnation.

d) More general research on the local elite and interactions among them. There are already many studies on this topic in the coastal areas of China (Xianqun Fu, 2003), but few in-depth studies in the multi-ethnic western part of China.

This study, designed on the basis of my previous studies in the same area, takes the conflict theory in sociology as its point of reference. It is based on the hypothesis that the Communist Party, village administration and religion, working among the same population in grass-roots society, have overlapping functions, and so they are rivals contending for dominance and this kind of conflict will lead to social confrontation or hostility in the local community.

This entire hypothesis was put to the true or false test in the course of my fieldwork. The study was conducted in a small village in the western region of China, where ethnic Tibetan people live. This village was selected as the site of fieldwork because it is a typical case where the three main functioning forces in rural grass-roots society—the Communist Party, the administration and religion—are to be seen, and it presents relatively simple and clear variables of social life. Though a single village may not be representative enough of the vast population and variety of local cultures in China, I believe that an in depth micro-study of one small village may provide good clues for further case studies and comparative analysis.

I employed the anthropological methods of participant observation and intensive interviews to conduct the fieldwork. The village selected had 45 households and 262 people and was composed of villagers' groups of T Administrative Village of T Township, L County. I simply named it as T Village. Methods of data collection involved taking part in collective activities such as roasting barley, watching videos collectively, mediating on some issues, visiting and seeking the views of some old and experienced people in the village, visiting the monastery and conducting interviews with the head of the monastery administration committee as well as with several monks. Forty questionnaires were used as a supplementary method to collect more background information, but observation and interview were the main methods.

Functions and Interactions of the Three Parts

In T Village, the three relatively most influential forces are the grass-roots unit of the Communist Party of China, the official administrative organistion at the grass-roots level (the villagers' committee) and religion (Tibetan Buddhist organisations).

In China's political system, villagers' committee is an organisation of villagers with some degree of autonomy, not regarded as a part of the organs of government. However, villagers' committee articulates with the xiang (township), the lowest level of government,[2] and has an obligation to carry out the orders and instructions of the township government.

Villagers' committees originated from the production teams under the commune system before the 1980s. The organisation at the village level was for a time a very loose and flexible institution, in charge of consultation and coordination of daily affairs among the villagers. Its functions were strengthened again with the spreading of village elections in China and it is now moving closer to a kind of government at the grass-roots level. But till now, the village committee in T Village still does not have a strong organisation and its operation depends largely on the leader's personal ability, ambition, style and social connections.

The Communist Party organisation here, following the general situation in China, has a branch at the village level—the smallest and lowest unit of the party organisation. Some members of this branch hold the leading posts of the village, while others are only common peasants without any special position. At the village level, the personnel of the Communist Party and administration are often interchangeable, but these two organs are separated in function.

In T Village, the activities of the Communist Party branch is mainly decided by a vertical 'from above to below' system; from provincial level autonomy committee, to city committee, to county committee, to township committee, to village branch. Relatively speaking, the Communist Party is a closed system, in which its own regulations and discipline decide personnel recruitment, appointments, examinations, rewards and punishments. Inside the Communist Party, a so-called democratic centralised principle is exercised, but members are generally recruited through a policy of consultative recommendation.

The relation between the Communist Party and administration in the village is not simply that of ruler and ruled, but is a much more complicated inter-dependent, inter-restraining relationship, with close connections with higher levels of the Communist Party and administrative organisations. In theory, administration cannot decide matters of party personnel, but in reality, most of the heads and some members of the village committee are Communist Party members, so that the relation between personnel of the Communist Party and committee are also reflected as the relationship of personnel inside the party. The party members in villagers' committee can also play important roles in the decision making inside the Communist Party branch. The personnel appraisal inside the party are often considered in light of a person's performance in administration. For example, the defeat of the former head of the villager's committee in the previous election will very likely result in his losing the party position later.[3]

On the committee front, the appointment of the head of a committee is decided through a Chinese-style election. The party can play an important role in the recommendation of the candidates, but not in the final decision. The villagers do not have to vote only for recommended candidates. The realisation of the Communist Party's intent can only be ensured by making an effort to win sufficient villager votes.

Most of the people in T Village are believers of Tibetan Buddhism. The local religious institution is a medium-sized monastery with a long and meaningful history. Local people have a lot of contact with it, but the monastery is responsible for not only this one area. According to local tradition, there is no concept of a geographical limit of the believers. All monasteries belong to all believers.

The monastery has regular relations with the Communist Party and the administration, but not at the village level. In terms of the bureaucratic hierarchy in China's administration, the *jibie* (administrative rank) of this monastery is higher than village level. The abbot of the monastery is also a leading member of the county congress and Political Consultative Conference (somewhat like the upper house in the West), as well as a responsible member in the higher city congress. Most issues between the monastery and the local administration are consulted and coordinated through these connections. In important religious ceremonies, county and township government are responsible for the preparation and services with some senior governmental officials also taking part. In most of the cases, it depends on the local government to maintain public order, security, traffic control, look into medical matters and provide some special financial support and infrastructure.

Another basic connection between the monastery and administration is the leading body of the monastery—the administrative committee of the monastery, which is composed of the living Buddhas, high-ranking religious leaders, monks' representatives and secular representatives from government. This is a system designed partly in accordance with the old government–religion unification system. The monks' representatives are elected from among the monks. The election is similar to the village election, presided over by religious leaders and governmental officials in charge of religious affairs.

The government, through consultation with the monastery appoints the secular representatives. Secular representatives avoid intervention in the religious affairs inside the monastery and only take part in the discussion and decision making relating to the Communist Party, the administration and other social organisations or institutions outside the monastery.

This system design makes the relationship between the monastery, administration and the Communist Party a clear administrative relation. At every level of government, there are organs in charge of religious affairs in administration and 'united–front work'[4] in the party. The administrative committee of the monastery merely maintains a direct working relation with them. Some other links between the monastery and local administration includes the businesses run by the monastery, such as land, real estate and shops owned by the monastery. They have relations with the government departments in charge of economic, financial and taxation affairs.

Villagers' Committee

Villagers' committee is the primary administrative institution of village. The head of the committee, called *druuren* (from the mandarin *zhuren*[5]), is elected by villagers. In T Village, the former druuren had just lost the election at the time of the fieldwork. The druuren is also the head (secretary) of the Communist Party branch of the village. Villagers elected him to be the druuren four years ago when he was already the party secretary and he still retains his party position.

People in the village elect their head through a method that is a mixture of Western-style voting and the local tradition of consultative recommendation. Expensive campaigning is forbidden in order to prevent plutocracy. Open electioneering is sensibly avoided because it is regarded as too agitational or threatening to social harmony. It is rare to see open face-losing criticism or tit-for-tat opposition. Things proceed indirectly and implicitly, with veiled communications and deals. The nature of primary social contact in traditional community is such that all villagers know each other well enough to elect even without a self-expressive campaign. In the normal procedure, the village voters first nominate the candidates. The committee[6] then examines and discusses the qualifications of the candidates nominated by villagers in accordance with the law and villagers' approval and chooses two of them as formal candidates. If the voters do not oppose the candidates, the candidates prepare speeches outlining their plans or programmes. However, voters can still cast the ballot for any other person whom they favour by writing his or her name in a blank space prepared on the ballot (though this has seldom happened).

Only when more than half of the legal voters take part in the voting, the election is effective. The candidate with more than half of the voters' support will be the winner and will take the post (in theory he still needs to be examined, approved and appointed by the higher level of administration, but this is a mere formality).

In practice,[7] the main functions of committee include:

a) To communicate information from the higher level, such as some new policies or regulations about agricultural and animal husbandry productions, and so on.
b) To conduct the annual economic and social statistics of every household.
c) To make or amend *cungui minyue* (regulations made by villagers for conducting daily life in the village).
d) Distribution and redistribution of land.
e) To help the peasants sell their grain and buy materials and equipment.
f) To help build a villagers' medical assurance system.
g) Other routine work such as registering marriages, issuing birth certificates, etc.

Because of the special tax-free preferential policies for ethnic Tibetan peasants, there is no taxation in the list of the basic work of the villagers' committees here as in other parts of China. Most of the work of villagers' committee is in line with the laws or regulations and give rise to little controversies.

The villagers' committee is mainly active in the internal affairs and not external relations of the village. Some villagers have built up strong connections with the urban world through business or relatives; some girls from this village have married workers from the eastern urban provinces of China and moved there; and some students from here have gone to middle schools in the coastal cities of China. However, most of these links with the outside world are privately set up, with few formally-organised channels through the committee.

Under the committee, the households of villagers are organised into several villagers' groups, which are the lowest and smallest units of grass-roots administration. The heads of villagers' groups fulfill all the concrete work and interact with the peasants face-to-face. But they are only operators, without real responsibility or power to decide anything. If some villager refuses to obey or cooperate with them, they can only turn to the members of the committee to solve the problem. In the two villagers' groups I stayed with and studied, one of the heads was a Communist Party member, while the other was not. But party member or not, both of them had the status of the head of the villagers' group.

The study in the village suggests that the real decisive meaning of the villagers' committee to the villagers does not lie in the practical functions of it, given the fact that common villagers actually do not have much to do with the committee. The real meaning of the committee seems to lie in the existence of this organisation itself, which provides identification for the villagers. In the interviews, peasants often said 'I will go to the committee if I have something' but when I asked 'what on earth do you really need to go there for?' they could hardly think of anything. It is an interesting phenomenon, suggesting that villagers need the committee mainly as a psychological and sentimental support to meet their needs of belonging and dependence. Under China's current system, traditional-style agricultural work is not counted as a vocation or profession. Accordingly, there are not any organisations such as farm companies or peasants guilds. So a peasant is an individual without membership of any formal work unit or social organisation. This vacuum of identity makes the villagers gravitate to the villagers' committee. As an embodied form of the community, the villagers' committee is the only organisation in the world to which peasants feel they belong. It is a significant identification of the villagers.

This psychology was reflected in my interviews with them. When I visited the households and talked with them, they always made it very clear as to which villagers' group they belonged to. When some boys asked me to take photos of them and wrote down their postal addresses, they shouted to me again and again after I walked away to confirm the number of the villagers' group to which each of them belonged.

The most practical result of the sense of belonging is an abstract or imagined sense of security. For the villagers, a half governmental, half self-government organisation like the villagers' committee suggests that there will be a strong backing force behind them to take the final responsibility if faced with some insurmountable difficulty. For instance, if natural disasters occur, there will be an organisation of their own, having the backing of the government, to arrange the salvage operations, provide relief and refuge, etc., though this kind of emergency has never really happened in this region. In some sense, the committee plays a role similar to that of the feudal manor in the old times, where people found dependence and stability.

The local people's psychology also indicates that the main stream of the local values and ideas is community-oriented rather than individual-oriented. The relationship between the individual and the collective is one where the community comes first and the individual second. The individual is thought to be born and to grow up and live in a community that has been in existence long before the individual. And the symbol of the community should be something more stable and eternal. But unfortunately, under today's committee election system, the leaders of the community must be elected once every three years, which is quite frequent as against the local rhythm of life and sense of time. The dream of most villagers is to have not an elected leader but an immortal saint, holy person, or superman who can hold the leading post forever, be responsible for everything and everybody in the community and provide absolute justice, without any mistake or corruption. People seem to feel that this dream is possible on earth and have a deep hope that it will happen someday. This is where Buddhism plays an important role in the lives of the villagers.

Under the influence of Buddhism, villagers seek not a worldly solution, but a thorough solution in a religious sense for their questions on life. In the secular realm, more attention is paid to basic livelihood instead of institutional concerns, because if they desire abstraction from basic life, they will not stop at the level of social institution, but will directly aspire to the spiritual level. It is a polarised mentality that seeks fulfillment of either one's basic or spiritual needs and this affects their attitude to local governance.

Villagers never attribute lofty meanings to their political activities, especially to the village elections. Similar to most parts of China, even the activist villagers here simply regard the election as a concrete solution for their concrete interests or difficulties and fail to grasp the associated abstract concepts such as 'democratic values', 'human rights', 'political reform', etc. (Jinping Wang, 2000).

Some other villagers, furthermore, are not interested to select or legalise the leaders of the village by voting. With a deep animistic and localised Buddhist tradition, many villagers regard the village as a 'super individual' complex of community, home, refuge, etc., that is linked with many deities, higher and more permanent than the individual's life. The village is one unit of the animistic world, rather than a geographical place or an administrative organisation. This kind of understanding of the village does not easily fit with the secular concept of election based on individualism, citizenship, or majority–minority game.

Many villagers do not show much interest in how a head is elected because they believe that no election in this world can produce the most suitable person as head of the village. *Samsara* (cycle of life) and *karma* (fruits of one's actions) should determine things. People are not yet accustomed to the idea of selecting a good leader from and by themselves, but believe in waiting for somebody different and higher than themselves to protect them. Adopting Max Weber's 'authority types', 'tradition' and 'charisma' are still the most popular qualities sought in a leader by the villagers. But in reality, the dominating discourses of the social elites are strongly promoting 'rational-legal types' of leaders and democracy as markers of progress, so that villagers have lost the confidence to justify and express their own feelings. Disintegration of the so-called 'two layer of skins'[8] could be discerned in interviews with villagers—a lack of fit between their reason and feeling—and the view that the right things are not always comfortable things.

The Party and the Village

Today the Communist Party plays a special role in Chinese society. It will not be so easy to find its parallel in conventional Western political science textbooks. The Communist Party is the only organised force without any distinguishable professional or class characteristics in the entire Chinese society. Party members hold completely diverse social positions, from senior officials, tycoons, millionaires, to scientists, intellectuals, students, media professionals, to the poorest peasants and laid-off workers, as well as some political dissidents. The 'party' has evolved into a network of uneven density stretching across almost all the social classes and social sectors. Undoubtedly, the 'party' as a whole is the 'ruling and leading' body of the country, but the functions and powers of its departments and branches can only be realised in combination with other social organisations or institutions.

In the T Village, the Communist Party branch and Communist Party members are in theory subordinated to the higher party organisation. But actually, Communist Party members also hold various roles in the village including that of common peasants, cadres, teachers, businesspersons, etc. At the grass-roots level, the Communist Party members engage in promotional work, such as publicising some new guideline or new policy of the party in the name of an abstract 'party'. So the concept 'party', in the minds of the villagers, stands for a larger and stronger 'abstract' entity with its center in cities, provincial capital or even Beijing. Villagers are forcefully reminded of the Communist Party as a concrete organisation or a group of people only when the Communist Party members specially announce that some concrete project is being pursued in the Communist Party branch's name. But these kinds of cases are decreasing by the day.

According to the Communist Party's constitution, the party at the village level should play the leading role in safeguarding the self-governance activities and democratic rights of villagers. But the party's constitution does not explain which part of the work in grass-roots governance the party's village branch should do. The county and township committees of the party have been given some guidelines and principles, based on the Communist Party and national constitutions, which define the party's functions as the following:

a) To transmit the new and important policies or instructions related to ideology or guidelines from the higher level, such as holding the Sixteenth National Congress of the Party[9] or 'Three Represents Theory'[10] policy.

b) To carry out important instructions or orders on some special political issues.

c) To carry out and implement policies related to the reform of the current economic, administrative or political system.

d) To suggest or recommend candidates for the villagers' committee election.

e) To pursue specific projects beyond the routine work, such as special construction projects, installation of new devices or facilities, introduction and popularisation of new technology, etc.

f) To solve abrupt and unexpected incidents, accidents, issues, etc., which fall outside the routine of administration and are difficult to decide by normal regulations.

Of these tasks of the party, the third one is the key to understanding the functions of the party at the village level. Projects of reform imply change of old habits, readjustment of some vested interest, such as redistribution or change in the use of lands, promotion of new agricultural technologies, construction of irrigation works, introduction of investment from outside and so on. This kind of work is often quite difficult for the villagers' committee to carry out. The Communist Party organisation can make good use of its political advantages (which includes power derived from the centre) to carry out work, such as directly ordering all Communist Party members to initiate the implementation of project work. For instance, excessive drinking used to be a serious problem in the village. The villagers' committee had for a long time failed to pass a restrictive regulation on it. Finally, a new village regulation was proposed by the Communist Party and passed by the committee. It forbids the villagers to drink too much and stipulates that if anybody causes trouble in a drunken bout, he will have to pay by doing extra labour for the entire village. It is still a controversial regulation in the higher-level legislatures because of its suspected violation of personal freedom. But few villagers speak against it because it actually solves one of the biggest problems in the villages. This regulation was publicised in the committee's name, but it was actually the will and resolution of the Communist Party that led to its implementation.

At the village level, the fifth task of the party as laid down in the constitution includes high risk projects, such as building long water channels to bring water to fields or better roads to remote villagers' groups, popularising solar electricity generators, spreading the use of new wheat seeds or other new agricultural technology, etc.

The promotion of change initiated by the Communist Party faces its own share of criticisms. While supporters are not as active in whipping up public opinion as opponents,[11] the Communist Party always has to bear the attacks of victims of change or anti-reform forces. However, in the village, the Communist Party being an abstract concept, a villager will not show hostility to the party members in the village even if he or she hates some policy of the party. As a result, common Communist Party members at the lower levels are often absolved of the responsibility of the policies of the party.

But the point here is that no other social force likes or dares to undertake the responsibility of reform.[12] The unique status and role of the Communist Party in China's political arena leaves it with no choice but to become the unlucky target of all the complaints.

Social progress as defined by mainstream Chinese society is not always realistic or appropriate when applied to local society.[13] Some of them prove to be not so meaningful, or may incur high costs through miscalculation.[14] Till now it has proved difficult to find a set of indices that can evaluate accurately the campaigns that the Communist Party has been launching in the name of development.

The sixth task of the Communist Party, that is, the solution of unexpected trouble, falls within the ambit of maintaining social order. In the village, the Communist Party's branch often handles disputes, conflicts, fighting, crimes, serious accident, etc. During my stay in the village, a serious fight between two close friends took place because of drunkenness in a 'lingka' (outdoor party). One of them was badly injured and the police were called in to intervene in the affair. But none of them actually wanted it to become a police matter. So the Communist Party (both at the township and the village level) took up the case. Finally, both sides reached an agreement about the incident and the friendship was restored.

In sum, the Communist Party at the village level is seen as a driving force behind the transformation of local society as well as the adjudicator of non-conventional affairs. However, the question that arises here is whether it is the best arrangement for the Communist Party alone to play the role of the social dynamic or whether some other organisation should share in this leading role. Till today, in a grass-roots community like T Village, it is still the Communist Party that works as the driving force. But it is only a result of natural evolution through a long series of trial-and-error processes rather than a product of intentional design.

Buddhism as a Buffer and Equilibrant

A discussion about the religious force in a grass-roots society is not only limited to the religious organisation. The monastery near the village has organisational connections with the Communist Party and administration at a higher level than the village. Here, the monastery is analysed as an organised embodiment of religion, but it is not the only form of the influence of religion.

The main functions of the monastery near the villages include:

a) As a physical embodiment of Buddhism, the monastery helps to produce a religious atmosphere that impacts on one's senses. The sight of beautiful buildings of the monastery and monks constantly reminds the villagers of their nearness to religion.

b) The monastery provides the villagers with a convenient condition to exercise religious activities. Villagers offer worship and also contribute their labour in the monastery as part of their religious activities. Some also visit the monastery to make vows and, later, to redeem the vows.

c) The Buddhist monks offer their service in accordance with the village customs and folklore. In wedding ceremonies, house building, travel, funerals etc., monks are invited to decide the lucky date, organise the rituals and chant the Buddhist scriptures.

d) During important religious festivals or special occasions such as visits by high-ranking monks or a living Buddha, the monastery organises large-scale rituals and ceremonies.

e) The monastery is the chosen place where people from this village perform 'chujia' (ceremonial renunciation of worldly ties to become monks or nuns). Since a fair number of monks come in this way from this village, there are many direct channels of communications between the village and monastery. The personal ties of monks to this village means a greater involvement of the monastery in the social life of the village.

Under the current circumstance of international politicisation and sensitivity of the so-called 'Tibet issue', the Chinese officials are very cautious about taking any initiative on religious reform. They try to abide by the official statement of 'maintaining the traditional form and content of the rituals or rules',[15] so as to prove that they 'respect' religion and would not consider 'violating the freedom of belief'. The negative side of this kind of caution is that the Communist Party and committee members themselves become the most 'conservative preservationists' in terms of adaptation of religion to the rapidly changing society.

Generally speaking, Buddhism does not have more or less anti-modernisation elements than other religions, and the real issue at present is not a clash between modernisation and religion. What is of concern is that more and more young villagers are being tempted by the modern and Western-style material prosperity and consumption shown in both media and cities, and are becoming estranged from the traditional Buddhist practices.

Compared with other villages in this region, the economic development and living standard in T Village is at an average level. Geographically, T Village is 40 km from a county town and 130 km from a big city. Although communication with the outside is still difficult, information and new products can reach here easily and freely. People in the village are exposed to all the changes and new fashions in the central cities almost simultaneously. In my fieldwork, I found that villagers and monks offered us instant noodles for lunch and dinner, instead of the old-style food such as *tsampa*, bread or potatoes. It is said that in the recent years, instant noodles has suddenly become one of the most popular food items because of its association with the modern world. As an observer from outside, I would say that the local daily food such as yak meat, butter, cheese and tsampa are much better than instant noodles in terms of both nutrition and market price, but the villagers understand it in another way. They feel that local food can be produced easily at home without much cost, while instant noodles is exotic for it comes from another world—a modern, industrialised society—for which there is no substitute at home. I unfortunately failed to understand to what extent villagers liked instant noodles for its taste and convenience and to what extent for its modernity and exoticism. This kind of impact from the outside world, though not as spectacular as some political or social movements, affects people's lives more deeply and fundamentally. The younger people are more drawn towards the new styles of consumption and entertainment.

It reflects a general tendency in the ethnic Tibetan population of China. The past decade has seen a growth of secular interests and concerns. Economic and social development is attracting more and more attention of the people. Religion is gradually withdrawing from some aspects of life, especially in the case of the young people and those more exposed to city life. A division of the secular and religious realms seems to be taking place. It is only a start, but the tendency seems quite clear.

In interviews, most of the middle school students expressed their strong identification with Buddhism, but their real knowledge of religion is limited to the most basic. In short, the strength and degree of people's identification with religion has not been exactly weakened, but the role of religion is shifting from concrete daily activities to the spiritual and psychological level. The main function of religion for villagers is to provide spiritual enrichment as a source of meaning and value of life in times of change.

Some villagers expressed that they worry about not being able to catch up with the rapid change and even to keep apace with their own children. I discerned a psychological tension among many that I interviewed. In this situation, religion plays a special role in alleviating tension. From the survey, we found some correlation between religiosity and personality or lifestyle. The strongest religious sense were found among two extreme personalities; those who are the quickest to follow the changing trends and those who feel hopeless or even refuse to keep up with the change.

An example of the former is a villager who has his own truck and is engaged in the transport trade. He earns a lot of money and in his home there is a big luxury shrine with many images of Buddha and several sets of religious instruments. He even set up a *mani khorlo* (fixed prayer wheel) at home, which is not common in the village. He openly admitted that he hoped to dedicate more to the monastery so that the Buddha keeps helping him with his business. Whenever he faces difficulties in his business, he first examines his own recent behaviour and tries to rule out the possibility that his own bad conduct may have led to failure in business.

The other extreme is a poor villager who struggles to make a basic livelihood by collecting and selling *jardzagunbu* (Chinese caterpillar fungus). He sometimes goes to the monastery to do voluntary work thereby hoping to accumulate good karma and gain a better life in his next reincarnation.

It may be concluded that, under the impact of development, Buddhism provides a psychological buffer and leeway in people's adjustment and adaptation to a changing society. In a social sense, religion is a necessary balance force to maintain a relatively stable moral foundation and social norms in a rapidly changing society.

The Beneficial Interaction and Problems

Party-Committee Relation: A Long Debate
The relation between the Communist Party's branch and villagers' committee reflects a more general party–administration relation of China's political system. The two crucial dimensions of developing societies are dynamic and order, or progress and stability. On one hand, the party–administration system cleverly solves the most difficult dilemma of these two dimensions, with the Communist Party acting as the dynamic of progress and the village administration acting to maintain stability. But on the other hand, its double function mechanism inevitably leads to internal tensions inside the system. This has been one of the most chronic problems of China's system and probably will continue until China completes its transitional phase and becomes a standardised country.

At village level, there do exist conflicts between the Communist Party and the villagers' committee (Song Yaowu, 2003; Bai Gang, 2003). Given these conflicts, many models have been designed and put forward as solutions. The central committee of the CCP and the State Council synthesised the various observations and gave an instruction manual titled 'A Notice on the Work of Further Improvement of the Election of Villagers' Committee' (2002). It recommends that during the election, the Party should help villagers to exercise their right properly, to safeguard against illegal actions and support the work of the newly elected committee…. Members of the Party should be encouraged to stand as candidates of the committee and villagers' group. It is also encouraged that the candidates of the head and leading members of Party branch are persons who have been elected by villagers in committee election. Members of committee, the heads of villagers' groups and villager representatives should be admitted into the Party.

However, in T village, there is, as far as I observed, not as serious a conflict as in most other cases in China. This fact itself should pose a question for researchers. One of the possible explanations[16] is that the existence of a third strong force—Buddhism—makes the Communist Party and the villagers' committee have relatively stronger feelings of 'we-ness' than that in other parts of China. In my view, it is the local cultural factors, the strong Buddhist cultural background, that objectively helps to realise a state that is an ideological ideal but rarely achieved in other cases.

Because of the existence of religion in T village, common people bracket the Communist Party and the villagers' committee in the single category of secular forces. Buddhism[17] leads to a simplification of worldly concerns. It does not encourage any complicated division of power and factionalism, leading to the feeling among villagers that 'village does not need so many officials', 'the less, the easier' and that 'it is simpler for the Communist Party secretary to take the position of head of committee, for they are one thing anyway' and so on. So both villagers and the party members have a tendency to combine the two systems by simply electing personnel of one system to be in the other. In fact, villagers elected the last head of the committee when he was also head of the Communist Party branch. He lost in the next election because villagers felt he was 'not competent enough', but the newly elected person was also a party leader. Thus, the tendency towards an all-purpose centralised authority is obviously stronger than that towards separated or specialised governance. In addition, in this village, the elected committee head does not have an inclination as in some other cases in China to hold on to all the power and exclude the party.[18] In fact, the committee is weak in handling affairs and depends on the Communist Party to a great extent.

This is probably because Buddhism [19] provides for people a much longer frame of reference for existence and so the social elites here, on an average, are less drawn to power than those in developed coastal regions of China. To a visitor from the outside world, people here appear loose, slow, careless, sloppy and lazy, but a deeper study reveals that it is the rich spiritual life here that make people more relaxed and aloof from the affairs involving power, interest, position, election, etc.

Relationship with Buddhism

In matters of ideology, the administration is at least in name 'neutral' of religion. The members of the committee and heads of villagers' groups may have their own religious beliefs but the committee as a 'superindividual' entity has no overt religious leaning.

In the past decades, the relation between the Communist Party and religion has experienced a long and complicated evolution. Today the official slogan is 'the adaptation of religion to (and)[20] socialism', which completely gives up the old dogma denying any positive effect of religion. It is one of the fundamental shifts in the Communist Party's ideological stance along with the opening up of China.

Party members at the grass-roots level have an obligation to do work that is termed 'united front work', which means making friends and keeping contact with non-communist social elites to enlarge the political foundation of the party. Party members sometimes take part in religious activities in course of such united front work.

There is also no clear dividing line between religion and folklore and some Communist Party members still follow religious customs in the name of traditional culture or folklore, within certain limits.

In T village, the sensitive point of local party organisation is not religion itself, but the political inclinations and involvement of the believers. In areas inhabited by ethnic Tibetans, the most sensitive political issue concerns the separatist activities. As long as the believers are not involved in such activities, the local Communist Party does not mind what and how people believe in spiritually.

It appeared from this study that the Communist Party and villagers' committee intentionally keep some distance from the religious sphere in order to avoid an open contrast between ideological orientations. As a result, people in this village unanimously feel that the government does not try to intervene or restrict religion. In interviews, what impressed me was that almost all the villagers immediately answered 'freedom of religious belief' when the question 'what do you know of the government's policy about religion?' was put to them.

Functionally too, there is no rivalry between religion and the Communist Party or villagers' committee, because at the village level, the party and committee mainly work as secular forces in charge of all worldly social concerns such as production, trade, technology, entertainment, education, justice, security, construction, etc, while religion functions at the super-social or spiritual level such as the life, fortune, birth, funeral, reincarnation, religious education, pilgrimage, unexplainable strange happenings, etc. In some fields, when the secular and religious concerns overlap, such as weather, natural disasters, treatment of illness, marriage, folk festivals and so on, people simply take both ways. When somebody is ill, it is very common for him or her to go to the doctor as well as to the monastery. Normally, an ill person will first try to be treated in the secular way (doctors and medicines), but if this fails, he will turn to religion to make vows or contributions. Religion is regarded as dealing with more fundamental issues of the supernatural or surrealistic level.

It is necessary to point out that the villagers do not make such a general division of secular and religious in their minds. This division is an analytical one for the author's understanding and expression.

Coexistence and its Reasons

The division of the functions of the Communist Party, villagers' committee and Buddhism in reality as well as in villagers' minds makes their relations not simple zero-sum conflicts. Common villagers accommodate all of them together in some order in their own minds, without difficulties of 'either this or that' options. The most common scene in villagers' homes is of the pictures of the Communist Party leaders Mao Zedong, Deng Xiaoping and Jiang Zemin put up on the wall together with Buddhist paintings around the home shrine for daily worship. It is funny to observe paintings with such strong official ideological colours mixed with images and figures of Buddha, but it is just a good case for us to understand the villagers' comprehension of what we call religion and politics in our parlance. The pictures on the wall indicate that they do not feel that the concept of party leaders is incompatible with the concept of Buddha, and that in their minds the government and religion may coexist without necessarily clashing with each other.

One of the main reasons of the relative compatibility between the Communist Party and religion is the secularisation of the Communist Party itself. Originally, the Communist Party was a political organisation united under a religion-like ideology (communism). With this kind of ideology-orientation, the Communist Party showed a strong anti-religion tendency before the 1970s because of the potential rivalry between the two ideologies. But the 20 years of opening up of China substantially changed the nature of the Communist Party from an organisation based on a specific exclusive belief into an association based on China's special social structure, cultural tradition and personal interests. The existence and survival of the Communist Party depends largely on whether it could successfully lead the Chinese people towards a national revival through the 'modernisation of China'.[21] The new pragmatic orientation of the Communist Party seeks to avoid any essential confrontation with religion.

Buddhism was also originally regarded by local people as part of folklore or custom, instead of a strong exclusive force. In the local context, it is sacred, but not necessarily mysterious or heavenly, as some outsiders tend to exaggerate. Politically, religion could be also classified in a broad sense as ideology. But for common villagers, religious activities such as regular pilgrimage and daily worship are nothing but a part of daily life learnt and inherited from the elders without question. The older villagers are more religious than the younger and most of the villagers older than 30 years regularly burn incense, change the sacred water before the Buddha's image, chant the scriptures and go on regular pilgrimage (usually twice a month). People younger than 30 years spend more time watching TV, videos, movies, going to parties, going out, etc. It is because of the relaxed religiosity of the villagers that they had no motivation for spontaneous antagonism against the ideology of the Communist Party or villagers' committee unless they were politically induced to.

An Embryonic Originality of a New System?

As far as this study tells, the essential relationship between the Communist Party, villagers' committee and Buddhism is non-destructive, if not complementary, instead of antagonistic as hypothesised before the study. The village administration fulfils the routine duties, keeps the regular operations running smoothly and maintains the basic integration and order. The Communist Party is primarily a dynamic system devoted to promoting reform, progress and handling exceptional crises. Religion provides spiritual support, moral guidelines and psychological leeway for the villagers struggling with social change. Hence, none of the three parts could be dispensed with.

Empirical research shows that it is unrealistic to wait until the scattered villagers, with limited modern knowledge and education, finally reach a consensus on development and organise themselves to build a modern social order. This practical situation justifies the Communist Party's role as the driving force of change.

But again, historical lessons from the past also strongly warns us of the possible danger of an unopposed dynamic force growing into an unrealistic radical power, which will also, ironically, cause social unrest by itself. Therefore, when social reform is being promoted, there must be a stabilising force. In T Village, the villagers' committee takes the role of the controlling device. Simultaneously, one of the biggest challenges to a developing society is the fracture of moral norms under the impact of new lifestyles and social norms from outside. And there are always many social problems relating to ethic, morality, psychology, etc. Religious functions in this situation act as a buffer and relaxing force.

The most interesting result of this study lies in its suggestions of the possibility that the Communist Party, the villagers' committee and Buddhism could constitute an optimum combination, in which all of them play their constructive and supportive roles. This mode of operation is still at a very initial stage. But we can see emerging from it, an embryonic form of a possible new system in future. There is still immense scope for further improvement. For instance, if spheres of influence are more clearly demarcated, then none of them would violate the line or interfere in the functions of others unnecessarily and there will be far less conflict among them. This necessitates a clear separation of politics and religion. The Communist Party and villagers' committee should avoid interfering in the purely religious affairs. On the other hand, history has proven repeatedly that religious enthusiasm often has a tendency towards politicisation, which, once stirred up, could lead to unexpected destructiveness. Thus if all preconditions are fulfilled, the three social forces in grass-roots society could form a sound structure of coalition.

In further improvement of the current system, it should be made clear that the separation of the three parts refers to separation of functions instead of personnel, which means that each part should be in charge of certain affairs no matter who are involved in it. Accordingly, each individual must have a clear understanding of his or her role in different affairs. If a monk has to discuss political matters, he could contact the villagers' committee or Communist Party in the status of a normal citizen instead of as a religious personnel. Similarly, if a party cadre has to invite a monk for some religious service for his family, he should go there not as a cadre, but as a layman.

Given a clear division of the functions of the three parts, it is possible to establish a supportive and cooperative relationship. Separation is to avoid destructiveness, while cooperation is to build a beneficial interaction. For instance, when some new reform policy is to be carried out, the three parts could discuss how to share the potential difficulties or consequences. Some kind of division of duties could be made by the three parts taking into account their strong points in their own realms in order to implement the policy effectively with the lowest social cost.

The major problem in the interactions between the three parts in the village lies in the lack of an automatic coordination mechanism. The relation between the Communist Party and villagers' committee is relatively mature, though the party-dynamic-committee-static pattern has never been openly justified or regularised. The relation between the religion and the party or committee is not mature yet. There is no normalised coordination mechanism among them. The contact between them at present is not really designed for the goal of coordination, but for some other consideration, such as political participation and representation. Most of the time, the religious leaders in congress only report the difficulties and demands of their monasteries and the central official in the monastery committee only helps to solve the practical difficulties or handles the issues between the monastery and other units. There is not yet any mechanism to coordinate the functions of the three parts to give maximum play to their constructiveness.

The other problem is that no clear dividing line has been drawn to define the spheres of the functions of the three parts. The villagers' committee tends to avoid responsibility and often passes the controversial decisions on to the Communist Party. But in fact, often a person holds posts in both the party and committee concurrently, and common villagers can hardly make out the difference. The relations between the party and committee is so close in form that any incompatibility between the party and committee will cause inefficiency and ineffectiveness of the leading group as a whole.

The relation between religion and politics has not been openly clarified or defined till now. It is still difficult in practical operation to judge what political activity for religious personnel could imply.

However, there is enough evidence to support an optimistic prospect. Under the current circumstance in China, the ultimate goals of the Communist Party (socialism and 'Three Represents Theory'), villagers' committee (development) and Buddhism (self-cultivation and helping others to overcome the samsara) do not directly conflict with one another. The difference only lies in the middle-level value in their outlook on the world, life, happiness, order, development, culture, tradition, etc. In my view, there exists the possibility that the three parts may constitute a more stable and normalised functional coalition through an innovation of the current system.

Conclusion

This case study in T Village is only one example of some aspects of a non-Western, developing society. Given their special and complicated histories, culture, population make-up, international status and other factors, people in China and India cannot achieve economic and social development simply by copying a ready-made model from the developed countries. History has proved that there is no free lunch in the world. We are destined to explore, try and find our own way of development, perhaps with a potential high risk and price.

In the past decades, China has sometimes intentionally and sometimes blindly developed some innovation of system, many of which were definitely not completely reasonable or perfect. What this chapter discussed is just a part of these tentative systems.

By studying this village, I conclude that the hypothesis I had before the fieldwork does not reflect the real points of that community. The hypothesis, primarily in terms of conflict theory, overestimated the conflicting sides of the relation among the three forces in grass-roots society and neglected the possibility that the three forces work at different levels of society. In fact, there is no overt conflict of interest because each of them is oriented towards specific aspects of life and not to life as a whole. Although the three forces are aimed at the same population, the individuals of this population group do not need to make a 'either this or that' choice. It is similar to the deities of some polytheistic religion, in which each god has its own realm and particular function, such as creation, maintenance, destruction or extermination. Not all the phenomena in this study can conform simply to the terms or categories in a standard political science textbook. When studying the local society in old and independent civilisations like China and India, we often have to be ready to overstep the limits of established mainstream academic discourses and to adjust ourselves to realise another logic. It is a challenge not only to conventional theories, but also to our personal mode of thinking and knowledge structure.

The community I studied reflects only one of many types of grass-roots societies in China and the developing world. In other places, there are other types as well. For instance, in most regions of China, the religion will not be Tibetan Buddhism, but some other. In many cases of eastern China, there will be more than one religion or folk belief coexisting together and the religious part will be much more complicated and less integrated than that in this study. In coastal regions where economical and social development is proceeding at a high speed, there appears some other social force besides the three in this study, such as newly rising entrepreneurs, NGOs and even some cults and underground societies, that makes the situation much more complicated for study. So this study is not a representative case for the whole country, but is one case of one type. But I hope that it will provide a comparable framework and reference for other case studies under the same topic.

Notes

1. It is a strong trend in 'reconstruction projects' of many cities of China, the dream and pride of local people, but ridiculed and condemned by Western observers and Chinese preservationists.
2. See The Organic Law on the Villagers' Committee (OLVC) of the People's Republic of China.
3. Here we only describe the current situation in T Village. There are many different models, discussions and new designs of this relation, which is, in fact, one of the 'hot topics' inside China.
4. 'United-front-work' is a political term of CPC formed during the revolutionary periods, referring to the work on building cooperation with non-CPC social forces in order to fight the 'common enemy'. An office or personnel in charge of it constitutes one of the basic organs of party in every level.
5. In Chinese, the word 'zhuren' is normally used to refer to an appointed head of some department such as 'director', instead of an elected post. The title itself suggests the subtle and ambiguous status of this post.
6. According to law, there should be an 'election committee', chosen by all villager voters or villagers' groups, to organise elections. But here villager voters let the current committee organise the election.
7. Here is the concrete work in this village. The general formal function of the committee is provided by law (OLVC).
8. From spoken Chinese, referring to the situation that 'the form is different from the substance'. People reasonably but superficially accept the slogan of 'democracy', but in practice misunderstand, distort or misuse it so much that what is produced is completely different from the original ideal.
9. The national party congress held every five years often means some new and important guidelines and policy making in central government.
10. A new and implicative guiding ideology formally written into the Communist Party Constitution in Sixteenth National Congress of the Communist Party, which is taken by some observers to mean 'social democracy'.
11. It is a typical phenomenon in China, probably because of its culture, that 'the positive' in public will never be as active as 'the negative'. Proponents, especially the beneficiaries, always tend to avoid expressing strong support openly for a policy as much as the opponents fight against it. This 'hitchhiking psychology' is one of the big difficulties in social operation.
12. In fact, some social forces are more active in making good use of public complaints for other political goals.

13. Inside China, the dominant tastes mostly come from eastern coastal regions. They are often imitations of Western models, but with distortion.

14. Some policies, it is said, are based on misunderstanding or prejudice of the mainstream society, not necessary or suitable for the local society. Some construction projects are alleged to be unsuccessful and a waste of money and time.

15. This policy originates from the disputes over the reincarnation of the living Buddha. The Chinese government insists on the traditional rule (from the Qing Dynasty) that only the central government of China, instead of any other living Buddha, should have the power of final approval of the new reincarnation.

16. It is a hypothesis by some co-researchers, not yet tested.

17. It is yet to be tested strictly if there is a logical relation between this inclination and common villagers' attitudes.

18. Some elected heads in coastal provinces of China, with a strong confidence of public support, tend to form a 'gang' of extreme localism or populism, confronting with any other generalising forces and often against modern social or economic order. It produces a situation satirically called by observers as 'self-governance of committee itself instead of villagers' (Song Yaowu, 2003).

19. It is only a hypothesis, not strictly tested.

20. In Chinese it is 'he', which has two meanings, 'and' and 'to', making the statement ambiguous with two possible literal meanings, implying different tendencies of policies.

21. The so-called 'Three Represents Theory' has been put forward by the CPC to try to 'theorise' as well as 'justify' these basic changes, in order to make a new ideological foundation which is both 'sacred' and 'effective' enough to unite society.

References

Bai, Gang. 2003. 'The Transformation of China's Grass-roots Governance' (Zhongguo de Jiceng Zhili de Bian'ge). Website of National Institute of law, Chinese Academy of Social Science, http://www.iolaw.org.cn/showarticle.asp?id=579

Bai, Gang and Shouxing Zhao. 2001. *Election and Ruling: A Study of Villagers' Self-Governance in China*. Beijing: China Social Science Press.

Constitution of Communist Party of China (CCPC). Website of Xinhua News Agency, http://news.xinhuanet.com/newscenter/2004-03/15/content_1367387.htm

Constitution of the People's Republic of China (CPRC). Website of Chinese Government, http://www.china.org.cn/chinese/2002/2002/nov/234227.htm

Fu, Xianqun. 2003. 'Research on the Integration of Political Resources in Villagers' Self-Governance' (Cunmin Zizhi Ziyuan Zhenghe Yanjiu). *Solicit Articles on Village Election and Self-Governance Mechanism*. NPC news website, http://www.wsjk.com.cn/gb/speical/class000000037/1/hwz237661.htm

General Office of Central Committee of CCP and General Office of the State Council. 2002. 'A Notice on the Work of Further Improvement of the Election of Villagers' Committee' (official document); website of Xinhua News Agency, http://news.xinhuanet.com/zhengfu/2002-08/19/content_529523.htm

Heberer, Thomas. 2001. 'Eastern Asia and West: Confrontation or Cooperation?' (Dongya he Xifang: Duikang haishi Hezuo?), in Rong Ma and Xing Zhou (eds), *21st Century: Culture Consciousness and Cross-cultural Communication* (21 shiji: Wenhua Zijue yu Kuawenhua Duihua). pp. 27–52, Beijing: Peking University Press.

Jing, Yaoji. 2001. 'The Debate on Modernity and the Location of Sociology of China' (Xiandaihua Lunbian yu Zhongguo Shehuixue zhi Dingwei), in Rong Ma and Xing Zhou (eds), *21st*

Century: Culture Consciousness and Cross-cultural Communication (21 shiji: Wenhua Zijue yu Kuawenhua Duihua). pp. 354–75, Beijing: Peking University Press.

Mukherji, Partha N. 2001. 'Generalization, Localization, Globalization: Sociology and Social Science'(Pubianhua, Bentuhua, Quanqiuhua: Shehuixue yu Shehuikexue), in Rong Ma and Xing Zhou (eds), *21st Century: Culture Consciousness and Cross-cultural Communication* (21 shiji: Wenhua Zijue yu Kuawenhua Duihua), pp. 165–78, Beijing: Peking University Press.

Song, Yaowu. 2003. 'Consideration of Innovation of the System of Villagers' Self-Governance' (Guanyu Cunmin Zizhi Zhidu de Sikao), *Solicit Articles on Village Election and Self-Governance Mechanism*. NPC news website, http://www.wsjk.com.cn/gf/special/class000000037/1/hwz237769.htm

The Organic Law on the Villagers' Committee (OLVC) of the People's Republic of China, NPC News Website, http://www. wsjk.com.cn/gb/paper12/1/class001200006/hwz64679.htm

Wang, Jinping. 2000. '"Killing with Hypercriticism" or "Killing with Extolling": Intellectuals' Attitude to Villagers' Self-governance' (Zhishi Fenzi dui Cunmin Zizhi de "Pengsha" yu "Bangsha"), website of *China Election and Governance*, http://www.chinaelections.org/newsinfo.asp?NewsID=69463

Wang, Xiaoyi. 2003. 'Village Structure and the Internal Tension of the Village' (Cunzhuang Jiegou yu Cunzhuang Neibu de Jinzhang), *Solicit Articles on Village Election and Self-governance Mechanism*. Website of Chinese Academy of Social Sciences, http://www.sociology.cass.net.cn/pws/wangxiaoyi/grwj_wangxiaoyi/t20030929_1154.htm

III

Comparative Reflections

20 Reconceptualising Local Democracy

Reflections on Democracy, Power and Resistance in the Indian and Chinese Countryside

MANORANJAN MOHANTY AND MARK SELDEN

Democratisation and Changing Power Relations

We reflect in this chapter on the institutional dynamics and socio-economic processes of local governance in India and China within the broader parameters of the political economy of local democracy. Our focus is the relationship between the forces of market dominance and global incorporation that are transforming many parts of the world including India and China and counter-pressures to enlarge the scope of individual and group autonomy at the grass-roots level. We assess the changing character of local politics in rural India and China in light of the trajectories of the political economy of the two nations since independence/liberation, with particular emphasis on emerging forces since the 1980s.[1]

In posing these large questions against a continental-scale social landscape, we highlight the interplay of two issues: pressures for democratisation understood to mean voice and demand for expanded power and rights for rural producers, and changing social structure, including class, caste, ethnic and gender relations, and patterns of inequality in the context of the expanding market forces, on the one hand, and changing state–society relations, on the other.

In addressing these issues we highlight the countryside not only because the literature on global change has been overwhelmingly preoccupied with states, cities and industry, generally seen as the 'cutting edge' of economic growth and progressive social change, but also because the specific gravity of population in both nations remains the countryside, as evident in rural unrest and discontent, because the problems of development and democracy are most intractable there *and* because we discern important changes underway there that affect national as well as global dynamics.

It is not surprising that in the course of taking stock of their economic reforms, the new leaderships of both India and China proclaimed a commitment to solving problems of farmers. The Manmohan Singh government of the United Progressive Alliance, which came to power in India in May 2004, defeating the National Democratic Alliance led by Atal Behari Vajpayee, announced its intention to pursue a policy of 'reforms with a human face'.

The fourth generation leadership of the Communist Party of China, Hu Jintao and Wen Jiabao, declared the three rural problems (*san nong*), namely, agriculture (*nongye*), peasant (*nongmin*) and countryside (*nongcun*) as the principal focus of their policies in 2004.[2] It is, however, one thing to proclaim a rural priority and quite another to deliver benefits that favour the countryside over the city from the interrelated perspectives of equity and environmentally-supportable development.

We begin by briefly assessing some of the major changes that took place at the time of Indian Independence and the formation of the People's Republic of China more than six decades ago, a moment when many took their trajectories as emblematic of democratic and socialist paths in the world's countrysides in a post-colonial era.

Different Trajectories?

The social and institutional—but not necessarily the political—changes appear to have been far deeper in China than in India both in the post-Liberation period of the 1950s and the post reform years of the 1980s?[3] After all China had an agrarian revolution encompassing a thorough-going redistributive land reform that broke the grip of landlord power, placed villages in the grip of the Communist Party and uplifted the poorest strata in the years 1947–52, followed by the collective transformation of rural economy and society in the years 1955–78. The rural reforms after 1978, with the introduction of a household responsibility system that retained equal land ownership while reverting to family farming, was also part of a far-reaching package including diversification of agriculture and vigorous promotion of rural industries, market-sensitive management, exports and foreign investment. Although India experienced substantial continuity in land tenure relations in the wake of Indian independence, the Green Revolution in the 1970s and the political changes mandated by the Seventy-third Constitutional Amendment in 1993 constituted significant changes in the prevailing situation in parts of rural India in terms both of income gains, growing inequality, but also the empowerment of women and poorer strata and castes through changes in the electoral process. China's 1940s and 1950s land reform and collectivisation appear to have had far deeper effects than India's 1950s zamindari abolition, and India never undertook the institutional transformation of agriculture on a comparable scale.

Of particular interest for comparative purposes is the success of the Green Revolution in Punjab, Haryana, western Uttar Pradesh, coastal Andhra, Tamil Nadu and parts of other states where substantial agricultural growth was accompanied by sharp socio-economic differentiation and class differentiation including the growth of a substantial class of landless and land-poor agricultural labourers. It made India self-sufficient in food grains but with gross inequality of land and vast disparities among regions. As a result, in today's India we see the paradox of over-flowing grain warehouses and starvation deaths existing simultaneously (Patnaik, 2004; 376–77).

China too, since the 1980s, has achieved significant growth of agricultural production fuelled by the use of modern inputs in tandem with rural industrialisation. In almost every respect the post-Mao Chinese leadership has reversed the social revolution of the 1940s and 1950s in industry, agriculture and commerce. An important exception, however, is land ownership rights. In contrast to post-revolutionary changes in Eastern Europe since the 1990s that reversed earlier land reform, China has retained equitable distribution of land while reverting from collective to household farming under the household contract system. Income and property inequality related to the growth of the market economy and rapid economic growth, however, have emerged with a vengeance. We assess the consequences of economic reforms for local democracy in both countries, with particular attention to recent decades that combine rapid growth with inequality.[4]

In the history of India's rural transformation, from community development in the 1950s to integrated rural development in the 1980s, the introduction of statutory panchayati raj in 1993 amounted to a break with the past in two ways. It entailed statutory elections every five years ending the long periods of suspension of panchayat elections, which had left rural administration in the hands of the state bureaucracy under the patronage of the ruling party of the state. With the Seventy-third Constitutional Amendment, one-third of seats were reserved for women in the rural local bodies, including the leading posts, in addition to provisions that set aside seats for the Scheduled Castes (SCs) and Scheduled Tribes (STs). The financial powers of the panchayat raj are still meagre. But the democratic aspirations that the law has released are momentous. On the 10th anniversary of panchayati raj, both the National Democratic Alliance (NDA) and the United Progressive Alliance (UPA) formations agreed on the need for constitutional amendments to strengthen local financial and administrative power. A successfully functioning panchayati raj system could constitute a break with the earlier political structure in the Indian countryside. If less radical than either China's land reform, collectivisation and subsequent decollectivisation under the household responsibility system, its consequences include initiating a political upsurge and mobilising women for expanded political roles.[5]

In the 1990s, both the Indian and Chinese states prioritised two tasks: integrating the rural economy through market liberalisation and globalisation, on the one hand, and political and institutional responses to demands from below for power and resources, on the other. We emphasise for both nations distinctive sets of conflicts and contradictions that generate patterns of resistance and produce winners and losers while structuring social change. Our reference point is the experience of different social groups in the changing power relations in the village. Keeping this in mind we can discern three trends in the developing political economy in the two countries: *emergence of a new rural elite, new challenges from below in response to institutional and social change, and altered priorities under globalisation.*

Emergence of a New Rural Elite

We note the emergence of a new and more assertive rural elite as a result of the Green Revolution and rural development programmes in India and de-collectivisation, the resurgence of the household economy, greater mobility of labour and capital resulting in new class formations and rural industrialisation in China. The results in both cases have included changing state–society relations, new patterns of inequality, stepped up demands for autonomy and power by emerging social classes constrained by the old order and growing demands from below.[6]

These are responses not only to local and nationally-generated patterns of social change, but also to the growing engagement of both nations, particularly China, in global economic and financial relationships driven by investment and trade and reinforced by exposure to television, film and other images from the global marketplace. Rapid social change has generated new political challenges both from the most privileged and most oppressed sectors of the social spectrum (including class, caste and nationality/ethnicity) with intellectuals and social activists—the latter more prominently in India—often playing a critical mediating role in the transmission of information and providing leadership.

The new rural elite often plays a dual role at once claiming greater autonomy from the centre or higher echelons of power even as it draws on its network ties to the political order, and securing benefits for itself while excluding poorer and disadvantaged rural strata from many of the gains associated with economic growth.[7] Electoral considerations compel Indian political leaders from the centre to the grass roots to appeal to the poor with welfare programmes.[8] In order to strengthen the legitimacy of the one-party state, the Chinese leadership has promoted local elections, launched anti-corruption drives and taken multiple measures designed to promote rural development and prosperity. These measures include reducing barriers to mobility, anti-poverty measures, tax reductions and steps to reduce regional disparity such as the Western Region Development Plan.[9] Chinese local elites face no organised challenge of the type confronting their Indian counterparts in a shifting multi-party system. Nevertheless, contradictions between the new rich and the lower strata have intensified in both nations.[10]

Institutional Changes

The process of change is in part the product of new institutional arrangements for local government brought about by major enactments, of which the Seventy-third Amendment of the Indian Constitution in 1992 and the Organic Law on Basic Level Local Government of 1998 in China are worth noting. Both the Indian and Chinese governments emphasise the development of local elections as the centrepiece of democratic governance. How have local political processes and the character of local government been affected by the institutionalisation of local elections and changes in electoral processes?

Panchayat elections are held in India every five years. In China, village committee elections, when and where held, were on a three-year cycle.[11] In India, the panchayat elections at the lowest level of village panchayat are legally conducted on a non-party basis. In other words, political parties do not formally endorse candidates and candidates do not run on party affiliations. However, in practice, the Indian party system has percolated right down to the village and hamlet levels. Therefore, while village-level elections ideally embody the community values of Gandhi's *sarvoday*, every election from the village upwards is fought on party lines. After the panchayat elections, the parties announce their victories or losses of the number of sarpanches at the village level, samiti chairpersons at the block level and zilla parishad presidents at the district level. In other words, Indian local elections are closely integrated with national politics in a multi-party system.

India's competitive grass-roots politics makes it possible for local people's organisations to influence decision making, especially with regard to the allocation of rural development funds. On the other hand, they confront political parties and powerful interest groups in every village. Gandhi's notion of gram swaraj as a self-governing village could not evolve in such an environment, since powerful interests left little space for autonomous functioning of the village community. Nevertheless, on balance the political landscape in the countryside is now more open for struggles involving the deprived sections than it was in the colonial or early post-independence years. In West Bengal and Kerala this process has been most pronounced, enabling sharecroppers and agricultural labourers to wield or share substantial power over local institutions. A whole new process of development planning from below has emerged in recent decades in Kerala with the interests of the rural poor and artisans to the fore. Because of the initiative taken by the Communist Party of India (Marxist) and its allies the voices and interests of the poor have found representation in West Bengal and Kerala, particularly in the wake of institutional changes that gave more power to the panchayats. It should be noted that in West Bengal and Karnataka, panchayats attained greater political role even before the central law was enacted.[12]

What is the character and scope of political democracy in village China?[13] China too, in recent decades, has emphasised multi-candidate elections for village councils, the most basic level of governance, and for village councils only. The political milieu in which the village council and panchayat elections take place is as different, however, as the character of competitive politics in the two countries. First, in contrast to India, Chinese elections remain limited to the village (cun) council, while township (xiang) elections continue to be held in the old style of the higher party leadership nominating from a panel drawn up by the township party leadership. Attempts at holding competitive elections at the township level have been firmly rejected by the Hu Jintao regime as they were by its predecessors.[14] Second, the multiple candidates in the contest for village committee are barred from representing different parties. Not even the six officially-recognised 'democratic parties', which are represented in the Political Consultative Conference, as an emblem of the continued united front politics that played a role in the Communist Party's rise more than six decades ago, may contest village elections.

This is formally comparable to the Indian case, which bars parties from competing in elections at the village panchayat level. But in practice, as we have observed, party competition takes place at every level in India, from the panchayat up. Chinese village committee elections are, in fact, monitored closely by the village Communist Party branch.[15] In some places, candidates are screened out by the local authorities on grounds of corruption or other offences. There is also no independent election commission to conduct elections—something that distinguishes the Indian situation from China.[16] The election process is under judicial review in India whereas the CCP leadership and the township government authorities implement the law and conduct the village committee elections. In practice, while the Discipline Commission has the authority to look into charges of corrupt practices, there can be no significant challenge to CCP leadership.

Moreover, in many localities, for example, in large areas of Hebei Province, no local elections have ever been held, or are held irregularly at best.[17] Finally, and most important, village politics are dominated not by the village committee but by the CCP branch, which is subject to party discipline and is selected by processes independent of the will of the village community.

Despite the fact that local elections are dominated by the CCP and are closely monitored to prevent the emergence of horizontal challenges of all kinds, multi-candidate contests in some localities have initiated an element of political competition at the local level. In the new environment of privatisation of rural enterprises this has meant the emergence of a new field of politics with entrepreneurs and workers, peasants and small traders trying to use the political space to pursue their interests. In China, as in India, the new economic dynamics of privatisation, market expansion, economic diversification, and labour mobility, have given rise to new social forces that compete for resources at the polls and through formal and informal ties to the state. But if elections provide one significant terrain for this competition under Indian conditions, the most important, and certainly the most intense and contested struggles, in rural China are fought in the rising number of local protests and court challenges, and in behind the scenes battles for control of resources. We take up this subject in the final section of this chapter.

In India, one outcome of demands for political representation was the guaranteed election of a proportion of representatives from lower castes, tribal people and women in decision-making bodies at all levels from the village upward to the centre. While the representation of the SCs and STs in proportion to their population was guaranteed from the beginning of the implementation of the Indian Constitution, reservation of one-third of seats for women at all levels of local government was achieved only in 1992 by the Seventy-third Amendment for rural and Seventy-fourth Amendment for urban bodies. No comparable system of reservation for women exists in China.[18] In minority areas and in the places where minority populations exist, there are clear guidelines for the composition of various local bodies including reservation of seats for minority candidates. In India, the women's representation has unleashed significant processes challenging the hold of patriarchy.[19] Yet, whether this amounts to 'women's empowerment' continues to be debated.[20]

The question of women's empowerment has had little place in the debate over village elections and village power in China. Rural women's representation at the village level throughout the PRC has largely consisted of the participation of a single 'women's representative' in the village committee. The most important task of the incumbent has always been implementing the party's policies, particularly those that affect women. Since the 1980s, this has above all meant assuring that village birth quotas were not exceeded under the rigorous birth control policies that have brought China's birth rates sharply downward.

The Fourth World Congress of Women held in Beijing in 1995 prompted discussion of policies pertaining to women's development, but this brought little discernible change to the countryside then or subsequently, with women's representation small and generally marginal in rural local governance.[21] There is no evidence that village elections have strengthened the position of women in rural society or that women's issues were among those prioritised in election campaigns.

Serious questions remain as to whether new forms of electoral politics signal a significant shift in the exercise of rural power, particularly in India. Have elections in general, and the reservation of women's seats in particular, shifted the power balance? Has the substantial increase in women's representation in panchayats significantly shifted gendered politics or the social and economic roles of women at the local level? Have new elites succeeded in using electoral politics to serve their economic and political interests to cement their grip on power? There is no doubt that Indian electoral and other reforms have brought about a new political environment at the grassroots level in which women's rights, the rights of farmers and workers and issues of unemployed youth are debated and candidates and leaders are called upon to respond to them.

The Global and the Local in the Era of Reform: Democracy and New Social Movements

The priorities of the Indian and Chinese states and dominant elites that have prioritised economic reforms and globalisation in recent decades have centred on achieving high growth rates. This has taken the form of institutional changes that are deemed to promote the growth of production, markets and mobility of people and capital. Economic growth has resulted in substantial income gains for broad segments of the rural population, notably in China, but this has gone hand in hand with rising income and opportunity inequality. Both the Indian and Chinese states have sought to ease the burdens of poor and vulnerable sectors, hundreds of millions of people in each, and in China in particular, there has been substantial reduction in the number of those living in extreme poverty. Nevertheless, in both societies, significant groups of rural poor have been bypassed both by reform and welfare measures.

For India, the most basic task for addressing rural poverty remains as elusive as it has been throughout the independence era, indeed it is not on the political agenda: that is, land reforms to provide the poor with greater access to productive assets. For China, where equal access to land is not a serious problem but rural poverty is, the priority task is to find means to reduce the constraints on rural people (particularly those on urban migration) and to subsidise poorer localities and households in ways that will lead to expanded economic opportunities for them.

Since joining the WTO—India in 1995 and China in 2001—both countries have accelerated neo-liberal reform programmes such as cutting subsidies to agriculture, privatising public enterprises, reducing tariffs on agricultural imports, removing trade barriers and reducing fiscal deficit.[22] These priorities have promoted growth in both agricultural output and (notably for China) rural industry, while exacerbating income inequalities, both intra-rural and urban-rural inequalities in both India and China. It is fair to say that the heaviest burdens of WTO membership and neo-liberal reform have fallen on the countryside, notably its poverty-stricken regions.

The new measures, while compatible with continued growth and income gains in both countries, imposed serious hardships on segments of their rural population.[23] In India, average farm incomes had fallen and rural indebtedness had risen—a phenomenon that was reflected in the frequent occurrence of farmers' suicides.[24]

China has achieved significant but uneven gains in rural per capita income and consumption in the course of three decades of reform, driven initially by gains in agricultural production, particularly in the early years of reform, 1978–84, when the state boosted purchasing prices for agricultural commodities and farmers responded. More important, and distinctive in the long run, have been China's burgeoning rural industry and commerce, a source of major export gains and higher rural incomes. China achieved rapid agricultural growth, but poverty alleviation programmes also contributed to rising rural incomes.[25] Nevertheless, substantial rural poverty exists in China, notably in inland and mountain areas remote from and largely bypassed by rural industrialisation, market and export growth, and foreign investment, all of which remain centred in coastal regions.

National household surveys conducted by the Chinese Academy of Social Sciences since the 1980s provide relatively robust data on rural income inequality. The data reveal that despite highly equal land distribution, between 1988 and 1995, China's rural income distribution changed from one of the most equal in the developing world to one of the most unequal in Asia, the gini coefficient rising from 0.30 in 1980 to 0.46 in 2003. By 2001, China's rural gini coefficient was 0.45 surpassing that of South Korea at 0.32 (1998) and Indonesia at 0.343 (in 2002).[26]

The story, however, is multidimensional and complex. First, because while China's rural ginis remain relatively high, as Khan and Riskin (2005) show, there was no significant increase between 1995 and 2002, during which time rural poverty and inequality declined in both intra- and inter-provincial terms. This was, in fact, a period of substantial rural income gains, with the advance coming almost entirely from rural wages, indicative of the surge in rural industry. At the same time, the urban–rural income gap continued to grow over the last quarter century and by 2004, by some estimates it stood at 6:1 if subsidies to urban dwellers are included.[27] To sum up, since the 1980s China's countryside has been transformed by decollectivisation, marketisation and rural industrialisation, bringing both substantial real income gains to many together with substantial and growing inequalities of income and opportunity.

Of particular interest for our purposes is the fact that Chinese rural income inequalities, which were far less prior to the 1980s, appear to have outstripped those of India. As of 2001, China's rural income gini of 0.43 may be compared with India's gini of 0.325 in 2000 (UNDP, 2004).

In comparing rural inequality, we recognise important differences in character, origins and trajectory. Of particular importance is the fact that through all the changes associated with decollectivisation and commodification in rural China, the original achievement of the Chinese revolution, an egalitarian land distribution, remains basically intact. By contrast, rural inequality in India rests in significant part on differences in land ownership reinforced in many instances by the caste order.[28] China's land revolution and collectivisation sharply reduced rural inequality by levelling processes of distribution of wealth and the elimination of major class distinctions. It also paved the way for much higher levels of urban–rural inequality than those found in India as a result of the combination of state transfer of the rural surplus to urban industry, and a distribution strategy that favoured workers and the city over collective farmers between 1947 and 1982 (Selden, 1993). We nevertheless note that the most dynamic sector of the Chinese economy, and an important source of rural income since the 1980s, has been rural industry, a situation that has no Indian parallel and is central to understanding both the character of Chinese development and popular responses to it (Patnaik, 2004).

Social Conflict and Social Movements in India and China

Was the expansion of grass-roots democratic movements since the 1990s in India and China a product of concessions by the ruling elite in both countries in order to push ahead with globalising reforms? Those who advance this view point out that this eased the path to integrating rural markets with the national and global economy.[29] Indeed, democratisation, building of civil society and promoting citizen and consumer empowerment were key components of the ideology of globalisation and reform in both countries.

We nevertheless emphasise two other factors. First, popular movements, which emerged in the course of the independence and liberation struggles, had long pressed for grass-roots democratic rights. In India, the resurgent people's movements of the 1970s and 1980s led to the legislative victories for local democracy in the 1990s. This was neither the invention of, nor a gift from, the state, but a product of social movements. In West Bengal and Karnataka, measures for decentralisation of power to the panchayat level had, moreover, already taken place in the late-1970s, long before the national reforms.[30] The movement for people's planning in Kerala was a result of protracted people's struggles which, if anything, constituted a challenge to globalisation.[31] In this context we have to stress the implications of India's relatively developed grass-roots democracy in key states for the legislation that would subsequently affect the entire countryside.

China's grass-roots democratic movements had goals and rhythms of its own. Its two peak periods, which have yet to be surpassed in intensity (and violence), were the late 1940s when villagers threw support to the Communist-led land reforms that broke the power of the landlord class and created a highly equitable pattern of landownership, and the late-1960s when the countryside joined in the Cultural Revolution attack on a range of party policies and entrenched leadership, at times verging on civil war. In contrast to the gains of land reform, however, the Cultural Revolution, coming on the heels of the Great Leap Forward, left the countryside scarred and its economy weakened by the assault on markets and the household economy. The consolidation of party power following both upsurges left villagers with few levers for the direct exercise of democratic rights.[32]

Since the 1980s, China's villagers have shared with their Indian counterparts growing involvement in the market and international economy, experiencing mounting class and spatial inequality in a period of rapid economic growth. This makes it worthwhile to take a fresh look at the comparison of Indian and Chinese democracy and social movements. We begin by noting three important differences between the two environments. China's Communist Party continues to monopolise political power, in contrast to India's multi-party democracy; the legacy of land reform provides a subsistence cushion for Chinese villagers that many Indians lack; and rural China has once again experienced rapid institutional change with the end of collectivisation and the rise of the household economy, rural industrialisation and large-scale labour migration.

In India, electoral and other reforms set the stage for a new phase in social movements with greater involvement of the backward classes, Dalits, women and tribal people against the overall backdrop of the radical peasant movement of the Naxalites. Decentralisation of power was one of the systemic responses to this trend even as the central leaderships of major political parties resisted conceding power to the grass-roots level.[33]

From time to time, the Indian central government had attempted to bypass state governments and directly reach out to the districts, blocks and panchayats.

This was often done in the name of efficiently implementing poverty-eradication and rural development policies for which the main funding came from the centre and on the plea that such intervention from the centre could counter the power of local elites and protect the interests of the dispossessed.[34] Other trends, however, were conducive to expanded local initiative. Regional political parties emerged to prominence in India in the 1980s and 1990s structuring the politics of federalism irreversibly—something the Indian Constitution had envisaged.

In China, the reform era that ushered in rising rural incomes and rising intra-rural and urban–rural inequality also facilitated the emergence of new social movements. In contrast to the literature, which has been mesmerised by the saga of village elections, we emphasise the fact that village elections have left intact local party-centred power structures in the one-party state. To understand the new political dynamics, we need to pay attention to the implications of other social, political and economic factors. Among the most important of these are: the relaxation of direct cadre control over villagers with the end of collective agriculture; the relaxation of population controls (the hukou system) that had long prevented rural migration, opening the way to the movement of well over one hundred million villagers to urban and suburban jobs (even as the permanent residence and registration of most remained their home villages); and the state's vigorous promotion of a legal culture in an attempt to bring local corruption under control and to redirect the antagonisms of rural people from protests and demonstrations to the courts.

Contradictory Pulls

The newly-initiated democratic structures in the rural areas of India and China are subjected to contradictory pulls reflecting, for example, contradictory central and local interests. In both electoral and legal reforms, the goals of national power are to reduce the potential for explosive conflicts that might be directed against the state in the form of rural protest and even rebellion, and to create channels that can mediate such conflict. At the same time diverse local actors, including both power-holders and the poor and oppressed, see the new institutional channels of local governance as potential means to enlarge spheres of autonomy and protect their interests. With this they can also challenge the arbitrary power of state (province) and local governments, appealing, for example, to the central government to rectify the abuses and corruption of the local state. On the other hand, many organisations of the poor in India regard the panchayat as local organs of the Indian state whose activities basically legitimise the power of the rulers.[35]

In other words, we note conflicting goals for, and perspectives on, democratising processes at the centre and the locality, with the centre stressing the contribution to the stability and maintenance of national power and the local bent on expanding the scope of autonomy and self-determination at the grass roots. The former frequently uses the framework of the new global ideology of *governance*, pointing to electoral processes as a vehicle for good governance and stability. The latter characteristically asserts that at every level—village, township/block, county/district, province to nation and transnational regions—constituents have a right to debate and make choices, including the right to challenge national policy.

Simultaneously, new local structures, including democratic and judicial institutions in both countries, provide sites for mediating local conflicts, specifically those among social classes and castes (in India), more generally struggles that pit the interests of local power-holders whether in the state or the private sector against the most vulnerable elements in the society, including the poor, minority nationalities, lower castes and women. We notice both groups of struggles emerging in the present conjuncture, that is those involving centre–local or spatial conflict and those at the local level with class, caste, gender and nationality dimensions, as well as in the arenas of intersection of the two. In India, the centre has at times made common cause with such dispossessed elements as tribals, Dalits and women as a result of accumulated pressures from people's movements. In China, too, both in the mobilisation era associated with Mao Zedong and the reform era in recent decades, the centre has often projected itself as the defender of rural people, especially the poorest strata, albeit in support of strikingly different policies during the two periods. In December 2005, for example, the centre floated proposals to eliminate agricultural tax, the basic tax on villagers from imperial China to the present. The problem, however, is that major burdens, from fees, both legal and illegal exacted by local officials, to restrictions on citizenship associated with the hukou system, have placed heavy burdens on rural people that are far greater than the agricultural tax. At a time when the countryside faces new burdens as a result of agricultural imports sanctioned by WTO rules, it is by no means clear whether the burden on the rural poor is increasing or decreasing.

What can be said with certainty is that the number and intensity of social conflicts, protests, legal challenges and diverse forms of rural resistance have increased in recent years. According to the Ministry of Public Security, nationwide there were 8,700 recorded 'disturbances' (*naoshi*) in 1993, rising to 11,000 in 1995, 32,000 in 1999 and 74,000 in 2004, and 87,000 'mass incidents' in 2005, the vast majority of these in the countryside (Ma, 2004).

A high-level government source revealed that in 1993 there were 6,236 incidents of resisting arbitrary taxation and levies, involving hundreds, and in some cases even thousands of villagers. In that year, more than 8,000 township and county officials were killed or injured and 560 county-level offices were ransacked. Waves of unrest were recorded in the years 1995–98 in agricultural provinces left behind as coastal area economies surged (Bernstein and Lu, 2000: 754–55). Riots centred in Sichuan, Hunan, Henan and Shanxi, agriculture-dependent regions in central and western China.

Until about 2000, the major grievances prompting mass action by villagers were state-imposed 'burdens', including taxes, levies, extraction of funds (for building public works or roads), penalties (particularly fines for exceeding birth quotas) and compulsory assessments. By the early 2000s, coercive land expropriation had become perhaps the most incendiary issue, notably in suburban areas in coastal provinces (Ho, 2005: 16). Local governments participated in the massive transfer of farmland into development zones, the most common pretext for depriving villagers of land ownership rights. Villagers were typically forced to accept a pittance for their land, while cadres cut deals with Chinese or foreign investors and pocketed millions of dollars. The results were often protracted confrontations, sometimes ending in violence, sometimes in court settlements (Guo, 2001; Perry and Selden, 2003).

With rural people on the move to the city and back to the countryside, and with the state encouraging legal challenges in the face of corruption and official abuse, villagers became familiar with many of the laws and regulations bearing on their interests and rights. Villagers now write complaint letters, visit higher officials, expose local violations of central policies in the media and mobilise fellow villagers to withhold payment of illegal and arbitrary fees and taxes in the face of official corruption and abuse. Confrontations between resisters and local cadres have resulted in protracted court battles and in small- and large-scale riots as well as violent crackdowns by local and provincial governments. In recent years, informal groups of rights activists have emerged in a number of localities. Shrewdly building networks across villages, occasionally even counties, relying on trust, reputation and verbal communication, they consciously avoid formal organisations with hierarchy, documents and memberships (Yu, 2003).

As tensions rise, the central government, mindful of the many peasant rebellions that toppled dynasties, has repeatedly issued sober warnings that rural discontent is a serious political problem. Since the mid-1980s, Beijing has repeatedly issued edicts urging local governments to lighten burdens and has sought to reduce central state taxation and abolish fees. Emphasising the centre's concern for the peasantry, and responding specifically to worsening conditions that precipitated rural riots in 1991–92, the national legislature in 1993 adopted the PRC Agricultural Law. It gave farmers the right to refuse payment of improperly authorised fees and fines and stipulated a 5 per cent cap on income tax. In 2000, the center inaugurated the tax for fee policy that aims at eliminating all fee exactions and retaining only a unified agricultural tax and in 2005 it moved ahead with plans to complete the process. Second, the central authorities passed laws to firm up farmers' land rights by extending their land contracts by 15 years in 1984 and then for another 30 years in 1998. Third, to enhance accountability, elections of rural committees have been instituted in many villages.

There is little evidence, however, that these efforts have had significant effect on curbing the arbitrary powers of local officials, still less that they have been effective in empowering villagers in the face of the party's monopoly on formal power. Township manipulation of village elections, where they do take place, is rife. In the event, village committees are incapable of providing a significant counterweight to officialdom in a system in which it is the party committee and not the village council that dominates village politics.

The state has frequently permitted local struggles to develop, sometimes resulting in challenges to officials, at times exploding in violence that has exacted casualties among villagers, police, and officials, at times ending in court. The strength of the Chinese state is manifest not in its ability to halt or reduce rural protest. As noted, quite the reverse has been the case as protests have spiralled in number and probably in intensity. It is rather that it has moved effectively to isolate and limit protest, to restrict if not prevent the emergence of horizontal movements that would challenge the state beyond the locality or enterprise, whether in the form of mass protest or new political parties. In this sense, the political rights of Chinese villagers remain far less institutionalised than those of their Indian counterparts: if the panchayats are the basic level of India's multi-party system, we suggest that village elections in China have little impact on the wielding of political power, still less on empowering villagers.

Reconceptualising Local Democracy

In the emerging context of expanding democratic consciousness in the face of globalisation and inequality, the concept of local democracy needs to be understood afresh. First, the new political economy perspective moves the focus of discourse beyond local governance to local democracy by treating local institutions not just as agencies for implementation of central policy, but as arenas for the exercise of autonomy and self-determination of local areas and local groups. Second, local institutions, which have generally served as institutions of domination by local elites, must be evaluated from the perspective of their contribution or obstacle to overcoming social as well as political inequality, that is, in terms of their facilitating or impeding the transfer of resources both material and cultural to the poor and the disadvantaged, including women, minorities and, in the Indian case, lower castes. We have told a story that is short of victories in these terms. But we attempted to highlight the emergence of new arenas and new forms of resistance linked to parallel movements in other sectors of society and beyond to international struggles. Struggles for the realisation of local democracy in India, China and beyond, seem certain to intensify as democratic consciousness continues to rise in the twenty-first century.

Notes

1. Even though Indian economic reforms are dated from 1991, there were initiatives launched during Indira Gandhi's regime in the early-1980s and Rajiv Gandhi's in the late-1980s.
2. The defeat of the NDA government in India in the Lok Sabha elections of 2004 was attributed to the hardships caused to the farmers in many parts of India symbolised by the farmers' suicides in Andhra Pradesh, Karnataka, Kerala and even in the prosperous state of Punjab. In China, the former premier, Zhu Rongji, often referred to the farmers' hardships as his main worry.
3. India–China comparative studies have gone through three stages or rather types—the cultural comparisons which focused on interaction through Buddhism, political system, comparisons of liberal democracy with a one-party state ruled by the Communist Party and the 'transition economies' pursuing economic reforms which have become rising powers. See Frankel (2005) and Friedman (2005). In our framework the comparison relates the two post-colonial societies seeking agrarian transformation to realise aspirations of their respective liberation struggles. See Deshpande and Acharya (2001) and Mohanty (1994).
4. According to the UNDP's Human Development Report of 2004, the gini coefficient of inequality in China is now higher than for India.
5. Studies on West Bengal and Karnataka where initiatives for statutory panchayat raj were taken in the late-1970s give adequate evidence of this.
6. G. Bhalla, G. K. Chadha, N. Krishnaji and P. C. Joshi on the emergence of rich farmers in India. See Manoranjan Mohanty et al. (1998).
7. To check this phenomenon, the West Bengal government introduced Operation Barga in 1977 registering sharecropping rights of the tenant. Yet, as shown in Chapter 3, this proved to be inadequate by the 1990s when a new elite emerged to take advantage of most of the privileges of rural development and panchyati raj.
8. In India, in August 2005, the UPA governments' initiative to provide 100 days assured employment to the rural poor was enacted into law as the National Employment Guarantee Act. The Indian Parliament also passed a national law to prevent taking over of tribal land by non-tribals. In both cases the panchayats were given a major role in implementation.
9. The Eleventh Five-Year Plan Outline document adopted by the Fifth Plenum of the CPC Central Committee in October 2005 highlights these policies. These were further emphasised by Premier Wen Jiabao in his Work Report to the Fourth Session of the Tenth National People's Congress on 4 March 2006.
10. The Andhra and Maharashtra studies in this volume bring out this phenomenon clearly. In case of China, the fourth generation leadership has stressed 'scientific concept of development' and the notion of building a 'harmonious society' mainly to address the issue of social inequality and regional disparity. The call for 'building a new socialist countryside' was given by Premier Wen Jiabao in his Government Work Report in March 2006.

11. See Article 111 of the *Constitution of the People's Republic of China* (Beijing: Foreign Languages Press, 2005) incorporating amendments till 2004.
12. See chapters 2 and 9 in this volume. Also see Mathew (2000).
13. An October 2005 government white paper offers an authoritative overview of the Chinese government's claims concerning democratic governance, including detailed discussion of the village council system. http://www.china.org.cn/english/2005/Oct/145718.htm.
14. See the discussion of the case of Buyun Township in Sichuan in Chapter 4, this volume. The experience in Taishi Township in Guangdong in 2005 also indicates the reluctance of the central leadership to allow competitive elections at the township level.
15. Studies of village committee elections in China make it evident.
16. Under the Constitution of India, every state has a state election commission, which is an autonomous body to conduct the local elections.
17. See, for example, Lianjiang Li, 'Popular Demands for Village Elections in Rural China', http://carnegiecouncil.org/viewMedia.php/prmTemplateID/8/prmID/564. Accessed 26 December 2005. John Pomfret, 'In China, Democracy Not All it Seems', *Washington Post*, 25 August 2001, notes that approximately 20 per cent of villages had held competitive elections. Pomfret drew on a survey conducted by Kevin O'Brien. http://www.hartford-hwp.com/archives/55/140.html accessed 26 December 2005.
18. India is not alone is establishing electoral quotas for women. The other main examples are parliamentary quotas implemented in African nations following civil wars (Rwanda, Eritrea, Mozambique, Somalia and Uganda) or liberation wars (South Africa and Namibia).See Schwartz (2005).
19. See Chapter 12, this volume.
20. For a critical view see Chapter 13, this volume. For a critical discussion on the concept of 'empowerment' see Mohanty (2000).
21. See, China: *Country Report 2005*, Beijing Plus Ten Conference (August 2005).
22. China was ahead of India in the reforms performance. See Bhattasali et al. (2004) and Ramesh (2005). Thomas Friedman, however, thinks that even though India may lag behind China in some respects including growth rate, India's liberal democratic institutions and market competence give it strength. Friedman (2005). Pranab Bardhan, however, noting the continued weight of the rural poor, observes that both countries have a long way to go. See Bardhan (2005).
23. India's agriculture minister, Sharad Pawar, repeatedly states that 'The Indian farmer is facing a serious crisis' (Sainath, 2005).
24. According to the Ninth Round of the National Sample Survey of India, the average monthly per capita expenditure (MPCE) of farm households in 2003 was only Rs 503 of which over 55 per cent was spent on food and some 18 per cent on clothing, fuel, footwear and electricity. Rural indebtedness had risen from 26 per cent of the farmers in 1991 to over 50 per cent (Sainath, 2005).
25. See Zhu Ling and Jiang Zhongyi (1996) and Bardhan (2005). See the debate in the *Economic and Political Weekly* on the effect of the reforms on poverty in India.
26. See Khan and Riskin (2005), *China Human Development Report 2005*, Chapter 2, 'The State of Equity in China: Wealth and Income'. Wen Tiejun (2005).
27. The Eleventh Five-Year Plan Outline addressed three gaps—peasant-workers, rural and urban and inland and coastal regions.
28. Francine Frankel (2005), restates the position in the new edition of *India's Political Economy*. See Chakravarti (2004).
29. In Chapter 7 of this volume this view is argued by Rajendra Vora citing the Maharashtra experience.
30. See chapters 2 and 9 in this volume.

31. See Chapter 8 in this volume.
32. See Edward Friedman et al. (1991, 2005), Selden (1993). The third major period of social transformation, the collectivisation of the years 1955–58 is not discussed here because the changes were essentially imposed from above in the absence of a significant social movement. Certainly there was no significant *autonomous* social movement.
33. The proposal for amending the Constitution further to give more financial powers to the panchayats did not materialise in 2005.
34. During 1984–1989, Prime Minister Rajiv Gandhi called meetings of district collectors nationally and in different zones and assigned them responsibilities. This was resented by many states, especially those ruled by non-Congress parties. As pointed out in Chapter 15, many Dalit groups worked for central intervention and were skeptical of the panchayats, which could be manipulated by the high castes in the village.
35. The Naxalite groups in India are divided on their approach to panchayati raj. The CPI ML (Liberation) takes part in elections and has come to power in many local bodies in Bihar and Jharkhand. The CPI (Maoist), the former People's War Group, treat the panchayat bodies as institutions of the semi-feudal compradore state. In the areas of their influence the rural development funds are utilised most effectively in the interest of the poor because the panchayat leaders and officers fear retaliation by the Maoists in the event of corruption or non-implementation. See Mohanty (2005).

References

Bardhan, Pranab. 2005. 'China, India Superpower? Not so Fast', *Yale Global* (25 October 2005).

Bernstein, Thomas and Xiaobo Lu. 2000. 'Taxation without Representation: Peasants, the Central and the Local States in Reform China', *The China Quarterly*, 163 (September): 742–63.

———. 2003. *Taxation without Representation in Contemporary China*. Cambridge: Cambridge University Press.

Bhattasali, Deepak, Shantong Li and Will Martin (eds). 2004. *China and the WTO: Accession, Policy Reform, and Poverty Reduction Strategies*. Washington: World Bank.

Chakravarti, Anand. 2004. 'Caste and Agrarian Class: A View from Bihar', in Manoranjan Mohanty (ed.), *Class, Caste, Gender*. New Delhi: Sage Publications.

Cheng, Tiejun and Mark Selden. 1994. 'City, Countryside and the Dialectics of Control: The Origins of China's Hukou System', *The China Quarterly*, 139: 644–68.

Deshpande, G.P. and Alka Acharya (eds). 2001. *Crossing the Bridge of Dreams: Fifty Years of India and China*. New Delhi: Tulika.

Frankel, Francine (ed.). 2005. *India's Political Economy 1947–2004—The Gradual Revolution*, second edition. New Delhi: Oxford University Press.

Friedman, Thomas. 2005. *The World is Flat: A Brief History of the Twenty-First Century*. New York: Random House Inc.

Friedman, Edward, Paul G. Pickowicz and Mark Selden. 1991. *Chinese Village, Socialist State*. New Haven: Yale University Press.

———. 2005. *Revolution, Resistance and Reform in Village China*. New Haven: Yale University Press.

Ho, Peter. 2005. 'Introduction', in Peter Ho (ed.), *Developmental Dilemmas: Land Reform and Institutional Change in China*, p. 16. London: Routledge.

Khan, Azizur Rahman and Carl Riskin. 2005. 'China's Household Income and Its Distribution, 1995 and 2002', *China Quarterly*, 182: 356–84.

Ma, Josephine. 2004. 'Three Million Took Part in Surging Protest Last Year', *South China Morning Post*, 8 June 2004 and also *International Herald Tribune*, 6 March 2006.

Mathew, George (ed.). 2000. *The Status of Panchayat Raj in the States and Union Territories of India*. New Delhi: Concept.

Mohanty, Manoranjan. 2000. *Contemporary Indian Political Theory*. New Delhi: Sanskriti.

———. 2005. 'The Course of Naxalism', *Himal Magazine* (Kathmandu, September–October 2005).

Mohanty, Manoranjan, Partha N. Mukherji and Olle Tornquist (eds). 1994. 'Swaraj and Jiefang: Freedom Discourse in India and China', in Neera Chandhoke (ed.), *Understanding the Post-colonial world: Theory and Method*. New Delhi: Sage Publications.

———. 1998. *People's Rights*. New Delhi: Sage Publications.

Patnaik, Utsa. 2004. 'The Republic of Hunger', *Social Scientist*, 5 (32): 376–77.

Perry, Elizabeth and Mark Selden (eds). 2003. *Chinese Society: Change, Conflict and Resistance*, 2nd edition. London: Routledge.

Ramesh, Jairam. 2005. *Making Sense of Chindia: Reflections on China and India*. New Delhi: India Research Press.

Sainath, P. 2005. 'Falling Farm Income, Growing Inequities', *The Hindu*, 18 November 2005.

Schwartz, Helle. 2004. 'Women's Representation in the Rwandan Parliament. An Analysis of Variations in the Representation of Womens' Interests Caused by Gender and Quota'. MA thesis, Department of Political Science, Gothenburg University, 2004, p. 6. http://www.quotaproject.org/news.cfm accessed 26 December 2005.

Selden, Mark. 1993. *The Political Economy of Chinese Development*. Armonk: M.E. Sharpe.

UNDP. 2004. *Human Development Report 2004*. New Delhi: Oxford University Press.

Unger, Jonathan. 2002. The Transformation of Rural China. Armonk: M.E. Sharpe.

Wen Tiejun. 2005. *Institutional Costs of China's Reforms*. Beijing: People's University, College of Agriculture and Rural Development.

Xiaolin Guo. 2001. 'Land Expropriation and Rural Conflicts in China', *The China Quarterly*, 166 (June): 422–39.

Yu Jianrong. 2003. 'Organized Peasant Resistance in Contemporary China', Lecture delivered at Fairbank Centre, Harvard University, 4 December 2003.

Zhu Ling and Jiang Zhongyi. 1996. *Public Works and Poverty Alleviation in Rural China*. New York: Nova Science Publishers.

Glossary

adhyaksha	chairperson
bage	administrative unit under a Banner in Inner Mongolia
bahujan	overwhelming majority in society—referring to the vast masses of cultivating castes, former untouchable castes and the tribal people.
banner	a county level unit in Inner Mongolia
benami	illegally registered in a wrong name
biaohui	rotating savings
brigade/production brigade	rural collective at the cun or village level which existed from 1958 till 1978
chowkidars	guards who also performed other functions in the village for the state
cungui minyue	regulations made by the village regarding villagers' daily life
cunmin weiyuanhui	villagers committee
dafadars	designated village guards reporting to police stations
dalit	scheduled castes, formerly untouchable
dengji guanli jiguan	registration management agency
Dharma	law of things (also loosely used for religion)
Dhobi	caste of those who wash clothes
foxiepa	manager of temple facilities and public property in Tajik village
Gaca	a former Brigade in Inner Mongolia
gaolidai	high interest lending
Gaote	Mutual Aid Team in Inner Mongolia
gongkai xuanba	method of open selection
gongtui gongxuan	method of open recommendation and selection
grama panchayat	village council
grama sabha	village assembly
grama swaraj	village self-rule
Grameen	rural self-development programme in Bangladesh—literally meaning rural
Guakao danwei	official sponsoring unit
haixuan	method of direct election or direct nomination of candidates by villagers

hangye xinyong	trade credit
hukou	household registration
Huzhuhui/Hehui	Mutual Aid Associations (for Credit)
Janmabhoomi	literally meaning motherland, it is a programme of rural activities launched by the Telugu Desam government of Andhra Pradesh.
jati	caste as it evolved over centuries into numerous formations
jotedar	land owner
kaxie/kaxiepa	village chief or village authority (Lahu language characters transliterated into Chinese)
kuoshi	second day of Lahu new year
Kutumbasree	a neighbourhood group development programme of clusters of families launched in Kerala in 1999–2000
liudong	migration without changing the *hukou*
mandal parishad	the layer of rural government above the *gram panchayat* in Andhra Pradesh but smaller in area than the erstwhile *panchayat samitis* at the Block or Taluka level which it replaced
minjian jiedai	interpersonal lending
mu	one-sixth of an acre of land
nagar panchayat	urban council/municipality
naxalite	Maoists of India who emerged as a Communist Stream after the peasant uprising in Naxalbari in West Bengal in 1967
non-Brahman	other than those who belong to the caste of priests ranked at the top in the Hindu caste order
nongcun hezuo jijinhui	rural cooperative foundation
palli Sabha	assembly at the level of the hamlet or a small natural village
panchayat samiti/ taluk samiti	block level rural council above the village panchayat but below the district
panchayat	rural local council (Panch or five-member council in traditional system in rural India)
panchayati raj	rural local self-government
Patwari	an official who maintains land records
People's Commune	rural collective at the Xiang or township level which existed from 1958 till 1978 and formally dissolved in 1983
Qianyi	permanent migration

sarpanch	head of the village panchayat
sarpanchpati	husband of the woman sarpanch
Shetkari Sanghatana	farmers organization
siren qianzhuang	private money houses (mostly illegal private banks)
Sumu	a former commune in Inner Mongolia
swaraj	self-rule/self-determination
Three arbitraries (san luan)	arbitrary taxation (luan shoufei), arbitrary fines (luan fakuan) and arbitrary expropriation (luan tanpei)
upadhyaksha	deputy chairperson
upsarpanch	deputy head of the village panchayat
Vana Samrakshana Samiti	Forest Conservation Society
varna	caste in the sense of the original four caste divisions in the Hindu caste order
ward sabha	assembly at the level of the ward or the segments of the village panchayat
xiang	township equivalent to the former commune
yipiao foujue	one vote rejects the whole election or decision making
zamindar	landlord
zhangli	who makes and repairs the farming tools in the Tajik village
zhen	xiang level town
zhongdian renkou	targeted people
Zhuang	village/rural area in pre-1949 Xinjiang
zhuoba	Buddhist priest who is part of the Tajik village administration
zhuren	director
zilla parishad/ zilla panchayat	district council

About the Editors and Contributors

The Editors

Manoranjan Mohanty is Co-Chairperson, Institute of Chinese Studies, Delhi. He is also a visiting professor at the Institute of Human Development, New Delhi. Formerly Professor of Political Science and Director, Developing Countries Research Centre, University of Delhi, his research interests are Chinese politics and comparative development studies. He has also been active in the peace and democratic rights movement. His most recent publications are *Class, Caste, Gender* (edited, 2004), *Contemporary Indian Political Theory* (2000) and *People's Rights* (co-edited with Partha Nath Mukherji, 1998).

Richard Baum is Professor of Political Science, University of Californi. at Los Angeles. He was also the director of the UCLA Center for Chinese Studies (1999–2005). A student of Chinese politics and foreign policy, he has written and edited eight books, including *Burying Mao: Chinese Politics in the Age of Deng Xiaoping* (1996) and *Reform and Reaction in Post-Mao China: The Road to Tiananmen* (1990).

Rong Ma is Professor and Chair, Department of Sociology and Director, Institute of Sociology and Anthropology, University of Beijing. He is a scholar of ethnic relations, migration, urbanisation, education and rural development. Besides having published a number of articles in various journals, he has authored *Introduction to Sociology of Ethnicity* (2005) in Chinese, *Population and Society in Tibet* (1996) and co-edited *On Development of China's Frontier Regions* (1993).

George Mathew is Director, Institute of Social Sciences, New Delhi. The founder of the Institute of Social Sciences, he has been on the forefront of research on and promotion of democratic decentralisation in India and has taken a leading role in the international forum on federalism. His major publications include *Panchayati Raj: From Legislation to Movement* (1994, 2002), *Communal Road to a Secular Kerala* (1990) and *Panchayati Raj in Jammu and Kashmir* (edited, 1990). He has also produced an award-winning feature film, *Swaraj: The Little Republic* (2002).

The Contributors

D. Bandyopadhyay, a civil servant, held many important positions in the State Government of West Bengal and in the Government of India. As Land Reform Commissioner of West Bengal, he led the landmark land reform project of the state, Operation Barga. He also served as Secretary to the Government of India in the ministries of Rural Development and Finance (Department of Revenue), besides being Executive Director of Asian Development Bank for three years. An acknowledged expert on land reform, Bandyopadhyay has written extensively on governance, decentralisation, land reform and rural development in national journals, newspapers and edited volumes. He was convenor of the Task Force on Panchayati Raj, Rajiv Gandhi Foundation for over a decade. Currently he is Executive Chairperson, Council for Social Development, New Delhi.

B.S. Bhargava, M.P.A. (The Hague) and Ph.D. (Pilani), was formerly a Professor of Development Administration at the Institute for Social and Economic Change, Bangalore, and currently is a Senior Fellow at the Institute of Social Sciences Bangalore Centre. His areas of interest include development administration, political behaviour and panchayati raj. His publications include *Lakshadweep: Towards Decentralised Governance* (co-author 2000) and *The Land Army and Rural Development: A study of organizational innovation in Karnataka* (1994).

Chung Siu Fung obtained an M.A. in Public Policy and Management from City University of Hong Kong and an M. Phil. in Community Medicine and Ph.D. from The University of Hong Kong. She was a teaching assistant in Division of Social Science, The Hong Kong University of Science and Technology. She is currently the director of the John Cathedral HIV Education Centre in Hong Kong.

Buddhadeb Ghosh served in the State Civil Service of West Bengal and held various positions in development administration including a stint as Director, State Institute of Panchayats. Currently he is Senior Fellow at the Institute of Social Sciences, New Delhi where he participates in research projects and consultancy assignments on governance, decentralisation and institutional issues of rural development. He has published several papers on decentralisation, local government and related matters in national journals and edited volumes. The books co-authored by him are *West Bengal Panchayat Election, 1993: A Study in Participation and State Politics* and *Panchayats in India*.

Saila K. Ghosh, Ph.D. is a retired Professor of the Indian Institute of Management, Calcutta. He has handled several national and international research projects in the areas of Indian labour and trade union, child labour, non-formal and primary organisation, rural development and rural self government sponsored by agencies like ILO, UNICEF, UNESCO, DFID etc. He was Research Adviser to the Second West Bengal Police Commission. His papers have been published in India and abroad. Currently he is engaged in projects relating to wasteland preservation and management.

G. Haragopal is Professor of Political Science and Dean, School of Social Sciences at the University of Hyderabad. A Ph.D. from Kakatiya University, he has worked in the areas of development administration, rural development, political economy and human rights. He is the Coordinator of the UGC Programme of Human Rights at the University of Hyderabad and Editor, *Indian Journal of Human Rights*. He has been closely associated with the Andhra Pradesh Civil Liberties Committee. His publications include, *The Political Economy of Human Rights* (1997), Gandhian Worldview—A *Civil Liberties Perspective* (1995), and *Administrative Leadership and Rural Development* (1980).

Shaoying He is Professor and Deputy President of Yunnan Minority University. He received his Masters degree in Minorities from Yunnan University. He has authored *Cultural History of Naxi* (2001).

T.M. Thomas Isaac is an economist and political worker since he was a student. He has been associated with the Kerala Shastra Sahitya Parishad from 1977; and Professor at the Centre for Development Studies, Thiruvananthapuram. He served on the State Planning Board from 1996 to 2001 and was elected to the Kerala Legislative Assembly in 2001. He has published a number of books and articles on economics, planning and politics in the leading regional, national and international journals and presented lectures and papers at conferences and seminars in India and abroad.

Besides, he has published many books in Malayalam and English including *Democracy at Work in an Indian Industrial Co-operative: The Story of Kerala Dinesh Beedi* (with Richard W. Franke and Pyaralal Raghavan) (1998); *Local Democracy and Development: People's Campaign for Decentralised Planning in Kerala* (with Richard W. Franke) (2000); *The Politics of People's Plan Campaign* (2005).

Tanzen Lhundup is Research Fellow and Deputy Director of the Institute of Social and Economic Development at the Chinese Center for Tibetological

Study. He received his Ph.D. from Beijing University. He has written extensively on Tibet.

Bidyut Mohanty is Head, Department of Women Studies at the Institute of Social Sciences, Delhi. A Ph.D. from Delhi School of Economics, she has worked in areas of famine studies, women's development and local government in India. Since 1994 she has organised the annual Women's Political Empowerment Day Programme of the ISS, assembling hundreds of elected women representatives from panchayats. She is the series editor of the *Proceedings on Women and Political Empowerment* from 1995 onwards. She has published many research articles on development, women and panchayats based on her extensive field level experience.

Tony Saich is the Daewoo Professor of International Affairs and Director of the Harvard University Asia Center. He is Faculty Chair of the Asia Program and the China Public Policy Program at the Kennedy School of Government, Harvard University. From 1994 until July 1999 he was the Representative for the China Office of the Ford Foundation. Prior to this he was the Director of the Sinological Institute, Leiden University, the Netherlands. His current research focuses on the interplay between state and society in China and the respective roles they play in the provision of public goods and services at the local level. He has written several books on developments in China, including; *China's Science Policy in the 80s* (1989); *Revolutionary Discourse in Mao's China* (with David E. Apter, 1994); *The Rise to Power of the Chinese Communist Party* (1996); *The Governance and Politics of China* (2004). He has just finished editing a book on reform of China's financial sector and on HIV/AIDS in China.

Mark Selden is Senior Fellow in the East Asia Program at Cornell University. His books include *Chinese Village, Socialist State*; *China in Revolution: The Yenan Way Revisited*; *War and State Terrorism: The United States, Japan, and the Asia-Pacific in the Long Twentieth Century* and, most recently, *Revolution, Resistance and Reform in Village China*. He is a coordinator of the Japan Focus e-journal on Japan and the Asia-Pacific.

K. Subha, a Ph.D. in Political Science from the University of Mysore is the Southern Regional Co-ordinator, Institute of Social Sciences. She has published research papers and articles in professional journals. Her publications include *Women in Local Governance* and *Karnataka Panchayat Elections 1995: Process, Issues and Membership Profile*. She has written extensively on women's political development and gender-related issues.

G. Sudarshanam is Professor of Political Science, School of Social Sciences at the University of Hyderabad where he has been working for over 20 years. He is also the Coordinator of Post Graduate Diploma in Human Rights and Associate Editor of *Indian Journal of Human Rights*. He has authored a number of books and published articles in reputed Journals and edited volumes. His areas of interest are Panchayati Raj, rural development, human rights and public administration.

Kellee S. Tsai, Ph.D. (Columbia University), is Associate Professor of Political Science at John Hopkins University. Her research interests include the political economy of development, informal finance, microfinance, and comparative democratisation with a focus on China. Her publications include *Back-Alley Banking: Private Entrepreneurs in China* (2002), *Rural Industrialization and Non-governmental Finance: Insights from Wenzhou* [in Chinese] (2004) and *Japan and China in the World Political Economy* (2005).

M. Vanamala taught Economics in various colleges of Andhra Pradesh government. Her areas of research are economics of backward classes and women's development. She has won the Best Teacher Award from the Government of Andhra Pradesh. She has a number of research publications on the SC, ST and Backward Classes Finance Corporation of AP and women labour under globalization.

Rajendra Vora is Lokmanya Tilak Professor of Politics and Public Administration at University of Pune. He is co-editor of *Region, Culture and Politics in India* (2006), *Indian Democracy: Meanings and Practices* (2004), *Home, Family and Kinship in Maharashtra* (1999) and editor of *Socio-Economic Profile of Rural India: Vol III: North-Central and Western India* (2005). He has contributed numerous papers on political process and political thought in Indian journals and edited volumes both in Marathi and English.

Fei-Ling Wang, Ph.D. (University of Pennsylvania), is Professor of International Affairs at Georgia Institute of Technology. He taught at the U.S. Military Academy (West Point), guest-lectured at universities in several countries, and held visiting and adjunct positions in five universities in China, Korea, Japan and Singapore. His most recent books are *China Rising: Power and Motivation in Chinese Foreign Policy* (co-editor, 2005) and *Organizing through Division and Exclusion: China's Hukou System* (2005).

Shengmin Yang is Professor and Dean, School of Ethnology and Sociology at the Central University of Minority Nationalities. He received his Ph.D. from the same University.

Xuedong Yang is a Fellow and Deputy Director of the China Center for Comparative Politics and Economics (CCCPE) and Assistant Director of China Local Governance Innovations Program. A Ph.D. from Beijing University, he was a visiting fellow in Kennedy School of Government, Harvard (2001–02). He has authored/co-authored books on Chinese local politics, including his doctoral dissertation 'Market Development, Society Growth and State Building: Taking the "county" as an analytical unit' (Zhengzhou 2002).

Changjiang Yu, Associate Professor, Department of Sociology, Beijing University received his Ph.D. from the same University. His publications in Chinese include *From Idea to Practice: The Theory and Process of the Founders of Chicago School of American Sociology* (2004); *Next to the Ruins of History: A Sociological Reflection of Yuanmingyuan Artists Community* (2005); *Meeting by Chance: Several Sociological Topics on Art*; *Art and Society: On the Redirection of Contemporary Chinese Art by 26 Famous Critics* (2005); *Other See Me Seeing Us: On Fei Xiaotong's Earthbound China and Three Villages in Yunnan* (2005); and 'Life in Lara Village, Tibet' (in English) in *Contemporary Tibet: Politics, Development, and Society in a Disputed Region* (2006).

Xin Zhang is a Ph.D. scholar in the Department of Political Science at UCLA. His main research interest includes relation between institutions (economic and political) and development. He is now conducting dissertation research on the contests over corporate property rights in Russia. He has published (with Richard Baum) in *The China Journal*.

Xiaohong Zhou is Dean and Professor of Sociology at Nanjing University and Director of Social Psychology Institute. He is the author of the *Survey of Chinese Middle Class* (2005) besides other books and articles.

David Zweig is Chair Professor, Division of Social Science and Director, Center on China's Transnational Relations, Hong Kong University of Science and Technology. He is also a Non-Resident Fellow, Pacific Council on International Policy, Los Angeles. He is the author of four books, most recently, *Internationalizing China: Domestic Interests and Global Linkages* (Cornell University Press, 2002). His most recent journal articles include: 'China's Global Search for Oil', *Foreign Affairs* (September–October 2005), 'Learning to Com-pete: China's Effort to Encourage a Reverse Brain Drain', *International*

Labour Review (January 2006) and 'Elections, Democratic Values, and Economic Development in Rural China', *Journal of Contemporary China* (Fall, 2007). His current research includes China's resource-based foreign policy, Chinese mainlanders with overseas education and Hong Kong's role in China's modernisation.

Index

linguistic and cultural differences, 265
livestock households, 153
loan, government-subsidised, 247; institutional, to local governments, 182; microfinance, from NGOs, 247; poverty alleviation, 233; sharking, 231; subsidised, 246
local administrative system, changes in, 146; in China, 141
local area development fund of MPs (MPLADS), 44, 67
local bodies, financial allotments to, 193
local finances, democratic management of, 78
local governance, Chinese, model, 15
local government, in Bengal, 53; under British Rule, 53; in China, 308; colonised, 55; in Constitution, 57; in independent India, 57–68; institutions in the villages, 55; introduced in India by the British Raj, 56; introduction of, in rural areas of Bengal, 53; perspectives on, 15; system in India and China, 33
local pastoral community (commune and brigade), 152
local self-government, 39; autonomy of, 186; in Kerala, 186; institutions, 22, 182; institutions of, in India's villages, 36; Lord Ripon's idea (1882) of, 40; planning function of, 183; resource mobilisation by, 204
local self-government, myth of, in British India, 53
local tax system of LSGIs, 204

Madras Village Panchayat Act, 1950, 210
Maharashtra Industrial Development Act, 177
Maharashtra Zilla Parishads and Panchayat Samitis Act of 1961, 162
Mahayana, 393
Mandal Parishad, 369
Mao's plan for national reconstruction, 75
Maoist and Post-Mao periods, rural political participation in, 73
Maoist period, rural participation in, 87
marriages, feudal system of arranged, 303
masculinisation of activities, 322
maternal mortality, 311
microcredit, an alternative model of, 197; in China, 332; interest rate controls on, 236

microfinance, facilities, 254; Grameen model of, 236; Grameen-style, in China, 236; institutions, 234; institutions, NGO and donor-managed, 234; local political economy of informal finance and, in rural China and India, 154, 229; NGOs, 235; programmes, 254; programmes, formal financial institutions and, 253; programmes run by NGOs, 232; rise of, 232; state-subsidised, in China, 233
microloans, government-sponsored, 245; subsidised, 232
migration, internal, in India, 278; new trend of seasonal, 152; seasonal, 153
militant movements in the north-east and in Punjab, 62
Minhe County Education Bureau—the SDA's official sponsoring unit (*guakao danwei*), 129
Minhe County Education, 129
minority nationalities, regional autonomy of, 427
modernity, definition of, 432; and exoticism, 445
monastery, connection between, and administration, 437
moneylenders, agricultural, 242; non-professional, 243; professional, 242, 248
more democratic nomination (MDN) systems and less democratic nomination (LDN) systems, 343
motivations for mobilising peasant political participation, 88
mutual aid group, 146
mutual benefit societies, 243
mutual finance, 250; groups, 249
Mydolalu Gram Panchayat, 215
Mysore Village Panchayat and District Board Act, 1952, 210
Mysore Village Panchayats and Local Boards Act 1959, 210

National Bank for Agriculture and Rural Development (NABARD), 235, 328
National People's Congress (NPC), 49, 94, 342
National People's Congress Standing Committee, 34–35
National Perspective Plan for Women in 1990, 162